P9-CKZ-163

Internet Routing Architectures, Second Edition

Sam Halabi with Danny McPherson

Cisco Press
201 West 103rd Street
Indianapolis, IN 46290 USA

Internet Routing Architectures, Second Edition

Sam Halabi with Danny McPherson

Published by:
Cisco Press
201 West 103rd Street
Indianapolis, IN 46290 USA

Printed in the United States of America 1 2 3 4 5 6 7 8 9 0

Library of Congress Cataloging-in-Publication Number: 00-105166

ISBN: 1-57870-233-X

Warning and Disclaimer

This book is designed to provide information about Internet Routing Architectures and the Border Gateway Protocol (BGP). Every effort has been made to make this book as complete and as accurate as possible, but no warranty or fitness is implied.

The information is provided on an "as is" basis. The author, Cisco Press, and Cisco Systems, Inc. shall have neither liability nor responsibility to any person or entity with respect to any loss or damages arising from the information contained in this book or from the use of the discs or programs that may accompany it.

The opinions expressed in this book belong to the author and are not necessarily those of Cisco Systems, Inc.

Trademark Acknowledgments

All terms mentioned in this book that are known to be trademarks or service marks have been appropriately capitalized. Cisco Press or Cisco Systems, Inc. cannot attest to the accuracy of this information. Use of a term in this book should not be regarded as affecting the validity of any trademark or service mark.

Feedback Information

At Cisco Press, our goal is to create in-depth technical books of the highest quality and value. Each book is crafted with care and precision, undergoing rigorous development that involves the unique expertise of members of the professional technical community.

Reader feedback is a natural continuation of this process. If you have any comments regarding how we could improve the quality of this book, or otherwise alter it to better suit your needs, you can contact us through e-mail at ciscopress@mcp.com. Please be sure to include the book title and ISBN in your message.

We greatly appreciate your assistance.

Publisher	John Wait
Editor-In-Chief	John Kane
Cisco Systems Program Manager	Jim LeValley
Managing Editor	Patrick Kanouse
Acquisitions Editor	Brett Bartow
Development Editor	Chris Cleveland
Production Editor	Marc Fowler
Copy Editor	Gayle Johnson
Technical Editors	Abha Ahuja, Shane Amante, Johnson Liu, Alvaro Retana, Alexei Roudnev
Team Coordinator	Amy Lewis
Book Designer	Gina Rexrode
Cover Designer	Louisa Klucznik
Compositer	Steve Gifford
Indexer	Tim Wright

Corporate Headquarters
Cisco Systems, Inc.
170 West Tasman Drive
San Jose, CA 95134-1706
USA
http://www.cisco.com
Tel: 408 526-4000
800 553-NETS (6387)
Fax: 408 526-4100

European Headquarters
Cisco Systems Europe s.a.r.l.
Parc Evolic, Batiment L1/L2
16 Avenue du Quebec
Villebon, BP 706
91961 Courtaboeuf Cedex
France
http://www-europe.cisco.com
Tel: 33 1 69 18 61 00
Fax: 33 1 69 28 83 26

Americas Headquarters
Cisco Systems, Inc.
170 West Tasman Drive
San Jose, CA 95134-1706
USA
http://www.cisco.com
Tel: 408 526-7660
Fax: 408 527-0883

Asia Headquarters
Nihon Cisco Systems K.K.
Fuji Building, 9th Floor
3-2-3 Marunouchi
Chiyoda-ku, Tokyo 100
Japan
http://www.cisco.com
Tel: 81 3 5219 6250
Fax: 81 3 5219 6001

Cisco Systems has more than 200 offices in the following countries. Addresses, phone numbers, and fax numbers are listed on the Cisco Connection Online Web site at http://www.cisco.com/offices.

Argentina • Australia • Austria • Belgium • Brazil • Canada • Chile • China • Colombia • Costa Rica • Croatia • Czech Republic • Denmark • Dubai, UAE Finland • France • Germany • Greece • Hong Kong • Hungary • India • Indonesia • Ireland • Israel • Italy • Japan • Korea • Luxembourg • Malaysia Mexico • The Netherlands • New Zealand • Norway • Peru • Philippines • Poland • Portugal • Puerto Rico • Romania • Russia • Saudi Arabia • Singapore Slovakia • Slovenia • South Africa • Spain • Sweden • Switzerland • Taiwan • Thailand • Turkey • Ukraine • United Kingdom • United States • Venezuela

About the Authors

Sam Halabi is one of the industry's foremost experts in the Internet Service Provider line of business. Mr. Halabi was recently Vice President of Marketing at an IP networking startup and has spent many years at Cisco Systems where he led the IP Carrier Marketing effort. Mr. Halabi is an expert in complex routing protocols and has specialized in the design of large-scale IP networks.

An active member in the industry, Halabi serves as a board member of the Optical Internetworking Forum and a member of the MPLS Forum.

Danny McPherson is currently Director of Architecture, Office of the CTO, at Amber Networks. Formerly, he held technical leadership positions with four Internet service providers (Qwest, GTE Internetworking, Genuity, and internetMCI), where he was responsible for network and product architecture, routing design, peering, and other business- and policy-related issues. McPherson is an active contributor to the Internet Engineering Task Force (IETF), as well as several other standards bodies. He is an acknowledged expert in Internet architecture and routing protocols.

About the Technical Reviewers

Alexei Roudnev is currently a Software System Engineer for Genesys Labs/Alcatel group in, San Francisco, California. He worked fir 10 years as a Network Engineer at Relcom Network, one of the creators of the Russian Internet, in Moscow, Russia. Alexei was also a UNIX based systems Software Developer in Moscow for 9 years.

Abha Ahuja is currently a Senior Network Engineer at Internap Network Services. She works on network design, architecture and operational issues. Previous to Internap, she worked at Merit Network, a leading network research institution where she worked on the Route Server Next Generation project, a nationwide deployment of routing servers at exchange points, and the Internet Performance Measurement and Analysis (IPMA) project. She continues to play an active role in the Internet community and pursues research interests including inter-domain routing behavior and protocols, network operations and performance statistics, and network security. She is a skilled network engineer, certified troublemaker and a classic Scorpio.

Dedications

Danny McPherson: To my wife, Heather, and my two daughters, Kortney and Ashli. You are my infrastructure.

Acknowledgments

This book would not have been possible without the help of many people whose comments and suggestions significantly improved the end result. First, we would like to thank Abha Ahuja, Shane Amante, Johnson Liu, Alvaro Retana, and Alexander Rudenev for their exceptional technical review of this manuscript. We would also like to explicitly acknowledge Henk Smit, Bruce Cole, Enke Chen, Srihari Ramachandra, Rex Fernando, Satinder Singh, and Ravi Chandra, as well as the entire Cisco "BGP Coders" group, and everyone else who provided any amount of input for the second edition. Also, we would like to acknowledge the overwhelming support and patience of Danny McPherson's present employer, Amber Networks, and previous employer, Qwest Communications, both of which had a significant impact on the value of the content. Finally, we would like to thank Christopher Cleveland, Tracy Hughes, Marc Fowler, Gayle Johnson, and the rest of the Cisco Press folks for keeping us on track and getting the book published.

Contents at a Glance

Contents

Introduction

The Internet, an upstart academic experiment in the late 1960s, struggles with identity and success today. From the ARPANET to the NSFnet to ANYBODYSNET, the Internet is no longer owned by a single entity; it is owned by anybody who can afford to buy space on it. Tens of millions of users are seeking connectivity, and tens of thousands of companies are feeling left out if they do not tap into the Internet. This has put network designers and administrators under a lot of pressure to keep up with networking and connectivity needs. Understanding networking, and especially routing, has become a necessity.

Some people are surprised when networks fail and melt down, but others are surprised when they don't. This seems to be the case because there is so little useful information out there. Much of the information on routing that has been available to designers and administrators up until now is doubly frustrating: The information makes you think you know how to build your network—until you try, and find out that you don't. The first edition of this book addressed real routing issues, using real scenarios, in a comprehensive and accessible way.

In addition to providing a thorough update to the original material, this edition introduces recent enhancements to the BGP protocol, discusses changes surrounding registration and allocation of Internet numbers, and provides additional information on research and educational networks.

Objectives

The purpose of this book is to make you an expert on integrating your network into the global Internet. By presenting practical addressing, routing, and connectivity issues both conceptually and in the context of practical scenarios, this book aims to foster your understanding of routing so that you can plan and implement major network designs in an objective and informed way. Whether you are a customer or a provider (or both) of Internet connectivity, this book anticipates and addresses the routing challenges facing your network.

Audience

This book is intended for any organization that might need to tap into the Internet. Whether you are becoming a service provider or are connecting to one, you will find all you need to integrate your network. The perspectives of network administrators, integrators, and architects are considered throughout this book. Even though this book addresses different levels of expertise, it progresses logically from the simplest to the most challenging concepts and problems, and its common denominator is straightforward, practical scenarios to which anyone can relate. No major background in routing or TCP/IP is required. Any basic or background knowledge needed to understand routing is developed as needed in text discussions, rather than assumed as part of the reader's repertoire.

Organization

The book is organized into four parts:

- **Part I: The Contemporary Internet**—Chapters 1 through 3 cover essential introductory aspects of the contemporary Internet with respect to its structure, service providers, and addressing. Even if you are already familiar with the general structure of the Internet, you are encouraged to read the portions of Chapter 1 concerning Network Access Points, the Routing Arbiter Project, and Network Information Services. The pressures that precipitated these components of the Internet have continuing practical implications for routing design problems faced by administrators. Chapter 2 provides valuable criteria by which to evaluate Internet service providers. If you represent such a provider, or are already a customer of one, some of the information might be familiar to you already. Chapter 3 discusses classless interdomain routing (CIDR), VLSM (variable-length subnet masks), IPv6, and other aspects of Internet addressing.

- **Part II: Routing Protocol Basics**—Chapters 4 and 5 cover the basics: properties of link-state and distance vector routing protocols and why interdomain routing protocols are needed and how they work. These topics are covered both generally and in the specific context of BGP (Border Gateway Protocol)—the de facto standard interdomain routing protocol used in the Internet today. BGP's particular capabilities and attributes are thoroughly introduced.
- **Part III: Effective Internet Routing Designs**—Chapters 6 through 10 delve into the practical, design-oriented applications of BGP. The BGP attributes introduced in Part II are shown in action, in a variety of representative network scenarios. BGP's attributes are put to work in implementing design goals such as redundancy, symmetry, and load balancing. The challenges of making intradomain and interdomain routing work in harmony, managing growing or already-large systems, and maintaining stability are addressed.
- **Part IV: Internet Routing Device Configuration**—Chapters 11 and 12 contain numerous code examples of BGP's attributes and of various routing policies. The code examples will make the most sense to you after you have read the earlier chapters, because many of them address multiple concepts and design goals. So that you can juxtapose textual discussions from earlier chapters with the code examples in Chapters 11 and 12, pointers called "Configuration Examples" appear in the earlier chapters. When you see one, you might want to fast-forward to the referenced page to see a configuration example of the attribute or policy being discussed.

Finally, several appendixes provide additional references for further reading, an up-to-date Cisco IOS™ BGP command reference, and information regarding IOS™ modifications intended to provide a more intuitive BGP command-line interface.

Approach

It is very hard to write about technical information in an accessible manner. Information that is stripped of too much technical detail loses its meaning, but complete and precise technical detail can overwhelm readers and obscure concepts. This book introduces technical detail gradually and in the context of practical scenarios whenever possible. The most heavily technical information—configuration examples in the Cisco IOS language—is withheld until the final two chapters of this book so that it is thoroughly grounded in the concepts and sample topologies that precede it.

Although your ultimate goal is to design and implement routing strategies, it is critical to grasp concepts and principles before applying them to your particular network. This book balances conceptual and practical perspectives by following a logical, gradual progression from general to specific, and from concepts to implementation. Even in chapters and sections that necessarily take a largely descriptive approach, hands-on interests are addressed through pointers to configuration examples, frequently asked questions, and scenario-based explanations.

The scenario-based approach is an especially important component of this book: it utilizes representative network topologies as a basis for illustrating almost every protocol attribute and routing policy discussed. Even though you might not see your exact network situation illustrated, the scenario is specific enough to facilitate learning by example, and general enough that you can extrapolate how the concepts illustrated apply to your situation.

Features and Text Conventions

This book works hard not to withhold protocol details and design-oriented information, while at the same time recognizing that building general and conceptual understanding necessarily comes first. Two features are included to help emphasize what is practical and design-oriented as underlying concepts are developed:

- Pointers to configuration examples—Located close to pertinent text discussions, these references point forward to places in Chapters 11 and 12 where related configuration examples can be found.
- Frequently Asked Questions—Located at the end of every chapter, these questions anticipate practical and design-oriented questions you might have, for your particular network, after having read the chapter.

Command Syntax Conventions

The conventions used to present command syntax in this book are the same conventions used in the IOS Command Reference. The Command Reference describes these conventions as follows:

- Vertical bars (|) separate alternative, mutually exclusive elements.
- Square brackets ([ ]) indicate optional elements.
- Braces ({ }) indicate a required choice.
- Braces within brackets ([{ }]) indicate a required choice within n optional elements.
- Boldface indicates commands and keywords that are entered literally as shown. In actual configuration examples and output (not general command syntax), boldface indicates commands that are manually input by the user (such as a show command).
- Italics indicates arguments for which you supply actual values.

Icons Used in This Book

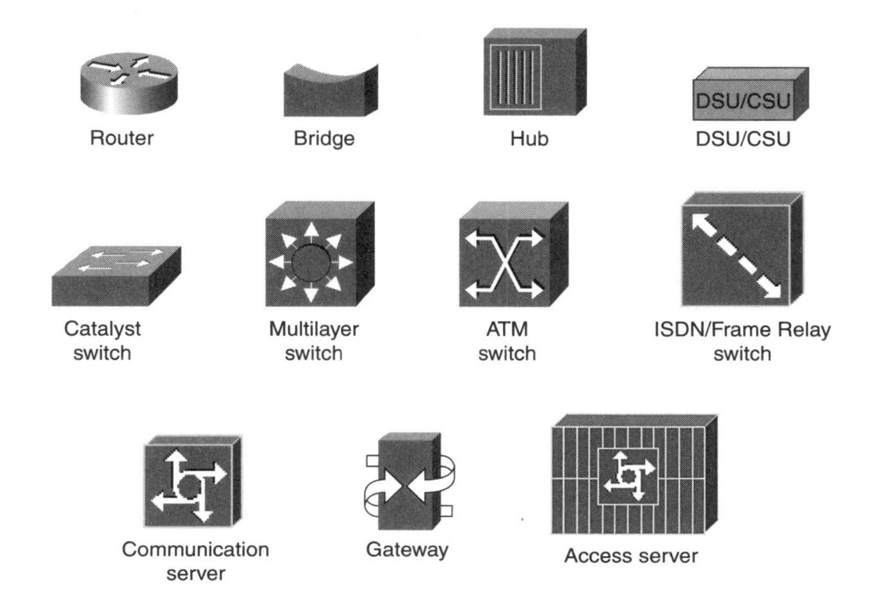

Throughout the book, you will see the following icons used for peripherals and other devices.

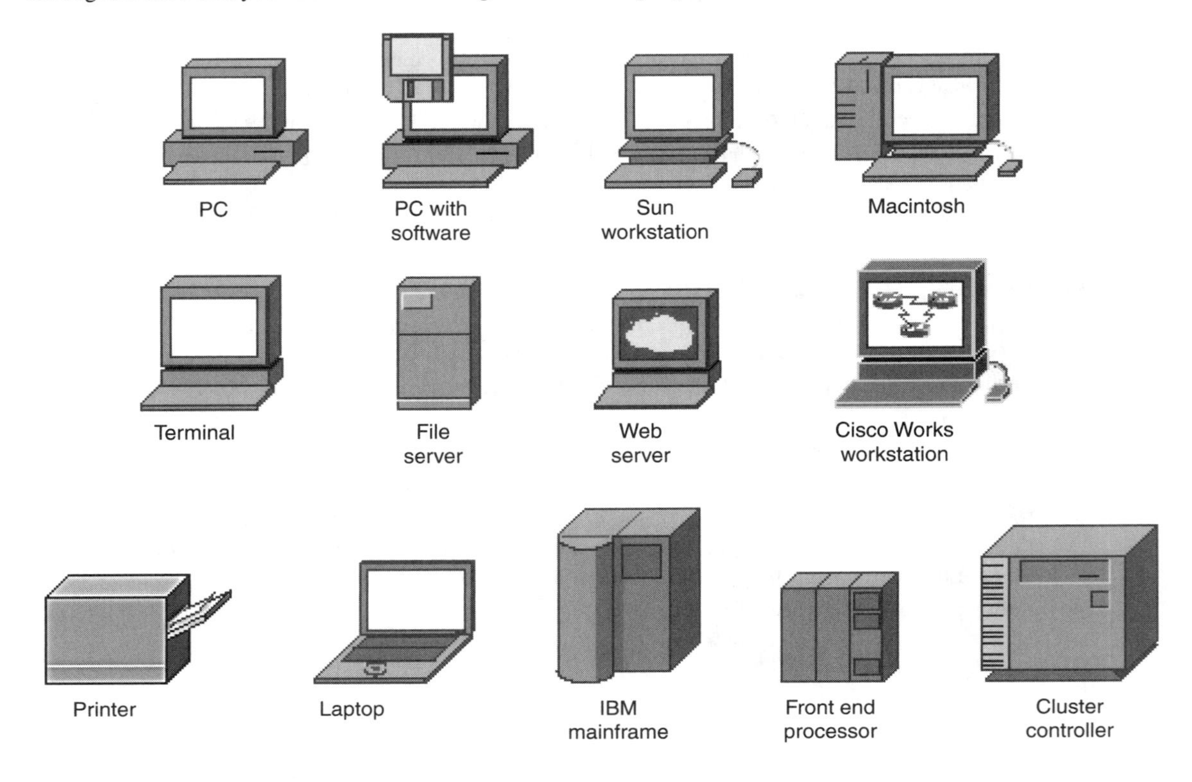

Throughout the book, you will see the following icons used for networks and network connections.

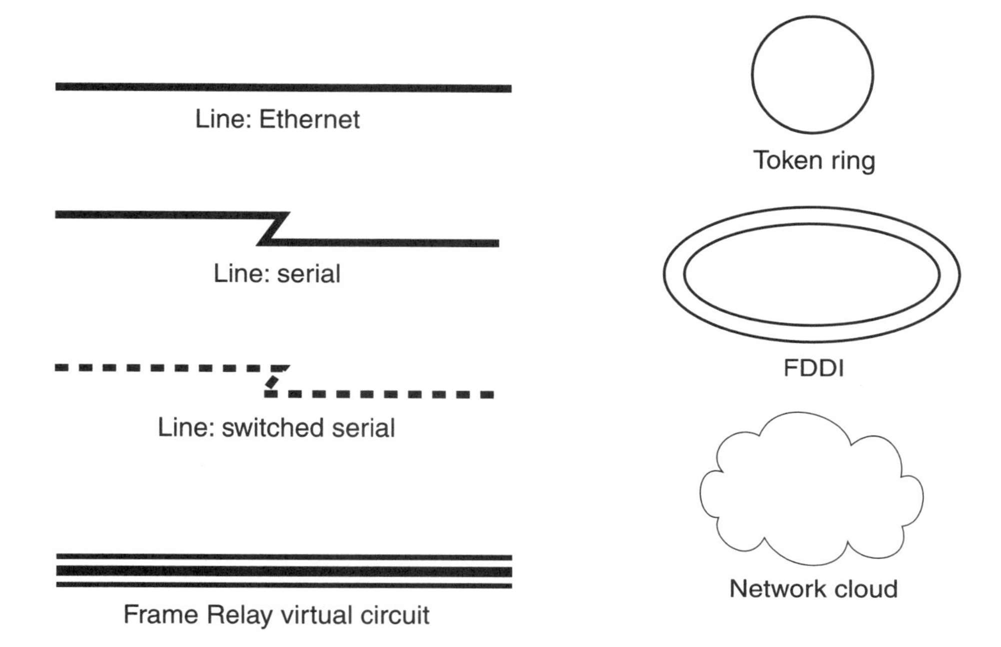

PART I

The Contemporary Internet

The complexity of routing problems and solutions is tied closely to the growth and evolution of the contemporary Internet. Thus, before delving into specifics about routing protocols, you will find it extremely useful to have some general perspective and background information. Such historical developments as the Route Arbiter project, Network Access Points, and Network Information Services, covered in Chapter 1, continue to have extremely practical implications for organizations that want to be connected to global networks. Chapter 2 introduces general and network topology issues associated with Internet service providers. Chapter 3 covers concepts of addressing and classless interdomain routing, which are needed to control the depletion of the IP address space

This chapter covers the following key topics:

- **Origins and recent history of the Internet**—A brief history of the early Internet, with emphasis on its implementers and users, as well as how it has evolved in the last decade. Includes an overview of several important NSF solicitations.
- **Network Access Points**—Internet service providers can connect, directly or indirectly, with Network Access Points (NAPs). You will need to know enough to evaluate how your ISP connects to the NAPs, as well as which NAPs are available in which regions of the world today.
- **Direct interconnections**—An alternative to NAPs, this connection model has gained popularity with large service providers in recent years, primarily because it overcomes some of the shortcomings of the public NAP connection model.
- **Routing arbiter project**—An overview of concepts central to the rest of this book: route servers and the Routing Arbiter Database. Route servers are architectural components of NAPs, Internet service providers, and other networks.
- **Regional providers**—Background on the current Internet layout with respect to regional connections.
- **Information services**—An overview of the information services and agencies that have evolved as a result of NSF solicitation and privatization of the Internet: the InterNIC, registration services, directory and database services, NIC support services, and the evolution of other Internet registries and the Internetworking Routing Registries.
- **The once and future Internet**—A survey of research efforts that point to the future of the Internet: The Next-Generation Initiative, Internet2, and Abilene.

CHAPTER 1

Evolution of the Internet

The structure and makeup of the Internet has adapted as the needs of its community have changed. Today's Internet serves the largest and most diverse community of network users in the computing world. A brief chronology and summary of significant components are provided in this chapter to set the stage for understanding the challenges of interfacing the Internet and the steps involved in building scalable internetworks.

Origins and Recent History of the Internet

The Internet started as an experiment in the late 1960s by the Advanced Research Projects Agency (ARPA, now called DARPA) of the U.S. Department of Defense[1]. DARPA experimented with the connection of computer networks by giving grants to multiple universities and private companies to get them involved in the research.

In December 1969, an experimental network went online with the connection of a four-node network connected via 56 kbps circuits. The new technology proved to be highly successful and led to the creation of two similar military networks—MILNET in the U.S. and MINET in Europe. Thousands of hosts and users subsequently connected their private networks (universities and government) to the ARPANET, thus creating the initial "ARPA Internet." Figures 1-1 and 1-2 illustrate the ARPANET in the early days, from its inception in 1969 to its growing number of connectors in 1976.

Figure 1-1 *ARPANET Architecture, December 1969*

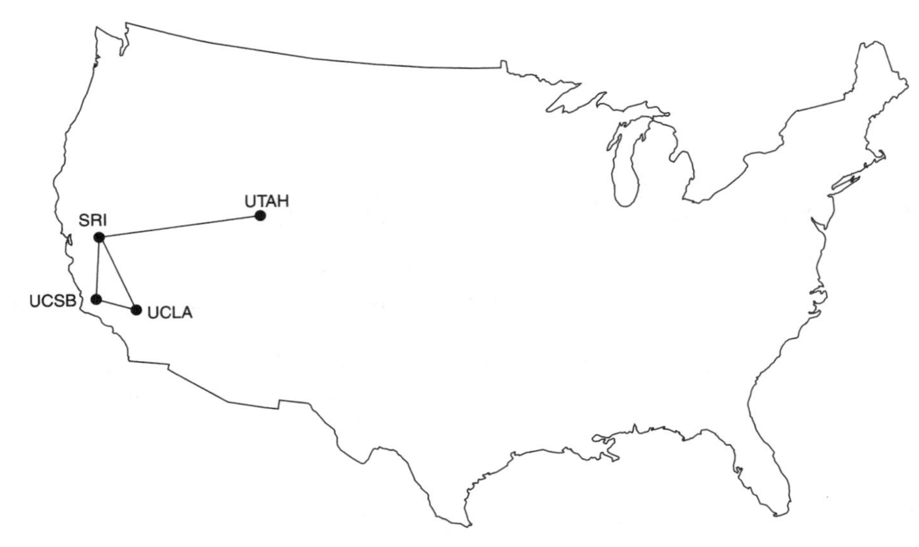

Figure 1-2 *ARPANET Architecture, July 1976*

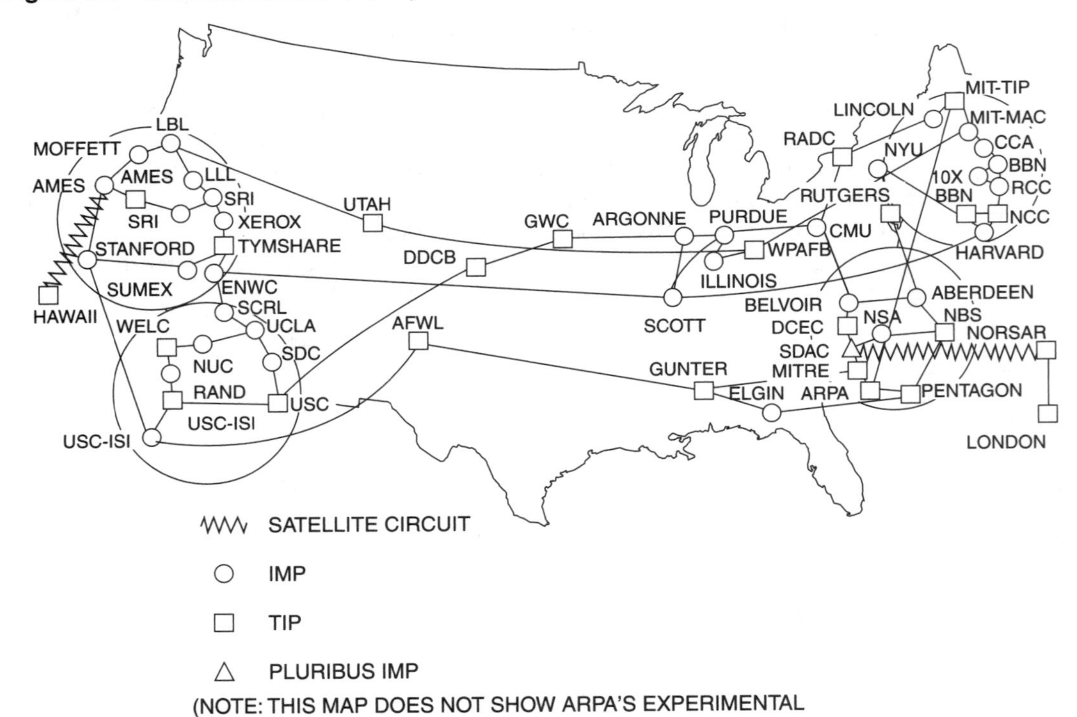

The conglomeration of research, academic, and government networks, combined with the ARPANET core network, was the beginning of what came to be known as the Internet. However, ARPANET had an Acceptable Usage Policy (AUP) that prohibited the use of the Internet for commercial purposes. Nonetheless, the usefulness of the ARPANET to its connectors resulted in scalability problems, the most apparent of which was link congestion. As a result, the National Science Foundation (NSF) began development of the NSFNET[2].

The ARPANET was decommissioned in 1989.

From ARPANET to NSFNET

By 1985, the ARPANET was heavily utilized and burdened with congestion. In response, the National Science Foundation initiated phase 1 development of the NSFNET. The NSFNET was composed of multiple regional networks and peer networks (such as the NASA Science Network) connected to a major backbone that constituted the core of the overall NSFNET.

In its earliest form, in 1986, the NSFNET created a more distributed, three-tiered network architecture. This architecture connected campuses and research organizations to regional networks, which in turn connected to a main backbone network linking six nationally funded supercomputer centers. The original links of 56 kbps were upgraded in 1988 to faster T1 (1.544 Mbps) links. This was a result of the 1987 NSF competitive solicitation for faster network service, awarded to Merit Network, Inc. and its partners MCI, IBM, and the state of Michigan. The NSFNET T1 backbone connected a total of 13 sites, including Merit, BARRNET, MidNet, Westnet, NorthWestNet, SESQUINET, SURAnet, NCAR (National Center for Atmospheric Research), and five NSF supercomputer centers.

In 1990, Merit[3], IBM, and MCI started a new organization known as Advanced Network and Services (ANS). Merit's Internet engineering group provided a policy routing database and routing consultation and management services for the NSFNET, whereas ANS operated the backbone routers and a Network Operation Center (NOC).

By 1991, data traffic had increased tremendously, which necessitated upgrading the NSFNET's backbone network service to T3 (45 Mbps) links. Figure 1-3 illustrates the original NSFNET with respect to the location of its core and regional backbones.

Figure 1-3 *The NSFNET-Based Internet Environment*

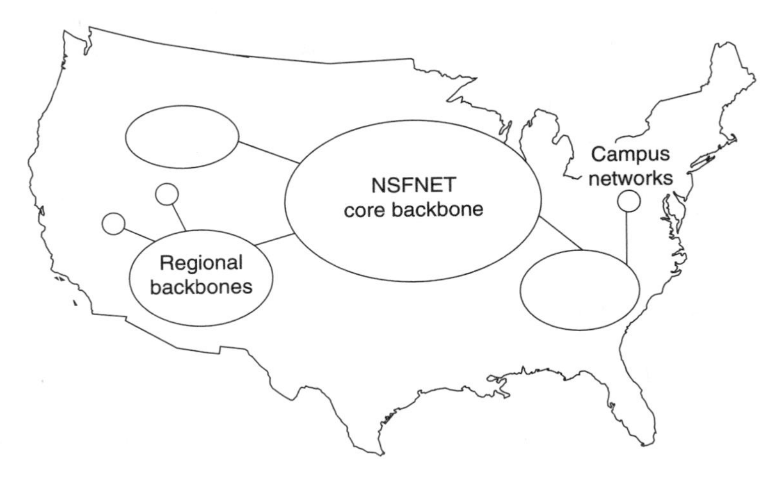

As late as the early 1990s, the NSFNET was still reserved for research and education applications, and government agency backbones were reserved for mission-oriented purposes. These and other emerging networks were feeling new pressures as different agencies needed to interconnect with one another. Commercial and general-purpose interests were clamoring for network access, and Internet service providers (ISPs) were emerging to accommodate those interests, defining an entirely new industry in the process. Networks in places other than the U.S. had developed, along with international connections. As the various new and existing entities pursued their goals, the complexity of connections and infrastructure grew.

In the United States, government agency networks interconnected at Federal Internet eXchange (FIX) points on both the east and west coasts. Commercial network organizations had formed the Commercial Internet eXchange (CIX) association, which built an interconnect point on the west coast. At the same time, ISPs around the world, particularly in Europe and Asia, had developed substantial infrastructures and connectivity.

To begin sorting out the growing complexity, Sprint was appointed by the NSFNET to be the International Connections Manager (ICM), responsible for providing connectivity between the U.S., European, and Asian networks. NSFNET was decommissioned in April 1995.

The Internet Today

The decommissioning of the NSFNET had to be done in specific stages to ensure continuous connectivity to institutions and government agencies that used to be connected to the regional networks. Today's Internet infrastructure is a move from a core network

(NSFNET) to a more distributed architecture operated by commercial providers such as UUNET, Qwest, Sprint, and thousands of others, connected via major network exchange points, as well as direct network interconnections. Figure 1-4 illustrates the general form of the Internet today.

Figure 1-4 *The General Structure of Today's Internet*

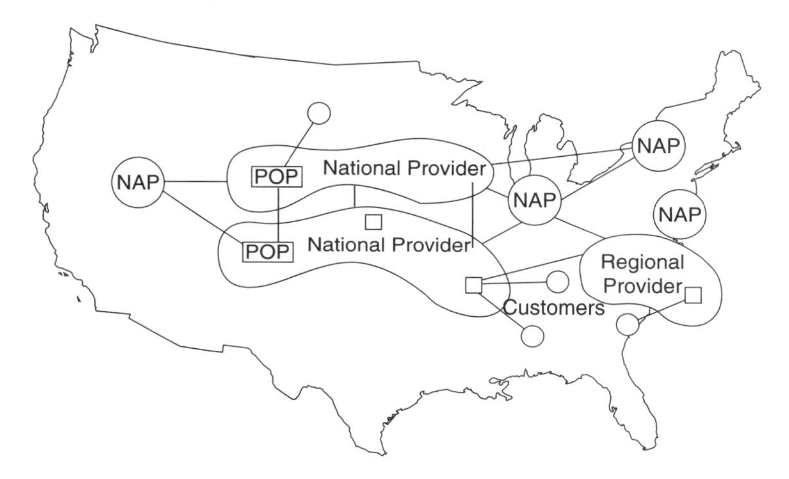

The contemporary backbone of the Internet is a collection of service providers that have connection points called POPs (points of presence) over multiple regions. Its collection of POPs and the infrastructure that interconnects them form a provider's network. Customers are connected to providers via access or hosting facilities in a service provider's POP. These customers can be service providers themselves. The prevalent service models employed by ISPs today are discussed in more detail in Chapter 2, "ISP Services and Characteristics."

Providers that have POPs throughout the U.S. are commonly referred to as *national providers*. Providers that cover specific regions, or *regional providers*, connect themselves to other providers at one or more points. To enable customers of one provider to reach customers connected to another provider, traffic is exchanged at public Network Access Points (NAPs) or via direct interconnections. The term ISP (Internet service provider) is commonly used to refer to anyone who provides Internet connectivity service, whether directly to the end user, or to other service providers. The term NSP (Network Service Provider) was traditionally used to refer to backbone network providers. However, NSP is now used much more loosely to refer to any service provider that has a presence at the NAPs and maintains a backbone network.

NSFNET Solicitations

NSF has supported data and research on networking needs since 1986. NSF also supported the goals of the High Performance Computing and Communications (HPCC) Program, which promoted leading-edge research and science programs. The National Research and Education Network (NREN) Program, which is a subdivision of the HPCC Program, called for gigabit-per-second (Gbps) networking for research and education to be in place by the mid-1990s. All these requirements, in addition to the April 1995 expiration deadline for the Cooperative Agreement for NSFNET Backbone Network Services, led NSF to solicit for NSFNET services.

As discussed, the first NSF solicitation, in 1987, led to the NSFNET backbone upgrade to T3 links by the end of 1993. In 1992, NSF wanted to develop a follow-up solicitation that would accommodate and promote the role of commercial service providers and that would lay down the structure of a new and more robust Internet model. At the same time, NSF would step back from the actual operation of the core network and focus on research aspects and initiatives. The final NSF solicitation (NSF 93-52) was issued in May 1993.

The final solicitation included four separate projects for which proposals were invited:

- Creating a set of NAPs where major providers interconnect their networks and exchange traffic.
- Implementing a Routing Arbiter (RA) project to facilitate the exchange of policies and addressing of multiple providers connected to the NAPs.
- Finding a provider of a high-speed Backbone Network Service (vBNS) for educational and government purposes.
- Transitioning existing and realigned networks to support interregional connectivity by connecting to NSPs that are connected to NAPs, or by directly connecting to NAPs themselves. Any NSP selected for this purpose must connect to at least three of the NAPs.

Each of these solicitations is covered as a major section in this chapter.

Network Access Points

The solicitation for the NSF project was to invite proposals from companies to implement and manage a specific number of NAPs where the vBNS and other appropriate networks could interconnect. These NAPs needed to enable regional networks, network service providers, and the U.S. research and education community to connect and exchange traffic with one another. They needed to provide for interconnection of networks in an environment that was not subject to the NSF Acceptable Usage Policy, a policy that was originally put in place to restrict the use of the Internet to research and education. Thus, general usage, including commercial usage, could go through the NAPs as well.

What Is a NAP?

In NSF terms, a *NAP* is a high-speed switch or network of switches to which a number of routers can be connected for the purpose of traffic exchange. NAPs must operate at speeds of at least 100 Mbps and must be able to be upgraded as required by demand and usage. The NAP could be as simple as an FDDI switch (100 Mbps) or an ATM switch (usually 45+ Mbps) passing traffic from one provider to another.

The concept of the NAP was built on the FIX and the CIX, which were built around FDDI rings with attached networks operating at speeds of up to 45 Mbps.

The traffic on the NAP was not restricted to that which is in support of research and education. Networks connected to a NAP were permitted to exchange traffic without violating the usage policies of any other networks interconnected via the NAP.

There were four NSF-awarded NAPs:

- Sprint NAP—Pennsauken, N.J.
- PacBell NAP—San Francisco, Calif.
- Ameritech Advanced Data Services (AADS) NAP—Chicago, Ill.
- MFS Datanet (MAE-East) NAP—Washington, D.C.

The NSFNET backbone service was connected to the Sprint NAP on September 13, 1994. It was connected to the PacBell and Ameritech NAPs in mid-October 1994 and early January 1995, respectively. The NSFNET backbone service was connected to the collocated MAE-East FDDI offered by MFS (now MCI Worldcom) on March 22, 1995.

Networks attaching to NAPs had to operate at speeds commensurate with the speed of attached networks (1.5 Mbps or higher) and had to be upgradable as required by demand, usage, and program goals. NSF-awarded NAPs were required to be capable of switching both IP and CLNP (Connectionless Networking Protocol). The requirements to switch CLNP packets and to implement IDRP-based procedures (Inter-Domain Routing Protocol, ISO OSI Exterior Gateway Protocol) could be waived, depending on the overall level of service provided by the NAP.

NAP Manager Solicitation

A NAP manager was appointed to each NAP with duties that included the following:

- Establish and maintain the specified NAP for connecting to vBNS and other appropriate networks.
- Establish policies and fees for service providers that want to connect to the NAP.
- Propose NAP locations subject to given general geographical locations.

- Propose and establish procedures to work with personnel from other NAPs, the Routing Arbiter (RA), the vBNS provider, and regional and other attached networks to resolve problems and to support end-to-end quality of service (QoS) for network users.
- Develop reliability and security standards for the NAPs, as well as accompanying procedures to ensure that the standards are met.
- Specify and provide appropriate NAP accounting and statistics collection and reporting capabilities.
- Specify appropriate physical access procedures to the NAP facilities for authorized personnel of connecting networks and ensure that these procedures are carried out.

Federal Internet eXchange

During the early phases of the transition from ARPANET to the NSFNET backbone, FIX-East (College Park, Md.) and FIX-West (NASA AMES, Mountain View, Calif.) were created to provide interconnectivity. They quickly became important interconnection points for exchanging information between research, education, and government networks. However, the FIX policy folks weren't very keen on the idea of allowing commercial data to be exchanged at these facilities. Consequently, the Commercial Internet eXchange (CIX) was created.

FIX-East was decommissioned in 1996. FIX-West is still used for interconnection of federal networks.

Commercial Internet eXchange

The CIX (pronounced "kicks") is a nonprofit trade association of Public Data Internetwork service providers that promotes and encourages the development of the public data communications internetworking service industry in both national and international markets. The creation of CIX was a direct result of the seeming unwillingness of the FIX operators to support nonfederal networks. Beyond just providing connectivity to commercial Internet service providers, the CIX also provided a neutral forum to exchange ideas, information, and experimental projects among suppliers of internetworking services. Here are some benefits CIX provided to its members:

- A neutral forum to develop consensus on legislative and political issues.
- A fundamental agreement for all CIX members to interconnect with one another. No restrictions exist in the type of traffic that can be exchanged between member networks.
- Access to all CIX member networks, greatly increasing the correspondence, files, databases, and information services available to them. Users gain a global reach in networking, increasing the value of their network connection.

Although today, in comparison to the larger NAPS, CIX plays a minor role in the Internet from a physical connectivity perspective, the coordination of legislative issues and the interconnection policy definition that it facilitated early on were clearly of great value.

Additional information on the CIX can be found on their Web server at www.cix.org.

Current Physical Configurations at the NAP

The physical configuration of today's NAP is a mixture of FDDI, ATM, and Ethernet (Ethernet, Fast Ethernet, and Gigabit Ethernet) switches. Access methods range from FDDI and Gigabit Ethernet to DS3, OC3, and OC12 ATM. Figure 1-5 shows a possible configuration, based on some contemporary NAPs. Typically, the service provider manages routers collocated in NAP facilities. The NAP manager defines configurations, policies, and fees.

Figure 1-5 *Typical NAP Physical Infrastructure*

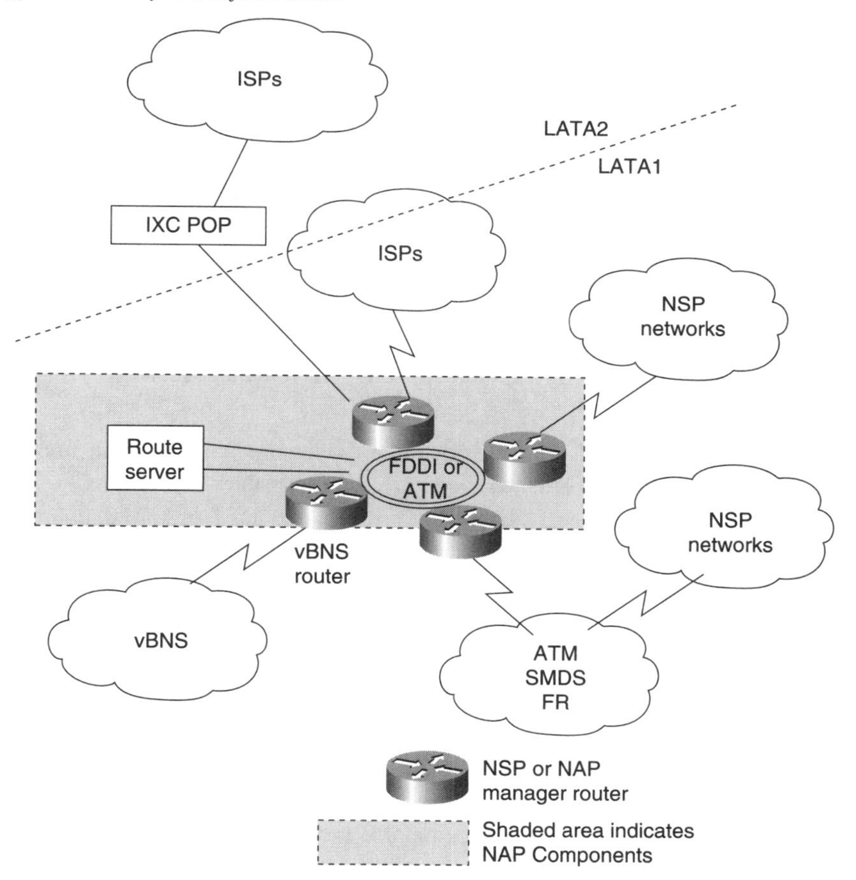

An Alternative to NAPs: Direct Interconnections

As the Internet continues to grow, the enormous amount of traffic exchanged between large networks is becoming greater than many NAPs can scale to support. Capacity issues at the NAPs often result in data loss and instability. In addition, large private networks and ISPs sometimes are reluctant to rely on seemingly less-interested third party NAP managers to resolve service-affecting issues and provision additional capacity. For these reasons, over the last few years an alternative to NAPs for interconnecting service provider networks has evolved—*direct interconnections*.

The idea behind direct interconnections is simple. By provisioning links directly between networks and avoiding NAPs altogether, service providers can decrease provisioning lead times, increase reliability, and scale interconnection capacity considerably. Link bandwidth and locations of direct interconnections usually are negotiated bilaterally, on peer-by-peer basis. Direct interconnections usually aren't pursued between two networks until one or both parties involved can realize the economic incentives associated with avoiding the NAPs.

Not only do direct interconnections provide additional bandwidth between the interconnecting networks, they also alleviate congestion and free up bandwidth at the NAPs, consequently improving throughput and performance there as well. Also, because market drivers usually result in large network topologies that closely mirror one another, the closeness of network topologies and interconnection requirements allows direct interconnections to provide a better geographical distribution for data exchange than do the NAPs. Direct interconnections can provide an architecture that will more optimally regionalize traffic exchange between networks, thereby increasing network throughput while decreasing latency between a given set of hosts.

Smaller regional providers and new service providers probably will not immediately be in a position to engage in direct interconnection agreements with larger providers, for a couple of reasons:

- The costs associated with existing providers maintaining large amounts of infrastructure in order to accommodate direct interconnections
- The increase in fees associated with the number of circuit facilities required from LECs (local exchange carriers) and IXCs (interexchange carriers)

Fortunately, most large providers continue to maintain a presence at the NAPs, utilizing NAP connections to exchange traffic with networks that cannot yet justify the additional costs of interconnecting directly.

Routing Arbiter Project

Another project for which the NSF solicited services is the Routing Arbiter (RA) project[4], which is charged with providing equitable treatment of the various network service providers with regard to routing administration. The RA provides for a common database of route information to promote stability and manageability of networks.

Multiple providers connecting to the NAP created a scalability issue because each provider had to peer with all other providers to exchange routing and policy information. The RA project was developed to reduce the requirement for a full peering mesh between all the providers. Instead of peering among each other, providers can peer with a central system called a route server. The route server would maintain a database of all information needed for providers to set their routing policies. Figure 1-6 shows the physical connectivity and logical peering between a route server and various service providers.

Figure 1-6 *Route Server Handling of Routing Updates in Relation to Traffic Routing*

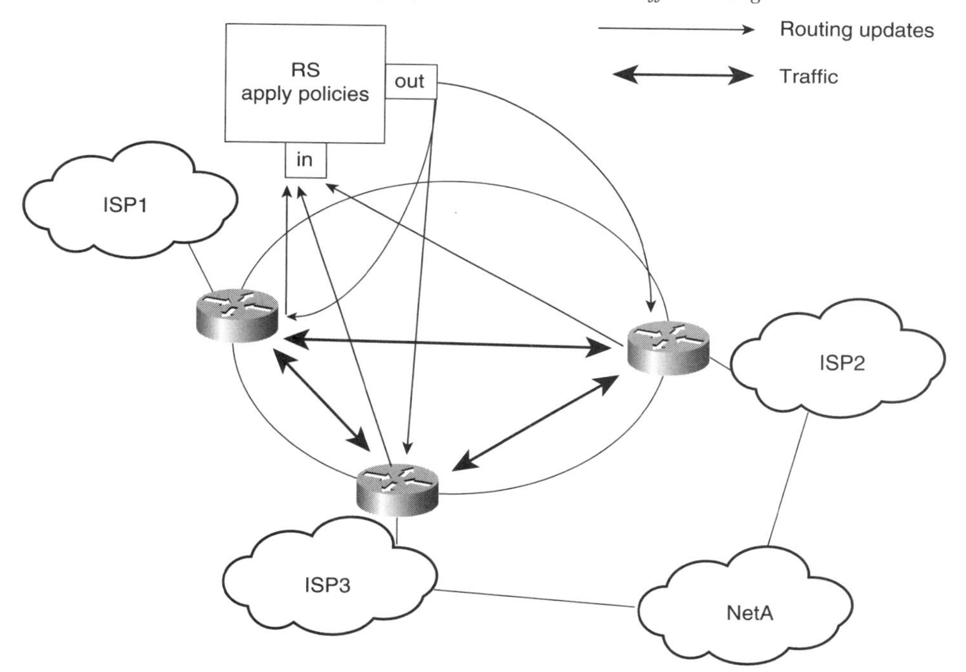

The following are the major tasks of the RA per the NSF proposal:

- Promote Internet routing stability and manageability. The route server accomplishes much of this task by reducing the number of BGP peers a router is required to maintain and by applying policy before passing routing information on to the peer, thereby alleviating the processing resources required by the router to filter the routing information.

- Establish and maintain network topology databases by such means as exchanging routing information with and dynamically updating routing information from the attached autonomous systems (ASs) using standard Exterior Gateway Protocols (EGPs), such as BGP (Border Gateway Protocol) and IDRP (support for IP and CLNP).
- Propose and establish procedures to work with personnel from the NAP manager(s), the vBNS provider, and regional and other attached networks to resolve problems and to support end-to-end connectivity and QoS for network users.
- Develop advanced routing technologies such as type of service and precedence routing, multicasting, bandwidth on demand, and bandwidth allocation services, in cooperation with the global Internet community.
- Provide for simplified routing strategies, such as default routing for attached networks.
- Promote distributed operation and management of the Internet.

The RA project was a joint effort of Merit Network, Inc., the University of Southern California Information Sciences Institute (USC ISI)[5], Cisco systems (as a subcontractor to ISI), and the University of Michigan ROC (as a subcontractor to Merit).

The RA service was comprised of four projects:

- **Route server (RS)**—The RS can be as simple as a Sun workstation deployed at each NAP. The route server exchanges only routing information with the service provider routers attached to the NAP. Individual routing policy requirements (RIPE 181)[6] for each provider are maintained. The route server itself does not forward packets or perform any switching function between service providers.

  The server facilitates interconnection between ISPs by gathering routing information from each ISP's predefined rules and policies and then redistributing the processed routing information to each ISP. This process saves each router from having to peer with every other router, thus decreasing the number of peers from (n–1) to 1, where n is the number of routers.

  In this configuration, the routers of the different providers concentrate on switching the traffic between one another and do relatively little filtering and policy application.
- **Network Management System**—This software monitors the performance of the RS. *Distributed rovers* run at each RS and collect information such as performance statistics. The central network management station (CNMS) at the Merit Routing Operations Center queries the rovers and processes the information.
- **Routing Arbiter Database (RADB)**[7]—This is one of several routing databases collectively known as the Internet Routing Registry (IRR). Policy routing in the RADB is expressed by using RIPE-181 syntax, developed by the RIPE Network

Coordination Center (RCC). The RADB was developed in dual mode with the Policy Routing Database (PRDB). The PRDB had been used to configure the NSFNET's backbone routers since 1986. With the introduction of the RIPE-181 language, which provided better functionality in recording global routing policies, the PRDB was retired in 1995 for full RADB functionality.

- **Routing engineering team**—This team works with the network providers to set up peering and to resolve network problems at the NAP. The Routing Engineering Team provides consultation on routing strategies, addressing plans, and other routing-related issues.

In practice, route servers play an important security role by verifying the authenticity of routing updates from participants, disallowing bogus routing information to be advertised to peers.

As you have already seen, the main parts of the Routing Arbiter concept are the route server and the RADB. The practical and administrative goals of the RADB apply mainly to service providers connecting to the NAP. Configuring the correct information in the RADB is essential in setting the required routing policies.

In the first edition of this book, Appendix A was devoted entirely to coverage of RIPE-181. However, most IRRs currently are transitioning to a new policy specification language, RPSL (Routing Policy Specification Language). RPSL is the next-generation language for defining policy in the IRRs. It was developed by the Internet Engineering Task Force (IETF)[8] Routing Policy System (RPS) Working Group. It was defined in RFC 2622 and explained in RFC 2650, with leadership from USC ISI. Because RPSL will quickly make RIPE-181 obsolete, Appendix A now includes information on RPSL from RFC 2650, "Using RPSL in Practice."

There are many reasons for the transition from RIPE-181 to RPSL, most of which were observed only after a considerable amount of deployment experience with the RIPE-181 language. RPSL enhancements include scalability of policy syntax and authentication mechanisms that promote integrity of addressing and policy information between network operators. For more information on RPSL, see Appendix A.

As a customer of a service provider, you may never have to configure RIPE-181 or RPSL. However, you should understand the reasoning behind the policies being defined with these languages. As you will see in this book, policies are the basis of routing architectures and behaviors.

On the other hand, the concept of a route server and peering with centralized routers is not restricted to providers at NAPs. It could be implemented in any architecture that needs it. As part of the implementation section of this book, the route server concept will come up as a means of creating a one-to-many relationship between peers. It's also worth noting that providers that are present at NAPs are not required to peer via the route servers, and providers that connect via direct interconnections are highly unlikely to use the route servers at all.

In March 1998, Merit successfully completed work on the Routing Arbiter project. Today, Merit and its RA project partner, the University of Southern California Information Sciences Institute, continue to carry out research in the areas surrounding the RA project.

Following recommendations from NSF, Merit completed work with ISI to transition the RA route servers to Route Server Next Generation (RSng), which commercialized the use of the Route Server services from Merit, allowing exchange point operators to purchase their services. NSF also recommended that, concurrent with commercialization of the router server services, NAP operations be commercialized, stating that they've accomplished the goal of establishing that ISPs can cooperate in a competitive market.

In 1997, Merit began NSF-funded work on Internet Performance Measurement and Analysis (IPMA). The goal of IPMA is to study the performance of networks and networking protocols through the collection and analysis of routing and network performance statistics in order to promote Internet stability. IPMA also develops tools to help facilitate network operations and engineering functions.

North American Network Operators Group (NANOG)[9] was initially funded by NSF during both the NSFNET and early RA days and originated from the NSFNET's regional technical meetings. It's now funded independently through conference registration fees, with Merit acting as the organizer. NANOG provides a forum for the discussion of technical issues associated with operating networks in North America.

Databases and tools created through the RADB projects are widely used by ISPs and have become an embedded part of the Internet today.

In order to provide stability and security to the global Internet routing scheme, there is still much work to be done in the interdomain policy specification and application space. Projects such as the RA provide a great deal of insight as to how Internet network architects should approach the issue.

The Very High-Speed Backbone Network Service

The very high-speed Backbone Network Service (vBNS)[10] project was created to provide a specialized backbone service for the high-performance computing users of the major government-supported SuperComputer Centers (SCCs) and for the research community.

On April 24, 1995, MCI and NSF announced the launch of the vBNS. MCI's duties include the following:

- Establish and maintain a 155 Mbps or higher transit network that switches IP and CLNP and connects to all NSFNET-funded NAPs.
- Establish a set of metrics to monitor and characterize network performance.
- Subscribe to the policies of the NAP and RA managers.
- Provide for multimedia services.

- Participate in the enhancement of advanced routing technologies and propose enhancements in both speed and quality of service that are consistent with NSF customer requirements.

The five-year, $50 million agreement between MCI and NSFNET tied together NSF's five major high-performance communications centers:

- Cornell Theory Center (CTC) in Ithaca, N.Y.
- National Center for Atmospheric Research (NCAR) in Boulder, Col.
- National Center for SuperComputing Applications (NCSA) at the University of Illinois at Champaign
- Pittsburgh SuperComputing Center (PSC)
- San Diego SuperComputing Center (SDSC)

The vBNS has been referred to as the research and development lab for the 21st century. The use of advanced switching and fiber-optic transmission technologies, Asynchronous Transfer Mode (ATM), and Synchronous Optical Network (SONET), enable very high-speed, high-capacity voice and video signals to be integrated.

The NSF has already authorized the use of the vBNS for "meritorious" high-bandwidth applications, such as supercomputer modeling at NCAR to understand how and where icing occurs on aircraft. Other applications at NCSA consist of building computational models to simulate the working of biological membranes and to show how cholesterol inserts itself into membranes.

The vBNS is accessible to select application sites through four NAPs in New York, San Francisco, Chicago, and Washington, D.C. Figure 1-7 shows the geographical relationships between the centers and NAPs. The vBNS is mainly composed of OC12 links connected via high-end routers, such as those supplied by Juniper Networks and Cisco Systems. The first OC48c trunk and Juniper routers were commissioned in January 1999.

Figure 1-7 *vBNS Backbone Network Map*

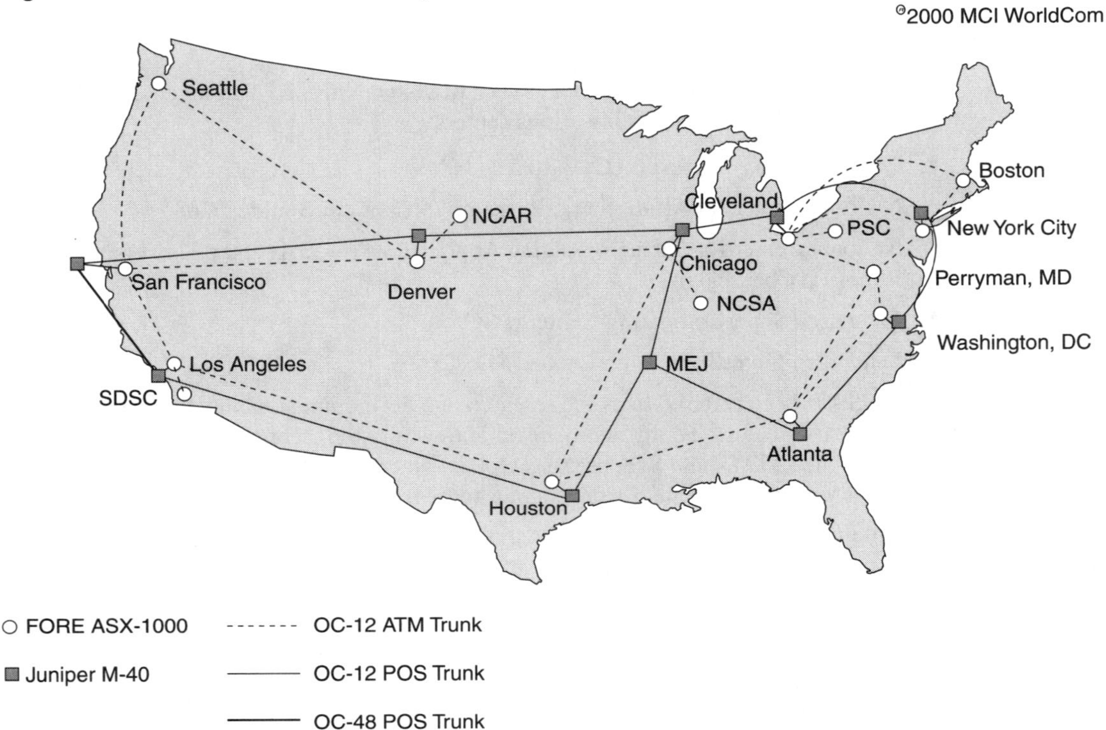

This material is based upon work supported by the National Science Foundation under Grant Number NCR 9321047. Any opinions, findings, conclusions, or recommendations expressed in this material are those of the author(s) and do not necessarily reflect the views of the National Science Foundation.

The vBNS is a specialized network that emerged due to the continuing need for high-speed connections between members of the research and development community, one of the main charters of the NSFNET. Although the vBNS does not have any bearing on global routing behavior, insight provided by preproduction deployment of new technologies does. The preceding brief overview is meant to give you a background on how NSFNET covered all its bases before being decommissioned in 1995.

Today, the vBNS hosts four SCCs and more than 80 universities at access speeds ranging from DS3 to OC12. Users have deployed IPv6, native multicast services, and MPLS. With April 2000 marking the expiration of the five-year agreement between NSF and MCI WorldCom, current plans are to continue post-April 2000 operation of the vBNS. Funding and support will be made possible by the commercialization of services without an Acceptable Use Policy (AUP), as well by creating a broader target community for services.

Because of its advanced research in QoS and traffic engineering, today it's more commonly referred to as the *very high-performance Backbone Network Service*. The vBNS continues the tradition begun by NSFNET in this field.

Transitioning the Regional Networks from the NSFNET

As part of the NSFNET solicitation for transitioning to the new Internet architecture, NSF requested that the regional networks (also called *mid-level networks*) start transitioning their connections from the NSFNET backbones to other providers.

Regional networks have been a part of the NSFNET since its creation and have played a major role in the network connectivity of the research and education community. Regional network providers (RNPs) connect a broad base of client/member organizations (such as universities), providing them with multiple networking services and with Inter-Regional Connectivity (IRC).

Here are the anticipated duties of the RNPs per the NSF 93-52 program solicitation:

- Provide for interregional connectivity by such means as connecting to NSPs that are connected to NAPs and/or by connecting to NAPs directly and making inter-NAP connectivity arrangements with one or more NSPs.
- Provide for innovative network information services for client/member organizations in cooperation with the InterNIC and the NSFNET Information Services Manager.
- Propose and establish procedures to work with personnel from the NAP manager(s), the RA, the vBNS provider, and other regional and attached networks to resolve problems and to support end-to-end connectivity and quality of service for network users.
- Provide services that promote broadening the base of network users within the research and communications community.
- Provide for (possibly in cooperation with an NSP) high-bandwidth connections for client/member institutions that have meritorious high-bandwidth applications.
- Provide for network connections to client/member organizations.

In the process of moving the regional networks from the NSFNET to the new ISP connections, the NSF suggested that they be connected either directly to the NAPs or to providers connected to the NAPs. During the transition, NSF supported, for one year, connection fees that would decrease and eventually cease (after the first term of the NAP Manager/RA Cooperative Agreement, which shall be no more than four years).

Table 1-1 lists some of the old NSFNET regional providers and their new respective regional providers under the current Internet environment. As you can see, most of the regional providers have shifted to either MCInet (now Cable & Wireless) or Sprintlink. Moving the regional providers to the new Internet architecture in time for the April 1995 deadline was one of the major milestones that NSFNET had to achieve.

Table 1-1 *Sample Regional Transitions to New Providers*

Old Regional Network	New Internet Provider
Argone	CICnet
BARRnet	MCInet
CA*net	MCInet
CERFnet	CERFnet
CICnet	MCInet
Cornell Theory Center	MCInet
CSUnet	MCInet
DARPA	ANSnet
JvNCnet	MCInet
MOREnet	Sprintlink
NEARnet	MCInet
NevadaNet	Sprintlink
SESQUINET	MCInet
SURAnet	MCInet
THEnet	MCInet
Westnet	Sprintlink

NSF Solicits NIS Managers

In addition to the four main projects relating to the architectural aspects of the new Internet, NSF recognized that information services would be a critical component in the even more widespread, freewheeling network. As a result, a solicitation for one or more Network Information Services (NIS) managers for the NSFNET was proposed. This solicitation invited proposals for the following:

- To extend and coordinate directory and database and information and services.
- To provide registration services for nonmilitary Internet networks. The Defense Information Systems Agency Network Information Center (DISA NIC) will continue to provide for the registration of military networks.

At the time of the solicitation, the domestic, nonmilitary portion of the Internet included the NSFNET and other federally sponsored networks such as NASA Science Internet (NSI) and Energy Sciences Network (ESnet). All these networks, as well as some other networks on the Internet, were related to the National Research and Education Network (NREN), which was defined in the president's fiscal 1992 budget. The NSF solicitations for database services, information services, and registration services were needed to help the evolution of the NSFNET and the development of NREN.

Network Information Services

At the time of the proposal, certain network information services were being offered by a variety of providers. Some of these services included the following:

- End-user information services were provided by NSF Network Services Center (NNSC), operated by Bolt, Beranek, and Newman (BBN). Other NSFNET end-user services were provided by campus-level computing and networking organizations.
- Information services for various federal agency backbone networks were provided by the sponsoring agencies. NASA, for example, provided NSI information services.
- Internet registration services were provided by DISA NIC, operated by Government Services, Inc. (GSI).
- Information services for campus-level providers were provided by NSFNET mid-level network organizations.
- Information services for NSFNET mid-level network providers were provided by Merit, Inc.

Under the new solicitation, NIS managers should provide services to end-users and to campus and mid-level network service providers. They should also coordinate with other mid-level and network organizations, such as Merit, Inc.

Creation of the InterNIC

In response to NSF's solicitation for NIS managers, in January 1993 the InterNIC was established as a collaborative project among AT&T, General Atomics, and Network Solutions, Inc.[11] It was to be supported by three five-year cooperative agreements with the NSF. During the second-year performance review, funding by the NSF to General Atomics stopped. AT&T was awarded the Database and Directory Services, and Network Solutions was awarded the Registration and NIC Support Services.

Directory and Database Services

The implementation of this service should utilize distributed database and other advanced technologies. The NIS manager could coordinate this role with respect to other organizations that have created and maintained relevant directories and databases. AT&T was providing the following services under the NSF agreement:

- Directory services (white pages):

  This provides access to Internet White Pages information using X.500, WHOIS, and netfind systems.

  The X.500 directory standard enables the creation of a single worldwide directory of information about various objects of interest, such as information about people.

  The WHOIS lookup service provides unified access to three Internet WHOIS servers for person and organization queries. It searches the InterNIC directory and Database Services server for nonmilitary domain and non-Point-of-Contact data. The search for MIL (military) domain data is done via the DISA NIC server, and the POC data is done via the InterNIC Registration Services server.

  Netfind is a simple Internet white pages directory search facility. Given the name of an Internet user and a description of where the user works, the tool attempts to locate information about the user.

- Database services:

  This should include databases of communications documents such as Request For Comments (RFCs), Internet Drafts (IDs), IETF Meeting Minutes, IETF Steering Group (IESG) documents, and so on. The service could also contain databases maintained for other groups with a possible fee.

  AT&T also offered a database service listing of public databases, which contains information of interest to the Internet community.

- Directory of directories:

  This service points to other directories and databases, such as those listed previously. This is an index of pointers to resources, products, and services accessible through the Internet. It includes pointers to resources such as computing centers, network providers, information servers, white and yellow pages directories, library catalogs, and so on.

  As part of this service, AT&T stores a listing of information resources, including type, description, how to access the resource, and other attributes. Information providers are given access to update and add to the database. The information can be accessed via different methods, such as Telnet, ftp, e-mail, and World Wide Web.

Registration Services

The NIS manager was required to act in accordance with RFC 1174, which states the following:

> The Internet system has employed a central Internet Assigned Numbers Authority (IANA)[12] for the allocation and assignment of various numeric identifiers needed for the operation of the Internet. The IANA function is performed by the University of Southern California's Information Sciences Institute. The IANA has the discretionary authority to delegate portions of this responsibility and, with respect to numeric network and autonomous system identifiers, has lodged this responsibility with an Internet Registry (IR).

The NIS manager would become either the IR or a delegate registry authorized by the IR. The Internet registration services included the following:

- Network number assignment
- Autonomous system number assignment
- Domain name registration
- Domain name server registrations

From 1993 to 1998, NSI was the only provider of domain name registration services for the .com, .net, and .org top-level domains, following the Cooperative Agreement with the U.S. Government. The agreement was amended in 1998, and NSI is now working to develop software supporting a "Shared Registration System" for these top-level domains.

Today the U.S. Government has begun to privatize the management of domain name space in hopes of introducing competition in order to benefit the global Internet community.

The Internet Corporation for Assigned Names and Numbers (ICANN)[13] is responsible for overseeing this process. ICANN is responsible for the registrar accreditation process. It also assumes responsibility for certain Internet domain name system functions, as set forth by the U.S. Government. ICANN is a nonprofit international organization.

NIC Support Services

The original solicitation for "Information Services" was granted to General Atomics in April 1993 and was taken away in February 1995. At that time, NSI took over the proposal, and it was renamed NIC Support Services.

The goal of the service was to provide a forum for the research and education community, Network Information Centers (NICs) staff, and the academic Internet community, within which the responsibilities of the InterNIC may be defined.

Other Internet Registries

With the privatization of registration services came a change in the way IP space and AS numbers are allocated. Currently, three Regional Internet Registries (RIRs) provide registration services to all regions around the globe: American Registry for Internet Numbers (ARIN), Reseaux IP Europeens Network Coordination Center (RIPE NCC), and Asian Pacific Network Information Center (APNIC).

ARIN

In late 1997, IANA transferred responsibility for IP number administration from Network Solutions, Inc. to ARIN[14]. ARIN officially opened for operation on October 22, 1997.

ARIN is responsible for the allocation of Internet Protocol (IP) numbers in the following geographical areas:

- North America
- South America
- The Caribbean
- Sub-Saharan Africa

ARIN currently manages allocation and registration services for IP numbers, AS numbers, IN-ADDR.ARPA, and IP6.INT inverse mappings. They also provide routing registry services where network operators can register, maintain, and retrieve router configuration information and WHOIS services to view specific information associated with a given allocation.

ARIN is a nonprofit organization. It recovers the costs of administration and management of IP numbers by charging fees for registration, transfer, maintenance, and membership.

RIPE NCC

Created in 1989, RIPE[15] is a collaborative organization that consists of European Internet service providers. It aims to provide the necessary administration and coordination to enable the operation of the European Internet. RIPE acts as an RIR for Europe and surrounding areas.

RIPE distributes Internet numbers, coordinates the Domain Name System (DNS), and maintains a network management database with information on IP networks, DNS and IP routing policies, and contact information. They also provide an Internet software repository, a RIPE document store, routing registry services, and interactive information services.

Like ARIN, RIPE is a nonprofit organization and obtains funding from fees associated with its services.

APNIC

APNIC[16] was created in 1993 and provides registration services similar to ARIN. APNIC provides these services to the Asian Pacific region, including 62 countries/regions in South and Central Asia, Southeast Asia, Indochina, and Oceania.

APNIC is currently not involved in the administration of DNS services, although it does work with others in the region involved with these services. APNIC provides other services, including training and education, policy development, and regional networking activities. Notably, APNIC helped found APRICOT (Asian Pacific Regional Internet Conference on Operational Technologies), which is now the premier regional forum for network operators and policy makers.

Internet Routing Registries

With the creation of a new breed of ISPs that want to interconnect with one another, offering the required connectivity while maintaining flexibility and control has become more challenging. Each provider has a set of rules, or policies, that describe what to accept and what to advertise to all other neighboring networks. Sample policies include determining route filtering from a particular ISP and choosing a particular path to a specific destination. The potential for various policies from interconnected providers to conflict with and contradict one another is enormous.

Internet Routing Registries (IRRs) also serve as a public database for accessing routing contact information used for coordination and troubleshooting.

To address these challenges, a neutral routing registry (RR) for each global domain had to be created. Each RR maintains a database of routing policies created and updated by each service provider. The collection of these different databases is known as the Internet Routing Registry (IRR).

The role of the RR is not to determine policies, but rather to act as a repository for routing policy and administration information. This should provide a globally consistent view of all policies used by all providers all over the globe. A large number of network operators use routing information obtained from the routing registries to dynamically generate routing policies.

Autonomous systems (ASs) use Exterior Gateway Protocols (EGPs) such as BGP to work with one another. In complex environments, there should be a formal way of describing and communicating policies between different ASs. Maintaining a huge database containing all registered policies for the whole world would be cumbersome and difficult. This is why a more distributed approach was created. Each RR maintains its own database and must coordinate extensively to achieve consistency between the different databases. Here are some of the different IRR databases in existence today:

- RIPE Routing Registry (European Internet service providers)
- Cable & Wireless Routing Registry (C&W customers)

- CA*net Routing Registry (CA*net customers)
- JPRR Routing Registry (Japanese Internet service providers)
- Routing Arbiter Database (public)
- ARIN Routing Registry (public)

Each of the preceding registries serves a specific service provider's customer base, with the exception of the Routing Arbiter Database (RADB) and ARIN, which provide registration services to anyone. As mentioned earlier, the RADB is part of the Routing Arbiter project.

Because of the flexibility and benefits of maintaining a local registry, other companies such as Qwest, Level(3), and Verio have developed RRs as well.

The Once and Future Internet

Surprisingly enough, although commercialization of the Internet has resulted in a phenomenal rate of growth over the past 10 years, it hasn't hindered innovation. Instead, it has inspired it. Development of new technologies by the commercial sector, as well as research and educational organizations, is occurring at an astounding rate. New technologies can no longer be immediately deployed in the now "production" Internet; they need to be thoroughly debugged and optimized for realistic conditions. Testbeds were created for early adoption of new technologies.

Next-Generation Internet Initiative

The federally funded Next-Generation Internet (NGI) Initiative[17] is a multiagency U.S. federal research and development program that is developing advanced network technologies and revolutionary applications and demonstrating these capabilities on testbeds that are 100 to 1,000 times faster end-to-end than today's Internet.

The NGI initiative began October 1, 1997, with the following participating agencies:

- DARPA (Defense Advanced Research Projects Agency)
- DoE (Department of Energy)
- NASA (National Aeronautics and Space Administration)
- NIH (National Institute of Health)
- NIST (National Institute of Standards and Technology)
- NSF (National Science Foundation)

The NGI initiative is managed by individual agency program managers and is coordinated by the Large-Scale Networking Working Group of the Subcommittee on Computing, Information, and Communications (CIC) R&D of the White House National Science and Technology Council's Committee on Technology.

NGI goals include the following:

- Conduct R&D in advanced end-to-end networking technologies
- Establish and operate two testbeds
- Conduct R&D in revolutionary applications

Conduct R&D in Advanced End-to-End Networking Technologies

The NGI is fostering early deployment of new technologies that will one day be an integral part of the commercial Internet. These technologies are focused on enhancing many aspects of computer networking, to include the following:

- Reliability
- Robustness
- Security
- Quality of service/differentiation of service (including multicasting and video)
- Network management (including allocation and sharing of bandwidth)

Establish and Operate Two Testbeds

Ensuring availability of capable testbeds is key to accomplishing the goals of the NGI. Two testbeds, referred to loosely as the "100x" testbed and the "1000x" testbed, will be developed for this purpose.

The "100x" testbed will connect at least 100 sites—universities, federal research institutions, and other research partners—at speeds 100 times faster end-to-end than today's Internet.

The testbed will be built on the following federal networks:

- NSF's very high-speed Backbone Network Service (vBNS)
- NASA's Research and Educational Network (NREN)
- DoD's Defense Research and Education Network (DREN)
- DoE's Energy Sciences network (ESnet)

The "1000x" testbed will connect about 10 sites with end-to-end performance at least 1,000 times faster than today's Internet. The "1000x" testbed will be built upon DARPA's SuperNet.

These testbeds will be used for system-scale testing of advanced technologies and services and for developing and testing advanced applications.

Conduct R&D in Revolutionary Applications

NGI research and development will focus on enabling applications and technologies such as these:

- Collaborative technologies
- Digital libraries
- Distributed computing
- Privacy and security
- Remote operation and simulation

It will also focus on disciplinary applications such as these:

- Basic science
- Crisis management
- Education
- The environment
- Federal information services
- Health care
- Manufacturing

Internet2

Internet2[18] is a project of the University Corporation for Advanced Internet Development (UCAID). It was announced in October 1996 by 34 research universities with a mission of helping to sustain U.S. leadership in development, deployment, and operation of next-generation network applications and infrastructure. The primary role of Internet2 is to provide focus on fostering the growth of advanced Internet applications and networking protocols that will strengthen the work of universities in their research and education roles. With the exponential growth of the Internet, commercial networks controlled by service providers are deploying bandwidth and technologies as rapidly as research and education networks. One of the primary goals of Internet2 is to re-create the leading-edge capabilities of testbed networks and then facilitate transfer of these technologies to the global Internet.

Internet2 is now a collaborative effort of more than 160 U.S. universities in partnership with more than 50 major corporations. UCAID's member universities and corporations fund Internet2. Many of the member institutions receive funding through competitively awarded grants from the NSF and other federal agencies participating in the NGI initiative. Funding is also made available through other initiatives such as the NSF's Knowledge and Distributed Intelligence (KDI) program.

Internet2's goal is not to replace the Internet, but rather to enhance it by making available technologies and experiences developed by Internet2 members. Member universities will still require commodity Internet connections from commercial service providers, and utilization of those connections will continue to grow.

Abilene

Abilene[19] is another project of UCAID. It's complementary to Internet2 in the sense that the main goal of Abilene is to provide a primary backbone network for the Internet2 project. UCAID, in partnership with Qwest Communications, Nortel Networks, and Cisco Systems, has developed the Abilene network. Abilene provides the high-performance interconnect services among the Internet2 regional aggregation points. The primarily OC48c (2.5 Gbps) POS (Packet Over SONET) Abilene network became operational in January 1999 and provides OC3 and OC12 access services.

Much like the vBNS, Abilene will continually explore emerging Internet technologies, but because of the importance of network stability, Abilene will develop a separate high-performance test network for support of applications that cannot yet be deployed on the leading-edge-but-stable Abilene network. Internet2 working groups are in the process of hashing out Abilene deployment details, focusing on native multicast services, optimizing routing configurations and policies, IPv6, and QoS. Abilene provides native multicast services and is planning deployment of IPv6 and QoS.

Figure 1-8 represents the current Abilene network.

Figure 1-8 *Abilene Network: Peering Map*

Looking Ahead

The decommissioning of the NSFNET in 1995 marked the beginning of a new era. The Internet today is a playground for thousands of providers competing for market share. Research networks such as Abilene and vBNS are struggling to stay ahead of the curve, as an evolving multibillion-dollar industry continues to exceed all expectations. For many businesses and organizations, connecting their networks to the global Internet is no longer a luxury, but a requirement for staying competitive.

The structure of the contemporary Internet has implications for service providers and their customers in terms of access speed, reliability, and cost of use. Here are some of the questions organizations that want to connect to the Internet should ask:

- Are potential providers (whether established or relatively new to the business) well versed in routing behaviors and architectures?
- How much do customers of providers need to know and do with respect to routing architectures?

- Do the customer and provider have a common definition of what constitutes a stable network?
- Is the bandwidth of the access connection the only thing customers need to worry about in order to have the "faster" Internet connection?

The next chapter is intended to help ISPs and their customers evaluate these questions in a basic way. Later chapters go into the details of routing architecture.

Although interdomain routing has been around for more than a decade, it is still new to everybody, and it continues to evolve every day. The rest of this book builds upon this chapter's overview of the structure of the Internet in explaining and demonstrating current routing practices.

Frequently Asked Questions

Q — *Are there other NAPs besides the four NSF-awarded NAPs?*

A — Yes. As connectivity needs to keep growing, more NAPs are being created. Many exchange points are spread over North America, Europe, Asia/Pacific, South America, Africa, and the Middle East.

Q — *If I am a customer of a provider, do I have to connect to a NAP?*

A — No. NAPs are mainly for interconnections between service providers. If you are a customer of a provider, your connection will be to the provider only. However, how your provider is connected to one or more NAPs, or via direct interconnections, can affect the quality of your service.

Q — *Is the function of the route server at the NAP to switch traffic between providers?*

A — No. The route server keeps a database of routing policies used by providers. Providers use the NAP physical media to exchange traffic directly between one another.

Q — *Do all providers that connect to a NAP have to peer with the route server?*

A — Although this is a recommended procedure, it is not a requirement, and most actually don't.

Q — *What is the difference between IRs and IRRs?*

A — Internet Registries (IRs) such as Network Solutions, Inc. are responsible for registration services such as registering Internet domain names. Internet Routing Registries (IRRs) such as RADB are responsible for maintaining databases of routing policies for service providers.

Q — *How are database services different from the Routing Arbiter Databases?*

A — Database services are part of the network information services. These databases include communication documents such as RFCs. The RADB is a database of routing policies.

References

[1]www.darpa.mil

[2]www.nsf.gov

[3]www.merit.edu

[4]www.ra.net

[5]www.isi.edu

[6]www.ietf.org/rfc/rfc1786.txt

[7]www.merit.edu

[8]www.ietf.org

[9]www.nanog.org

[10]www.vbns.net

[11]www.internic.net

[12]www.iana.org

[13]www.icann.org

[14]www.arin.net

[15]www.ripe.net

[16]www.apnic.net

[17]www.ngi.gov

[18]www.internet2.edu

[19]www.internet2.edu/abilene

This chapter covers the following key topics:

- **ISP services**—A basic categorization of Internet service providers in terms of physical access methods, basic services, and security options.
- **ISP service pricing**—An overview of issues that affect pricing of ISP services.
- **ISP backbone selection criteria**—Criteria for evaluating ISPs in terms of their network topology and traffic exchange agreements.
- **Demarcation point**—Distinguishing the provider's network, equipment, and responsibilities from those of the customer.

CHAPTER 2

ISP Services and Characteristics

Before we go deeper into the technical subject of interdomain routing, it is important for you to be familiar with some basic provider services and characteristics that affect the quality of Internet connections. Anyone who can offer Internet connectivity could claim to be a service provider; the term "service provider" covers everything from a provider with a multimillion-dollar backbone and infrastructure to a provider with a single router and access server in his garage.

Price should not be the main factor on which you base your decision to select an ISP. What you should really be concerned with are factors such as the provider's services, backbone design, fault tolerance, redundancy, stability, bottlenecks, provider/customer equipment arrangements, and so on.

Routing behaviors on the Internet are affected by how routing protocols and data traffic behave over an already established physical infrastructure. Good infrastructure design and maintenance are primary factors in achieving healthy routing on the Internet.

ISP Services

Different ISPs offer different services, depending on how big they are and the infrastructure of their networks. Mainly, providers can be categorized by their method of physical Internet access, the applications they provide to customers, and the security services they provide.

The following sections cover the service models that are most common throughout the Internet service provider market today. As you'll see, these services range from providing dial-up access via a telephone line in your home to data center hosting facilities where you collocate your equipment and obtain connectivity locally.

Dedicated Internet Access

Dedicated Internet access is commonly provided at speeds of 56 kbps or 64 kbps up to T1/E1 lines (1.5 and 2 Mbps, respectively) on the lower end and T3/E3 (45 and 34 Mbps, respectively) and OC3 (155 Mbps) on the higher end. Dedicated Internet access providers are also beginning to provide OC12 (622 Mbps) and even OC48 (2.5 Gbps) high-speed access services. Dedicated access connections are used when bandwidth utilization is predictable and the frequency of network access is high enough to justify a line's being up 24 hours a day. Of course, the trade-off for dedicated access is cost, which is usually higher than for other access methods.

Dedicated Internet access usually involves termination of the physical circuit on the CPE (customer premises equipment) device, as well as direct circuit termination on an IP router on the service provider side. Link layer protocols such as PPP or Cisco HDLC (a derivative of PPP) are used for signaling and frame transfer across the connection. Figure 2-1 illustrates a typical dedicated Internet access configuration.

Figure 2-1 *Dedicated Internet Access Configuration*

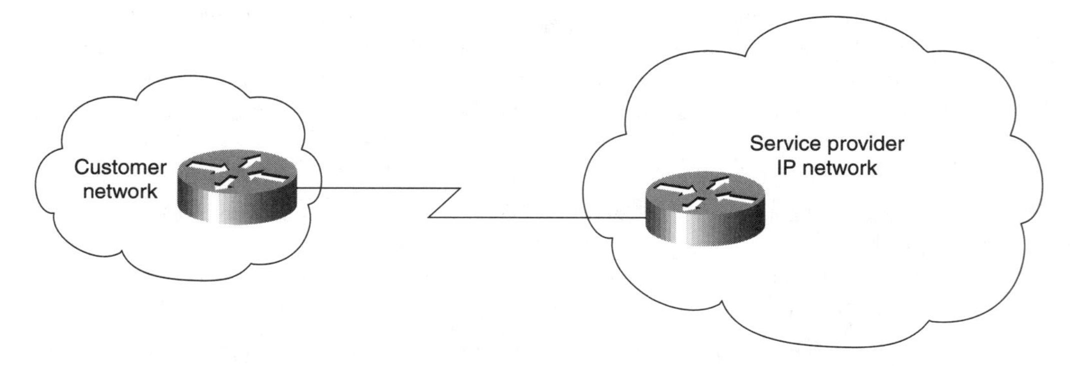

Frame Relay and ATM Internet Access

Frame Relay and ATM (Asynchronous Transfer Mode) connections are among the most economical ways for corporations to connect to the Internet. Purchasing dedicated access connections with sufficient capacity can be prohibitively expensive for many companies, in which case they might consider connecting via existing Frame Relay or ATM services. With these alternative access methods, corporations can purchase enough bandwidth to meet their existing needs while providing a practical expansion path as bandwidth requirements increase.

Because service providers can statistically multiplex data from multiple subscribers over a single link and then backhaul the data to an IP network, prices associated with Frame Relay and ATM Internet access services are usually much lower than dedicated access. Figure 2-2 illustrates a typical Frame Relay Internet access model.

Figure 2-2 *Frame Relay Internet Access*

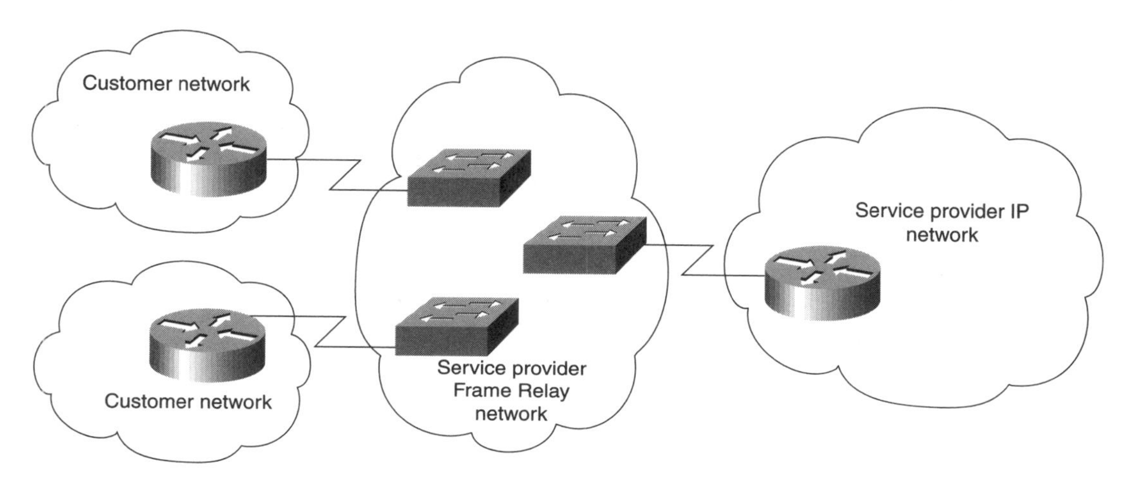

Frame Relay and ATM access services are particularly appealing to corporations that have existing Frame Relay and ATM networks. This is because service providers often provision access gateways from these networks to their IP networks, thereby requiring no additional infrastructure by the customer to accommodate the new connection.

Although Frame Relay, ATM, and dedicated Internet access all utilize the same underlying physical layer technologies, it's important to understand that ATM and Frame Relay services, in contrast to dedicated access, perform statistical multiplexing before providing access to the IP network. This statistical multiplexing is what allows service providers to perform an additional layer of service aggregation, thereby reducing the service's cost.

Understanding the amount of aggregation performed by the Frame Relay or ATM network, in addition to the Internet Gateway's capacity and resiliency design, is important. For example, an oversubscribed Internet Gateway could result in significant performance degradation on your Internet access circuit.

Dialup Services

Dialup services include traditional modem access, with speeds up to 56 kbps. They also include ISDN (Integrated Services Digital Network), BRI (Basic Rate Interface) of up to 128 kbps, and PRI (Primary Rate Interface) with speeds up to 1.5 Mbps. Dialup services range from servicing individual users to providing services to corporations that are subcontracting with providers to obtain all their remote login needs. ISDN, BRI, and PRI services have experienced tremendous growth over the past few years, primarily because of their on-demand (utilize only when needed) nature and their capability to carry digital signals used by multimedia applications such as video teleconferencing.

Digital Subscriber Line

Digital Subscriber Line (DSL) services provide high-speed, low-cost Internet access. They fit nicely between dialup and dedicated access services in terms of both price and speed. DSL service types vary based on which DSL technology is employed. The term *xDSL* is commonly used to refer to generic DSL services, where *x* can represent any of a number of different encoding techniques used across the physical line at Layer 1. Table 2-1 lists some of the more common types of DSL technologies and their characteristics.

Table 2-1 *DSL Technologies*

DSL Technology	Upstream Rates	Downstream Rates	Symmetric/ Asymmetric	POTS Coexist-ence	Standardization
ADSL (Asymmetrical Digital Subscriber Line)	16 kbps to 640 kbps	1.5 to 8 Mbps	Asymmetric	Yes	Yes
HDSL (High-bit-rate Digital Subscriber Line)	Fixed 1544, 2048 kbps	Fixed 1544, 2048 kbps	Symmetric	No	Yes
SDSL (Symmetric Digital Subscriber Line)	1.5 or 2.048 Mbps	1.5 or 2.048 Mbps	Symmetric	Yes	No
VDSL (Very high-bit-rate Digital Subscriber Line)	1.6 to 19.2 Mbps; distance-dependent	12.96 Mbps at 4500 feet 55.2 Mbps at 1000 feet	Both	Yes	Under development

A key benefit of DSL technology is that it can utilize existing twisted-pair copper loops in the Plain Old Telephone System (POTS) infrastructure, making it a popular residential and small-business access technology. Available DSL services usually vary significantly between providers and regions, with speeds ranging from 64 kbps up to 52 Mbps (VDSL). The quality of cable plants and the distance from the serving central office (CO) can have significant bearing on performance and throughput characteristics of a DSL connection. Over half a million DSL lines were deployed in the U.S. in 1999.

Cable Modems

Much like DSL, cable modems are a fast-growing access technology. Cable modems leverage the high-bandwidth potential of cable TV lines to provide data access services.

Because cable modem services were designed to utilize the existing fiber and coaxial cable TV infrastructure, which was optimized to carry one-way broadcasts, available bandwidth is usually very asymmetric in nature. For example, typical services provide capacity close to 2 Mbps downstream (to the subscriber's location) and 64 kbps upstream (to the service provider's network).

In addition, unlike DSL, which is a point-to-point technology, the downstream bandwidth is shared among multiple users of the service, thereby creating challenging security issues for manufacturers, service providers, and consumers.

Despite these challenges, cable modem services have been deployed for several years, and the number of subscribers and service availability is growing rapidly. There are nearly 2 million cable modem subscribers in the U.S. today, with projections as high as 16 million by the end of 2003.

Dedicated Hosting Services

Although hosting has been around almost as long as dedicated access services, it has become very popular over the past few years, with many service providers specializing in this market. Large providers that focus on dedicated hosting are commonly referred to as *content providers*. These providers usually develop highly fault-tolerant data center facilities that house cabinets or racks in which both enterprise and Web hosting customers can lease space and collocate servers and other computer equipment. Providers then sell Internet access to the collocating devices locally via technologies such as Fast Ethernet (100 Mbps) and Gigabit Ethernet (1 Gbps). Pricing models vary, and both usage-based and fixed-rate services are available.

Hosting providers often use high-end Ethernet switches to aggregate traffic from hundreds or thousands of collocated servers. Consumers should be concerned about upstream oversubscription ratios and fail-over mechanisms used by the provider. Also, because of security implications with large switched networks, consumers should be aware of if and how (usually with virtual LANs) the provider separates broadcast domains. In a shared switched network, common in the content-hosting model, understanding these issues is extremely important in order to prevent potential Denial of Service (DoS) attacks, unauthorized access to and visibility of data, and other security and management problems.

Hosting is definitely becoming very popular and is already a multibillion-dollar business by itself. It's also a market where consumers should be very cautious of what, where, and how their services are being provided. For more details about switches, VLANs, and broadcast domains, read *Interconnections: Bridges, Routers, Switches, and Internetworking*

Protocols, Second Edition (Addison-Wesley, 1999) by Radia Perlman, or *Cisco LAN Switching* (Cisco Press, 1999) by Kennedy Clark and Kevin Hamilton.

Other ISP Services

Other higher-layer services include e-mail and news services, VPNs (Virtual Private Networks), and IP Multicast. As these and other new services continue to evolve, customers need to weigh their costs and benefits against proven available options. Be especially concerned with how the services are provisioned and managed, as well as the knowledge base of the associated support and engineering personnel.

Many ISPs also offer consulting and other value-added services, such as security. The simplest security services involve packet filters at the access device. Other evolving services include data encryption and virus scanning.

Prices can vary significantly based on a given provider's reliance on an access method (this is discussed further in the next section). Prices also vary significantly based on a given provider's investment in infrastructure and operations and engineering resources.

ISP Service Pricing, Service-Level Agreements, and Technical Characteristics

In addition to evaluating the availability of services, customers should consider pricing and technical characteristics of an offered service before selecting a service provider. Although technical characteristics in particular might seem intimidating, they have enormous implications for the reliability and ease of use of the provider that you eventually select. Technical issues that this section addresses include backbone characteristics, circuit demarcation, and dedicated hosting.

ISP Service Pricing

Prices for services can vary dramatically between ISPs, even for the same services and within the same geographical regions. The provider's relative strength and amount of investment in a particular area often determine the price of a given service. For example, a provider that has established Frame Relay service will probably give you a much better price than a provider that has just begun deploying Frame Relay service. On the other hand, the new provider might be more competitive because it doesn't have an investment in legacy infrastructure required to accommodate the service and can take advantage of new platform densities and provided service capabilities.

Because of this and many other factors, getting the same price from different providers does not necessarily mean you're getting the same services. For example, with dedicated access, some providers include the CPE (discussed in more detail later in this chapter), such as a router and CSU/DSU (Channel Service Unit/Data Service Unit), as part of the product. Others charge you an extra fee for the CPE, or require that you arrange for it yourself, which can make the bottom line substantially different. You might find that you'll save a significant amount of money if you supply CPE yourself, or perhaps it might be more appealing for you to pay the provider to supply and/or manage the CPE.

Large companies often purchase national and international Internet and other communications services from a single provider. A bundled solution from a single provider usually means better control and coordination of services between the different regions of the same network. Some providers offer consolidated billing plans for all their services, national and international, and often provide significant discounts to clients who purchase multiple services, such as long distance and Internet access. This bill consolidation means one invoice and one check, which is considered a plus for many companies. Of course, if the convenience of consolidated billing or common services is not an important issue, companies might find better deals for national and international services from different service providers.

Service-Level Agreements

Many service providers today are also creating very competitive SLA/SLGs (Service-Level Agreements/Service-Level Guarantees) that define a basis for guaranteed performance and availability when using their services. Ensure that the details of these agreements, as well as penalties for failure to comply, are clearly defined. Also, ask the provider how the guarantees are currently monitored and whether exception reports (failure to comply with the guaranteed level of service) are automatically generated and followed through on, or whether notifying the provider of exceptions is the customer's responsibility.

These guarantees usually address acceptable percentages of packet loss and delay incurred on their network, as well as access circuit availability and maintenance and/or outage notification time lines.

Commitments a service provider makes in SLAs can be a true service differentiator; however, identifying violations and collecting penalties might prove quite challenging.

ISP Backbone Selection Criteria

An ISP's backbone network encompasses many important technical characteristics, including the following:

- Physical network topology
- Network bottlenecks and subscription ratios

- Level of network and individual network element redundancy
- Interconnections with other networks, including distance to destinations and traffic exchange agreements

This section is aimed at both customers and designers of ISP networks. Customers should certainly evaluate these characteristics when choosing a provider; they are far more important than pricing when attempting to predict service quality. Architects should consider the potential benefits and pitfalls associated with these characteristics when setting up or expanding their networks.

Physical Connections

Customers should investigate the provider's physical network topology, and the provider should be able to provide a recent map of the network with every connection indicated. With respect to connections, a healthy physical topology is one that can provide consistent, adequate bandwidth for the entire traffic trajectory, even in the event that single or multiple connections become unavailable. The existence of high-speed backbone links such as OC12 and OC48 does not by itself guarantee high-speed access for the customers. Your traffic might enter the provider's network from a low-speed backbone connection, or a high-speed but severely oversubscribed backbone connection. These are all things that will affect the quality of your connection.

Potential ISP Bottlenecks and Subscription Ratios

The provider's network is only as strong as its weakest link. There are two potential ISP bottlenecks: oversubscription of backbone trunks and small tail circuits leading to a POP or downstream customer. A provider should not recklessly oversubscribe its connections. ISPs that attempt to save money by overloading their routers or connections will end up losing credibility in the long run.

Oversubscription occurs when the cumulative utilization of multiple links exceeds the bandwidth of the pipe used to carry the traffic to its destination. A provider selling 20 T1s at a POP and connecting to a NAP via a T1 link will experience a bottleneck at the NAP connection. As illustrated in Figure 2-3, a common rule of thumb is a 5:1 ratio—there should be no more than five T1 links for each T1 backbone connection. Subscription ratios vary based on the product being offered. Typically, dedicated hosting providers often use 8:1 or even 10:1 ratios. These values are usually based on past experiences and projected utilization, but if they are not carefully selected and managed, they can quickly result in congestion.

Figure 2-3 *An ISP's Weakest Link Limits Performance*

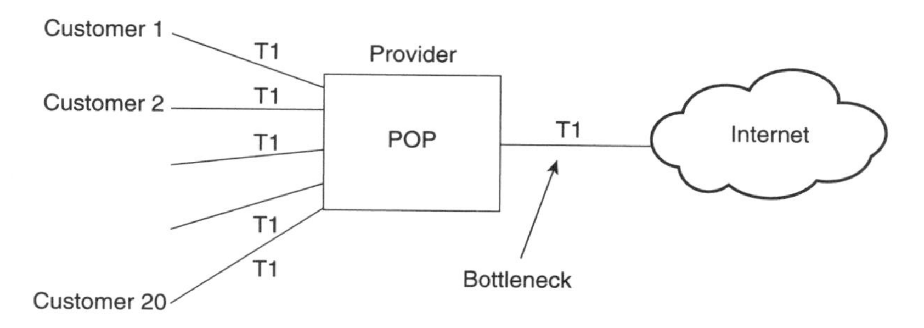

Another example of a potential bottleneck is high-speed sites trying to access information from low-speed sites. A Web server located at a site connected to the Internet via a 56 kbps link can be accessed at a maximum aggregate speed of only 56 kbps, regardless of the speed of the links used by the persons accessing the site. Figure 2-4 illustrates a client with T3 access to the Internet that will be limited to no more than 56 kbps when accessing the Web server. Also note that if other users are attempting to access the site at the same time, everyone must share the 56 kbps connections.

Figure 2-4 *Access Speed Is Limited by the Smallest Bandwidth*

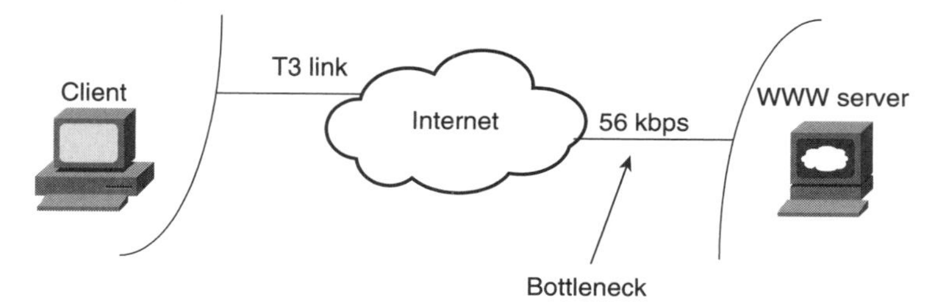

It's important that providers monitor and manage link utilization in their networks. Before committing to purchasing services from an ISP, customers should ask potential providers the following questions:

- How do you manage link utilization?
- At what thresholds do you begin to provision additional capacity?
- What are typical subscription ratios (available capacity:utilized capacity) for this service?
- What are typical subscription ratios for your backbone network and interconnection points?
- What is the theoretical bottleneck for this service?

Level of ISP Internet Access Redundancy

Murphy is out there, ready to make your life miserable. Whether because of bad weather, carrier problems, or just plain bad luck, an ISP's connection to a NAP, another provider, or another POP will become unavailable at some point, potentially resulting in the inability to reach all or a set of destinations. A redundant network enables traffic to utilize an alternative path to reach those destinations until the problem has been corrected. A well-designed ISP network has POPs connected to multiple NAPs, other provider networks, and multiple other POPs, as illustrated in Figure 2-5.

Figure 2-5 *A Redundant Network Provides More Reliable Connectivity*

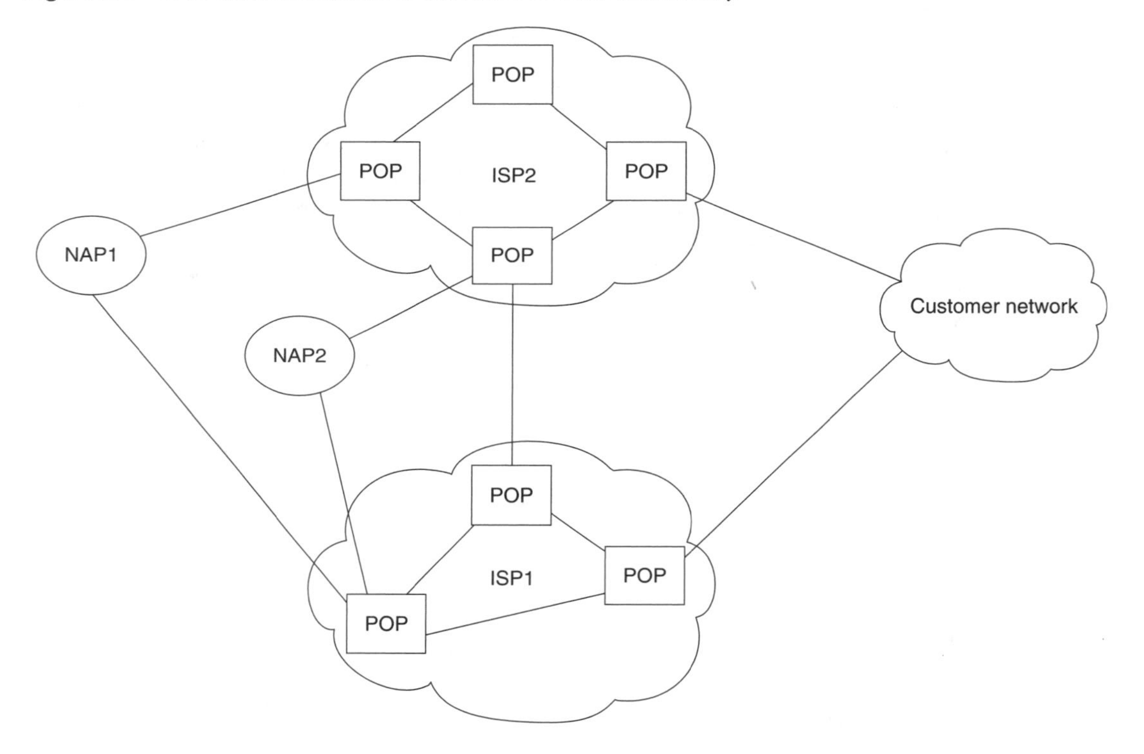

It's important to understand that peering and interconnection redundancy to other networks are usually provided on a global basis. In other words, if a connection to a provider becomes unavailable via the primary traffic exchange point, the next closest exchange point will be selected. The idea behind this is to not provision redundant capacity from the same location to another network, but to ensure that enough spare interconnection and backbone capacity exists to accommodate failures in one (or more) locations in the network. With this approach, provisioning more interconnection and NAP circuits in more geographically optimal locations can offset costs of the redundant connections, benefiting the network during both normal operation and failure scenarios by providing this redundancy on a global versus POP-by-POP basis. Figure 2-6 illustrates a less-than-optimal connectivity model, and 2-7 illustrates a redundant interconnection model.

Figure 2-6 *Less-Than-Optimal Connectivity Model*

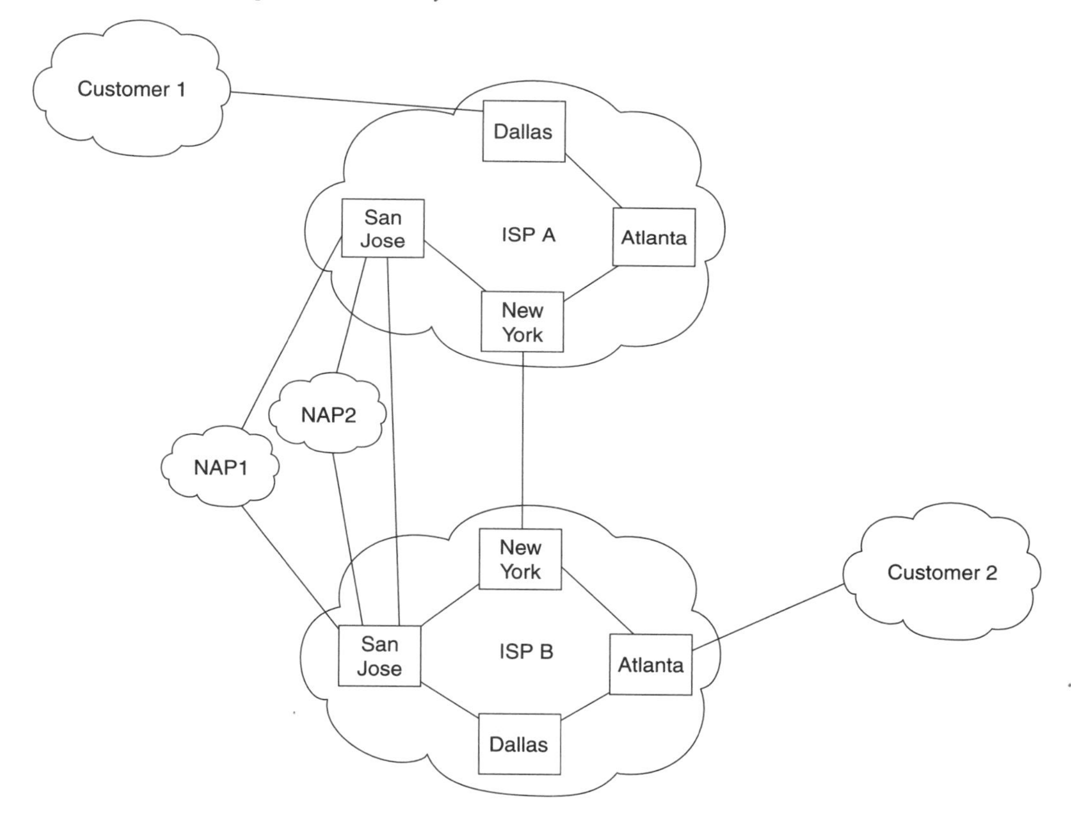

Figure 2-7 *Redundant Interconnection Model*

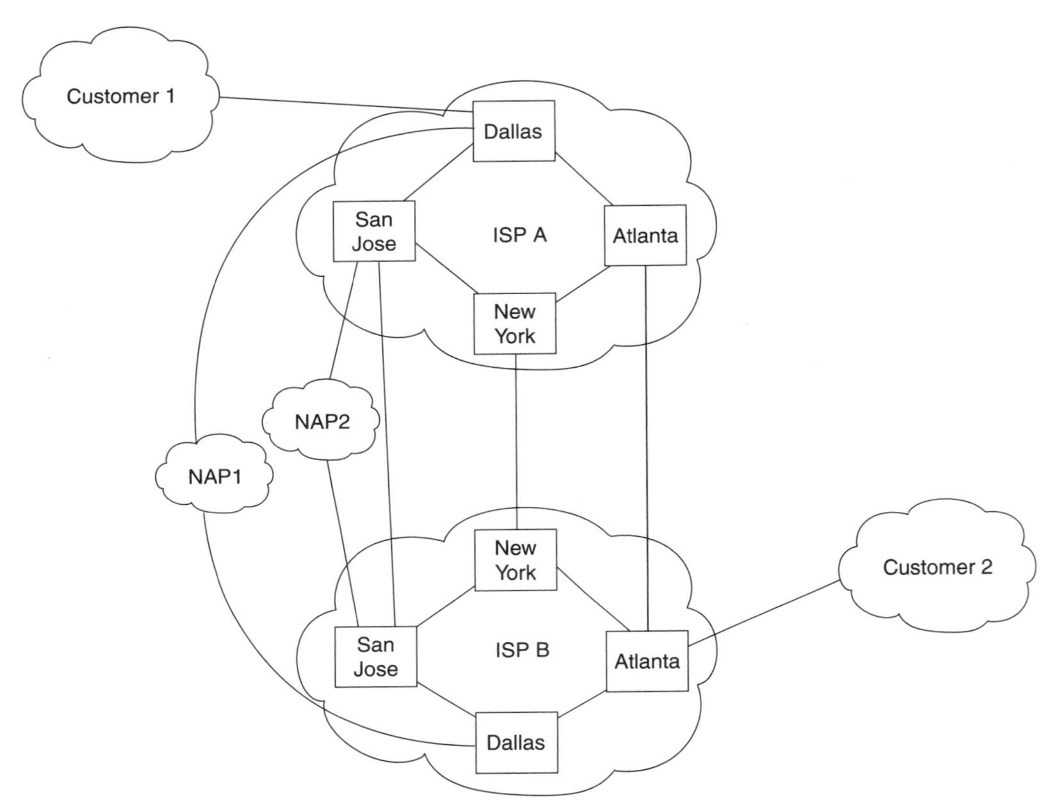

A provider's sparing plan should also be considered when discussing redundancy. Most providers keep an on-site supply of critical hardware components and manage spare equipment as a ratio of working:spare. The number of spare components usually depends on the critical nature of the component, as well as the component's theoretical 4848MTBF (Mean Time Between Failures).

Some providers choose to outsource the sparing services, normally to vendors who maintain geographically dispersed depots and share the inventory among several customers. Although this approach does potentially increase MTTR (Mean Time To Repair) when problems occur—and sometimes results in availability constraints of popular components—it's certainly better than no sparing plan at all.

Distance to Destinations

A typical misconception is that customers should be concerned only with the number of *IP hops*—that is, the number of IP routers—required to reach a given destination network through their ISP. In the past, it was somewhat true that more IP hops tended to introduce more potential for packets to be delayed, misdirected, or garbled. Today, however, many ISP backbone networks are based on MPLS (Multiprotocol Label Switching), ATM, or Frame Relay technologies, which result in many device hops at Layer 2 but are transparent to IP path-detection tools such as traceroute.

A smaller number of IP hops to a destination via a given network may very well indicate a better path to the destination than via a network with more IP hops. However, understanding what technologies intermediate networks are based upon is important before making any such assumptions. For example, it might be more desirable to take several through high-speed links than to travel over a single low-speed link.

As you know by now, the Internet is a conglomeration of overlapping backbone networks connected via exchange points and direct interconnections. Evaluating the number of *network* or *AS hops* (the number of routing domains traversed) to a given set of destinations is a reasonably good idea. The distance to destinations will depend on how many destination networks purchase connectivity from the provider and how well the provider is connected to other networks. Smaller providers might connect to only one NAP, or they might not connect to any NAPs at all. Larger providers often connect to other networks via both the NAPs and direct interconnections.

Traffic Exchange Agreements

It's an absolute requirement that ISPs be part of traffic exchange agreements, which are usually negotiated bilaterally on a peer-by-peer basis. Given the architecture of the Internet today and the little regulation governing who should interconnect how (directly or at which NAPs), it's entirely up to ISPs how to approach the traffic exchange model.

For years, ISPs have tossed around ideas regarding settlements associated with interconnecting networks, but arguments about who pays whom and how the costs should be measured have produced little consensus. As discussed in Chapter 1, "Evolution of the Internet," larger ISPs are beginning to move more and more traffic to a more distributed direct interconnection model, utilizing NAPs only to connect to smaller providers. Larger ISPs are also becoming much more strict regarding whom they'll peer with at the NAPs. That information is often protected by a mutual NDA (Nondisclosure Agreement) executed between both parties.

Although potential providers likely won't be very keen about the idea of releasing specifics of traffic exchange agreements with other networks, they usually are willing to provide aggregate available capacity numbers and other useful information regarding interconnections and peering policies. How a provider connects to other networks could be the single most important piece of information regarding potential throughput characteristics of a connection you purchase.

Demarcation Point

Finally, in addition to pricing, backbone, and interconnection issues, customers should consider demarcation point (DP) issues when selecting an ISP and executing an agreement. A *demarcation point* is the point that differentiates the provider's network and responsibilities from the customer's network and responsibilities. This is particularly true in a service provider's dedicated hosting environment. It is important to understand the difference between the responsibilities of the provider and those of the customer. Demarcation points are defined down to the cables and connectors to make sure that no disagreements occur in case of equipment or network problems. Figure 2-8 illustrates a typical demarcation point between an ISP network and a customer network.

Figure 2-8 *Demarcation Point*

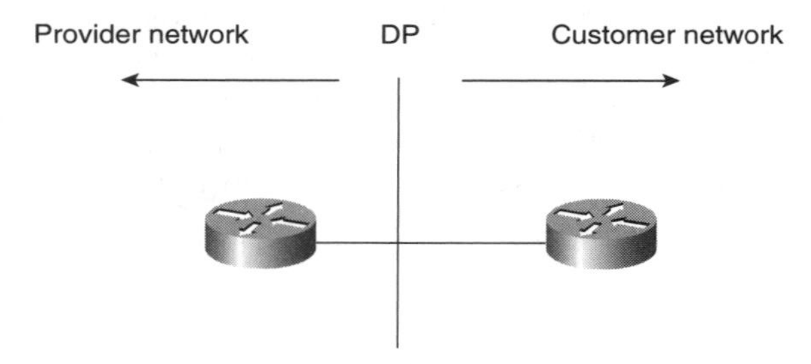

Different providers define the demarcation point differently, usually depending on who is paying for the equipment and access line, where the equipment is located, and who manages it.

Customer Premises Equipment

Customer premises equipment (CPE) usually includes the router, the CSU/DSU, the cabling, and often an analog modem for OOB (out-of-band) access for monitoring and management. ISPs typically offer the customer a choice of buying the CPE and access line, buying just the access line, or just paying a monthly fee with all equipment and access needs taken care of by the ISP. As with most everything, any arrangement is available at the right price. ISPs usually are responsible for maintaining equipment or packages that they provide. ISPs usually have predefined packages that include the CPE and/or access. If the customer does not want to take the package, he would be required to choose equipment that has been preapproved by the ISP. The customer would then be responsible for troubleshooting and maintaining his own equipment. The provider is always available to solve problems, usually for an extra fee. Figures 2-9 through 2-11 illustrate some examples of ISP packages.

In the scenario illustrated in Figure 2-9, the ISP is responsible for the access line and the CSU/DSU all the way up to the CSU's serial connector at the customer location. Restrictions might be imposed on the customer premises router to meet some memory or software revision guidelines.

Figure 2-9 *Example: ISP Provides Access and CSU/DSU; Customer Provides Router*

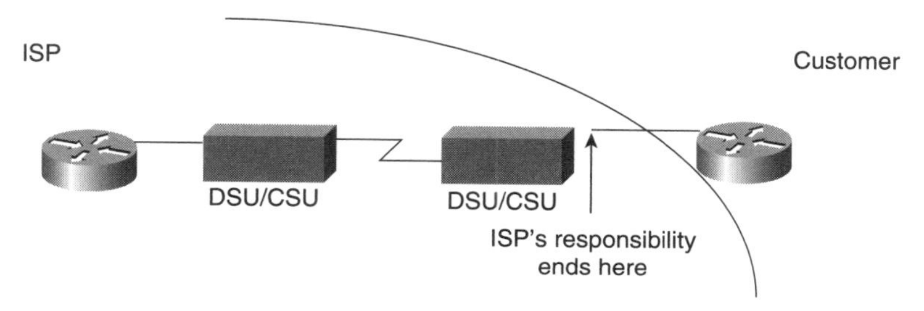

In the scenario illustrated in Figure 2-10, the ISP has provided everything, and its responsibility ends at the LAN port on the router at the customer's premises.

Figure 2-10 *Example: ISP Provides Access, Router, and CSU/DSU*

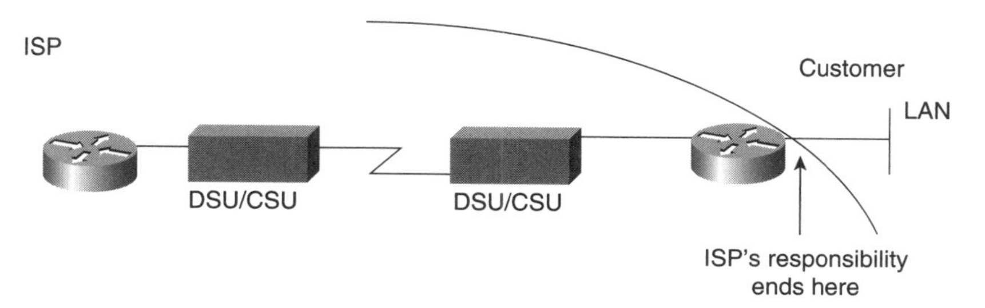

In the scenario illustrated in Figure 2-11, the customer provides the CPE and the access line. The provider's responsibility ends at the POP's wiring closet, where the ISP interconnects with the carrier's central office.

Figure 2-11 *Example: Customer Provides Everything*

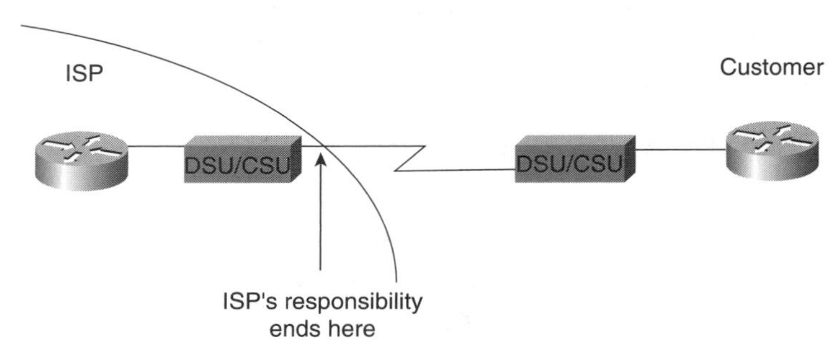

Router Collocation

Collocation is the act of placing one party's equipment on another party's premises. An example of collocation is putting the customer's router at the provider's site or hosting center, as illustrated in Figure 2-12. The customer motivations for such a collocation scheme would be to have the ISP provide faster access speeds or local monitoring of the equipment, or perhaps to give the customer better control of access bandwidth utilization.

Figure 2-12 *Collocation Example: Customer Router Located at ISP Site*

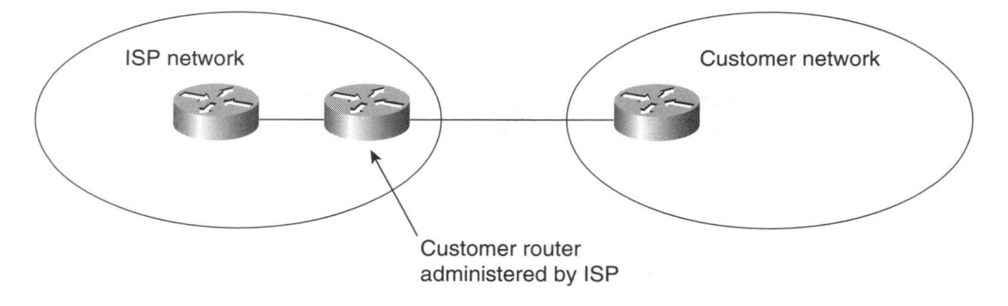

The opposite of the situation described in Figure 2-12 is for the ISP to collocate its own POP router at the customer's site, as illustrated in Figure 2-13. Usually in this case, the ISP would purchase the access line and the router and would charge the customer a fee for the entire service.

Figure 2-13 *Collocation Example: ISP Router Located at Customer Site*

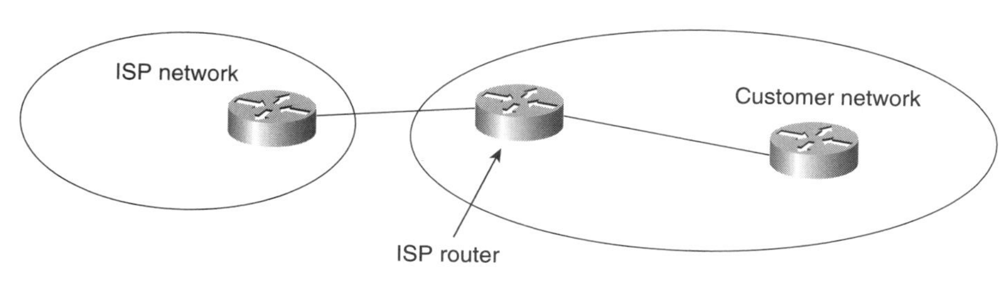

Looking Ahead

The technical characteristics of an ISP's network have significant repercussions for the customer's service, including the quality of routing architecture. Because the customer might not have direct control over some of these characteristics, it is critical that the customer at least evaluate them and ensure that they will deliver the required connectivity and quality.

If you are an ISP customer whose demarcation point and collocation agreements stipulate that you are running and maintaining equipment on your premises—even if you do not own it outright—you are likely to be taking a significant hands-on role in developing the routing policies and architecture for your network. Even if you are not running and maintaining the equipment, there are decisions you will need to make and understand with respect to routing architecture.

The next chapter completes the foundational part of the book by discussing fundamentals of Internet addressing and address space depletion. After that groundwork has been established, Part II of this book provides an in-depth discussion of routing protocols.

Frequently Asked Questions

Q — *Is higher pricing an indication that I will receive a faster, better connection from an ISP?*

A — Not necessarily. Higher prices sometimes reflect the provider's having invested in fast connections, such as OC12 or OC48 backbone links. The mere presence of such links, however, does not necessarily mean that your connections will be faster. A poorly designed combination of high-speed links and low-speed clouds, for example, might negatively affect the provider's overall performance. The bottom line is that price is just one factor to consider. Even more important is a sound network topology that offers enough redundancy and adequate bandwidth to fit your needs.

Q — *What causes bottlenecks in the ISP's backbone?*

A — Bottlenecks are caused by oversubscription or overutilization of bandwidth on a physical link.

Q — *When I connect to an ISP, should I buy my own equipment?*

A — There are pros and cons to buying your own equipment; only you can decide whether this is the optimal approach for your organization's needs. First, find out whether your ISP insists on your using its equipment (some do). Even if the ISP will let you purchase your own CPE, it probably will stipulate certain hardware and software that conform to its system. Cost issues are likely to factor significantly in your decision. Can your organization afford the capital investment, including upgrades and expansion as needed? By buying the equipment, you might also be committing yourself to maintaining it, although some ISPs will agree to maintain (for a fee) equipment owned by the customer.

In many countries, government regulations impose strict limitations on the equipment used. Understanding the available options is important.

Q — *If my connection to an ISP goes down because of equipment failure, who is responsible for what?*

A — It all depends on the service you are getting from the ISP. The preset demarcation point defines the line of responsibility between you and the provider.

This chapter covers the following key topics:

- **Overview of Internet addressing**—Provides an overview of IPv4 Class A/B/C addressing and basic subnetting concepts.
- **Variable-length subnet masks (VLSMs)**—Provides a description of variable-length subnet masks and how they can be used in efficient assignment of the IP address space.
- **IP address space depletion**—Discusses how the problem of IP address space depletion is being managed through creative address allocation, supernetting, private addressing, and next-generation protocols.
- **Private addressing and Network Address Translation (NAT)**—Discusses how NAT software is used to map between private and global IP addresses.
- **IP version 6 (IPv6)**—Provides an overview of the IP next generation (IPng) addressing scheme and how it maps to the hierarchical model offered by CIDR and IPv4.

CHAPTER 3

IP Addressing and Allocation Techniques

This chapter begins with a brief history of Internet addressing, providing information on traditional IP version 4 (IPv4) addressing and subnetting models. From there, you'll learn about some of the issues surrounding address space depletion on the Internet. Then we'll examine IP addressing techniques and allocation strategies such as variable-length subnet masking (VLSM), classless interdomain routing (CIDR), and Network Address Translation (NAT). The chapter finishes with a brief introduction to IP version 6 (IPv6).

Addressing strategies are of direct and fundamental relevance to routing architecture in any network. One of the basic functions of routing architecture and routers is to accommodate addresses for all the traffic they direct. With the explosive growth of the Internet, the sheer number of addresses and the evolution of new addressing strategies have presented new challenges for routing architectures. An understanding of the history and fundamentals of IP addressing will no doubt play a key role in your ability to quickly grasp routing protocol concepts.

History of Internet Addressing

The addressing scheme that is used today in the Internet is based on version 4 of the Internet Protocol (IPv4)[1], usually referred to simply as *IP*. This section discusses the following:

- Basic IP addressing
- Basic IP subnetting[2]
- Variable-length subnet mask (VLSM)[3]

Basic IP Addressing

An IP address is a unique 4-octet (32-bit) value expressed in dotted-decimal (or dotted-quad) notation of the form W.X.Y.Z, where periods (dots) are used to separate each of the 4 octets of the address (for example, 10.0.0.1). The 32-bit address field consists of two parts: a *network* or *link number* (which represents the network portion of the address) and a *host number* (which identifies a host on the network segment).

The network and host boundaries were traditionally defined based on the class of the IP address, with five defined classes (three of which are used for unicast addressing): A, B, C, D, and E. Table 3-1 illustrates the different classes of address space and their functions.

Table 3-1 *IP Address Classes and Functions*

Class	Address Range	High-Order Bits	Network Bits	Host Bits	Function
A	0.0.0.0 to 127.255.255.255	0	7	24	Unicast
B	128.0.0.0 to 191.255.255.255	10	14	16	Unicast
C	192.0.0.0 to 223.255.255.255	110	21	8	Unicast
D	224.0.0.0 to 239.255.255.255	1110			Multicast
E	240.0.0.0 to 255.255.255.255	1111			Reserved

Notice that only Class A, B, and C addresses are used for unicast. Class D addresses are used for multicast, and Class E address space is reserved. Several addresses within these classes are reserved for special use. Table 3-2 lists some of these addresses.

Table 3-2 *Special-Purpose IP Addresses*

Address Range	Purpose
0.0.0.0	Unknown network; commonly represents default
10.0.0.0 - 10.255.255.255	Reserved for private use (RFC 1918)
127.0.0.0 - 127.255.255.255	Reserved for loopback/local address
172.16.0.0 - 172.31.255.255	Reserved for private use (RFC 1918)
192.168.0.0 - 192.168.255.255	Reserved for private use (RFC 1918)
255.255.255.255	Limited broadcast

This class-based addressing scheme is often referred to as the *classful model*. The different classes lend themselves to different network configurations, depending on the desired ratio of networks to hosts. The full implications of the different classes will become more apparent as this chapter proceeds. The next few sections focus on the basic definitions of each class.

Class A Addressing

Class A networks are represented by a 0 in the leftmost bit position of the address. The first octet (bits 0 to 7) of the address, beginning from the leftmost bit, represents the network number, and the remaining 3 octets (bits 8 to 31) represent a host number on that network. An example of a Class A network is 124.0.0.1, where 124.0.0.0 represents the network number and the host number is 1. The outcome of this representation, illustrated in Figure 3-1, is 128(2^7) Class A network numbers. However, because 0.0.0.0 is not a valid network number, only 127(2^7–1) Class A addresses are possible.

Figure 3-1 *General Class A Address Format*

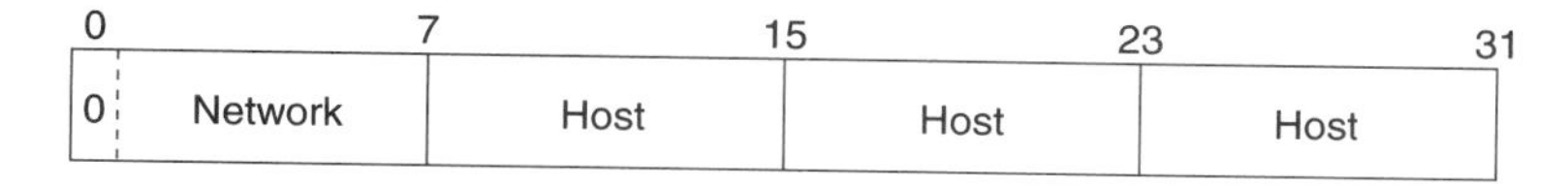

After the network is defined, the first and last host addresses within the network serve special functions. The first address (124.0.0.0 in the previous example) is used to represent the network number, and the last address of the network is used to represent the directed broadcast address of the network (124.255.255.255). Therefore, Class A addresses have only 16,777,214 (2^{24}–2) hosts per network, rather than 16,777,216 (2^{24}) hosts per network.

Class B Addressing

Class B networks are represented by a 1 and a 0 in the leftmost two bits of the address. The first two octets of the address (bits 0 to 15) represent the network portion of the address, and the remaining two octets (bits 16 to 31) represent the host number of that network. The outcome of this representation, illustrated in Figure 3-2, is 16,384 (2^{14}) network numbers, with 65,534 (2^{16}–2) hosts per network. An example of a Class B address is 172.16.0.1, where 172.16.0.0 is the Class B network and 1 is the host.

Figure 3-2 *General Class B Address Format*

0 1
7
15
23
31
1 0
Network
Network
Host
Host

Class C Addressing

Class C networks are represented by 1, 1, and 0 in the leftmost three bits of the address. The first three octets (bits 0 to 23) represent the network number, and the last octet (bits 24 to 31) represents the host number in that network. The outcome of this representation, as illustrated in Figure 3-3, is 2,097,152 (2^{21}) network numbers with 254 (2^8–2) hosts per network. An example of a Class C network is 192.11.1.1, where 192.11.1.0 is the network number and the host number is 1.

Figure 3-3 *General Class C Address Format*

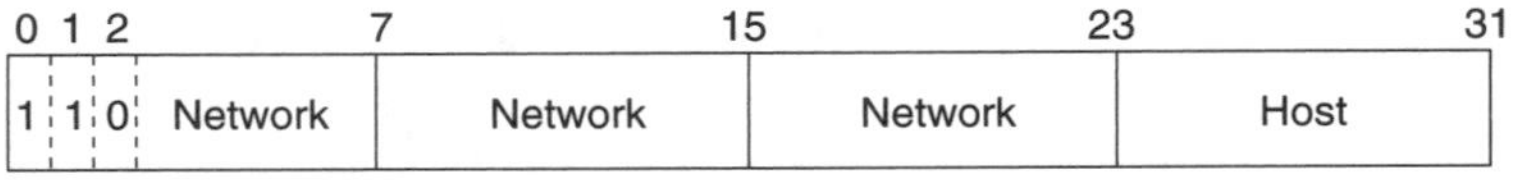

0 1 2	7	15	23	31
1 1 0	Network	Network	Network	Host

Class D Addressing

Class D networks are represented by 1, 1, 1, and 0 in the leftmost 4 bits of the address. The Class D address space is reserved for multicast, used to represent multicast group numbers.

Class E Addressing

Class E networks are represented by 1, 1, 1, and 1 in the leftmost 4 bits of the address. Class E address space is currently reserved for experimental use.

Basic IP Subnetting

Basic subnetting and variable-length subnets are often misunderstood. This section gives a brief introduction to how subnetting works, and the next section discusses variable-length subnet masks (VLSMs).

A *subnet*, or *subnetwork,* is a subset of a Class A, B, or C network. To better understand subnetting, it helps to take a closer look at IP addresses that are not subnetted. As explained earlier, IP addresses are comprised of a network portion and a host portion, representing a static two-level hierarchical addressing model (networks and hosts). IP subnetting[2] introduces a third level of hierarchy with the concept of a network mask, or netmask. The netmask serves as a bitmask with bits set corresponding to the bits used to the classful IP network number, as well as additional bits set corresponding to the subnet number.

In Figure 3-4, the network mask 255.0.0.0 is applied to network 10.0.0.0. The mask in binary notation is a series of contiguous 1s followed by a series of contiguous 0s. The 1s portion represents the network portion of the address, and the 0s represent the host portion. This provides a mechanism to split the IP address of host 10.0.0.1 into a network portion of 10 and a host portion of 1.

Figure 3-4 *Basic Network Masking*

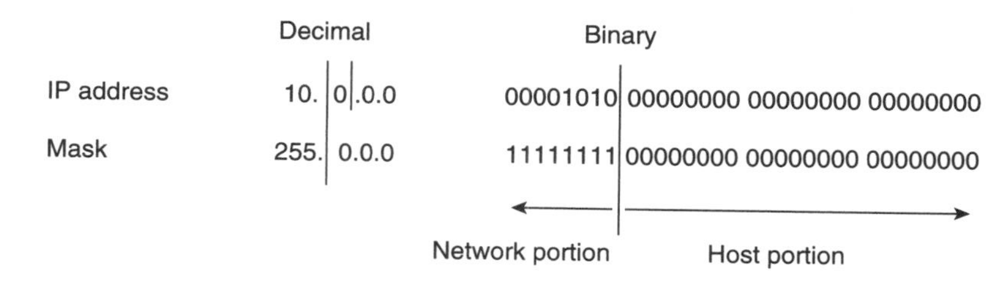

Class A, B, and C addresses each have what is referred to as a natural mask, which is the mask created by the very definition of the network and host portions of each class. The natural masks for Class A, B, and C addresses are as follows:

- Class A natural mask is 255.0.0.0
- Class B natural mask is 255.255.0.0
- Class C natural mask is 255.255.255.0

By separating the network and host portions of the IP address, masks facilitate the creation of subnets. Without subnets, network numbers would be very limited in use. Each physical segment, such as an Ethernet, Token Ring, or FDDI segment, is normally associated with one or more network numbers. If subnetting were not available, a Class A network of the form 10.0.0.0 would accommodate only one physical segment with about 16 million hosts on it, as shown in Figure 3-5.

Figure 3-5 *Unsubnetted Class A Address Space*

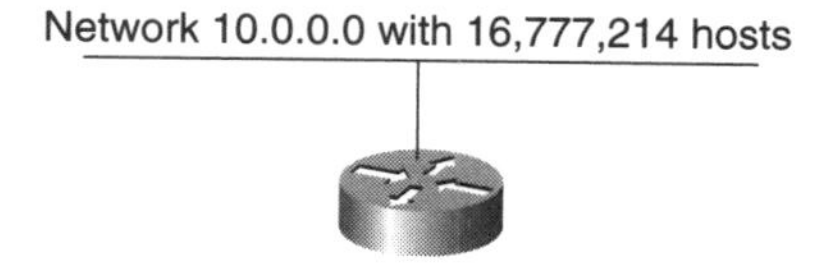

With the use of masks, networks can be divided into smaller subnetworks by extending the network portion of the address into the host portion. The subnetting technique provides a larger number of subnetworks while reducing the number of hosts on each network.

In Figure 3-6, a mask of 255.255.0.0 is applied to network 10.0.0.0. This divides the IP address 10.0.0.1 into a network portion of 10, a subnet portion of 0, and a host portion of 1. The 255.255.0.0 mask has borrowed a portion of the host space and has applied it to the network space. As a result, the classful ten-network space has increased from a single large network to 256 subnetworks ranging from 10.0.0.0 to 10.255.0.0. This would decrease the number of hosts per each subnet from 16,777,214 to 65,534.

NOTE Note that in this example, 10.0.0.0 represents the zero subnet. Some legacy router software does not allow the zero subnet address space to be used, nor is it used by default in Cisco routers. In order to enable the use of zero subnets in IOS, you must configure **ip subnet-zero**.

Figure 3-6 *Basic Subnetting*

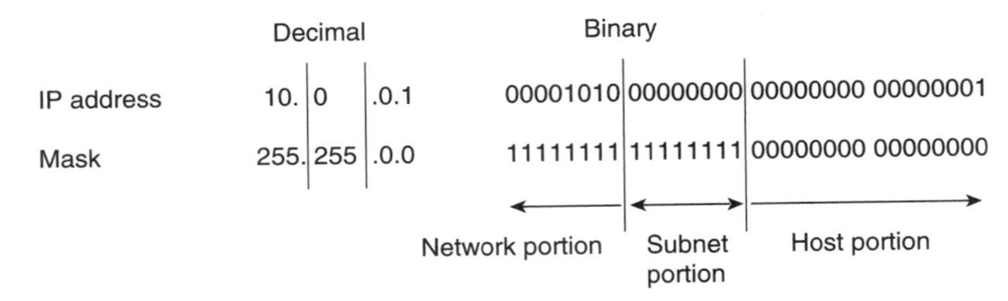

VLSMs

The term *variable-length subnet mask (VLSM)* refers to the fact that one network can be configured with different masks. The basic idea behind VLSMs[3] is to offer more flexibility in dividing a network into multiple subnetworks while being able to optimally allocate variable amounts of host space among the subnetworks. Without VLSM, only one subnet mask can be applied to an entire network. This would restrict the number of hosts given the number of subnets required. If you select the mask so that you have enough subnets, you might not be able to allocate enough host numbers in each subnet. The same is true of hosts; a mask that allows enough hosts might not provide enough subnet space. VLSM provides the capability to allocate subnetworks with variable numbers of hosts, allowing the network administrator to better utilize the address space.

Suppose, for example, that you are assigned a Class C network 192.214.11.0 and you need to divide it into three subnets. One subnet will require 100 host numbers, and the other two will require 50 host numbers each. Ignoring the two network end limits of 0 (network number) and 255 (directed broadcast address), you theoretically have 256 host numbers available, 192.214.11.0 through 192.214.11.255. The desired subnet division cannot be accomplished without VLSM, as you will see.

To determine the available subnet options associated with the 192.214.11.0 network, you first need to identify the network mask, which in the case of this traditional Class C network is represented by 255.255.255.0 (all 1s in the first three octets). A handful of subnet masks of the form 255.255.255.X can be used to divide the Class C network 192.214.11.0 into more subnets. A mask must have a contiguous number of 1 bits, starting from the leftmost bit, and the remaining bits must be 0s.

NOTE Initially, masks were not required to be a contiguous group of 1s followed only by 0s. For example, some implementations used the "middle bits" to identify the host portion of the address and the low-order bits to identify the subnetwork. Although this flexibility provided little benefit to network administrators, it introduced a significant amount of complexity to routing. Because of this complexity, the specification was updated to require that the mask be a contiguous group of 1s.

Table 3-3 lists potential masks that could be used to segment the 256 available addresses into additional subnets.

Table 3-3 *Potential Class C Subnets*

Last Octet	Binary Representation	Number of Subnets	Number of Hosts*
128	1000 0000	2	128
192	1100 0000	4	64
224	1110 0000	8	32
240	1111 0000	16	16
248	1111 1000	32	8
252	1111 1100	64	4

*Note that the Number of Hosts field includes the network number and directed broadcast addresses.

Prior to VLSM, a traditional network would have to be divided using a single contiguous netmask over the whole network. In this case, you have the choice of using a mask 255.255.255.128 and dividing the address into two subnets with 128 hosts each or using 255.255.255.192 and dividing the addresses into four subnets with 64 hosts each. Neither of these options will accommodate the requirement of having 100 hosts on one segment and 50 hosts on each of the other two segments.

By using variable-length masks, you can accomplish the stated goal. For example, assume you have been given network 192.214.11.0. First, use the mask 255.255.255.128 to divide the network address into two subnets with 128 hosts each. These two subnets would be represented as 192.214.11.0 (.0 to .127), the bottom half of the Class C network, and 192.214.11.128 (.128 to .255), the top half of the Class C network. Next, further subnet the 192.214.11.128 network using a mask of 255.255.255.192, creating two subnets with 64 hosts each—subnet 192.214.11.128 (.128 to .191) and subnet 192.214.11.192 (.192 to .255). Figures 3-7 and 3-8 illustrate how to divide the address space accordingly. (Note that the network number and directed broadcast addresses are included in the host counts.)

Figure 3-7 *Example of a Class C Network Divided into Three Subnets*

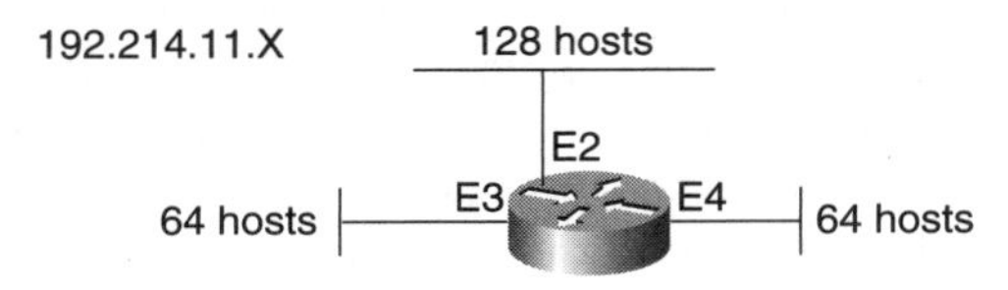

Figure 3-8 *Use of VLSM to Split Network Space into Subnets of Unequal Size*

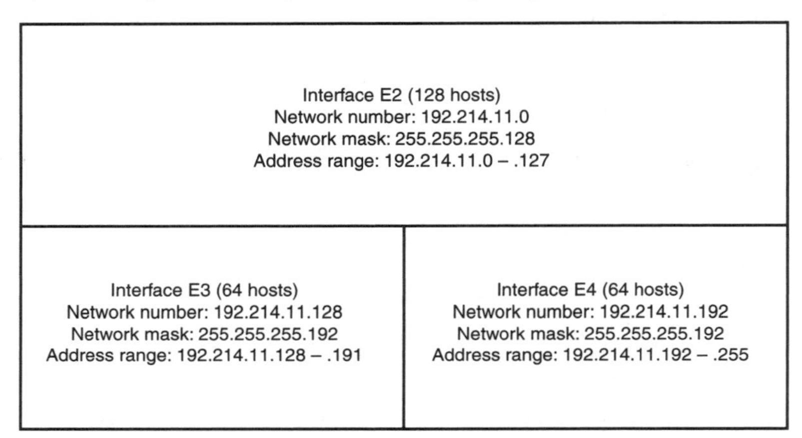

Of course, not all routing protocols can support VLSM. Routing Information Protocol version 1 (RIP-1) and Interior Gateway Routing Protocol (IGRP) do not carry network masks in routing updates and hence cannot correctly deal with variably subnetted networks. Today, even with the deployment of routing protocols such as Open Shortest Path First (OSPF), Enhanced IGRP (EIGRP), Routing Information Protocol version 2 (RIP-2), and Intermediate System-to-Intermediate System (IS-IS), which do support VLSM, administrators still have difficulties adapting to this technique. Most early networks built on RIP-1 and IGRP do not have their IP addresses allocated in a manner that would enable them to be more optimally grouped into blocks. Rather, their IP addresses are scattered, and administrators would have to renumber their hosts to make them conform to the new addressing scheme. Such renumbering is difficult, and administrators often consider it out of the question. This coexistence is a challenge, and administrators have resorted to much maneuvering and static routing to accommodate it.

IP Address Space Depletion

The growing demand for IP addresses has put a severe strain on the classful model. Most companies requesting Class B addresses have estimated that a Class B address would best accommodate their requirements because of the balance between the number of networks and the number of hosts. A Class A was overkill, with more than 16 million hosts, and a Class C had too few hosts per network. By 1991, it was becoming obvious that the Class B consumption was not slowing and actions needed to be taken to prevent its depletion.

Some of the measures consisted of creative assignment of IP addresses and promoting the use of private addresses for organizations that did not have global Internet connectivity. Other measures resulted in the initiation of working groups and directorates such as the Routing and Addressing (ROAD) working group and the IP next generation (IPng) directorate. In 1992, the ROAD working group proposed the use of classless interdomain routing (CIDR) as a measure to move away from classful IP addressing. At the same time, the IPng directorate was working on developing a new and improved IP addressing scheme that uses IP version 6 (IPv6), which would eventually solve the utilization problems that IPv4 addressing has encountered.

The measures to handle IP address depletion can be grouped into the following four categories:

- Creative IP address allocation
- Classless interdomain routing (CIDR)[4]
- Private IP addressing and Network Address Translation (NAT)[5, 7]
- IP version 6 (IPv6)[8]

Accompanying concerns of depletion, growing IP address demand generated a need to convert the IP addressing allocation process from a central registry. Originally, the IANA and the Internet Registry (IR) had complete control of address assignment. IP addresses were assigned to organizations sequentially without consideration of geographical factors and of how or where an organization would be connecting to the Internet. This method had the effect of punching holes in the IP address space—segregating individual or small numbers of IP addresses and eliminating large, contiguous ranges of numbers.

A different approach was needed in which large, contiguous ranges of addresses are given to different administrations (such as service providers), and those service providers in turn allocate customer addresses from their own space. In general, this funnel-down method of address allocation predicts a more controlled and hierarchical method of IP address distribution. It is somewhat similar to the approach employed by the telephone network allocation scheme, where area codes are associated with regions (service provider networks), prefixes with subsets of those regions (service provider customers), and the remainder with individual customers (hosts).

IP Address Allocation

Class A network numbers are limited resources, and the allocation from this space is restricted. Although Class A space will continue to be distributed, it's now being allocated on a subnetwork basis, rather than in entire classful boundaries. Class B addresses are restricted as well, and are allocated on a subnetwork basis. Class C addresses are usually allocated from the upstream service provider's address space. Table 3-4 summarizes the current allocation of Class C address space.

Table 3-4 *Class C Address Assignment Summary*

Organization Requirement	Address Assignment
Fewer than 256 addresses	1 Class C network
Fewer than 512 but more than 256 addresses	2 contiguous Class C networks
Fewer than 1,024 but more than 512 addresses	4 contiguous Class C networks
Fewer than 2,048 but more than 1,024 addresses	8 contiguous Class C networks
Fewer than 4,096 but more than 2,048 addresses	16 contiguous Class C networks
Fewer than 8,192 but more than 4,096 addresses	32 contiguous Class C networks
Fewer than 16,384 but more than 8,192 addresses	64 contiguous Class C networks

Regional Internet Registries such as the American Registry for Internet Numbers (ARIN) are now hesitant to allocate space directly to end-user networks. In order to obtain address space directly from ARIN, a network must first justify allocation of at least 16 Class C addresses, or 4,096 hosts. Even with justification, administrators with requests of these sizes are encouraged to obtain address space from their providers.

Suggested user assignment guidelines, current allocation policies, request templates, and other related information can be found on ARIN's Web server (www.arin.net).

As far as geographic allocation of address space is concerned, there are four major areas: Europe, North America and sub-Saharan Africa, the Pacific Rim, and South and Central America. Table 3-5 summarizes allocations reserved for these regions. The multiregional area represents network numbers that were assigned prior to the implementation of this plan.

Table 3-5 *Address Space Allocation among Major Geographic Areas*

Address Space	Area of Allocation	Date Allocated
61.0.0.0 to 61.255.255.255	APNIC—Pacific Rim	April 1997
62.0.0.0 to 62.255.255.255	RIPE NCC—Europe	April 1997
63.0.0.0 to 63.255.255.255	ARIN	April 1997

Table 3-5 *Address Space Allocation among Major Geographic Areas (Continued)*

Address Space	Area of Allocation	Date Allocated
64.0.0.0 to 64.255.255.255	ARIN	July 1999
128.0.0.0 to 191.255.255.255	Various Registries	May 1993
192.0.0.0 to 192.255.255.255	Multiregional	May 1993
193.0.0.0 to 195.255.255.255	RIPE NCC—Europe	May 1993
196.0.0.0 to 198.255.255.255	Various registries	May 1993
199.0.0.0 to 199.255.255.255	ARIN—North America	May 1993
200.0.0.0 to 200.255.255.255	ARIN—Central and South America	May 1993
201.0.0.0 to 201.255.255.255	Reserved—Central and South America	May 1993
202.0.0.0 to 203.255.255.255	APNIC—Pacific Rim	May 1993
204.0.0.0 to 205.255.255.255	ARIN—North America	March 1994
206.0.0.0 to 206.255.255.255	ARIN—North America	April 1995
207.0.0.0 to 207.255.255.255	ARIN—North America	November 1995
208.0.0.0 to 208.255.255.255	ARIN—North America	April 1996
209.0.0.0 to 209.255.255.255	ARIN—North America	June 1996
210.0.0.0 to 210.255.255.255	APNIC—Pacific Rim	June 1996
211.0.0.0 to 211.255.255.255	APNIC—Pacific Rim	June 1996
212.0.0.0 to 212.255.255.255	RIPE NCC—Europe	October 1997
213.0.0.0 to 213.255.255.255	RIPE NCC—Europe	March 1999
216.0.0.0 to 217.255.255.255	ARIN—North America	April 1998

Classless Interdomain Routing

In recent years, the global IP routing tables have grown in a way that caused routers to start becoming saturated due to processing power and memory allocation. Statistics and growth rate projections suggest that routing tables have doubled in size every 10 months between 1991 and 1995 and have grown significantly since 1998. Figure 3-9 illustrates this growth.

Figure 3-9 *The Growth of Internet Routing Tables*

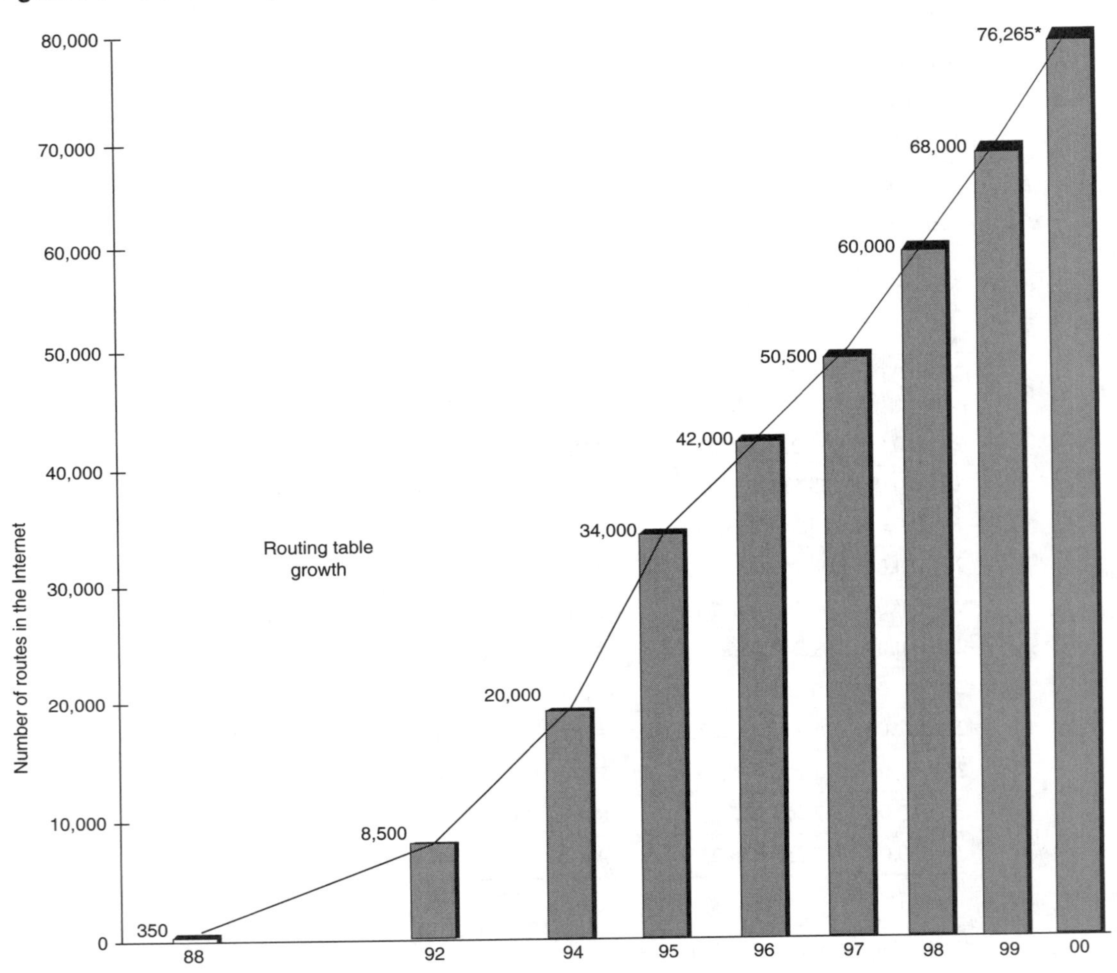

*2000 information taken from CIDR Report on May 25, 2000

Without any plan of action, the routing table would have grown to about 80,000 routes in 1995. Actual data in early 2000, however, showed that the routing table size was around 76,000 routes. This reduction in growth is due to the IP address allocation scheme discussed in the previous section and to the adoption of CIDR.

CIDR was an evolutionary step beyond traditional classful IP addresses—namely, Class A, B, and C networks. In CIDR, an IP network is represented by a prefix, which is the IP address of a network, followed by a slash and, lastly, an indication of the number of leftmost contiguous bits corresponding to the network mask to be associated with that network address. For example, consider network 198.32.0.0 with a prefix of /16, written as 198.32.0.0/16. The /16 indicates that there are 16 bits of mask counting from the far left. This is synonymous to IP network 198.32.0.0 with a netmask of 255.255.0.0.

A network is referred to as a *supernet* when a prefix netmask boundary contains fewer bits than a network's natural mask. A Class C network 198.32.1.0, for example, has a natural mask of 255.255.255.0, which corresponds to a /24 in CIDR notation. The representation 198.32.0.0 255.255.0.0 can also be represented as 198.32.0.0/16, both of which have a shorter mask than the natural mask (16 is less than 24); hence, the network is referred to as a supernet. Figure 3-10 illustrates these address schemes.

Figure 3-10 *CIDR-Based Addressing*

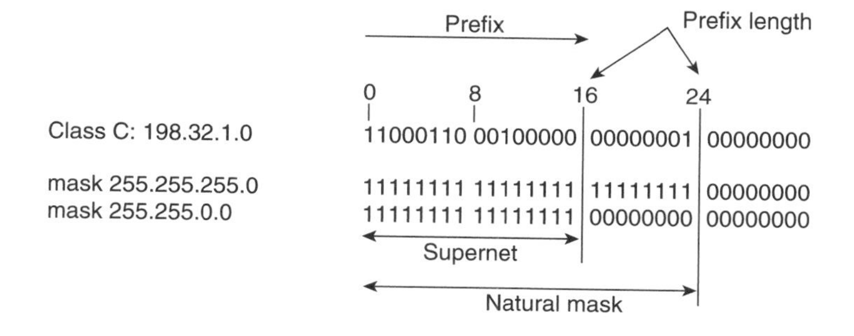

198.32.1.0 255.255.255.0 <==> 198.32.1.0/24

198.32.0.0 255.255.0.0 <==> 198.32.0.0/16

This notation provides a mechanism to easily lump all the more-specific routes of 198.32.0.0/16 (such as 198.32.0.0, 198.32.1.0, 198.32.2.0, and so on) into one advertisement referred to as an *aggregate*.

It is easy to be confused by all the terminology, especially because the terms aggregate, CIDR block, and supernet are often used interchangeably. Generally, these terms all indicate that a group of contiguous IP networks has been summarized into one route announcement. More precisely, CIDR is represented by the <prefix/length> notation, supernets have a prefix length shorter than the natural mask, and aggregates represent any summary route.

All the networks that are a subset of an aggregate or CIDR block are usually referred to as more specific because they provide more information about the location of a network. More specific prefixes have a longer prefix length than the aggregate:

- 198.213.0.0/16 has an aggregate of length 16
- 198.213.1.0/20 has a more-specific prefix with a length of 20

Routing domains that are CIDR-capable are referred to as *classless*, in contrast to the traditional classful routing domains. CIDR has depicted a new, more hierarchical Internet architecture, where each domain takes its IP address from a higher hierarchical level. This offers tremendous savings in route propagation, especially when summarization is done close to leaf or stub networks. Leaf or stub networks are end points on the global networks; they do not, in turn, provide Internet connectivity to other networks. An ISP that supports numerous leaf networks subdivides its subnets into many smaller blocks of addresses to serve those customers. Aggregation permits an ISP to advertise one IP network, generally represented as a supernet, rather than many individual advertisements, thus resulting in more efficient routing strategies and propagation, as well as introducing stability of route advertisements. Figure 3-11 illustrates the efficiency of aggregation.

Figure 3-11 *Classful Addressing Versus CIDR-Based Addressing*

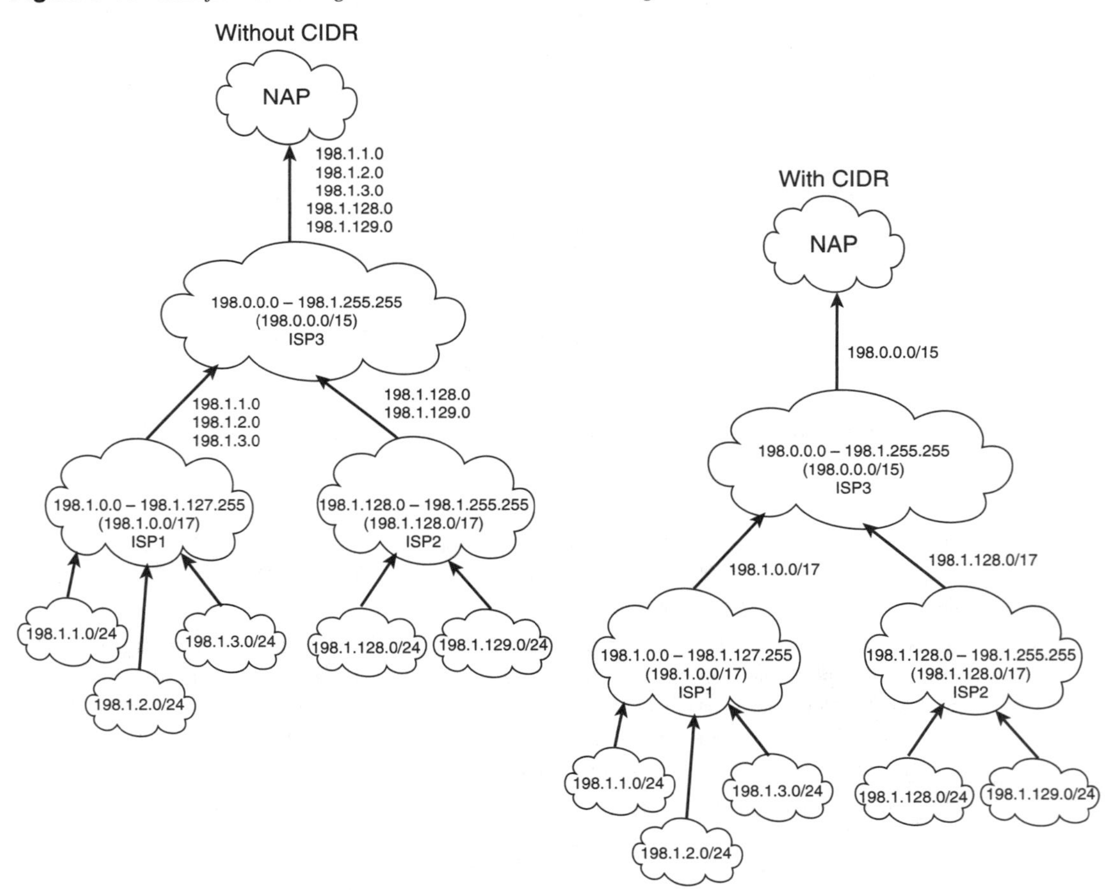

In this example, ISP3 has been given the block 198.0.0.0 through 198.1.255.255 (198.0.0.0/15). ISP3 then allocates two smaller blocks of its addresses to ISP1 and ISP2. ISP1 is allocated the range 198.1.0.0 through 198.1.127.255 (198.1.0.0/17), and ISP2 is allocated the range 198.1.128.0 through 198.1.255.255 (198.1.128.0.0/17). In the same manner, ISP1 and ISP2 allocate their own customers a block of addresses from their own ranges. The left-side instance of Figure 3-11 shows what happens if CIDR is not used: ISP1 and ISP2 advertise all subnets from their customers, and ISP3 passes all these advertisements to the outside world. This results in a major increment in the global IP routing table size.

The right-side instance of Figure 3-11 portrays the same scenario when CIDR is applied. ISP1 and ISP2 perform aggregation in their customer subnets, ISP1 advertises the aggregate 198.1.0.0/17, and ISP2 advertises the aggregate 198.1.128.0/17. In the same manner, ISP3 performs aggregation on its customer subnets, ISP1 and ISP2, and sends only one aggregate (198.0.0.0/15) to its peer networks. This results in tremendous savings in the global IP routing tables.

As you can see, aggregation results in more significant efficiency gains when done close to the leaf node because the majority of the subnets to be aggregated are deployed on the customer network. Aggregation at higher levels, such as ISP3, results in a further reduction because it is dealing with fewer networks that are learned from downstream customer networks.

Aggregation works optimally if every customer connects to its provider via one connection only, which is referred to as single-homing, and also if the customer has taken its IP addresses from its provider's CIDR blocks. Unfortunately, this is not always the case in the real world. For example, situations arise where customers already have IP addresses that were not allocated from their provider's address space. As another example, some customers (who could be providers themselves) have found the need to connect to multiple providers at the same time, a scenario referred to as *multihoming*. These situations result in further complications and less flexibility in aggregation.

The Longest Match Routing Rule

Routing to any destination is always done on a longest match basis: A router that has to decide between two different length prefixes of the same network will always follow the longer mask. Suppose, for example, that a router has the following two entries in its routing table:

198.32.1.0/24 via path 1
198.32.0.0/16 via path 2

When attempting to deliver traffic to host 192.32.1.1, the router tries to match the destination that has the longest prefix and will deliver the traffic via Path 1 in the example.

Figure 3-12 illustrates the longest match routing rule. Domain C is receiving the two updates 198.32.1.0/24 and 198.32.0.0/16, and traffic toward 198.32.1.1 is following Path 1.

Figure 3-12 *Following the Longest Match*

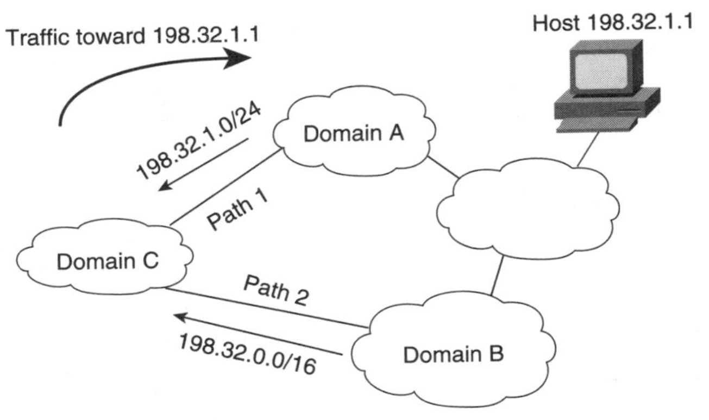

If Path 1 were to become unavailable for some reason, traffic would utilize the next closest match in the routing table, which in this case is Path 2. In cases where Domain C is receiving identical routing updates with masks of equal length coming from Domain A and Domain B, Domain C would select one path or the other, or perhaps both, depending on the load-balancing techniques offered by the specific routing implementation running in the domain.

The longest match rule implies that a destination connected to multiple domains must always be explicitly announced—that is, announced in its most specific nonaggregate form—by these domains. In Figure 3-12, because Domain B does not explicitly advertise route 198.32.1.0/24, traffic from the customer toward the host must always prefer the path via the longest prefix match, through Domain A. Such a routing configuration might place an unacceptable burden on Domain A.

Less-Specific Routes of a Network's Own Aggregate

A specific rule of routing states that, for the sake of preventing routing loops, a network must not follow a less-specific route for a destination that matches one of its own aggregated routes. A *routing loop* occurs when traffic circles back and forth between network elements, never reaching its final destination. Default routes 0.0.0.0/0 are a special case of this rule. A network should not follow the default route to reach destinations that are part of its aggregated advertisements. This is why routing protocols that handle aggregation of routes should always keep a bit bucket (Null0 route in Cisco parlance) to the aggregate route itself. Traffic sent to the bit bucket will be discarded, which prevents potential looping situations.

TIP Avoid loops in default routing by using a bit bucket.

Figure 3-13 illustrates ISP1 aggregating its domain into a single route 198.32.0.0/13.

Figure 3-13 *Following Less-Specific Routes of a Network's Own Aggregate Causes Loops*

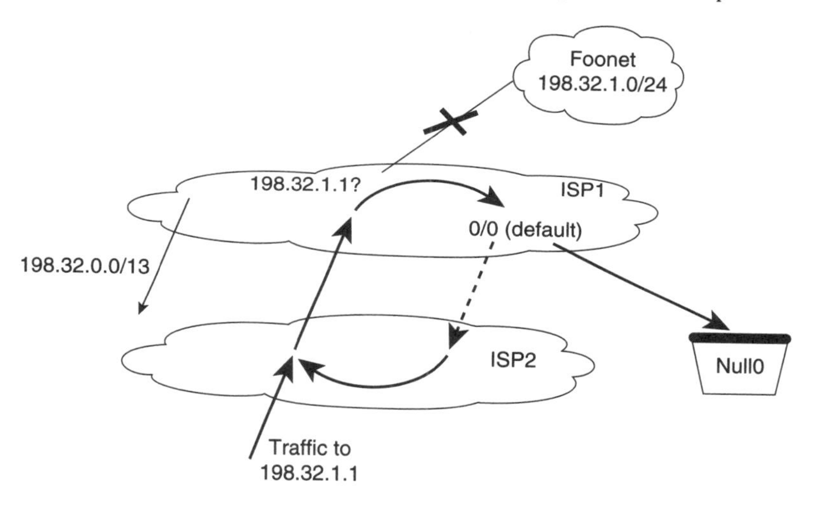

Assume that the connection between ISP1 and its customer Foonet (where network 198.32.1.0/24 exists) becomes unavailable. Suppose also that ISP1 has a default route 0.0.0.0/0 that points to ISP2 for addresses not known to ISP1. Traffic toward 198.32.1.1 following the aggregate route to ISP1 will not find the destination and will follow the default route back to ISP2. The traffic will loop back and forth between ISP1 and ISP2. To prevent such a loop, a null entry to the aggregate route, 198.32.0.0/13, is installed in ISP1's routers. The null route entry will drop all packets bound for an unreachable destination that is less specific than the aggregate route.

Aggregation, if not properly applied, can result in routing loops or *black holes*. A black hole occurs when traffic reaches and stops at a destination that is not its intended destination and from which it cannot be forwarded. These and other routing challenges will become more apparent as you learn about multiple address allocation schemes and how they interact with aggregation.

Single-Homing Scenario: Addresses Taken from Outside the Provider's Address Space

The routing rules discussed so far, along with the nature of a network's address space and whether it is single-homed or multihomed, have implications for whether and how the network can aggregate addresses. This section and the next three sections examine several scenarios.

In the single-homing scenario, the customer is connected to a single provider and has IP address space totally different from the provider's. This could have occurred because the customer changed providers and kept the addresses of the previous provider. Usually in this situation, customers are encouraged or forced to renumber into new address space. If renumbering does not take place, the new provider cannot aggregate the customer's addresses. Moreover, the old provider cannot aggregate as efficiently as it once did because a hole has been punched in its address space. The overall effect of using an old provider's address space is that more routes must be installed in the global Internet routing tables.

This scenario is discussed further in future chapters, but for now, network administrators should keep in mind that if their network is single-homed, the best routing option is usually the simplest one. In the single-homed case, pointing default to your provider and having the provider statically route your address space to you is usually the most trouble-free approach available. Only when multiple connections and redundancy become an issue should you consider more-complicated solutions.

The KISS (Keep It Simple, Stupid) principle, which every designer, architect, engineer, and administrator should practice, suggests that the simplest solution available is very often the best solution.

Multihoming Scenario: Addresses Taken from One Provider

In this scenario (depicted in a moment in Figure 3-14), customers are connected to multiple providers. Customers are small enough that they need to take IP addresses from only one of their multiple providers, or they were allocated the addresses while they were single-homed. We will consider two ISPs (ISP1 and ISP2) and their customers: Onenet, Twonet, and Stubnet. For each domain, Table 3-6 lists the IP address ranges, corresponding aggregates, and providers.

Table 3-6 *List of Customers and Corresponding Providers*

Domain	Address Range	Aggregate	Provider	Address Taken From
ISP1	198.24.0 to 198.31.255.255	198.24.0.0/13		
Onenet	198.24.0.0 to 198.24.15.0	198.24.0.0/20	ISP1, ISP2	ISP1
Stubnet	198.24.16.0 to 198.24.23.0	198.24.16.0/21	ISP1	ISP1
Twonet	198.24.56.0 to 198.24.63.0	198.24.56.0/21	ISP1, ISP2	ISP1
ISP2	198.32.0.0 to 198.39.255.255	198.32.0.0/13		

Note that Onenet and Twonet are multihomed to ISP1 and ISP2 with their address ranges taken from ISP1 (see Figure 3-14).

Figure 3-14 *Advertising the Wrong Aggregate Causes Black Holes*

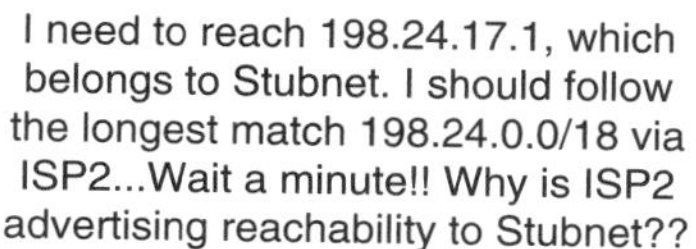

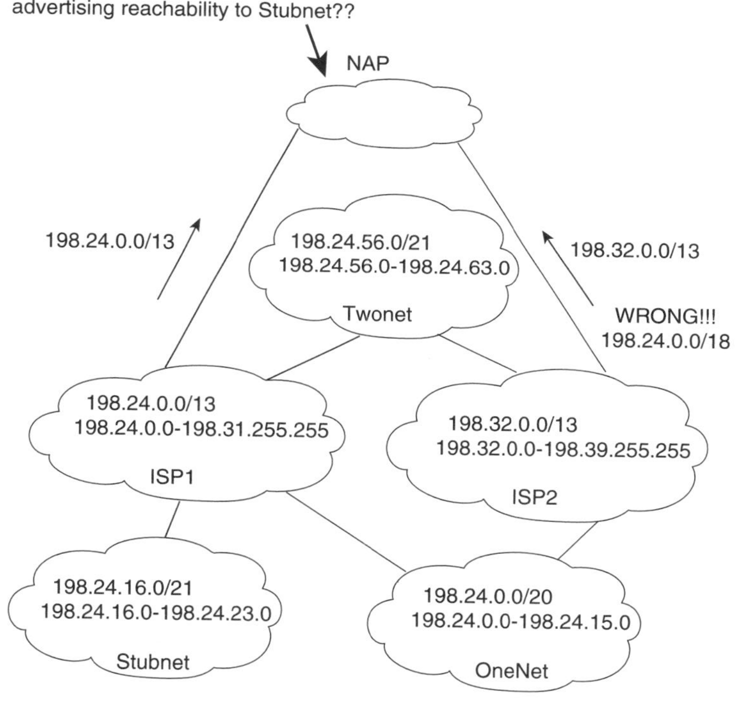

Advertising aggregates is a tricky business. Customers and ISPs have to be careful about the IP address ranges that the aggregate covers. No one is allowed to aggregate someone else's routes (proxy aggregation) unless the aggregating party is a supernet of the other party or both parties are in total agreement. In the following example, you will see how ISP2 can cause a routing black hole by aggregating the ranges coming from Onenet and Twonet.

NOTE Black holes result from inappropriate aggregation of others' routes.

If ISP2 were to send an aggregate that summarizes Onenet and Twonet into one update (198.24.0.0/18), as shown in Figure 3-14, a routing black hole would occur. For example, Stubnet, which is a customer of ISP1, has an IP address space that falls inside the aggregate 198.24.0.0/18. If ISP2 were to advertise the aggregate, traffic to Stubnet would follow the longest match of an IP prefix and end up blackholed in ISP2. This is why ISP2 must specifically announce each of the IP address ranges of its downstream customers that are not part of its own address space that it has in common with ISP1 (198.24.0.0/20 for Onenet and 198.24.56.0/21 for Twonet). In addition, ISP2 must announce its own address space of 198.32.0.0/13.

Figure 3-15 shows the correctly advertised aggregates. ISP2 has advertised the aggregates from Onenet and Twonet explicitly. This way, traffic destined for Stubnet will never go to ISP2.

Figure 3-15 *Correctly Advertised Aggregates Prevent Black Holes*

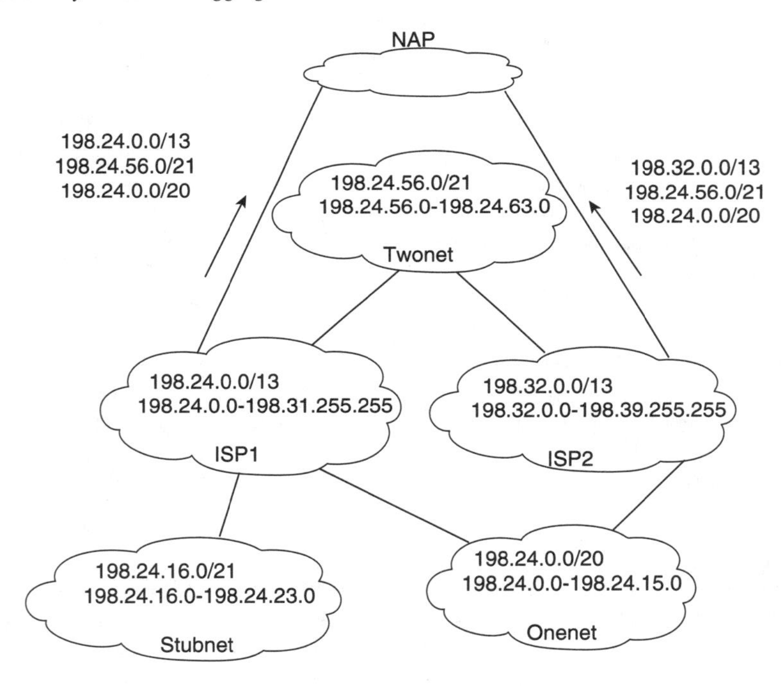

Note in Figure 3-15 that ISP1 is also advertising explicit aggregates of Onenet and Twonet. If ISP1 were to advertise only the less-specific aggregate 198.24.0.0/13, all traffic toward Onenet and Twonet would prefer the more-specific longest match path via ISP2.

Multihoming Scenario: Addresses Taken from Different Providers

One possibility for large domains is to take IP addresses from different providers based on geographic location. Consider Figure 3-16. Largenet has taken its IP addresses from two different providers, ISP1 and ISP2. With this design, each provider will be able to aggregate its own address space without having to list specific ranges from the other provider. ISP1 would advertise the aggregate 198.24.0.0/13, and ISP2 would advertise the aggregate 198.32.0.0/13. Both aggregates are supersets of IP address blocks given to Largenet.

Figure 3-16 *Multihomed Environment with Addresses from Different Providers*

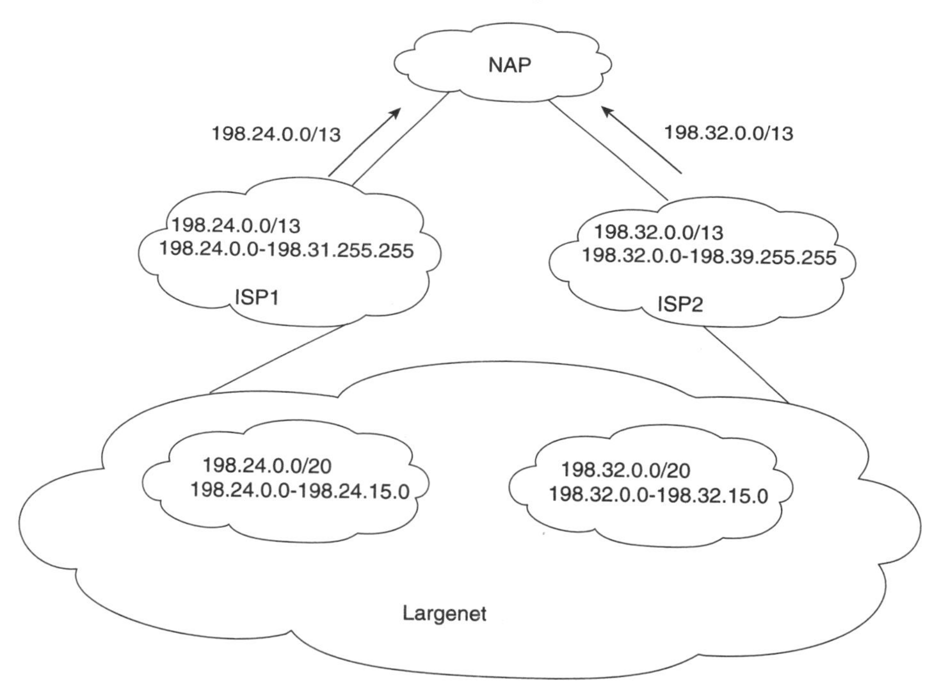

The major drawback with the design illustrated in Figure 3-16 is that backup routes to multihomed organizations are not maintained. ISP2 is advertising only its block of addresses and not the block taken from ISP1. In case ISP1 has problems and the 198.24.0.0/13 is lost, traffic to Largenet destined for 198.24.0.0/20 will be affected because it is not advertised anywhere else. The same reasoning applies to Largenet's addresses taken from ISP2. If the link to ISP2 fails, accessibility of the 198.32.0.0/20 range will be impaired. To remedy this situation, ISP1 has to advertise 198.32.0.0/20, and ISP2 has to advertise 198.24.0.0/20.

Multihoming Scenario: Addresses Taken from None of the Providers

Figure 3-17 illustrates a situation in which addresses are taken from a range totally different from ISP1 or ISP2's address space. In this case, both ISP1 and ISP2 advertise a specific aggregate (202.24.0.0/20) in addition to their own ranges (198.24.0.0/13 and 198.32.0.0/13). The drawback of this method is that all routers in the Internet must have a specific route to the new range introduced. Too many such instances would result in a significant increase in the global Internet routing table size.

Figure 3-17 *Addresses Obtained Outside ISP Address Space*

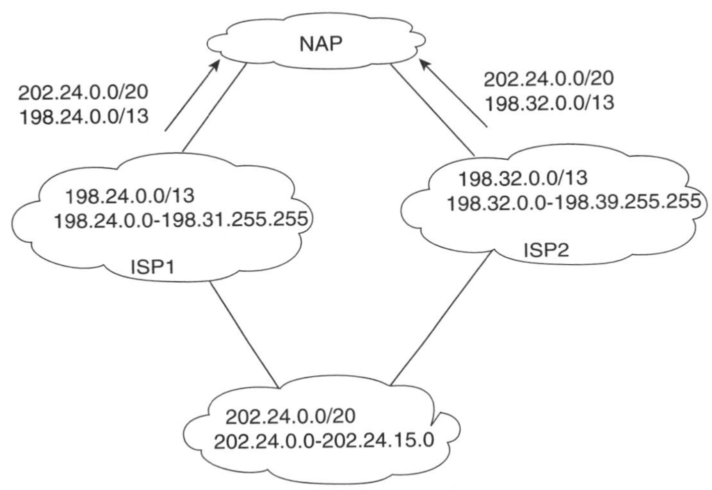

Aggregation Recommendations

In conclusion, a domain that has been allocated a range of addresses has the sole authority (and responsibility) for aggregation of its addresses. When a domain performs aggregation, it should aggregate as much as possible without introducing ambiguity, which is possible in the case of multihomed networks.

Different situations require different designs. No single specific solution can handle all cases. It is recommended that single-homed customers obtain a single contiguous prefix from their direct provider and perform static routing to their ISP if possible, thereby avoiding potential problems with more-complicated, unnecessary configurations. If single-homed customers change providers, they should plan to transition to the new provider's address space. For multihomed customers, address assignments should be conducted in such a way that aggregation is maximized as much as possible. In the case where aggregation impacts redundancy, redundancy should prevail even if extra networks have to be listed.

The introduction of CIDR has helped dampen the explosion of global Internet routing tables tremendously over the last few years. Border Gateway Protocol version 4 (BGP-4) is the interdomain routing protocol of choice on the Internet, in part because it so efficiently handles route aggregation and propagation between domains. As this book progresses, you will see more examples of the importance of CIDR in controlling traffic behavior and stability.

For additional information on CIDR, current and historical Internet routing table sizes, and some other interesting information, follow the references provided in Appendix A.

Private Addressing and Network Address Translation

To find ways to slow down the pace at which IP addresses were being allocated, it was important to identify different connectivity requirements and to try to assign IP addresses accordingly.

Most organizations' connectivity needs fall into the following categories:

- Global connectivity
- Private connectivity

Global Connectivity

Global connectivity means that hosts inside an organization have access to both internal and Internet hosts. In this case, hosts have to be configured with globally unique IP addresses that are recognized inside and outside the organization. Organizations requiring global connectivity must request IP addresses from their service providers.

Private Connectivity

Private connectivity means that hosts inside an organization have access to internal hosts only, not Internet hosts. Examples of hosts that require only private connectivity include bank ATM machines, cash registers in a retail store, or any hosts that do not require connectivity to hosts outside the company. Private hosts need to have IP addresses that are unique inside the organization. For this type of connectivity, the IANA has reserved the following three blocks of the IP address space for what are referred to as "private internets":

- 10.0.0.0 through 10.255.255.255 (a single Class A network number)
- 172.16.0.0 through 172.31.255.255 (16 contiguous Class B network numbers)
- 192.168.0.0 through 192.168.255.255 (256 contiguous Class C network numbers)

Additional information on their use, as well as other reserved network numbers, can be found in Internet RFC 1918[5].

An enterprise that picks its addresses from the preceding ranges does not need to get permission from IANA or an Internet Registry. Hosts that get a private IP address can connect with any other host inside the organization, but they cannot connect to hosts outside the organization without going through a proxy gateway device. The reason is that IP packets leaving the internal network will have a source IP address that is ambiguous outside the company and that cannot be reached via external networks. Because multiple companies building private networks can use the same private IP address, fewer unique global IP addresses need to be assigned.

Hosts having private addresses can coexist with hosts having global addresses. Figure 3-18 illustrates such an environment.

Figure 3-18 *General Private Connectivity Environment*

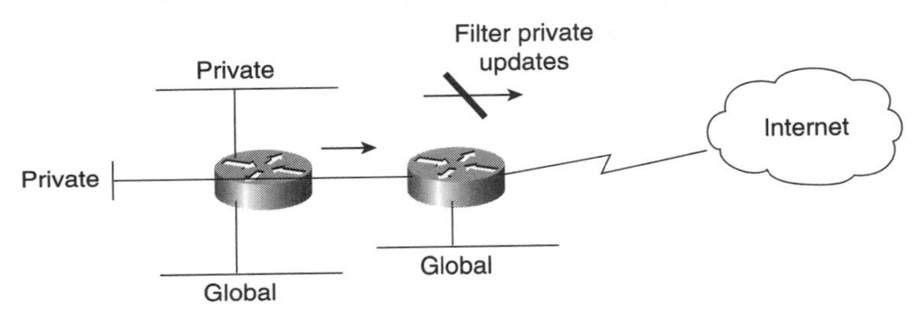

Companies may choose to make most of their hosts private and still keep particular segments with hosts having global addresses. The latter hosts can reach the Internet as usual. Companies that use private addresses and still have connectivity to the Internet have the responsibility of applying routing filters to prevent the private addresses from being leaked to the Internet. Most service providers, however, should apply explicit policies to incoming routing updates from customers that permit only their global IP space.

The drawback of this approach is that if an organization later decides to open its hosts to the Internet, the private IP address will have to be renumbered to use the new global IP space. With the introduction of new protocols such as the Dynamic Host Configuration Protocol (DHCP)[6], this task has become much simpler. DHCP provides a mechanism for transmitting configuration parameters (including IP addresses) to hosts using the TCP/IP protocol suite. If the hosts are DHCP-capable, hosts can get their new addresses dynamically from a central server.

A second option is to install a bastion host that acts as a gateway between the private network and the global Internet. Host A in Figure 3-19 has a private IP address. If it wants to Telnet to a destination outside the company, it can do so by first logging in to Host B and then Telnetting from Host B to the outside. Packets leaving the company would now have Host B's source IP address, which is globally reachable. A third option is to use a Network Address Translator.

Figure 3-19 *Privately Addressed Hosts Accessing Internet Resources*

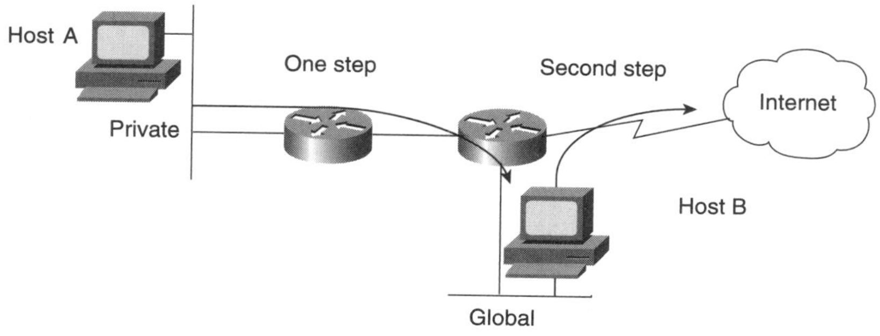

Network Address Translator

Companies migrating from a private address space to a global address space can do so with the help of Network Address Translator (NAT)[7] technology. NAT technology lets private networks connect to the Internet without resorting to renumbering IP addresses. A NAT router is placed at the border of a domain; it translates the private addresses into global addresses, and vice versa, when internal hosts need to communicate with destinations on the Internet.

In Figure 3-20, Hosts A and B have private IP addresses 10.1.1.1 and 10.1.1.2, respectively.

Figure 3-20 *Network Address Translator Example*

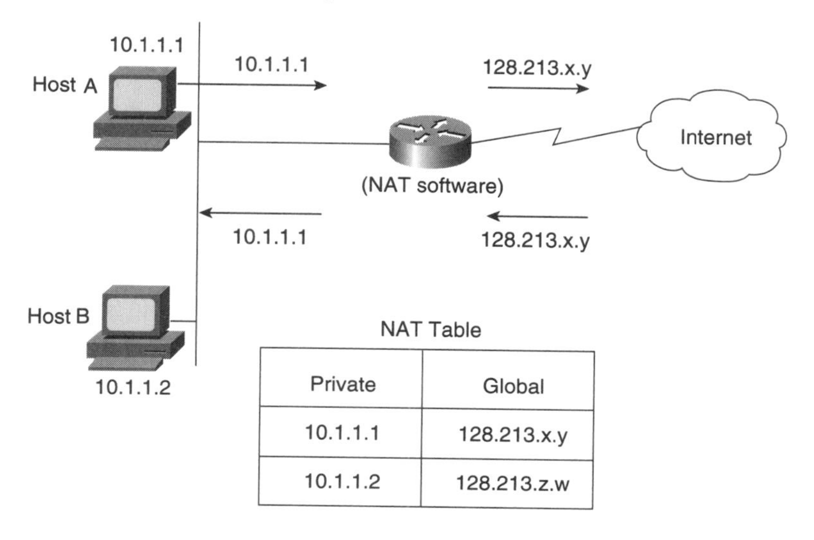

Private	Global
10.1.1.1	128.213.x.y
10.1.1.2	128.213.z.w

If Hosts A and B want to reach a destination outside the company, the NAT device will convert the source IP addresses of the packets according to a predefined (or dynamic) mapping in the NAT table on the device. Packets from Host A will reach an outside destination as coming from source IP address 128.213.x.y. Hosts in the global domain will be unaware that the address translation is taking place, and they will reply to the global address. Packets returning from an outside host will have the destination address of the packets mapped back to the private IP address of the internal source host of the conversation.

A detailed discussion of NAT devices is beyond the scope of this book primarily because they have to handle many "corner cases" and more-involved situations. Such cases include enterprises that have used addresses that are not part of the IANA private addresses. In this case, an IR could have already assigned the address space used to some other company. Other situations involve enterprises that are assigned fewer global addresses than their number of internal hosts. In this case, the NAT must dynamically map private IP addresses to a smaller pool of global addresses.

NAT functionality doesn't always require a dedicated device, and it is often available in router software already deployed in a network. For example, Cisco Systems offers NAT as part of Cisco Internetwork Operating System (IOS).

IP Version 6

IP version 6 (IPv6)[8], also known as IP next generation (IPng), is a move to improve the existing IPv4 implementation.

The IPng proposal was released in July 1992 at an Internet Engineering Task Force (IETF) meeting in Boston, and a number of working groups were formed in response. IPv6 tackles issues such as IP address depletion, quality of service capabilities, node auto-configuration, authentication, and security capabilities.

IPv6 is still in the experimental stage. It is not easy for companies and administrators who are deeply invested in the IPv4 architecture to migrate to a totally new architecture. As long as the IPv4 implementation keeps providing hooks and techniques (as cumbersome as they might seem) to tackle all the major issues that IPv6 is expressly designed to solve, adopting IPv6 does not seem very compelling to many companies. How soon or how late people will migrate to IPv6 is yet to be seen. This book touches on only part of the IPv6 addressing scheme and how it compares to what you have already seen with IPv4.

IPv6 addresses are 128 bits long, compared to 32 bits in IPv4. This should provide ample address space to handle address depletion and scalability issues in the Internet. 128 bits of addressing translates to 2^{128}, which is a large number of addresses!

The types of IPv6 addresses are indicated by the leftmost bits of the address in a variable-length field referred to as the Format Prefix (FP) (see Figure 3-21).

Figure 3-21 *IPv6 Prefix and Address Format*

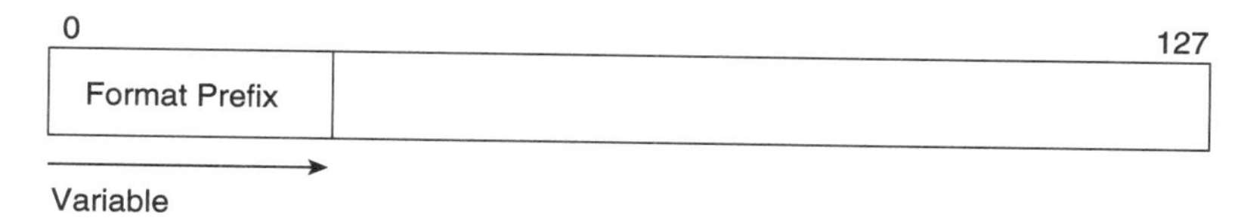

Table 3-7 outlines the initial allocation of those prefixes. IPv6 has defined multiple types of addresses. For the sake of this discussion, we are interested in the provider-based unicast addresses and the local use addresses for companies with IPv4 techniques.

Table 3-7 *Allocation of IPv6 Prefixes*

Description	Format Prefix
Reserved	0000 0000
Unassigned	0000 0001
Reserved for NSAP allocation	0000 001
Reserved for IPX allocation	0000 010
Unassigned	0000 011
Unassigned	0000 1
Unassigned	0001
Unassigned	001
Provider-based unicast addresses	**010**
Unassigned	011
Reserved for geographic unicast addresses	100
Unassigned	101
Unassigned	110
Unassigned	1110
Unassigned	1111 0
Unassigned	1111 10
Unassigned	1111 110
Unassigned	1111 1110 0
Link-local-use addresses	**1111 1110 10**
Site-local-use addresses	**1111 1110 11**
Multicast addresses	1111 1111

Provider-Based Unicast Addresses

Provider-based unicast addresses are similar to IPv4 global addresses. Figure 3-22 illustrates their format.

Figure 3-22 *IPv6: Provider-Based Unicast Address Format*

3	x bits	y bits	z bits	w bits	48-x-y-z-w bits
010	REGISTRY ID	PROVIDER ID	SUBSCRIBER ID	SUBNET ID	INTERFACE ID

Descriptions of the fields for the provider-based unicast addresses are as follows:

- **Format prefix**—The first three bits are 010, indicating a provider-based unicast address.
- **REGISTRY ID**—Identifies the Internet address registry that assigns the PROVIDER ID.
- **PROVIDER ID**—Identifies the service provider responsible for the address.
- **SUBSCRIBER ID**—Identifies which subscriber is connected to the service provider.
- **SUBNET ID**—Identifies the physical link to which the address belongs.
- **INTERFACE ID**—Identifies a single interface among interfaces that belong to the SUBNET ID. For example, this could be the traditional 48-bit IEEE-802 Media Access Control (MAC) address.

IPv6 global addresses incorporate the CIDR functions of the IPv4 scheme. Addresses are defined in such a way as to allow hierarchy, where each entity takes its portion of the address from an entity above it (see Figure 3-23).

Figure 3-23 *IPv6 Address Assignment Hierarchy*

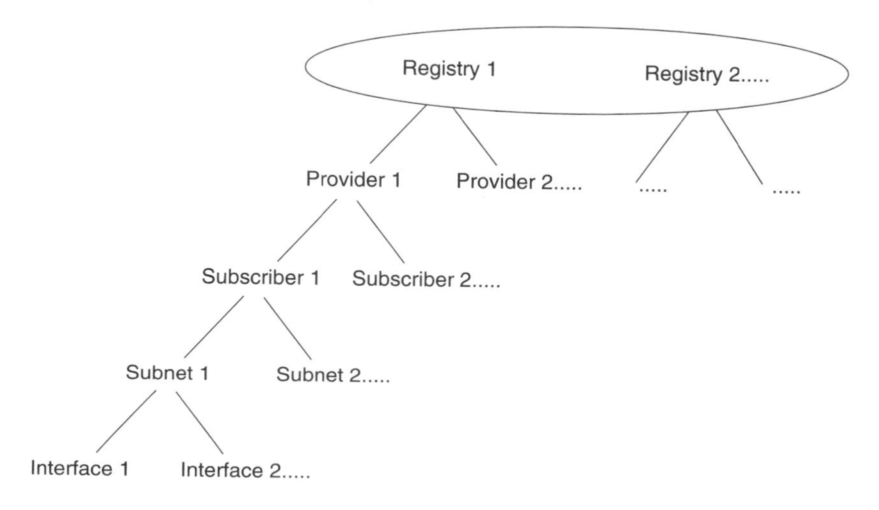

Local-Use Addresses

Local-use addresses are similar to the IPv4 private addresses defined in RFC 1918. Local-use addresses are divided into two types:

- Link-local-use (prefix 1111111010), which are private to a particular physical segment
- Site-local-use (prefix 1111111011), which are private to a particular site

Figure 3-24 illustrates the format of these local-use addresses.

Figure 3-24 *Local-Use Address Formats*

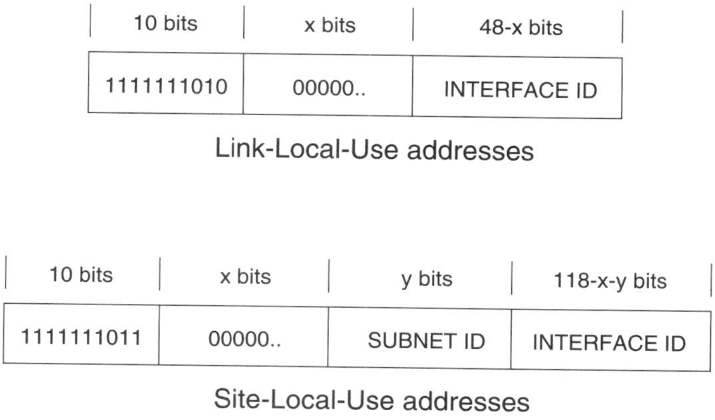

10 bits	x bits	48-x bits
1111111010	00000..	INTERFACE ID

Link-Local-Use addresses

10 bits	x bits	y bits	118-x-y bits
1111111011	00000..	SUBNET ID	INTERFACE ID

Site-Local-Use addresses

Local-use addresses have local meaning. Link-local addresses have local meaning to a particular segment, and site-local addresses have local meaning to a particular site.

Companies that are not connected to the Internet can easily assign their own addresses without a need for requesting prefixes from the global address space. If the company later decides to connect to the global Internet, a REGISTRY ID, PROVIDER ID, and SUBSCRIBER ID will be assigned with the already assigned local addresses. This is a major advantage over having to replace all private addresses with global addresses or using NAT tables to get things working in the IPv4 addressing scheme.

Looking Ahead

IP addresses and addressing issues are basic elements of interdomain routing. IP addressing defines where certain information can be found, but it does not give any indication of the pathway by which the information is to be accessed. Hosts need a mechanism to exchange information about destinations and to calculate the optimal path to reach a given destination. This mechanism, of course, is routing.

This chapter concludes all the fundamental material required before proceeding to further study of Internet routing architectures. The next chapter covers the basics of interdomain routing, building on the concepts of addressing, global networks, and domains that have already been discussed. Routing protocols in general, and BGP in particular, will be discussed, with implementation details on BGP to follow in Chapter 5 and beyond.

Frequently Asked Questions

Q — *How is VLSM different from subnetting?*

A — It is not. VLSM is an extension of basic subnetting whereby the same Class A, B, or C address is subnetted by using masks of different lengths.

Q — *Why do I need VLSM?*

A — VLSM provides a more efficient way to assign IP addresses. It provides more flexibility in assigning adequate numbers of hosts and subnets given a limited number of IP addresses.

Q — *What is the difference between CIDR and supernetting?*

A — Classless inter-domain routing is the mechanism that allows networks to advertise both supernets and subnets outside the normal bounds of a classful network number. Supernetting is a representation that allows masks that are shorter than the natural masks, hence creating supernets.

Q — *Is the classful model the cause of the growth in the global routing tables?*

A — No. The growth of the routing tables is due to more organizations connecting to the Internet. The classful model does not offer a scalable solution to cope with such growth.

Q — *I have a network that uses older protocols such as RIP-1 and IGRP. What issues should I consider in deciding whether to upgrade to newer protocols that support VLSM and CIDR?*

A — If you feel that implementing VLSM and CIDR can help you utilize your address space more efficiently and will give you better route summarization capabilities, you should upgrade. One issue could be whether your current hardware is capable of running newer protocols that might need extra processing or memory requirements. Of course, this depends on the protocol to which you are upgrading. Other issues involve the coexistence of new and old protocols. Because network upgrades are usually done in stages, you will be faced with situations where both older and newer protocols are running concurrently. Because older classful routing protocols cannot deal with VLSM or CIDR, you should not be surprised that extensive use of static routing might be required to ensure connectivity in your domain during the transition period.

Q — *Can I aggregate any routes in my routing table?*

A — You can aggregate only routes that you administer. Aggregating routes that are not an extension of your domain could create black holes.

Q — *If I leave my provider, can I keep my IP addresses?*

A — For the purposes of better aggregation, today's routing practices recommend (sometimes require) that you return the old addresses and get addresses from your new provider. Ask your provider for its policies.

Q — *I have some hosts that require Internet connectivity and others that do not. Can I use private addresses on some hosts and not others?*

A — Yes, you can use both private and global addresses in the same network. When advertising routes to your provider, you advertise only the legal (nonprivate) networks.

Q — *I need to connect to the Internet, and not all my addresses are registered. I can't afford to renumber. What should I do?*

A — You could use Network Address Translation (NAT) to map your invalid address to a legitimate pool of addresses that you get from your provider.

References

[1]RFC 791, "Internet Protocol (IP)," www.isi.edu/in-notes/rfc791.txt

[2]RFC 917, "Internet Subnets," www.isi.edu/in-notes/rfc917.txt

[3]RFC 1878, "Variable Length Subnet Table for IPv4," www.isi.edu/in-notes/rfc1878.txt

[4]RFC 1519, "Classless Inter-Domain Routing (CIDR)," www.isi.edu/in-notes/rfc1519.txt

[5]RFC 1918, "Address Allocation for Private Internets," www.isi.edu/in-notes/rfc1918.txt

[6]RFC 1541, "Dynamic Host Configuration Protocol," www.isi.edu/in-notes/rfc1541.txt

[7]RFC 1631, "The IP Network Address Translator," www.isi.edu/in-notes/rfc1631.txt

[8]RFC 1884, "IP Version 6 Addressing Architecture," www.isi.edu/in-notes/rfc1884.txt

PART II

Routing Protocol Basics

Although this book is primarily concerned with exterior gateway protocols—routing between different autonomous systems—it makes sense to look at internal gateway protocols as a first step because, conceptually and in practice, the two will affect each other's behavior. Thus, Chapter 4 begins with a consideration of protocols intended for routing within an autonomous system before moving into exterior gateway protocols. Chapter 4 concludes with an overview of the particular exterior gateway protocol, Border Gateway Protocol (BGP), which we will focus on. Chapter 5 contains provides an overview of how BGP Version 4 (BGP-4) operates and how and what it negotiates with neighboring routers. In addition, Chapter 5 covers the multiprotocol extensions to BGP-4, Capabilities Negotiation with BGP-4, and the TCP MD5 Signature Option for BGP. Understanding the basics of BGP, as described in Part II, is necessary before we can put the protocol's capabilities to use in practical routing design problems throughout the rest of the book.

This chapter covers the following key topics:

- **Overview of routers and routing**—Provides a brief consideration of basic routing and interior gateway protocols (IGPs) as a point of contrast for the next chapter's more in-depth deliberation of exterior gateway protocols.
- **Routing protocol concepts**—This section provides an overview of the distance vector and link-state distributed routing algorithms.
- **Segregating the world into autonomous systems**—An autonomous system is a set of routers that shares the same routing policies. Various configurations for autonomous systems are possible, depending on how many exit points to outside networks are desired and whether the system should permit transit traffic.

CHAPTER 4

Interdomain Routing Basics

The Internet is a conglomeration of autonomous systems that define the administrative authority and the routing policies of different organizations. Autonomous systems are made up of routers that run Interior Gateway Protocols (IGPs) such as Routing Information Protocol (RIP), Enhanced Interior Gateway Routing Protocol (EIGRP), Open Shortest Path First (OSPF), and Intermediate System-to-Intermediate System (IS-IS) within their boundaries and interconnect via an Exterior Gateway Protocol (EGP). The current Internet de facto standard EGP is the Border Gateway Protocol Version 4 (BGP-4), defined in RFC 1771[1].

Overview of Routers and Routing

Routers are devices that direct traffic between hosts. They build routing tables that contain collected information on all the best paths to all the destinations that they know how to reach. The steps for basic routing are as follows:

Step 1 Routers run programs referred to as *routing protocols* to both transmit and receive route information to and from other routers in the network.

Step 2 Routers use this information to populate routing tables that are associated with each particular routing protocol.

Step 3 Routers scan the routing tables from the different routing protocols (if more than one routing protocol is running) and select the best path(s) to each destination.

Step 4 Routers associate with that destination the next-hop device's attached data link layer address and the local outgoing interface to be used when forwarding packets to the destination. Note that the next-hop device could be another router, or perhaps even the destination host.

Step 5 The next-hop device's forwarding information (data link layer address plus outgoing interface) is placed in the router's forwarding table.

Step 6 When a router receives a packet, the router examines the packet's header to determine the destination address.

Step 7 The router consults the forwarding table to obtain the outgoing interface and next-hop address to reach the destination.

Step 8 The router performs any additional functions required (such as IP TTL decrement or manipulating IP TOS settings) and then forwards the packet on to the appropriate device.

Step 9 This continues until the destination host is reached. This behavior reflects the hop-by-hop routing paradigm that's generally used in packet-switching networks.

EGPs, such as BGP, were introduced because IGPs do not scale well in networks that go beyond the enterprise level, with thousands of nodes and hundreds of thousands of routes. IGPs were never intended to be used for this purpose. This chapter touches on basic IGP functionality.

Basic Routing Example

Figure 4-1 describes three routers—RTA, RTB, and RTC—connecting three local area networks—192.10.1.0, 192.10.5.0, and 192.10.6.0—via serial links. Each serial link is represented by its own network number, which results in three additional networks, 192.10.2.0, 192.10.3.0, and 192.10.4.0. Each network has a metric associated with it, indicating the level of overhead (cost) of transmitting traffic on that particular link. The link between RTA and RTB, for example, has a cost of 2,000, much higher than the cost of 60 of the link between RTA and RTC. In practice, the link between RTA and RTB might be a 56 Kbps link with much larger delays than the T1 link between RTA and RTC and the T1 link between RTC and RTB combined.

Figure 4-1 *Basic Routing Behavior*

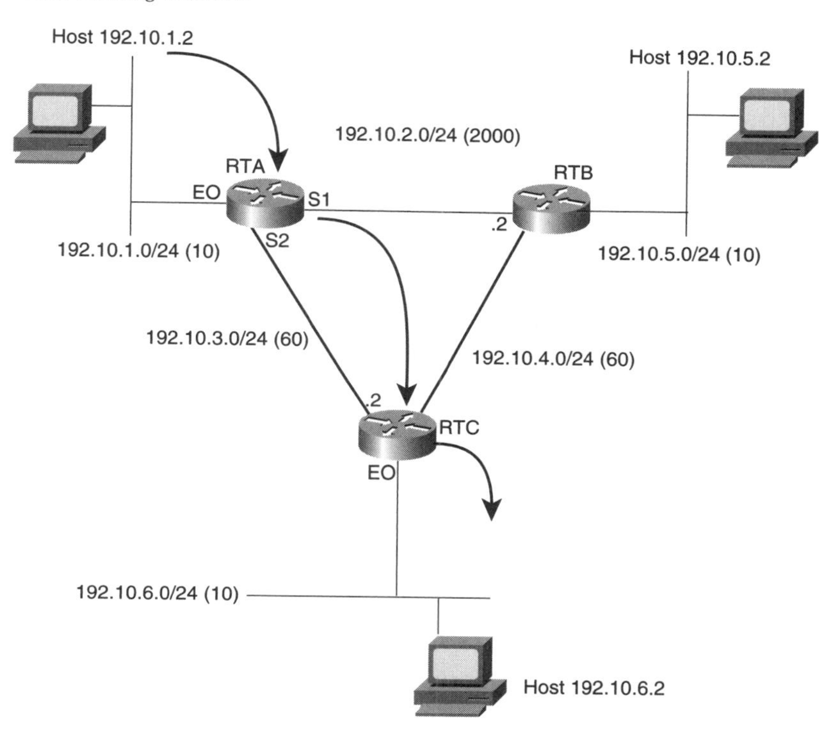

RTA IP Routing Table (RIP)

Destination	Next Hop	Hop Count
192.10.1.0	Connected (E0)	-
192.10.2.0	Connected (S1)	-
192.10.3.0	Connected (S2)	-
192.10.4.0	192.10.2.2 (S1) 192.10.3.2 (S2)	1 1
192.10.5.0	192.10.2.2 (S1)	1
192.10.6.0	192.10.3.2 (S2)	1

RTA IP Routing Table (OSPF)

Destination	Next Hop	Hop Count
192.10.1.0	Connected (E0)	-
192.10.2.0	Connected (S1)	-
192.10.3.0	Connected (S2)	-
192.10.4.0	192.10.3.2 (S2)	120
192.10.5.0	192.10.3.2 (S2)	130
192.10.6.0	192.10.3.2 (S2)	70

Routers RTA, RTB, and RTC would exchange network information via some IGP and build their respective IP routing tables. Figure 4-1 shows examples of RTA's IP routing table for two different scenarios; the routers are exchanging routing information via RIP in one scenario and OSPF in another.

As an example of how traffic is passed between end stations, if host 192.10.1.2 were trying to reach host 192.10.6.2, it would use its local manually installed default route to first send the traffic to RTA. RTA would look in its IP routing table for any network that matches this destination and would find that network 192.10.6.0 is reachable via next-hop 192.10.3.2 (RTC) on serial line 2 (S2). RTC would receive the traffic and would try to look for the destination in its IP routing table (not shown). RTC would discover that the host is directly connected to its Ethernet 0 interface (E0) and would send the traffic to 192.10.6.2.

In this example, the routing is the same whether RTA is using the RIP or OSPF scenario. RIP and OSPF, however, fall into different categories of IGP protocols—distance vector protocols and link-state protocols, respectively. For a different routing example in Figure 4-1, the results might be different depending on whether you are looking at the RIP or OSPF scenario. It is useful at this point to consider characteristics of both IGP protocol categories to see how protocols generally have evolved to meet increasingly sophisticated routing demands.

Routing Protocol Concepts

Generally speaking, most routing protocols used today are based on one of two types of distributed routing algorithms: link-state or distance vector. In the next few sections, we'll discuss the different properties of distance vector and link-state routing algorithms.

Distance Vector Routing Protocols

Distance vector protocols are sometimes referred to as Bellman-Ford protocols, named after the person who invented the algorithm used for calculating the shortest paths[2] and for the people who first described a distributed use of the algorithm[3]. The term *distance vector* is derived from the fact that the protocol includes a vector (list) of distances (hop counts or other metrics) associated with each destination prefix routing message.

Distance vector routing protocols, such as Routing Information Protocol (RIP), utilize a distributed computation approach to calculating the route to each destination prefix. In other words, distance vector protocols require that each node separately calculate the best path (output link) to each destination prefix.

After selecting the best path, a router then sends distance vectors to its neighbors, notifying them of the reachability of each destination prefix and of the corresponding metrics associated with the path it has selected to reach the prefix. In parallel, its neighbors also calculate the best path to each available destination and then notify their neighbors of the available path (and associated metrics) they've selected to reach the destination. Upon the receipt of messages from neighbors detailing the destination and associated metrics that the neighbor has selected, the router might determine that a better path exists via an alternative neighbor. The router will again notify its neighbors of its selected paths (and associated metrics) to reach each destination. This cycle continues until all the routers have converged upon a common understanding of the best paths to reach each destination prefix.

Initial specifications of distance vector routing protocols such as RIP Version 1 (RIP-1) had several drawbacks. For example, hop count was the only metric RIP-1 used to select a path. This imposed several limitations. Consider, for example, the RTA routing tables shown in Figure 4-1. One table represents routing information considered when using RIP, and the other when using OSPF. (OSPF is a link-state routing protocol that will be discussed in more detail in the following sections.)

When using RIP-1, RTA would select the direct link between RTA and RTB to reach network 192.10.5.0. RTA prefers this link because the direct path requires just one hop via the RTB path versus two hops via the RTC-RTB path. However, RTA has no knowledge that the RTA-RTB link is actually a very low-capacity, high-latency connection and that using the RTC-RTB path would provide a better level of service.

On the other hand, when using OSPF and metrics other than hop count alone for path selection, RTA will realize that the path to RTB via RTC (cost: 60 + 60 = 120; 2 hops) is actually more optimal than the direct path (cost: 2000; 1 hop).

Another issue with hop counts is the count to infinity restriction. Traditional distance vector protocols (for example, RIP-1) have a finite limit of hops, often 15, after which a route is considered unreachable. This would restrict the propagation of routing updates and would cause problems for large networks (those with more than 15 nodes in a given path). The reliance on hop counts is one deficiency of distance vector protocols, although newer distance vector protocols (that is, RIP-2 and EIGRP) are not constrained as such.

Another deficiency is the way that the routing information is exchanged. Traditional distance vector protocols work on the concept that routers exchange all the IP network numbers they can reach via periodic exchange of distance vector broadcasts—broadcasts that are sent when a "refresh timer" associated with the message exchange expires. Because of this, if the refresh timer expires and a fresh set of routing information is broadcast to your neighbors, the timer is reset, and no new information is sent until the timer expires again. Now, consider what would happen if a link or path became unavailable just after a refresh occurred. Propagation of the path failure would be suppressed until the refresh timer expired, thereby slowing convergence considerably.

Fortunately, newer distance vector protocols, such as EIGRP and RIP-2, introduce the concept of *triggered updates*. Triggered updates propagate failures as soon as they occur, speeding convergence considerably.

As you might have realized, in large networks, or even small networks with a large number of destination prefixes, periodic exchange of the routing table between neighbors might become very large and very difficult to maintain, contributing to slower convergence. Also, the amount of CPU and link overhead consumed by periodic advertisement of routing information can become quite large. Another property that newer distance vector protocols have adopted is to introduce reliability to the transmission of the distance vectors between neighbors, eliminating the need to periodically readvertise the entire routing table.

Convergence refers to the point in time at which the entire network becomes updated to the fact that a particular route has appeared, disappeared, or changed. Traditional distance vector protocols worked on the basis of periodic updates and hold-down timers: If a route is not received in a certain amount of time, the route goes into a hold-down state and gets aged out of the routing table. The hold-down and aging process translates into minutes in convergence time before the whole network detects that a route has disappeared. The delay between a route's becoming unavailable and its aging out of the routing tables can result in temporary forwarding loops or black holes.

Another issue in some distance vector protocols (for example, RIP) is that when an active route disappears, but the same route reappears with a higher metric (presumably emanating from another router, indicating a possible "good" alternative path), the route is still put into a hold-down state. Thus, the amount of time for the entire network to converge is still increased.

Another major drawback of first-generation distance vector protocols is their classful nature and their lack of support for VLSM or CIDR. These distance vector protocols do not exchange mask information in their routing updates and are therefore incapable of supporting these technologies. In RIP-1, a router that receives a routing update on a certain interface will apply to this update its locally defined subnet mask. IGRP does the same thing as RIP-1 but falls back to Class A, B, and C network masks if a portion of the transmitted network address does not match the local network address. This would lead to confusion (in case the interface belongs to a network that is variably subnetted) and a misinterpretation of the received routing update. Newer distance vector protocols, such as RIP Version 2 (RIP-2) and EIGRP, overcome the aforementioned shortcomings.

Several modifications have been made that alleviate deficiencies associated with traditional distance vector routing protocol behaviors. For example, RIP-2 and EIGRP support VLSM and CIDR. Also, IGRP and EIGRP have the capability to factor in composite metrics used to represent link characteristics along a path (such as bandwidth, utilization, delay, MTU, and so forth), which allows them to calculate more optimal paths than using a hop count alone.

The simplicity and maturity of distance vector protocols has led to their popularity. The primary drawback of traditional implementation of distance vector protocols is slow convergence, a property that can be a catalyst for introducing forwarding loops and/or black-holing traffic during topological changes. However, newer distance vector protocols—most notably, EIGRP—actually converge quite well.

This section wouldn't be complete without mentioning that BGP falls into the distance vector category. In addition to the standard distance vector properties, BGP employs an additional mechanism referred to as the *path vector*, used to avoid the count to infinity problem previously discussed. Essentially, the path vector contains a list of routing domains

(AS numbers) through which the route has traversed. If a domain receives a route for which its domain identifier is already listed in the path, the route is ignored. This path information provides a mechanism that allows routing loops to be pruned. It can also be used to apply domain-based policies. This path attribute, and many other path attributes, are discussed in detail in the following chapters.

Link-State Routing Protocols

Link-state routing protocols, such as Open Shortest Path First (OSPF)[4] and Intermediate System-to-Intermediate System (IS-IS)[5], utilize a replicated distributed database model and are considered to be more-complex routing protocols. Link-state protocols work on the basis that routers exchange information elements, called *link states*, which carry information about links and nodes in the routing domain. This means that routers running link-state protocols do not exchange routing tables as distance vector protocols do. Rather, they exchange information about adjacent neighbors and networks and include metric information associated with the connection.

One way to view link-state routing protocols is as a jigsaw puzzle. Each router in the network generates a piece of the puzzle (link state) that describes itself and where it connects to adjacent puzzle pieces. It also provides a list of the metrics corresponding to the connection with each piece of the puzzle. The local router's piece of the puzzle is then reliably distributed throughout the network, router by router, via a flooding mechanism, until all nodes in the domain have received a copy of the puzzle piece. When distribution is complete, every router in the network has a copy of every piece of the puzzle and stores the puzzle pieces in what's referred to as a *link-state database*. Each router then autonomously constructs the entire puzzle, the result of which is an identical copy of the entire puzzle on each router in the network.

Then, by applying the SPF (shortest path first) algorithm (most commonly, the Dijkstra Algorithm) to the puzzle, each router calculates a tree of shortest paths to each destination, placing itself at the root.

Following are some of the benefits that link-state protocols provide:

- **No hop count**—There are no limits on the number of hops a route can take. Link-state protocols work on the basis of link metrics rather than hop counts.

  As an example of a link-state protocol's reliance on metrics rather than hop count, turn again to the RTA routing tables shown in Figure 4-1. In the OSPF case, RTA has picked the optimal path to reach RTB by factoring in the cost of the links. Its routing table lists the next hop of 192.10.3.2 (RTC) to reach 192.10.5.0 (RTB). This is in contrast to the RIP scenario, which resulted in a suboptimal path.

- **Bandwidth representation**—Link bandwidth and delays may be (manually or dynamically) factored in when calculating the shortest path to a certain destination. This leads to better load balancing based on actual link cost rather than hop count.
- **Better convergence**—Link and node changes are immediately flooded into the domain via link-state updates. All routers in the domain will instantly update their routing tables (some similar to triggered updates).
- **Support for VLSM and CIDR**—Link-state protocols exchange mask information as part of the information elements that are flooded into the domain. As a result, networks with variable-length subnet masks can be easily identified.
- **Better hierarchy**—Whereas distance vector networks are flat networks, link-state protocols provide mechanisms to divide the domain into different levels or areas. This hierarchical approach better scopes network instabilities within areas.

Although link-state algorithms have traditionally provided better routing scalability, which allows them to be used in bigger and more complex topologies, they still should be restricted to interior routing. Link-state protocols by themselves cannot provide a global connectivity solution required for Internet interdomain routing. In very large networks and in case of route oscillation caused by link instabilities, link-state retransmission and recomputation will become too large for any single router to handle.

Although a more detailed discussion of IGPs is beyond the scope of this book, two excellent references that discuss the different link-state and distance vector routing protocols are *Interconnections, Second Edition: Bridges, Routers, Switches and Internetworking Protocols*[6] by Radia Perlman and *OSPF: Anatomy of an Internet Routing Protocol*[7] by John T. Moy.

Most large service providers today use link-state routing protocols for intra-AS routing, primarily because of its fast convergence capabilities. The two most common protocols deployed in this space are OSPF and IS-IS.

Many older service providers have selected IS-IS as their IGP, and some newer providers select OSPF or IS-IS. Initially, it might seem that older networks use IS-IS rather than OSPF because the U.S. Government required support of ISO CLNP by networks in order for the networks to be awarded federal contracts. (Note that IS-IS is capable of carrying both CLNP and IP Network layer information, while OSPF is capable of carrying only IP information.) However, Internet folklore suggests that the driving factor was that IS-IS implementations were much more stable than OSPF implementations when early providers were selecting which routing protocol to use. This stability obviously had a significant impact on which IGP service providers selected.

Today, both IS-IS and OSPF are widely deployed in ISP networks. The maturity and stability of IS-IS has resulted in its remaining deployed in large networks, as well as its being the IGP of choice for some more recently deployed networks.

Segregating the World into Autonomous Systems

Exterior routing protocols were created to control the expansion of routing tables and to provide a more structured view of the Internet by segregating routing domains into separate administrations, called *autonomous systems (ASs)*, which each have their own independent routing policies and unique IGPs.

During the early days of the Internet, an exterior gateway protocol called EGP[8] (not to be confused with Exterior Gateway Protocols in general) was used. The NSFNET used EGP to exchange reachability information between the backbone and the regional networks. Although the use of EGP was widely deployed, its topology restrictions and inefficiency in dealing with routing loops and setting routing policies created a need for a new and more robust protocol. Currently, BGP-4 is the de facto standard for interdomain routing in the Internet.

NOTE Note that the primary difference between intra-AS and inter-AS routing is that intra-AS routing is usually optimized in accordance with the required technical demands, while inter-AS usually reflects political and business relationships between the networks and companies involved.

Static Routing, Default Routing, and Dynamic Routing

Before introducing and looking at the basic ways in which autonomous systems can be connected to ISPs, we need to establish some basic terminology and concepts of routing:

- *Static routing* refers to routes to destinations being listed manually, or statically, as the name implies, in the router. Network reachability in this case is not dependent on the existence and state of the network itself. Whether a destination is active or not, the static routes remain in the routing table, and traffic is still sent toward the specified destination.
- *Default routing* refers to a "last resort" outlet. Traffic to destinations that is unknown to the router is sent to that default outlet. Default routing is the easiest form of routing for a domain connected to a single exit point.
- *Dynamic routing* refers to routes being learned via an interior or exterior routing protocol. Network reachability is dependent on the existence and state of the network. If a destination is down, the route disappears from the routing table, and traffic is not sent toward that destination.

These three routing approaches are possibilities for all the AS configurations considered in forthcoming sections, but usually there is an optimal approach. Thus, in illustrating different autonomous systems, this chapter considers whether static, dynamic, default, or some combination of these is optimal. This chapter also considers whether interior or exterior routing protocols are appropriate. However, a more detailed exploration of routing choices for different AS topologies will not be discussed until Chapter 6, "Tuning BGP Capabilities."

Always remember that static and default routing are not your enemy. The most stable (but sometimes less flexible) configurations are based on static routing. Many people feel that they are not technologically up to date just because they are not running dynamic routing. Trying to force dynamic routing on situations that do not require it is a waste of bandwidth, effort, and money. Recall the KISS principle introduced in the preceding chapter!

Autonomous Systems

An *autonomous system* (AS) is a set of routers that has a single routing policy, that run under a single technical administration, and that commonly utilizes a single IGP (the AS could also be a collection of IGPs working together to provide interior routing). To the outside world, the entire AS is viewed as a single entity. Each AS has an identifying number, which is assigned to it by an Internet Registry, or a service provider in the instance of private ASs. Routing information between ASs is exchanged via an exterior gateway protocol such as BGP-4, as illustrated in Figure 4-2.

Figure 4-2 *Routing Information Exchange Between Autonomous Systems*

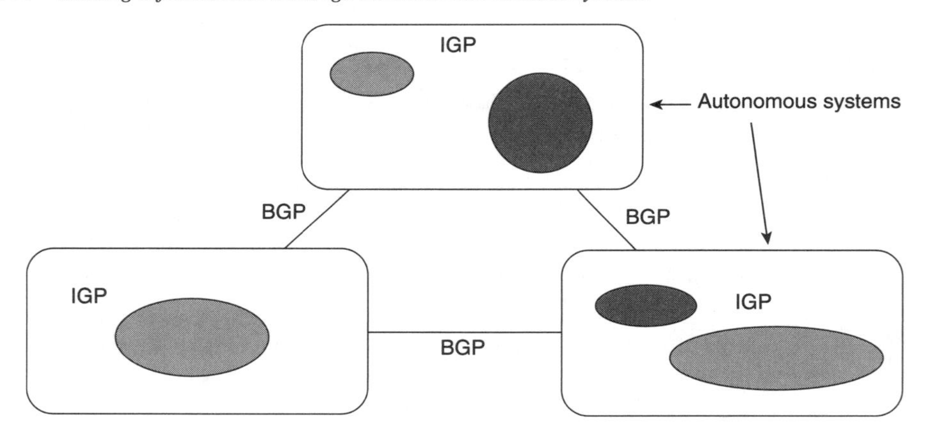

What we have gained by segregating the world into administrations is the capability to have one large network (in the sense that the Internet could have been one huge OSPF or IS-IS network) divided into smaller and more manageable networks. These networks, represented as ASs, can now implement their own set of rules and policies that will uniquely distinguish their networks and associated service offerings from other networks. Each AS can now run its own set of IGPs, independent of IGPs in other ASs.

The next few sections discuss potential network configurations with stub (single-homed) networks, multihomed nontransit networks, and multihomed transit networks.

Stub AS

An AS is considered stub when it reaches networks outside its domain via a single exit point. These ASs are also referred to as *single-homed* with respect to other providers. Figure 4-3 illustrates a single-homed or stub AS.

Figure 4-3 *Single-Homed (Stub) AS*

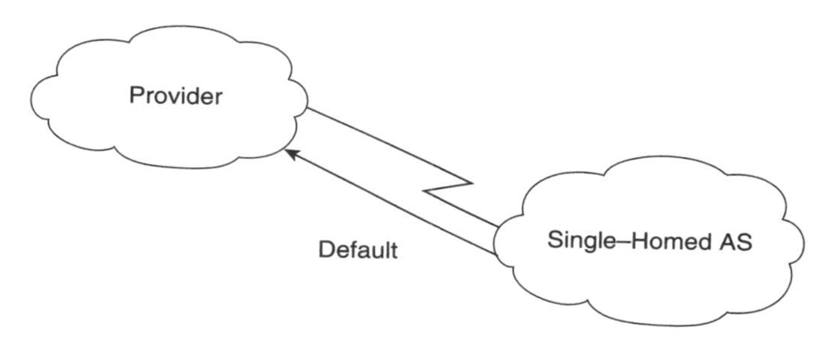

A single-homed AS does not really have to learn Internet routes from its provider. Because there is a single way out, all traffic can default to the provider. When using this configuration, the provider can use different methods to advertise the customer's routes to other networks.

One possibility is for the provider to list the customer's subnets as static entries in its router. The provider would then advertise these static entries toward the Internet via BGP. This method would scale very well if the customer's routes can be represented by a small set of aggregate routes. When the customer has too many noncontiguous subnets, listing all these subnets via static routes becomes inefficient.

Alternatively, the provider can employ IGPs for advertising the customer's networks. An IGP can be used between the customer and provider for the customer to advertise its routes. This has all the benefits of dynamic routing where network information and changes are dynamically sent to the provider. This is very uncommon, however, primarily because it doesn't scale well because customer link instability can result in IGP instabilities.

The third method by which the ISP can learn and advertise the customer's routes is to use BGP between the customer and the provider. In the stub AS situation, it is hard to get a registered AS number from an IRR because the customer's routing policies are an extension of the policies of a single provider.

NOTE RFC 1930[9] provides a set of guidelines for the creation, selection, and registration of autonomous system numbers.

Instead, the provider can give the customer an AS number from the private pool of ASs (65412-65535), assuming that the provider's routing policies have provisioned support for using private AS space with customers, as described in RFC 2270[10].

Quite a few combinations of protocols can be used between the ISP and the customer. Figure 4-4 illustrates some of the possible configurations, using just stub ASs as an example. (The meaning of EBGP and IBGP will be discussed in upcoming sections.) Providers might extend customer routers to their POPs, or providers might extend their routers to the customer's network. Note that not every situation requires that a customer run BGP with its provider, as mentioned earlier.

Figure 4-4 *Stub ASs: Sample Protocol Implementation Variations*

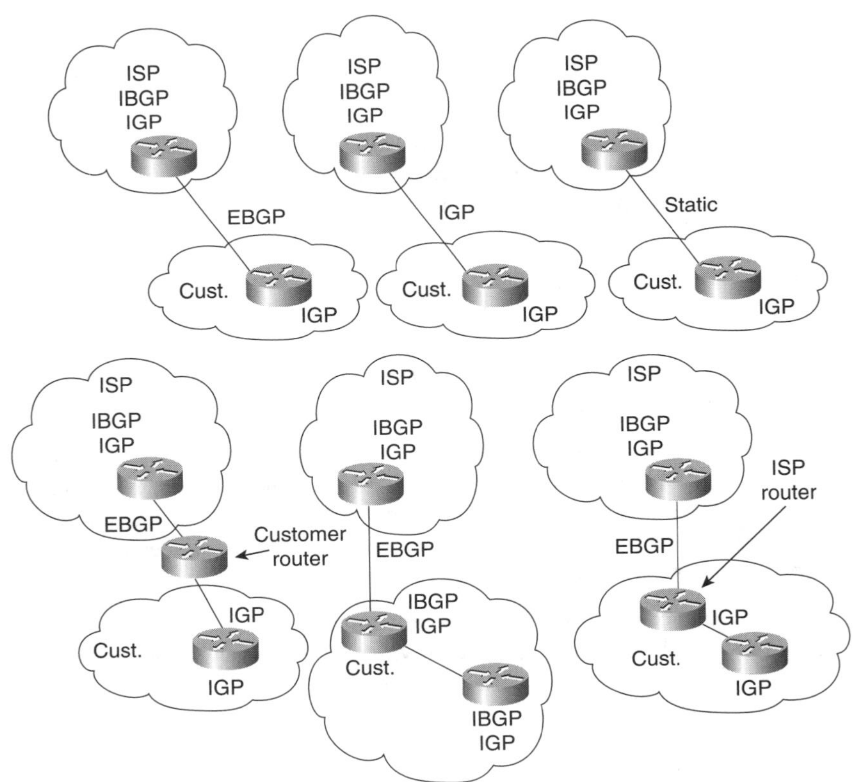

Multihomed Nontransit AS

An AS is multihomed if it has more than one exit point to the outside world. An AS can be multihomed to a single provider or multiple providers. A nontransit AS does not allow transit traffic to go through it. *Transit traffic* is any traffic that has a source and destination outside the AS. Figure 4-5 illustrates an AS (AS1) that is nontransit and multihomed to two providers, ISP1 and ISP2.

Figure 4-5 *Multihomed Nontransit AS Example*

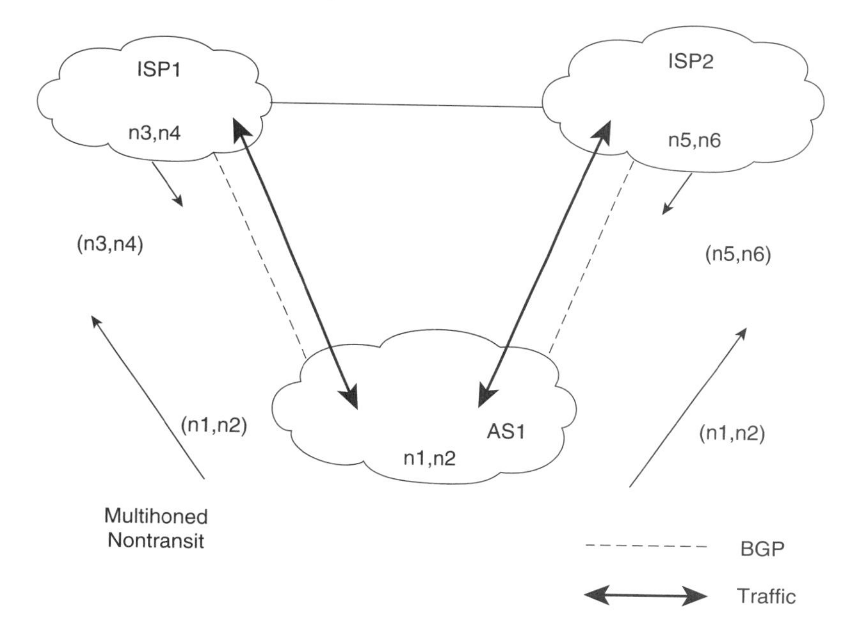

A nontransit AS would only advertise its own routes and would not propagate routes that it learned from other ASs. This ensures that traffic for any destination that does not belong to the AS would not be directed to the AS. In Figure 4-5, AS1 learns about routes n3 and n4 via ISP1 and routes n5 and n6 via ISP2. AS1 advertises only its local routes (n1,n2). It does not pass to ISP2 the routes it learned from ISP1 or to ISP1 the routes it learned from ISP2. This way, AS1 does not open itself to outside traffic, such as ISP1 trying to reach n5 or n6 and ISP2 trying to reach n3 and n4 via AS1. Of course, ISP1 or ISP2 can force its traffic to be directed to AS1 via default or static routing. As a precaution against this, AS1 could filter any traffic coming toward it with a destination not belonging to AS1.

Multihomed nontransit ASs do not really need to run BGP with their providers, although it is recommended and most of the time is required by the provider. As you will see later in this book, running BGP-4 with the providers has many advantages as far as controlling route propagation and filtering.

Multihomed Transit AS

A *multihomed transit AS* has more than one connection to the outside world and can still be used for transit traffic by other ASs (see Figure 4-6). Transit traffic (relative to the multihomed AS) is any traffic that has an origin or destination that does not belong to the local AS.

Although BGP-4 is an exterior gateway protocol, it can still be used inside an AS as a pipe to exchange BGP updates. BGP connections between routers inside an autonomous system are referred to as *Internal BGP (IBGP)*, whereas BGP connections between routers in separate autonomous systems are referred to as *External BGP (EBGP)*. Routers that are running IBGP are called *transit routers* when they carry the transit traffic going through the AS.

A transit AS would advertise to one AS routes that it learned from another AS. This way, the transit AS would open itself to traffic that does not belong to it. Multihomed transit ASs are advised to use BGP-4 for their connections to other ASs and to shield their internal nontransit routers from Internet routes. Not all routers inside a domain need to run BGP; internal nontransit routers could run default routing to the BGP routers, which alleviates the number of routes the internal nontransit routers must carry. In most large service provider networks, however, all routers usually carry a full set of BGP routes internally.

Figure 4-6 illustrates a multihomed transit autonomous system, AS1, connected to two different providers, ISP1 and ISP2. AS1 learns routes n3, n4, n5, and n6 from both ISP1 and ISP2 and in turn advertises all that it learns, including its local routes, to ISP1 and ISP2. In this case, ISP1 could use AS1 as a transit AS to reach networks n5 and n6, and ISP2 could use AS1 to reach networks n3 and n4.

Figure 4-6 *Multihomed Transit AS Using BGP Internally and Externally*

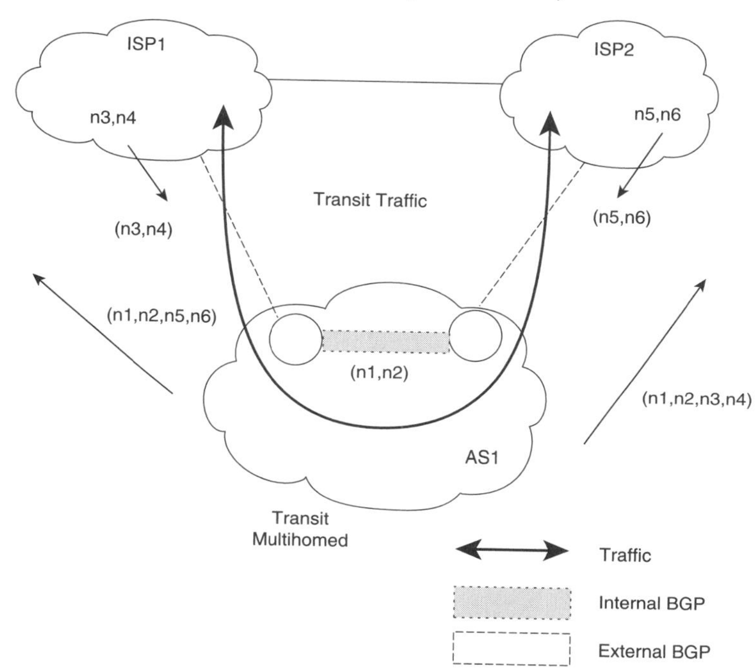

Looking Ahead

The Border Gateway Protocol has defined the basis of routing architectures in the Internet. The segregation of networks into autonomous systems has logically defined the administrative and political borders between organizations. Interior Gateway Protocols can now run independently of each other, but networks can still interconnect via BGP to provide global routing.

Chapter 5, "Border Gateway Protocol Version 4," is an overview of how BGP-4 operates, including detailed discussions of its message header formats.

Frequently Asked Questions

Q — *What is the difference between a domain and an autonomous system?*

A — Both terms are used to indicate a collection of routers. The domain notation is usually used to indicate a collection of routers running the same routing protocol, such as a RIP domain or an OSPF domain. The AS represents one or more domains under a single administration that have a unified routing policy with other ASs.

Q — *My company is connected to an ISP via RIP. Should I use BGP instead?*

A — If you are thinking of connecting to multiple providers in the near future, you should start discussing the option of using BGP with your provider. If your traffic needs do not require multiple provider connectivity, you should be okay with what you have.

Q — *I have a single IGP connection to a provider. I am thinking of connecting to the same provider in a different location. Can I connect via an IGP, or should I use BGP?*

A — This depends on the provider. Some providers will let you connect via IGP in multiple locations; others prefer that you use BGP. Practically speaking, when you use BGP, you will be in better control of your traffic, as you will see in the following chapters.

Q — *I thought that BGP is to be used between ASs. I am a bit confused about using BGP inside the AS.*

A — Think of BGP inside the AS (IBGP) as a tunnel through which routing information flows. If your AS is a transit AS, IBGP will shield all your internal nontransit routers from the potentially overwhelming number of external routing updates. On the other hand, even if you are not a transit AS, you will realize as this book progresses that IBGP will give you better control in choosing exit and entrance points for your traffic.

Q — *You talk about BGP-4, but is anybody still using BGP-1, -2, or -3? What about EGP?*

A — BGP-4 is the de facto interdomain routing protocol used on the Internet. EGP and BGP-1, 2, and 3 are obsolete. BGP-4's support of CIDR, incremental updates, and better filtering and policy-setting capabilities have prompted everybody to shift gears into using this new protocol.

Q — *I'm planning to install a second connection to my current Internet service provider. Should I get an AS number from my RIR?*

A — Getting an AS number is indeed an option, although you might first see if your provider has provisions in place to support the use of private ASs for customers multihomed to a single provider. In addition, you should check with your RIR to ensure that it will allocate AS numbers to networks connected to only a single provider.

References

[1]RFC 1771, "A Border Gateway Protocol 4 (BGP-4)," www.isi.edu/in-notes/rfc1771.txt

[2]Bellman, R. *Dynamic Programming* (Princeton University Press, 1957)

[3]Ford, L. R., Jr. and D. R. Fulkerson. *Flows in Networks* (Princeton University Press, 1962)

[4]RFC 1583, "OSPF Version 2," www.isi.edu/in-notes/rfc1583.txt

[5]ISO 10589, "Intermediate System to Intermediate System"; RFC 1195, "Use of OSI IS-IS for Routing in TCP/IP and Dual Environments," www.isi.edu/in-notes/rfc1195.txt

[6]Perlman, Radia. *Interconnections, Second Edition: Bridges, Routers, Switches, and Internetworking Protocols* (Boston, Mass.: Addison-Wesley Longman, Inc., 1999)

[7]Moy, John. *OSPF: Anatomy of an Internet Routing Protocol* (Boston, Mass.: Addison-Wesley Longman, Inc., 1998)

[8]RFC 904, "Exterior Gateway Protocol Formal Specification," www.isi.edu/in-notes/rfc904.txt

[9]RFC 1930, "Guidelines for creation, selection, and registration of an Autonomous System (AS)," www.isi.edu/in-notes/rfc1930.txt

[10]RFC 2270, "Using a Dedicated AS for Sites Homed to a Single Provider," www.isi.edu/in-notes/rfc2270.txt

This chapter covers the following key topics:

- **How BGP works**—An overview of how the Border Gateway Protocol (Version 4) operates, including its message header format, and how and what it negotiates with neighboring routers. We'll cover the formats and purposes of BGP's four main message types—OPEN, NOTIFICATION, KEEPALIVE, and UPDATE.
- **Multiprotocol extensions to BGP-4**—We'll discuss Multiprotocol BGP, which was originally designed expressly for interdomain multicasting but can accommodate other protocols as well.
- **Capabilities Negotiation with BGP-4**—BGP Capabilities Negotiation provides a mechanism to cleanly introduce new features to BGP. I'll discuss its operation and then detail some of these features in later chapters.
- **TCP MD5 Signature Option for BGP**—The TCP MD5 Signature Option was added to BGP to protect BGP from spoofed TCP segments, particularly TCP resets. I'll discuss its operation and some associated caveats.

CHAPTER 5

Border Gateway Protocol Version 4

The Border Gateway Protocol (BGP) has gone through several phases and improvements since its original version, BGP-1, in 1989. BGP-4 deployment began in 1993. It is the first BGP version that handles aggregation (classless interdomain routing [CIDR]) and supernetting, as discussed earlier in this book.

BGP imposes no restrictions on the underlying network topology. It assumes that routing within an autonomous system is done via an intra-autonomous system routing protocol (Interior Gateway Protocol [IGP]). For the purposes of this book, *intra* means within an entity, and *inter* means between entities. BGP constructs a graph of autonomous systems based on the information exchanged between BGP routers. This directed graph environment is sometimes referred to as a *tree*. As far as BGP is concerned, the whole Internet is a graph of ASs, with each AS identified by a unique AS number. Connections between two ASs together form a path, and the collection of path information forms a route to reach a specific destination. BGP uses the path information associated with a given destination to ensure loop-free interdomain routing. Figure 5-1 illustrates this general path tree concept.

Figure 5-1 *Sample AS_PATH Tree*

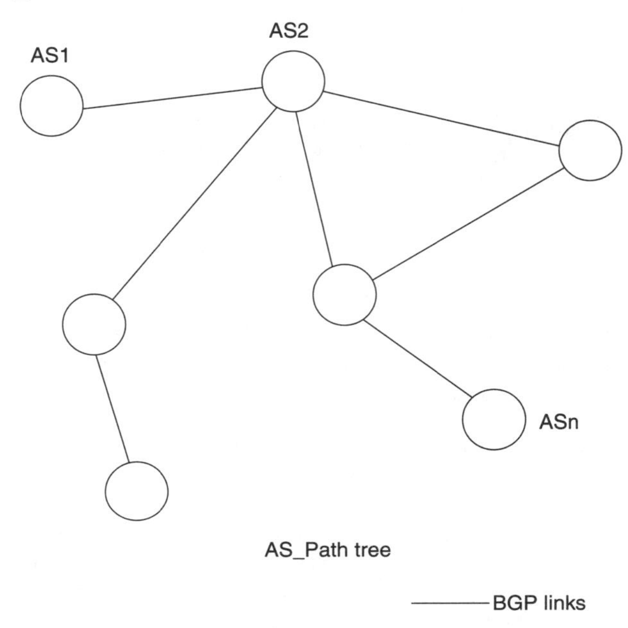

How BGP Works

BGP is a path vector protocol used to carry routing information between autonomous systems. The term *path vector* comes from the fact that BGP routing information carries a sequence of AS numbers that identifies the path of ASs that a network prefix has traversed. The path information associated with the prefix is used to enable loop prevention.

BGP uses TCP as its transport protocol (port 179). This ensures that all the transport reliability (such as retransmission) is taken care of by TCP and does not need to be implemented in BGP, thereby simplifying the complexity associated with designing reliability into the protocol itself.

Routers that run a BGP routing process are often referred to as *BGP speakers*. Two BGP speakers that form a TCP connection between one another for the purpose of exchanging routing information are referred to as *neighbors* or *peers*. Figure 5-2 illustrates this relationship. Peer routers exchange open messages to determine the connection parameters. These messages are used to communicate values such as the BGP speaker's version number.

Figure 5-2 *BGP Routers Become Neighbors*

BGP also provides a mechanism to gracefully close a connection with a peer. In other words, in the event of a disagreement between the peers, be it resultant of configuration, incompatibility, operator intervention, or other circumstances, a NOTIFICATION error message is sent, and the peer connection does not get established or is torn down if it's already established. The benefit of this mechanism is that both peers understand that the connection could not be established or maintained and do not waste resources that would otherwise be required to maintain or blindly reattempt to establish the connection. The graceful close mechanism simply ensures that all outstanding messages, primarily NOTIFICATION error messages, are delivered before the TCP session is closed.

Initially, when a BGP session is established between a set of BGP speakers, all candidate BGP routes are exchanged, as illustrated in Figure 5-3. After the session has been established and the initial route exchange has occurred, only incremental updates are sent as network information changes. The incremental update approach has shown an enormous improvement in CPU overhead and bandwidth allocation compared with complete periodic updates used by previous protocols, such as EGP.

Figure 5-3 *Exchanging All Routing Updates*

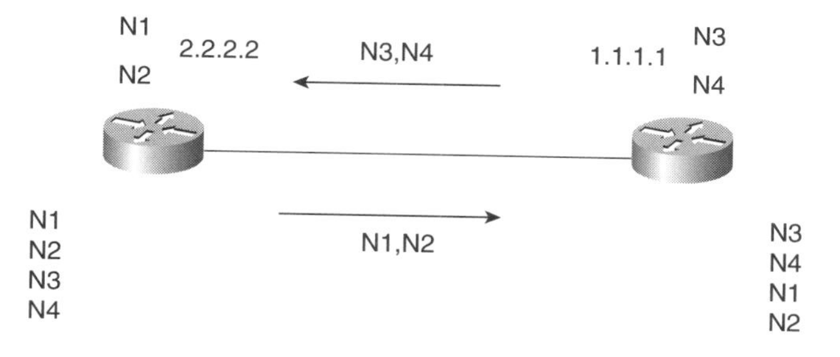

Routes are advertised between a pair of BGP routers in UPDATE messages. The UPDATE message contains, among other things, a list of <length, prefix> tuples that indicate the list of destinations that can be reached via a BGP speaker. The UPDATE message also contains the path attributes, which include such information as the degree of preference for a particular route and the list of ASs that the route has traversed.

In the event that a route becomes unreachable, a BGP speaker informs its neighbors by withdrawing the invalid route. As illustrated in Figure 5-4, withdrawn routes are part of the UPDATE message. These routes are no longer available for use. If information associated with a route has changed, or a new path for the same prefix has been selected, a withdrawal is not required; it is enough to just advertise a replacement route.

Figure 5-4 *N1 Goes Down; Partial Update Sent*

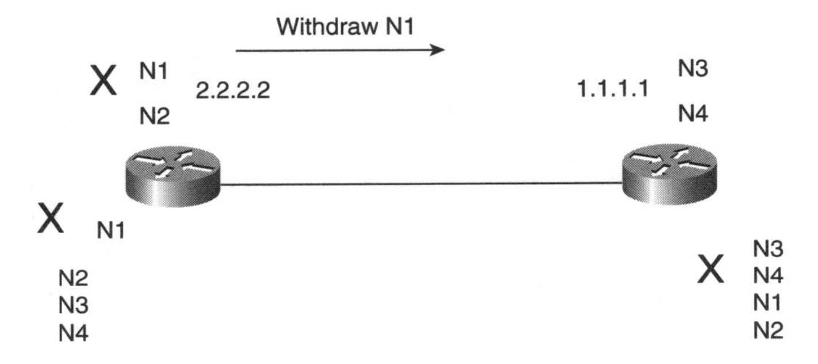

Figure 5-5 illustrates a *steady state* situation: If no routing changes occur, the routers exchange only KEEPALIVE packets.

Figure 5-5 *Steady State; N1 Is Still Down*

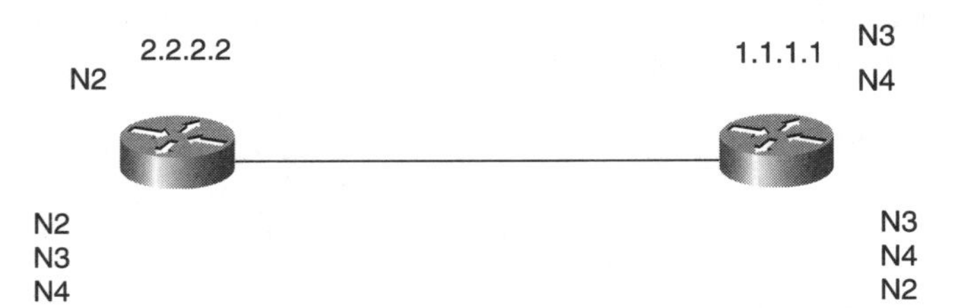

KEEPALIVE messages are sent periodically between BGP neighbors to ensure that the connection is kept alive. KEEPALIVE packets (19 bytes each) should not cause any strain on the router CPU or link bandwidth, because they consume a minimal amount of bandwidth (one instantaneous 152-bit packet every 60 seconds, or about 2.5 bps per peer for a periodic rate of 60 seconds).

BGP keeps a table version number to keep track of the current instance of the BGP routing table. If the table changes, BGP increments the table version number. A table version that increments rapidly is usually an indication of network instability (although this is quite common in large Internet service provider networks). Because of this, instability introduced by Internet-connected networks anywhere in the world will result in the table version number incrementing on every BGP speaker that has a full view of the Internet routing tables. Route flap dampening and other provisions (discussed in detail in Chapter 10, "Designing Stable Internets") have been designed to scope the effects of this instability.

BGP Message Header Format

The BGP message header format is a 16-byte Marker field, followed by a 2-byte Length field and a 1-byte Type field. Figure 5-6 illustrates the basic format of the BGP message header.

Figure 5-6 *BGP Message Header Format*

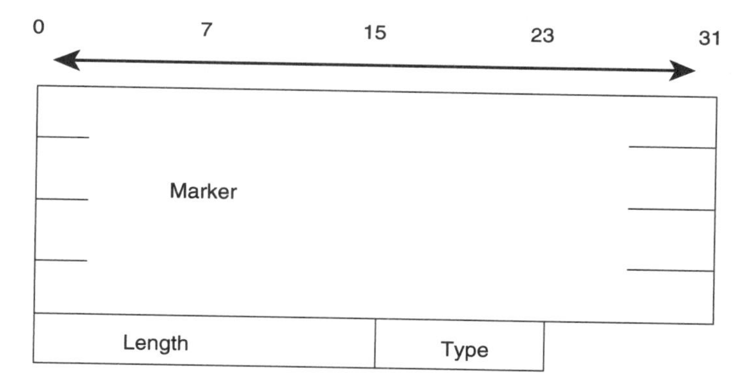

Depending on the message type, there might or might not be a data portion following the header. KEEPALIVE messages, for example, consist of the message header only, with no following data.

The 16-byte Marker field is used to either authenticate incoming BGP messages or detect loss of synchronization between two BGP peers. The Marker field can have one of two formats:

- If the type of the message is OPEN, or if the OPEN message has no authentication information, the Marker field must be all 1s.
- Otherwise, the Marker field will be computed based on part of the authentication mechanism used. Later in this chapter, I will discuss the TCP MD5 Signature Option's use of this marker.

The 2-byte Length field is used to indicate the total BGP message length, including the header. The smallest BGP message is no less than 19 bytes (16+2+1) and no greater than 4,096 bytes.

The 1-byte Type field indicates the message type, with the following possibilities:

- OPEN
- UPDATE
- NOTIFICATION
- KEEPALIVE

The following sections examine the purpose and format of each of the four message types in more detail.

BGP Neighbor Negotiation

One of the basic steps of the BGP protocol is establishing sessions between BGP peers. Without successful completion of this step, the exchange of updates will not occur. Neighbor negotiation is based on the successful completion of a TCP transport connection, the successful processing of the OPEN message, and periodic detection of the UPDATE or KEEPALIVE messages.

OPEN Message Format

Figure 5-7 illustrates the format of the OPEN message.

Figure 5-7 *Open Message Format*

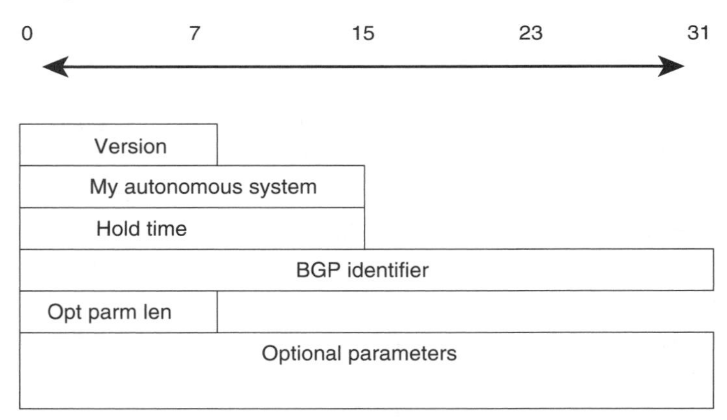

The following descriptions summarize each of the OPEN message fields:

- **Version**—A 1-byte unsigned integer that indicates the version of the BGP message, such as BGP-3 or BGP-4. During the neighbor negotiation, BGP peers agree on a BGP version number. BGP peers try to negotiate the highest common version that they both support. They reset the BGP session and renegotiate until a common supported version is determined by the peers. Cisco Systems provides the option of predefining the version negotiated to cut down on the negotiation process. The version is usually set statically when the versions of the BGP peers are already known, although most implementations begin and default to BGP-4.

- **My Autonomous System**—A 2-byte field that indicates the AS number of the BGP speaker.
- **Hold Timer**—The Hold Timer is a 2-byte unsigned integer that indicates the maximum amount of time in seconds that may elapse between the receipt of successive KEEPALIVE or UPDATE messages. The Hold Timer is a counter that increments from 0 to the hold time value. Receipt of a KEEPALIVE or UPDATE message causes the Hold Timer to reset to 0. If the hold time for a particular neighbor were exceeded, the neighbor would be considered dead.

  The BGP router negotiates with its neighbor to select the hold time at whichever value is lower—its own Hold Timer or its neighbor's. The Hold Timer could be 0, in which case the Hold Timer and the KEEPALIVE timers are never reset. In other words, these timers never expire, and the connection is considered to be always up. If it isn't set to 0, the minimum Hold Timer is 3 seconds.

  Note that the negotiation done for the Version Number (by actually resetting the session until both nodes agree on a common Version) and the one for the Hold Timer (use the minimum value of the two BGP speakers) are very different. In both cases, only the OPEN message is sent by each router. However, if the values don't match (in the case of Hold Timer), the session is not reset.

- **BGP Identifier**—A 4-byte unsigned integer that indicates the value of the sender's BGP ID. In Cisco's implementation, this is usually equal to the Router ID (RID), which is calculated as the highest IP address on the router or the highest loopback address at BGP session startup. A *loopback address* is a representation of the IP address of a virtual software interface that is considered to be up at all times, irrespective of the state of any physical interface.
- **Optional Parameter Length (Opt Parm Len)**—This is a 1-byte unsigned integer that indicates the total length in bytes of the Optional Parameters field. A length value of 0 indicates that no Optional Parameters are present.
- **Optional Parameters**—This is a variable-length field that indicates a list of optional parameters used in BGP neighbor session negotiation. This field is represented by the triplet <Parameter Type, Parameter Length, Parameter Value> with lengths of 1 byte, 1 byte, and variable length, respectively. An example of optional parameters is the authentication information parameter (type 1), which is used to authenticate the session with a BGP peer.

Finite State Machine Perspective

BGP neighbor negotiation proceeds through different stages before the connection is fully established. Figure 5-8 illustrates a simplified finite state machine (FSM) that highlights the major events in the process with an indication of messages (OPEN, KEEPALIVE, NOTIFICATION) sent to the peer in the transition from one state to the other.

Figure 5-8 *BGP Neighbor Negotiation Finite State Machine*

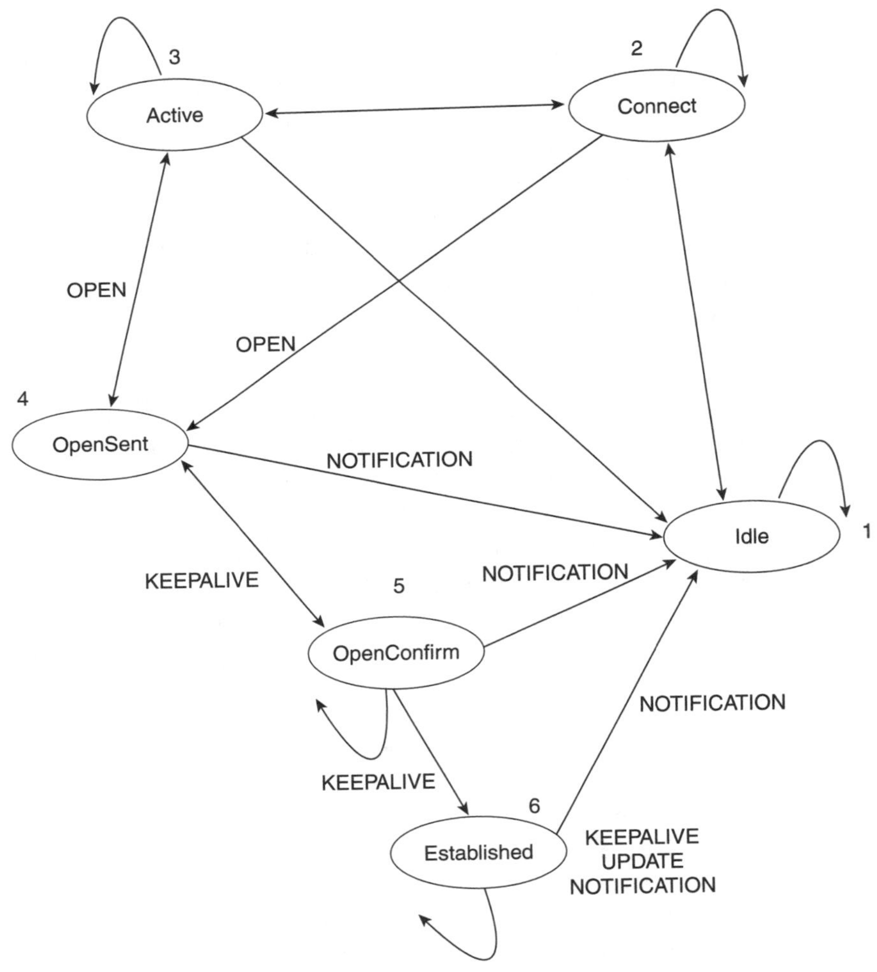

The following list summarizes the key states in the FSM example illustrated in Figure 5-8:

1 **Idle**—This is the first stage of the connection. BGP is waiting for a Start event, which is initiated by an operator or the BGP system. An administrator establishing a BGP session through router configuration or resetting an already existing session usually causes a Start event. After the Start event, BGP initializes its resources, resets a ConnectRetry timer, initiates a TCP transport connection, and starts listening for a connection that may be initiated by a remote peer. BGP then transitions to a Connect state. In case of errors, BGP falls back to the Idle state.

2 **Connect**—BGP is waiting for the transport protocol connection to be completed. If the TCP transport connection is successful, the state transitions to OpenSent (this is where the OPEN message is sent). If the transport connection is unsuccessful, the state transitions to Active. If the ConnectRetry timer expires, the state remains in the Connect stage, the timer is reset, and a transport connection is initiated. In case of any other event (initiated by system or operator), the state goes back to Idle.

3 **Active**—BGP tries to acquire a peer by initiating a transport protocol connection. If the transport connection is established, it transitions to OpenSent (an OPEN message is sent). If the ConnectRetry timer expires, BGP restarts the ConnectRetry timer and falls back to the Connect state. In addition, BGP continues to listen for a connection that might be initiated from another peer. The state might go back to Idle in case of other events, such as a Stop event initiated by the system or the operator.

   In general, a neighbor state that is oscillating between Connect and Active indicates that something is wrong with the TCP transport connection. It could be because of many TCP retransmissions or the inability of a neighbor to reach the IP address of its peer.

4 **OpenSent**—BGP is waiting for an OPEN message from its peer. The OPEN message is checked for correctness. In case of errors, such as a bad version number or an unacceptable AS, the system sends an error NOTIFICATION message and goes back to Idle. If there are no errors, BGP starts sending KEEPALIVE messages and resets the KEEPALIVE timer. At this stage, the hold time is negotiated, and the smaller value is taken. In case the negotiated hold time is 0, the Hold Timer and the KEEPALIVE timer are not restarted.

   At the OpenSent state, the BGP recognizes, by comparing its AS number to the AS number of its peer, whether the peer belongs to the same AS (Internal BGP) or to a different AS (External BGP).

   When a TCP transport disconnect is detected, the state falls back to the Active state. For any other errors, such as an expiration of the Hold Timer, the BGP sends a NOTIFICATION message with the corresponding error code and falls back to the Idle state. Also, in response to a stop event initiated by the system or the operator, the state falls back to the Idle state.

5 **OpenConfirm**—BGP waits for a KEEPALIVE message. If a KEEPALIVE is received, the state goes to Established, and the neighbor negotiation is complete. If the system receives a KEEPALIVE message, it restarts the Hold Timer (assuming that the negotiated Hold Time is not 0). If a NOTIFICATION message is received, the state falls back to the Idle state. The system sends periodic KEEPALIVE messages at the rate set by the KEEPALIVE timer. In case of any transport disconnect notification or in response to any stop event (initiated by the system or the operator), the state falls back to Idle. In response to any other event, the system sends a NOTIFICATION message with an FSM (Finite State Machine) error code and returns to the Idle state.

6 **Established**—This is the final stage in the neighbor negotiation. At this stage, BGP starts exchanging UPDATE packets with its peers. Assuming that it is nonzero, the Hold Timer restarts at the receipt of an UPDATE or KEEPALIVE message. If the system receives any NOTIFICATION message (if an error has occurred), the state falls back to Idle.

   The UPDATE messages are checked for errors, such as missing attributes, duplicate attributes, and so on. If errors are found, a NOTIFICATION message is sent to the peer, and the state falls back to Idle. If the Hold Timer expires, or a disconnect notification is received from the transport protocol, or a Stop event is received, or in response to any other event, the system falls back to the Idle state.

NOTIFICATION Message

From the preceding examination of the Finite State Machine, it should be apparent that many opportunities exist among the various states for errors to be detected. A NOTIFICATION message is always sent whenever an error is detected. After that, the peer connection is closed. Network administrators need to evaluate these NOTIFICATION messages to determine the specific nature of errors that emerge in the routing protocol. Figure 5-9 illustrates the general message format.

Figure 5-9 *NOTIFICATION Message Format*

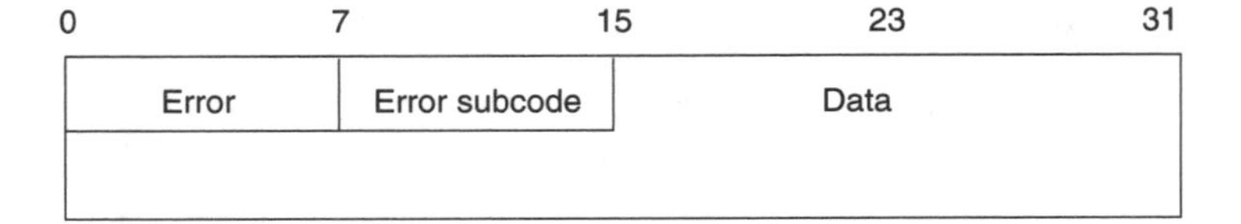

The NOTIFICATION message is composed of the Error code (1 byte), the Error subcode (1 byte), and the Data field (variable).

The Error code indicates the type of the notification, and the Error subcode provides more specific information about the nature of the error. The Data field contains data relevant to the error, such as a bad header, an illegal AS number, and so on. Table 5-1 lists possible errors and their subcodes.

Table 5-1 *Possible BGP Error Codes*

Error Code	Error Subcode
1—Message header error	1—Connection Not Synchronized
	2—Bad Message Length
	3—Bad Message Type
2—OPEN message error	1—Unsupported Version Number
	2—Bad Peer AS
	3—Bad BGP Identifier
	4—Unsupported Optional Parameter
	5—Authentication Failure
	6—Unacceptable Hold Timer
	7—Unsupported Capability
3—UPDATE message error	1—Malformed Attribute List
	2—Unrecognized Well-Known Attribute
	3—Missing Well-Known Attribute
	4—Attribute Flags Error
	5—Attribute Length Error
	6—Invalid Origin Attribute
	7—AS Routing Loop
	8—Invalid NEXT_HOP Attribute
	9—Optional Attribute Error
	10—Invalid Network Field
	11—Malformed AS_PATH
4—Hold Timer expired	N/A
5—Finite State Machine error (for errors detected by the FSM)	N/A
6—Cease (for fatal errors besides the ones already listed)	N/A

KEEPALIVE Message

KEEPALIVE messages are periodic messages exchanged between peers to determine whether peers are reachable. As discussed earlier, the hold time is the maximum amount of time that may elapse between the receipt of successive KEEPALIVE or UPDATE messages. The KEEPALIVE messages are sent at a rate that ensures that the hold time will not expire (the session is considered alive). A recommended KEEPALIVE rate is one-third of the Hold Timer value. If the Hold Timer value is 0, periodic KEEPALIVE messages are not sent. As previously mentioned, the KEEPALIVE message is a 19-byte BGP message header with no data following it, or it can be suppressed during an interval if an UPDATE message is sent.

UPDATE Message and Routing Information

Central to the BGP protocol is the concept of routing updates. Routing updates contain all the necessary information that BGP uses to construct a loop-free picture of the network. The following are the basic blocks of an UPDATE message:

- Network Layer Reachability Information (NLRI)
- Path Attributes
- Unfeasible Routes

Figure 5-10 illustrates these components in the context of an UPDATE message format.

Figure 5-10 *BGP UPDATE Message*

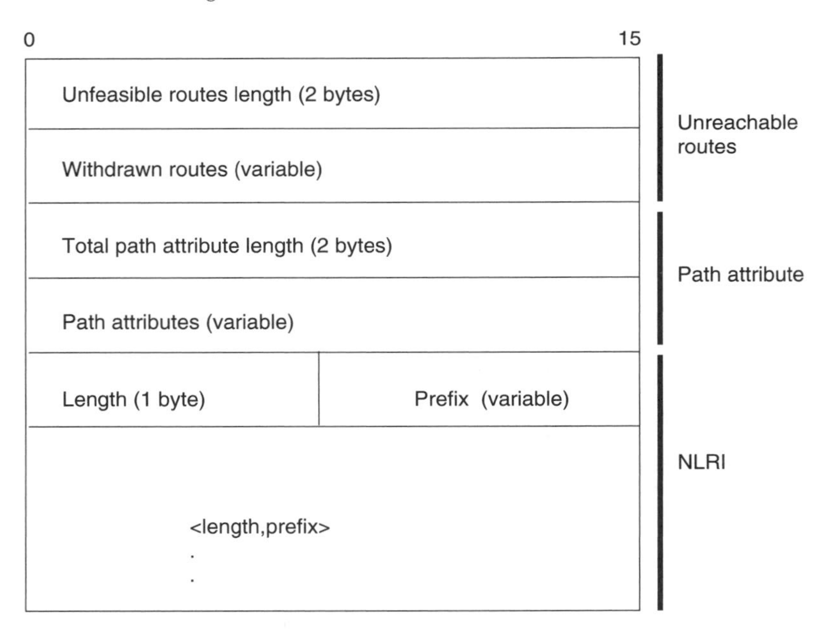

The NLRI indicates, in the form of an IP prefix route, the networks being advertised. The Path Attribute list enables BGP to detect routing loops and gives it the flexibility to enforce local and global routing policies. An example of a BGP Path Attribute is the AS_PATH attribute, which is a sequence of AS numbers that a route has traversed before reaching the BGP router.

In Figure 5-11, for example, AS3 receives BGP UPDATEs from AS2, indicating that network 10.10.1.0/24 (NLRI) is reachable via two AS hops—first AS2 and then AS1. Based on this information, AS3 can direct its traffic to 10.10.1.0/24 via transit AS, AS2 to the destination AS, AS1.

Figure 5-11 *BGP Routing Update Example*

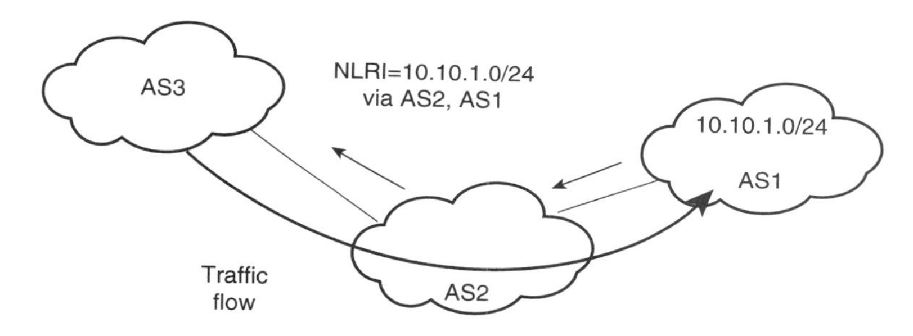

The third part of the UPDATE message is a list of routes that have become unreachable or, in BGP terminology, withdrawn. In Figure 5-11, if 10.10.1.0/24 is no longer reachable, or if it experiences a change in its attribute information, BGP in any of the three ASs can withdraw the route it advertised by sending an UPDATE message that lists the new path attribute information or the network as being unreachable.

Network Layer Reachability Information

One of the primary enhancements of BGP-4 over previous versions is that it provides a new set of mechanisms for supporting classless interdomain routing (CIDR). As discussed in Chapter 3, "IP Addressing and Allocation Techniques," the concept of CIDR is a move from the traditional IP classful (A, B, C) model toward a concept of IP prefixes and a classless model.

The IP prefix is an IP network address that indicates the number of bits (left to right) that constitute the network number. The Network Layer Reachability Information (NLRI) is the mechanism by which BGP supports classless routing. The NLRI is the part of the BGP UPDATE message that lists the set of destinations about which BGP is trying to inform its other BGP neighbors. The NLRI consists of one or more instances of the 2-tuple format <length, prefix>, where length is the number of masking bits that a particular prefix has.

Figure 5-12 illustrates the NLRI <19, 198.24.160.0>. The prefix is 198.24.160.0, and the length is a 19-bit mask (counting from the far left of the prefix).

Figure 5-12 *NLRI Example*

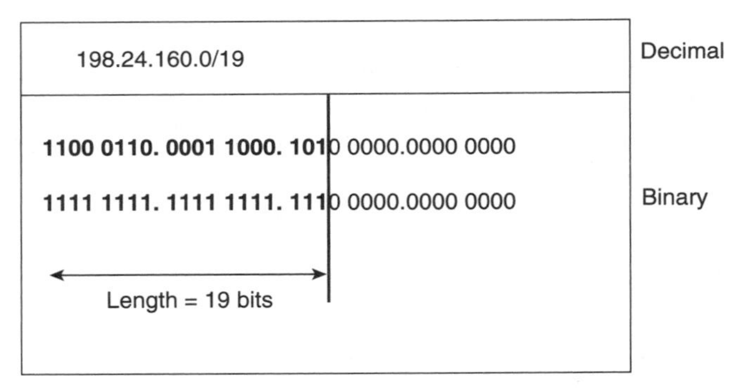

Withdrawn Routes

Withdrawn routes provide a list of routing updates that are not feasible or that are no longer in service and need to be withdrawn (removed) from the BGP routing tables. The withdrawn routes have the same format as the NLRI: an IP address and the number of bits in the IP address, counting from the left, as illustrated in Figure 5-13.

Figure 5-13 *General Form of the Withdrawn Routes Field*

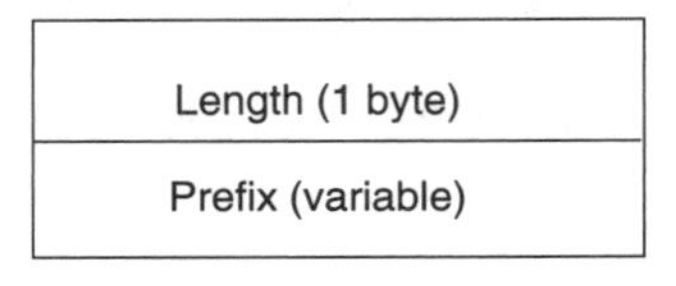

Withdrawn routes are also represented by the 2-tuple <length, prefix> format. A tuple of the form <18, 192.213.128.0> indicates a route to be withdrawn of the form 192.213.128.0 255.255.192.0 or 192.213.128.0/18 in CIDR format.

The Unfeasible Routes Length field in the UPDATE message represents the length in bytes of the total withdrawn routes. An UPDATE message can list multiple routes to be withdrawn at the same time or no routes to be withdrawn. An Unfeasible Routes Length of 0 indicates that no routes are to be withdrawn. On the other hand, an UPDATE message can advertise at most one route, which can be described by multiple path attributes. An UPDATE message that has no new NLRI or Path Attribute information is used to advertise only routes to be withdrawn from service.

Path Attributes

The BGP attributes are a set of parameters used to keep track of route-specific information such as path information, degree of preference of a route, NEXT_HOP value of a route, and aggregation information. These parameters are used in the BGP filtering and route decision process. Every UPDATE message has a variable-length sequence of path attributes. A path attribute is a triple of the form <attribute type, attribute length, attribute value>. The attribute type is a 2-byte field that consists of a 1-byte attribute flag and a 1-byte attribute type code. Figure 5-14 illustrates the general form of the Path Attributes type field.

Figure 5-14 *Path Attribute Type Format*

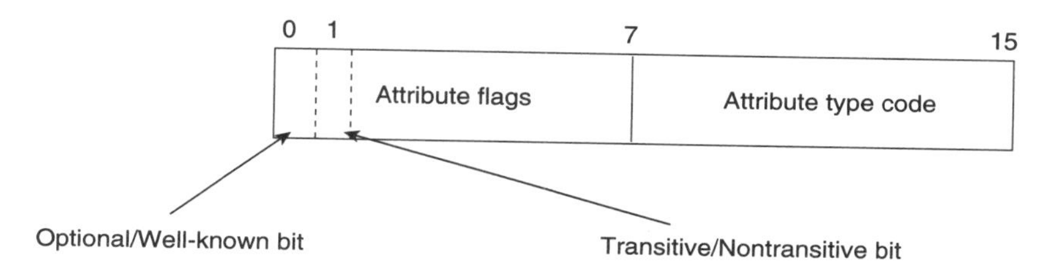

Path attributes fall under four categories: well-known mandatory, well-known discretionary, optional transitive, and optional nontransitive. These four categories are described by the first two bits of the Attribute Flags field:

- The first bit (bit 0) of the Attribute Flags field indicates whether the attribute is well-known (0) or optional (1).
- The second bit (bit 1) indicates whether the optional attribute is nontransitive (0) or transitive (1). Well-known attributes are always transitive, so the second bit is always set to 1.
- The third bit (bit 2) indicates whether the information in the optional transitive attribute is complete (0) or partial (1).
- The fourth bit (bit 3) defines whether the attribute length is 1 byte (0) or 2 bytes (1).
- The low-order four bits (4 to 7) in the Attribute Flags field are currently unused and are always set to 0.

The following descriptions elaborate on the significance of each attribute category:

- **Well-known mandatory**—An attribute that has to exist in the BGP UPDATE packet. It must be recognized by all BGP implementations. If a well-known attribute is missing, a NOTIFICATION error is generated, and the session is closed. This is to make sure that all BGP implementations agree on a standard set of attributes. An example of a well-known mandatory attribute is the AS_PATH attribute.

- **Well-known discretionary**—An attribute that is recognized by all BGP implementations but that might or might not be sent in the BGP UPDATE message. An example of a well-known discretionary attribute is LOCAL_PREF.

In addition to the well-known attributes, a path can contain one or more optional attributes. Optional attributes are not required to be supported by all BGP implementations. Optional attributes can be transitive or nontransitive:

- **Optional transitive**—If an optional attribute is not recognized by the BGP implementation, that implementation looks for a transitive flag to see whether it is set for that particular attribute. If the flag is set, which indicates that the attribute is transitive, the BGP implementation should accept the attribute and pass it along to other BGP speakers.
- **Optional nontransitive**—When an optional attribute is not recognized and the transitive flag is not set, which means that the attribute is nontransitive, the attribute should be quietly ignored and not passed along to other BGP peers.

The Attribute Type Code byte contains the attribute code. Currently, the following attributes are defined as documented in Table 5-2.

Table 5-2 *Attribute Type Codes*

Attribute Number	Attribute Name	Category/Type Code	Related RFC/ Internet Draft
1	ORIGIN	Well-known mandatory, Type code 1	RFC 1771
2	AS_PATH	Well-known mandatory, Type code 2	RFC 1771
3	NEXT_HOP	Well-known mandatory, Type code 3	RFC 1771
4	MULTI_EXIT_DISC	Optional nontransitive, Type code 4	RFC 1771
5	LOCAL_PREF	Well-known discretionary, Type code 5	RFC 1771
6	ATOMIC_AGGREG ATE	Well-known discretionary, Type code 6	RFC 1771
7	AGGREGATOR	Optional transitive, Type code 7	RFC 1771
8	COMMUNITY	Optional transitive, Type code 8	RFC 1997[1]
9	ORIGINATOR_ID	Optional nontransitive, Type code 9	RFC 1966[2]
10	Cluster List	Optional nontransitive, Type code 10	RFC 1966

Table 5-2 *Attribute Type Codes (Continued)*

Attribute Number	Attribute Name	Category/Type Code	Related RFC/ Internet Draft
11	DPA	Destination Point Attribute for BGP	Expired Internet Draft
12	Advertiser	BGP/IDRP Route Server	RFC 1863[3]
13	RCID_PATH/ CLUSTER_ID	BGP/IDRP Route Server	RFC 1863
14	Multiprotocol Reachable NLRI	Optional nontransitive, Type code 14	RFC 2283[4]
15	Multiprotocol Unreachable NLRI	Optional nontransitive, Type code 15	RFC 2283
16	Extended Communities		draft-ramachandra-bgp-ext-communities-00.txt, "work in progress"
256		Reserved for development	

BGP Capabilities Negotiation

While the BGP Capabilities Negotiation specification is still being developed by the IETF IDR (Inter-Domain Routing) Working Group[5], we'll touch on its usefulness here in order to foster understanding for future discussions of new mechanisms that utilize the facilities it provides in order to introduce new features to BGP.

The Capabilities Negotiation with BGP-4 specification is currently in draft form and is still a "work in progress." The purpose of this specification is to introduce a new optional parameter to BGP-4 called Capabilities. It is expected to facilitate the introduction of new features in BGP by providing graceful capability negotiation without requiring that the BGP peering be terminated.

If a BGP speaker supports capabilities negotiation, when it sends an OPEN message to a BGP peer, the message may include an Optional Capabilities parameter. A BGP speaker examines the information contained in the Capabilities parameter of an OPEN message in order to determine which capabilities the peer supports. If a BGP speaker determines that a peer supports a given capability, the speaker can use the capability with the peer.

A BGP speaker determines that a peer doesn't support capabilities negotiation if, in response to an OPEN message that carries the new Optional parameter, the speaker receives a NOTIFICATION message that contains an Error Subcode set to "Unsupported Optional Parameter." If this occurs, the BGP speaker should attempt to reestablish the connection without sending the Capabilities Optional parameter to the peer.

BGP Capabilities is of Parameter Type 24 and contains one or more triples <Capability Code, Capability Length, Capability Value>, where each triple is encoded as illustrated in Figure 5-15.

Figure 5-15 *BGP Capabilities Optional Parameter Format*

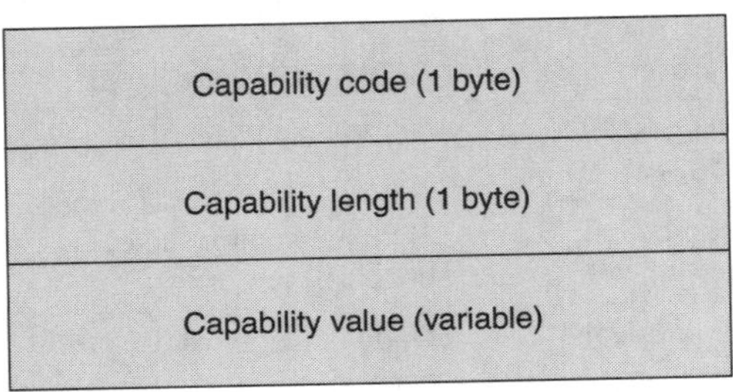

The uses and meanings of the three fields are as follows:

- **Capability Code**—A 1-byte field that unambiguously identifies individual capabilities.
- **Capability Length**—A 1-byte field that contains the length of the Capability Value Field in bytes.
- **Capability Value**—A variable-length field that is interpreted according to the value of the Capability Code field.

Capability Code 0 is currently reserved. Capability codes 128 through 255 are also currently reserved for vendor-specific applications.

Cisco IOS already uses BGP Capabilities Negotiation to introduce two new features to BGP—BGP Route Refresh and Outbound Request Filter (ORF), both of which have already been implemented and will be discussed in more detail in later chapters.

BGP Capabilities provides a great deal of potential when attempting to introduce new features to BGP. It should be noted, however, that many such features might very well remain vendor-proprietary.

Multiprotocol Extensions for BGP

Multiprotocol BGP (MBGP), also referred to as BGP-4+ and often erroneously expanded to Multicast BGP, is defined in RFC 2283 and is negotiated via BGP capabilities. MBGP provides backward-compatible extensions to the BGP-4 protocol that let it carry information for network layer protocols other than IPv4, such as IPv6 and IPX. Although we won't spend a great deal of time on MBGP, we will cover the new attribute types, as well as touch on where MBGP is most often used today.

In order to support multiprotocol capabilities in BGP-4, two new attributes were introduced: Multiprotocol Reachable NLRI (MP_REACH_NLRI) and Multiprotocol Unreachable NLRI (MP_UNREACH_NLRI).

Multiprotocol Reachable NLRI (MP_REACH_NLRI) is an optional nontransitive attribute that can be used for three purposes:

- To advertise a feasible route to a peer
- To permit a router to advertise the network layer address of the router that should be used as the next hop to the destination listed in the NLRI field of the MP_NLRI attribute
- To allow a given router to report some or all of the Subnetwork Points of Attachment (SNPAs) that exist within the local system

Multiprotocol Unreachable NLRI (MP_UNREACH_NLRI) is an optional nontransitive attribute that can be used to withdraw one or more unfeasible routes from service.

These new attributes introduced by MBGP provide the capability to associate a particular network layer protocol with the next-hop information, as well as associate a particular network layer protocol with NLRI. The Address Family information defined in RFC 1700[6] is used to identify particular network layer protocols.

Interdomain multicast routing is the most common use of BGP's multiprotocol extensions today. It's probably the reason that folks often expand MBGP to Multicast BGP rather than Multiprotocol BGP. When using MBGP for multicast, BGP carries two sets of routes: one for unicast routing and one for multicast routing. The routes associated with multicast routing are then used by PIM (Protocol-Independent Multicast) for RPF (Reverse Path Forwarding) checks to build data distribution trees.

Prior to MBGP, interdomain multicast routing used the unicast BGP infrastructure and required that unicast and multicast topologies be congruent. MBGP introduces greater flexibility to interdomain multicasting and gives the network administrator more control over network resources.

For more information on IP multicast routing, associated protocols, and their behaviors, refer to Beau Williamson's *Developing IP Multicast Networks*[7].

TCP MD5 Signature Option

The TCP MD5 Signature Option, defined in RFC 2385 [8], is used to help BGP protect itself from spoofed TCP segments and, particularly, TCP resets. The TCP MD5 Signature Option employs MD5's message digest algorithm, defined in RFC 1321[9]. More details regarding the usefulness of the TCP MD5 Signature Option can be found in the specification.

The extension provides a mechanism for TCP to carry a digest message in each TCP segment, where the digest utilizes information known only to the connection end points and acts as a signature for the segment.

Applying the MD5 algorithm to the following items, in the order listed, produces the digest created for a given segment:

1. TCP pseudo-header, in this order: source IP address, destination IP address, zero-padded protocol number, and segment length
2. TCP header, excluding options and assuming a checksum of zero
3. TCP segment data
4. Independently specified key or password, known to both TCP sender and receiver

When TCP receives a signed segment, the receiver must validate it by using its local key to calculate its own digest and compare the value with that of the received digest. If the comparison results in unequal values, the segment should be discarded and must not produce any response to the sender.

If a receiver is configured to utilize the option, the absence of a signature from a sender should not result in the receiver's disabling its use of the option.

The MD5 option appears in every segment and is always 16 bytes in length. (Recall the available 16 bytes in the BGP message header that were reserved for this purpose.) The format is shown in Figure 5-16.

Figure 5-16 *MD5 Option Format*

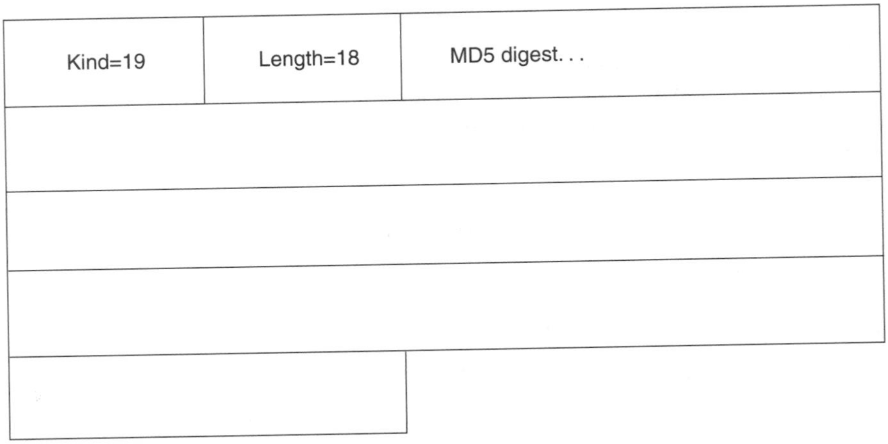

Kind=19
Length=18
MD5 digest. . .

The MD5 option results in potentially hostile TCP resets being ignored by the receiver of the reset if the sender doesn't know the key value. Note that the key is never exchanged via the connection and that only the end points should be aware of the value.

Several issues are associated with using this option. Most notably, the MD5 algorithm has been found to be vulnerable to collision search attacks and is therefore considered by some to be insufficient for this application. Fortunately, the current specification does not prevent the deployment of an alternative-hashing algorithm.

There are also performance implications associated with calculating the digest value. This is because each TCP segment requires that both the sender and receiver perform the hashing function to generate the key value, and the receiver must compare the two values before accepting a message. The result is significantly increased delay with BGP message processing and generation.

Despite these offshoots, this option has already been widely deployed in both the interdomain and intradomain routing space.

Looking Ahead

BGP as a protocol presents some basic elements of routing that are flexible enough to allow total control from the administrator's perspective. The power of BGP lies in its attributes and its route-filtering techniques. Attributes are simply parameters that can be modified to affect the BGP decision process. Route filtering can be done on a prefix level or a path level. A combination of filtering and attribute manipulation can achieve the optimal routing behavior. Because traffic follows a road map laid out by routing updates, modifying the routing behavior will eventually modify the traffic trajectories. The next chapter provides a hands-on approach to understanding the basics of setting routing policies with BGP.

Frequently Asked Questions

Q — *Does BGP send periodic updates like RIP?*

A — No. BGP exchanges routing information once, when the BGP session is being established. After that, only network changes are exchanged between BGP peers.

Q — *Does the BGP session become "established" after all the routing updates have been exchanged between BGP neighbors?*

A — No. It is the other way around. No routing exchange can take effect until both BGP neighbors agree on all parameters and the session becomes established.

Q — *Is the Network Layer Reachability Information (NLRI) the actual BGP routing update?*

A — No. The NLRI is one of the elements that is carried in a BGP UPDATE message. Other elements are the attributes and the unreachable networks.

Q — *You talk about authentication as an example of the BGP optional parameters. How important is authentication?*

A — Authentication is a means to validate the BGP peer. This is to prevent hackers from assuming the identity of one of your peers and feeding you wrong routing information. With authentication, both peers validate the connection via password mechanisms.

Q — *Where does BGP carry information about AS numbers?*

A — AS numbers are listed as part of the AS_PATH attribute carried in the UPDATE message.

Q — *Is BGP connection symmetrical, or does it utilize a master/slave relationship?*

A — The BGP protocol has no master and slave roles. At the transport layer, the connection is always initiated by one side and appears as a client (with the source TCP port number greater than 2048) that connects to a server (port 179), but it does not have any influence at the protocol level.

Q — *The link to my provider has a firewall. What must be done in order for BGP to work?*

A — The firewall must be configured to allow a TCP connection to port 179 in at least one direction (from the provider to you, or from you to the provider). Use caution, because some providers use passive BGP mode (their router does not attempt to establish the BGP connection).

References

[1]RFC 1997, "BGP Communities Attribute," www.isi.edu/in-notes/rfc1997.txt

[2]RFC 1966, "BGP Route Reflection: An alternative to full mesh IBGP," www.isi.edu/innotes/rfc1966.txt

[3]RFC 1863, "A BGP/IDRP Route Server alternative to a full mesh routing," www.isi.edu/in-notes/rfc1863.txt

[4]RFC 2283, "Multiprotocol Extensions for BGP-4," www.isi.edu/in-notes/rfc2283.txt

[5]IETF Inter-Domain Routing Working Group, www.ietf.org/html.charters/idr-charter.html

[6]RFC 1700, "Assigned Numbers," www.isi.edu/in-notes/rfc1700.txt

[7]Williamson, Beau. *Developing IP Multicast Networks* (Indianapolis, Ind.: Cisco Press, 1999)

[8]RFC 2385, "Protection of BGP Sessions via the TCP MD5 Signature Option," www.isi.edu/in-notes/rfc2385.txt

[9]RFC 1321, "The MD5 Message-Digest Algorithm," www.isi.edu/in-notes/rfc1321.txt

PART III

Effective Internet Routing Designs

You are now in a position to begin applying the attributes and functionality of BGP to practical routing problems. Chapter 6 begins this process by examining BGP's attribute manipulation techniques and the use of route filtering in influencing the BGP decision process. Chapter 7 introduces three fundamental design criteria—redundancy, symmetry, and load balancing—that network architects frequently must implement and balance in developing their routing policies. Chapter 8 considers how to integrate BGP with interior protocols, and Chapter 9 considers how to tap BGP's potential for managing large and growing networks. Chapter 10 takes up the problem of network stability, and increasingly challenging design goals in the wake of the ever-expanding Internet. BGP includes a number of built-in functions designed to help build stability. Part III takes an example-oriented approach, using specific topologies and scenarios to illustrate routing design concepts and applications.

This chapter covers the following key topics:

- **Building peer sessions**—A walk-through of the negotiation process between BGP and its neighbors.
- **Sources of routing updates**—The source and method by which routes are injected into BGP have implications for the accuracy and stability of routing information.
- **Overlapping protocols: backdoors**—When alternative routes into and out of a network are offered by overlapping protocols, a method of ranking them by preference is available.
- **The routing process simplified**—The decision model by which BGP receives, filters, selects for usage, and advertises routes, as a continuous process.
- **Controlling BGP routes**—At the core of BGP is a collection of attributes that administrators can apply to control routing according to their networks' needs.
- **Route filtering and attribute manipulation**—An example-oriented, systematic look at how BGP permits or denies routes, applies filters, and manipulates attributes to define the set of routing updates that enter and exit an autonomous system.
- **BGP-4 aggregation**—Several specific scenarios involving different aggregation choices and how BGP-4 accommodates them.

CHAPTER 6

Tuning BGP Capabilities

Up to this point, this book has been concerned primarily with general definitions of interior and exterior gateway protocols and an overview of their respective and interconnected tasks. The Border Gateway Protocol (BGP) was also presented from the technical perspective of its functional elements. With this chapter, you will begin to consider more practical implementation details for BGP as part of the overall design problem in building reliable Internet connectivity. This chapter examines specific attributes of BGP and how they are applied individually and together to address this design problem. Although the terminology, attributes, and details of this chapter are specific to BGP, the general concepts and problems raised are pertinent to routing architecture design, regardless of what specific protocols are being utilized.

Building Peer Sessions

The previous chapter examined the process of BGP neighbor negotiation at a fairly technical level. It emphasized the formats of messages exchanged during negotiation. This chapter now expands the examination to consider additional subtleties of the negotiation process. In addition, this section introduces distinctions between internal and external BGP, which have practical implications in building peer sessions.

Although BGP is most commonly used to provide a loop-free interdomain topology, BGP is also used internal to an autonomous system (AS) to provide internal routers with external destination reachability information. A *neighbor connection* (also referred to as a *peer connection*) between two routers can be established within the same AS, in which case BGP is called internal BGP (IBGP). Likewise, a peer connection between routers in different ASs is referred to as external BGP (EBGP). Figure 6-1 contrasts these environments.

Figure 6-1 *Internal and External BGP Implementations*

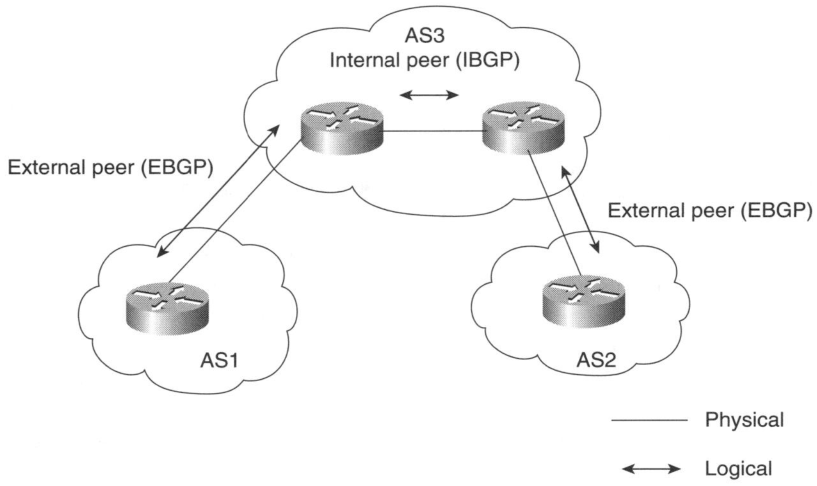

Upon neighbor session establishment and during the OPEN message exchange negotiation, peer routers compare AS numbers and determine whether they are peers in the same AS or in different ASs. The difference between EBGP and IBGP manifests itself in how each peer would process the routing updates coming from the other peer and in the way different BGP attributes are carried on external connections versus internal connections.

The neighbor negotiation process is mainly the same for internal and external neighbors as far as building the TCP connection at the transport level. It is essential to have IP connectivity between the two neighbors for the transport session to be established. IP connectivity must be achieved via a protocol different from BGP; otherwise, the session will be in a race condition, an example of which follows:

> Neighbors can reach one another via some Interior Gateway Protocol (IGP), the BGP session is established, and BGP messages are exchanged. The IGP connection goes away for some reason, but the BGP TCP session is still up because neighbors can still reach each other via BGP. Eventually, the session will go down because the BGP session cannot depend on BGP itself for neighbor connectivity—the underlying substrate provides NEXT_HOP reachability. Another example is if a route more specific than that used to established the peer connection is learned via BGP.

Most commonly for IBGP peering sessions, an Interior Gateway Protocol (IGP) or static route can be configured to achieve IP connectivity. In essence, a ping packet, containing a source IP address (the IP address of one BGP peer) and a destination IP address (the IP address of the second peer), must succeed for a transport session to initiate. Generally, for external BGP sessions, a route through a directly connected interface establishes IP reachability.

Physical Versus Logical Connections

External BGP neighbors have a restriction in that they must be physically connected, adjacent to one another. BGP drops any UPDATE message from its external BGP peer if the peer is not physically connected, unless otherwise specified. However, some situations arise in which external neighbors cannot be on the same physical segment. Such neighbors are logically connected (multiple IP hops away) but not physically connected. An example would be running BGP between external neighbors across non-BGP routers. In this situation, Cisco (and most other vendors) offers an extra knob to override this restriction. BGP would require some extra configuration to indicate that its external peer is not physically attached.

NOTE Indirectly connected external neighbors require extra configuration.

A BGP session formed between external BGP peers that are not physically connected is referred to as *multihop EBGP*. In Figure 6-2, RT2 can't run BGP, but RT1 and RT3 can. Thus, external neighbors RT1 and RT3 are logically connected and peer with one another via multihop EBGP. (Note, however, that RT2 must somehow learn the appropriate routing information to avoid potential forwarding loops or black-holing packets.)

Figure 6-2 *External BGP Multihop Environment*

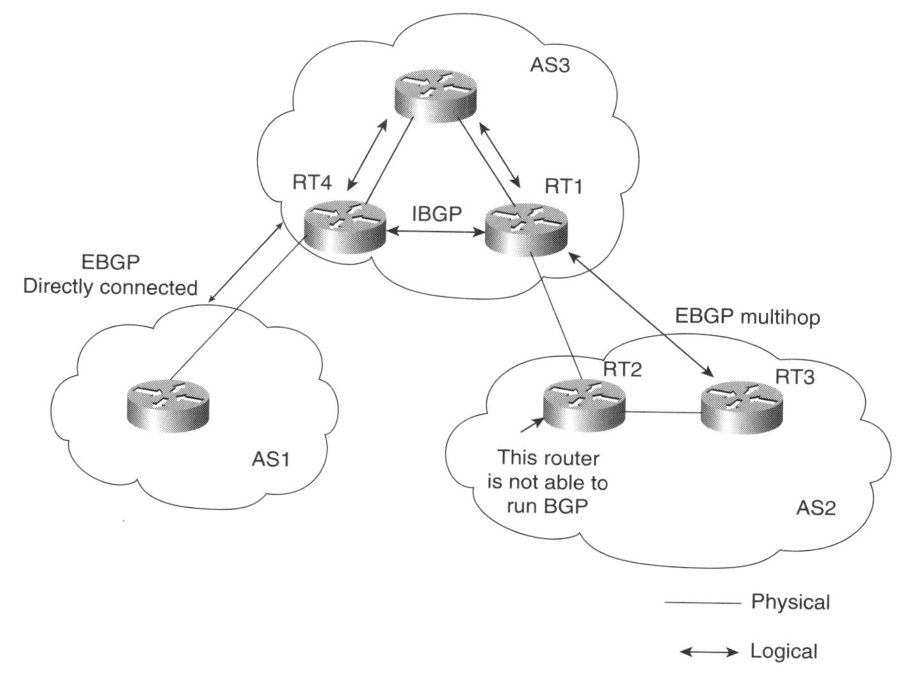

On the other hand, neighbors within the same autonomous system (internal neighbors) have no restrictions whatsoever on whether the peer is physically connected or separated by multiple IP hops. As long as there is IP connectivity between the two neighbors, BGP requires no additional configuration. In Figure 6-2, RT1 and RT4 are logically, but not physically, connected. Because both are in the same AS, no additional configuration is required for them to run IBGP.

Obtaining an IP Address

The neighbor's IP address could be the address of any of the routers' interfaces, such as Ethernet, Token Ring, or serial. Keep in mind that the stability of the neighbor connection depends on the stability of the IP address you choose.

NOTE Session stability depends on the stability of neighbor IP addresses.

If the IP address belongs to an Ethernet card that has some hardware problems and is shutting down every few minutes, the neighbor connection and the stability of the routing system will suffer. Cisco provides the capability to configure a virtual interface, referred to as a *loopback interface*, that is supposed to be up at all times. Tying the BGP neighbor connection to a loopback interface will ensure that the BGP session is not reliant on any hardware interface that might be problematic.

Adding loopback interfaces is not necessary in every situation (it actually requires more configuration). If external BGP neighbors are directly connected and the IP addresses of the directly connected segment are used for the neighbor negotiation, a loopback address is of no added value. If the physical link between the two peers is problematic, the session will break with or without loopback.

TIP See the section "Building Peering Sessions" in Chapter 11, "Configuring Basic BGP Functions and Attributes," on page 301.

Authenticating the BGP Session

As you saw in Chapter 4, "Interdomain Routing Basics," the BGP message header allows for authentication. Authentication is a precaution against hackers who might present themselves as one of your BGP peers and feed invalid routing information into your AS. Authentication between two BGP peers provides the capability to validate the session between you and your neighbor by using shared secret keys. A neighbor that attempts to establish a session without using the proper key will be ignored. The current authentication features available in BGP-4 use the message-digest version 5 (MD5) algorithm. A detailed discussion of the MD5 authentication algorithm is beyond the scope of this book, but as previously discussed, it can provide added security to the underlying TCP transport connection.

BGP Continuity Inside an AS

Aside from the special case of route reflection, in order to avoid routing information loops inside an AS, BGP does not readvertise to internal BGP peers routes that are learned from other IBGP peers. Thus, it is important to maintain a full IBGP mesh within the AS. In other words, every BGP router in the AS has to establish a BGP session with all other BGP routers inside the AS. Figure 6-3 illustrates one of the common mistakes administrators make when setting BGP routing inside the AS.

Figure 6-3 *Common BGP Continuity Mistake*

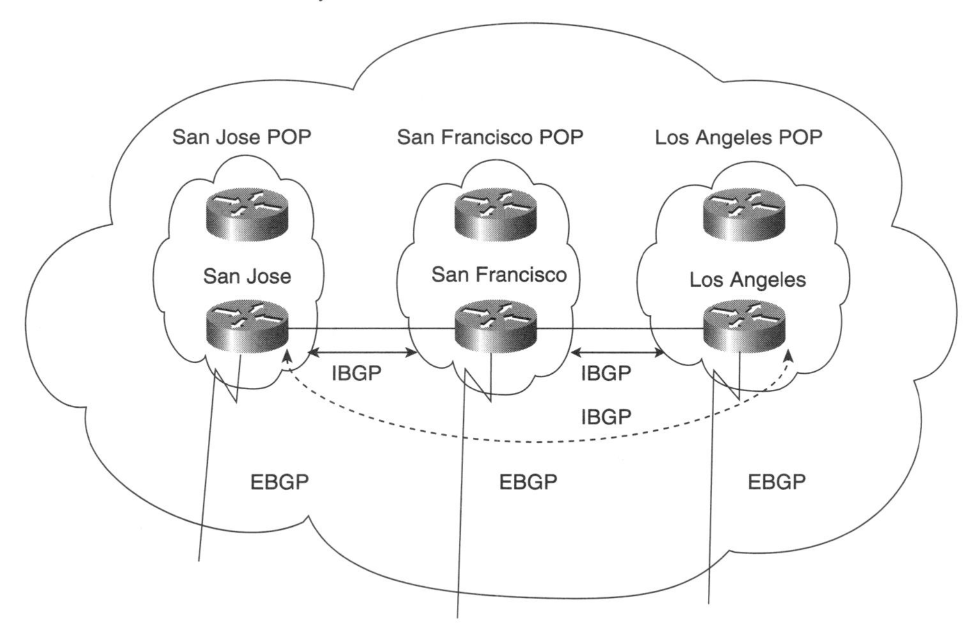

In the situation illustrated in Figure 6-3, an ISP has points of presence (POPs) in San Jose, San Francisco, and Los Angeles. Each POP has multiple non-BGP routers and a BGP border router running EBGP with other ASs. The administrator configures an IBGP connection between the San Jose border router and the San Francisco border router. He configures another IBGP connection between the San Francisco border router and the Los

Angeles border router. In this configuration, EBGP routes learned via San Jose will be given to San Francisco, EBGP routes learned via San Francisco are given to San Jose and Los Angeles, and EBGP routes learned via Los Angeles are given to San Francisco. Routing in this picture is not complete: EBGP routes learned via San Jose will not be given to Los Angeles, and EBGP routes learned via Los Angeles will not be given to San Jose. This is because the San Francisco router will not pass on IBGP routes between San Jose and Los Angeles. What is needed is an additional IBGP connection between San Jose and Los Angeles (shown via the dotted line). You will see in Chapter 9, "Controlling Large-Scale Autonomous Systems," how this situation could be handled by using the concept of route reflectors, an option that scales much better in cases where the AS has a large number of IBGP routers.

Synchronization Within an AS

By definition, the default behavior of BGP requires that it must be synchronized with the IGP before BGP may advertise transit routes to external ASs. It is important that your AS be consistent about the routes it advertises to avoid unnecessarily black-holing traffic. For example, if an IBGP speaker were to advertise a route to an external peer before all routers within your AS had learned about the route through the IGP, your AS could receive traffic to destinations for which some of the routers might not yet have the information to reach.

Whenever a router receives an update about a destination from an IBGP peer, the router tries to verify internal reachability for that destination before advertising it to other EBGP peers. The router does this by checking the destination prefix first to see if a route to the next-hop router exists and second to see if a destination prefix in the IGP exists. This router check indicates whether non-BGP routers can deliver traffic to that destination. Assuming that the IGP recognizes that destination, the router announces it to other EBGP peers. Otherwise, the router treats the destination prefix as not being synchronized with the IGP and does not advertise it.

Consider the situation illustrated in Figure 6-4. ISP1 and ISP2 use ISP3 as a transit AS. ISP3 has multiple routers in its AS and is running BGP only on the border routers. (Even though RTB and RTD are carrying transit traffic, ISP3 has not configured BGP on these routers.) ISP3 is running an Interior Gateway Protocol inside the AS for internal connectivity.

Figure 6-4 *BGP Route Synchronization*

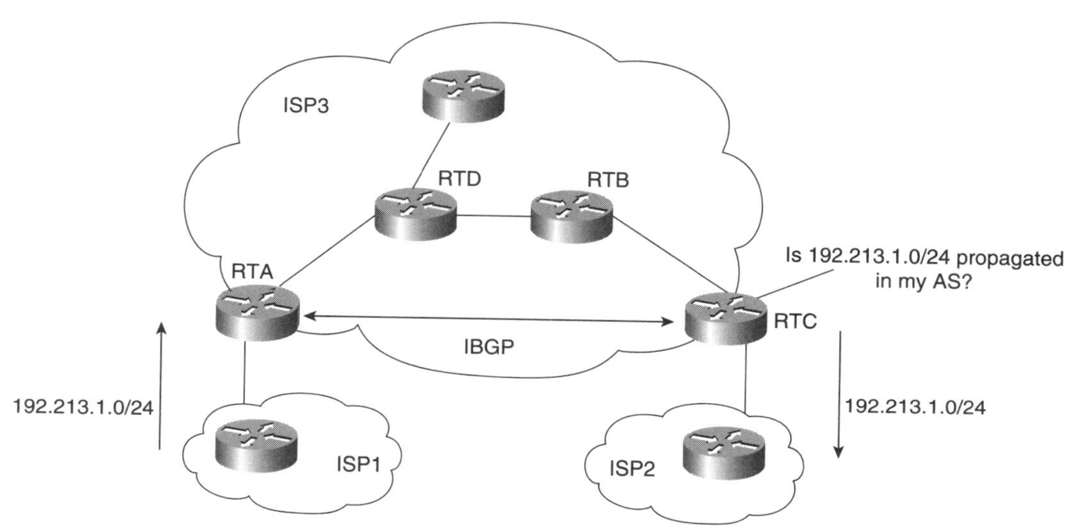

Assume that ISP1 is advertising route 192.213.1.0/24 to ISP3. Because RTA and RTC are running IBGP, RTA propagates the route to RTC. Note that other routers besides RTA and RTC are not running BGP and have no knowledge so far of the existence of route 192.213.1.0/24.

In the situation illustrated in Figure 6-4, if RTC advertises the route to ISP2, traffic toward the destination 192.213.1.0/24 will start flowing toward RTC. RTC will perform a lookup in its IP routing table and will direct the traffic toward RTB. RTB, having no visibility to the BGP routes, will drop the traffic because it has no knowledge of the destination. The traffic is dropped because BGP and the IGP are not synchronized.

The BGP rule states that a BGP router should not advertise to external neighbors destinations learned from IBGP neighbors unless those destinations are also known via an IGP. This is known as synchronization. If a router knows about these destinations via an IGP, it assumes that the route has already been propagated inside the AS, and internal reachability is ensured.

The consequence of injecting BGP routes inside an IGP is costly. Redistributing routes from BGP into the IGP will result in major overhead on the internal routers, primarily from an IGP scalability perspective, because (as discussed earlier) IGPs are not designed to handle that many routes. Besides, carrying all external routes inside an AS is not necessary. Routing can easily be accomplished by having internal non-BGP routers default to one of the BGP routers. Of course, this will result in suboptimal routing because there is no guarantee that the shortest path for each route will be used, but this cost is minimal compared to maintaining thousands of routes inside the AS. Of course, managing default routes in a situation such as this can be extremely complex and may very well result in routing loops.

Most BGP implementations, however, offer a software knob that lets the network operator disable synchronization. As you might suspect, configuring the Cisco BGP subcommand **no synchronization** will tell BGP to override the synchronization requirement and allow it to advertise routes learned via IBGP, irrespective of the existence of an IGP route. In practice, most situations allow synchronization to be safely turned off on border routers, assuming that all transit routers in the AS are running fully meshed IBGP. In this situation, internal reachability is guaranteed because a route that is learned via EBGP on any border router will automatically be passed on via BGP to all transit routers.

That said, by far the most common configuration in Internet-connected networks is to disable BGP synchronization and rely on a full mesh of IBGP routers. The thought of injecting tens of thousands of routes into an IGP is quite frightening.

Sources of Routing Updates

In networks as complex as today's Internet, route stability is a big issue. With respect to route fluctuations, there is a close correspondence between the stability of the Internet access links and how the routing information was injected into the Internet via BGP. Information can be injected into BGP dynamically or statically. Dynamically injected routes come and go from the BGP routing table, depending on the status of the networks they identify. Statically injected routes are constantly maintained by the BGP routing tables, regardless of the status of the networks they identify. Thus, although a dynamic advertisement will cease if the network being advertised no longer exists, a static advertisement would not. Each method has its pros and cons, as you will see next.

TIP See the section "Sources of Routing Updates" in Chapter 11 on page 318.

Injecting Information Dynamically into BGP

Dynamically injected information can be further divided into purely dynamic, in which all the IGP routes are redistributed into BGP (via the **redistribute** BGP subcommand), and semidynamic, in which only certain IGP routes are to be injected into BGP (via the **network** BGP subcommand). This distinction reflects both the level of user intervention and the level of control in defining the routes to be advertised.

Information is injected dynamically into BGP by allowing all the IGP routes to be automatically redistributed into BGP. A variety of IGPs are used in autonomous systems these days, including Routing Information Protocol (RIP), Interior Gateway Routing Protocol (IGRP), Enhanced IGRP (EIGRP), Open Shortest Path First (OSPF), and the

Intermediate System-to-Intermediate System (IS-IS) routing protocol. What dynamic redistribution offers is ease of configuration: All internal IGP routes will dynamically flow into BGP, regardless of what particular protocols are being used.

TIP See the section "Injecting Information Dynamically into BGP" in Chapter 11 on page 318.

Another method of injecting information into BGP that isn't quite as dynamic is to manually specify a subset of IGP networks to be advertised by individually listing them for injection into BGP by using the **network** BGP subcommand. This method is less than completely dynamic, because a list of all the prefixes that need to be advertised must be maintained in the router. The router does not automatically inject all IGP routes into BGP. If the list of prefixes were large, maintaining it would be impractical.

BGP assumes that networks defined with the **network** command are existing networks and will try to verify that by checking in the IP routing table. If BGP does not find an exact match for these networks, they will not be advertised. Note that if an accompanying **mask** is not specified with the **network** command (for example, **network 10.10.0.0 mask 255.255.0.0**) and auto-summarization is enabled (the default), existence of any subset of the classful prefix specified by the **network** command (for example, **network 10.0.0.0** with the existing 10.10.10.0/24) will result in advertisement of the classful prefix. (In this case, 10.0.0.0/8 will be advertised.) This intelligent verification step increases the robustness of BGP so much that other, external networks will not be misled due to a router advertising a network not connected to or otherwise unknown by it.

Injecting routes into BGP via the **network** command offers more-controlled route advertisement. Injecting IGPs into BGP via redistribution might result in the side effect of leaking unwanted or faulty information into BGP, as you will see next.

Injection of Unwanted or Faulty Information

Redistributing the whole IGP into BGP could result in some unwanted information being leaked into BGP. Such information could be private addresses, or illegal (unregistered) internal addresses that are supposed to be used within the AS only. Other information could include routes that have a prefix length that does not comply with the provider's aggregation policies; a host route with a prefix length of /32 is an example. Careful filtering is required in order to guard against undesired consequences. Also, in more recent IOS releases, auto-summarization of routes (on classful boundaries) is enabled by default.

TIP See the section "Sources of Routing Updates" in Chapter 11 on page 318.

Faulty information can also be injected into BGP due to the mutual exchange of routes between BGP and the IGP. In the same way that an IGP can be redistributed into BGP, BGP routes can be injected into an AS via redistribution into the IGP. When redistribution occurs in both directions, it is called *mutual redistribution*. In mutual redistribution, information that was injected from the outside into the AS could be sent back to the Internet as having originated from the AS. Figure 6-5 illustrates the danger of mutual redistribution between protocols.

Figure 6-5 *Mutual Redistribution Example*

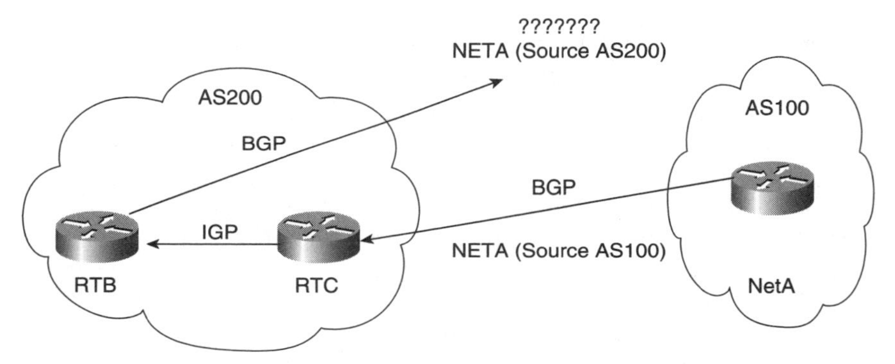

In Figure 6-5, AS100 is the source of NetA and is sending this information via BGP to AS200. The border router, RTC, injects that BGP information into the IGP. RTB learns about AS100's information through the IGP. RTB is configured to redistribute the IGP information into BGP. With respect to most IGPs, RTB has no means of differentiating AS100's prefixes from its own internal prefixes because that type of information is not conveyed in the IGP. Hence, NetA will end up being advertised via BGP back to the Internet as if it originated from AS200. This is very misleading to ASs connected to the Internet, because NetA now has two sources rather than one source (AS100).

Again, to remedy this situation, special filtering should be put on the border routers to specify what particular networks should be injected from the IGP into BGP. This would have stopped NetA from being redistributed back into BGP by RTB. For protocols that differentiate between internal and external routes such as OSPF, the administrator can configure the protocol to ensure that it will redistribute only internal routes into BGP. (In the Cisco implementation, external OSPF routes are automatically blocked from being redistributed into BGP; the administrator has the option of overriding this behavior.) For protocols (such as RIP or IGRP) that do not distinguish between internal and external routes, special route tagging should be performed to differentiate between external routes and internal routes.

Unstable Routes

Injecting the IGP routes into BGP dynamically or semidynamically is based on the dependency of the BGP routes on the IGP routes. Although you could argue that this is good because it reflects the actual status of networks, it can have drawbacks as well. Remember that with today's global network connectivity, route fluctuation within your AS will have a ripple effect through other networks attached to the Internet that communicate via BGP. The IGP route you advertise will translate into a BGP route. If that route goes down, a WITHDRAWN message will be sent via BGP, requesting peers to remove that route from their BGP routing tables. A route constantly going up and down in your AS has the effect of being constantly sent and withdrawn by other ASs. The example of one fluctuating route is very simplistic; imagine having hundreds of these routes fluctuating in hundreds of ASs. Internet stability will be affected very negatively.

Strict measures are being put into place to try to mitigate the effect of route fluctuation on the Internet. As you will see in Chapter 10, "Designing Stable Internets," a process called route dampening penalizes and ultimately discontinues advertisement of fluctuating routes, depending on their degree of instability. Route advertisements may be suppressed for minutes or even hours (until they stabilize).

Controlling route instability is not an easy matter because it usually depends on factors that are beyond your control. Such factors could be unstable access links or faulty hardware. One way to minimize route instability is through aggregation. When an aggregate route announcement represents more than one route, the fluctuation of any single route does not cause fluctuation in the aggregate itself. Aggregation could be done on the customer boundary or the provider boundary, depending on the level of information exchanged between the customer and the provider. If done on the customer boundary, this would alleviate the provider from seeing the fluctuations of individual customer routes. If aggregation is used on the provider boundary, the customer fluctuation would leak to the provider but would not be propagated to the Internet. BGP-4 aggregation is discussed near the end of this chapter, after the discussion of many of the techniques used in BGP tuning.

Another way of controlling route instability is to decouple route advertisement from the existence of the route itself. This is called *static injection of routes* into BGP, and it is described in the following section.

Injecting Information Statically into BGP

Today, injecting information statically into BGP has proven to be the most effective method of ensuring route stability. Of course, this method also has drawbacks.

TIP See the section "Injecting Information Statically into BGP" in Chapter 11 on page 325.

To statically inject information into BGP, IGP routes (or aggregates) that need to be advertised to other peers are manually defined as static routes. This ensures that these routes will never disappear from the IP routing table and hence will always be advertised. Because administrators are often uncomfortable advertising routes to networks that might be down or unreachable, the appropriateness of injecting information statically depends on the particular situation.

For example, if the route is advertised to the Internet from a single point, advertising a route that is actually down is not a big issue. Hosts trying to access that destination will fail irrespective of whether the route is advertised.

On the other hand, if a route is advertised to the Internet from multiple points, advertising the route statically at all times might end up black-holing the traffic. If problems inside the AS prevent the border router from being able to reach the network it is advertising, traffic to that destination will be dropped even though it could have been reached from some other interconnection point.

The actual advertisement of the static route can be done with either of the methods described in the section "Injecting Information Dynamically into BGP." Advertisement can be done by redistributing all the static routes via the **redistribute** command or a subset of the static routes via the **network** command. The latter of the two methods provides for a more controlled route injection model because redistribution might cause some unwanted static routes to be conveyed via BGP, although filtering of redistributed routes can also accomplish this.

ORIGIN of Routes

BGP considers the networks advertised via the **network** command or via aggregation as being internal to the AS and will include the ORIGIN attribute in each route as being IGP(i). On the other hand, whenever a route is injected into BGP via redistribution (whether statically or dynamically), the ORIGIN of the route will be INCOMPLETE because the redistributed routes could have come from anywhere.

Finally, if the route was learned via EGP, that ORIGIN value will be assigned. Note also that aggregated routes will assume the worst ORIGIN value of all the component routes.

Figure 6-6 illustrates these issues. In Scenario 1, all networks have been listed under the BGP process via the **network** command. Note that BGP considers 10.0.0.0 and 11.0.0.0 as having a known origin of IGP. Network 12.0.0.0 is the only network that is not known to the router (that does not exist in the IP routing table). As you can see, 12.0.0.0 is not being advertised via BGP, even though it has been listed via the **network** command.

Figure 6-6 *Behavior Comparison for the ORIGIN Attribute*

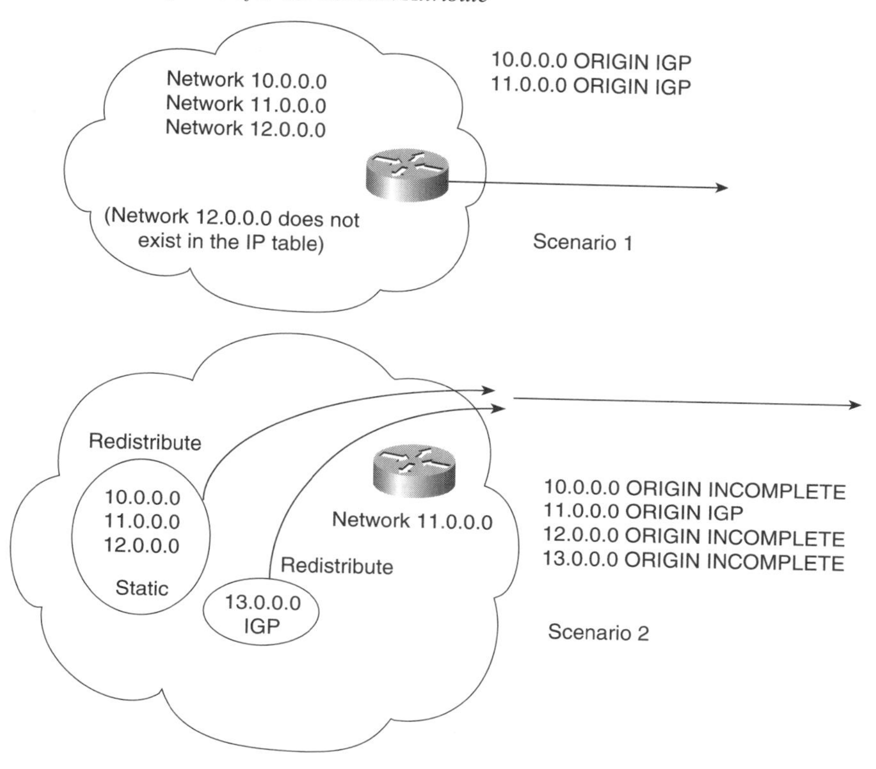

In Scenario 2, networks 10.0.0.0, 11.0.0.0, and 12.0.0.0 have been defined through static routes. Network 11.0.0.0 has also been defined via the **network** command. Finally, network 13.0.0.0 is learned dynamically by the router via an IGP. All these networks have been injected into BGP via redistribution. As a result, networks 10.0.0.0, 12.0.0.0, and 13.0.0.0 have been advertised with an ORIGIN of INCOMPLETE because these networks have been injected into BGP via redistribution.

Although network 11.0.0.0 has been injected into BGP via explicit redistribution of static routes, it is also defined natively to BGP via the **network** command, which is why it is sent out with an ORIGIN of IGP(i). If network 11.0.0.0 had not been defined with a static **network** command, it would have been sent out with an ORIGIN of INCOMPLETE. It should be noted that network 11.0.0.0 did not need to be redistributed because defining it statically and listing it via the **network** command would suffice to inject it into BGP.

Although the ORIGIN attribute is immaterial at this point, it is used by the BGP decision process to favor one route over another.

An Example of Static Versus Dynamic Routing: Mobile Networks

It is common in the military for units to be mobile; this creates a problem for assigning IP addresses. Usually these mobile units want to deploy their subnets and IP addresses wherever they go and operate as if they had never moved. If these networks are part of a global network and advertised via BGP, announcing them statically will not work well. The static commands would have to be removed from the border router of an AS in one location and installed in the border router of another AS in the new location every time the unit moves.

To avoid such complications, injecting these networks dynamically into BGP becomes mandatory. One solution is to inject the IGP into BGP in all locations. This way, whenever the IP addresses are moved from one location to another, the announcements will disappear from one location and reappear in the new one. In some cases, network administrators are not comfortable with this solution for reasons discussed earlier, such as mutual redistribution problems and the mandate for extensive filtering.

Another possibility is to define these networks in all the border routers of all the locations via the **network** command. Because BGP checks for the existence of these routes in the IP routing table before announcing them, BGP will announce only the routes in the location of the mobile unit. All other locations will automatically cease from announcing the routes because they are not part of the IGP of that particular AS.

Overlapping Protocols: Backdoors

With different IGPs and EGPs working together to achieve routing, routes can be learned via different protocols; choosing one protocol over another affects how the traffic flows. For example, if traffic follows a RIP route, it might traverse one link, whereas if it follows an external BGP route, it might end up on another link. Backdoor links offer an alternative IGP path that can be used instead of the external BGP path. IGP routes that can be reached over the backdoor link are called *backdoor routes*. With the existence of such alternative routes, a mechanism that gives one protocol preference over other protocols is needed. Cisco Systems offers a preference parameter called the *administrative distance* of a protocol. The lower a routing protocol's administrative distance, the higher the preference for the protocol.

It should be noted that administrative distance is a parameter that is relative only to the locally configured router and is not known by or communicated to any other routers in the AS. Thus, if you intend to modify the administrative distance of one router in the AS, it is highly recommended that the administrative distance be changed similarly on all routers in the AS in order to guarantee a consistent routing decision. Table 6-1 lists distances according to the Cisco implementation.

TIP

See the section "Overlapping Protocols: Backdoors" in Chapter 11 on page 326.

Table 6-1 *Protocol Distance Default Values*

Protocol	Distance
Directly connected	0
Static	1
EBGP	20
EIGRP (internal)	90
IGRP	100
OSPF	110
ISIS	115
RIP	120
EGP	140
EIGRP (external)	170
IBGP	200
BGP local	200
Unknown	255

Table 6-1 indicates that a directly connected route is generally preferred over a static route, which in turn is preferred over an EBGP route, and so on. Note that EBGP routes with a distance of 20 are preferred over all the other IGP routes.

Figure 6-7 illustrates the use of backdoor routes. In the figure, AS1 is receiving updates about NetA from two different sources. AS1 is receiving routes via EBGP on the link to AS3 and via the backdoor link running RIP between AS1 and AS2. According to Table 6-1, the router will automatically give a distance of 20 to the EBGP route and a distance of 120 to the RIP route. In AS1, the routers that learn the route via EBGP (AS border routers) will install the lower distance in the routing table. Hence, traffic toward NetA will follow the indirect BGP route via AS3 and then AS2, rather than the direct RIP route via AS2.

Figure 6-7 *Backdoor Routing Conflicts*

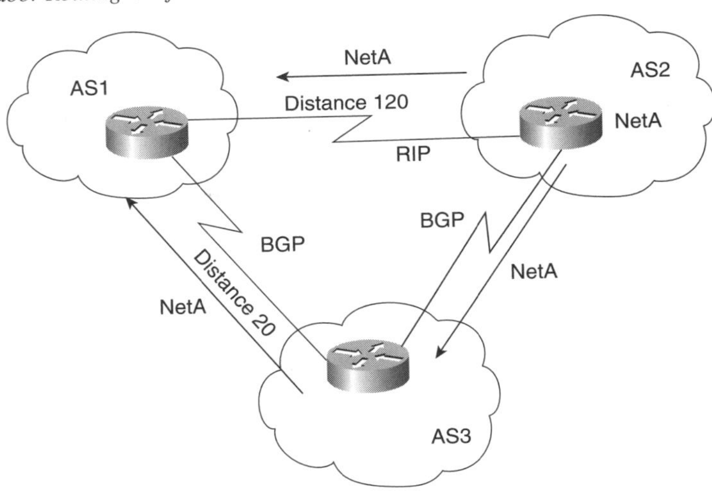

Cisco provides a way to force IGP routes to take precedence over EBGP routes. The concept is simple. Specific EBGP routes can be tagged as backdoor routes, which sets the distance of these routes to be the same as the "BGP local" route's distance (the default is 200). According to Table 6-1, this distance is higher than any IGP learned route, and the backdoor IGP route will be preferred.

Alternatively, as previously discussed, another option is to use the **distance** BGP subcommand to alter the administrative distance of all the BGP prefixes learned by the router.

The Routing Process Simplified

Until now, this chapter has examined discrete aspects of routing—specifically, peer negotiation and static versus dynamic routing. Before diving into details of routing configuration, it makes sense to pause here and briefly overview the BGP routing process in its entirety.

BGP is a fairly simple protocol, which is why it's so flexible. Routes are exchanged between BGP peers via UPDATE messages. BGP routers receive the UPDATE messages, run some policies or filters over the updates, and then pass the routes to other BGP peers. An implementation is required to keep all BGP updates in a BGP routing table separate from the IP routing table. In case multiple routes to the same destination exist, BGP does not flood its peers with all those routes; rather, it picks the best route and sends it. In addition to passing along EBGP routes from peers or IBGP routes from route reflector clients, a BGP router can originate routing updates to advertise internal networks that belong to its own autonomous system. Valid local routes originated in the system and the best routes learned from BGP peers are then installed in the IP routing table. The IP routing table is the final routing decision and is used to populate the forwarding table.

To model the BGP process, imagine that each BGP speaker has different pools of routes and different policy engines applied to the routes (although in reality only one pool may exist). The model would involve the following components:

- A pool of routes that the router receives from its peers
- An Input Policy Engine that can filter the routes or manipulate their attributes
- A decision process that decides which routes the router itself will use
- A pool of routes that the router itself uses
- An Output Policy Engine that can filter the routes or manipulate their attributes
- A pool of routes that the router advertises to other peers

Figure 6-8 illustrates this model. The subsequent discussion provides more details about each component.

Figure 6-8 *Routing Process Overview*

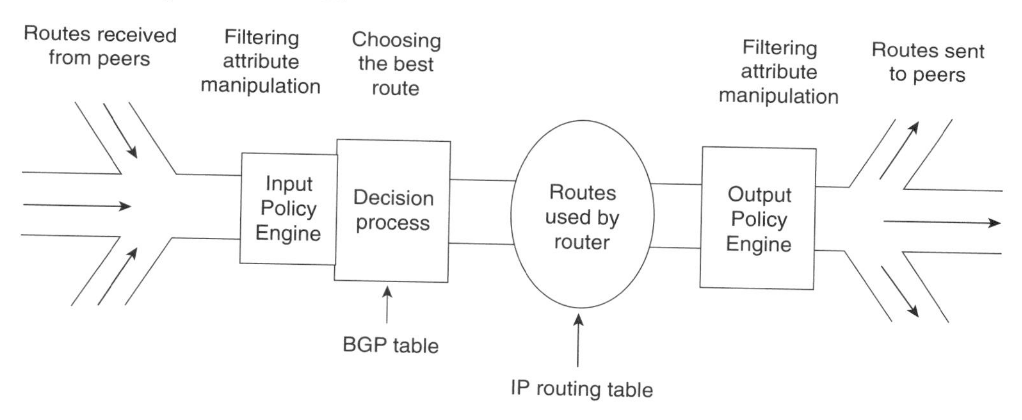

BGP Routes: Advertisement and Storage

As specified in RFC1 771:

> For the purpose of this protocol, a route is defined as a unit of information that pairs a destination with the attributes of a path to that destination:
>
> Routes are advertised between a pair of BGP speakers in UPDATE messages: the destination is the system whose IP addresses are reported in the Network Layer Reachability Information (NLRI) field, and the path is the information reported in the path attributes field of the same UPDATE message.
>
> Routes are stored in the Routing Information Bases (RIBs): namely, the Adj-RIBs-In, Loc-RIB, and the Adj-RIBs-Out. Routes that will be advertised to other BGP speakers must be present in the Adj-

RIB-Out; Routes that will be used by the local BGP speaker must be present in the Loc-RIB, and the next hop for each of these routes must be present in the local BGP speakers forwarding information base (FIB); and routes that are received from other BGP speakers are present in the Adj-RIBs-In.

If a BGP speaker chooses to advertise a route, it may add to or modify the route's path attributes before advertising it to the peer.

Note that from this point forward, the term *route* used in the context of BGP will represent a unit of information that pairs a destination with the attributes of a path to that destination, as just defined.

The BGP Routing Information Bases

As illustrated in Figure 6-9, the BGP routing table consists of three distinct parts: Adj-Routing Information Base (RIB)-In, Loc-RIB, and Adj-RIB-Out.

Figure 6-9 *Logical Representation of BGP Routing Table*

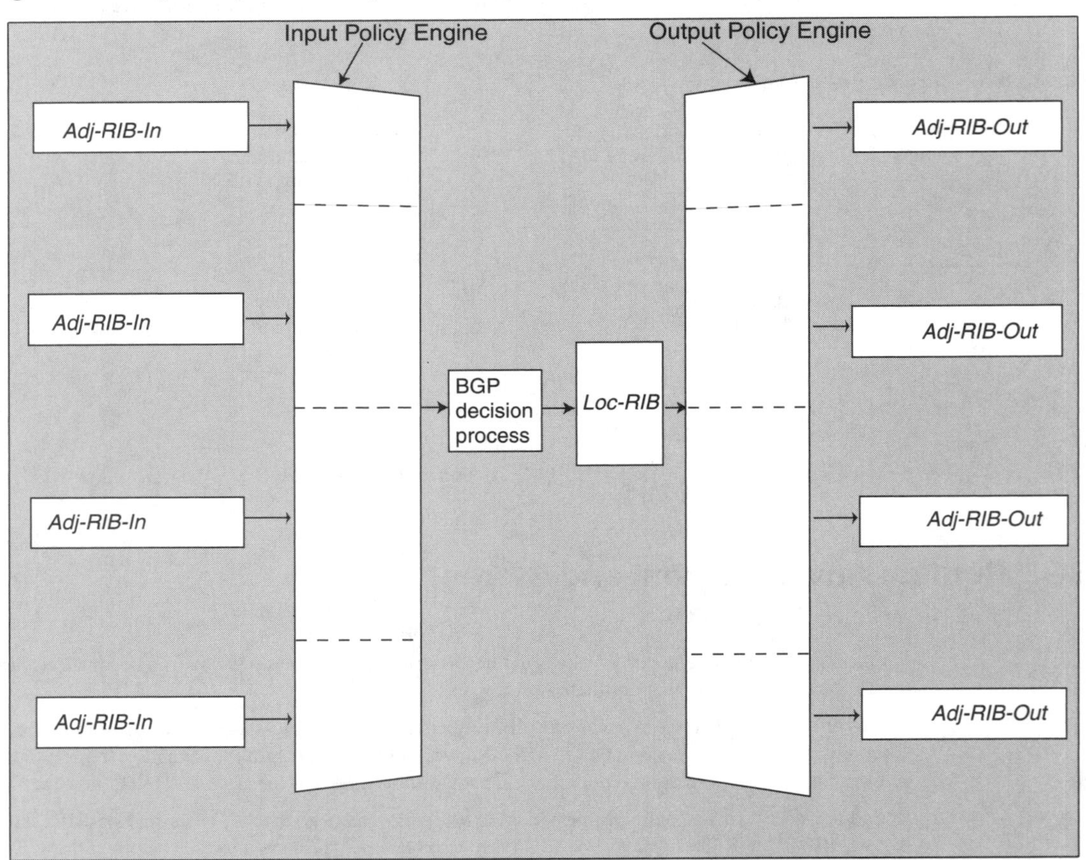

An Adj-RIB-In is logically associated with each individual peer of a BGP speaker. It stores routing information that has been learned from the peer via inbound UPDATE messages. The contents of all the Adj-RIBs-In are available as input to the BGP decision process after being manipulated or perhaps even filtered by the Input Policy Engine associated with the peer.

The Loc-RIB contains only the preferred routes that have been selected as the best path to each available destination. The Loc-RIB is the result of the BGP decision process after incoming local policies have been applied by the Input Policy Engines.

An Adj-RIB-Out is logically associated with each individual peer of a BGP speaker. It stores routing information that the BGP speaker has selected for advertisement to the peer. The Adj-RIB-Out contains information from the Loc-RIB to be advertised to the peer after the associated Output Policy Engine has been applied.

Although the conceptual model presented here distinguishes between Adj-RIBs-In, Loc-RIB, and Adj-RIBs-Out, storing three separate copies of the routing information is not a requirement. In reality, most implementations actually store one copy of the information with pointers in order to conserve memory.

Routes Received from Peers

A BGP speaker receives routes (and their associated attributes) from external and/or internal peers via UPDATE messages. Depending on what is configured in the Input Policy Engines, some or all of these routes will make it into the Loc-RIB.

Input Policy Engine

The Input Policy Engine handles route filtering and attribute manipulation. Filtering is done based on different parameters such as IP prefixes, AS_PATH, and other BGP attribute values. BGP also uses the Input Policy Engine to manipulate the path attributes in order to influence its own decision process and hence affect what routes it will actually use to reach a given destination. For example, if BGP chooses to filter a certain prefix coming from a given peer, this indicates that BGP does not want to reach that destination via that peer. Or, if BGP gives a certain prefix a better LOCAL_PREF value, this indicates that BGP prefers the prefix from a specific peer to a similar prefix from other peers. The Input Policy Engine applies incoming policies configured by the operator.

Routes Used by the Router

The best routes, as identified by the decision process, are placed in the Loc-RIB. These routes become candidates that can be advertised to other peers or placed in the IP routing table. If a route is not placed in the Loc-RIB, it cannot be placed in the Adj-RIB-Out for advertisement to peers.

In addition to routes passed on from other peers, the router (if configured to do so) originates updates about the networks inside its autonomous system. This is how an AS advertises its internal networks to the outside world.

Output Policy Engine

This is the same engine as the Input Policy Engine, applied on the output side. Routes used by the router (the best routes) in addition to routes that the router generates locally are given to this engine for processing. The Output Policy Engine might apply filters and might change some of the BGP attributes (such as AS_PATH or metric) before sending the update.

The Output Policy Engine also differentiates between internal and external peers; for example, routes learned from one internal peer cannot be passed on to another internal peer.

Routes Advertised to Peers

The set of routes advertised to peers consists of those routes that successfully pass through the Output Policy Engine and are advertised to the BGP peers, internal or external.

Sample Routing Environment

Figure 6-10 illustrates the process applied to BGP routes in a sample environment. In the figure, AS5 receives routes from both AS1 and AS2 and originates its own routes (172.16.10.0/24). To simplify, consider just the flow of updates in one direction, left to right.

Figure 6-10 *Sample Routing Environment*

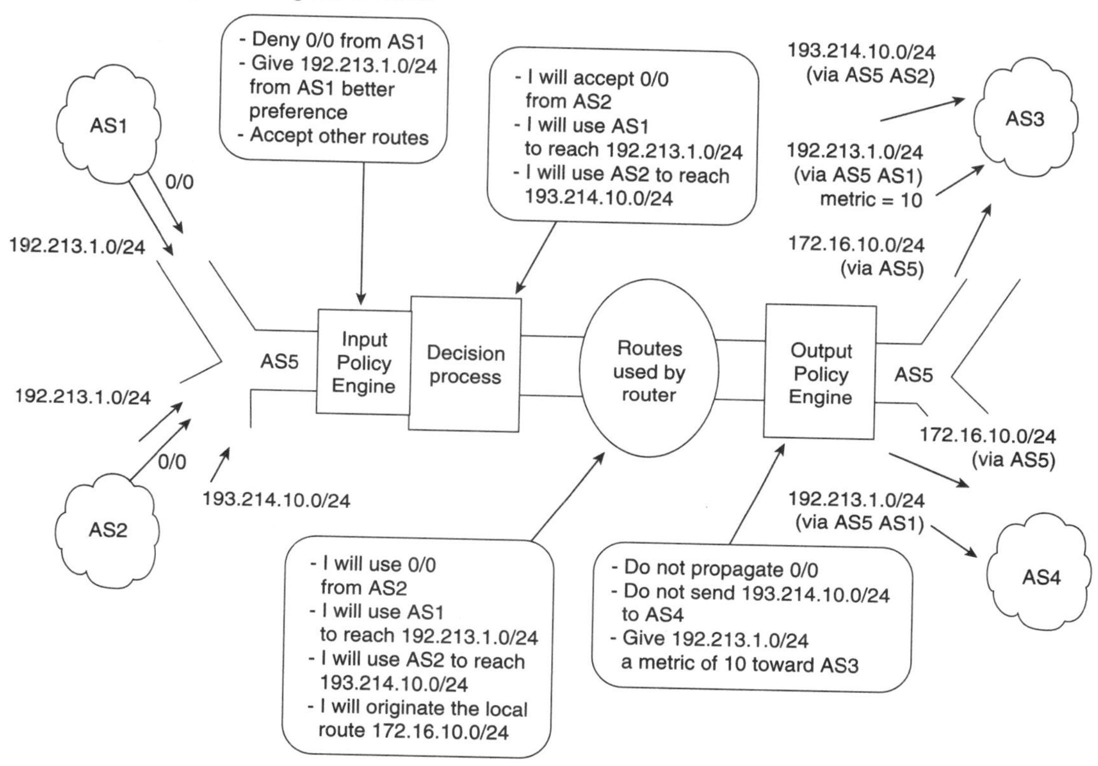

By applying the engine model to AS5, you will get these results.

Routes received from peers (the routes coming from AS1 and AS2) consist of the following:

- 192.213.1.0/24 via AS1
- 0/0 (this is a default route) via AS1
- 193.214.10.0/24 via AS2
- 0/0 (this is a default route) via AS2
- 192.213.1.0/24 via AS2

Input Policy Engine criteria dictate the following:

- Do not accept default route 0/0 from AS1.
- Give route 192.213.1.0/24 coming from AS1 better preference than route 192.213.1.0/24 coming from AS2.
- Accept all other routes (this will accept 193.214.10.0/24).

The decision process concludes the following:

- Because 192.213.1.0/24 has better preference via AS1, I will reach 192.213.1.0/24 via AS1.
- I will reach 193.214.10.0/24 via AS2.
- I will accept 0/0 via AS2.

Routes used by the router conclude the following:

- I will use 0/0 as the default from AS2.
- I can reach 192.213.1.0/24 via AS1.
- I can reach 193.214.10.0/24 via AS2.
- Network 172.16.10.0/24 is one of my local networks that I want to advertise.

Output Policy Engine criteria dictate the following:

- Do not propagate the default route 0/0.
- Do not advertise 193.214.10.0/24 to AS4.
- Give 192.213.1.0/24 a metric of 10 when sent to AS3.

Routes advertised to peers toward AS3 consist of the following:

- 192.213.1.0/24 (via AS5 AS1) (this means first AS5 and then AS1) with a metric of 10
- 172.16.10.0/24 (via AS5)
- 193.214.10.0/24 (via AS5 AS2)

Routes advertised to peers toward AS4 consist of the following:

- 192.213.1.0/24 (via AS5 AS1)
- 172.16.10.0/24 (via AS5)

BGP Decision Process Summary

BGP bases its decision process on the attribute values. When faced with multiple routes of the same prefix length to the same destination, BGP chooses the best route for routing traffic toward the destination. The following process summarizes how BGP chooses the best route:

1. If the next hop is inaccessible, the route is ignored. (This is why it is important to have an IGP route to the next hop.)
2. Prefer the path with the largest weight. (Weight is a Cisco proprietary parameter, local to the router.)
3. If the weights are the same, prefer the route with the largest local preference value.

4 If there are no locally originated routes and the local preference is the same, prefer the route with the shortest AS_PATH.

5 If the AS_PATH length is the same, prefer the route with the lowest origin type (where IGP is lower than EGP and EGP is lower than INCOMPLETE).

6 If the origin type is the same, prefer the route with the lowest MED value if the routes were received from the same AS (or if **bgp always-compare-med** is enabled).

7 If the routes have the same MED value, prefer EBGP paths to IBGP paths.

8 If all the preceding scenarios are identical, prefer the route that can be reached via the closest IGP neighbor—that is, take the shortest internal path inside the AS to reach the destination. (Follow the shortest path to the BGP NEXT_HOP.)

9 If the internal path is the same, the BGP ROUTER_ID will be a tiebreaker. Prefer the route coming from the BGP router with the lowest RID. With Cisco IOS, the RID is the loopback address if one is configured; otherwise, it's the highest IP address on the router. RID determination is vendor-specific.

Note that if BGP Multipath is enabled (discussed in Chapter 11), Steps 7 through 9 could be bypassed, and all paths with the same AS_PATH length and MED value could be installed into the routing table. Some implementations have also been known to bypass Step 9 and use the "first installed" routes as the active routes.

Controlling BGP Routes

The preceding section discussed the existence of policy engines, which provide attribute manipulation and route filtering. This section discusses in detail attribute manipulation and route filtering, which are the keys to controlling routing information. Each BGP attribute is examined to illustrate what is manipulated.

Traffic inside and outside an AS always flows according to the road map laid out by routes. Altering the routes translates into changes in traffic behavior. Here are some of the more common questions that organizations and service providers ask about controlling routes:

- How do I prevent my private networks from being advertised?
- How do I filter routing updates coming from a particular neighbor?
- How do I make sure that I use this link or this provider rather than another one?

As you will see, BGP provides the necessary hooks and attributes to address all these questions and more.

BGP Path Attributes

The BGP attributes are a set of parameters that describe the characteristics of a prefix (route). The BGP decision process couples these attributes with the prefix they describe, compares all the paths available to reach a given destination, and then selects the best routes to be used to reach the destination. Remember that attributes are part of each BGP UPDATE packet and describe the path information of the associated prefix. The next few sections cover these attributes and how they can be manipulated to affect the routing behavior.

Before I describe the BGP path attributes, let's take a brief look at the four separate categories of path attributes:

- Well-known mandatory
- Well-known discretionary
- Optional transitive
- Optional nontransitive

The following section was extracted from RFC 1771:

> Well-known attributes must be recognized by all BGP implementations. Some of these attributes are mandatory and must be included in every UPDATE message. Others are discretionary and may or may not be sent in a particular UPDATE message.
>
> All well-known attributes must be passed along (after proper updating, if necessary) to other BGP peers.
>
> In addition to well-known attributes, each path may contain one or more optional attributes. It is not required or expected that all BGP implementations support all optional attributes. The handling of an unrecognized optional attribute is determined by the setting of the Transitive bit in the attribute flags octet. Paths with unrecognized transitive optional attributes should be accepted. If a path with unrecognized transitive optional attribute is accepted and passed along to other BGP peers, then the unrecognized transitive optional attribute of that path must be passed along with the path to other BGP peers with the Partial bit in the Attribute Flags octet set to 1. If a path with recognized transitive optional attribute is accepted and passed along to other BGP peers and the Partial bit in the Attribute Flags octet is set to 1 by some previous AS, it is not set back to 0 by the current AS. Unrecognized non-transitive optional attributes must be quietly ignored and not passed along to other BGP peers.
>
> New transitive optional attributes may be attached to the path by the originator or by any other AS in the path. If they are not attached by the originator, the Partial bit in the Attribute Flags octet is set to 1. The rules for attaching new non-transitive optional attributes will depend on the nature of the specific attribute. The documentation of each new non-transitive optional attribute will be expected to include such rules. (The description of the MULTI_EXIT_DISC attribute gives an example.) All optional attributes (both transitive and non-transitive) may be updated (if appropriate) by ASs in the path.

The currently defined BGP attributes are described in the following list. More-detailed information is provided in the associated sections thereafter.

- **ORIGIN (Type Code 1)**—A well-known mandatory attribute that defines the origin of the path information. The data octet can assume the following values:
  - **0: IGP**—Network Layer Reachability Information that is interior to the originating AS

— **1: EGP**—Network Layer Reachability Information learned via EGP
— **2: INCOMPLETE**—Network Layer Reachability Information learned by some other means

- **AS_PATH (Type Code 2)**—A well-known mandatory attribute that is composed of a sequence of AS path segments. Each AS path segment is represented by a triple <path segment type, path segment length, path segment value>.
- **NEXT_HOP (Type Code 3)**—A well-known mandatory attribute that defines the IP address of the border router that should be used as the next hop to the destinations listed in the Network Layer Reachability field of the UPDATE message.
- **MULTI_EXIT_DISC (Type Code 4)**—An optional nontransitive attribute that is a four-octet nonnegative integer. The value of this attribute may be used by a BGP speaker's decision process to discriminate among multiple exit points to a neighboring autonomous system.
- **LOCAL_PREF (Type Code 5)**—A well-known discretionary attribute that is a four-octet nonnegative integer. It is used by a BGP speaker to inform other BGP speakers in its own autonomous system of the originating speaker's degree of preference for an advertised route.
- **ATOMIC_AGGREGATE (Type Code 6)**—A well-known discretionary attribute of length 0. It is used by a BGP speaker to inform other BGP speakers that the local system selected a less-specific route without selecting a more-specific route that is included in it.
- **AGGREGATOR (Type Code 7)**—An optional transitive attribute of length 6. The attribute contains the last AS number that formed the aggregate route (encoded as two octets), followed by the IP address of the BGP speaker that formed the aggregate route (encoded as four octets).
- **COMMUNITY (Type Code 8)**—An optional transitive attribute of variable length. The attribute consists of a set of four octet values, each of which specifies a community. All routes with this attribute belong to the communities listed in the attribute.

TIP See the section "BGP Attributes" in Chapter 11 on page 328.

The ORIGIN Attribute

The ORIGIN attribute is a well-known mandatory attribute (Type Code 1) that indicates the origin of the routing update with respect to the autonomous system that originated it. BGP considers three types of origins:

- **IGP**—The Network Layer Reachability Information (NLRI) is internal to the originating AS.
- **EGP**—The Network Layer Reachability Information is learned via the Exterior Gateway Protocol (EGP).
- **INCOMPLETE**—The Network Layer Reachability Information is learned by some other means.

BGP considers the ORIGIN attribute in its decision-making process to establish a preference ranking among multiple routes. Specifically, BGP prefers the path with the lowest origin type, where IGP is lower than EGP and EGP is lower than INCOMPLETE. For more details on how the ORIGIN attribute is calculated, see the earlier section "ORIGIN of Routes."

The AS_PATH Attribute

The AS_PATH attribute is a well-known mandatory attribute (Type Code 2) that contains a sequence of autonomous system numbers that represent the path a route has traversed. Internally to an AS, routes passed among BGP speakers leave the AS_PATH information intact; however, when sending routes to external BGP peers, the AS that originates the route adds its own AS number. Thereafter, each AS that receives the route and passes it on to other EBGP peers will prepend its AS number to the list. *Prepending* is the act of adding the AS number to the beginning of the list. The final list represents all the AS numbers that a route has traversed. The AS number of the AS that originated the route is at the end of the list (just before the ORIGIN code). This type of AS_PATH list is referred to as an *AS_SEQUENCE*, because all the AS numbers are ordered sequentially.

TIP See the section "The AS_PATH Attribute" in Chapter 11 on page 332.

BGP uses the AS_PATH attribute as part of the routing updates (UPDATE packet) to ensure a loop-free topology on the Internet. Each route that is passed between BGP peers carries a list of all AS numbers that the route has traversed. If the route is advertised to an AS whose AS number is already present in the AS_SEQUENCE, the UPDATE is ignored. BGP speakers prepend their AS numbers when advertising routing updates to other ASs. When the route is passed to a BGP speaker within the same AS, the AS_PATH information is left intact.

Figure 6-11 illustrates the AS_PATH attribute at each instance of the route 172.16.10.0/24, originating in AS1 and passed to AS2, then AS3 and AS4, and back to AS1. Note how each AS that passes the route to other external peers adds its own AS number to the beginning of the list. When the route gets back to AS1, the AS1 BGP border router realizes that this route has already been through its AS (AS number 1 appears in the list) and will not accept the route.

Figure 6-11 *Sample Loop Condition Addressed by the* AS_PATH *Attribute*

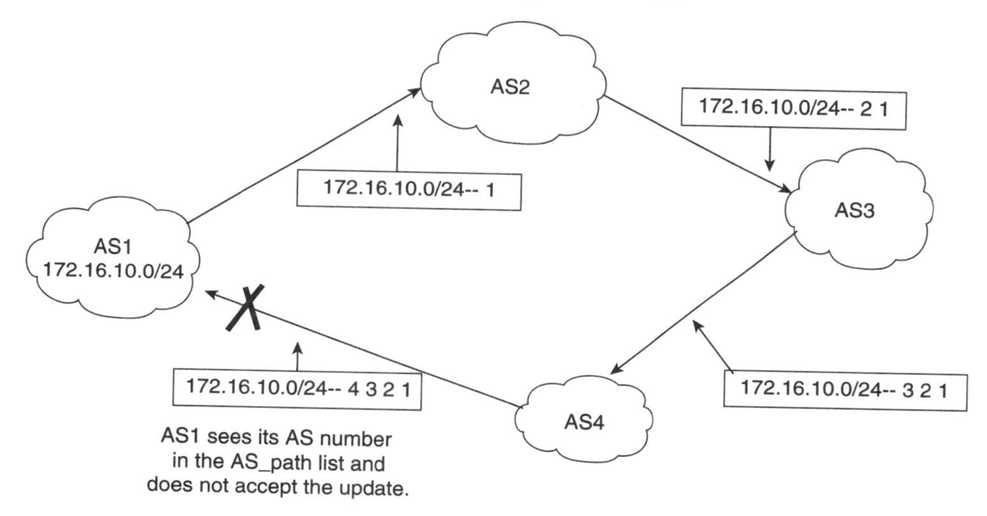

AS_PATH information is one of the attributes BGP uses to determine the best route to take to reach a destination. In comparing two or more different routes, given that all higher-priority attributes are equal, a shorter AS_PATH is always preferred over a longer one. In case of a tie, other attributes are used to determine the best path to the destination. (See the earlier section "BGP Decision Process Summary.")

The NEXT_HOP Attribute

The NEXT_HOP attribute is a well-known mandatory attribute (Type Code 3). This varies slightly when used in the context of an IGP, where the next hop to reach a destination is the IP address of the connected interface of the router that has announced the route.

TIP See the section "The NEXT_HOP Attribute" in Chapter 11 on page 331.

The next-hop concept with BGP is slightly more elaborate. It takes one of the following four forms:

- For EBGP sessions, the next hop is the IP address of the neighbor that announced the route.
- For IBGP sessions, for routes originated inside the AS, the next hop is the IP address of the neighbor that announced the route.
- For routes injected into the AS via EBGP, the next hop learned from EBGP is carried unaltered into IBGP. The next hop is the IP address of the EBGP neighbor from which the route was learned.
- When the route is advertised on a multiaccess medium (such as Ethernet, Frame Relay, and so on), the next hop is usually the IP address of the interface of the router connected to the medium that originated the route.

Figure 6-12 illustrates the BGP NEXT_HOP attribute environment.

Figure 6-12 BGP NEXT_HOP *Example*

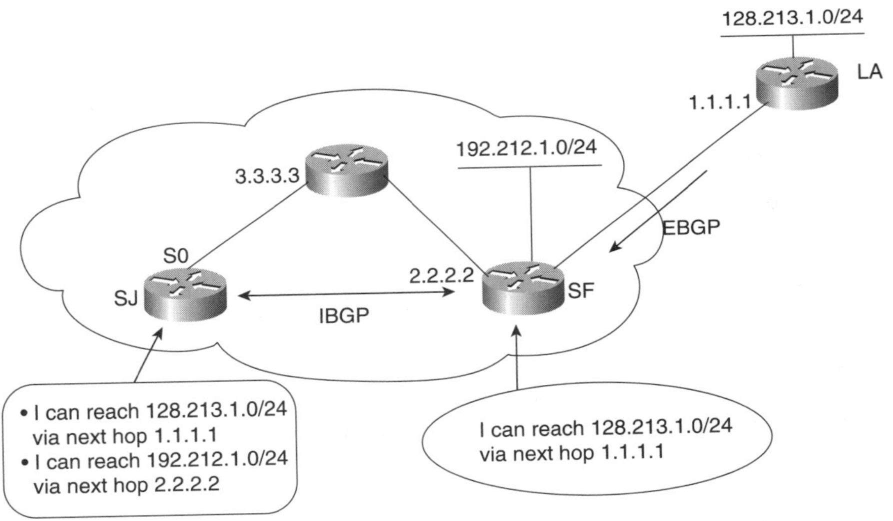

The SF router is running an EBGP session with the LA router and an IBGP session with the SJ router. The SF router is learning route 128.213.1.0/24 from the LA router. In turn, the SF router is injecting the local route 192.212.1.0/24 into BGP.

The SJ router learns route 192.212.1.0/24 via 2.2.2.2, the IP address of the IBGP peer announcing the route. Thus, 2.2.2.2 is the next hop, according to the definition, for SJ to reach 192.212.1.0/24. Similarly, the SF router sees 128.213.1.0/24 coming from the LA router via next hop 1.1.1.1. When it passes this route update to the SJ router via IBGP,

SF includes the next-hop information, unaltered. Thus, the SJ router would receive the BGP update about 128.213.1.0/24 with next hop 1.1.1.1. This is an example of the EBGP next hop being carried into IBGP.

As you can see from this example, the next hop is not necessarily reachable via a direct connection. For example, SJ's next hop for 128.213.1.0/24 is 1.1.1.1, but reaching it requires a pathway through 3.3.3.3. Thus, the next-hop behavior mandates a recursive IP lookup for a router to know where to send the packet. To reach the next hop 1.1.1.1, the SJ router will recursively look into its IGP routing table to see if and how 1.1.1.1 can be reached. This recursive search continues until the router associates destination 1.1.1.1 with an outgoing interface. The same recursive behavior is performed to reach next hop 2.2.2.2. If a hop can't be reached, BGP considers the route inaccessible.

The following is an example of how IP recursive lookup is used to direct the traffic toward the final destination. Tables 6-2 and 6-3 list the BGP and IP routing tables for the SJ router illustrated in Figure 6-12.

Table 6-2 *BGP Table of the SJ Router*

Destination	Next Hop
192.212.1.0/24	2.2.2.2
128.213.1.0/24	1.1.1.1

Table 6-3 *IP Routing Table of the SJ Router*

Destination	Next Hop
192.212.1.0/24	2.2.2.2
2.2.2.0/24	3.3.3.3
3.3.3.0/24	Connected; Serial 0
128.213.1.0/24	1.1.1.1
1.1.1.0/24	3.3.3.3

Table 6-2 indicates that 128.213.1.0/24 can be reached via next hop 1.1.1.1. Looking into the IP routing table, network 1.1.1.0/24 can be reached via next hop 3.3.3.3. Another recursive lookup in the IP routing table indicates that network 3.3.3.0/24 is directly connected via Serial 0. This indicates that traffic toward next hop 1.1.1.1 should go via Serial 0. The same reasoning applies to delivering traffic toward next hop 2.2.2.2.

Care must be taken to make sure that reachability of the BGP NEXT_HOP is provided via some IGP or static routing. If the IBGP NEXT_HOP cannot be reached, the BGP route is considered inaccessible.

The MULTI_EXIT_DISC Attribute

The BGP Multiexit Discriminator (MULTI_EXIT_DISC or MED) attribute is an optional nontransitive attribute (Type Code 4). It is a hint to external neighbors about the preferred path into an AS that has multiple entry points. The MED is also known as the external metric of a route. A lower MED value is preferred over a higher MED value.

Unlike LOCAL_PREF, the MED attribute is exchanged between ASs, but a MED attribute that is received by an AS does not leave the AS. When an update enters the AS with a certain MED value, that value is used for decision making within the AS. When BGP passes the routing update to another AS, the MED is reset to 0 (unless the outgoing MED is explicitly set to a specific value).

When the route is originated by the AS itself, the most common practice is for the MED value to follow the internal IGP metric of the route. This becomes useful when a customer has multiple connections to the same provider. The IGP metric within the customer's AS reflects how close to or how far from a certain entrance point to that AS a network is. A network that is closer to entrance point A than to entrance point B will have a lower IGP metric in the border router connected to A. When the IGP metric is translated to MED, traffic received by the AS should enter from the link closest to the destination. This behavior is the result of a lower MED being preferred to reach the same destination. MEDs can be used by both providers and customers to balance the traffic over multiple links between two ASs.

Unless otherwise specified, the router compares MED attributes for paths from external neighbors that are in the same AS. MEDs from different ASs are not comparable because the MED associated with a route usually gives some indication of the AS's internal topology, routing policies, and routing protocol. Comparing MEDs from different ASs is like comparing apples and oranges. Still, for administrators who have a reason to do so, Cisco offers the **bgp always-compare-med** router command, which tells BGP to compare MEDs from different ASs for the same route.

TIP See the section "The MULTI_EXIT_DISC Attribute" in Chapter 11 on page 337.

In the example illustrated in Figure 6-13, the MED shows how an AS can influence the outbound decision of another AS. In Figure 6-13, ANET and YNET try to influence XNET's outbound traffic by sending it different MED values.

Figure 6-13 *Effects of the MED Attribute*

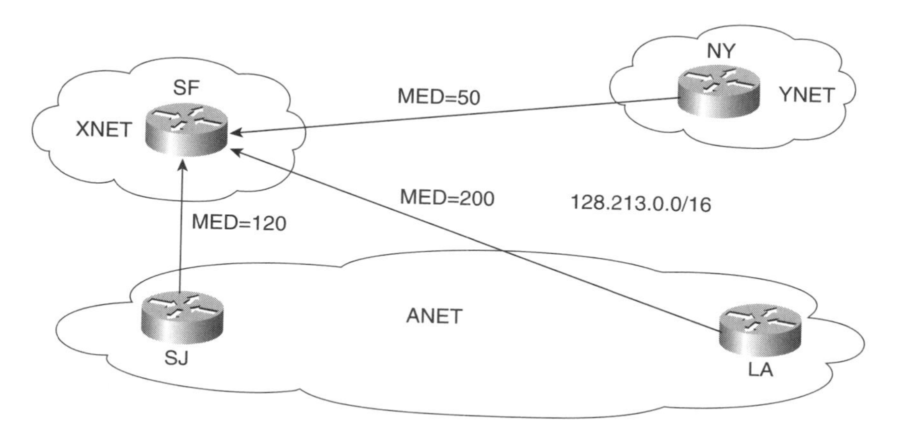

XNET is receiving routing updates about 128.213.0.0/16 from three different sources: SJ (metric 120), LA (metric 200), and NY (metric 50). SF will compare the two metric values coming from ANET and will prefer the SJ router because it is advertising a lower metric (120). When the **bgp always-compare-med** command is used on the SF router, it will compare metric 120 with metric 50 coming from NY and will prefer NY to reach 128.213.0.0/16. Note that SF could have influenced its decision by using the LOCAL_PREF attribute inside XNET to override the metrics coming from outside ASs. Nevertheless, MED is still useful in case XNET prefers to base its BGP decisions on outside factors to simplify router configuration on its end. Customers who connect to the same provider in multiple locations could exchange metrics with their providers to influence each other's outbound traffic, which leads to better load balancing.

MEDs are somewhat handicapped by aggregation in scenarios in which providers announce a given CIDR block from multiple locations in their network and suppress the smaller routes from the block. Utilizing MEDs in this scenario could potentially result in suboptimal routing because the more-specific routes of the CIDR block could be scattered throughout the AS and MEDs associated with more-granular routes are no longer available.

When using MEDs to perform what's commonly referred to as *best-exit* routing, some providers leak the more-specifics of their CIDR blocks to select peers to remove the offshoots introduced by aggregation. The problem with this is that controlling the more-specific announcements is sometimes complex, and failure to do so can result in some very suboptimal routing situations.

MEDs are not always accepted by peers, not only because of the potential suboptimal routing situations introduced by aggregation, but also because many networks either don't derive the MED values from some intelligent IGP metric or don't provide consistency of MED values across all prefixes announced from their AS. In either case, for ASs depending on reasonable MEDs, the likely result is little more than poor decision-making.

When providers don't use MEDs or other attribute manipulation techniques to prefer the best-exit path, it's often referred to as *closest-exit* or *hot potato* routing. The many offshoots of using manipulation techniques have resulted in closest-exit routing currently being the most prevalent interdomain routing model in the traffic exchange points today.

The Local_Preference Attribute

The local preference (LOCAL_PREF) attribute is a well-known discretionary attribute (Type Code 5). The local preference attribute is a degree of preference given to a route to compare it with other routes for the same destination. A higher local preference value indicates that the route is more preferred. Local preference, as indicated by the name, is local to the autonomous system and is exchanged between IBGP peers only. An AS connected via BGP to several other ASs will get routing updates about the same destinations from different ASs. Local preference is usually used to set the exit point of an AS to reach a certain destination. Because this attribute is communicated within all BGP routers inside the AS, all BGP routers will have a common view of how to exit the AS.

TIP See the section "The LOCAL_PREF Attribute" in Chapter 11 on page 335.

Consider the environment illustrated in Figure 6-14. Suppose that company ANET has purchased Internet connections via two service providers, XNET and YNET. ANET is connected to YNET via a primary T3 link and to XNET via a backup T1 link.

Figure 6-14 *Local Preference Attribute Example*

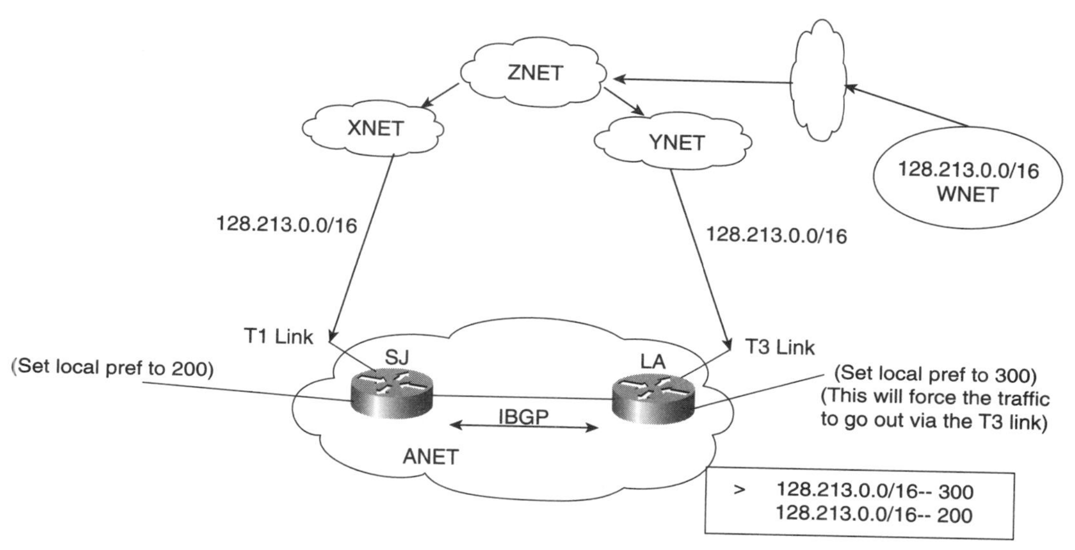

It is important for ANET to decide what path its outbound traffic will take. Of course, ANET prefers to use the T3 link via YNET in normal operation because it is a high-speed link.

This is where local preference comes into play: The LA router assigns a local preference of 300 to the routes received from YNET. The SJ router designates a lower value of, say, 200 to the routes received from XNET. Because both the LA and SJ routers exchange routing updates via IBGP, they both agree that the exit point of the AS will be via YNET because of the higher local preference. In Figure 6-14, ANET learns route 128.213.0.0/16 via XNET and YNET. The SJ and LA routers agree on using YNET as the exit point for destination 128.213.0.0/16 because of the higher local preference value of 300. Because local preference is local only to the AS (ANET), manipulations discussed in this case affect outbound traffic of the AS and not inbound traffic to the AS. Inbound traffic can still enter via the T1 link.

Cisco's proprietary **weight** parameter is similar to the local preference in that it gives higher preference to the route that has a higher weight. The difference is that the weight parameter is local to the router and is not exchanged between routers, even internal to an AS. The **weight** parameter influences routes received from different providers by the same router (for example, one router with multiple connections to two or more providers). The **weight** parameter has a higher precedence than any other BGP attribute; it is used as a proprietary switch to determine route preference.

The ATOMIC_AGGREGATE Attribute

Route aggregation causes a loss of information because the aggregate is coming from different sources that have different attributes. The ATOMIC_AGGREGATE attribute is a well-known discretionary attribute (Type Code 6) that gets set as an indication of information loss. Basically, if a system propagates an aggregate that causes loss of information, it is required to attach the ATOMIC_AGGREGATE attribute to the route.

The ATOMIC_AGGREGATE should not be set when the aggregate carries some extra information that indicates from where the aggregated information came. An example is an aggregate with the AS_SET parameter, as discussed earlier. An aggregate that carries the set of ASs that form the aggregate is not required to attach the ATOMIC_AGGREGATE attribute.

TIP See the section "Aggregate Only, Suppressing the More-Specific" in Chapter 11 on page 343.

The AGGREGATOR Attribute

The AGGREGATOR attribute is an optional transitive attribute (Type Code 7). It specifies the autonomous system and the router that has generated an aggregate. A BGP speaker that performs route aggregation might add the AGGREGATOR attribute, which contains the speaker's AS number and IP address. In Cisco's implementation, the IP address is actually the ROUTER_ID (RID), which is the loopback address of the router if one exists. If there is no loopback address, the highest IP address on the router becomes the RID. The loopback interface is the virtual interface discussed earlier in this chapter. Figure 6-15 illustrates the AGGREGATOR attribute.

Figure 6-15 *AGGREGATOR Implementation Example*

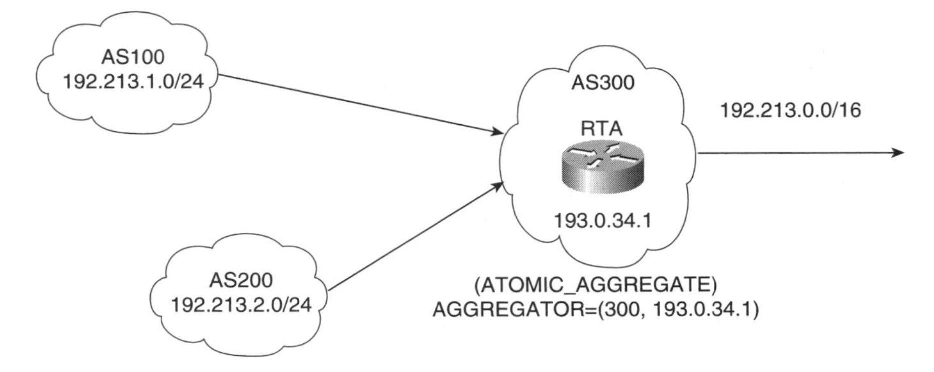

AS300 receives routes 192.213.1.0/24 and 192.213.2.0/24 from AS100 and AS200, respectively. When RTA generates aggregate 192.213.0.0/16, it has the option of including the AGGREGATOR attribute, which consists of the AS number 300 and the RID 193.0.34.1 of the router (RTA) that originated the aggregate.

The COMMUNITY Attribute

In the context of BGP, a *community* is a group of destinations that share some common property. A community is not restricted to one network or one autonomous system; it has no physical boundaries. An example is a group of networks that belong to the educational or government communities. These networks can belong to any autonomous system. Communities are used to simplify routing policies by identifying routes based on a logical property rather than an IP prefix or an AS number. A BGP speaker can use this attribute in conjunction with other attributes to control which routes to accept, prefer, and pass on to other BGP neighbors.

TIP See the section "The COMMUNITY Attribute" in Chapter 11 on page 340.

The COMMUNITY attribute (Type Code 8) is an optional transitive attribute. It is of variable length and consists of a set of 4-byte values. Communities in the range 0x00000000 through 0x0000FFFF and 0xFFFF0000 through 0xFFFFFFFF are reserved. These communities are well-known—that is, they have a global meaning. Here are some examples of well-known communities:

- **NO_EXPORT (0xFFFFFF01)**—A route carrying this community value should not be advertised to peers outside an AS.
- **NO_ADVERTISE (0xFFFFFF02)**—A route carrying this community value, when received, should not be advertised to any BGP peer.

Besides well-known community attributes, private community attributes can be defined for special uses. So can those defined in RFC 1998[1], which describes a mechanism by which communities can be used to manipulate BGP path selection in service provider networks.

A common practice is to use the first 2 bytes of the community attribute for the AS number and the last 2 bytes to define a value in relation to that AS. For example, a provider (AS256) who wants to define a private community called my-peer-routers could use the community 256:1 represented in decimal notation. The 256 indicates that this particular provider has defined the community. The 1 has special meaning to the provider. In this case, it is my-peer-routers.

A route can have more than one community attribute. A BGP speaker that sees multiple community attributes in a route can act based on one, some, or all of the attributes. A router has the option of adding or modifying community attributes before passing routes on to other internal and external peers.

Figure 6-16 shows a simple use of the COMMUNITY attribute. XNET is sending toward YNET routes X and Y with a NO_EXPORT community attribute, and route Z with no modification. The BGP router in YNET will propagate only route Z toward ZNET. Routes X and Y will not be propagated because of the NO_EXPORT community attribute.

Figure 6-16 *Simple Application of the COMMUNITY Attribute*

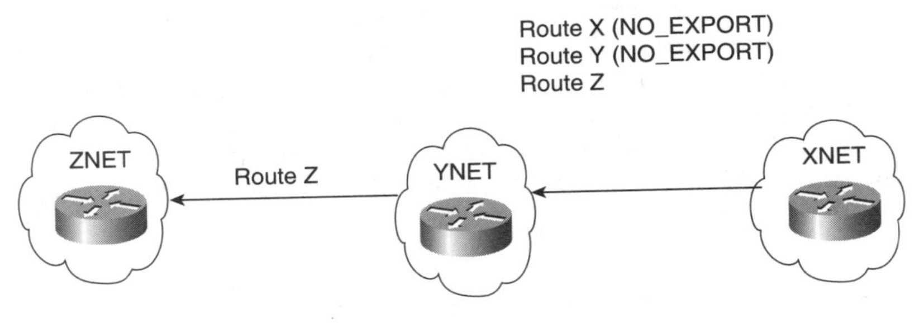

As you'll see in later chapters, communities provide a great deal of flexibility when defining routing policies.

Other Attributes

NOTE The ORIGINATOR_ID, CLUSTER_ID, and CLUSTER_LIST attributes are discussed in Chapter 9, "Controlling Large-Scale Autonomous Systems."

NEXT_HOP Behavior on Multiaccess Media

A medium is considered multiaccess (MA) if routers connected to that medium can exchange data in a many-to-many relationship. Routers on an MA medium share the same IP subnet and can physically access all other routers on the medium in one hop (directly connected). Ethernet, FDDI, Token Ring, Frame Relay, and ATM are examples of multiaccess media.

The rule that IP has on MA media is that a router should always advertise the actual originator of the route in case the route's source is on the same MA medium as the router that has just learned the route. In other words, if RTA (router A) is advertising a route learned from RTB and if RTA and RTB share a common MA medium, when RTA advertises the route, it should specify RTB as the source of the route. If not, other routers, such as RTC, on the same medium would have to make an unnecessary hop via RTA to get to a router, RTB, that is sitting in the same segment.

In Figure 6-17, RTA, RTB, and RTC share a common multiaccess medium. RTA and RTC are running EBGP, and RTC and RTB are running OSPF. RTC has learned network 11.11.11.0/24 from RTB via OSPF. RTC is advertising that prefix to RTA via EBGP. Because RTA and RTB are running different routing protocols, you might think that RTA would consider RTC (10.10.10.2) as its next hop to reach 11.11.11.0/24, but this is incorrect. The correct behavior is for RTA to consider RTB (10.10.10.3) as the next hop because RTB shares the same medium with RTC.

Figure 6-17 *Sample Multiaccess Media Environment*

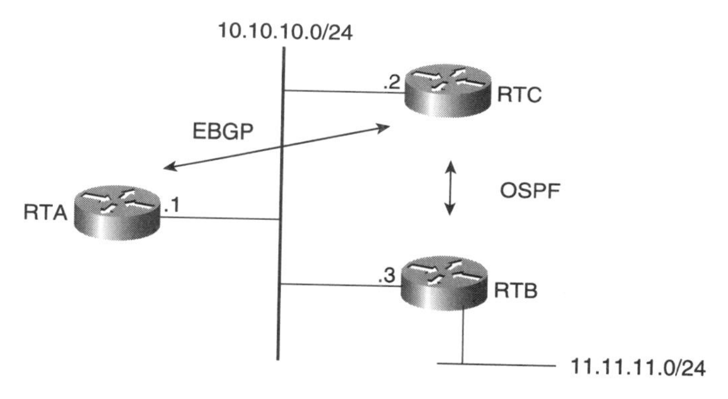

In situations where the medium is broadcast, such as Ethernet and FDDI, physical connectivity is a given, and the next-hop behavior is no problem. In situations where the medium is nonbroadcast, such as Frame Relay and ATM, special care should be taken, as described in the following section.

NEXT_HOP Behavior Over Nonbroadcast Multiaccess Media

Media such as Frame Relay and ATM are referred to as nonbroadcast multiaccess media. The many-to-many direct interaction between routers is not guaranteed unless virtual circuits are configured from each router to all other routers. This is referred to as a *full-mesh* topology, and it is not always implemented for a number of reasons. In practice, Frame Relay or ATM virtual circuits are provided by the access carrier at a certain dollar amount per circuit, and additional circuits translate into extra money. In addition to this prohibitive cost, many organizations use a hub and spoke approach, in which multiple remote sites have virtual circuits built to one or more concentration routers at a central site (the hub site) where information resides. Figure 6-18 illustrates an example of next-hop behavior in a nonbroadcast multiaccess environment.

Figure 6-18 *Nonbroadcast Multiaccess NEXT_HOP Example*

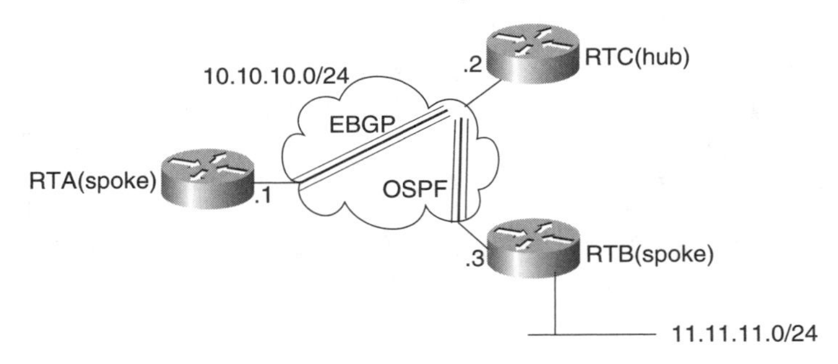

The only difference between the environments illustrated in Figure 6-17 and Figure 6-18 is that the medium in Figure 6-18 is a Frame Relay cloud that is NBMA. RTC is the hub router, and RTA and RTB are the spokes. Notice how the virtual circuits are laid out between RTC and RTA, and between RTC and RTB, but not between RTA and RTB. This is called a *partial-mesh* topology.

RTA gets a BGP routing update about 11.11.11.0/24 from RTC, which in turn learns about the prefix from the originator RTB. RTA will try to use RTB (10.10.10.3) as the next hop (the same behavior as on MA media). Packet forwarding will fail because no virtual circuit exists between RTA and RTB.

Cisco IOS software supports a special-case parameter that remedies this situation. The **next-hop-self** parameter (configured as part of the BGP **neighbor** command) forces the router (in this case, RTC) to advertise 11.11.11.0/24 with itself as the next hop (10.10.10.2). RTA would then direct its traffic to RTC to reach destination 11.11.11.0/24.

Use of next-hop-self versus Advertising DMZ

The demilitarized zone (DMZ) defines a shared network between ASs. The IP subnet used for the DMZ link might or might not be owned by any of the networked ASs. As you have already seen, the next-hop address learned from the EBGP peer is preserved within IBGP. It is important for the IGP to be able to reach the IP address denoted via the NEXT_HOP attribute in the UPDATE message. One way to do this is for the DMZ subnet to be part of the IGP and have the subnet advertised in the AS. The other method is to override the next-hop address by forcing the next hop to be the IP address of the border IBGP neighbor.

In Figure 6-19, the SJ router is receiving updates about 128.213.1.0/24 with next hop 1.1.1.1 (part of the DMZ). For the SJ router to be able to reach this next hop, one option is for network 1.1.1.0/24 to be advertised inside the AS by the SF border router.

Figure 6-19 *Using the* **next-hop-self** *Parameter*

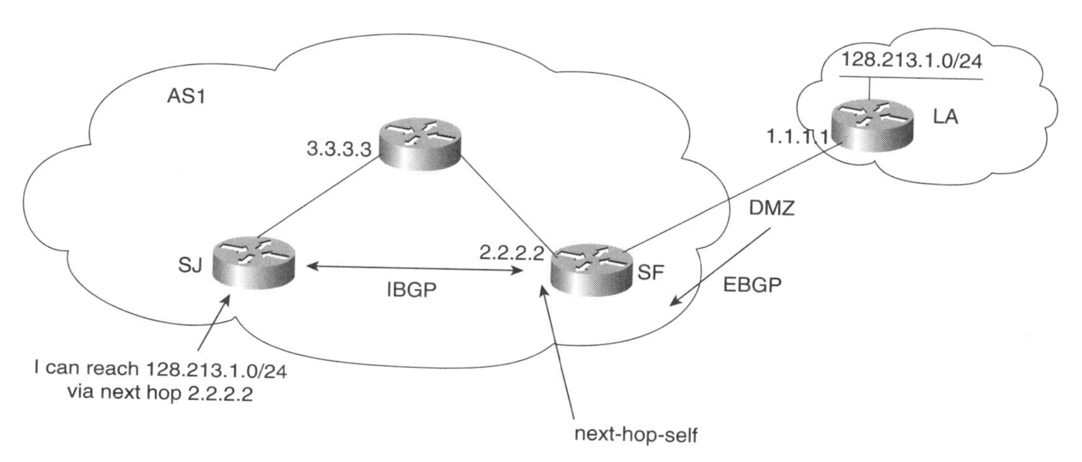

The other option is to have the SF router set the **next-hop-self** parameter as part of the IBGP neighbor connection to the SJ router. This will set the next-hop address of all EBGP routes to 2.2.2.2, which is already part of the IGP. The SJ router can now reach the next hop with no problem.

Choosing one method over another depends on whether you want to reach the DMZ. An example could be an operator trying to do a **ping** from inside the AS to a router interface that belongs to the DMZ. For the **ping** to succeed, the DMZ must be injected into the IGP. In other cases, the DMZ might be reachable via some suboptimal path external to the AS. Instead of reaching the DMZ from inside the AS, the router might attempt to use another EBGP link to reach the DMZ. In this case, using **next-hop-self** ensures that the next hop can be reached from within the AS. In all other cases, both methods are similar as far as the BGP routing functionality.

Also, it is important to understand that Internet exchange point participants often require that the BGP NEXT_HOP specified in UPDATE messages be that of the peer's IP address, as a matter of policy.

Using Private ASs

To conserve AS numbers, the InterNIC generally does not assign a legal AS number to customers whose routing policies are an extension of the policies of their provider. Thus, when a customer is single-homed or multihomed to the same provider, the provider generally requests that the customer use an AS number taken from the private pool of ASs (64512 to 65535). As such, all BGP updates that the provider receives from its customer contain private AS numbers.

TIP See the section "Using Private ASs" in Chapter 11 on page 334.

Private AS numbers cannot be leaked to the Internet because they are not unique. For this reason, Cisco has implemented a feature to strip private AS numbers out of the AS_PATH list before the routes are propagated to the Internet, thereby performing a type of proxy advertisement function. Figure 6-20 demonstrates how private AS numbers are stripped from the AS_PATH list.

Figure 6-20 *Stripping Private AS Numbers*

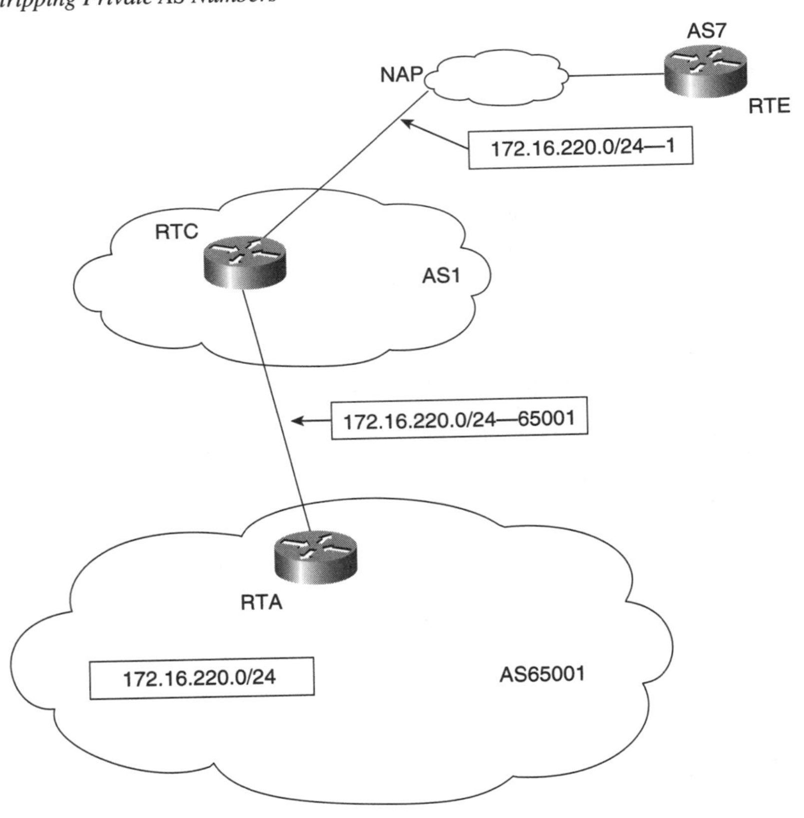

NOTE Chapter 1, "Evolution of the Internet," introduced Network Access Points (NAPs) and their role in interconnecting multiple providers. BGP connections to the NAP are sometimes done via a route server where multiple ASs peer via EBGP into a single system. The route server would have its own AS number. In Figure 6-20, the NAP is represented by the route server RTE having AS number 7. The route server concept could apply any time multiple ASs rely on a single point for exchanging EBGP updates.

In Figure 6-20, AS1 is providing Internet connectivity to its customer AS65001. Because the customer has only this provider and has no plans to add another provider in the near future, the customer has been allocated a private AS number by the provider. If the customer later needs to connect to another provider, the appropriate Internet Registry should assign a globally unique AS number.

Prefixes originating from AS65001 have an AS_PATH of 65001. Note prefix 172.16.220.0/24 in Figure 6-20 as it leaves AS65001. For AS1 to propagate the prefix to the Internet, it has to strip the private AS number. When the prefix reaches the Internet, it will look as though it originated from the provider's AS. Note how prefix 172.16.220.0/24 has reached the NAP with AS_PATH 1.

BGP will strip private ASs only when propagating updates to the external peers. This means that the AS stripping would be configured on RTC as part of its neighbor connection to RTE.

Private ASs should be connected to only a single provider. If the AS_PATH contains a mixture of private and legal AS numbers, BGP will view this as an illegal design and will not strip the private AS numbers from the list, and the update will be treated as usual. Only AS_PATH lists that contain at least one private AS number in the range of 64512 to 65535 are stripped.

For additional information describing a routing architecture using private ASs, see RFC 2270[2], "Using a Dedicated AS for Sites Homed to a Single Provider."

AS_PATH and Route Aggregation Issues

Route aggregation involves summarizing a range of prefixes into one or more aggregates or CIDR blocks to minimize the number of routes in the routing tables. A drawback of route aggregation is the loss of granularity that exists in the specific routes that form the aggregate. For example, the AS_PATH information that exists in multiple routes will be lost when these routes are summarized into a single advertisement. This could lead to routing loops, because a route that has passed through an AS might be accepted by the same AS as a new route.

In order to avoid this unwanted behavior, BGP defines another type of AS_PATH object called an AS_SET, where the ASs are listed in an unordered set. This set includes the ASs that a route has traversed. Aggregates carrying the AS_SET information would have a collective set of the attributes that form the individual routes they summarize.

In Figure 6-21, AS1 is advertising 192.213.1.0/24, and AS2 is advertising 192.213.2.0/24. AS3 is aggregating both routes into 192.213.0.0/16. An AS that advertises an aggregate considers itself the originator of that route, irrespective of where that route came from. When AS3 advertises the aggregate 192.213.0.0/16, the AS_PATH information would be just 3. This would cause a loss of information because the originators of the routes AS1 and AS2 would no longer be listed in the AS_PATH. In the situation where some other AS somehow advertises the aggregate back to AS1 and AS2, AS1 and AS2 would accept the route. This could lead to routing loops.

Figure 6-21 *Effects of the* **AS_SET**

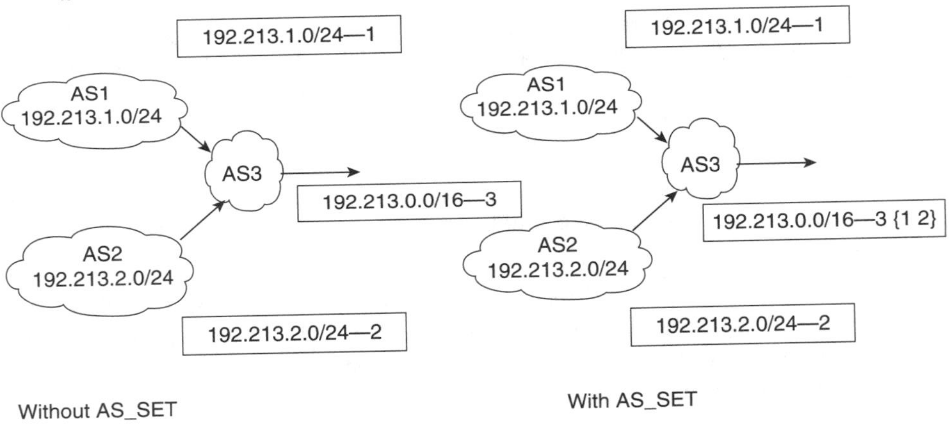

With the notion of AS_SET, it is possible to have AS3 advertise the aggregate 192.213.0.0/16 while keeping information about the components of the aggregate. The set {1 2} indicates that the aggregate has come from both of these ASs in no particular order. The AS_PATH information of the aggregate with the AS_SET option would be 3 {1 2}.

Specifying the **AS_SET** parameter before an **aggregate-address** statement will automatically generate an AS_SET associated with the aggregate.

AS_PATH Manipulation

AS_PATH information is often manipulated to affect interdomain routing behavior. Because BGP prefers a shorter AS_PATH path to a longer one, network operators are tempted to change the path information by including dummy AS_PATH entries that would increase the path length to influence or deter the traffic trajectory. Cisco's implementation lets a user prepend AS numbers at the beginning of an AS_PATH to make the path length longer. The following example shows how this feature can be used.

TIP See the section "AS_PATH Manipulation" in Chapter 11 on page 333.

In Figure 6-22, AS50 is connected to two providers, AS200 and AS100. AS100 is directly connected to the NAP, whereas AS200 has to go through an extra hop via AS300 to reach the NAP.

Figure 6-22 *Routing Environment Before Dummy AS Is Prepended*

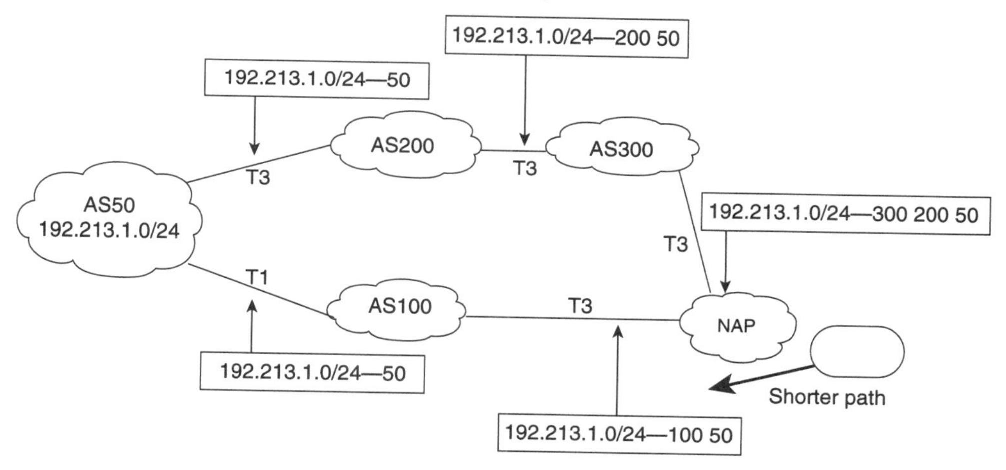

Figure 6-22 shows instances of prefix 192.213.1.0/24 as it traverses the ASs on its way to the NAP. When the 192.213.1.0/24 prefix reaches the NAP via AS300, it has an AS_PATH of 300 200 50. If the same prefix reached the NAP via AS100, it would have an AS_PATH of 100 50, which is shorter than the path via AS300. ASs upstream from the NAP will prefer the shorter AS_PATH length and will direct their traffic toward AS100 for destination 192.213.1.0/24.

AS50 is unhappy about this behavior, because it prefers the traffic to be directed inbound via its higher-bandwidth T3 link to AS200. AS50 will manipulate the AS_PATH information by inserting dummy AS numbers when sending routing updates to AS100. One common practice is for AS50 to repeat its AS number as many times as necessary to tip the balance and make the path via AS200 shorter.

In Figure 6-23, AS50 inserts the two AS numbers 50 50 only at the front of the AS_PATH of prefix 192.213.1.0/24, which is advertised to AS100. When the prefix 192.213.1.0/24 reaches the NAP via AS100, it will have the AS_PATH 100 50 50 50, which is longer than the AS_PATH 300 200 50 via AS300. ASs upstream of the NAP will prefer the shortest path and will direct the traffic toward AS300 for destination 192.213.1.0/24.

Figure 6-23 *Routing Environment After Dummy AS Is Prepended*

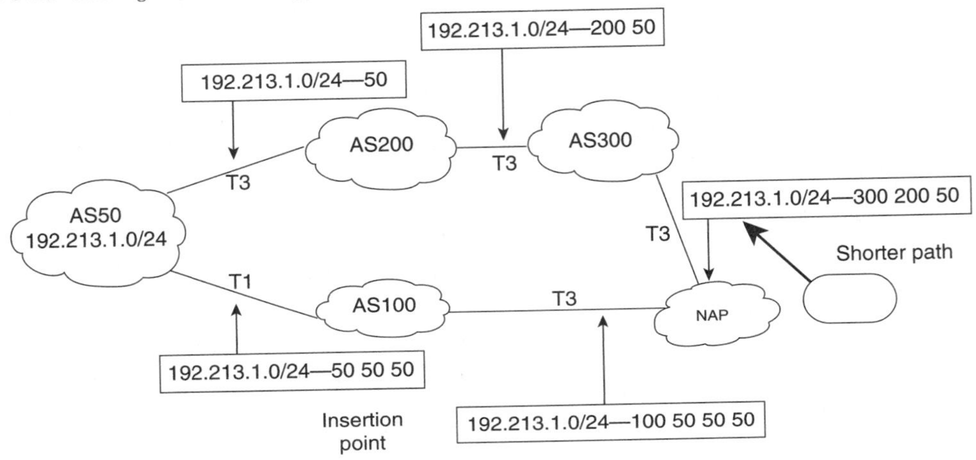

In practice, the bogus number should always be a duplicate of the AS announcing the route or the neighbor the route is learned from (in case an AS is increasing the path length for incoming updates). Adding any other number is misleading and could potentially lead to routing loops or black holes. Note the insertion point in Figure 6-23.

Route Filtering and Attribute Manipulation

The concept of route filtering is straightforward. A BGP speaker can choose what routes to send and what routes to receive from any of its BGP peers. Route filtering is essential in defining routing policies. An autonomous system can identify the inbound traffic it is willing to accept from other neighbors by specifying the list of routes it advertises to its neighbors. Conversely, an AS can control what routes its outbound traffic uses by specifying the routes it accepts from its neighbors.

TIP See the section "Route Filtering and Attribute Manipulation" in Chapter 11 on page 308.

Filtering is also used on the protocol level to limit routing updates flowing from one protocol to another. Earlier, this chapter discussed the possibility of injecting BGP routes in the IGP as well as injecting the IGP or static routes into BGP. Cisco's terminology for this process is *redistributing* between protocols. This chapter has also discussed the dangers of mutual redistribution between protocols. Filtering is essential in specifying exactly what goes from BGP into the IGP and vice versa.

Routes permitted through a filter can have their attributes manipulated. Manipulating the attributes affects the BGP decision process used to identify the best routes to a given destination.

Inbound and Outbound Filtering

Both the inbound and outbound filtering concepts can be applied to the peer and protocol levels. Figure 6-24 illustrates this behavior.

Figure 6-24 *Inbound/Outbound Filtering Example*

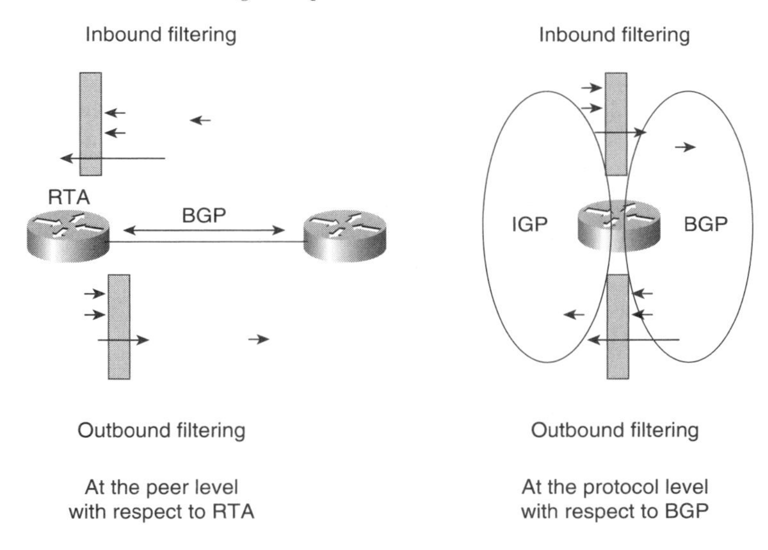

From the perspective of routes exchanged between BGP peers, inbound filtering indicates that the BGP speaker is filtering routing updates received from other peers, whereas outbound filtering limits the routing updates advertised from the BGP speaker to other peers. Filtering behavior is the same whether the BGP peers are external (EBGP) or internal (IBGP).

At the protocol level, inbound filtering limits the routing updates being injected into a protocol. Outbound filtering limits the routing updates being injected from this protocol.

With respect to BGP, for example, inbound filtering limits the updates being redistributed from other protocols such as the IGP and static routes into BGP. Outbound filtering limits the updates being redistributed from BGP into IGP.

The Route Filtering and Manipulation Process

Filtering and manipulating a route or a set of routes involves three actions:

Step 1 Identifying the routes

Step 2 Permitting or denying the routes

Step 3 Manipulating attributes

Cisco uses access lists, prefix lists, or as-path access lists to accomplish only filtering. Cisco also uses the concept of route maps to achieve both filtering and attribute manipulation. Route maps are discussed in Chapter 11.

Identifying Routes

Identifying routes is the process of setting criteria to differentiate routes from each other. Such criteria could be based on the route's IP prefix, the autonomous system from which a route was originated, a list of ASs that a route has passed through, a specific attribute value inside the route, and so on. A list of criteria instances is contained in the filtering rules, and a route is compared to the first instance in the list. If the route does not match the first instance, it is checked against the next instance in the list. After a route matches an instance, it is considered identified and will not be compared to any further instances.

If the route proceeds to be compared against the entire list of instances and there is still no match, the route is discarded.

Identifying routes based on the Network Layer Reachability Information (NLRI), the AS_PATH, or both is the most common way of identifying routes. Each of these methods is discussed in more detail in the following sections.

Identifying Routes Based on the NLRI

A BGP route could be identified by its NLRI, which is the prefix and the mask, as discussed in Chapter 4. For filtering purposes, a prefix or a range of prefixes is defined. If the route falls within the range, it will be identified.

TIP See the section "Identifying and Filtering Routes Based on the NLRI" in Chapter 11 on page 312.

Figure 6-25 illustrates filtering criteria of 10.1.0.0 0.0.255.255, which represents a range of routes identified by a prefix 10.1.0.0 and an inverse mask 0.0.255.255. The 0s in the mask indicate a match, whereas the 1s indicate a do-not-care-bit. The 10.1.0.0 0.0.255.255 range will identify all routes of the form 10.1.X.X. Presented with the prefixes shown in Figure 6-25, this filter will identify 10.1.1.0/24, 10.1.2.0/24, and 10.1.2.2/30 and will exclude 11.2.0.0/16 and 12.1.1.0/24. Prefix-based filtering will be discussed in detail in later chapters.

Figure 6-25 *NLRI Filtering Criteria Example*

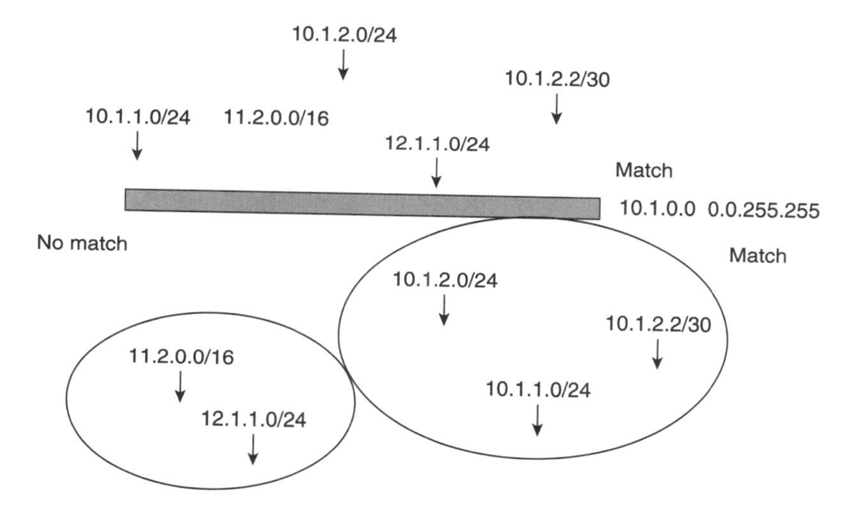

Prefix lists are currently the preferred mechanism to be used for filter routing information. Introduced to IOS only recently, they provide several benefits in comparison to traditional access lists.

Prefix lists employ a more efficient lookup structure, providing a significant reduction in resources required to process routing updates. At this time, prefix lists cannot be used for functions other than filtering routing protocol information.

One of the key benefits of prefix lists is the capability to perform incremental updates. In other words, you can add, delete, or modify a list without having to completely rebuild it. Also, the syntax used for configured prefix lists is much more intuitive than that used for traditional access lists. Chapter 11 provides configuration guidelines for prefix lists.

Identifying Routes Based on the AS_PATH

Identifying routes based on the AS_PATH information is a bit more involved. As you know by now, the AS_PATH is a list of ASs that a route has traversed before reaching a BGP peer. The list itself is a character string that contains characters from the following set:

- Numbers 0 through 9
- Space
- Left brace {
- Right brace }
- Left parenthesis (
- Right parenthesis)
- Beginning of the input string
- End of the input string
- Comma ,

The AS_PATH list 10 2, for example, is actually a beginning-of-string character followed by character 1 followed by a 0 followed by a space followed by a 2 followed by an end-of-string character.

TIP See the section "Identifying and Filtering Routes Based on the AS_PATH" in Chapter 11 on page 315.

Trying to identify the AS_PATH list consists of comparing the list to what is called a *regular expression*. A regular expression is just a pattern of characters represented by a formula such as ^200 100$. This is a regular expression representing a list that starts with 200, that is followed by a space, and that ends with 100. The ^ and $ are representations of the beginning-of-string and end-of-string characters, respectively.

NOTE A regular expression can be formed by using single-character patterns or multiple-character patterns.

Permitting or Denying Routes

After the route has been identified, actions can be taken on it. The route is permitted or denied, depending on what filtering rules have been established for that juncture. The criteria for permitting or denying routes depend on the policies an AS is setting. If the route is permitted, it is either accepted "as is" or is submitted for modification of attributes. Again, this depends on what attributes are to be modified. If the route is denied, that route is discarded, and no further processing is required.

Manipulating Attributes

If a route is permitted, its attributes can be changed to affect the decision process. In earlier sections, you saw how attributes such as local preference and MED can be added or made larger or smaller to prefer one route to another. As you will see later, attribute manipulation is key to establishing route policies, load balancing, and route symmetry.

Figure 6-26 shows in detail how multiple instances can be applied on a set of routes to find a match.

Figure 6-26 *Summary Example of the Route Filtering and Manipulation Process*

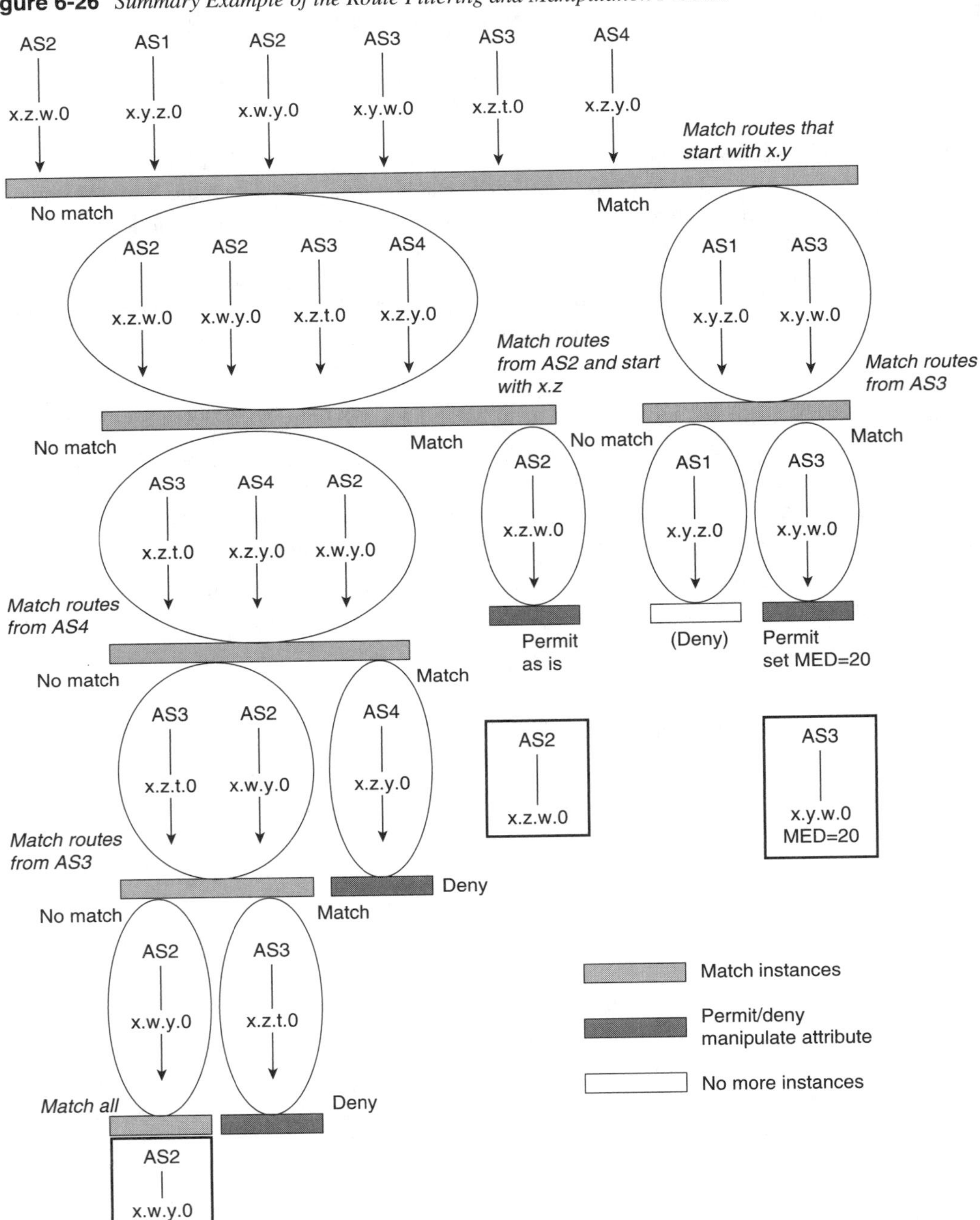

Note that each instance could have one or more criteria. A route could be checked based on its prefix and its AS_PATH information, for example, and it must meet all criteria before a match occurs.

Also note that after a route matches, it is not compared to any more instances. Hence, the order in which the instances are checked is important. For example, if it's put at the beginning of the list, an instance that permits all routes will override all the other instances.

Single-Character Patterns

A single-character pattern tries to match a single character. The single-character regular expression 3 tries to match the character 3 in an input string. You can specify a range of single characters to match against a string. Ranges are included within brackets ([]). The order in which the characters forming the range are listed is not important. The regular expression consisting of the range [efghEFGH], for example, tries to match any of the bracket-enclosed characters in an input string. Given two input strings, "hello" and "there", the regular expression matches both of these lists because they both contain the character e.

Ranges can be listed by typing the end points of a range. For example, ranges [a-z] and [0-9] indicate any lowercase character from a to z and any numeric character between 0 and 9, respectively.

You can also reverse or negate the pattern matching by including a caret (^) at the beginning of the range. The range [^a-dA-D], for example, matches any character except a, b, c, d, A, B, C, or D. Some characters have a special meaning, such as the dollar sign $ and the underscore _ (see Table 6-4).

To list the special characters as part of an input list, precede them with a backslash (\). The range [abc\$], for example, will match an input string that contains the characters a, b, c, and $. Table 6-4 lists the special characters used in regular expressions.

Table 6-4 *Regular Expression Special Characters*

Character	Symbol	Special Meaning
Period	.	Matches any single character, including white space.
Asterisk	*	Matches zero or more sequences of the pattern.
Plus sign	+	Matches one or more sequences of the pattern.
Question mark	?	Matches zero or one occurrences of the pattern.
Caret	^	Matches the beginning of the input string. Also used to negate a pattern match if used inside the beginning of a range of characters—for example, [^range].
Dollar sign	$	Matches the end of the input string.

continues

Table 6-4 *Regular Expression Special Characters (Continued)*

Character	Symbol	Special Meaning
Underscore	_	Matches a comma (,), left brace ({), right brace (}), left parenthesis, right parenthesis, the beginning of the input string, the end of the input string, or a space.
Brackets	[range]	Designates a range of single-character patterns.
Hyphen	-	Separates the end points of a range.

Multiple-Character Patterns

Multiple-character regular expressions are just an ordered sequence of single-character patterns. The pattern is a combination of letters, numbers, any keyboard characters, and special-meaning characters. Here is an example of a multiple-character regular expression: 100 1[0-9]. This regular expression matches any string that contains the exact sequence 100, followed by a space, followed by a 1, followed by any number between 0 and 9. Any of the following input strings will match the regular expression: 123 **100 10** 11, or **100 19**, or 19 **100 11** 200, and so on.

Building Complex Regular Expressions

The special characters listed in Table 6-4 can be used to build complex but very practical regular expressions. The caret (^) and dollar sign ($) are used to match the regular expression pattern against the beginning and end of the input string. Other characters, such as the asterisk (*), the plus sign (+), and the question mark (?), let you repeat the patterns inside the regular expression.

The following example matches any number of occurrences of the letter a, including none:

> a* is equivalent to any of the following: (nothing), a, aa, aaa, aaaa, and so on.

The following example requires that at least one letter a be present in the string to be matched:

> a+ is equivalent to a, aa, aaa, aaaa, and so on.

The following is an example of a list that may or may not contain the letter a:

> ba?b is equivalent to bb or bab.

To repeat instances of multiple-character patterns, the pattern is enclosed in parentheses. For example, the expression (ab)+ is equivalent to ab or abab.

The underscore character (_) matches the beginning of a string (^), the end of a string ($), parentheses, space, braces, comma, or underscore. The dot character (.) matches a single character, including a white space. Figure 6-27, Table 6-5, and Table 6-6 illustrate how characters can be strung together to create a useful regular expression.

Consider the network topology illustrated in Figure 6-27. AS400, AS300, AS200, AS100, and AS50 are originating the routes NetA, NetB, NetC, NetD, and NetE, respectively. RTA in AS50 is receiving updates about all these networks from its neighbors AS100 and AS300. After running its BGP decision process, RTA has picked the best path to reach these networks according to Table 6-5.

Figure 6-27 *Sample Network Topology for Complex Regular Expression*

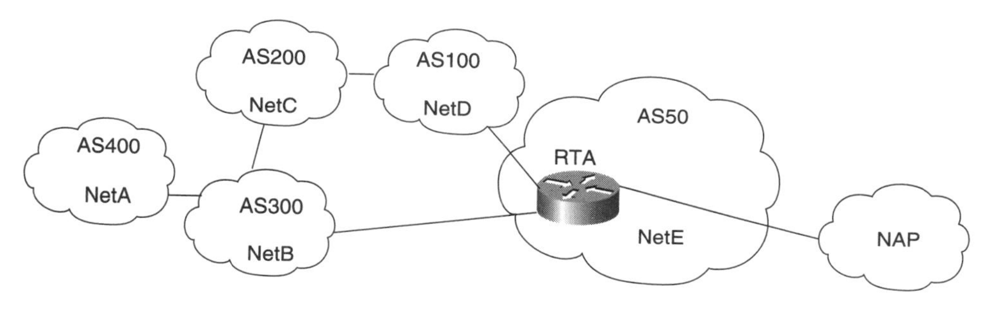

Table 6-5 *Best BGP Route Selection for RTA*

Network	AS_PATH
NetA	300 400
NetB	300
NetC	100 200
NetD	100
NetE	Empty

Table 6-6 reflects the regular expressions that would be used to create possible route filtering arrangements that RTA could apply when propagating routes to the NAP.

Table 6-6 *Sample Table Expressions and Resulting Outcomes for Regular Expressions*

Routes to Be Advertised from RTA to the NAP	Expression	Path Info	Outcome
Local routes only	^$	Empty	NetE
All routes	.*	All paths	NetA, NetB, NetC, NetD, NetE
Routes that originated from directly connected customers	^300$ ^100$	300 100	NetB, NetD
Connected customer routes and their customers' routes	^300_ ^100_	300 400 300 100 200 100	NetA, NetB, NetC, NetD
Routes that originated in AS200	_200$	100 200	NetC
Routes that passed via AS100	_100_	100 200 100	NetC, NetD

The ^$ expression indicates an empty path list, which is actually the local routes. (Recall that the local AS is not attached to the path until advertisement to an EBGP occurs, so it's null.) The ^ and $ characters define the border of the string. The underscore, as in _200$, limits the AS number to being exactly 200 and not 1200 or 2200.

Filtering based on AS_PATH information is quite effective because it filters all the routing updates that belong to the AS_PATH at the same time. Without this type of filtering, thousands of routes would have to be listed individually or perhaps be members of an already identified BGP community.

Peer Groups

A BGP *peer group* is a group of BGP neighbors that share the same update policies. Instead of defining the same policies for each individual neighbor, you define a peer group name and assign policies to the peer group itself. For example, an administrator setting policies toward its BGP peers will probably set the same policies toward the majority of its peers and therefore will define them as a peer group.

Not only do peer groups save the operator from repetitive configuration of each BGP peer, they save the BGP router itself from the effort of parsing the policies sequentially for each neighbor. With peer groups, the router formulates the update once, based on the policies of the peer group, and then floods the same update to all the neighbors that fall within the group.

In Figure 6-28, RTA has three internal peers with which it has the same internal policies. RTA also has three external peers with which it has the same policies. RTA's configuration includes two sets of peer groups—one for inside the AS and one for outside the AS. Each peer group contains the set of policies that RTA has toward its peers. These policies could be a set of IP prefix filters or AS_PATH filters and possibly other attribute manipulations. After the peer groups have been defined, these policies are applied to the neighbors that make up the peer group.

Figure 6-28 *Peer Group Implementation*

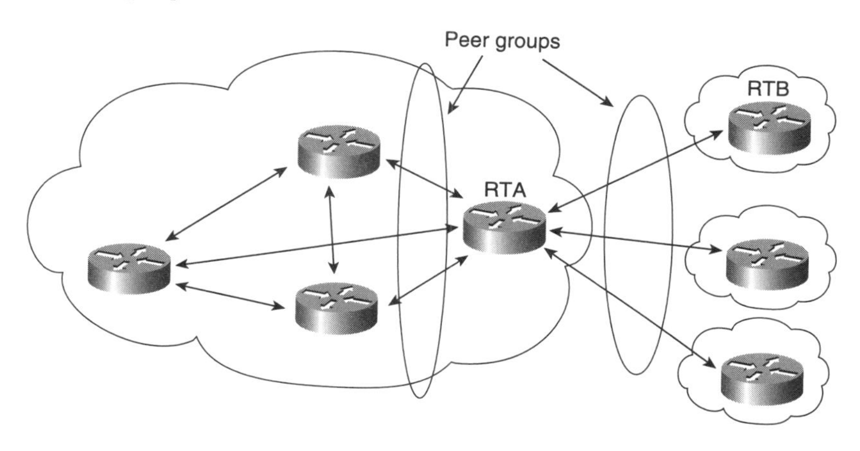

At one time, Cisco IOS imposed some restrictions on EBGP neighbors residing in the same peer group. Enhancements have since removed these restrictions. Therefore, we won't consume additional time discussing those restrictions. However, note that if you're using older versions of IOS, some of these restrictions might still be present. Consult Cisco documentation associated with your specific version of IOS for additional information.

Peer Group Exceptions

Exceptions occur when some neighbors inside a peer group have slightly different policies from other neighbors. Additional policies can be added to the neighbor to complement the set of policies that fall within the peer group. Assume in the scenario presented in Figure 6-28 that RTA requires an additional set of filters to be set toward its peer RTB. RTA can apply the extra filters toward RTB while still keeping RTB within the external peer group.

TIP See the section "Peer Groups" in Chapter 11 on page 316.

BGP-4 Aggregation

One of BGP–4's main improvements over previous versions of BGP is its capability to handle CIDR and supernetting. CIDR and supernetting were first discussed in Chapter 3, "IP Addressing and Allocation Techniques," in the section "IP Address Space Depletion," as a means to control the growth of IP routing tables and the depletion of the IP address space.

Aggregation applies to routes that exist in the BGP routing table. This is in contrast to the **network** command, discussed earlier in this chapter, which applies to routes that exist in the IP routing table. Aggregation can be performed if at least one more-specific route of the aggregate exists in the BGP routing table.

Cisco Systems offers a variety of ways to manipulate aggregates to make sure that every need on the Internet is fulfilled. This section first examines simple aggregation techniques and then moves on to more complicated (but fun) scenarios.

Aggregate Only, Suppressing the More-Specific Routes

This scenario illustrates a case in which an aggregate is advertised and all its specific routes are suppressed. This is usually done when the more-specific routes do not offer any extra benefits, such as making better decisions in forwarding traffic.

TIP See the section "Aggregate Only, Suppressing the More-Specific" in Chapter 11 on page 343.

Figure 6-29 illustrates a situation in which all the routing updates are lumped into a single aggregate. Suppose that AS100 has the subnet ranges 172.16.0.0/24 to 172.16.15.0/24. This includes 172.16.0.X, 172.16.1.X, and so on. The list of specific prefixes can be summarized in the range 172.16.0.0/20. The aggregate 172.16.0.0/20 is sent out, and all the more-specific prefixes are suppressed.

Figure 6-29 *BGP-4 Aggregation Example: Suppressing Specific Routes*

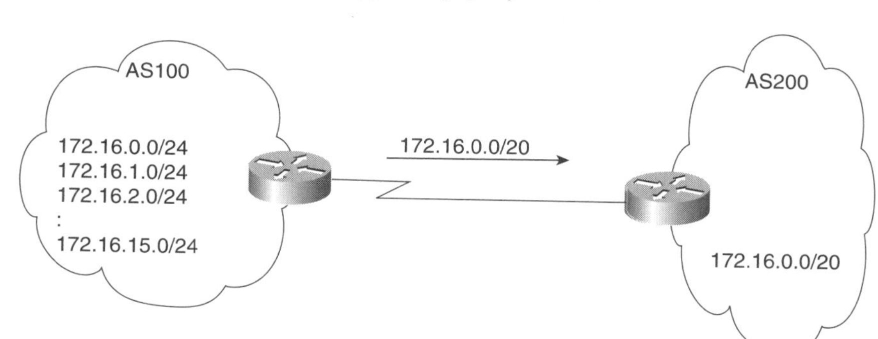

Aggregate Plus More-Specific Routes

A number of situations exist in which an AS will send out an aggregate as well as its more-specific routes. This usually occurs in situations where the customer is multihomed to a single provider. The provider would use the more-specific routes to make better decisions when sending traffic toward the customer. At the same time, the provider can propagate the aggregate only toward the NAP to minimize the number of routes propagated to the Internet. This is illustrated in Figure 6-30.

Figure 6-30 *BGP-4 Aggregation Including Specific Routes*

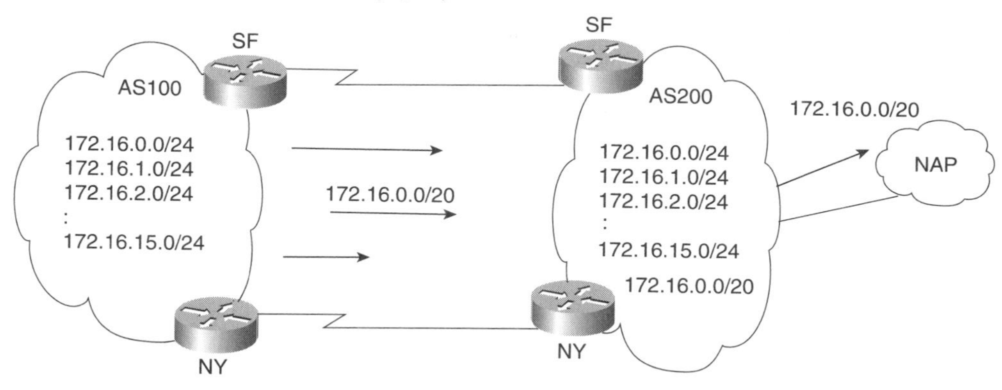

AS100 is multihomed with provider AS200 via the SF and NY links. AS100 can send AS200 the aggregate 172.16.0.0/20 only, or it can send the aggregate and all the more-specific routes. If the aggregate only is sent over both the SF and NY links, traffic from AS200 toward AS100 will always take one link or the other. This arrangement creates an unbalanced traffic load. (Balanced loading is discussed further in Chapter 7, "Redundancy, Symmetry, and Load Balancing.") To balance the load, AS100 sends the aggregate and all the more-specific routes. Different metrics could be sent for different routes on each of the links. This way, based on the specific network number, AS200 can decide whether to use the SF or NY link when trying to reach AS100.

TIP See the section "Aggregate Plus More-Specific Routes" in Chapter 11 on page 346.

To avoid complicating routing tables beyond the provider level, more-specific routes from customers are usually stopped at the provider level. AS200 would propagate only the aggregate 172.16.0.0/20 toward the NAP and suppress the more-specific routes.

Usually providers like to minimize configuration and administration. In this situation, a dynamic approach can be used to stop all the more-specific routes from being propagated to the NAP. This is done by having AS100 tag all the more-specific updates with the community attribute **NO_EXPORT** while leaving the aggregate as is. This is illustrated in Figure 6-31.

Figure 6-31 *Community* **No_Export** *Route Aggregation Example*

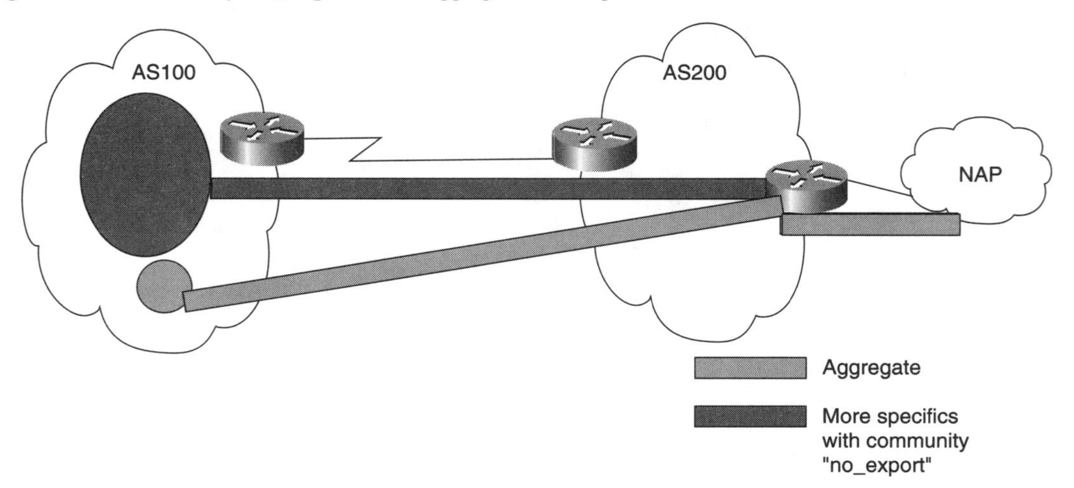

When AS200 gets the updates from AS100, it will recognize the community assigned to AS100's specific routes as a request not to forward the updates to its external peers. The aggregate will be propagated as usual to the NAP and other peers.

Aggregate with a Subset of the More-Specific Routes

In some situations, a subset of the more-specific routes needs to be advertised in addition to the aggregate. Figure 6-32 illustrates a situation in which this might be useful.

Figure 6-32 *Aggregation Example Including a Subset of Specific Routes*

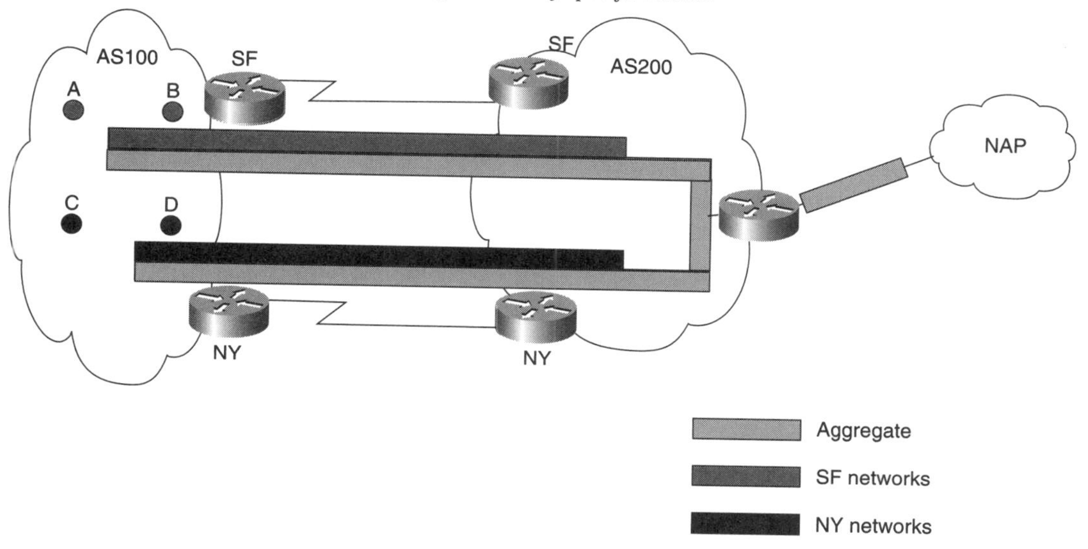

In Figure 6-32, AS100 is multihomed to AS200. AS100 would like the networks near SF to be accessed via the SF link and the networks near NY to be accessed via the NY link. This could be achieved in the following manner:

- On the SF link, advertise the aggregate and the SF networks only.
- On the NY link, advertise the aggregate and the NY networks only.

In this case, AS200 can only reach the SF networks via the SF link and the NY networks via the NY link. Networks in other locations could be sent on both links or either link. In case of a link failure, all networks can still be reached by following the aggregate route, which is advertised on both links. The no-export technique, discussed in the previous example, can be used to propagate only the aggregate to the NAP.

TIP See the section "Aggregate with a Subset of the More-Specific Routes" in Chapter 11 on page 350.

Loss of Information Inside Aggregates

Aggregation causes loss of information because the attributes of individual routes that form the aggregate will be lost. As already discussed in this chapter, BGP defines an AS_SET, which is a mathematical set consisting of all elements contained in all paths that are being summarized. Examples of such elements are the AS_PATH and community attributes. Using AS_SET with the aggregate will cause additional route instabilities due to the fact that changes in the attributes of the individual routes being summarized will now translate into changes of the aggregate itself and will cause the aggregate to be constantly withdrawn and updated.

TIP See the section "Loss of Information Inside Aggregates (AS_SET)" in Chapter 11 on page 354.

Changing the Attributes of the Aggregate

Some situations require that the attributes of the aggregate be changed. One such situation is when the aggregate contains some unwanted attributes that it inherited from the routes it is summarizing (in case of AS_SET). An example could be a NO_EXPORT community attribute that the aggregate got from one of the more-specific routes and that causes the aggregate not to be exported to other ASs. Another situation that calls for changing the attributes of the aggregate is to reflect a level of preference for a certain aggregate. An example would be a customer's advertising an aggregate via multiple links to a certain provider. The customer might like to have the aggregate go out with different MEDs on different links to influence the entrance point into the AS. Cisco has developed techniques to let the user modify the attributes of an aggregate accordingly.

TIP See the section "Changing the Aggregate's Attributes" in Chapter 11 on page 357.

Forming the Aggregate Based on a Subset of the More-Specific Routes

You have seen that with AS_SET the aggregate will contain a set of all attributes (including AS numbers) that exist in the individual routes being summarized. If the aggregate is summarizing routes that come from different ASs, it becomes useful to specify which routes are being included in forming the aggregate. This would help in a hub and spoke situation in which each of the leaf ASs contains a separate subset of the aggregate that is originated by the hub. When forming the aggregate, the hub AS would exclude the more-specific routes that belong to the leaf AS that needs to receive the aggregate. The aggregate received by the leaf AS would not contain the AS number of the leaf AS, so it would not be discarded. Figure 6-33 gives an example of where this could be used.

Figure 6-33 *Forming the Aggregate Based on a Subset of More-Specific Routes*

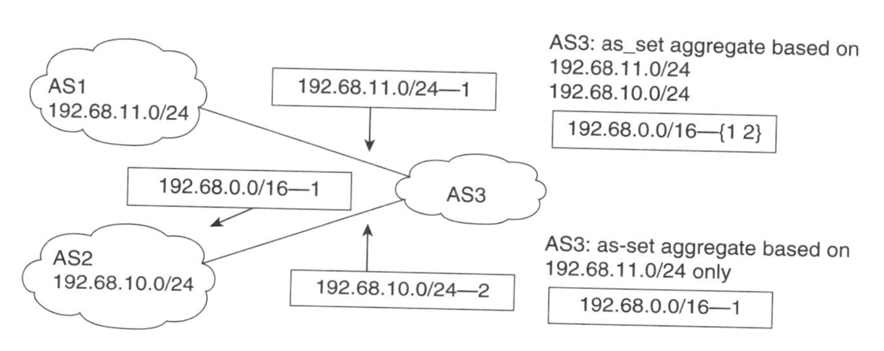

AS3 is a hub AS receiving routes 192.68.11.0/24 and 192.68.10.0/24 from the leaf ASs AS1 and AS2. Prefix 192.68.11.0/24 has an AS_PATH of 1, and 192.68.10.0/24 has an AS_PATH of 2. When the AS_SET aggregate is being formed by AS3 based on all the more-specific routes, the AS_PATH information would be {1 2}. The aggregate itself, if sent back to either AS1 or AS2, would be discarded for loop prevention. AS1 would see its AS number in the AS_PATH information and would drop the update; the same is true for AS2. If you could specify which more-specific routes can form the aggregate, you could, for example, specify that the aggregate is to be formed based on 192.68.11.0/24 only. This way, the AS_PATH information would be 1 and would not contain AS2. The aggregate could now be sent back to AS2 with no problem. AS2 can use this aggregate to forward traffic to all destinations in AS1.

TIP See the section "Forming the Aggregate Based on a Subset of More Specific Routes" in Chapter 11 on page 359.

Looking Ahead

Having mastered the basics of routing protocols and examined the particular attributes of BGP, you are now in a position to begin applying these tools to specific internetworking topologies. In doing so, you will be juggling a number of overarching design goals—redundancy, symmetry, and load balancing—that are of varying importance depending on a particular network's needs. Sometimes these needs conflict with one another. The meaning of these design goals is discussed in more detail in the next chapter. The attributes covered in this chapter are used in the following chapter to achieve the desired routing design goals.

Tuning BGP capabilities to satisfy a network's needs involves looking both outside and inside the AS. In other words, the policies set by the networks to which you are interconnected, although usually outside your direct control, have practical implications for how you configure BGP at your end. All this becomes clearer in the next chapter, which covers multiple redundancy, symmetry, and balancing scenarios by presenting architectures commonly used on the current Internet.

Frequently Asked Questions

Q — *If my IBGP peers are not directly connected, do I have to use EBGP multihop?*

A — No. There is no restriction on IBGP peers to be connected. EBGP multihop is for EBGP only.

Q — *Should I inject my BGP routes into the IGP for synchronization to take effect?*

A — No. Injecting the BGP into your IGP is not recommended. You should turn the BGP synchronization off. Make sure that this will not result in reachability problems inside your AS.

Q — *Will listing my IGP routes via the* **network** *command rather than redistributing the IGP into BGP give my BGP routes more stability?*

A — No. In both methods, the fluctuation of your IGP routes will translate into fluctuation in your BGP routes. The **network** command only gives you better control and less worry about what your IGP might distribute into BGP if you use redistribution. Combine it with static routes (with distance 254, for example) to Null0 if you want to prevent route fluctuation even if your IGP routing is not stable.

Q — *Do I have to list my connected interfaces by using the* **network** *command?*

A — If you want the directly connected subnets to be reachable via BGP, you can advertise them. If not, you don't have to.

Q — *I have two border routers talking EBGP to my provider and IBGP internally. If I list my IGP routes via the* **network** *command on both routers, would that create a loop on the IBGP session?*

A — No, you will not create a loop. Actually, doing so gives you more redundancy. If one of your border routers fails, the other border router will still announce the same networks.

Q — *I need to receive only a few routes from my neighbor. Can I filter on my side of the link?*

A — Yes, you can. However, you should ask your neighbor to send you only the routes you need to minimize unnecessary link bandwidth usage and unnecessary route fluctuations. At the same time, use filtering on your end to protect yourself from potential accidents in which your neighbor sends you more routes than you are expecting.

Q — *My provider needs me to send him different local preference on different links. Is that possible?*

A — No. Local preference is defined inside the AS and is not carried on EBGP sessions. However, a more optimal solution might be to ask your provider to set up a route map that does a match based on BGP community strings (such as those defined in RFC 1998), on his side of the peering session, to set the local preference for your routes in his AS. You will have to tag your routes with the appropriate community string in order for the local preference to be set correctly by his peer session. You could also use MEDs for this.

Q — *I am receiving a MED from my provider that is influencing my traffic in a way that conflicts with my IGP. What should I do?*

A — If receiving MEDs is causing you problems, call your provider and ask him to stop sending MEDs. Or, you can set MED to 0 on your end of the session.

Q — *I am connected to multiple providers. On some occasions, my AS is hit with an enormous amount of traffic that does not belong to my AS. What could be wrong?*

A — You might be advertising routes that you receive from one provider to other providers. Other ASs might be using your AS as transit for their traffic. Make sure that you advertise only your routes to your providers.

Q — *I am multihomed to the same provider. Do I have to worry about advertising the routes I learn from one link back on the second link?*

A — Presumably, BGP policies on your provider's end will detect the routes it is receiving from you that have already passed through its AS and will ignore them. Nevertheless, this is bad practice. By doing so, you're unnecessarily consuming CPU and link resources with useless information; if possible, make sure that you send your own routes only.

Q — *I am a provider, and I have given one of my customers a private AS number. Now, the customer wants to have a different connection with another provider. What would happen if he keeps using the private AS number?*

A — Though this does occur in the Internet today, it is considered a very undesirable configuration. After you advertise this customer's network to the Internet, you are stripping the private AS number and announcing the routes as if they originated from your own AS. If the second provider does the same thing, the customer's networks will be originated from two unique ASs, potentially resulting in routing loops. Also, if any type of aggregation is performed on the customer address before it is announced to other networks, it could result in a more-specific route's being available via one of the two providers, thereby removing the potential for load sharing between the connections. If the customer cannot obtain a global AS number from the appropriate RIR, he should ensure that both providers thoroughly coordinate and provide adequate details regarding load sharing and failover scenarios associated with the configuration.

Q — *I am connected to one provider in San Francisco, and I am advertising my routes via BGP. I am connecting to another provider in LA. Should I get a different AS number?*

A — If both the SF and LA networks fall under the same administration and have the same policies with other ASs, they belong in the same AS. Remember that dividing networks via BGP is to define the boundaries of administration and policy. Network topology and connectivity should be the driving factor.

References

[1]RFC 1998, "An Application of the BGP Community Attribute in Multi-home Routing," www.isi.edu/in-notes/rfc1998.txt

[2]RFC 2270, "Using a Dedicated AS for Sites Homed to a Single Provider," www.isi.edu/in-notes/rfc2270.txt

This chapter covers the following key topics:

- **Redundancy**—Building stability by providing alternate (default) routes in case of link failure is an important design goal of routing architecture.
- **Setting default routes**—Configuring default routes is the fundamental way to build redundancy into network connections. When multiple default routes exist, methods of ranking them by preference are needed.
- **Symmetry**—Configuring routes so that certain traffic enters and exits an AS at the same point is often a design goal of routing architecture.
- **Load balancing**—Dividing traffic over multiple links for optimal network perfomance
- **Specific scenarios**—Several representative network designs are explored with respect to developing redundancy, symmetry, and load balancing. Examples of attribute configuration to achieve these design goals for the different scenarios are offered.

CHAPTER 7

Redundancy, Symmetry, and Load Balancing

Redundancy, symmetry, and load balancing are crucial issues facing anyone implementing high-throughput connections to the Internet. Internet service providers (ISPs) and corporations connected to ISPs require adequate control over how traffic enters and exits their respective autonomous systems (ASs).

Redundancy is achieved by providing multiple alternative paths for the traffic, usually by having multiple connections to one or more ASs. *Symmetry* means having traffic that leaves the AS from a certain exit point return through the same point. *Load balancing* is the capability to divide traffic optimally over multiple links. Putting these three requirements together, you can imagine how challenging it is to achieve an optimal routing solution.

No single switch exists that you can turn on to give you all you need. On the Internet, multiple providers can control and manipulate traffic that transits any AS. Any provider along the way can direct the traffic. The art of balancing traffic depends on coordination between multiple entities.

The general design problem of how best to implement redundancy, symmetry, and load balancing is common to every network. The specific answer, however, depends on the needs and configuration of each particular network. This chapter considers the general design problem within the context of several specific network configurations. You might not see your exact network configuration in these examples, but the general issues and implementation methods they raise provide a model for your analysis and design of your own routing needs.

Before examining specific network scenarios, it is necessary to establish some basic concepts and definitions concerning redundancy.

Redundancy

Although corporations and providers would prefer uninterrupted connectivity, connectivity problems occur for one reason or another from time to time. Connectivity is not the responsibility of one entity. A router's connection to the Internet involves the router, the CSU/DSU, power, cabling, physical access line, and numerous administrators—each with influence over different parts of the connection. At any time, human error, software errors, physical errors, or adverse unforeseen conditions (such as bad weather or power outages) can jeopardize connectivity.

For all these reasons, redundancy is generally desirable. Finding the correct balance between redundancy and symmetry, however, is critical. Redundancy and symmetry can be conflicting design goals: The more redundancy a network has, the more unpredictable the traffic entrance and exit points are. If a customer has multiple connections—one to a Point Of Presence (POP) in San Francisco and another to a POP in New York—traffic leaving San Francisco might come back from New York. Adding a third connection to a POP in Dallas makes connectivity even more reliable, but it also makes traffic symmetry more challenging. Network administrators must consider these trade-offs in implementing routing policies.

Geographical Restrictions Pressure

In addition to the reliability motivation, companies might feel geographical pressure to implement redundancy. Many contemporary companies are national, international, or multinational in nature. For them, the autonomous system is a logical entity that spans different physical locations. A corporation with an AS that spans several geographical points can take service from a single provider or from different providers in different regions. In Figure 7-1, the San Francisco office of AS1 connects to the San Francisco POP of ISP1, and the New York office connects to the New York POP of ISP2. In this environment, traffic can take a shorter path to reach a destination by traveling via the geographically adjacent POP.

Figure 7-1 *Geographically Based Multihoming Situation*

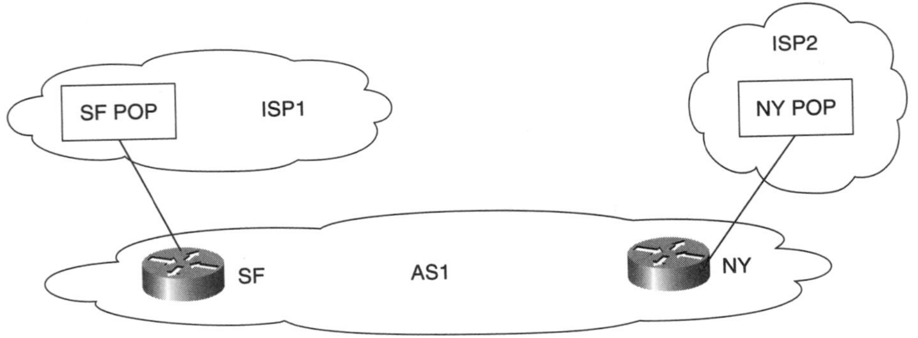

Because redundancy refers to the existence of alternate routes to and from a network, this translates into additional routing information that needs to be kept in the routing tables. To avoid the extra routing overhead, default routing becomes an alternative practical tool. Default routing can provide you with backup routes in case primary connections fail. The next section attempts to define the different aspects of default routing and how it can be applied to achieve simple routing scenarios.

Setting Default Routes

Following defaults is a powerful technique in minimizing the number of routes a router has to learn and providing networks with redundancy in the event of failures and connectivity interruptions. Cisco calls the default path the *gateway of last resort*. It is important to understand how default routing works. Although it makes life easier when configured correctly, life is more difficult when routing is configured incorrectly.

By definition, a default route is a route in the IP forwarding table that is used if a routing entry for a destination does not exist. In other words, a default route is a last resort in case specific route information for a destination is unknown.

Dynamically Learned Defaults

The universally known default route is usually represented by the network mask combination 0.0.0.0/0.0.0.0 (also represented as 0/0). This route can be exchanged as a dynamic advertisement between routers. Any system advertising this route represents itself as a gateway of last resort for other systems. Figure 7-2 illustrates such an advertisement.

Figure 7-2 *Dynamic Default Advertisement*

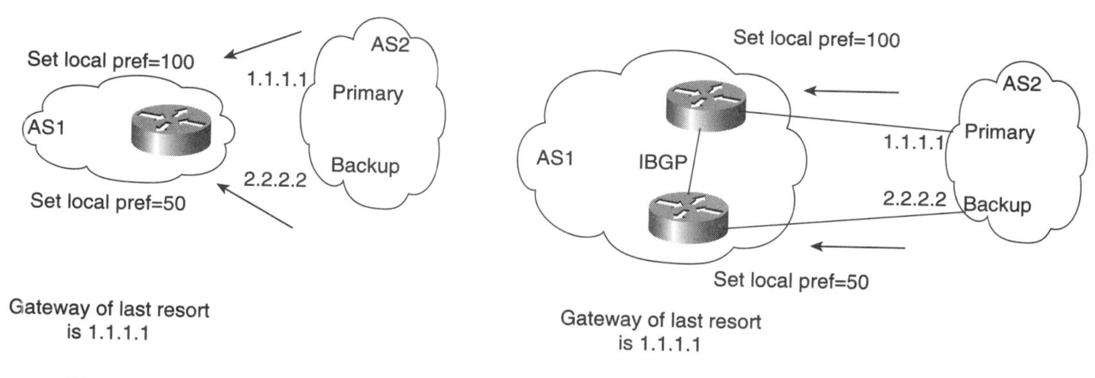

Dynamic defaults (0/0) can be learned via BGP or IGP, depending on what protocol is running between two domains. For redundancy purposes and to accommodate potential failures, you should receive defaults from multiple sources. In the context of BGP, the local preference can be set for the default to give a degree of preference over which default is primary and which is backup. If one default goes away, the other will take its place.

In the left instance of Figure 7-2, a single router connects AS1 to AS2 via two connections. If AS1 chooses to accept as few routes as possible from AS2, AS1 can accept only the 0/0 default route. In this example, AS1 learns 0/0 from two links and gives preference by setting the local preference to 100 on the primary link and 50 (or any number smaller than 100) on the backup link. During normal operation, this would set the gateway of last resort to 1.1.1.1.

In the multiple routers scenario (the right instance of Figure 7-2), the same behavior can be achieved with multiple routers as long as IBGP is running inside the AS. Local preference, which is exchanged between IBGP routers, determines the primary and backup links.

TIP See the section "Dynamically Learned Defaults" in Chapter 12, "Configuring Effective Internet Routing Policies," on page 365.

Statically Set Defaults

Many operators choose to filter dynamically learned defaults to avoid situations in which traffic ends up where it is not supposed to be. Thus, it is also possible for an AS to statically set its own defaults by setting its own 0/0 route. Statically set defaults provide more control over routing behaviors because the operator has the option of defining his last resort rather than having it forced on him by some outside entity. Many operators choose to filter dynamically learned defaults to avoid situations in which traffic ends up where it is not supposed to be.

TIP See the section "Statically Set Defaults" in Chapter 12 on page 367.

An operator can statically set the default route 0/0 to point to the following:

- The IP address of the next-hop gateway
- A specific router interface
- A network number

Figure 7-3 illustrates the first two possibilities. On the left, a router statically points its own 0/0 default toward the IP address 1.1.1.1. On the right, the same router points its default toward an Ethernet interface. In the latter of the two approaches, further processing is needed to figure out to whom on the segment the traffic should be sent. Such processing usually involves sending Address Resolution Protocol (ARP)[1] packets to identify the physical address of the next-hop router.

Figure 7-3 *Statically Set Defaults*

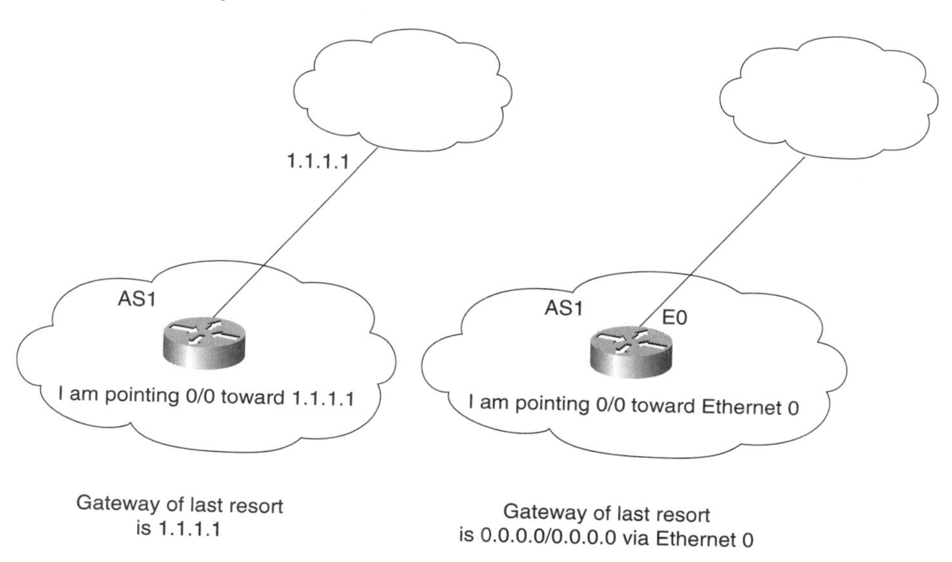

A system can also set its default based on a network number it learns from another system. In Figure 7-4, AS1 dynamically learns route 192.213.0.0/16 from AS2. If AS1 points its default to 192.213.0.0/16, that network automatically becomes the gateway of last resort. This approach uses recursive route lookup to find the IP address of the next-hop gateway. In this example, the recursive lookup determines that 192.213.0.0/16 was learned via the next hop 1.1.1.1, and traffic would be directed accordingly.

Figure 7-4 *Pointing Default Toward a Network Number*

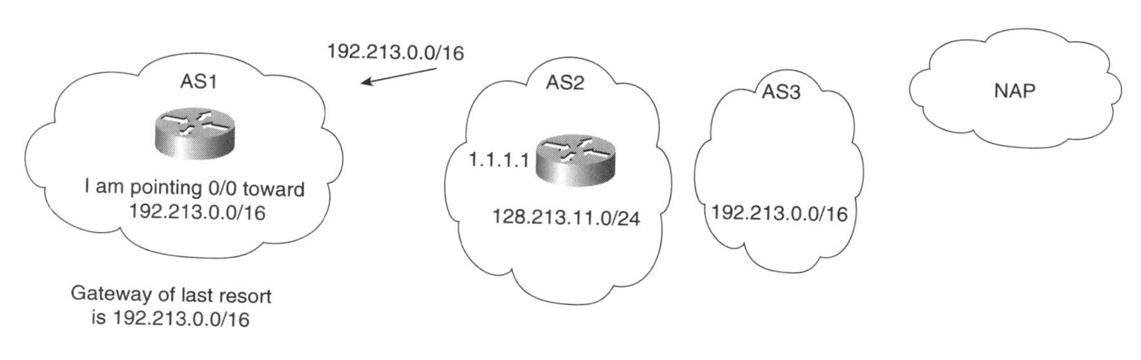

It is important for defaults to disappear dynamically if what they point to disappears. Cisco lets a statically defined default follow the existence of the entity to which it is pointing. For example, if the default is pointing to a network number and that network can no longer be reached (it does not show in the IP routing table), the default will also disappear from the IP routing table. This behavior is needed in situations in which multiple defaults exist. One default can be used as primary and others as a backup in case the primary default is no longer valid.

Default networks should be selected as far upstream (close to the Internet) as possible so that they are more representative of the whole link toward the NAP or other service provider interconnections rather than a portion. This is important if the AS you are connected to has a single connection toward the NAP. In Figure 7-4, AS1 can set the default toward its provider, AS2, by pointing to prefix 128.213.11.0/24 or the supernet 192.213.0.0/16. Pointing the default to 128.213.11.0/24 makes it dependent on the stability of a portion of the link (AS1 to AS2) and not the whole link (AS1 to AS3) toward the NAP. If the link between AS2 and AS3 goes down, AS1 will still send traffic toward AS2 rather than directing it to some other default (assuming that AS1 has other providers). A better default choice would be the supernet, 192.213.0.0/16, because its existence is more representative of the whole link toward the NAP and is no longer dependent on any intervening links.

Selected default networks should not be specific subnets. A subnet that is flip-flopping might cause your default to come and go constantly. It is much better to point the default to a major aggregate or supernet that reflects the stability of a whole provider rather than a particular link.

Multiple static defaults can be used at the same time. One way to set multiple static defaults is to point to multiple networks (using aggregates if possible for stability reasons) and establish a degree of preference by using the local preference BGP attribute. This would apply to a single router connected to the provider via multiple connections or to multiple routers running IBGP inside the AS. Both scenarios are illustrated in Figure 7-5. These are similar to the scenarios you saw in Figure 7-4. The only difference is that the customer sets its own default rather than relying on the provider to send the 0/0 default route. In this example, the customer chooses 128.213.0.0/16 with the local preference of 100 via the upper link. The lower link is used as a backup, based on a local preference of 50 for the default in case of failure in the primary link.

Figure 7-5 *Statically Pointing to Multiple Network Defaults*

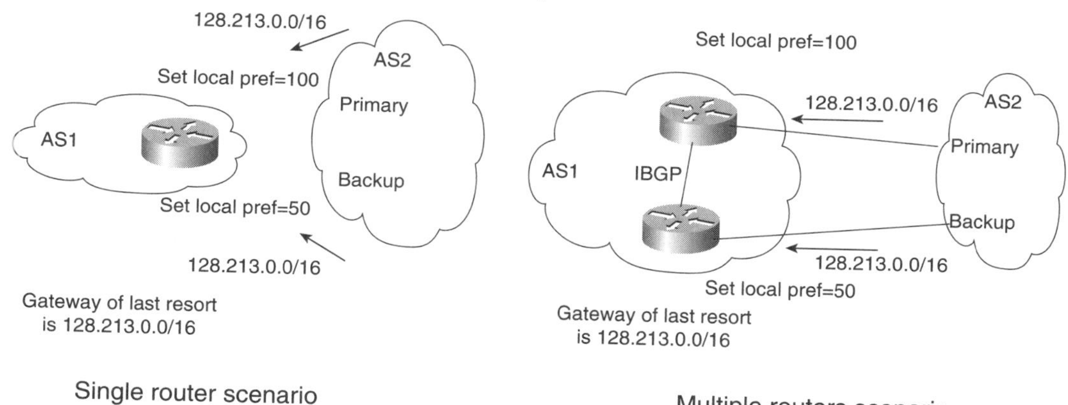

Another way of setting defaults statically involves using the Cisco distance parameter (as described in Table 6-1 in Chapter 6, "Tuning BGP Capabilities") to establish a degree of preference. Because the distance parameter is not exchanged between routers, this would work only in the case of one router connected via multiple connections.

If two static default entries are defined with different distances, the default with the lower distance wins. If the better default goes away, the second default becomes available. If both defaults have the same distance, traffic will be balanced between the two default paths using mechanisms provided by the underlying switching mode utilized.

Figure 7-6 illustrates the use of the distance parameter in setting multiple defaults. AS1 is connected to AS2 via two links and sets its own defaults toward AS2. AS1 uses one link as primary by giving the static default a distance of 50, lower than the distance of 60 given to the backup link. In case of failure in the primary link, traffic will shift toward the backup.

Figure 7-6 *Static Defaults Pointing to Multiple Connections*

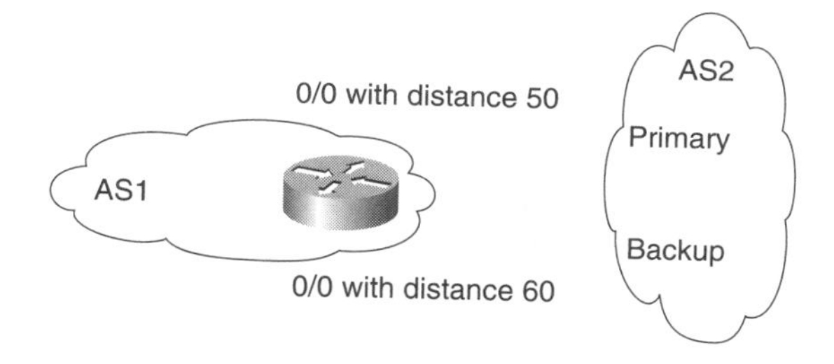

Understand that if a route is associated with an interface, the interface must be unavailable before the route becomes invalid. For example, Cisco HDLC by default exchanges keepalive messages across the connection. If the keepalives are not received within a specified interval, the interface protocol connection is dropped. This results in the route's being removed. On the other hand, a Frame Relay or ATM virtual circuit doesn't exchange keepalive messages with the remote router. This means that if the virtual circuit fails, the interface will still be active, as will the associated route.

Symmetry

Symmetry refers to when traffic leaving the AS from a given exit point comes back through the same point. This is easy to achieve if a single exit and entrance point exist. However, given the mandates of redundancy and the presence of multiple connections, traffic tends to be asymmetrical. When traffic is asymmetrical, customers and providers notice a lack of control over how traffic flows into and out of their ASs. Traffic leaving the AS from the East Coast might end up taking the "scenic route," coming back from the West Coast and traveling inside the AS multiple hops before returning to its origin. This is usually the result of closest-exit routing, as discussed in Chapter 6.

In reality, this is not as bad as it sounds. In some situations, asymmetrical traffic is acceptable, depending on the applications being used and the overall physical topology as far as the speed of the links and the number of hops between locations. In general, customers and providers would like to see their traffic come back close to or at the same point it left the AS to minimize potential delays that could be incurred otherwise. Then again, customers might want to carry the traffic as far as possible on their network to avoid latency or congestion on the peer network.

To accommodate symmetry, you should designate a primary link and make the utmost effort to direct the majority of traffic to flow on this link. Although I will discuss several methods of attaining symmetry via policy specification, it's important to understand that in practice, asymmetry is observed more often than not, and it usually doesn't pose significant problems.

Load Balancing

Load balancing deals with the capability to divide data traffic over multiple connections. A common misconception about balancing is that it means an equal distribution of the load. Equal distribution of traffic is elusive enough even in situations in which traffic flows in a network that is under a single administration. Given the multiple players that traffic has to touch, equal distribution of traffic is difficult to achieve in most scenarios. Load balancing tries to achieve a traffic distribution pattern that will best utilize the multiple links that provide redundancy. Achieving this requires a good understanding of what traffic you are trying to balance, incoming or outgoing.

It is important not to think of traffic as a single entity. Traffic should be thought of as two separate entities, inbound and outbound. With respect to an autonomous system, inbound traffic is received from other ASs, whereas outbound traffic is sent to other ASs.

Suppose that you are connected to two ISPs and traffic is overloading your link to ISP1. Your first question should be: Which traffic, inbound or outbound? Are you receiving all your traffic from ISP1, or are you sending all your traffic toward ISP1?

The patterns of inbound and outbound traffic go hand-in-hand with the way you advertise your routes and the way you learn routes from other ASs. Inbound traffic is affected by how the AS advertises its networks to the outside world, whereas outbound traffic is affected by the routing updates coming in from outside ASs. Make sure that you fully understand this behavior, because it will be the basis of all future discussions. From now on, whenever we talk about taking steps to affect inbound traffic, we are really talking about applying attributes to outbound routing announcements because how our routes are learned by others affects how traffic is routed inbound. Similarly, whenever we talk about taking steps to affect outbound traffic, we are talking about applying attributes to inbound routing announcements because how our network learns routes affects how outbound traffic is routed. Figure 7-7 illustrates how inbound and outbound traffic behaves.

Figure 7-7 *Inbound and Outbound Decisions*

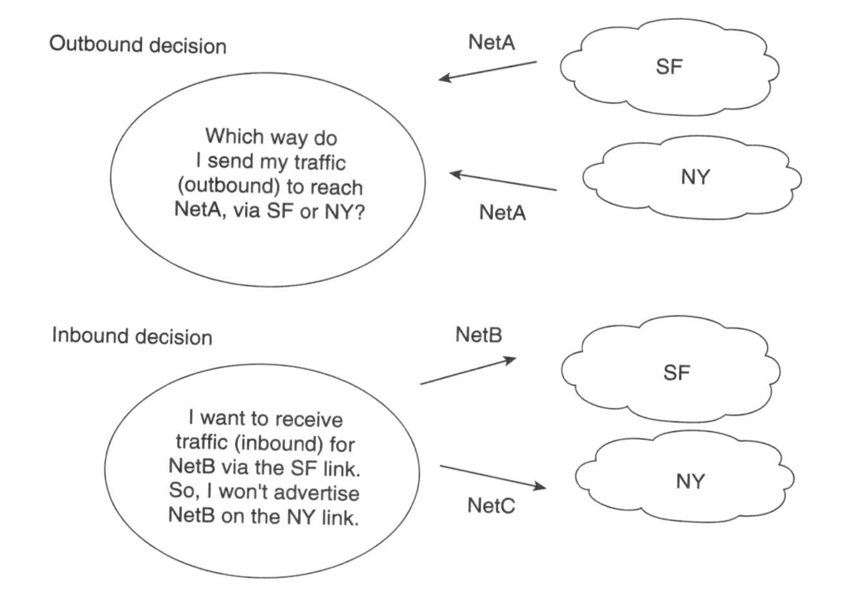

As you can see, the path for outbound traffic to reach NetA depends on where NetA is learned. Because NetA is received from both SF and NY, your outbound traffic toward NetA can go via SF or NY.

On the other hand, the path for inbound traffic to reach your local networks, NetB and NetC, depends on how you advertise these networks. If you advertise NetC over the NY link only, incoming traffic toward NetC will take the NY link. Similarly, if you advertise NetB over the SF link only, traffic toward NetB will take the SF link. Although this scenario appears optimal for traffic entering the AS, there is no provision for redundancy for the two advertised networks.

Specific Scenarios: Designing Redundancy, Symmetry, and Load Balancing

By now you recognize the general ways in which the design goals of redundancy, symmetry, and load balancing intersect with and potentially conflict with one another. How is it possible to balance traffic among multiple links and still achieve a single entrance and exit point as symmetry mandates? This becomes even more difficult when multiple links are spread out over multiple routers in the autonomous system. The routing attributes described in Chapter 6 are the tools for implementing the desired redundancy, symmetry, and load balancing. It is the responsibility of the operator to choose and configure the correct attributes and filtering to achieve the desired outcome.

This section presents specific scenarios and attempts to configure them in such a way as to optimize redundancy, symmetry, and load balancing. The scenarios are not representative of every possible network configuration, and the design solutions shown here are not the only ones possible. However, the lessons they illustrate can be applied to other scenarios and will help you understand and implement better and more efficient designs.

The first scenario is a simple case; the scenarios that follow are increasingly complex. Note that there is a fine line between a customer and provider in many cases because a provider can be the customer of another provider. The principal distinction is this: Customers obtain Internet connectivity by connecting to providers but do not themselves offer connectivity to other customers. Providers offer Internet connectivity services and can themselves be customers of other providers.

The scenarios to be considered in the following sections are further divided depending on whether the customer is receiving minimal or no routes, partial routes, full routes, or some combination of these from the providers. In the case in which the customer is accepting minimal or no routes (called *default only*), you can assume that the customer can still learn the 0/0 route or a couple of aggregate routes that allow the customer to statically set a default. *Partial routing* usually consists of the provider's local routes and the provider's other customers' routes. *Full routing* refers to all Internet routes in existence—about 75,000 routes in early 2000. A combination of these scenarios can occur in which a customer can receive a default route and partial routes from the same provider, or partial routes from one provider and full routes from another, and so on.

Scenario 1: Single-Homing

Single-homed customers have sites that connect to the Internet via a single connection to a service provider. Figure 7-8 illustrates such a situation.

Figure 7-8 *Simple Single-Homed Site Situation*

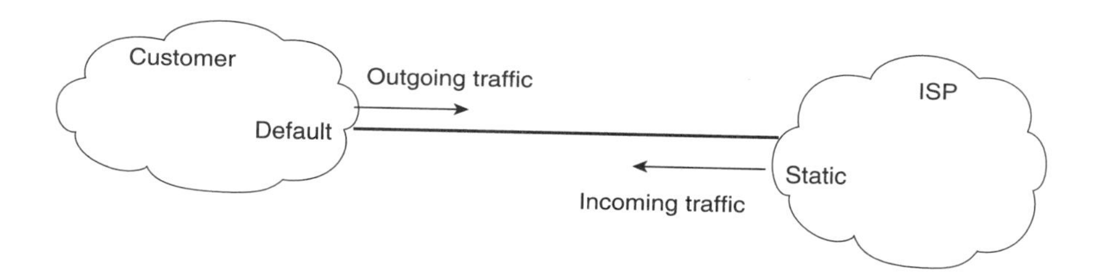

These customers usually can be adequately served by pointing defaults toward the provider. The provider can also install static routing to reach the customer. This method is the least expensive and the most effective. Technically, neither the customer nor the provider needs to run BGP. Thus, the customer router does not need to learn any of the Internet routes. This substantially reduces memory usage and processing overhead. In this case, there is no issue of route symmetry because traffic has a single entrance and exit point.

Single-homed sites generally rely on a single connection to the Internet. Backup is not an issue. If the connection is lost, the customer can tolerate the outage until it is fixed. Obviously, such an arrangement would not satisfy mission-critical data communication requirements. A single-homed site with no backup access would not be appropriate for applications needing high levels of reliability. It should also be noted that in this situation, utilizing a standard static/default routing configuration would reduce complexity even more.

Scenario 2: Multihoming to a Single Provider

A customer that has multiple connections to the Internet via the same provider is considered to be multihomed to a single provider. For multihoming to a single provider, assume that BGP is used as a routing protocol. Although it is not necessary in all cases, it will probably provide the most flexibility. Moreover, it is possible to use a private AS in this case (multihoming to a single provider), so there is no need to request the AS number. As suggested in Chapter 6, see RFC 2270 for additional information.

We'll discuss the following topics in the next few sections:

- Default only, one primary link, and one backup link
- Default, primary, and backup, plus partial routing
- Default, primary, and backup, plus full and partial routing
- Automatic load balancing
- Balancing between two routers sharing multiple paths

Default Only, One Primary Link, and One Backup Link

In this scenario, the customer configures default routing toward the provider and does not accept partial or full routes. The customer can run default to both connections. In Figure 7-9, the customer wants to use one link as the primary traffic conduit and the other as a backup in case the primary link goes down. If there were more than two connections to the provider, the customer could set up multiple defaults with varying preference levels.

Figure 7-9 *Basic Multihoming/Single Provider Scenario*

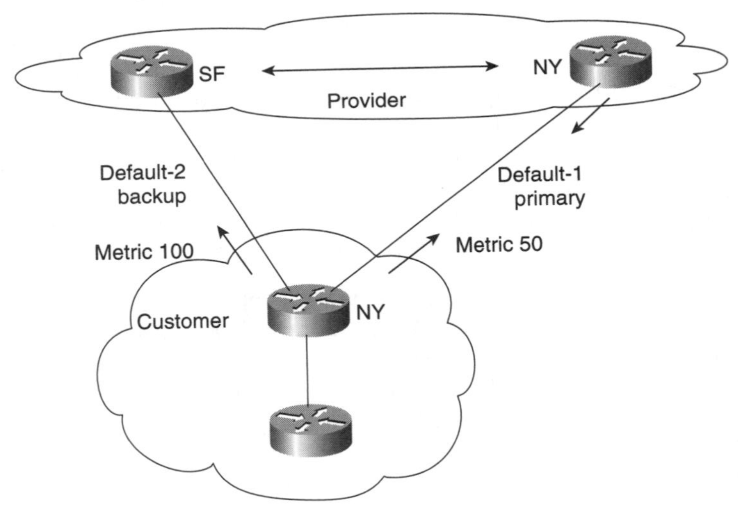

TIP See the section "Default Only, One Primary Link, and One Backup Link" in Chapter 12 on page 371.

In the following two sections, we'll discuss control of both inbound and outbound traffic.

Customer's Outbound Traffic

In the scenario of Figure 7-9, where a single router is used to connect to the provider in multiple locations, multiple static defaults with different distance values can be used. The default with the lower distance will be the primary. The 0/0 default route or few aggregate routes can also be learned dynamically from the provider to let the customer set the default. Local preference can be used to prefer one default over the other.

Assume in Figure 7-9 that the default to NY is preferred over the default to SF. In normal operations, the customer will use the NY link as the primary link and the SF link as a backup.

For outbound traffic, load balancing is not an option because all traffic is sent over the primary line, and the secondary is kept as backup.

Absence of load balancing is offset by the fact that the customer's router requires less memory and processing power.

Customer's Inbound Traffic

The customer can advertise its networks to the provider via BGP. The provider will have two paths to reach the customer. Which path the provider chooses affects the customer's inbound traffic. Usually, the provider's natural behavior (assuming that all BGP attributes it receives are the same) is for traffic to flow through the provider's nearest exit point to the customer's AS. If traffic toward the customer is closer to the NY link, it will enter the customer's AS via NY. If traffic is closer to SF, it will enter via SF.

All of these factors are out of the customer's control. Customers who want to override these influences and control incoming traffic via one path or the other can do so by advertising their routes with different metrics. The provider will direct its traffic toward the customer based on the metric value. In Figure 7-9, the customer is advertising its routes with a metric of 50 toward NY and a metric of 100 toward SF. As such, traffic toward the customer will take the NY route.

Default, Primary, and Backup, Plus Partial Routing

This is the same scenario as the default, primary, and backup case, except that the customer can accept partial routing from the provider. Figure 7-10 illustrates this environment.

Figure 7-10 *Multihoming/Single Provider Scenario with Partial Routing*

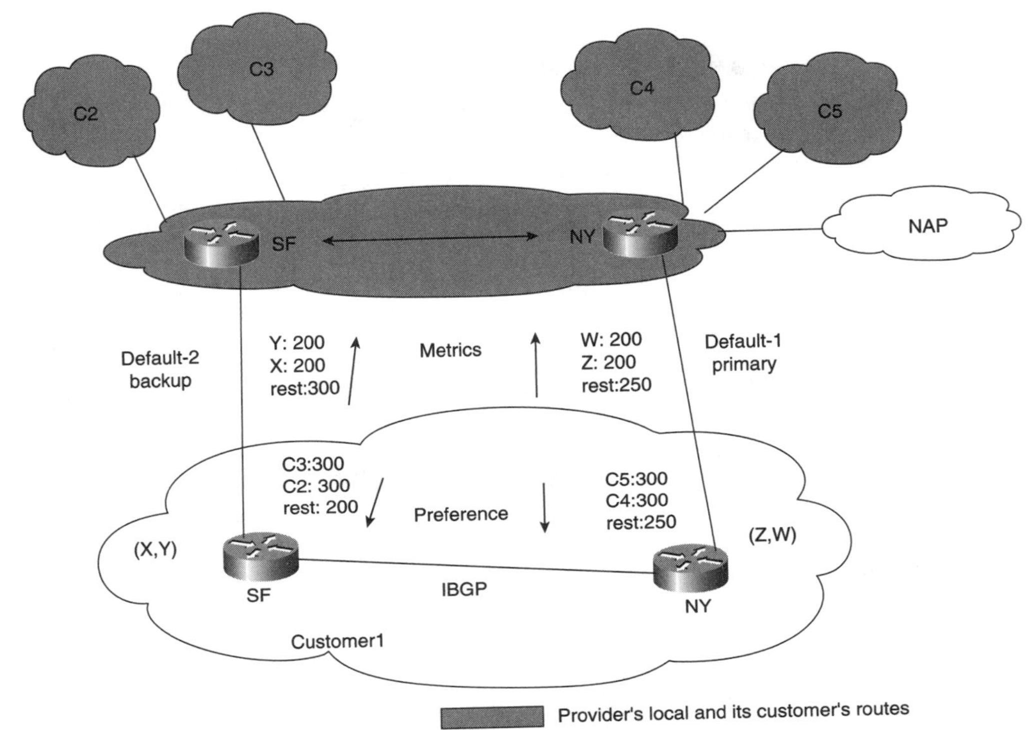

The approach illustrated in Figure 7-10 gives the customer better flexibility in choosing its exit point because more routing information is provided. Both inbound and outbound traffic patterns will be discussed.

TIP See the section "Default, Primary, and Backup Plus Partial Routing" in Chapter 12 on page 373.

Customer's Outbound Traffic

Consider a situation in which customer 1 is connected to the provider via two separate routers. The customer has the option of deciding which path to take for each of the partial routes it accepts from the provider. Setting different local preferences for different routes coming into the customer's AS usually does this. Local preference can be set on an AS path, a prefix basis, or both. If set based on an AS path, the local preference will apply to all prefixes contained in a particular AS. In case routing decisions need to be made on a prefix basis, the local preference can be set based on each prefix. In Figure 7-10, based on the physical location of certain ASs or prefixes with respect to the provider's AS, the customer can choose to forward traffic to customer 2 and customer 3 (C2 and C3) on the SF link and to C4 and C5 on the NY link. The customer can achieve this by doing the following:

- For routes being learned on the NY link, assign a local preference of 300 for the C4 and C5 routes. Give all other routes a preference of 250. (This would include C2 and C3.)
- For routes being learned on the SF link, assign a local preference of 300 for the C2 and C3 routes. Give all other routes a preference of 200. (This would include C4 and C5.)

When presented with multiple routes for the same destination (via external and internal BGP), the customer will prefer the C4 and C5 routes via the NY link (300 is greater than 200). In the same manner, the customer will prefer the C2 and C3 routes via the SF link (300 is greater than 250). For customers other than C2, C3, C4, and C5, the NY link will be preferred (250 is greater than 200).

For all other Internet routes not known to customer 1, default will be taken in the primary and backup default manner. The 0/0 default route could be dynamically learned from the provider via both links, or it could be statically configured to point to one of the provider's networks (as discussed in the "Setting Default Routes" section of this chapter). Local preference could be used to choose a primary default versus a backup default. Based on the way local preference was set for the C2, C3, C4, and C5 customers, all other routes including the 0/0 will be preferred via the NY link (250 is greater than 200).

A totally different approach that doesn't require as much configuration on the customer's side is for the provider to send its metrics toward the customer. This option was discussed in the section "The MULTI_EXIT_DISC Attribute" in Chapter 6. If metrics coming from the provider are representative of the relative distance that networks are from the entrance points to the customer networks (for example, C2, C3, C4, C5), the customer (C1) will be able to load balance its outbound traffic accordingly. Traffic toward C4 and C5 will exit via the NY link, and traffic toward C2 and C3 will exit via the SF link. Other traffic will exit C1's AS depending on the associated metrics learned from routes on each link. Although this method requires less configuration, it is also less deterministic because C1's traffic trajectory is totally dependent on the provider's delivering accurate MEDs. Recall that this type of routing is referred to as *best-exit routing*. The most desirable results might be achieved by a combination of both approaches.

Customer's Inbound Traffic

The customer can influence inbound traffic by advertising different metrics on different links. Some providers encourage their customers to send their internal IGP metrics as BGP metrics (also discussed in Chapter 6). This way, the provider will deliver traffic to the customer via the link closer to the destination. In Figure 7-10, the customer has decided to manually set the metrics to force the following behavior:

- For routes being sent on the NY link, send the Z and W prefixes with a MED of 200. Give all other prefixes a metric of 250. (This includes X and Y.)
- For routes being sent on the SF link, send the X and Y prefixes with a MED value of 200. Give all other prefixes a MED value of 300. (This includes Z and W.)

When presented with multiple routes for the same destinations, the provider will access the Z and W prefixes over the NY link (200 is less than 300). In the same manner, the provider will access the X and Y prefixes over the SF link (200 is less than 250). For all prefixes other than X, Y, W, and Z, the provider will choose the NY link (250 is less than 300).

RFC 1998[2] defines another method for influencing inbound traffic. Although I won't discuss this scenario here, I encourage you to review the approach suggested therein.

Default, Primary, and Backup, Plus Full and Partial Routing

For customers multihomed to a single provider, the customer can get full routes on all its connections to the provider, or the customer can have a combination of full routes on one link and no routes (default) or partial routes on the other links. The same techniques discussed in the preceding sections would apply here—local preference is used to control the customer's outbound traffic, and the metric (or RFC 1998-type approach) is used to control the inbound traffic. Also, if internal metrics are exchanged between customer and provider, a certain level of load balancing can be achieved.

CAUTION When dealing with outbound traffic, manipulating exit points for specific routes is dangerous. Routing loops can occur if outbound traffic following an IGP default toward the customer's BGP router is directed toward another router following default to the BGP router. In other words, when using default routers, all routers in the domain must behave the same, especially during failures. This might seem confusing now, but it will become more clear in the next chapter.

Automatic Load Balancing

As is probably clear from the previous scenarios, load balancing is not a very intuitive task and requires extensive planning. To help, Cisco IOS software supports dynamic load balancing on a single router for identical destinations learned via EBGP that are sourced from the same autonomous system. This will reduce configuration efforts.

NOTE Again, note that the actual effects of load balancing are as dependent on the underlying packet-switching modes that are enabled as they are on the routing protocols. Although further discussion of switching is beyond the scope of this discussion, understanding these switching modes is strongly encouraged.

Figure 7-11 illustrates an example in which the same router (NY) is connected to its provider via two links and is receiving identical routing updates on both links.

Figure 7-11 *Router Receiving Identical Routes from Two Sources*

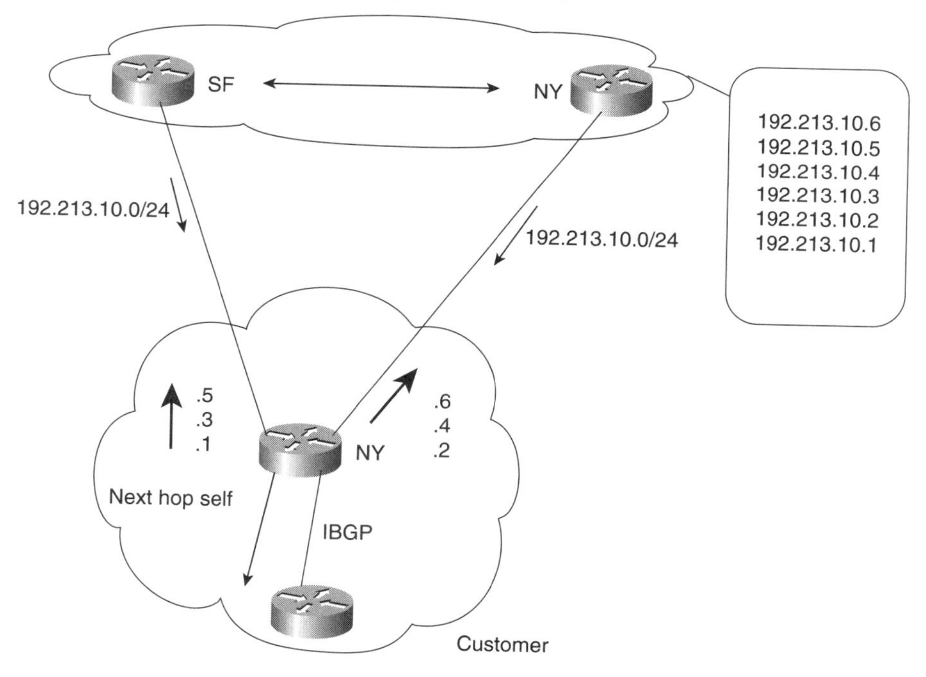

A Cisco router will keep (locally in its IP routing table) up to six identical BGP routes to the same destination. When passing on the EBGP updates to the IBGP peers, however, the router will pass only its singular best route for a particular destination. The next-hop address of the route will automatically be changed to reflect the NY router's own IP address instead of having the EBGP next-hop address carried into IBGP. Note that this is done automatically only in the case where load balancing is configured dynamically.

By default, a Cisco router will load balance on a per-destination (host) basis. Balancing on a per-destination basis is performed in a round-robin fashion. One host will be locked to one path (interface), the next host will be locked to the other path (interface), and so on.

Figure 7-11 assumes that the customer is getting two identical routes to network 192.213.10.0/24. Without automatic load balancing, the BGP process prefers one path only. The network administrator is responsible for modifying BGP attributes to balance traffic between paths.

TIP See the section "Load Balancing with BGP Multipath" in Chapter 12 on page 378.

With automatic balancing, BGP keeps two entries for the 192.213.10.0/24 prefix—one via the SF link and one via the NY link. Outbound traffic from the customer network is then split over the two links on a round-robin basis, assuming that the customer needs to send traffic to the destinations 192.213.10.1 through 192.213.10.6. Destination 10.1 will be reached via the SF link, destination 10.2 will go over the NY link, destination 10.3 will go over the SF link, and so on.

NOTE As discussed, BGP by default installs only a single best route to each destination in the IP routing table. However, BGP Multipath can be used to install multiple paths in the IP routing table if the paths are learned via the same neighboring AS. The **maximum-paths** router configuration command can be used to have the router install up to six paths to a single destination network. Chapter 12 provides additional configuration information regarding BGP Multipath.

NOTE Load balancing in this manner works only when dealing with identical routing updates coming into the same router from the same provider. This method does not work to load balance in a multiprovider environment.

Balancing Between Two Routers Sharing Multiple Paths

In some situations, two routers share multiple physical paths for backup or higher-bandwidth services, as illustrated in Figure 7-12. Although automatic load balancing works well for outbound traffic, for inbound traffic, you must resort to manipulating metrics to influence the provider's decision.

Figure 7-12 *Load Balancing Between Two Routers Sharing Multiple Paths*

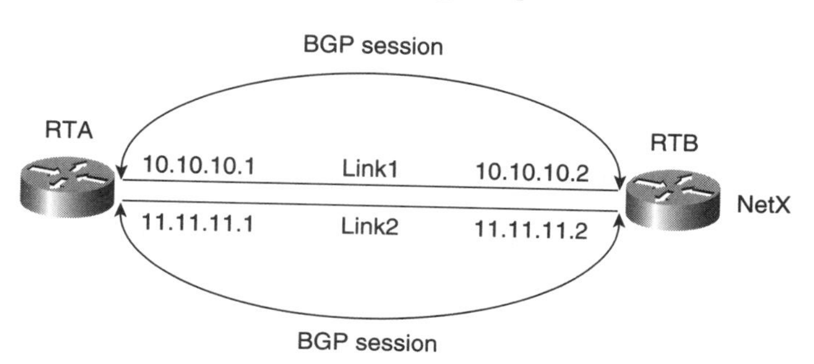

To balance traffic in the environment depicted in Figure 7-12, one option is to implement dynamic balancing. This is simply a special situation of the previous automatic load-balancing case. Dynamic load balancing, however, would result in extra overhead for the routers. Each router would receive duplicate update messages from the other router. In the case of full routing, the result would be approximately 70,000 routes arriving on each link. Instead, it is possible (and preferable) to achieve load balancing for the situation illustrated in Figure 7-12 by using a static route approach.

During normal behavior, BGP keeps the best next hop for each prefix it learns. As shown in Table 7-1, RTA receives two identical BGP routes for NetX.

Table 7-1 *RTA's BGP Table—NetX Is Reachable Via 10.10.10.2*

Destination	Next Hop
NetX	10.10.10.2 (best)
NetX	11.11.11.2

BGP will pick the best route and install it in its IP routing table. In this case, BGP has picked the route via next hop 10.10.10.2. Table 7-2 illustrates RTA's IP routing table, where the next hop 10.10.10.2 is reachable via Link1. As a result of this configuration, all traffic toward networks learned from RTB will be sent over Link1. Hence, no load balancing is achieved.

Table 7-2 *RTA's IP Routing Table—NetX Is Reachable Via Link1*

Destination	Next Hop
NetX	10.10.10.2
10.10.10.0/24	Link1

TIP See the section "Balancing Between Two Routers Sharing Multiple Paths" in Chapter 12 on page 381.

To enable more intelligent load balancing, you can fool BGP by setting the next hop to a virtual interface rather than the physical link. Then, the IP routing table is used to perform the actual load balancing by mapping the virtual interface IP address (next hop) to multiple directly connected interface IP addresses. In Figure 7-13, RTB can be assigned a loopback interface (virtual interface), and RTA can use that address to set up the BGP neighbor connection. This way, the loopback interface itself and not the IP address of the physical link will be used as a next hop. Either dynamic IGP or static routing can be used to load balance between the links independent of BGP.

Figure 7-13 *A Single BGP Session Across Multiple Physical Links*

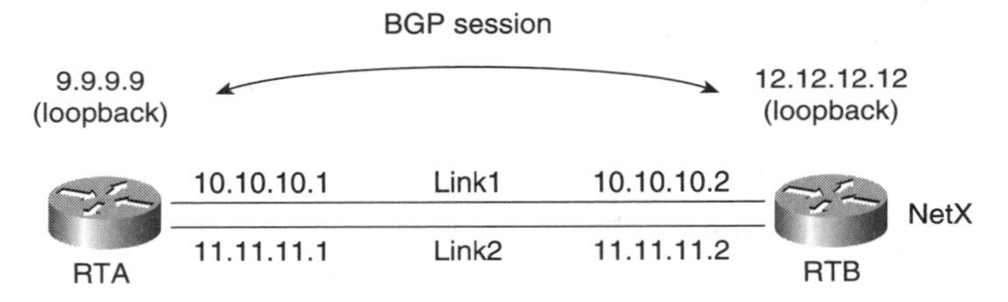

As shown in Table 7-3, RTA will receive its BGP routes from its neighbor 12.12.12.12 and will be able to reach NetX via the next-hop 12.12.12.12.

Table 7-3 *RTA's BGP Table—NetX Is Reachable Via 12.12.12.12*

Destination	Next Hop
NetX	12.12.12.12

Table 7-4 illustrates RTA's IP routing table. Next-hop 12.12.12.12 can be reached via Link1 and Link2. Reachability of the 12.12.12.0/24 network can be achieved via IGP or by pointing multiple static routes toward Link1 and Link2. The router can now load balance the traffic. Due to the recursive route lookup in this scenario, load balancing is done per network rather than per destination. Traffic to networks learned from RTB can now be round-robin load balanced over multiple links.

Table 7-4 *RTA's Routing Table—NetX Is Reachable Via Link1 or Link 2*

Destination	Next Hop
NetX	12.12.12.12
12.12.12.0/24	Link1
12.12.12.0/24	Link2

Scenario 3: Multihoming to Different Providers

A customer connected to multiple providers is considered to be multihomed to different providers. Redundancy and geographical restrictions are strong motivations for multihoming. The outbound traffic behavior of each iteration of this scenario will be considered on a case-by-case basis. For all cases, the inbound traffic behavior is the same and will be covered at the end of this section.

In the following sections, we'll cover these topics related to multihoming to different providers:

- Default Only, Primary, and Backup
- Default, Primary, and Backup, Plus Partial Routing
- Default, Primary, and Backup, Plus Full and Partial Routing
- Customer Inbound Traffic (AS_PATH Manipulation)

Default Only, Primary, and Backup

In this case, the customer can follow defaults toward the provider. One link is used as primary, and the second link is used as backup. Figure 7-14 illustrates a relevant situation.

Figure 7-14 *Multihoming to Two Providers*

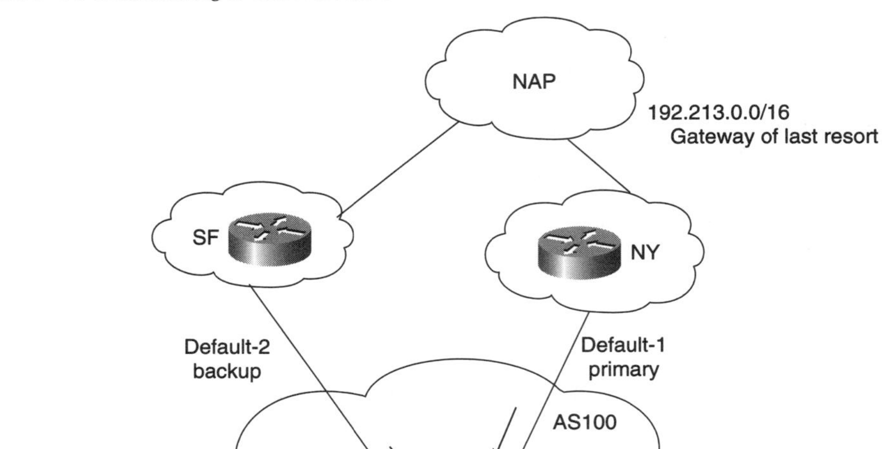

A customer can set or learn the default routes to the two providers either through static routes or through both providers' dynamic advertisements of default routes. The customer can prefer one default over another by using administrative distance or local preference. A good method of pointing defaults to both providers is to accept the same network from both providers. The customer will configure its 0/0 default based on that network and can manipulate local preference to choose one link versus the other. If one default is withdrawn because of a link failure toward one provider, the other default will take its place. The customer can negotiate with the providers to send only the one network entry, or the customer can filter all updates on its side except for the one required entry.

In Figure 7-14, the customer is pointing default toward the 192.213.0.0/16 prefix it is receiving from both providers. The NY link will be the primary link, and the SF link will be the backup. Thus, the customer is setting the local preference on the NY link highest (200).

Default, Primary, and Backup, Plus Partial Routing

The addition of partial routing to the environment introduced in the previous discussion changes the outbound traffic behavior. Figure 7-15 illustrates the new situation. The customer can accept partial routing from one or both providers. In addition, the customer must accept or configure default toward both providers, with one default preferred over the other.

Figure 7-15 *Multihoming to Two Providers Plus Partial Routing*

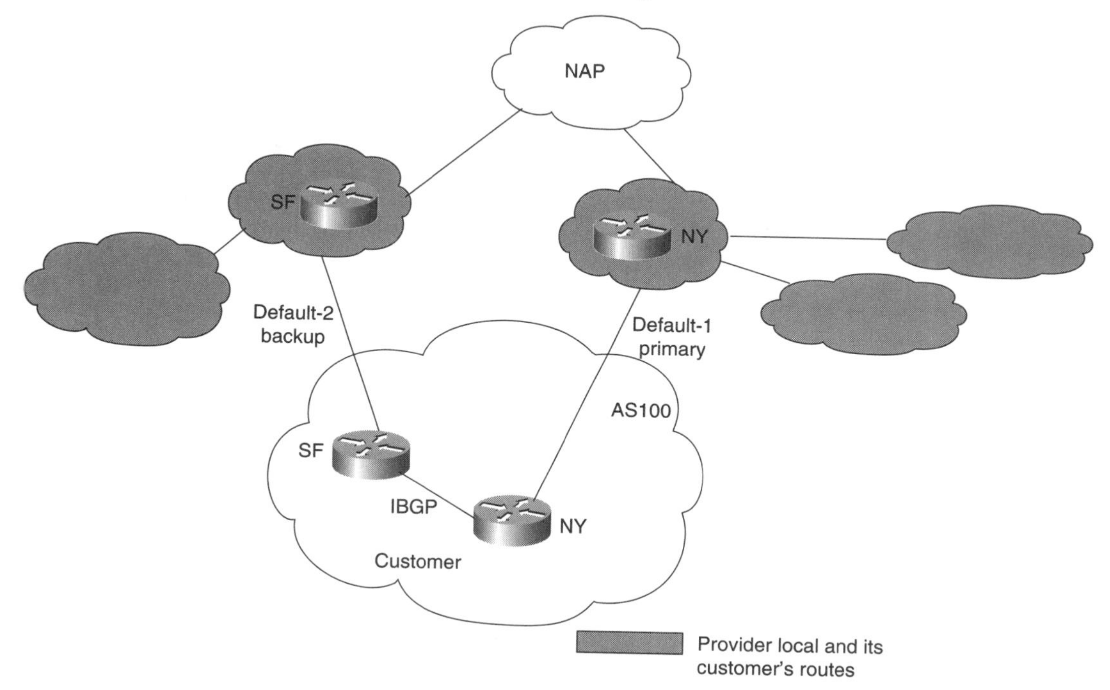

By accepting partial routing from the providers, a customer does not need to see all Internet routes and can still make the best route decision when routing toward its direct providers. (For some major providers, partial routes could represent a substantial number of routes.) In the case illustrated in Figure 7-15, BGP will make the right choice, and the customer will choose the provider link closest to the destination network (shortest AS path). For other Internet routes, the basic principle of primary and backup can be used. The customer can point to a specific network to be the default, accept that network from both providers, and use local preference to prefer one link over the other.

Default, Primary, and Backup, Plus Full and Partial Routing

In multihoming to different providers, accepting full routes from either or both providers is not really necessary unless the customer plans to be a provider itself and pass along full routes to its customers (act as a transit AS). Figure 7-16 illustrates a relevant environment.

Figure 7-16 *Multihoming to Two Providers with Full and Partial Routing*

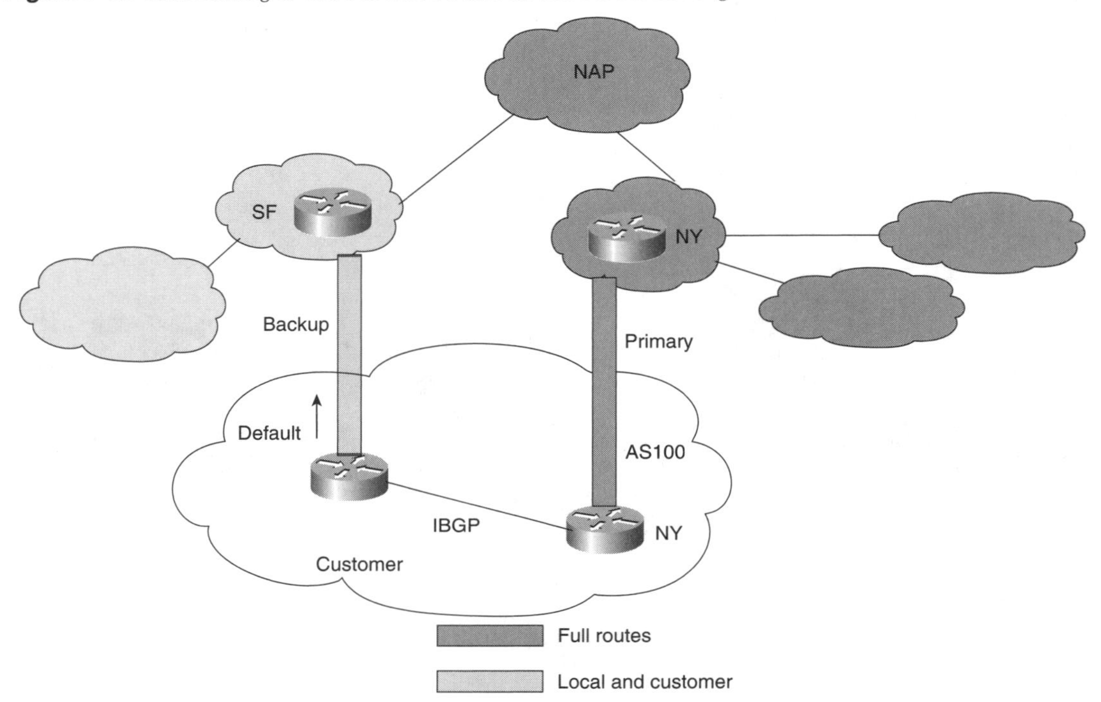

The customer can accept full routing from one or both providers, depending on whether the customer requires effective load balancing. In the case of full routing from both (or multiple) providers, the customer can use local preference to decide what networks can be accessed via which provider. Decisions can be made based on AS, prefix, or, possibly, community-string information. In some cases, the customer might want to accept full routing from one provider and implement partial/default routing with the other provider. This way, the customer can get the best of both worlds without having to deal with managing full routes from different links. As you will see later, Internet instabilities caused by any provider are very CPU-intensive on routers.

In Figure 7-16, the customer is receiving full routes from the NY provider and partial routes from the SF provider. The customer is also pointing default toward the SF provider. For the SF local and customer routes, the SF link will be used because of the shorter AS path. For all other routes, the NY link will be used because the SF link provides only partial routes. In case the SF link goes down, all networks can be reached via NY. In case the NY link goes down, the customer can still reach all Internet routes by following a default toward the SF link.

TIP See the section "Multihoming to Different Providers" in Chapter 12 on page 384.

Customer Inbound Traffic

Inbound traffic is affected by how the customer advertises its networks to the providers. Note that with the multiprovider scenario, sending different metrics from the customer's end will not have any effect. This is because the MED value is nontransitive. In other words, the MED value is learned only by the customer's direct upstream providers and is not passed from provider to provider.

To affect the providers' behavior dynamically, the customer can manipulate the AS path attribute by inserting bogus entries in the AS path to affect the AS path length. The providers will receive the same prefix information with different path length and will pick the path that has the shortest length (assuming that all higher-priority attributes are the same). Note that in a multiprovider environment, it is not enough to influence the direct provider only because there is no guarantee that the adjacent provider will itself receive traffic from other providers for that customer's networks. Path manipulation will have to influence providers all the way up to the exchange point because this is where the balance (as far as path length) will be tipped one way or the other.

Figure 7-17 illustrates how bogus entries in the AS path affect routing. The customer (AS100) has inserted a bogus entry (100) in its AS path toward AS300. Providers at the NAP will get the same prefixes with different path length (300 100 100 versus 200 100) and will pick the shorter path via AS200 (assuming that higher-priority attributes are the same). The bogus entry should be a repeat of the AS that originated the entry (in this case, 100).

Figure 7-17 *Using Bogus AS Path Entries to Affect Routing*

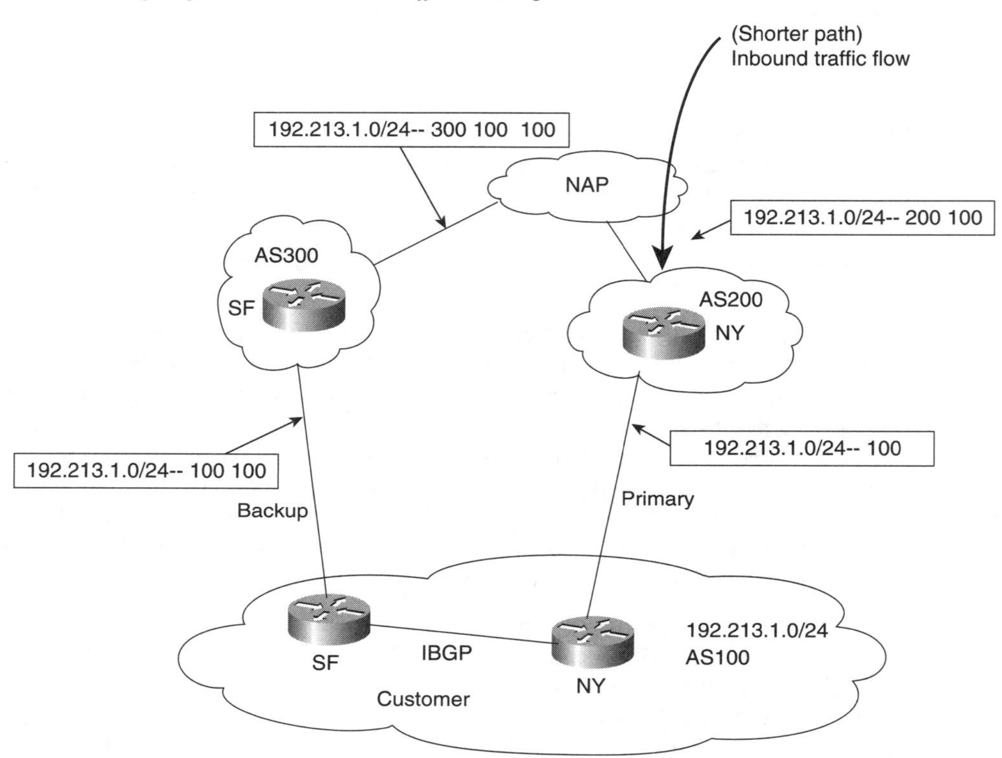

Scenario 4: Customers of the Same Provider with a Backup Link

In some cases, customers with common interests agree to provide each other with internal connectivity and backup connectivity to the Internet. The customers are connected to the same provider and at the same time have an alternative private link to each other. Two scenarios might typically arise:

- The private link can be used as a secondary (backup) link when an Internet link fails.
- The private link can be used as a primary link for internal traffic between the two companies and as a backup link in case of an Internet link failure. If a backup strategy is to work, customers must advertise each others' networks to the provider. One customer must be able to act as a transit AS for the other customer when the other customer's Internet link fails.

Private Link Used as a Pure Backup

Figure 7-18 illustrates a scenario in which AS2 and AS3 are connected to the same provider—AS1. AS2 and AS3 have a private link that will be used only for backup. AS2 and AS3 will have the same policies.

Figure 7-18 *Private Link Used as Backup*

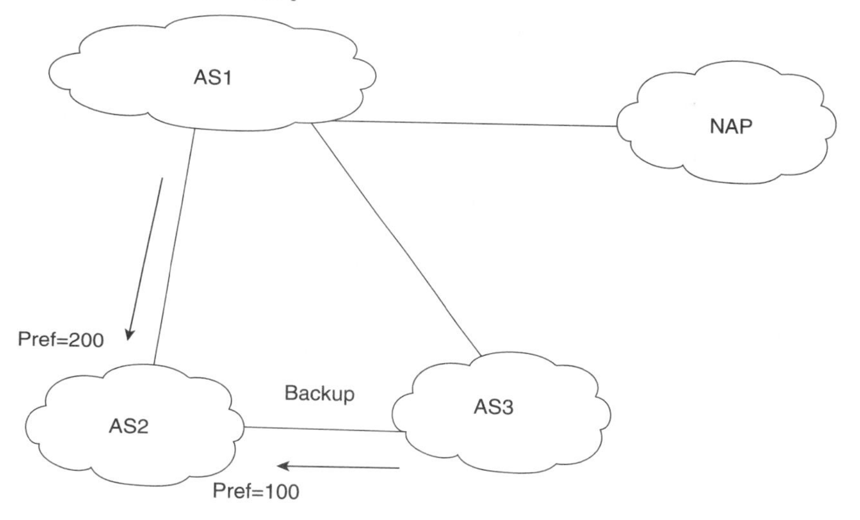

For the backup environment illustrated in Figure 7-18, AS2's outbound traffic considerations are of particular interest. Whether AS2 is getting full routing or a combination of default, full, and partial routing from the provider and AS3, AS2 will have to set its local preference for routes coming from AS1 to be higher (200) than the ones coming from AS3 (100). As a result, provider AS1 is always preferred, and the private link acts as a backup only. In case of partial routing being accepted by AS2, AS2 can set defaults to both the provider (AS1) and AS3. Setting a higher local preference ensures that all the traffic will be sent toward the provider. If AS2 is getting full routing from the provider and partial routing from AS3, AS2 can keep a default route to AS3 to be used if the provider link fails. The default route AS2 is learning from AS3 should not need to be set at a lower local preference than the full routing AS2 learns from the provider.

Private Link Used as Primary Between AS2 and AS3

Figure 7-19 illustrates a case in which the link between AS2 and AS3 is used as a primary link for all traffic to AS3's local networks or to AS3's customers. For all other traffic, the link to the provider AS1 should be used. The two links (provider and private) should back up one another.

Figure 7-19 *Private Links Used as Primary AS Interconnection*

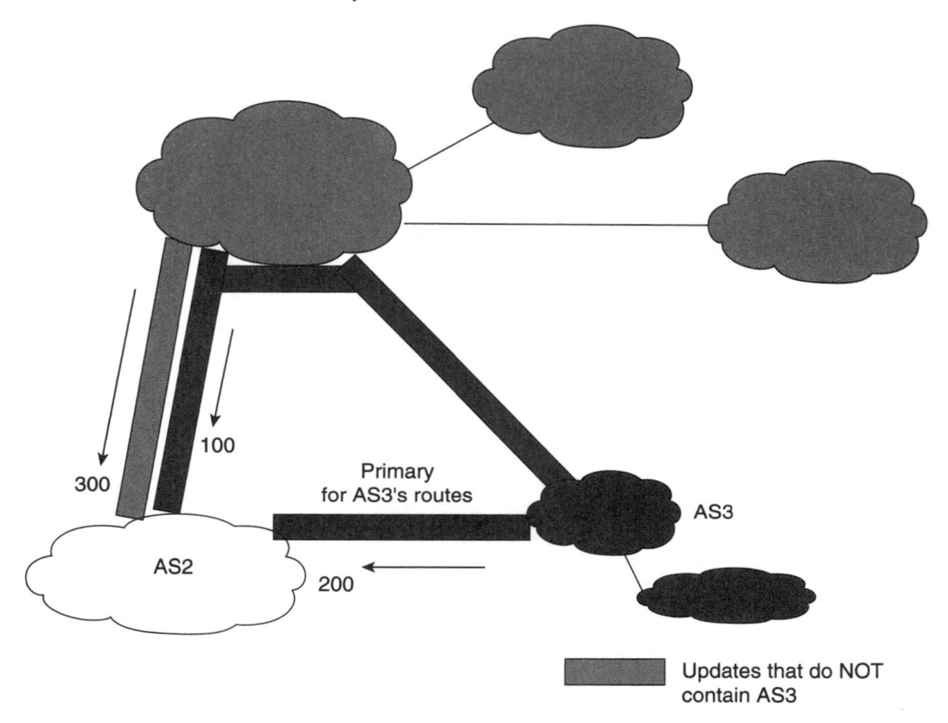

Assume that the environment illustrated in Figure 7-19 features default, full, and partial routing; the following discussions focus on outbound and inbound traffic implications from AS2's perspective. This scenario is usually handled by the default BGP behavior. Because the shortest path is always preferred (assuming that higher-priority attributes are the same), AS2 and AS3 will always use the private link to reach one another's networks. For the sake of experimenting with BGP policies, we will attempt to address this scenario by manipulating the local preference attribute to affect outbound traffic.

TIP See the section "Customers of the Same Provider with a Backup Link" in Chapter 12 on page 388.

AS2's Outbound Traffic

Whether AS2 is accepting default, full, or partial routing from the provider and AS3, AS2 should set the local preference of all updates that do not contain AS3 to be higher than all other updates. In the case illustrated in Figure 7-19, all non-AS3-originated routes are given a local preference of 300. Updates sent by AS3 across the private link to AS2 (including AS3-originated routes) are given a local preference of 200. Updates from the provider containing AS3-originated routes are, in turn, forwarded to AS2, which keeps them at a default local preference of 100. This ensures that the private link between AS2 and AS3 is taken (200 is greater than 100).

For all other traffic, AS2 accepts defaults or sets its own defaults to the provider and AS3, with the provider being preferred.

It is also possible for AS2 to accept only locally originated routes from AS3 and not accept any routes from the provider. AS2 then defaults to both, with the provider declared as the preferred egress. This way, any traffic destined for AS3 will take the private link; any other traffic will take the link to the provider (because of the better default). In case of the provider's link failure, the default to the private link will be activated.

AS2's Inbound Traffic

All the cases discussed so far in Scenario 4 have the same inbound traffic behavior. Because of the shorter path length, incoming traffic from the Internet will always take the provider-to-AS2 link. For all traffic originating from AS3 or its customers, the private link will be taken also because of the shorter path. This is the desired behavior.

Scenario 5: Customers of Different Providers with a Backup Link

It is not unusual for separate ASs to require Internet interconnection and to have different Internet service providers. Whenever multiple providers are involved and the customers of these providers agree to back up one another, support can get complicated. This section takes the previous discussions one step further by discussing how this backup connectivity is addressed from the provider's point of view.

In Figure 7-20, AS1 is the customer of ISP1, and AS2 is the customer of ISP2. AS1 and AS2 have also entered a bilateral agreement under which the private link between the two ASs will be used as a backup in case of a failure of either primary Internet link.

Figure 7-20 *Customers of Multiple Providers with a Backup Link*

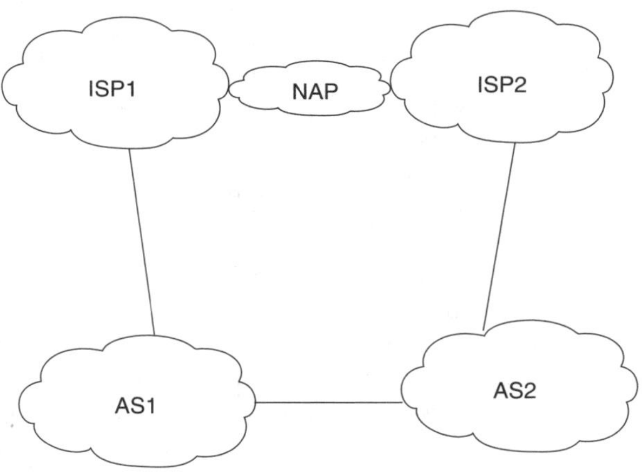

Normally, an individual AS does not want to be used as transit for another AS. In the case illustrated in Figure 6-20, AS1 wants ISP1 to set its routing configuration so that ISP1 reaches AS2 via ISP2. Similarly, AS2 would prefer that ISP2 set its routing configuration so that ISP2 reaches AS1 via ISP1. In this scenario, for the backup link to work, AS1 advertises AS2's networks to ISP1, and AS2 advertises AS1's networks to ISP2.

TIP See the section "Customers of Different Providers with a Backup Link" in Chapter 12 on page 391.

The discussions about primary and backup are the same as with the scenario discussed in the earlier section "Scenario 4: Customers of the Same Provider with a Backup Link." The private link can be a pure backup or can be used for interior traffic between customers.

The requirement to have the provider not use one customer to reach the other customer is more complicated. ISP1 will have to set the local preference for AS2 routes coming from ISP2 to be higher than the AS2 routes coming from AS1. This would cause ISP1 to use ISP2 under normal operational conditions to reach AS2. The same strategy might be deployed for ISP2.

Providers like to minimize configuration of their network as much as possible. In cases where a provider has multiple customers coming online every day, manually manipulating the local preference for each could be cumbersome. Providers also like to set their policies based on AS numbers rather than specific networks.

You can use a couple of approaches to implement the required policies. The first approach, which requires coordination between providers and their customers, is the BGP community approach. The second approach is the AS path manipulation approach. AS path manipulation is easier to implement but might not be available in all vendor products. In addition, AS path manipulation might require coordination between a provider and its customers if the provider has restrictive AS path filters.

The Community Approach

The use of the community approach is very effective. Providers want to map certain community values to corresponding local preference values (that is, RFC 1998). The provider will automatically assign customers routing updates tagged with a specific community to a corresponding local preference value.

To keep this scenario manageable, only routing and policy setting from ISP1's point of view are addressed. An identical discussion would apply to ISP2. Traffic flow for the case illustrated in Figure 7-21 can be divided into a minimum of three patterns.

Figure 7-21 *Community Approach Solution*

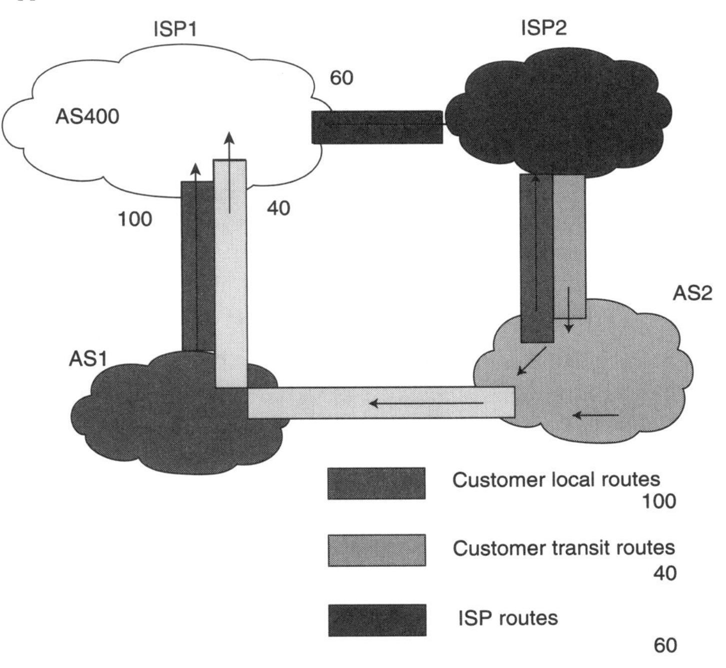

There can be more flow patterns, depending on how many connections a customer has to its provider, but the basic set of three illustrates required considerations.

Flow patterns from ISP1's point of view can be summarized as follows:

- **Pattern 1**—Routes originated by the customer AS1, or customer local routes.
- **Pattern 2**—Routes transiting via AS1. These routes come from AS2 and consist of AS2's routes and all other routes that AS2 is receiving from ISP2. ISP1 uses this information to reach AS2 via AS1 as a backup in the event that AS2's link to ISP2 fails. This pattern is referred to as customer transit routes.
- **Pattern 3**—All other routes coming from ISP2, or ISP routes. These can include routes learned from AS2.

Having divided the routes into different categories, ISP1 will assign a community value to each pattern and will dynamically map it to the local preference. These are listed in Table 7-5.

Table 7-5 *Dynamic Mapping of Local Preference*

Pattern	Community	Local Preference
Customer local routes	None	100
Customer transit routes	400:40	40
ISP routes	400:60	60

ISP1 will inform all its customers and connected ISPs that its local preference values are dynamically set according to Table 7-5. Customers can then dynamically influence the ISP's decision by sending the corresponding community values. In Figure 7-21, AS1 will send its local routes with no community and the transit routes with community 400:40. ISP2 will send its routes with community 400:60.

According to the preferences summarized in Table 7-5, ISP1 prefers AS1's local routes via its direct link to AS1 (preference 100 is the highest). ISP1 prefers all other routes, including AS2 routes, via ISP2 (preference 60 is higher than 40.)

TIP See the section "Customers of Different Providers with a Backup Link" in Chapter 12 on page 391.

The AS Path Manipulation Approach

The AS path manipulation approach is the same as the one discussed for multihoming to different providers in the section "Customer Inbound Traffic (AS Path Manipulation)." It is straightforward and has proven to be one of the most efficient methods of influencing a provider's routing decisions. Figure 7-22 illustrates an environment in which AS path manipulation is used to direct routing processes.

Figure 7-22 *AS Path Manipulation Example*

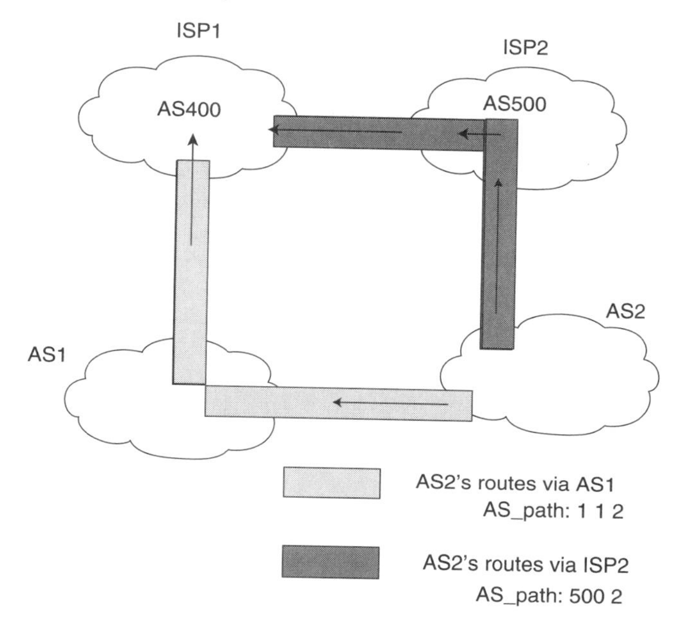

For the case illustrated in Figure 7-22, assume that all local preference attributes are kept at their default values to avoid overriding the AS path attribute. With this assumption in mind, the AS path attribute will be manipulated such that ISP1 will use the direct link to AS1 for traffic destined for AS1 and the direct link to ISP2 for traffic destined for ISP2. These decisions are made based on the shortest AS path.

For traffic going to AS2, ISP1 has an equal path via ISP2 and AS1. ISP1's AS path to AS2 via AS1 is 1 2, and the AS path via ISP2 is 500 2, which are of equivalent length.

To influence ISP1's decision, AS1 must increase the AS path length when advertising AS2's routes to ISP1 by prepending an additional AS number to the AS path list. Normally, AS1 will repeat its own AS number. ISP1's new AS path to reach AS2 via AS1 will be 1 1 2, which is longer than ISP1's AS path to reach AS2 via ISP2 500 2. As a result, under normal conditions, ISP1 will use ISP2 to reach AS2.

TIP See the section "The AS Path Approach" in Chapter 12 on page 394.

Looking Ahead

Mastering routing at the edges of your domain gives you full control over traffic into and out of your autonomous system. Another piece of the puzzle is how the traffic flows inside the AS before it gets out. Not all routers inside the AS run BGP. IGP-only routers usually do not carry a full list of Internet routes due to memory constraints. Running defaults inside the AS to reach external routes is one of the most common ways for internal routers to reach destinations outside the AS. With defaults comes the threat of routing loops if conflicting policies exist between your BGP and your IGP. The following chapter discusses these issues of how to make BGP policies flow hand-in-hand with IGP defaults. That chapter also discusses the use of policy routing in achieving total control over routing behaviors based on the sources of IP addresses rather than the traditional destination-based routing.

Frequently Asked Questions

Q — *I statically defined a default toward my provider by pointing toward a network I am learning via BGP. What happens if that network goes up and down?*

A — Your default will appear and disappear. That is why you should not point your default to a specific subnet. Always point to an aggregate or supernet, because they are less likely to flip-flop.

Q — *I have the option of getting the 0/0 default via BGP or defining a static default. Which do you think is best?*

A — For the border router, both methods are the same as long as the aggregate you are pointing to is stable. On the other hand, after you receive the 0/0 via BGP, it will get flooded to all your IBGP peers, and there is a chance that you will end up sending it to your other EBGP peers. When you define the default statically, you will have better control.

Q — *My AS is connected to two providers, one in SF and one in NY. I want the traffic from and toward my SJ site to go in and out on the SF link. All other traffic should flow over the NY link. What do I need to do to achieve this behavior?*

A — Because there are two different providers, MEDs should be used. The only methods are AS path manipulation (or perhaps methods such as those proposed in RFC 1998) for inbound traffic and local preference manipulation for outbound traffic. For your inbound traffic toward San Jose, you can use the AS path manipulation technique to make your path longer for all SJ routes advertised on the NY link. The problem is with your outbound traffic. If you know exactly what networks the SJ users are trying to reach, you can give those destinations better local preference on the SF exit. If the SJ site needs to reach any destination, setting a better local preference on the SF link will cause all your outbound traffic to leave via the SF link. However, that doesn't meet your requirement for the NY link to carry all other traffic.

Another way of dealing with this scenario is policy routing, in which a router can track source addresses and direct traffic accordingly. This is described in Chapter 8, "Controlling Routing Inside the Autonomous System."

Q — *I am prepending AS numbers to my routes to tip the balance of my traffic. I am not seeing any effect. Why?*

A — Remember that your updates are exchanged by multiple providers. A provider along the way can use local preference to override your path length. Check with your provider.

Q—*Do I have to set BGP policies? Why can't I leave it to BGP to figure out the correct path?*

A — You do not have to set policies. Remember, though, that BGP is not taking into account the speed of your links and your user traffic requirements. If you are happy with your traffic pattern the way it is, you do not need to change any attributes.

References

[1]RFC 826, "Address Resolution Protocol (ARP)," www.isi.edu/in-notes/rfc826.txt

[2]RFC 1998, "An Application of the BGP Community Attribute in Multi-home Routing," www.isi.edu/in-notes/rfc1998.txt

This chapter covers the following key topics:

- **Interaction of non-BGP routers with BGP routers**—A brief overview of the methods by which non-BGP routers inside an AS can reach the outside world.
- **Defaults inside the AS: primary/backup policy**—Different methods by which to avoid potential loops when default routing inside an AS conflicts with the goal of providing a primary and a backup link to outside the AS.
- **Defaults inside the AS: other BGP policies**—An overview of routing policies other than primary/backup, which can lead to routing loops within the AS.
- **Policy routing**—A definition and sample of a method of controlling routes, based on traffic source IP addresses or source and destination IP addresses rather than destination only.

CHAPTER 8

Controlling Routing Inside the Autonomous System

The preceding chapter focused on the interaction between different ASs and how BGP attributes can be manipulated to address symmetry, redundancy, and load balancing. The discussion concentrated on the behavior of the BGP border routers that connect the AS to other ASs.

ISPs usually have most of their routers running BGP, perhaps with some leaf nodes running only Interior Gateway Protocols (IGPs). On the other hand, most customers have few routers running BGP, and the majority of their internal IGP routers default routing toward the BGP routers. In these scenarios, it is important to have the BGP policies go hand-in-hand with routing inside the AS. Conflicting policies might result in routing loops if the AS's physical layout does not complement the logical layout. This chapter discusses the interaction of BGP routes with IGPs inside the AS and presents the options of controlling routes via policy routing.

Interaction of Non-BGP Routers with BGP Routers

Non-BGP routers inside the AS can reach the outside world by using the following two methods:

- Injecting BGP into the IGP
- Following default routes inside the AS

Injecting BGP into the IGP

Injecting full BGP routes into an IGP is not recommended; doing so will add excessive routing overhead to any IGP. Interior routing protocols were never meant to handle more than the networks inside your AS, perhaps in addition to a small number of exterior routes from other IGPs.

This does not mean that BGP routes should never be injected into IGPs. Depending on the number of BGP routes and how critical it is for them to be in the IGP, injecting partial BGP routes into IGP might be appropriate. If you follow this course, you should exercise caution to control routes leaked into the IGP. Discussing all the potential issues associated with BGP redistribution into IGPs is beyond the scope of this book. However, here are some things worthy of consideration: the amount of available memory, CPU resources available for calculating paths and processing routing updates, link utilization from routing control traffic, impact on convergence, IGP limitations, and network topology. All of these factors, and numerous others, should be considered.

Injecting partial BGP routes into the IGP from specific points of the AS can help direct the corresponding outbound traffic toward specific exit points. Outbound traffic toward other Internet routes will still have to follow defaults toward the BGP routers. Although injecting BGP routes into the IGP seems like the optimal routing solution, it has its drawbacks. For instance, if the IGP is classful (such as RIP-1 or Interior Gateway Routing Protocol [IGRP]), information about classless interdomain routing (CIDR) blocks will be lost. The other major problem is the potential for instability in the injected BGP routes, causing further instability of the IGP. Some major network meltdowns have been caused by IGPs failing due to fluctuations of a large number of external routes.

Following Defaults Inside an AS

The more practical solution for non-BGP routers inside the AS to reach the outside world is to follow defaults inside your AS to the closest exterior gateway router that can get you outside the AS. A default route can be injected into the AS from each autonomous system border router. Each IGP router might receive the default route from one or multiple routers. Each IGP router chooses the best path to an exterior destination based on the internal cost or metric to reach the default. After the traffic reaches the BGP routers, the traffic propagates according to how BGP has determined the best path. Figure 8-1 illustrates non-BGP routers inside an AS following defaults to reach the closest BGP router.

Figure 8-1 *Example of Following Defaults*

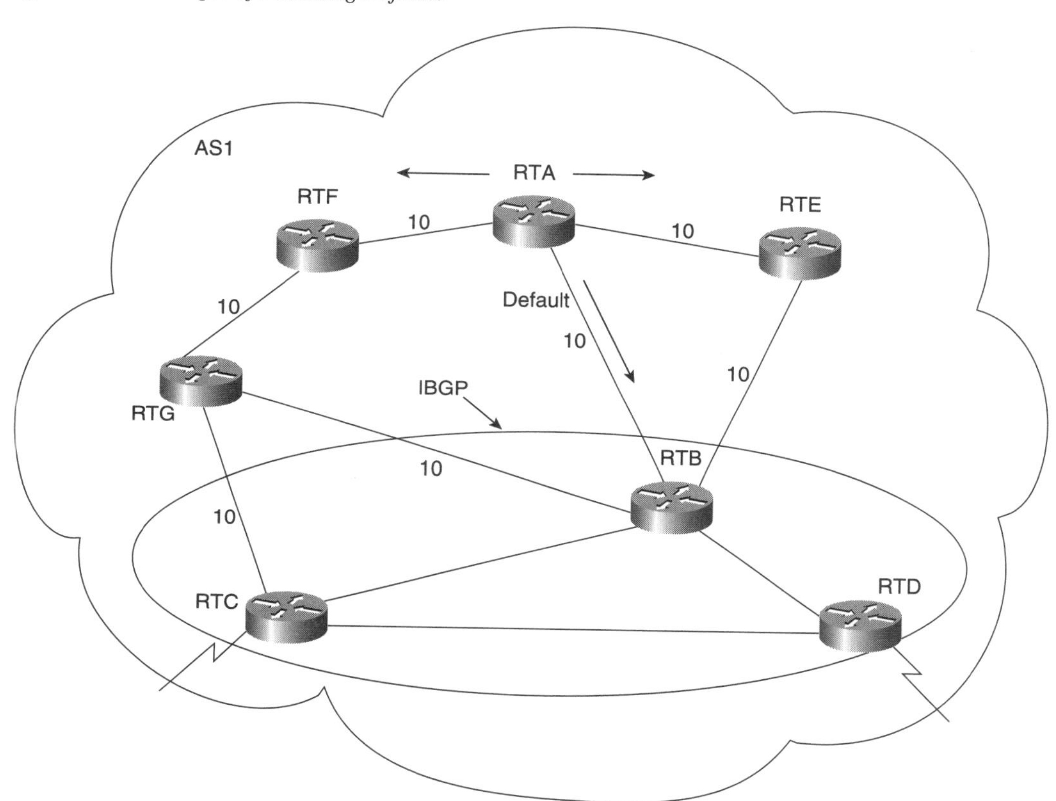

RTC and RTD are BGP border routers that are injecting the default 0/0 inside AS1. RTB is an internal BGP transit router running a full IBGP mesh with RTC and RTD. Internal non-BGP routers, such as RTA, receive the default from different IGP sources; they prefer the default with the smallest IGP metric. In Figure 8-1, RTA is receiving the 0/0 from RTB with a metric of 10, from RTE with a metric of 20 (RTA-to-RTB: 10 + RTB-to-RTE: 10), and from RTF with a metric of 30 (RTA-to-RTF: 10 + RTF-to-RTG: 10 + RTG-to-RTB or RTC: 10). RTA prefers the default via its link to RTB because it has the lowest internal metric (10). After traffic arrives at RTB, the BGP routing table of RTB is used to reach external destinations of the AS.

TIP See Examples 12-38 through 12-41, "Following Defaults Inside an AS," beginning on page 397.

Running IBGP inside the AS is an important element both to help direct traffic that must exit the AS and to carry transit traffic in previously mentioned cases such as a partner AS providing backup transit during failures. Also, most of the symmetry techniques discussed in the preceding chapter cannot be implemented if multiple BGP routers are not running IBGP.

BGP Policies Conflicting with Internal Defaults

Depending on the physical topology of an AS and how BGP policies are set, some nonoptimal situations might arise. For instance, traffic inside the AS following IGP defaults to reach a BGP border router might loop if the BGP border routers have contradictory BGP policies that result in the traffic's being sent back inside the AS.

TIP See the section "Policy Routing" in Chapter 12 on page 411.

This section discusses situations in which loops might occur and experiments with possible solutions to the problems. The following two cases will be considered:

- Defaults inside the AS in conjunction with a primary/backup BGP policy
- Defaults inside the AS in conjunction with other BGP policies

Defaults Inside the AS: Primary/Backup BGP Policy

Consider the routing scenario shown in Figure 8-2. AS1 is connected to the Internet via two connections. RTC in SF is running Exterior Border Gateway Protocol (EBGP) with one provider, whereas RTD in NY is running EBGP with another provider. Inside the AS, RTC and RTD are running IBGP; however, they are not physically connected. As a result, traffic between RTC and RTD must flow through routers RTA and RTB.

Figure 8-2 *Following Defaults: Loop Situation*

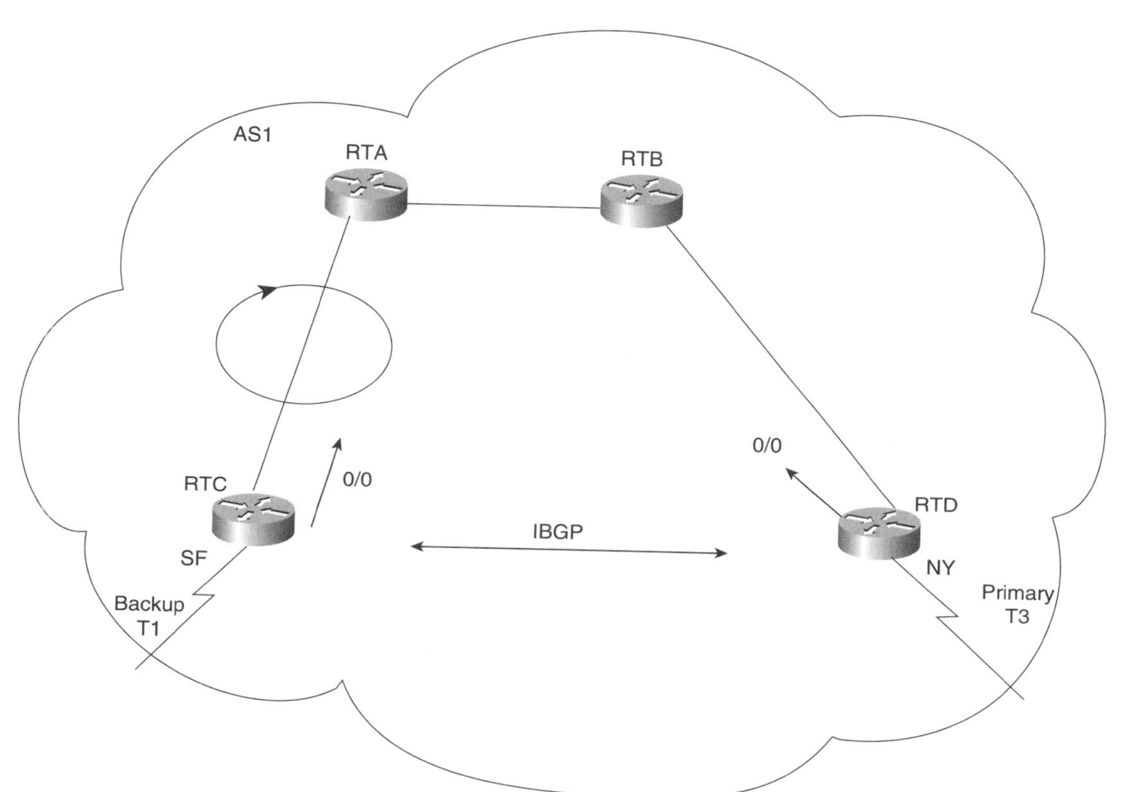

Assume that RTC and RTD are both receiving full routes from their respective providers. RTC and RTD are also injecting a 0/0-default route into the IGP inside AS1. Also assume that AS1 wants to run the primary/backup technique to enable the NY T3 link to be the primary. AS1 would set the local preference higher for routes coming across the NY T3 link, which makes that link primary. The SF T1 link will be used as backup, so all outbound traffic that reaches RTC will be directed back toward RTD.

RTA and RTB are interior non-BGP routers. They exchange routes via IGP with all other routers in the AS. RTA and RTB do not see any of the exterior routes. They follow defaults toward RTC or RTD according to which one has the lower IGP metric. Traffic for outside networks reaching RTA will end up following the default toward RTC, whereas traffic reaching RTB will end up following the default toward RTD.

When RTC receives the traffic, it diverts it toward RTD because of the BGP policy that makes NY the primary link. Because RTC has no direct connection to RTD, it sends the traffic toward RTA. RTA receives the traffic and sends it back toward RTC, resulting in a routing loop between RTA and RTC.

Next, multiple scenarios are examined for avoiding the potential looping behavior when using defaults within the AS for primary/backup routing.

Scenario 1: Manipulating the IGP Metric

In this scenario, we want to try to avoid a loop condition by having all traffic for external destinations follow the default toward RTD. This could be done by having RTC inject the 0/0 default inside the IGP with a very high metric to make the 0/0 default injected by RTD shorter for any internal router. Traffic should never go to RTC to reach unknown (external) destinations unless the NY link goes down.

Scenario 2: The IBGP Path Is Shorter Than the IGP Path

The existence of a shorter path between the IBGP routers ensures that traffic will not go back over the IGP-only routers to reach its destination. This is required only if BGP policies necessitate the redirection of traffic from one BGP router to the other. Such situations occur when an IBGP router does not have an external link to send the traffic. If it does have an external link, that link is not used as the best path (RTC's situation in Figure 8-2).

In the scenario shown in Figure 8-2, a loop can be avoided if the border routers RTC and RTD that run IBGP also share a physical segment such as a serial link. Traffic coming toward RTC from RTA would be redirected over a physical link (not shown in the figure), which provides a shorter, direct path between RTC and RTD, and connectivity in the event that one of the other links becomes unavailable.

Scenario 3: Running BGP on Transit Routers

Running BGP on all transit routers ensures that when traffic reaches any of these routers, it can be directed outside the AS. In Figure 8-2, if RTA and RTB were to run an IBGP full mesh with RTC and RTD, all traffic that reaches RTA or RTB would be able to intelligently determine the appropriate path out of the network. Although it is easiest to load full BGP routes on RTA and RTB, with more care you could also implement only partial routes and/or BGP defaults on RTA and RTB. Note that although AS1 might not be a transit AS, RTA and RTB are still used to carry traffic between border routers. Internal IGP-only routers will use the IBGP cloud to reach the outside world, as shown in Figure 8-2.

Scenario 4: Who Generates the Default, and How Is It Generated?

In this scenario, a loop can be avoided if the primary router generates the default into IGP while the secondary router does not. In this example, RTD would inject the 0/0 into the IGP, and RTC would not. All the traffic would follow the default toward RTD.

This solution works only in normal conditions and fails in backup situations. If the NY link fails, the IGP routers lose the 0/0 default. Because RTC is not generating any default, traffic to destinations outside the AS will fail.

The ideal situation is for RTC to inject the default into the IGP only when the NY link fails. If the NY link goes down, RTD should stop injecting the default into the IGP and RTC should start injecting the default into the IGP. For this mechanism to take place, the routers must engage in the following behaviors:

- **A BGP router should stop injecting the default into the IGP if the router's external link fails**—This is easily achieved if the IGP allows redistribution of the external default 0/0 into the IGP. Whenever the external 0/0 ceases to exist, the IGP default disappears with it. The availability and behavior of redistribution depends on what IGP you are running and on the particular vendor implementation. Cisco's method of redistribution could differ from that of other vendors.
- **A BGP router should inject the default into the IGP only if the default will use the locally attached external link**—This mandates that any router should stop generating a default route if the default it prefers comes from inside rather than outside the AS. The reason is that when the secondary router prefers the default from inside the AS, this means that the primary link is still up and it should be used. However, when the primary link goes down, the secondary router will prefer the default from outside the AS and will inject the default into IGP. This situation is easier to explain and understand with an example.

TIP See the section "Following Defaults Inside an AS" in Chapter 12 on page 395.

The next two examples examine the difference between a RIP- and OSPF-generated default in a Cisco implementation.

RIP-Generated Default

In Figure 8-3, RTC and RTD can learn a 0/0 default or statically configure a 0/0 default toward their respective providers. Under normal conditions, RTD automatically (or via controlled redistribution) injects the 0/0 into RIP. RTC detects the presence of a default originating from RTD, causing RTC to stop generating a default. All traffic is directed toward RTD.

Figure 8-3 *Injecting the 0/0 Default into RIP*

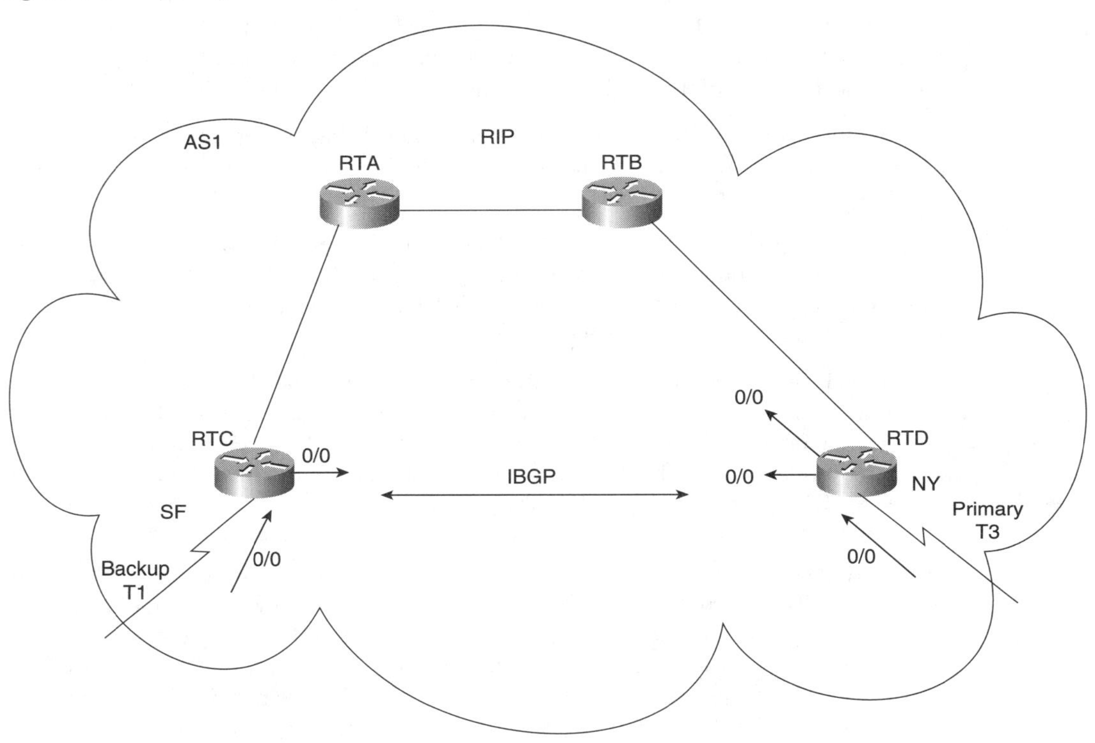

In case of a failure in the NY link, RTD stops generating the default into RIP. RTC detects the loss of 0/0 via RIP and injects its own default. Note that RTC receives the 0/0 default via EBGP (from the locally attached external network), RIP, and possibly IBGP if RTD is passing the 0/0 in the IBGP session. Because of the higher local preference via RTD, RTC prefers the 0/0 via IBGP. Because RTC's IBGP administrative distance is 200, higher than the RIP distance of 120 (see Table 6-1), the 0/0 default via RIP is preferred because it has the lowest administrative distance.

OSPF-Generated Default

OSPF behaves differently from RIP. The BGP 0/0 route cannot be passed into OSPF via redistribution. OSPF has different hooks to let the protocol generate the 0/0 into the OSPF at any time, or even better, if the presence of a 0/0-default route is detected in the IP routing table. Now apply this behavior to the example shown in Figure 8-4.

Figure 8-4 *Injecting the 0/0 default into OSPF*

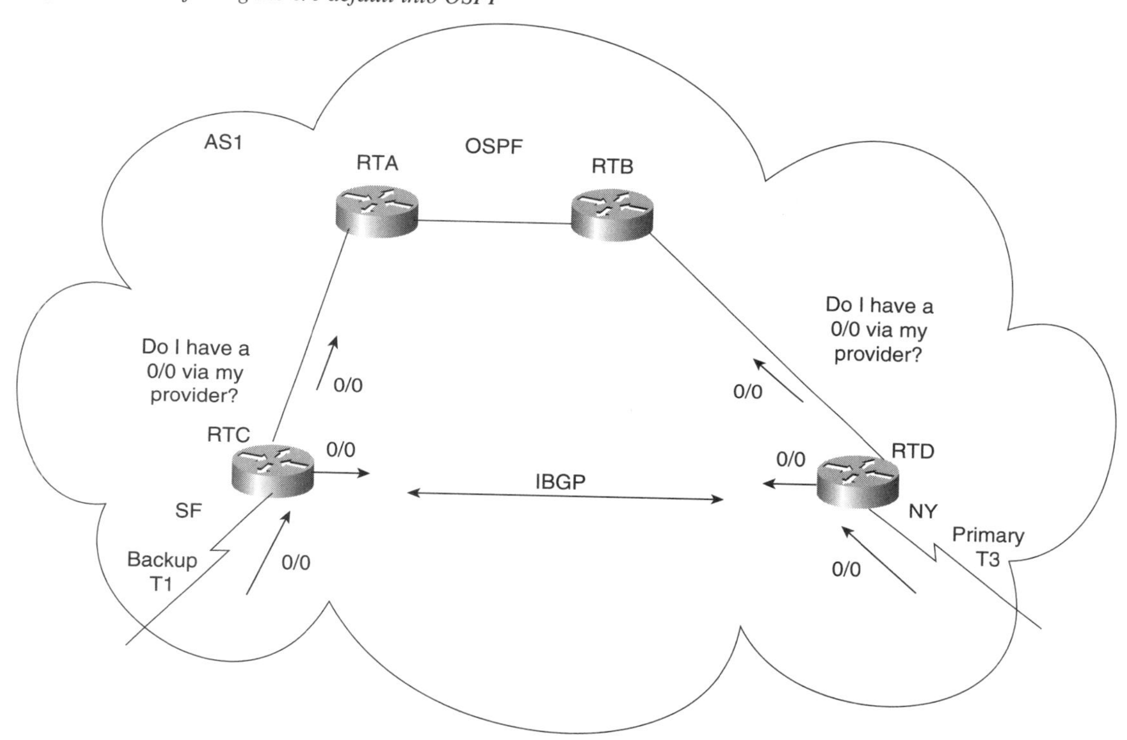

RTD and RTC receive the 0/0 route via EBGP or point a static default toward their respective providers. If RTD and RTC are configured such that the 0/0-default route is injected into OSPF as long as they themselves have a 0/0 route in their IP routing table, the primary/backup model will fail. The primary/backup model fails because both RTD and RTC are receiving the 0/0 route via IBGP from each other. RTC will always inject the 0/0 prefix into OSPF whether the NY link is up or down. In addition, unlike the RIP scenario, RTC will ignore the OSPF default coming from RTD because RTC is also configured to generate its own default route.

To remedy this situation, further configuration is needed to instruct the routers RTC and RTD to generate the 0/0 route into OSPF only if their own default points to their respective providers.

TIP See the section "Using OSPF as the IGP" in Chapter 12 on page 400.

In essence, if RTD chooses the default that points to its provider over all other defaults, RTD will inject the 0/0 route into OSPF. In the same manner, if RTC prefers the default that points to its provider, RTC will inject the 0/0 route into OSPF.

With this new model, the following will occur:

- In normal operation, the NY link is up.
- RTD prefers the external default to any other default and injects the 0/0 route into OSPF.
- RTC receives the 0/0 via EBGP (from its own provider), IBGP, and OSPF. It ignores the OSPF default, as mentioned earlier.
- RTC prefers the 0/0 coming from RTD via IBGP because of the higher local preference.
- Because the 0/0 is not learned via RTC's provider, RTC does not inject any default into OSPF.
- If the NY link goes down, RTD loses the 0/0 route from its provider and continues to receive a 0/0 route via IBGP and generates a 0/0 route into OSPF because the 0/0 route was not learned via RTD's provider.
- RTC stops receiving the 0/0 route via IBGP and prefers the 0/0 route via its provider. RTC then starts injecting the 0/0 route into OSPF.

Defaults Inside the AS: Other BGP Policies

As you have already seen, loop situations can occur at any time if the IGP defaults conflict with the BGP policies. In the primary/backup scenarios, you could control which border router should generate the default because you decided in advance which should be the primary router for all traffic external to the AS. In some situations, routing policies might be imposed on your AS by outside factors. In other cases, normal IBGP/EBGP routing makes the exit point from your ASs unspecified, which would conflict with your own defaults.

Consider Figure 8-5. AS1 is connected to its provider AS2 and learns full or partial routes in two locations—SF and NY. AS1 injects defaults from both its SF router RTC and its NY router RTD in such a way that internal locations will exit from the closest exit point.

Figure 8-5 *Policies Inflicted from Outside Sources*

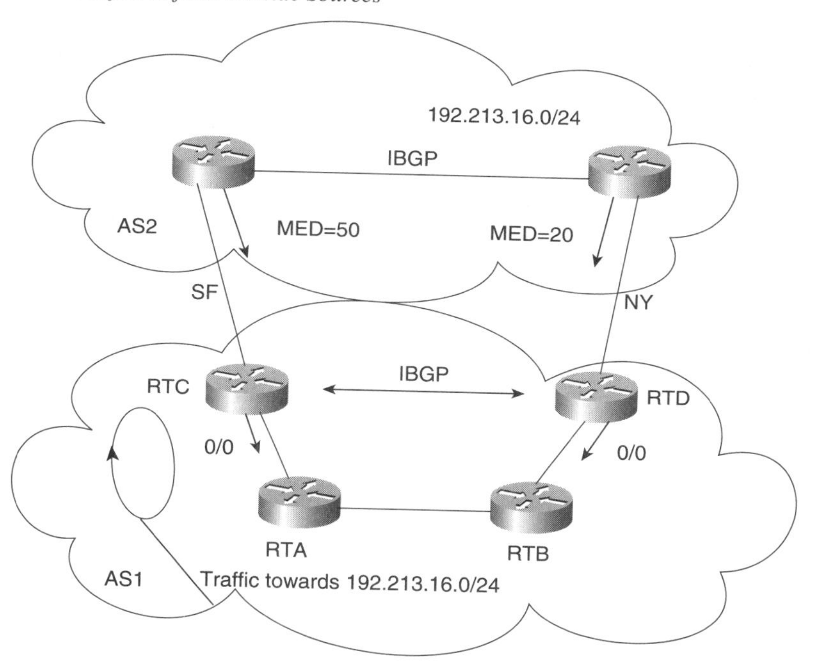

Assume also that AS1 is very careful about injecting defaults. The SF router will never inject a default if the SF link is down, and the NY router will never inject a default if the NY link is down. All is well and working great until provider AS2 starts advertising metrics (MED) toward AS1.

Assume in Figure 8-5 that AS2 is sending its updates toward AS1 with the internal IGP metrics as the MED values. AS1 receives the same networks on both the SF and NY links with different MED values. For each network, BGP follows the path with the lowest metric. If, for example, RTC receives network 192.213.16.0/24 with MED 50 on the SF link and MED 20 on the NY link, RTC will prefer the NY link. This would mean that to reach 192.213.16.0/24, RTA might follow the interior default toward RTC and then be instructed to instead go toward RTD. Similarly, RTB might follow a default toward RTD and then be directed toward RTC. In both cases, a loop will occur.

As you can see, the exit point for all networks cannot be predetermined as in the primary/backup case. To deal with this situation, you have the following options:

- Ignore the MED and base the routing on a primary/backup scenario.
- Have a shorter path connection between RTC and RTD so that traffic redirected between exit points follows the shortest path between the IBGP routers.
- Run an IBGP mesh between RTA, RTB, RTC, and RTD.

Other normal situations can also cause loops. You could end up in a looping situation whenever you have multiple links and you are running defaults inside the AS. If you are connected to two providers, you might prefer some destinations via one provider and others via the second provider. If your IGP is following defaults, you might end up at the wrong exit point with no way to go back.

As you can see by now, the solution to looping problems is to either have BGP and IGP be more deterministic about where to exit the AS or prevent traffic between IBGP routers from going back over IGP-only routers. The more you are aware of your traffic behavior, the better you can avoid loop situations.

Policy Routing

Policy routing is a means of controlling routes that rely on the source, or source and destination, of traffic rather than destination alone. Policy routing can be used to control traffic inside an AS as well as between ASs. Policy routing is a glorified form of static routing. It is used when you want to force a routing behavior different from what the dynamic routing protocols dictate.

Static routing lets you direct traffic based on the traffic destination. Traffic toward destination 1 can be transmitted via point A, and traffic toward destination 2 can be transmitted via point B.

Policy routing, on the other hand, lets you direct traffic based on traffic source or a combination of source and destination (or perhaps even other attributes) rather than standard destination-based routing. Traffic originating from network 1 can be transmitted via point A, or traffic originating from network 1 destined for network 2 can be transmitted via point B.

TIP See Example 12-6, "Policy Routing," on page 412.

The following sections examine policy routing based on traffic source and traffic source/ destination, as well as the other applications of policy routing.

Policy Routing Based on Traffic Source

Consider the example shown in Figure 8-6. Assume that AS1 was assigned network numbers from two different providers. The 10.10.10.0/24 range was taken from AS3, and the 11.11.11.0/24 range was taken from AS4. AS1 wants to have any traffic originated from its 10.10.10.0/24 networks to be directed toward AS3 and traffic from its 11.11.11.0/24 networks to be directed to AS4, irrespective of the traffic's final destination. AS1 could use policy routing to achieve this requirement by forcing all traffic with a source IP address belonging to 10.10.10.0/24 to have a next hop of 1.1.1.1 and traffic with a source IP belonging to 11.11.11.0/24 to have a next hop of 2.2.2.2.

Figure 8-6 *Policy Routing Scenario Based on Source*

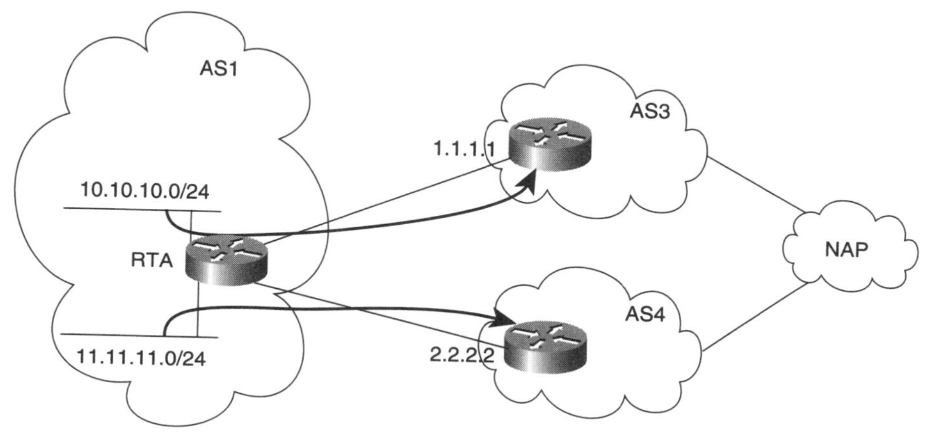

Policy Routing Based on Traffic Source/Destination

Policy routing can also be based on a source/destination combination, as illustrated in Figure 8-7.

Figure 8-7 *Policy Routing Scenario Based on Source and Destination*

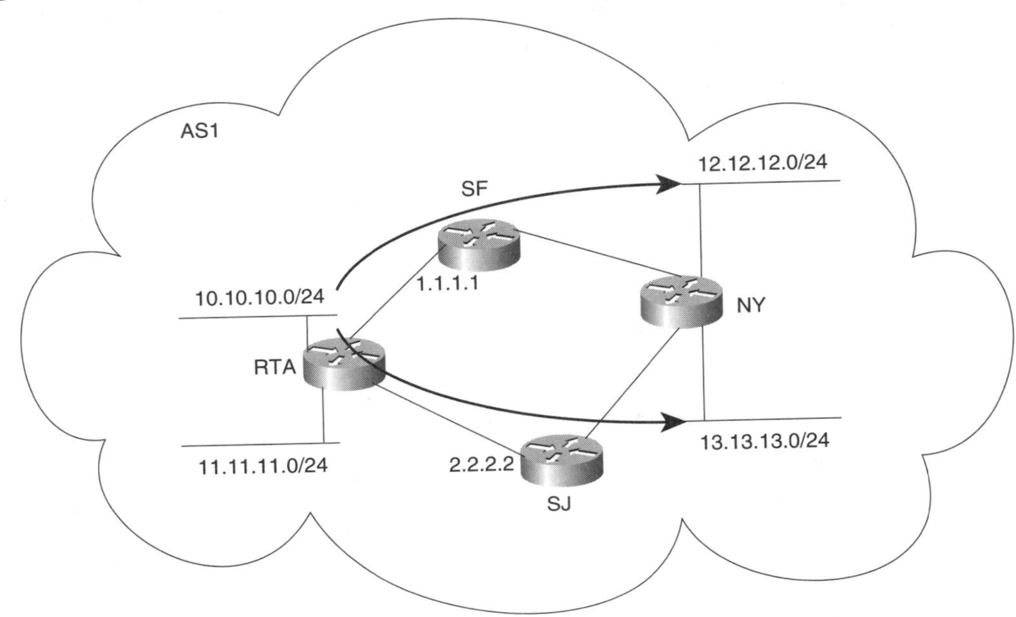

Assume that RTA wants to use the SF link for any traffic originating from network 10.10.10.0/24 and reaching network 12.12.12.0/24 in NY. Also, RTA wants to use the SJ link for any traffic originating from network 10.10.10.0/24 and reaching network 13.13.13.0/24 in NY. Policy routing can be used to set the next hop for the traffic combination (source = 10.10.10.0/24, destination = 12.12.12.0/24) to be 1.1.1.1. The traffic combination (source = 10.10.10.0/24, destination = 13.13.13.0/24) will trigger the next hop to be set to 2.2.2.2.

Policy Routing Defaults to Dynamic Routing

Whenever static behavior is enforced, backup becomes an issue. It is important to make sure that if policy-routed traffic cannot be delivered because the next hop is down, some other alternative is available. Cisco offers a creative way of executing policy routing by offering multiple next hops for policy-routed traffic. If the first next hop is down or unavailable, the second next hop is tried, and so on. If none of the statically defined next hops are available, the router can be configured to send traffic according to the normal dynamic routing (that is, based on destination), as illustrated in Figure 8-8.

Figure 8-8 *Policy Routing Defaults to Dynamic Routing*

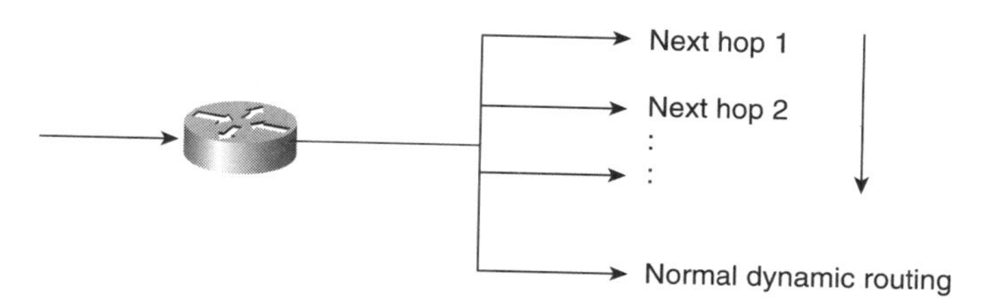

Other Applications of Policy Routing

One practical application of policy routing is its use with firewalls. *Firewalls* are devices that apply security requirements to traffic. Firewall implementations include packet filtering, authentication, and encryption. Depending on the network setup, administrators might want to direct some or all incoming (or outgoing) traffic toward a firewall device, as shown in Figure 8-9.

Figure 8-9 *Incoming or Outgoing Traffic Can Be Routed to a Firewall*

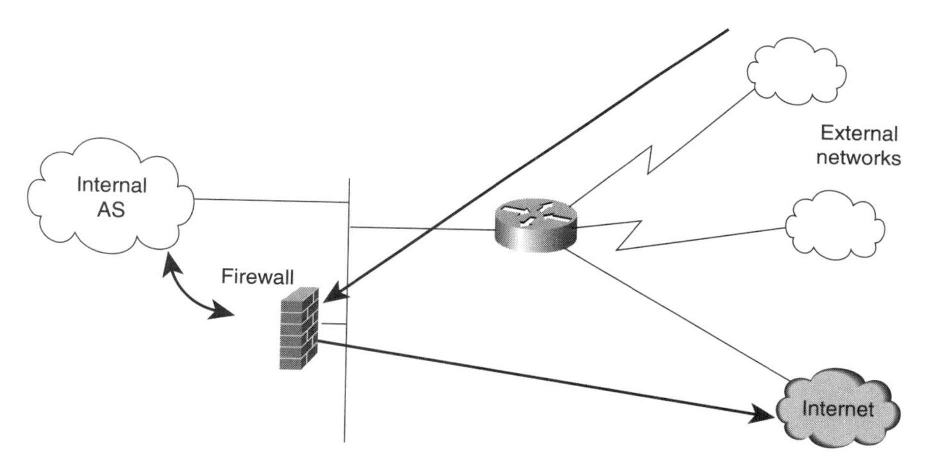

An applicable situation might involve traffic entering an organization through dialup services. Perhaps the organization requires that the dialup users from remote sites pass through a firewall before reaching the Internet. If the firewall is in the traffic trajectory, this is not a problem. Any inbound or outbound traffic will pass through the firewall on its way to a destination. In some cases, however (such as that shown in Figure 8-9), traffic bypasses the firewall in its normal path. Policy routing can be configured on a router bordering external networks to force the incoming dialup traffic to be directed to the firewall. After the firewall applies its policies or encryption, dialup traffic is sent to its final destination.

NOTE Policy routing does not change the traffic destination. It affects only the next hop to which traffic is directed prior to being sent toward its ultimate destination.

Policy routing can also be used with dialup services for better traffic balancing, as shown in Figure 8-10.

Figure 8-10 *Balancing Dialup Traffic Based on Source*

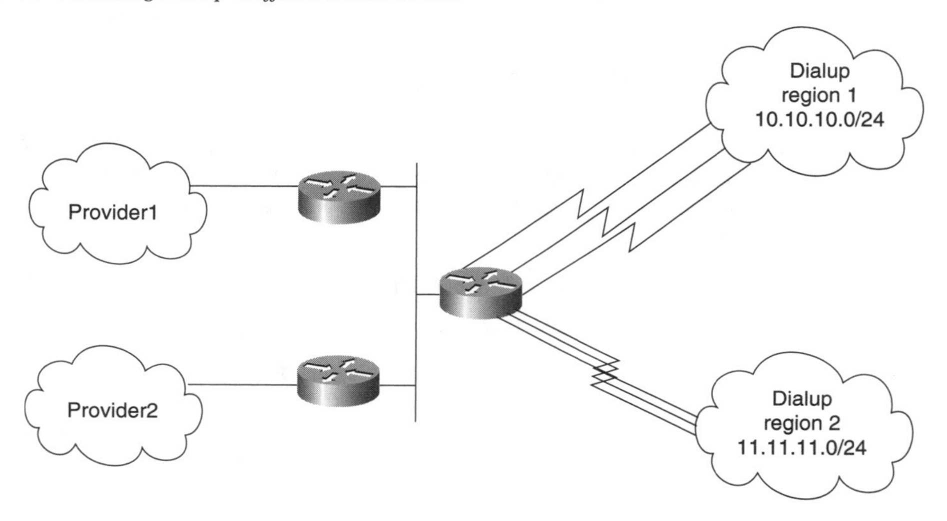

Dialup users accessing a certain point of presence can be directed toward certain providers based on their source IP address. As illustrated in Figure 8-10, dialup users in region 1 can be directed toward Provider1, whereas dialup users from region 2 can be directed toward Provider2.

Policy routing should not replace dynamic routing, but instead should complement it. Policy routing has its own set of drawbacks:

- Extra static configuration is needed to identify sources of traffic or a combination of source and destination. Care should be taken not to disrupt other traffic and to specify other alternatives for traffic in case of backup situations.
- Policy routing is CPU-intensive because it is based on the source IP addresses, unlike dynamic and static routing, which are based on the destination IP addresses. Sophisticated caching and switching techniques have been implemented all along based on the traffic's destination. Most implementations have not yet optimized routing and caching techniques based on the source of the IP packet. As such, policy

routing takes additional CPU cycles to detect source addresses. This behavior should change as implementations attain a better understanding of IP traffic flows that let caches keep track of source and destination information. This new caching methodology would alleviate routers from disruptive processing on matching sources of IP traffic and make policy routing much more effective and practical.

Looking Ahead

Autonomous systems can grow in size beyond the control of administrators. Service providers might find themselves with a large internal BGP mesh that is both cumbersome and inefficient to control. On the other hand, enterprise networks might grow in a manner that causes internal gateway protocols to struggle in keeping up with instabilities. Controlling large-scale autonomous systems lies in the art of dividing these large domains into smaller, more manageable entities. The following chapter offers concepts and techniques that can help providers and customers apply architectural designs to achieve structured routing inside their domains.

Frequently Asked Questions

Q — *I am not running IBGP between my border routers. Do I need to worry about routing loops?*

A — As far as the interaction between IGP and BGP, loops cannot occur. If your internal routers are following a default toward the BGP border routers, after the traffic reaches the border router, it has only one way out via the EBGP session.

Q — *I have two BGP border routers running IBGP and connected via a serial link. I am using local preference to control my exit points. What happens if the serial line goes down?*

A — If you are setting BGP policies that cause traffic to be directed between BGP border routers, this would be the same scenario as if you did not have a link between the border routers. While the serial line is down, your traffic might end up looping inside the AS.

Q — *If I use a serial link between my IBGP border routers to direct traffic from one router to the other, should that link be as fast as my links to my providers?*

A — The only traffic that line will carry is outbound traffic that is redirected between border routers and a portion of incoming traffic. Try to figure out what percentage of your total traffic that constitutes to estimate the appropriate link bandwidth.

Q — *I need to direct traffic toward destination X over my serial line and toward destination Y over my Ethernet line. Can I do that via policy routing?*

A — What you have just described can be done via static routing, which works based on destination. There is no need for policy routing, which works based on source or source and destination combined.

Q — *Do I apply policy routing over my outbound or inbound router interface?*

A — Policy routing checks source addresses coming into an interface. Configure on the inbound interface.

This chapter covers the following key topics:

- **Route reflectors**—A method of managing expanding mesh requirements in large autonomous systems (ASs) by using selected routers as focal points for internal BGP sessions.
- **Confederations**—A method of managing expanding mesh requirements in large ASs by creating sub-ASs.
- **Controlling IGP expansion**—Methods of managing networks in which expansion is characterized by the use of multiple IGPs.
- **Virtual private networks with route reflectors**—A method of developing restricted network access within an AS using route reflectors.

CHAPTER 9

Controlling Large-Scale Autonomous Systems

Autonomous systems consisting of hundreds of routing nodes can pose a serious routing management problem to network administrators. Service providers and customers each have their own set of problems when dealing with large networks. On the service provider side, the majority of routers run Border Gateway Protocol (BGP). Because of the BGP rule that states that one Interior Border Gateway Protocol (IBGP) speaker can't advertise a route learned from another IBGP speaker to a third IBGP speaker, the IBGP mesh can quickly grow beyond the provider's control. On the customer side, however, the majority of routers run Interior Gateway Protocols (IGPs), which also might grow beyond the customer's control.

This chapter discusses methods and techniques that can be used to better control the deployment of BGP and IGPs inside large autonomous systems. There are no absolute rules that say a provider or customer should or should not use one of the methods discussed in this chapter, or which method is best. Keep in mind that any new technique brings with it its own complexities. Imposing complex techniques on situations that do not really need them could hurt more than help, but in contrast, planning ahead can save you a considerable number of headaches down the road.

Route Reflectors

In some Internet service provider (ISP) networks, the internal BGP mesh can become quite large (more than 100 internal BGP sessions per router), which strongly suggests that some new peering mechanism be implemented. The *route reflector*[1] concept is based on the idea of specifying a *concentration* router to act as a focal point for internal BGP sessions. Multiple (client) BGP routers can peer with a central server (the route reflector), and then route reflectors peer with one another. Although the BGP rule states that routes learned via one IBGP speaker can't be advertised to another IBGP speaker, route reflection allows the route reflector servers to "reflect" routes as described later, thereby relaxing the IBGP full-mesh constraints.

Route reflectors are recommended only for ASs that have a large internal BGP mesh. The route reflector concept introduces processing overhead on the route reflector server and, if configured incorrectly, might introduce routing loops and routing instability. As a result, route reflectors are not recommended for every topology.

That said, route reflection does introduce some advantages on both the route reflector servers and their clients. For example, a route reflector server implementation could be optimized to simply copy UPDATE messages when sending to multiple peers, rather than generating unique messages per peer. In addition, the clients normally peer with only the local route reflector server, thereby significantly decreasing the number of sessions they're required to maintain.

TIP See the section "Route Reflectors" in Chapter 12 on page 415.

Internal Peers Without Route Reflectors

Without route reflectors, BGP speakers in an AS will have a logical full mesh. We discussed this behavior earlier in this book; the following illustration is just a reminder. In Figure 9-1, RTA, RTB, and RTC form an internal BGP logical full mesh. Each router acts as a BGP peer with the other two routers. RTA and RTB are physically connected, as are RTB and RTC. No physical connection exists between RTA and RTC.

Figure 9-1 *Internal Peers in a Normal Full-Mesh Environment*

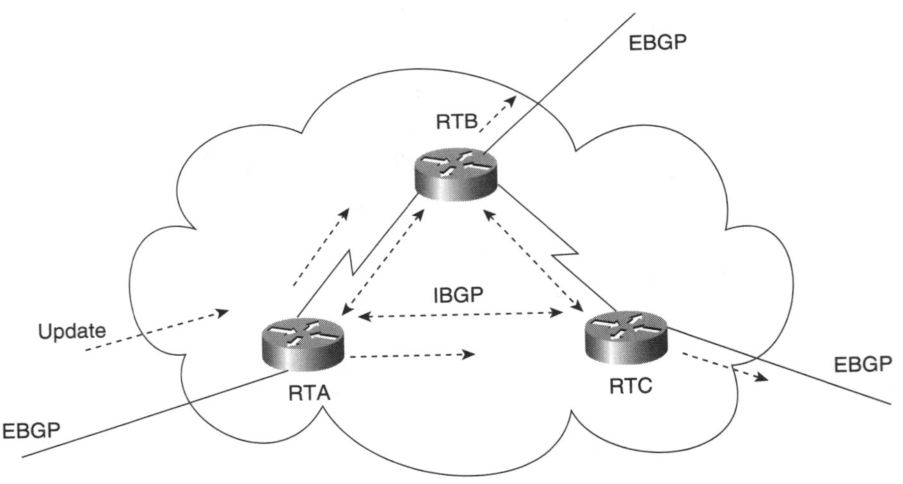

When RTA receives an update from an external peer, it forwards the update to its two internal peers, RTB and RTC. Note that although there is no physical connectivity between RTA and RTC, RTA manages to pass the update to RTC via the BGP peering session. RTB and RTC, in turn, pass the update to their external peers.

The UPDATE message that RTB receives from RTA is not readvertised to RTC because RTC is an internal peer, and the UPDATE message RTB received was from an internal peer (RTA). Without the internal BGP session between RTA and RTC, RTC would never get the update; hence, the full IBGP mesh is required.

Internal Peers with Route Reflectors

The route reflector acts as a concentration point for other routers referred to as *clients*. The clients peer with the route reflector and exchange routing information with it. In turn, the route reflector passes (or reflects) the information between clients and to other IBGP and Exterior Border Gateway Protocol (EBGP) peers.

In Figure 9-2, RTB is configured as a route reflector with two clients, RTA and RTC. RTA gets an update from an external peer and forwards it to RTB. RTB reflects the update from client RTA to client RTC. In this configuration, a peering session between RTA and RTC should not be configured, because the route reflector is propagating the BGP information from RTA to RTC.

Figure 9-2 *Internal Peers Using a Route Reflector*

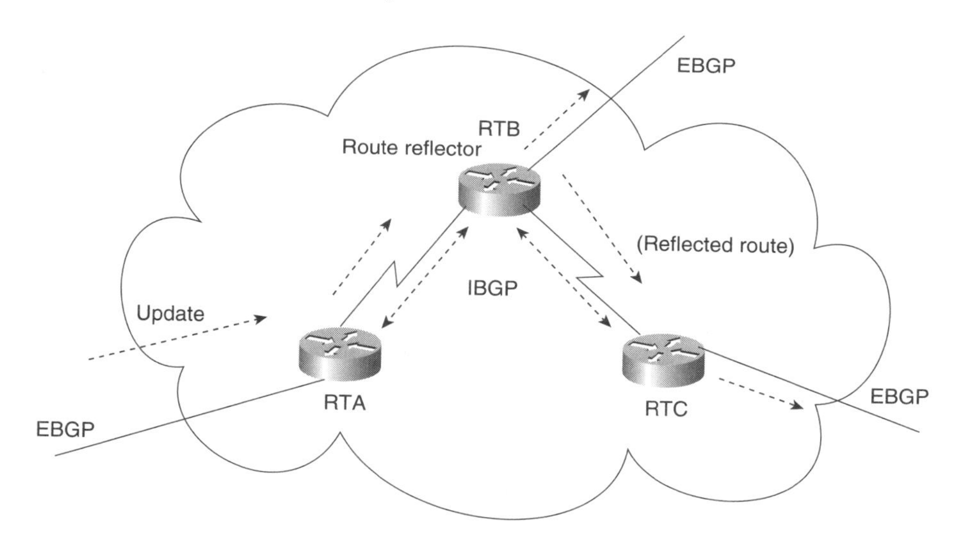

In an AS where the administrator would have to build a substantial number of BGP sessions between routers, the route reflector concept provides a very helpful and scalable solution to the problem.

Naming Conventions and Rules of Operation

The route reflector is a router that performs the route reflection function. The IBGP peers of the route reflector fall under two categories—*clients* and *nonclients*. A route reflector and its clients form a *cluster*. All peers of the route reflector that are not part of the cluster are nonclients. Figure 9-3 illustrates these components.

Figure 9-3 *Route Reflection Process Components*

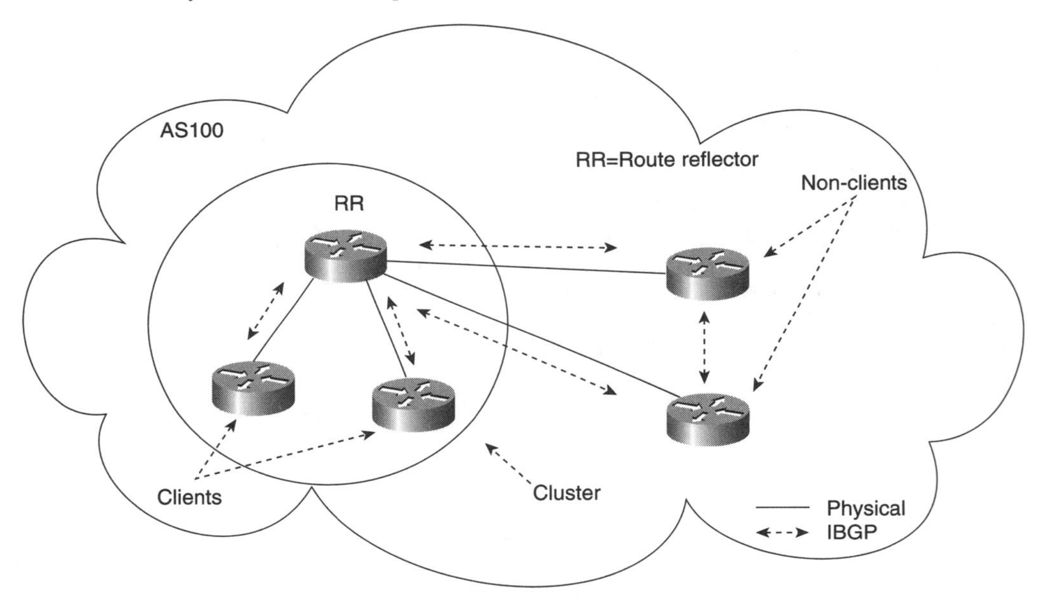

Nonclients (standard IBGP speakers) are still required to be fully meshed with one another and the route reflector because they follow the normal IBGP advertisement rules, although they no longer need to peer with the clients of the route reflectors. Clients should not peer with internal speakers outside their associated cluster. As you can see, these conditions have been met for the clients and nonclients in Figure 9-3.

The route reflector function is implemented only on the route reflector; all clients and nonclients are normal BGP peers that have no notion of the route reflector. Route reflector clients are considered as such only because the route reflector lists them as clients.

Any route reflector that receives multiple routes for the same destination employs the usual BGP decision process to pick the overall best path. The best path would be propagated inside the AS based on the following rules of operation:

- If the route is received from a nonclient peer, reflect to clients only.
- If the route is received from a client peer, reflect to all nonclient peers and also to client peers.
- If the route is received from an EBGP peer, reflect to all client and nonclient peers.

Because route reflection is a concept that applies only internally to an AS, routers external to the AS, which would receive UPDATEs via EBGP, are considered nonclients and follow normal nonclient behavior with respect to sending and receiving UPDATEs.

Redundancy Issues and Multiple Route Reflectors in an AS

With the lack of a full BGP mesh inside the AS, redundancy and reliability become issues. If a route reflector fails, clients will be isolated. Redundancy requires the existence of multiple route reflectors in a cluster where clients can simultaneously peer with multiple routers. If one route reflector fails, the other(s) should still be available.

The importance of complementing logical redundancy with physical redundancy cannot be overstated. It does not make sense to build route reflector redundancy if the physical redundancy itself does not exist. The logical redundancy arrangement on the left in Figure 9-4 shows RTA as the client of both RR1 and RR2. (RR stands for route reflector in this figure and those that follow.) RTA is peering with both route reflectors in an effort to create a redundant link. Unfortunately, if the connection to RR1 is broken, or if RR1 itself fails, RTA is isolated. The logical connectivity between RTA and RR2 is of no practical use; it is simply more memory and processing overhead.

Figure 9-4 *Comparison of Logical and Physical Redundancy Solutions*

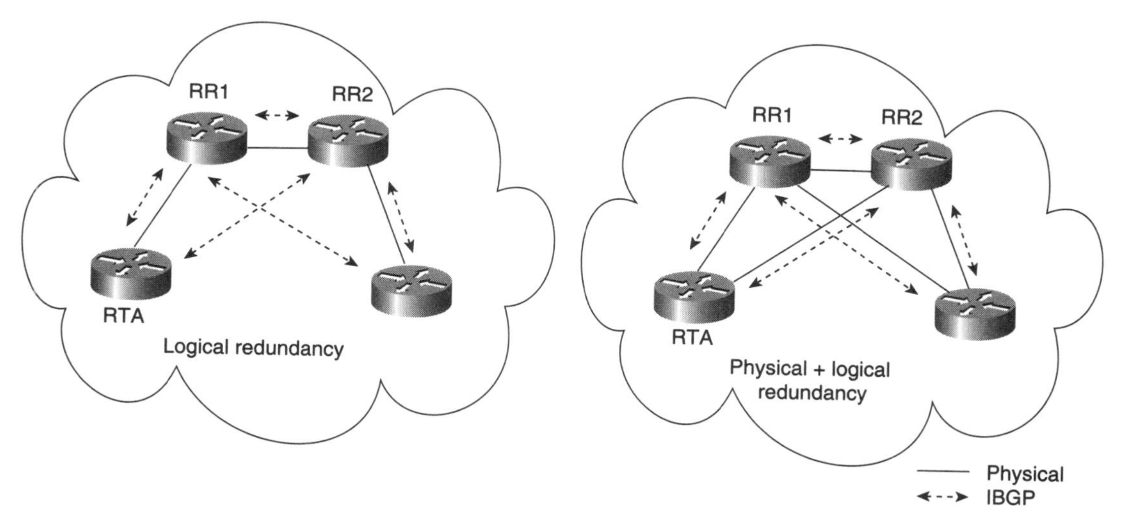

The physical redundancy configuration on the right in Figure 9-4 illustrates how logical redundancy can be backed up with physical redundancy. In the event of a failure in the link to RR1, RTA can reach RR2.

Route Reflection Topology Models

National networks are usually laid out in concentration points across geographical regions. Providers have points of presence (POPs), sometimes called *hubs*, in different regions in the U.S. with high-speed links connecting different locations in a partial-mesh topology. The route reflector concept can be used to logically interconnect the routers running BGP in a pattern that follows the physical topology. Figure 9-5 illustrates a complex arrangement featuring route reflectors.

Figure 9-5 *Complex Multiple Route Reflector Environment*

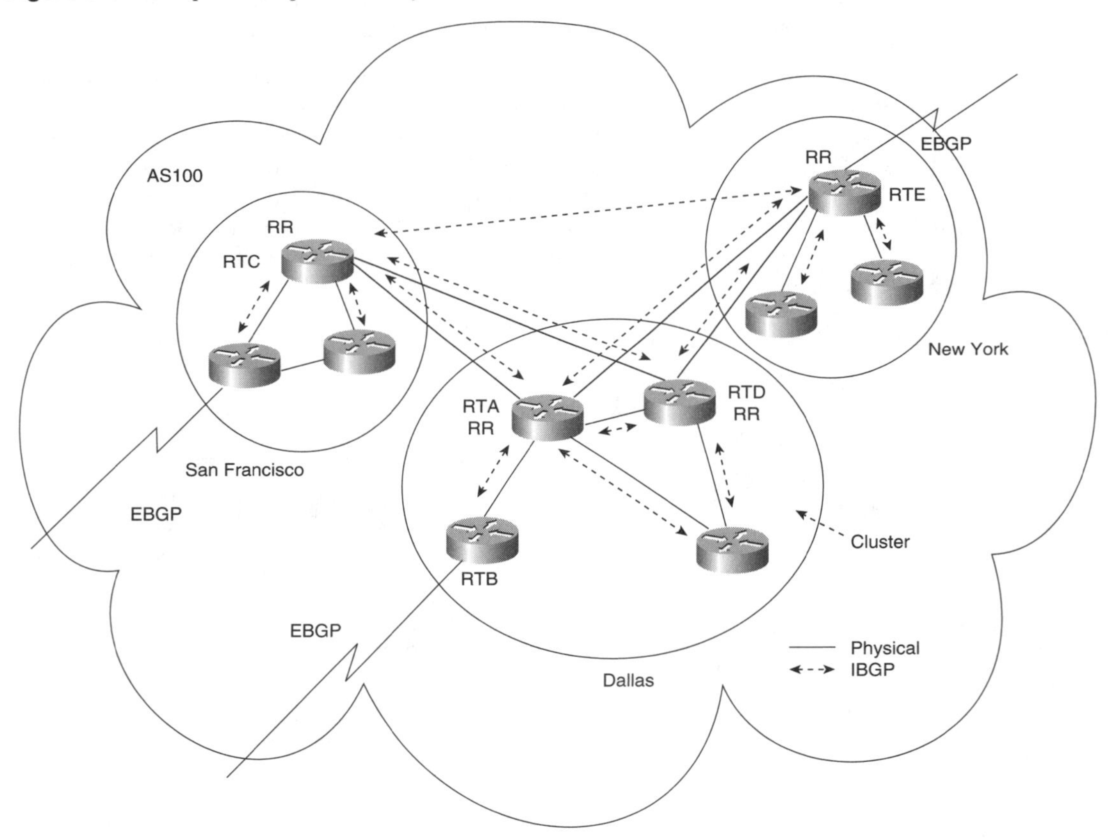

Except for the fact that the route reflector needs to keep up with more IBGP sessions than client routers, any router could be configured as a route reflector. Your physical topology should be the main indicator of which router would be the best route reflector. Also, because the clients aren't required to peer with lots of other IBGP routers, more resources are available for handling EBGP connections.

In Figure 9-5, AS100 is divided into three clusters: San Francisco, Dallas, and New York. The Dallas cluster has multiple RRs for redundancy. RTA and RTD physically connect San Francisco to New York. It makes sense to follow the actual physical traffic flow in selecting RRs, so RTA and RTD are the obvious choices for RRs in the Dallas cluster.

In San Francisco, router RTC physically connects San Francisco to Dallas, so RTC would be the best candidate to become a RR. The same reasoning applies for the New York cluster: RTE physically connects New York to Dallas and is the best candidate for a RR.

The Route Reflector Preserves IBGP Attributes

The route reflector concept does not change IBGP behavior—the route reflector is not allowed to modify the attributes of the reflected IBGP routes. The NEXT_HOP attribute, for example, remains the same when an IBGP route is exchanged between RRs. This is necessary to avoid loops inside the AS.

Figure 9-6 illustrates why the RR should not modify the attributes of the reflected IBGP routes. The NEXT_HOP attribute is used as an example. Figure 9-6 focuses on the portion of the network where Dallas connects to San Francisco.

Figure 9-6 *The Route Reflector Preserves IBGP Attributes*

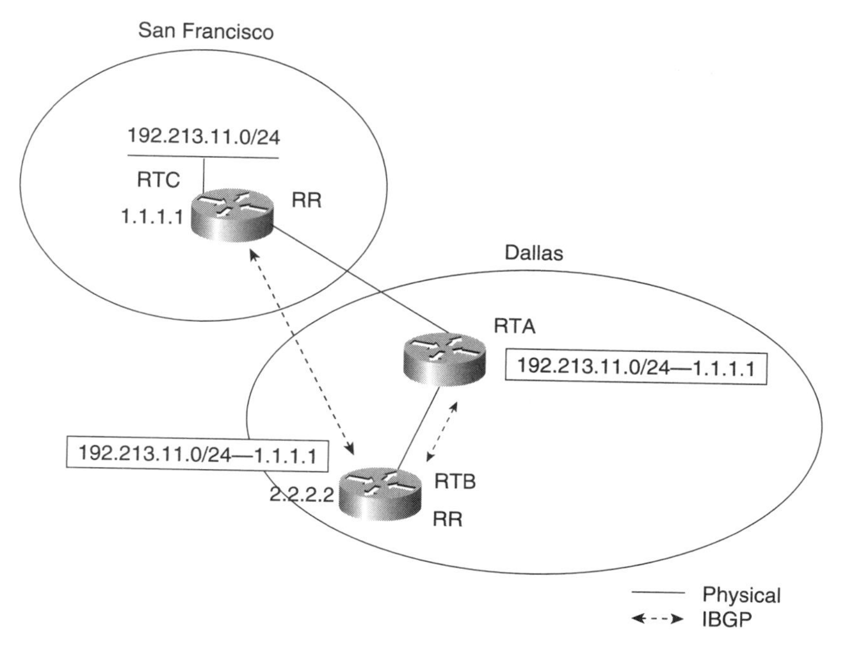

Although the route reflection rules state that a route reflector should not modify any of the attributes, many implementations do permit this and/or filtering to occur. In practice, use care if you must perform actions of this nature.

Assume that RTB rather than RTA is specified as the route reflector and that an IBGP session is configured between RTB (2.2.2.2) and RTC (1.1.1.1). This looks odd, because RTA is physically passing the traffic, while logically RTB is reflecting the BGP routes between RTA and RTC. RTB will receive the prefix 192.213.11.0/24 from its IBGP neighbor RTC with a next hop of 1.1.1.1. RTB will reflect the route to its client RTA with the next hop 1.1.1.1 also. This is the standard, desired behavior for route reflection.

On the other hand, if RTB were to change the next hop to its IP address, 2.2.2.2, RTA would try to use RTB to reach destination 192.213.11.0/24. A loop would occur between RTA and RTB, because RTA will use the next hop of RTB. The result is that RTA will forward traffic to RTB. Subsequently, RTB will forward the traffic back to RTA to reach the final destination. This hypothetical situation exemplifies why the route reflector must not change IBGP attributes.

It is worth mentioning again that route reflectors propagate only the best route to a given destination. In other words, if a route reflector learns the same prefix from multiple client peers, only one path will be propagated to other peers. Therefore, when route reflectors are used, the number of paths available to reach a given destination will likely be lower than that of a full-mesh configuration. Due to this behavior, it is again advised that route reflector topologies resemble that of the physical topology, or the potential for suboptimal routing might occur.

Avoiding Loops

BGP relies on the information in the AS path to facilitate loop detection. A BGP update that attempts to reenter the AS it was originated from will be dropped by the border router of the source AS.

With the introduction of route reflectors, there is a potential for routing loops within an AS. A routing update that leaves a cluster may reenter the cluster. Loops inside the AS cannot be detected by the traditional AS path approach because routing updates do not have an originating AS path signature. Therefore, when route reflectors are deployed, BGP offers two extra measures for loop avoidance inside the AS—using an ORIGINATOR_ID and using a CLUSTER_LIST.

Using an ORIGINATOR_ID

The *ORIGINATOR_ID* is a 4-byte, optional, nontransitive BGP attribute (type code 9). This attribute carries the ROUTER_ID of the route's originator in the local AS and is to be added to the UPDATE message by the route reflector. If the update comes back to the originator because of poor configuration, the originator should discard it.

The CLUSTER_LIST

The *CLUSTER_LIST* is an optional, nontransitive BGP attribute (type code 10). Each cluster is represented with a CLUSTER_ID.

A CLUSTER_LIST is a sequence of CLUSTER_IDs that contain path information regarding the list of clusters that an UPDATE has traversed. When a route reflector sends a route from its clients to nonclients outside the cluster, it appends the local CLUSTER_ID to the CLUSTER_LIST, or creates the list if one is not present. If the route reflector receives an UPDATE whose CLUSTER_LIST contains the local CLUSTER_ID value, the UPDATE message should be discarded. Thus, the CLUSTER_LIST provides loop avoidance inside an AS, whereas the AS_PATH list, discussed earlier, facilitates loop avoidance for UPDATEs traversing multiple, external ASs.

See the configuration guidelines in the section "Route Reflectors" in Chapter 12.

Route Reflectors and Peer Groups

Recall from Chapter 6, "Tuning BGP Capabilities," that a peer group is a group of BGP neighbors that share similar routing policies. Previously, route reflectors could be used only in conjunction with peer groups when all route reflector clients within a cluster were fully meshed. The reason can best be described through the following example. In a typical route reflection situation, Router A learns a prefix from Router B. Subsequently, Router A sends an UPDATE message containing WITHDRAWN ROUTES information back to Router B to poison that route. In other words, Router A informs Router B that this prefix is unreachable via A. This prevents a route loop situation in which A claims that a prefix is reachable via B, and B claims it is reachable via A.

In a peer group, the same UPDATE message (with subsequent WITHDRAWN ROUTES information) is sent to all members of the group. In a peer group/route reflector situation, a route reflector that learns a prefix from one of the clients and attempts to poison that route ends up withdrawing that prefix from all the other clients. Because the clients are not talking to one another via BGP, that prefix is lost. Therefore, an IBGP mesh between the clients of a route reflector is necessary so that other clients will learn the prefix directly from the originator. Even with this design, the network administrator avoids building a full IBGP mesh between all IBGP routers in the AS by concentrating the mesh between route reflectors and clients (versus between clients within a cluster).

Fortunately, IOS has removed the full-mesh requirement on route reflector clients. Currently, clients of a route reflector configured under a peer group are not required to be fully meshed.

With the use of peer groups, the AS design would look like rings of fully meshed BGP speakers. Route reflectors are fully meshed among each other, and clients are only required to peer with the route reflectors. Figure 9-7 illustrates such an environment; each circled area represents a distinct peer group and route reflector cluster. In contrast, Figure 9-8 demonstrates what would be required without the use of route reflectors.

Figure 9-7 *Typical BGP Route Reflection Topology*

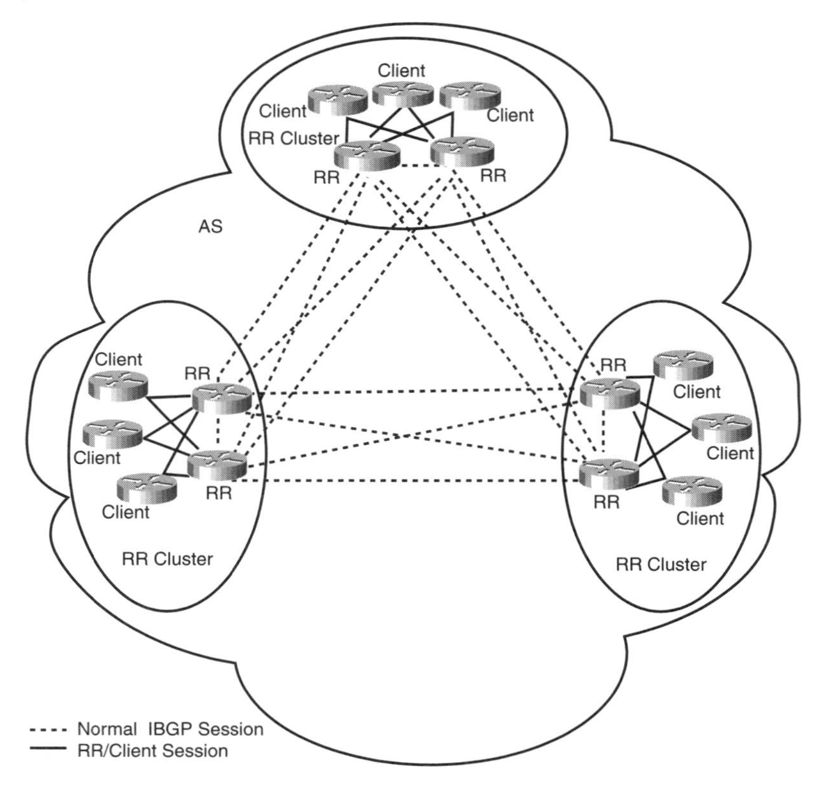

Figure 9-8 *Full-Mesh BGP Topology*

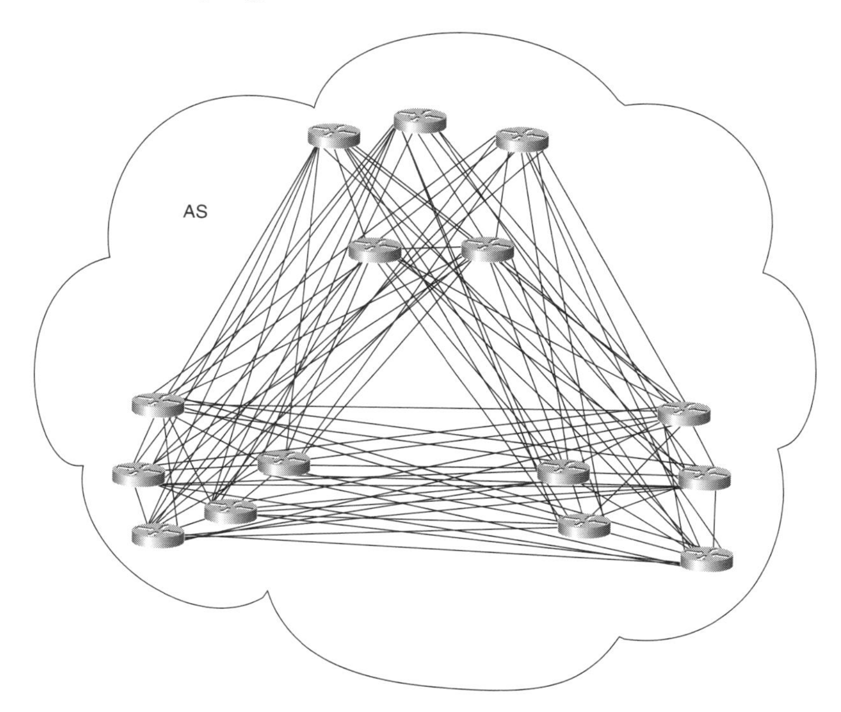

In conclusion, the route reflector concept is growing in popularity for large networks because it is both a simple and a scalable approach that does not require substantial overhead. Furthermore, migrating from a nonroute reflector to a route reflector design is easy. Only those routers intended to be route reflectors need to be modified; all other routers operate as usual. In addition, routers that do not implement the route reflector behavior, such as clients or nonclients, could be part of the AS with no loss of BGP routing information.

Confederations

A *confederation*[2] is another way to deal with the explosion of an IBGP mesh within an AS. As with route reflection, confederations are recommended only for cases in which IBGP peering involves a large number of IBGP peering sessions per router.

TIP See the section "Confederations" in Chapter 12 on page 419.

BGP confederations are based on the concept that an AS can be broken into multiple sub-ASs. Inside each sub-AS, all the rules of IBGP apply. All BGP routers inside the sub-AS, for example, must be fully meshed. Because each sub-AS has a different AS number, external BGP must run between them. Although EBGP is used between sub-ASs, routing inside the confederation behaves like IBGP routing in a single AS. In other words, the next hop, MED, and local preference information is preserved when crossing the sub-AS boundaries. To the outside world, a confederation looks like a single AS. Figure 9-9 shows an example of a confederation.

Figure 9-9 *Sample Confederation of Sub-AS Constructs*

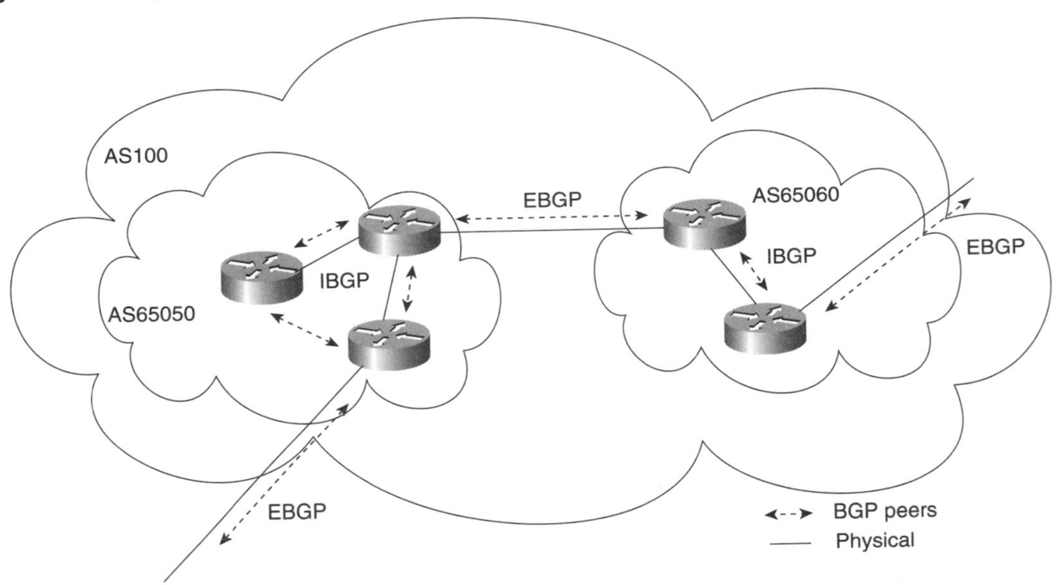

In Figure 9-9, AS100 is split into two sub-ASs: AS65050 and AS65060. The AS, as a whole, is now one large confederation, identified by a single confederation number, 100. All the sub-ASs are shielded from the outside world and can be given any AS numbers. The numbers could be chosen from the private AS range (64512 to 65534, as designated in RFC 1930[3]) in order not to use up any formal AS numbers.

As mentioned previously, inside the sub-AS an IBGP full mesh is used. EBGP is used between the sub-ASs as well as between the confederation itself and outside ASs. Confederations can easily detect routing loops inside the whole AS because EBGP is run between sub-ASs. The AS path list is a loop-avoidance mechanism used to detect routing updates leaving one sub-AS and attempting to reenter the same sub-AS. A routing update that tries to reenter a sub-AS it originated from will be detected because the sub-AS will see its own sub-AS number listed in the update's AS path.

Confederation Drawbacks

The drawback of confederations is that migration from a nonconfederation to a confederation design requires major reconfiguration of the routers and a major change in the logical topology. In addition, routing through a confederation might not take an optimal path without manually setting BGP policies. Figure 9-10 illustrates this issue.

Figure 9-10 *AS Confederation Internal and External Routing*

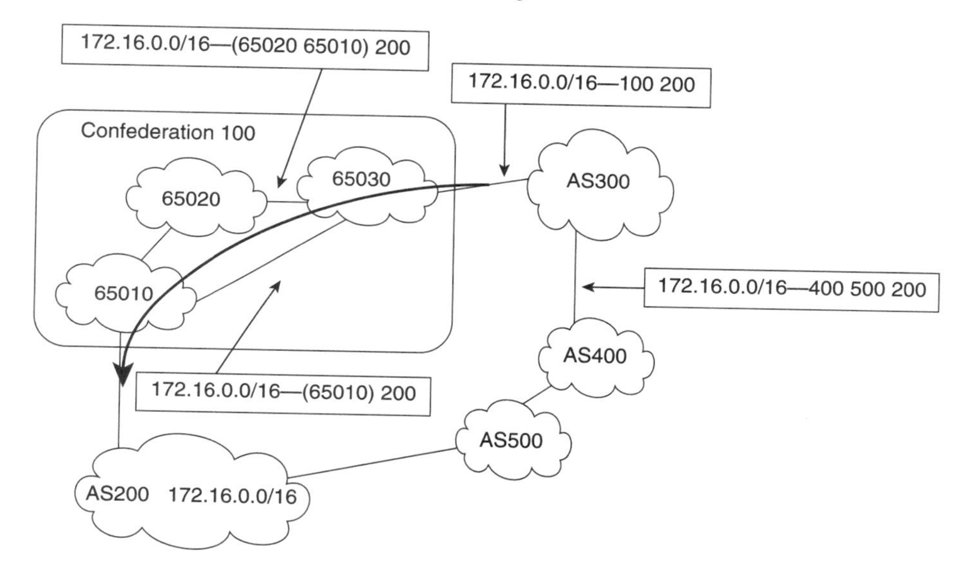

Confederation 100 is composed of three sub-ASs: 65010, 65020, and 65030. The AS path within confederation 100 is represented by the sequence of ASs and sub-ASs the route has traversed. In standard BGP, the shortest AS path determines the best path traffic will pass through. However, in a confederation, sub-ASs do not influence the overall AS path length. For instance, one prefix composed of two equal-length AS paths that each have different-length sub-AS paths could introduce suboptimal routing inside the AS because it is unclear which is the better path. From the point of view of sub-AS 65030, AS path (65010) is the same length as AS path (65020 65010); traffic inside the confederation may take either path. Additional policies would have to be set to affect routing behavior appropriately. For example, the local preference can be configured to make the AS path (65010) preferred over (65020 65010).

Because the confederation is a single AS, the path taken by external ASs through a confederation is unknown. This is misleading for ASs that base their routing policies on the AS path length. To reach AS200, AS300 will most likely prefer to go via confederation 100 because the path looks shorter than the path through AS400 and AS500. In actuality, of course, confederation 100 is not the shortest path because it includes a path via three sub-ASs (65030 65020 65010), whereas the alternative (AS400 AS500) includes only two. AS300 will never know of this pitfall unless the AS100 confederation design is disclosed.

Route Exchange and BGP Decisions with Confederations

Even though routes are exchanged between sub-ASs of a confederation via EBGP, all the IBGP rules still apply in order for the whole AS to still behave as a single routing domain. The EBGP NEXT_HOP is still carried within the AS, as is the MED and LOCAL_PREF values.

As far as the BGP decision algorithm, the only changes are in the way BGP routes to outside the confederation compared to how BGP routes inside the confederation. Without confederations, EBGP routes are preferred over IBGP routes. With confederations, we have introduced a new type of EBGP route between the sub-ASs—a confederation external route. BGP prefers routes in the following manner:

> EBGP routes to outside the confederation > confederation exterior routes > IBGP routes

Therefore, if BGP has a choice between two paths to the same destination—one leading outside the confederation and one leading inside the whole confederation—BGP will pick the exterior path. Furthermore, if BGP has a choice between two paths to the same destination—one inside the sub-AS and one outside the sub-AS—BGP will pick the exterior path leading out of the sub-AS. This is, of course, assuming that all other attributes are the same.

Recommended Confederation Design

Choosing and connecting the sub-ASs randomly inside the confederation will lead to problems. Unnecessary processing might occur because each sub-AS can end up getting similar information from other sub-ASs via a single path. Besides, suboptimality will be introduced because all paths inside the AS have exactly the same length, as already discussed.

Experience has proven that a centralized confederation architecture results in the most optimal routing behavior. The centralized design means that all sub-ASs exchange information with each other through a central sub-AS backbone.

In Figure 9-11, each sub-AS interacts with only one other sub-AS. The result will be more uniform routing with respect to AS path length and route exchange within the confederation.

Figure 9-11 *Centralizing Confederation*

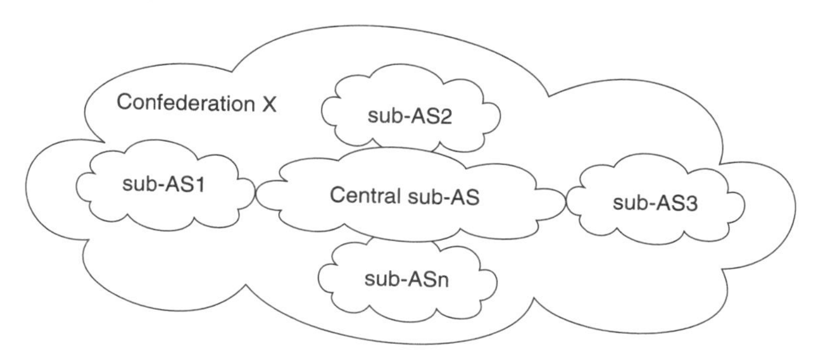

Confederations Versus Route Reflectors

Determining whether to use route reflectors or confederations is not a simple decision. Although different organizations have experienced various levels of stability with these approaches, Cisco recommends the use of the route reflector technique to solve IBGP mesh scalability issues. Actual deployments have proven that route reflectors are more flexible to implement and maintain. On the other hand, confederations could be used to run an IGP in one sub-AS independently of IGPs in other sub-ASs, which would help control the instability of large IGPs.

In some situations, route reflectors can be used in conjunction with confederations. In particular, an AS can be divided into sub-ASs that each run route reflectors internally.

Whichever approach you use, you should always understand the restrictions and behavior of each method and design your network accordingly.

Controlling IGP Expansion

One of the ways in which administrators push their networks to the limit is by letting them grow in such a way that the IGP will be hard to manage. Whether the IGP is as outdated as RIP version 1 or as advanced as Open Shortest Path First (OSPF) and Intermediate System-to-Intermediate System (IS-IS), the issue of scalability will arise. So far, this chapter has discussed route reflectors and confederations as ways of managing IBGP growth. A scalable way of managing IGP expansion is to segment the AS into multiple regions, each running a single, distinct IGP. The individual regions, in turn, must be connected via BGP. With this design, the stability of one region would not affect the stability of another.

What criteria should network designers and architects follow in deciding whether their networks need segmentation? One thing is for sure: The Internet is one huge network that cannot be handled by running an IGP, and that is why it is segmented by BGP.

So what constitutes a large or small network? Is it the number of routers or the number of routes, and, if so, what number? You will hear different answers based on different administrators' experiences. The general answer to this question depends mainly on the robustness of the IGP, what tools it can offer to control the route explosion and instability, and whether BGP segmentation represents a more beneficial, less costly (in dollars and effort) method than relying on the IGP's tools.

Protocols such as OSPF and IS-IS offer certain hierarchical methods that can control route instabilities and provide means for route summarization. But even with these methods, the IGP can grow beyond control. A working guideline for today's networks is that IP routing tables that have 2,000 to 3,000 IGP interior routes might have reached a limit and need a closer look to make sure that they do not grow further. It is not the number of routes that causes problems, because BGP transit routers today carry more than 75,000 Internet routes with no problem. What causes problems is situations (such as hardware and access line instabilities) in which these routes end up bouncing and trying to converge, causing what is known as a network "meltdown."

Does this mean that networks with 3,000 IGP routes need to be segmented via BGP? Not necessarily. In most cases, a redesign of the IGP itself with more emphasis on using IGP segmentation and summarization techniques can bring down the number of routes to a manageable level.

To understand why the decision to control growth with BGP segmentation should be approached with caution, you need to understand what is compromised when ASs are segmented. The main strength of IGPs, especially IGPs based on link-state protocols, has always been convergence—their capability to quickly adapt to network changes. Another strength is their capability to develop a level of redundancy and load balancing.

BGP, on the other hand, was created to implement policies across AS boundaries, with no major emphasis on convergence. When segmenting routing domains with BGP, convergence is enhanced within the newly created smaller segments, but it might diminish when crossing locally administered AS boundaries because of the dependency of BGP on TCP sessions to carry routing updates.

Another drawback is the additional user intervention needed to control and manage the BGP policies that are imposed on this segmented, sub-AS design. As has been illustrated in this book, attribute manipulation is so far the only tool to manipulate the routing behavior of BGP. It should be obvious that controlling routing policies of multiple sub-ASs is more difficult than the routing policy of a single IGP. Understanding all these issues should help network architects use rational judgment when designing their networks. Although further discussion of these issues is beyond the scope of this book, *Large-Scale IP Network Solutions*[4] provides some useful insight into how to identify and deal with these issues.

This section discusses two methods of segmenting the AS:

- Multiple regions separated by IBGP
- Multiple regions separated by EBGP

Segmenting the AS with Multiple Regions Separated by IBGP

The AS can be divided into multiple regions, each running different and independent IGPs. Regions are logically interconnected via a full IBGP mesh. For better redundancy, regions could also be physically interconnected in a fully meshed topology, as illustrated in Figure 9-12.

Figure 9-12 *Multiple Regions Via IBGP*

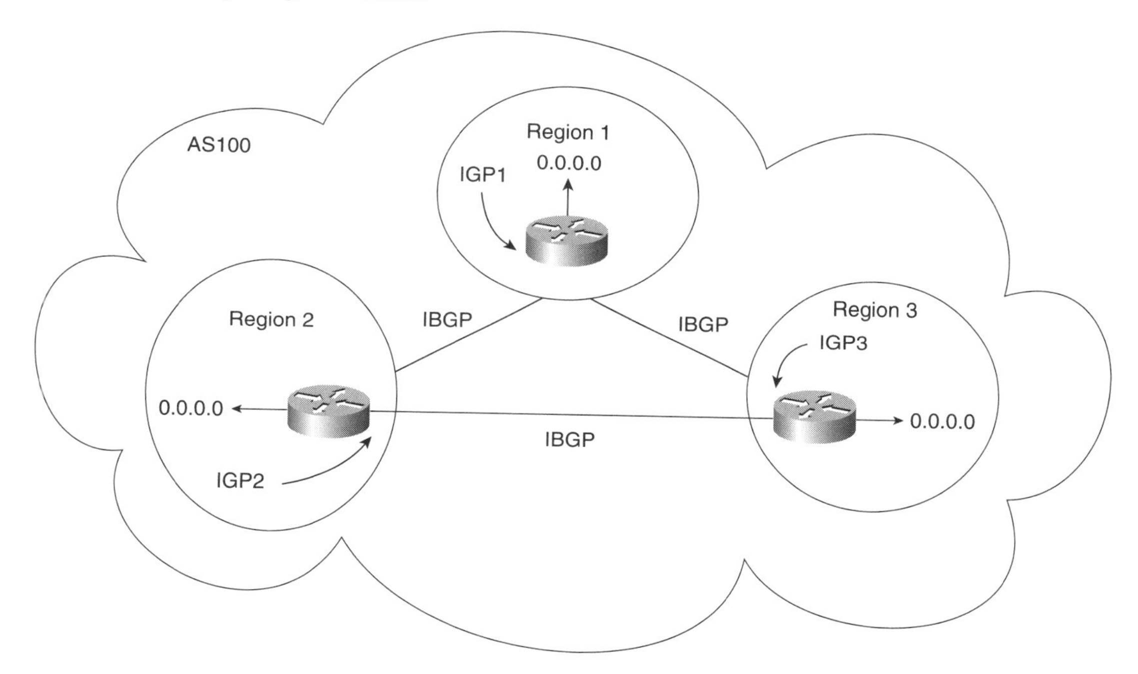

Each region will both inject its IGP routes into IBGP and announce a default route inside the region. As a result, each region will default to the BGP border router for destinations that do not belong to the region. Regional border routers will carry all routes from all regions (exchanged via IBGP) and will be able to direct the traffic accordingly. Each region is totally shielded from the instabilities of all the other regions because the internal non-BGP routers are exposed only to routes that comprise their respective region. You can use a separate IGP in case there is a need for a dynamic routing protocol to establish reachability between regional border routers participating in the full IBGP mesh.

This design is still missing one important piece—Internet connectivity. Connecting to the Internet in this scenario requires further planning. As illustrated in Figure 9-12, each region already follows a default route to reach other regions inside the AS. The problem occurs if the BGP border router (for the region) does not maintain continuous synchronization with the actual routes learned at the connection point to the Internet. In this case, internal non-BGP routers have to choose between the default to the Internet and the default to other regions, as illustrated in Figure 9-13.

Figure 9-13 *Multiple Conflicting Defaults*

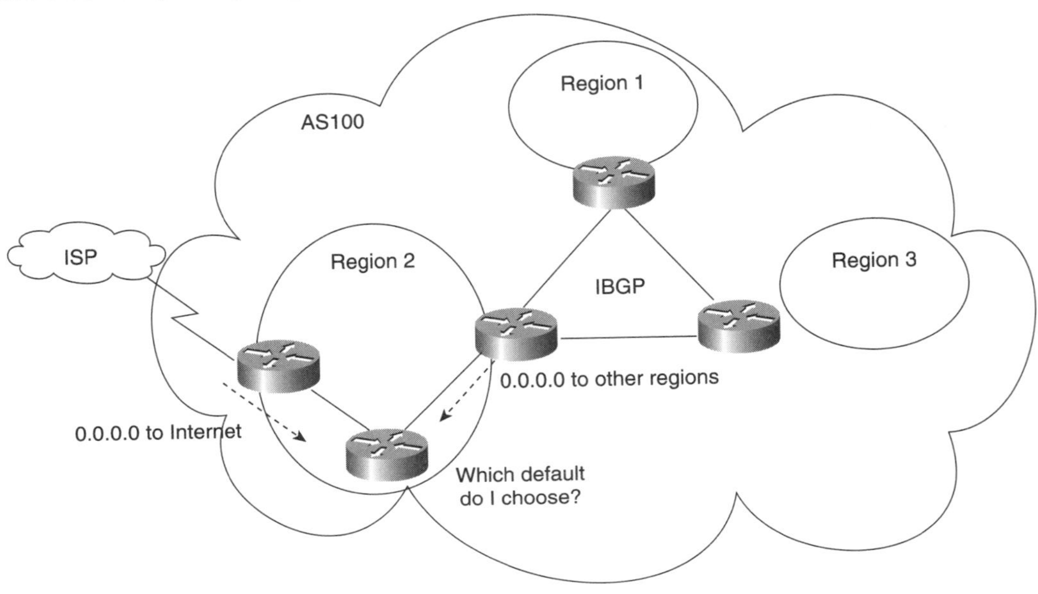

To remedy this situation, all regions should always point to the regional BGP border router for the default, whether attempting to reach destinations on the Internet or in other intra-AS regions. This would require the Internet connections to be part of a central IBGP mesh, as illustrated in Figure 9-14.

Figure 9-14 *Multiple Regions with Internet Connectivity*

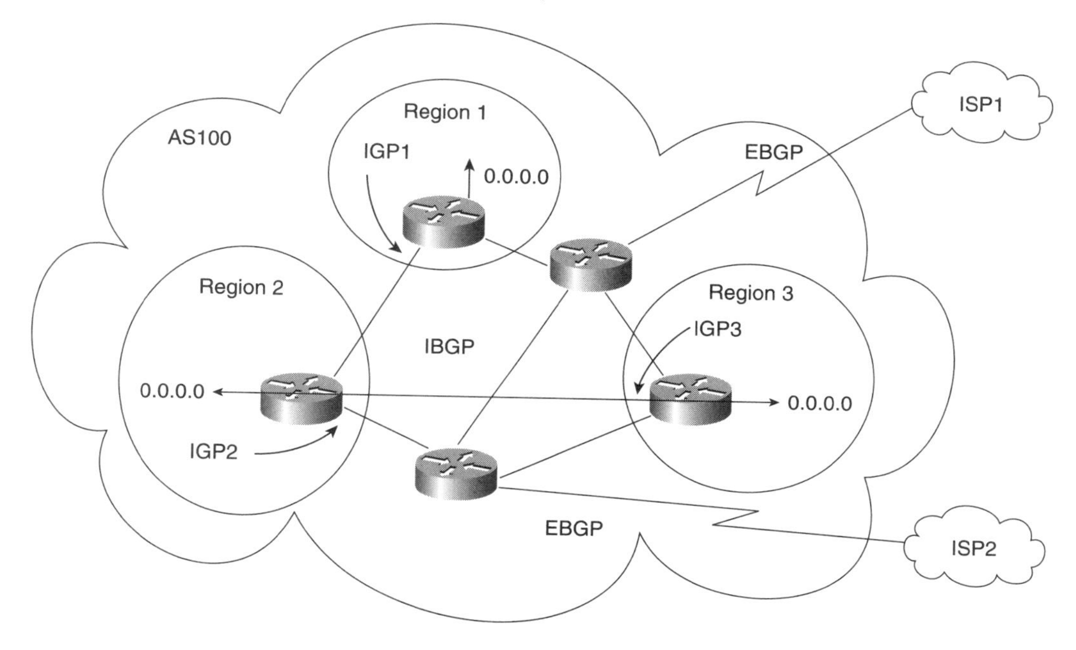

Regions 1, 2, and 3 are interconnected via an IBGP mesh, which also provides Internet connectivity. Internal non-BGP routers in each region default to the BGP border router, which contains all routes. If the destination belongs to any other region, the traffic is directed to that region. Otherwise, the traffic will be sent to the Internet connections according to BGP policies.

This method does not have the flexibility to set policies for each region. Because all regions run under the same autonomous system, prefixes from each region cannot be easily differentiated from those in another region by BGP. Designs that are more complex could utilize the "community" attribute to differentiate prefixes between regions. This could be used in conjunction with a hierarchical route reflection configuration to create large virtual private networks, as you will see at the end of this chapter.

Segmenting the AS with Multiple Regions Separated by EBGP

If flexible policies are required between regions to direct traffic accordingly, for instance, each region can be represented as a separate autonomous system. EBGP operates between ASs, and IBGP is run within each AS. You can use a separate IGP if there is an additional requirement for a dynamic routing protocol to establish reachability between EBGP peers. Figure 9-15 illustrates this AS segmentation method.

Figure 9-15 *Multiple Regions Separated by EBGP*

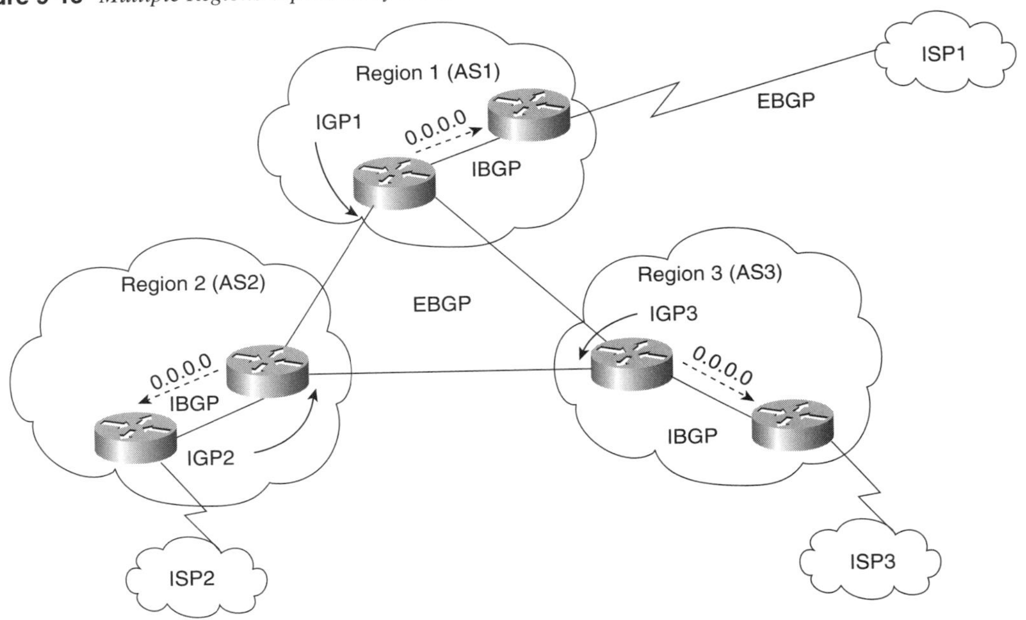

At first glance, this seems to be the most scalable solution for managing the growth of a large IGP. The AS is now divided into multiple ASs, with each region represented by a separate AS number and having a preferred connection to the Internet. Each AS injects its IGP routes into BGP so that they are propagated to all other regions and the Internet. Internal non-BGP routers in each region default to the regional BGP border routers, which contain all routes. BGP policies can set local preference of prefixes so that regional BGP border routers prefer interior company links, instead of exterior Internet connections, for communication between regions. With respect to external connectivity to the Internet, each region prefers its own external provider for Internet connectivity; if the link to its preferred provider fails, external providers from other regions can be used.

This design looks good on paper until you try to implement it. It's very difficult to justify all the AS numbers from American Registry for Internet Numbers (ARIN) or other Regional Internet Registries (RIRs) required for such a network. AS numbers are a finite resource that is quickly being depleted. ARIN and the other RIRs would likely require substantial justification before they would allocate multiple AS numbers to one network administrator. Unfortunately, using multiple ASs for better IGP stability is usually not a good-enough justification. You should consult your local RIR for information on precisely what "enough justification" entails.

Other alternatives include using private AS numbers or BGP confederations to control IGP expansion. We'll discuss these options in the following sections.

Using Private AS Numbers

Using private AS numbers is another way to divide a large AS into multiple regions, interconnected by EBGP. Regions will run IBGP internally and interconnect to each other via EBGP. In addition, each regional domain will inject its local prefixes into BGP to facilitate interregional connectivity. Internal non-BGP routers in each region will default to the regional BGP border routers, which contain all routes. Finally, you can run a separate IGP in case a dynamic protocol is needed to establish EBGP connectivity among regions.

This scenario works well without Internet connectivity. However, private AS numbers will have to be hidden from the outside world in order to connect to the Internet. Hiding private AS numbers requires a more involved design. Figure 9-16 illustrates a method that can be used to remedy the situation of private ASs with Internet connectivity.

Figure 9-16 *Private ASs in a Multiprovider Environment*

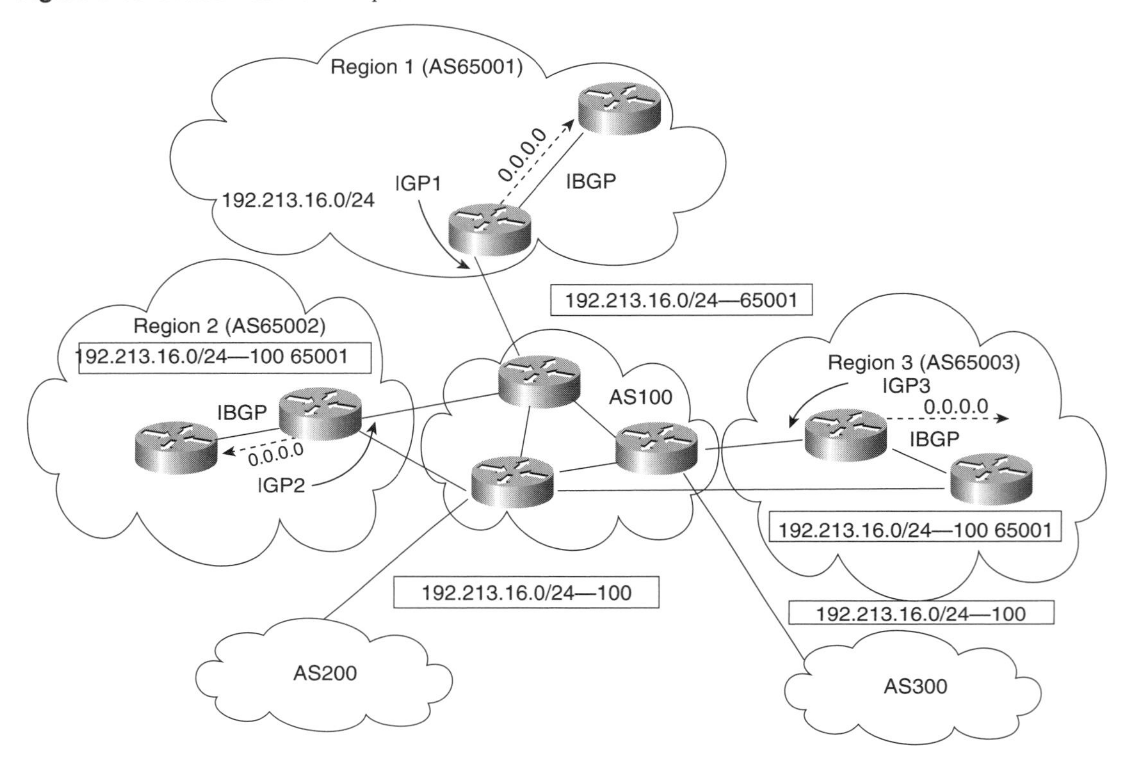

Figure 9-16 shows an AS that is broken into multiple private sub-ASs. Region 1 is now AS65001, region 2 is AS65002, and region 3 is AS65003. Different mutually exclusive IGPs are running in each private AS.

In order to facilitate multiple external Internet provider connectivity, AS100 is introduced as an interconnection point between all private ASs. It is important to note that this central backbone AS is a legal AS number. All private ASs will EBGP peer with backbone AS100 for interregional and Internet connectivity.

To prevent private AS numbers from leaking to external Internet providers, the network administrator uses the AS path-stripping technique discussed in Chapter 6. AS100 strips private AS numbers from each region before propagating those BGP updates to external Internet providers.

In Figure 9-16, AS65001 is originating prefix 192.213.16.0/24. To all other private ASs, this prefix is seen with AS path 100 65001. When the prefix is propagated to the two external

ASs, AS200 and AS300, the private AS number is stripped, and the remaining AS path is 100. To the Internet, all your networks will be advertised as if they originated from AS100.

Using Confederations to Control IGP Expansion

Confederations can also be used to control the expansion of IGPs. You have already seen how a confederation can divide the AS into multiple smaller sub-ASs. If each sub-AS is running a different IGP, the centralized design described in Figure 9-16 would be a viable approach. The IGPs are now running independently of one another, and the whole AS is still considered a single entity to the outside world. Each IGP will be injected into BGP for interregional connectivity. Internal non-BGP routers in each region will default to the BGP border router, which contains all routes. Internet connectivity can be provided via the central AS to provide a central default for all the different regions. This is similar to the scenario shown in Figure 9-16.

On the negative side, confederations require extra configuration and do not provide the same capabilities for setting policies between the sub-ASs because the whole AS is still considered one entity. In addition, any confederation design that is not centralized could introduce complications such as suboptimal routes that indiscriminately direct traffic within the confederation.

Looking Ahead

So far you have seen so far how BGP can be a powerful tool in giving routing a more structured look. You have learned how to manipulate traffic and how to segment the AS into more controlled elements. One more aspect that needs discussion is route instability on the Internet. Many factors induce route fluctuations and, in turn, traffic fluctuations. Some of these elements can be avoided, and others are beyond your control. The Internet has become a necessity for everyday operations; it is in your best interest to respect and protect its integrity. The following chapter discusses the causes of route instability and some of the measures that can be taken to stop it or at least dampen its effect.

Frequently Asked Questions

Q — *I have an SF hub and an SJ hub. Do you think it is better to separate them into different ASs and run BGP instead of running an IGP in between?*

A — This doesn't sound like a candidate for segmentation via BGP. Remember that even though segmentation gives better hierarchy and control, it introduces more routing policies dictated by BGP's behavior. In small networks such as yours, you could achieve the same stability by performing adequate hierarchical routing using an IGP.

Q — *I do not have enough BGP peers to justify using route reflectors. What happens if I use them anyway?*

A — You will achieve normal routing. You just need to understand that with this model, you need to rely on the centralized routers to forward BGP routes to another part of your network. Not only does the RR have to do more processing, but it also becomes a single point of failure. Therefore, additional provisioning will have to be performed to ensure at least two RRs for redundancy. You also have to deal with the potential for other issues, such as peer groups and attribute modification, as described in this chapter. If you think that the overhead is not an issue, configuring RRs is no problem.

Q — *With confederations, an EBGP external route is more preferred than a confederation external route. Does this mean that I can never use another sub-AS as an exit point?*

A — No. You could always use attributes such as local preference to prefer whichever exit point you want.

Q — *Because local preference is not passed between ASs, it won't be passed between sub-ASs inside a confederation, will it?*

A — That is not true. Using additional configuration, the sub-AS will know that it is talking to an external peer inside a confederation and will maintain all attributes that are normally maintained by IBGP.

Q — *I need to configure route reflectors, but the current software on my routers does not support it. Do I need to upgrade all my routers at the same time?*

A — No. You need to upgrade only the routers that will become RRs. Other routers will behave as a conventional IBGP speaker. This will help you cautiously migrate your network to the new design.

References

[1]RFC 1966, "BGP Route Reflection: An Alternative to Full Mesh IBGP," www.isi.edu/in-notes/rfc1966.txt

[2]RFC 1965, "Autonomous System Confederations for BGP," www.isi.edu/in-notes/rfc1965.txt

[3]RFC 1930, "Guidelines for Creation, Selection, and Registration of an Autonomous System (AS)," www.isi.edu/in-notes/rfc1930.txt

[4]Raza, Khalid and Mark Turner. *Large-Scale IP Network Solutions* (Indianapolis, Ind.: Cisco Press, 2000)

This chapter covers the following key topics:

- **Route instabilities on the Internet**—Briefly examines the most common causes of route instability.
- **Controlling route and cache invalidation**—Cisco offers a soft configuration feature that enables administrators to reconfigure attributes on the fly with minimal repercussions for routes and cache.
- **BGP route refresh**—Border Gateway Protocol (BGP) route refresh provides a mechanism to apply new policies by requesting a fresh set of routes from a peer without having to reset the BGP connection or flap the route announcements.
- **Route dampening**—BGP's route dampening feature identifies and suppresses unstable routes for better reliability within and outside the autonomous system (AS).

CHAPTER 10

Designing Stable Internets

Establishing and maintaining route stability within and among networks is crucial to ensuring reliable Internet connectivity. A number of design flaws and problems can contribute to destabilizing connections to the Internet. This chapter explores some of the causes of route instability and techniques for reducing it.

Route Instabilities on the Internet

The central symptom of route instability is the disappearance of a route that previously existed in the routing table. This route might disappear and reappear intermittently, a condition sometimes referred to as *flapping*. What occurs at the routing protocol level is that BGP sends a routing update and then quickly withdraws it. A router that receives UPDATE or WITHDRAWN messages must propagate those messages to its peers. These messages are visible to all Border Gateway Protocol (BGP) networks connected to the global Internet. If this behavior continues to cascade, routing performance suffers.

Here are some factors that affect route instabilities on the Internet:

- Interior Gateway Protocol (IGP) instability
- Faulty hardware
- Software problems
- Insufficient CPU power
- Insufficient memory
- Network upgrades and routine maintenance
- Human error
- Link congestion

IGP Instability

Dynamically injecting IGPs into BGP can cause unnecessary route flapping. Problems that occur inside a domain can translate into problems outside the domain. As already discussed in Chapter 6, "Tuning BGP Capabilities," static injection of routing into BGP can alleviate this problem.

Route aggregation at border or core routers can also reduce the potential unpleasant side effects associated with IGP injection into BGP. With aggregation, multiple route entries are injected into BGP as a summary aggregate. Single route instability in any single element of the aggregate does not affect the stability of the aggregate itself.

Still, some network designers are forced to rely on dynamic routing for valid reasons:

- BGP implementations can handle only a fixed number of network entries to be advertised statically. The number of static routes permitted varies from vendor to vendor. Whatever that limit is, networks that want to go beyond this limit require that administrators inject the IGP into BGP.
- Some administrators are not comfortable with the fact that the networks they are statically advertising might become unreachable by the router advertising them. This is understandable, especially in cases where routes are advertised from different points of the AS. Advertising a route that is not reachable can create black holes.

Faulty Hardware

Faulty interfaces, faulty systems, or faulty lines can affect route stability. An interface that is intermittently available might cause routing information to transition. Hardware failures are, to a certain degree, beyond the control of service users. System and link redundancy are important tools for reducing connectivity loss due to failures, but when a physical failure occurs, routing is interrupted, and any interruption initiates some kind of cascade effect down the routing path.

Software Problems

Software problems (bugs) can cause system failures and network instability. Routing protocol development teams try their best to catch these problems before the software is released to customers. Nevertheless, it is almost impossible to foresee every situation that might occur in live networks. Administrators should experiment with new software or new features in test labs and low-impact portions of their networks in order to get some level of confidence before the software is deployed in a production environment.

Insufficient CPU Power

The more routing updates and peering sessions the router handles, the more CPU power that is required. Think of the router as your basic 4×4 truck, and think of the routing and traffic overhead as the load you carry. Would you be surprised if the truck had trouble moving while carrying a 20-ton load? Picking the correct system with the correct CPU power is very important to satisfy your particular routing needs.

At the initial stages of building BGP tables after the BGP sessions are established, a system's processor can spend more than 90 percent of its time processing updates. When links become unstable and overloaded, the router might end up in a race condition: the CPU is too busy handling updates, which causes BGP sessions to drop, which in turn triggers more instability.

Insufficient Memory

In addition to the memory needed by a router to run its own operating system, a router must store routing tables, cache tables, databases, and other bits of software to permit operation. A router that reaches its memory limit might stop functioning, which causes all routes it knows of or advertises to be lost.

In BGP terms, a routing entry consists of the entry in the IP forwarding table and whatever corresponding information is available in the BGP routing table. Today, the Internet routing tables include more than 75,000 routes, and this number increases every month. Systems that take full routes from the Internet from one or more providers are barely keeping up (if they are keeping up at all) with 32 MB of memory (for storing BGP and other routing information). Most providers have upgraded their systems to 96, 128, and even 256 MB of routing table memory. Insufficient memory itself often results in instability, because when a router runs out of memory once, it often can't collect the heap of fragmented memory back and becomes a permanent (until rebooted) source of route flaps.

Network Upgrades and Routine Maintenance

Networks are dynamic. Performance improvement, site consolidation, and support expansion all require changes and adaptations. Changes might include upgrades to new versions of software or hardware, additions of more links, additions of more bandwidth, or reconfiguration of a network's layout.

For obvious reasons, administrators prefer to bring a system down for upgrading during a period when it usually experiences minimal usage. The downtime for some networks cannot exceed an hour, even at night, because of time zone differences. Despite these difficulties, the upgrade period itself is not usually the time when errors are most significant, because administrators usually develop a backup plan and can revert to the old setup if the new setup does not work. In case of configuration or software/hardware problems, network instability will take effect the next day when everybody is back online. At that point, reverting to the old setup is not likely to be a viable option. Unfortunately, to rectify the situation, administrators sometimes start adding or changing the configuration on the fly, potentially making the situation even worse.

To reduce the likelihood of causing disruptions, network changes should first be simulated in nonproduction environments if possible. In addition, multiple major changes should not be deployed at the same time. For example, it is unwise for a provider to perform major router software upgrades, switch hardware, and change cabling all at the same time. Good planning and network simulation are the keys to successful network upgrades.

Human Error

Most of the network instabilities caused by human error occur because an administrator circumvents an administration policy or makes a change without knowledge of possible effects. It is easy to make mistakes in complex network configurations. One wrong filter, and an entire AS can be isolated. Administrators should anticipate problems before they occur.

Here's an example of the kinds of errors that can happen: Any router can send the default 0.0.0.0 via BGP to its neighbors. If you are not careful, traffic will take the wrong route. As much as it is somebody else's responsibility to send appropriate default routes, it is your responsibility to protect yourself by making sure that you filter any unwanted routes, default or otherwise, that come your way. The list of possible human errors is long: someone might advertise somebody else's networks, a provider might stop advertising your networks, or somebody summarizes the wrong networks. The point is, don't expect everyone else to play by your rules. Other administrators can (usually inadvertently) deploy rules that directly conflict with your rules, which can lead to serious performance and connectivity degradation.

Link Congestion

In some cases, a link failure causes another link to be overloaded with traffic. This occurs because the link is handling all the additional traffic that is now being routed its way on top of its normal traffic. Even if the link can support the throughput, a router might not be able to handle the additional load, depending on its horsepower. This can result in major performance degradation for the end user.

In the process of trying to get a handle on network instability, BGP implementations have introduced several helpful features. Although these features do not provide a complete solution, they are significant preventative measures of route instability.

BGP Stability Features

Of course, developing effective routing policies and configuring them correctly is at the core of building stability. BGP's attribute selections, as discussed throughout this book, are tools for building that core stability. In addition, here are some BGP functions that can help provide a buffer against route instability effects:

- Controlling route and cache invalidation
- BGP route refresh
- BGP route dampening

Controlling Route and Cache Invalidation

The basis of any BGP conversation is the transport protocol connection that takes place between two neighbors. The neighbor connection itself is based on the OPEN message, which contains parameters such as the BGP version number. In addition, exchanged routing updates carry different attributes such as the metric, communities, and AS_PATH. Whenever an administrator changes attributes or policies, traditional BGP implementations require that a BGP TCP session with its neighbor be reset (broken and restarted) before the modified routing behavior will take effect.

Unfortunately, every time the TCP session is reset, routing is interrupted. When a session is reset, the routing cache is invalidated, routes disappear, and route instability cascades throughout the Internet. By the time the session is back online and routes and caches are reestablished, real damage could result.

Cisco Systems introduced a mechanism called *soft reconfiguration* that enables administrators to reconfigure attributes on the fly without killing an already established TCP session or manually introducing a route flap. Therefore, the routing cache is not cleared, and the impact on the route is minimal.

TIP See the section “Controlling Route and Cache Invalidation” in Chapter 12 on page 424.

The offshoot of using soft reconfiguration is that it requires a set of unmodified routes (the respective Adj-RIB-In, which should be inline with the peer’s Adj-RIB-Out) from the specified peer(s) to be stored in local memory. The memory consumption required for utilizing soft reconfiguration with large peers can be quite significant. A rule of thumb is that for each route learned from the peer, assume that 250 bytes of memory is required to store it.

BGP Route Refresh

Another solution was introduced recently that removes the memory consumption offshoot associated with using soft reconfiguration. This alternative approach, referred to as *route refresh capability*, utilizes BGP-4 Capabilities Negotiation (discussed in Chapter 5, "Border Gateway Protocol Version 4") to facilitate a means of dynamically requesting that a peer readvertise all the prefixes learned from the peer (its Adj-RIB-Out).

This behavior is enabled by default in newer versions of IOS and must be supported by the BGP peer router in order to use the feature. BGP route refresh removes the overhead of memory and CPU consumption required when using soft reconfiguration. It also allows all the prefixes learned from the peer to be examined and subjected to the new policy without requiring the BGP session to be reset.

TIP See the section "BGP Route Refresh" in Chapter 12 on page 429.

Route Dampening

Another mechanism for controlling route instability is *route dampening*. A route that appears and disappears intermittently causes BGP UPDATE and WITHDRAWN messages to be repeatedly propagated on the Internet. The tremendous amount of routing traffic generated can use up all the link's bandwidth and drive up CPU utilization of routers.

TIP See the section "Route Dampening" in Chapter 12 on page 432.

Dampening categorizes routes as well either *behaved* or *ill behaved*. A well-behaved route shows a high degree of stability during an extended period of time. On the other hand, an ill-behaved route experiences a high level of instability in a short period of time. Ill-behaved routes should be penalized in a way that is proportional to the route's expected future instability. An unstable route should be suppressed (not advertised) until there is some degree of confidence that the route has become stable.

A route's recent history is used as a basis for estimating future stability. To track a route history, it is essential to track the number of times the route has flapped over a period of time. Under route dampening, each time a route flaps, it is given a penalty. Whenever the penalty reaches a predefined threshold, the route is suppressed. The route can continue to accrue penalties even after it is suppressed. The more frequently a route oscillates in a short amount of time, the faster the route is suppressed.

Similar criteria are put in place to unsuppress a route and start readvertising it. An algorithm is implemented to decay (reduce) the penalty value exponentially. The algorithm bases its configuration on a user-defined set of parameters. The following set of terms and parameters applies to the Cisco implementation:

- **Penalty**—An incremented numeric value that is assigned to a route each time it flaps.
- **Half-life**—A configurable numeric value that describes the amount of time that must elapse to reduce the penalty by one-half.
- **Suppress limit**—A numeric value that is compared with the penalty. If the penalty is greater than the suppress limit, the route is suppressed.
- **Reuse limit**—A configurable numeric value that is compared with the penalty. If the penalty is less than the reuse limit, a suppressed route that is up will no longer be suppressed.
- **Suppressed route**—A route that is not advertised, even if it is up. A route is suppressed if the penalty value is greater than the suppressed limit.
- **History entry**—An entry used to store flap information. For the purposes of monitoring and calculating a route's oscillation level, it is important to store this information in the router when the route oscillates. When the route stabilizes, the history entry becomes useless and must be flushed from the router.

Figure 10-1 illustrates the process of assessing a penalty to a route every time it flaps. The penalty is exponentially decayed according to parameters such as the half-life. The half-life parameter can be changed by the administrator to reflect the oscillation history of a route: A longer half-life might be desirable for a route that has a habit of oscillating frequently. A larger half-life value would cause the penalty to decay more slowly, which translates into a route's being suppressed longer.

Figure 10-1 *Route Dampening Penalty Assessment*

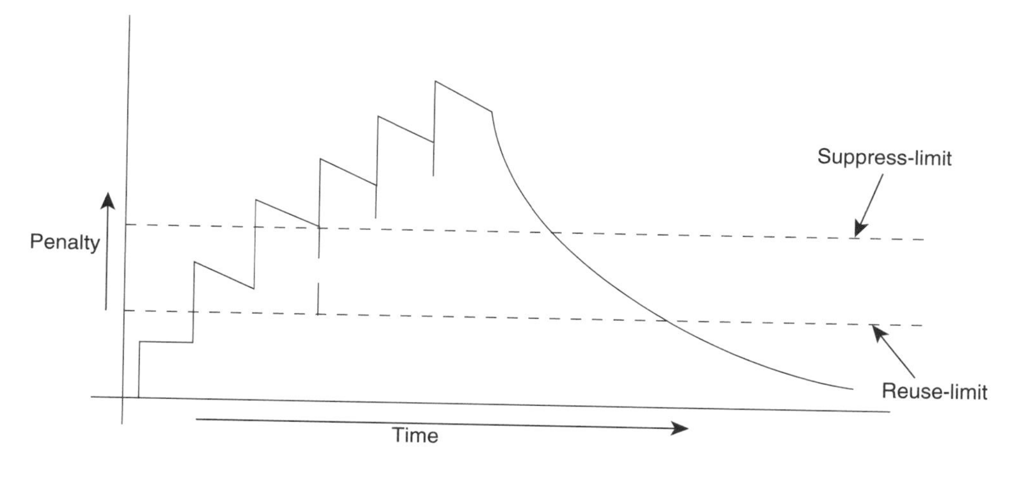

Stability Inside the AS

The benefits of route dampening are noticed inside as well as outside an autonomous system. When BGP is redistributed (injected) into an IGP, it is important that BGP instability does not affect internal routing in such a way as to cause a meltdown inside the AS. This is where route dampening can be useful. Routes that are flapping will be suppressed and prevented from being injected into the AS until they show some degree of stability. Figure 10-2 compares the effects of EBGP flapping on an IGP with and without route dampening.

Figure 10-2 *Effects of EBGP Flapping on an IGP*

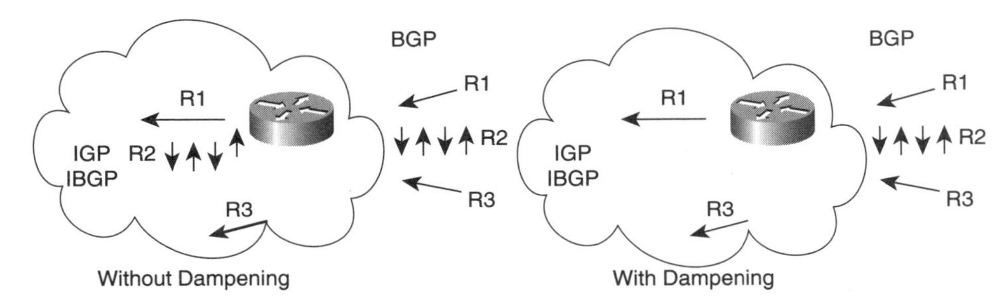

In Figure 10-2, routes R1, R2, and R3 are injected from BGP into the AS. The up and down arrows next to R2 indicate that it is flapping. The routes are carried via IBGP and/or IGP depending on how the administrator is injecting the routes into the AS. In either case, the oscillations of R2 create major overhead for the border router and on the interior routers. IGPs will flood and remove the route as long as the route is unstable. With route dampening, the ill-behaved route will be suppressed (after reaching the suppress limit) and will be prevented from entering the AS.

Instabilities Outside the AS

Route dampening can prevent unstable EBGP routes from being propagated to other peers. This can save on link bandwidth usage and processing overhead within border routers. If you are a provider with multiple customers using your services, it is important not to burden your own network (and the outside world) with instabilities that go on inside a customer's network. In the case where a provider advertises a customer's network as part of an aggregate, this is not an issue. The aggregate will be stable (always advertised) even if most of its elements are not. Nonetheless, within the provider's AS, a customer's instabilities are a concern. When a customer's network cannot be aggregated (due to multi-homing or addresses not being part of the provider's address space), instabilities will be carried to the outside world.

With dampening, the provider's border router suppresses customer routes that are flapping. Suppression will take effect according to the dampening rules and parameters discussed earlier in this section. Figure 10-3 illustrates route dampening in an ISP environment.

Figure 10-3 *Route Dampening: ISP Environment*

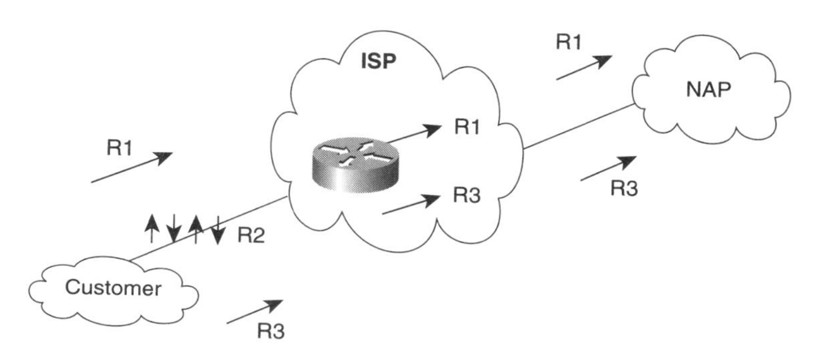

One possible side effect of route dampening is that the customer will experience some short outages even if his routes become stable. In Figure 10-3, route R2 in the customer network is flapping. When the customer's ISP is running route dampening, R2 will be penalized and suppressed according to its level of oscillation. R2 could be dampened for minutes. Even if R2 stops oscillating, the penalty it had accumulated still might be far above the reuse limit, and it has to be decayed before the route can be used. In the meantime, some poor soul on the customer's network is pulling out his or her hair trying to figure out why some subnets can't be reached from the outside world. If administrators are unaware that their routes are being dampened, they might try to remedy the situation by some other means, which makes their routes flap even more and become more penalized. The better approach is to ask the provider whether he is receiving the routes, and if he is, check why they are not being advertised. Providers have strict policies and might not change the dampening behavior per the customer's request. What the provider can do is "flush" the history information of the routes being dampened to advertise the route. This is, of course, under the condition that the customer will investigate the routing problems causing the routes to fluctuate.

On the other hand, instabilities can be caused by the providers themselves, and the effect can be much larger. If a link carrying full routes between a provider and customer or a provider and another provider oscillates, the border routers will feel the impact.

Suppose that you are getting full Internet routes (currently about 75,000 routes) from multiple providers. Now imagine that 5 percent of these routes (about 3,750 routes) are toggling every 2 minutes. Your border router will be unable to handle this load.

Without route dampening, it is difficult to determine what is really happening. All you know is that the process utilization on your border router is increasing rapidly. With route dampening, all the unstable routes generate a history entry that shows the routes' level of stability. After the unstable routes are identified, it is easy to determine where they are coming from by looking at the next-hop address. Although route dampening in this case did not help solve the problem, it helped identify who was causing the problem. After you identify the culprit, you can temporarily remove your BGP session with the ISP at fault. Pick up the telephone, call the ISP, and start complaining.

In conclusion, route instabilities in the Internet will affect everybody one way or the other. It is everyone's responsibility to minimize route oscillation by being more aware of the things they do and why they do them. Providers are becoming tougher on culprits; some providers apply harsher penalties to routes with longer masks, for example. This might sound like overkill, but it is getting harder to control the Internet. Having a "routing patrol" issue tickets whenever someone breaks the rules might become necessary.

Looking Ahead

We have talked enough about architectures and routing behaviors. If you want to put things into perspective by learning actual routing implementations, the best is yet to come. The following chapters touch upon important designs and architectures already discussed in this book by presenting actual configuration using the Cisco IOS software language.

The configuration examples are accompanied by complete explanations of why a certain action is taken and what outcome results from it. Actual displays are taken from Cisco routers to point out multiple BGP attributes and how the configuration has affected the routing tables. By going through the examples in the next two chapters, I hope you will achieve a high level of expertise in integrating your networks in the global Internet.

Frequently Asked Questions

Q — *If I specify the maximum number of prefixes that will be accepted from a peer as 100, for example, and enable soft reconfiguration inbound for that peer, will this limit the number of unaltered routes to be stored in memory to 100?*

A — No. All the routes learned from the peer (the Adj-RIB-In before the Input Policy Engine is applied) will be stored in memory.

Q — *My border router is having problems because the link to my provider is oscillating, causing routes to flip-flop. Will configuring route dampening stabilize my router?*

A — To a certain extent. In this case, configuring route dampening might help stabilize your AS if you are injecting the BGP routes into your IGP. Your border router will still experience the instabilities caused by your provider. A better approach is to call your provider.

Q — *I am advertising my IGP routes into BGP. My IGP routes are very unstable, which causes the BGP routes I am advertising to fluctuate. Will route dampening solve the problem?*

A — No. Configuring route dampening on your border router will prevent your routes from being advertised. This will help others but will cause you outages. What you need to do is address the source of your IGP's instability.

Q — *Some of my internal routes are flip-flopping, which is causing my provider to dampen them. I can't figure out the problem. What should I do in the meantime?*

A — You can always define these routes statically and inject them into BGP. This way, they will always be advertised, irrespective of their up or down state. Even better (if possible), you can define your routes as part of an aggregate route. The aggregate route will not disappear unless all the more-specific routes it represents disappear.

Q — *I am a provider. I don't want to penalize all prefixes in the same manner. Is there a way to assign different dampening parameters to different prefixes?*

A — Yes. Cisco offers you the flexibility to selectively apply the dampening parameters depending on certain criteria such as IP prefixes, AS_PATH, or community.

PART IV

Internet Routing Device Configuration

In previous chapters, we developed concepts and approaches, but withheld the details of configuration code. In chapters 11 and 12, you will find code examples for most of the concepts and functions described in Part II and Part III. Chapter 11 focuses on configuration examples of basic BGP attributes, and Chapter 12 focuses on configuration examples for some of the more complex, realistic design problems faced by administrators developing routing policies. You cannot simply plug these code examples into your own network routing policies. Rather, they are models for the particular routing decisions you are likely to have to make as you develop, maintain, and extend routing policies to accommodate your evolving network and connectivity needs. You will need to extrapolate from and adjust the models to suit your particular situation.

This chapter covers the following key topics:

- **Building peering sessions**—Configuration examples for the first step in the routing task. This section covers basic syntax used in configuration code.
- **Route filtering and attribute manipulation**—BGP route maps, filtering based on NLRI, and filtering based on AS_PATH.
- **Peer groups**—Configuration examples of defining and utilizing peer groups.
- **Sources of routing updates**—Dynamic and static configuration for injecting information into BGP.
- **Overlapping protocols (backdoors)**—Configuration examples for changing the distance parameter to favor certain routes over others.
- **BGP attributes**—Configuration examples for NEXT_HOP, AS_PATH, local preference, MED, and community attributes.
- **BGP-4 aggregation**—Configuration examples for various aggregation scenarios.

CHAPTER 11

Configuring Basic BGP Functions and Attributes

This is the first of two chapters consisting primarily of configuration examples. Having covered all the important prerequisite concepts, you can delve into these examples of how to write code for basic BGP functions and attributes. This chapter focuses on those basics, and the next chapter considers some of the more complex design-oriented configuration problems.

Even if you have been using the references in previous chapters to flip ahead to these configuration examples, you are encouraged to reexamine them now, with the benefit of having read and assimilated all the concept-oriented chapters. In addition to the configuration code itself, be sure to look at the many routing tables that are included; they are intended to solidify your understanding of what results to expect.

Chapters 11 and 12 are not intended to replace Cisco manuals and do not cover every command and scenario. They present configurations for common situations that are encountered in connecting networks to the Internet. Your particular network might require a combination of scenarios—or a different approach—to achieve the most effective policies.

In the following discussions, an AS could play the role of a customer, provider, or both. Do not get confused by having AS numbers and AS roles switched around, or by IP address numbering not being too realistic. These are just exercises that will help you understand BGP so that you can apply it accordingly in your own environment.

Building Peering Sessions

This example demonstrates the different types of BGP peering sessions you will encounter. Consider Figure 11-1.

Figure 11-1 *Building Peering Sessions*

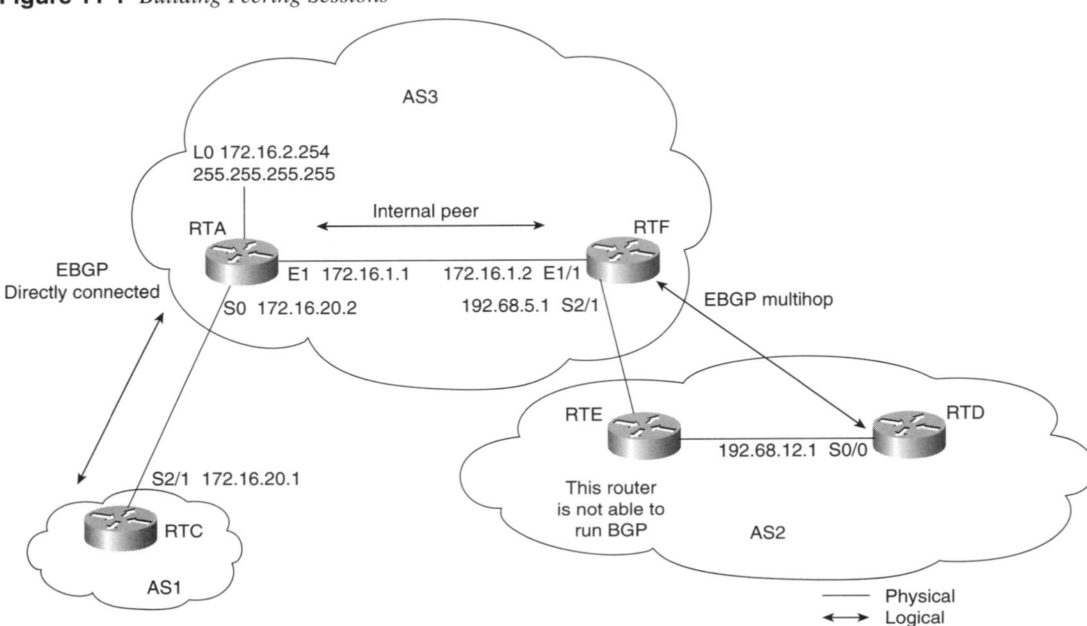

An IBGP peering session is formed within AS3, between RTA's loopback address and RTF's physical address. EBGP sessions are also formed between AS3 and AS1 by using the two directly connected IP addresses of RTA and RTC. Another EBGP session is formed between RTF in AS3 and RTD in AS2, using IP addresses that are not on the same segment (multihop).

It is important to remember that the BGP TCP connection will not become established unless there is IGP connectivity between the two peers or the two peers are directly connected. We will use OSPF as an IGP to establish the required underlying connectivity internally. Example 11-1 shows the configuration for RTA.

Example 11-1 *RTA Configuration*

```
ip subnet-zero

interface Loopback0
 ip address 172.16.2.254 255.255.255.255

interface Ethernet1
 ip address 172.16.1.1 255.255.255.0

interface Serial0
 ip address 172.16.20.2 255.255.255.0
```

Example 11-1 *RTA Configuration (Continued)*

```
router ospf 10
 network 172.16.0.0 0.0.255.255 area 0

router bgp 3
 no synchronization
 neighbor 172.16.1.2 remote-as 3
 neighbor 172.16.1.2 update-source Loopback0
 neighbor 172.16.20.1 remote-as 1
 no auto-summary

ip classless
```

The configuration for RTA in Example 11-1 shows some syntax that might be unfamiliar to you. All the syntax is explained in Table 11-1 generically, as well as in relation to the particular routing scenario of Figure 11-1. In subsequent examples throughout this chapter, however, the router's configuration focus on the relevant commands required to configure BGP, the IGP, or static routing. Commands that assign IP addresses to interfaces will be omitted in many instances due to space limitations.

Table 11-1 *Example 11-1 Configuration Commands*

Command	Explanation
ip subnet-zero	This global configuration command is necessary in case you are configuring interfaces that fall in subnet-zero subnets (that is, 192.168.1.0/30). With the introduction of classless routing, using subnet-zero is very common and is a recommended default configuration.
interface ***type slot/port***	This command configures an interface type and number on the router. Any configuration that appears under the command will be specific to that particular interface. (The actual ***slot/port*** syntax might vary slightly across different platforms.) Note that RTA has three interface commands—one for each of its three connections. The ***loopback*** interface is a software-only interface that emulates an interface that is always up.
ip address ***ip-address mask*** **[secondary]**	This is an interface command that configures an interface with an IP address/mask tuple. RTA's Ethernet IP address, for example, is configured by **ip address** 172.16.1.1 255.255.255.0.
router ***process*** ***[process-id]***	This is a global command that defines a process such as OSPF, RIP, or BGP and gives the process a process ID. Some processes, such as RIP, do not require a process ID. For example, in RTA's configuration, **router ospf 10** indicates an OSPF process with ID 10, whereas **router bgp 3** indicates a BGP process in autonomous system 3.
network	This command indicates the networks or, in the case of OSPF, the interfaces that will participate in a specific routing process.

continues

Table 11-1 *Example 11-1 Configuration Commands (Continued)*

Command	Explanation
inverse mask	In RTA's **network** command, you will notice a representation of the form 0.0.255.255—basically, a number of 0s followed by a number of 1s. This is an inverse mask, in which the 0s are an exact match, and the 1s are referred to as *do-not-care bits*. For example, 172.16.0.0 0.0.255.255 indicates any IP address or network of the form 172.16.X.X. Inverse masks can be applied to access lists as well as the **network** command. Table 11-2 provides a dotted decimal/inverse mask reference chart.
area *area-number*	This represents an OSPF area with a specified area number.
neighbor	This command is used to define the BGP neighbor connection parameters and policies between this router and its peers. In RTA's configuration, **neighbor 172.16.1.2 remote-as 3** indicates that a BGP peer session is to be established between RTA and peer 172.16.1.2 in autonomous system 3.
no synchronization	This command turns off the synchronization between BGP and IGP, as explained in Chapter 6, "Tuning BGP Capabilities."
no auto-summary	This command turns off the BGP classful automatic summarization at the major net boundary. Without this command, BGP will not send the subnets of a major net that are redistributed into BGP. In other words, updates about 172.16.1.0/24, 172.16.2.0/24, and so on will be sent as a single major class B 172.16.0.0/16. Summarization at the major net boundary should be done only if the AS owns the whole major net. Unless summarization is explicitly required, the recommended configuration is to disable it.
ip classless	This command lets the router forward packets that are destined for unrecognized subnets of directly connected networks. By default, when a router receives packets for a subnet that falls numerically within its subnetwork addressing scheme, if there is no such subnet number in the routing table and there is no network default route, the router discards the packets. When the **ip classless** command is enabled, however, the router forwards those packets to the best supernet route. Unless classful behavior is explicitly required, the recommended configuration is to disable it.
update-source *interface*	This command, when associated with the BGP **neighbor** statement, specifies the interface to be used as a source IP address of the BGP session with the neighbor. In RTA's configuration, for example, the second **neighbor** statement indicates that Loopback 0 is to be used as a source IP address.
remote-as	This command, when associated with the BGP **neighbor** statement, specifies the AS number of the remote BGP peer. In RTA's configuration, the first **neighbor** statement indicates that the internal BGP neighbor 172.16.1.2 belongs to the local AS3. The third **neighbor** statement indicates that the external BGP peer 172.16.20.1 belongs to AS1.

Table 11-2 *CIDR-to-Dotted Decimal Notation Chart*

CIDR	Dotted Decimal	Inverse Dotted Decimal
/1	128.0.0.0	127.255.255.255
/2	192.0.0.0	63.255.255.255
/3	224.0.0.0	31.255.255.255
/4	240.0.0.0	15.255.255.255
/5	248.0.0.0	7.255.255.255
/6	252.0.0.0	3.255.255.255
/7	254.0.0.0	1.255.255.255
/8	255.0.0.0	0.255.255.255
/9	255.128.0.0	0.127.255.255
/10	255.192.0.0	0.63.255.255
/11	255.224.0.0	0.31.255.255
/12	255.240.0.0	0.15.255.255
/13	255.248.0.0	0.7.255.255
/14	255.252.0.0	0.3.255.255
/15	255.254.0.0	0.1.255.255
/16	255.255.0.0	0.0.255.255
/17	255.255.128.0	0.0.127.255
/18	255.255.192.0	0.0.63.255
/19	255.255.224.0	0.0.31.255
/20	255.255.240.0	0.0.15.255
/21	255.255.248.0	0.0.7.255
/22	255.255.252.0	0.0.3.255
/23	255.255.254.0	0.0.1.255
/24	255.255.255.0	0.0.0.255
/25	255.255.255.128	0.0.0.127
/26	255.255.255.192	0.0.0.63
/27	255.255.255.224	0.0.0.31
/28	255.255.255.240	0.0.0.15
/29	255.255.255.248	0.0.0.7
/30	255.255.255.252	0.0.0.3

continues

Table 11-2 *CIDR-to-Dotted Decimal Notation Chart (Continued)*

CIDR	Dotted Decimal	Inverse Dotted Decimal
/31	255.255.255.254	0.0.0.1
/32	255.255.255.255	0.0.0.0

We turn now to RTF's configuration in Example 11-2.

Example 11-2 *RTF Configuration*

```
ip subnet-zero

interface Ethernet1/1
 ip address 172.16.1.2 255.255.255.0

interface Serial2/1
 ip address 192.68.5.1 255.255.255.0

router ospf 10
 network 172.16.0.0 0.0.255.255 area 0
 network 192.68.0.0 0.0.255.255 area 0

router bgp 3
no synchronization
 neighbor 172.16.2.254 remote-as 3
 neighbor 192.68.12.1 remote-as 2
 neighbor 192.68.12.1 ebgp-multihop 2
 no auto-summary

ip classless
```

In RTF's configuration, you can see the **ebgp-multihop 2** command being used as part of the neighbor configuration. This indicates that the exterior BGP peer is not directly connected and can be reached at a maximum of two hops away. Remember that **ebgp-multihop** is applicable with only EBGP, not IBGP. Also, the value at the end (2 in this example) represents the TTL (Time To Live) value to be configured in the IP packet header. Example 11-3 and Example 11-4 show the configurations for RTC and RTD, respectively.

Example 11-3 *RTC Configuration*

```
ip subnet-zero

interface Serial2/1
 ip address 172.16.20.1 255.255.255.0

router bgp 1
 neighbor 172.16.20.2 remote-as 3
 no auto-summary

ip classless
```

Example 11-4 *RTD Configuration*

```
ip subnet-zero

interface Serial0/0
 ip address 192.68.12.1 255.255.255.0

router ospf 10
  network 192.68.0.0 0.0.255.255 area 0

    router bgp 2
 neighbor 192.68.5.1 remote-as 3
 neighbor 192.68.5.1 ebgp-multihop 2
 no auto-summary

ip classless
```

Example 11-5 shows how the peer connection will look after the neighbors are in an established state.

Example 11-5 *RTF Peer Connection*

```
RTF#show ip bgp neighbor
BGP neighbor is 172.16.2.254,  remote AS 3, internal link
  BGP version 4, remote router ID 172.16.2.254
  BGP state = Established, table version = 2, up for 22:36:09
  Last read 00:00:10, hold time is 180, keepalive interval is 60 seconds
  Minimum time between advertisement runs is 5 seconds
  Received 1362 messages, 0 notifications, 0 in queue
  Sent 1362 messages, 0 notifications, 0 in queue
  Connections established 2; dropped 1
Connection state is ESTAB, I/O status: 1, unread input bytes: 0
Local host: 172.16.1.2, Local port: 11008
Foreign host: 172.16.2.254, Foreign port: 179

BGP neighbor is 192.68.12.1,  remote AS 2, external link
  BGP version 4, remote router ID 192.68.5.2
  BGP state = Established, table version = 2, up for 22:13:01
  Last read 00:00:00, hold time is 180, keepalive interval is 60 seconds
  Minimum time between advertisement runs is 30 seconds
  Received 1336 messages, 0 notifications, 0 in queue
  Sent 1336 messages, 0 notifications, 0 in queue
  Connections established 1; dropped 0
  External BGP neighbor may be up to 2 hops away.
Connection state is ESTAB, I/O status: 1, unread input bytes: 0
Local host: 192.68.5.1, Local port: 11016
Foreign host: 192.68.12.1, Foreign port: 179
```

From RTF's point of view, neighbor 172.16.2.254 is an internal neighbor that belongs to AS3. The neighbor connection is running BGP-4 with a table version of 2. The table version changes every time the BGP table is updated.

RTF's other neighbor 192.68.12.1 is also in an established state. This external neighbor belongs to AS2. Note that the display indicates that this neighbor is two hops away (as configured in the **ebgp-multihop**).

Route Filtering and Attribute Manipulation

Route filtering and attribute manipulation are the basis of implementing BGP policies. This section describes the following:

- BGP route maps
- Prefix lists
- Identifying and filtering routes based on the NLRI
- Identifying and filtering routes based on the AS_PATH

In order for new BGP policies such as attribute manipulation or filtering to be applied, a fresh set of the relevant routes must be presented to the Input Policy Engine. This can be accomplished in a number of ways. The brute-force way is to simply reset the BGP session by using the following command:

```
clear ip bgp [* | address | peer-group][soft [in|out]]
```

However, soft reconfiguration or BGP Route Refresh provide solutions that are much more elegant. Refer to Chapter 12, "Configuring Effective Internet Routing Policies," for more details.

BGP Route Maps

Route maps are used with BGP to control and modify routing information and to define the conditions by which routes are redistributed between routers and routing processes.

The format of a route map is as follows:

```
route-map map-tag [permit | deny] [sequence-number]
```

The *map-tag* is nothing more than a name that identifies the route map, and the *sequence-number* indicates the position that an instance of the route map is to have in relation to other instances of the same route map. (Instances are ordered sequentially.)

For example, you might use the commands demonstrated in Example 11-6 to define a route map named MYMAP.

Example 11-6 *Route Map MYMAP*

```
route-map MYMAP permit 10
! First set of conditions goes here.
route-map MYMAP permit 20
! Second set of conditions goes here.
```

When BGP applies MYMAP to routing updates, it applies the lowest instance first (in this case, instance 10). If the first set of conditions is not met, the second instance is applied, and so on, until either a set of conditions has been met or there are no more sets of conditions to apply.

The condition portion of a route map is set by using the **match** and **set** commands. The **match** command specifies criteria that must be matched, and the **set** command specifies an action that is to be taken if the routing update meets the conditions defined by the **match** command.

The configuration in Example 11-7 demonstrates a simple route map.

Example 11-7 *Route Map Configuration*

```
Router bgp 3
Neighbor 1.1.1.1 route-map MYMAP in
!
route-map MYMAP permit 10
match ip address 1
set metric 5
!
route-map MYMAP permit 20
set local-preference 200
!
ip access-list 1 permit 1.1.1.0 0.0.0.255
```

The statements in Example 11-7 subject routes learned from neighbor 1.1.1.1 to route map MYMAP. If 1.1.1.0/24 is advertised from neighbor 1.1.1.1, the metric is set to 5 (as specified in sequence 10), and no further action will occur. Any other prefixes received from the neighbor will also be subjected to route map MYMAP sequence 10. However, because they won't match sequence 10, they continue to sequence 20. Because no match statement is present, the LOCAL_PREF attribute for all prefixes presented will be set to 200.

There are two types of access lists—standard and extended. The main difference is that a standard access list is applied to the source IP address, whereas an extended access list is applied to source and destination or source and network mask. The following global command defines a standard access list; the extended access list will be covered in this chapter at the point it is used in context.

access-list *access-list-number* {**deny** | **permit**} *source* [*source-wildcard*]

A standard access list is used to match on a particular source IP network or host, to permit or deny a specific route. Consider the standard access list in Example 11-8.

Example 11-8 *Standard Access List*

```
Router bgp 3
Neighbor 1.1.1.1 route-map MYMAP in
!
route-map MYMAP permit 10
match ip address 1
set metric 5
!
ip access-list 1 permit 1.1.1.0 0.0.0.255
```

In Example 11-8, access list 1 identifies all routes of the form 1.1.1.X. (Note the inverse mask notation 0.0.0.255 versus the explicit 1.1.1.0/24 in the previous example, which permits only that exact prefix length.) A route of the form 1.1.1.X will match the access list and will be propagated (because of the **permit** keyword) with a metric attribute set to 5. The logic will then break out of the list of route map instances because a match has occurred. Prefix lists are a newer, more intuitive, more efficient way of filtering routes. We'll discuss these in more detail later.

When an update does not meet the criteria of a route map instance, BGP applies the next instance, and so on, until an action is taken or there are no more route map instances to apply. If the update does not meet any criteria, the update is not redistributed or controlled; it is silently discarded.

The route map can be applied on the incoming (in) or the outgoing (out) BGP updates. Example 11-9 demonstrates the route map MYMAP applied on the outgoing updates toward BGP neighbor 172.16.20.2.

Example 11-9 *Route Map MYMAP Applied to Outgoing Updates*

```
router bgp 1
neighbor 172.16.20.2 remote-as 3
neighbor 172.16.20.2 route-map MYMAP out
```

Prefix Lists

As discussed in Chapter 6, the prefix list is a newer, more efficient, more intuitive way to identify routes for matching and filtering of routing protocols. Let's take a moment to provide some prefix list configuration guidelines.

In addition to being a much more intuitive interface, and unlike access lists, prefix lists can be updated incrementally. This means that each entry of a prefix list is identified with a sequence number. If you want to add, remove, or modify a given sequence of a prefix list, you only need to specify the sequence number, as discussed in a moment. The primary benefit of this is that, unlike access lists, you need not delete and then reconfigure an entire list in order to make a modification.

Prefix lists are still order-dependent—that is, the first match wins. Like access lists, they allow you to **permit** or **deny** the associated prefix. Prefix lists also allow you to filter on both exact matches and ranges of prefixes.

Some configuration guidelines for prefix lists are discussed next. Note that these guidelines should not replace the IOS configuration documentation provided for your specific version(s) of IOS.

Prefix lists can be named by any alphanumeric string and can also be configured with a description. The description is configured like this:

```
ip prefix-list list-name description text
```

To add or remove entries from the prefix list, you would use the following syntax:

```
ip prefix-list list-name seq seq-value deny | permit network/len [ge ge-value][le
le-value]
```

list-name is an alphanumeric string. You could use a standard number scheme, or perhaps something more intuitive:

```
ip prefix-list CustomerA description <up to 80 characters, spaces permitted>
```

Table 11-3 documents some examples of filtering specific prefixes.

Table 11-3 *Filtering Specific Prefixes*

Filtering Criteria	Command to Execute
Permit exact prefix 192.68.0.0/16	**ip prefix-list sample permit 192.68.0.0/16**
Deny a default route	**ip prefix-list sample deny 0.0.0.0/0**
Permit all	**ip prefix-list sample permit 0.0.0.0/0 le 32**
Deny all	**ip prefix-list sample deny 0.0.0.0/0 le 32**
Deny /25+, in all address space	**ip prefix-list sample deny 0.0.0.0/0 ge 25**
In 192.68.0.0/24, deny /25+	**ip prefix-list sample deny 192.68.0.0/24 ge 25**
Permit all addresses from /8 to /24	**ip prefix-list sample permit 0.0.0.0/0 ge 8 le 24**

Note that sequence numbers are not included in Table 11-3. If you do not specify a sequence number, the initial sequence value will default to 5 and will be incremented by 5 each entry thereafter unless explicitly specified otherwise.

To perform incremental configuration of a prefix list, you simply specify the sequence number of the entry you want to add, remove, or modify. For example, consider the prefix list in Example 11-10.

Example 11-10 *Sample Prefix List*

```
ip prefix-list sample seq 5 permit 1.1.1.0/24
ip prefix-list sample seq 10 permit 2.2.2.0/24
ip prefix-list sample seq 15 permit 3.3.3.0/24
ip prefix-list sample seq 20 deny 0.0.0.0/0 le 32
```

The sample prefix list in Example 11-10 permits 1.1.1.0/24, 2.2.2.0/24, and 3.3.3.0/24, and then denies all other routes. Let's assume that you now want to permit 4.4.4.0/24 also. Configuring the following entry would accomplish this:

```
ip prefix-list sample seq 18 permit 4.4.4.0/24
```

This entry would result in a prefix list that looks like Example 11-11.

Example 11-11 *Prefix List After Permitting 4.4.4.0/24*

```
ip prefix-list sample seq 5 permit 1.1.1.0/24
ip prefix-list sample seq 10 permit 2.2.2.0/24
ip prefix-list sample seq 15 permit 3.3.3.0/24
ip prefix-list sample seq 18 permit 4.4.4.0/24
ip prefix-list sample seq 20 deny 0.0.0.0/0 le 32
```

Now let's assume that you want to deny the 4.4.4.0/24 as well. The following command would accomplish this:

```
no ip prefix-list sample seq 18
```

The prefix list would look like Example 11-12.

Example 11-12 *Prefix List After Denying 4.4.4.0/24*

```
ip prefix-list sample seq 5 permit 1.1.1.0/24
ip prefix-list sample seq 10 permit 2.2.2.0/24
ip prefix-list sample seq 15 permit 3.3.3.0/24
ip prefix-list sample seq 20 deny 0.0.0.0/0 le 32
```

As you can see, the incremental update capabilities of prefix lists provide a significant advantage over traditional access lists. Although most of the examples in the remainder of this chapter will continue to use access lists versus prefix lists, real-world examples of prefix lists will be supplied in the next chapter.

Identifying and Filtering Routes Based on the NLRI

To restrict the routing information that the router learns or advertises, you can filter based on routing updates to or from a particular neighbor. The filter consists of a prefix list (or access list) that is applied to updates to or from a neighbor. In Figure 11-2, RTD in AS2 is originating network 192.68.10.0/24 and is sending it to RTF. RTF will pass the update to RTA via IBGP, which in turn will propagate it to AS1. By doing so, AS3 could become a transit AS, advertising reachability of network 192.68.10.0/24.

Figure 11-2 *Identifying and Filtering Prefixes*

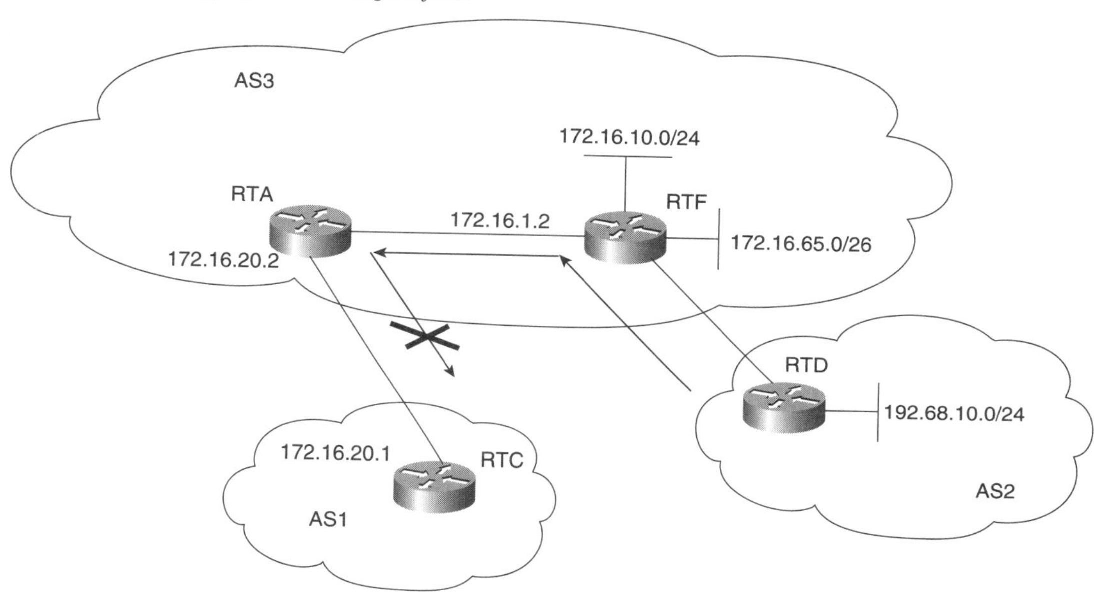

To prevent this situation, RTA will configure a filter to prevent prefix 192.68.10.0/24 from propagating to AS1. Example 11-13 demonstrates the following configuration for RTA to prevent prefix 192.68.10.0/24 from propagating to AS1.

Example 11-13 *RTA Prefix Filter*

```
router bgp 3
 no synchronization
 neighbor 172.16.1.2 remote-as 3
 neighbor 172.16.20.1 remote-as 1
 neighbor 172.16.20.1 prefix-list 1 out
 no auto-summary
!
ip prefix-list 1 seq 5 deny 192.68.10.0/24
ip prefix-list 1 seq 10 permit 0.0.0.0/0 le 32
```

In Example 11-13, the combination of the **neighbor prefix-list** router configuration command and prefix list 1 prevents RTA from propagating prefix 192.68.10.0/24 to AS1. The prefix list portion of the configuration identifies the prefixes, and when used in conjunction with the BGP **neighbor** subcommand, it applies the filtering on the outgoing updates associated with the specified neighbor (note the **out** keyword). Note that prefix list 1 ends with a logic that permits all updates (**permit 0.0.0.0/0 le 32**). When you use prefix lists or access lists for filtering, if no action is specified at the end of the access list statements, the logic of "deny everything else" applies implicitly. This means that anything that did not match any of the preceding instances will be denied. This is why it is important to specify the default action; in this example, 192.68.10.0/24 will be denied, and everything else will be allowed. For this reason, explicitly configuring the "deny everything else" – if you actually intend to– could save you some headaches down the road.

Although it isn't demonstrated here, the best current practice (if possible) is to supply a list of routes that will be permitted and then configure an explicit deny. This assures that you won't accept routing information from a peer if it's not included in the filter. Of course, this might not be practical if a large number of routes are learned from the peer.

Route maps (which reference access lists or prefix lists, and perhaps other policies) could have been used to filter updates in the previous example. The direct prefix list method was chosen to give you different options for filtering.

Using access lists to filter supernets or ranges of updates is trickier. Assume, for example, that RTF in Figure 11-2 has different subnets of 172.16.X.X, and you want to advertise an aggregate of the form 172.16.0.0/16 only. The following standard access list:

```
access-list 1 permit 172.16.0.0 0.0.255.255
```

would not work because it permits more than is desired. The standard access list looks at the source IP address only and cannot check the length of the network mask. The preceding access list will permit 172.16.0.0/16, 172.16.0.0/17, 172.16.0.0/18, 172.16.1.0/24, and so on.

To restrict the update to 172.16.0.0/16 only, you have to use an extended access list of this form:

```
access-list access-list-number {deny | permit} protocol source source-wildcard
destination destination-wildcard | mask mask-wildcard
```

This defines an extended access list that matches on a source destination or a source mask tuple to permit or deny a specific routing update. The access list number falls between 100 and 199. In the case where the protocol is IP and you are checking on a source/mask tuple, this would translate into the following:

```
access-list access-list-number permit ip network-number network-do-not-care-bits
mask mask-do-not-care-bits
```

For example:

```
access-list 101 permit ip 172.16.0.0 0.0.255.255 255.255.0.0 0.0.0.0
```

A 0 is an exact match bit, and a 1 is a do-not-care bit.

The preceding extended access list indicates that aggregate 172.16.0.0/16 is to be sent only because you have indicated that the mask should match 255.255.0.0 exactly. An update of the form 172.16.0.0/17 will not be allowed.

You could also accomplish this a couple of other ways. For example:

```
access-list 101 permit ip host 172.16.0.0 host 255.255.0.0
```

Or you could use a prefix list:

```
ip prefix-list 1 seq 5 permit 172.16.0.0/16
```

Remember that an ending implicit deny is assumed unless it is explicitly overridden.

Identifying and Filtering Routes Based on the AS_PATH

Filtering routes based on AS_PATH information becomes handy when filtering is needed for all routes of the same or multiple ASs. It is an efficient alternative to listing hundreds of routes one-by-one, as might be required when filtering on a prefix basis. You can also specify a prefix list on both incoming and outgoing updates based on the value of the AS_PATH attribute.

Looking again at Figure 11-2, if AS3 wanted to prevent itself from becoming a transit AS for other ASs, AS3 could configure its border routers RTA and RTF to advertise only local networks. Local networks originated from the AS itself. This can be accomplished with the RTA configuration in Example 11-14; RTF will be configured in the same manner.

Example 11-14 *Preventing AS3 from Becoming a Transit AS for Other ASs: RTA Configuration*

```
router bgp 3
 no synchronization
 neighbor 172.16.1.2 remote-as 3
 neighbor 172.16.20.1 remote-as 1
 neighbor 172.16.20.1 filter-list 1 out
 no auto-summary

ip as-path access-list 1 permit ^$
```

In Example 11-14, the AS_PATH access list 1 identifies only updates that originate from AS3. The filter list works in conjunction with the AS_PATH access list to filter the updates. In this example, the filter list is applied on the outgoing updates (note the **out** keyword). The regular expression **^$** indicates an AS_PATH that is empty. The caret symbol (^) indicates the beginning of the AS_PATH, and the $ symbol indicates the end of the AS_PATH. Because all networks originating from AS3 have an empty AS_PATH list (recall that the local AS number is not attached to the path until the route is passed to an EBGP peer), they will be advertised. All other prefixes will be denied.

If you want to verify that your regular expression works as intended, use the following EXEC command:

```
show ip bgp regexp regular-expression
```

The router displays all the paths that match the specified regular expression. Refer to Table 6-4 in Chapter 6 for a list of regular expression characters with special meanings.

NOTE Route maps (referencing AS_PATH access lists) also could have been used to filter updates in the previous example. The filter list was chosen to give you a different option for filtering.

Peer Groups

A BGP *peer group* is a group of BGP neighbors that share a common set of update policies. Update policies are usually defined by route maps, distribution lists, prefix lists, and filter lists. Instead of defining the same policies for each individual neighbor, you define a peer group name and assign policies to the peer group.

The network shown in Figure 11-3 demonstrates the use of BGP peer groups.

Figure 11-3 *BGP Peer Groups*

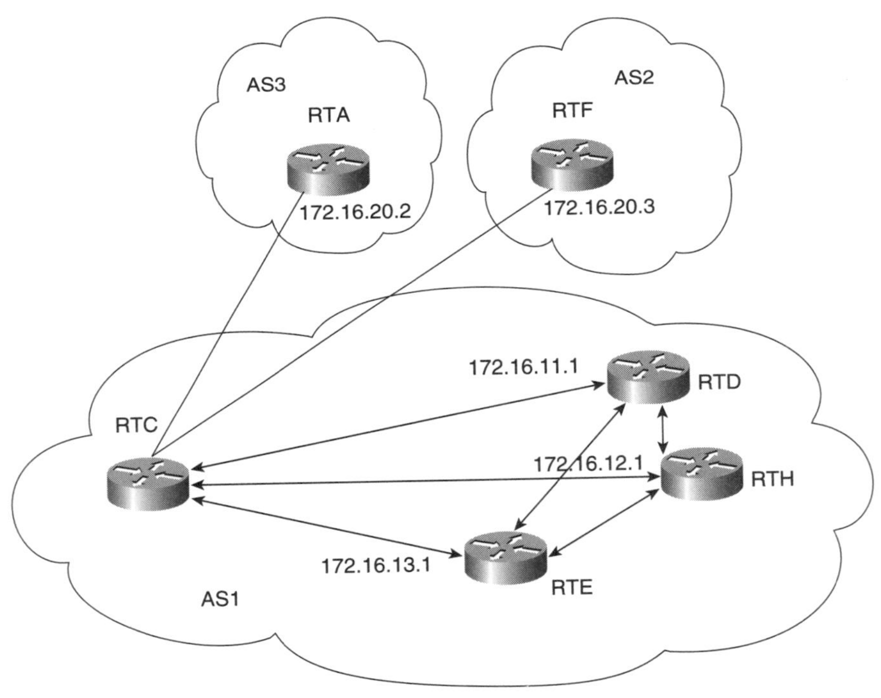

RTC forms similar internal peering sessions with RTD, RTE, and RTH. Instead of formulating and applying similar policies for each neighbor individually, RTC defines a peer group that contains the policies and configures all the internal neighbors as members of the peer group. Example 11-15 illustrates this.

Example 11-15 *Configuring a BGP Peer Group*

```
router bgp 1
 neighbor INTERNALMAP peer-group
 neighbor INTERNALMAP remote-as 1
 neighbor INTERNALMAP route-map INTERNAL out
 neighbor INTERNALMAP filter-list 1 out
 neighbor INTERNALMAP filter-list 2 in
 neighbor 172.16.11.1 peer-group INTERNALMAP
 neighbor 172.16.13.1 peer-group INTERNALMAP
 neighbor 172.16.12.1 peer-group INTERNALMAP
 neighbor 172.16.12.1 filter-list 3 in
```

The configuration in Example 11-15 defines a peer group called INTERNALMAP that contains the following policies. (Note that INTERNALMAP is an arbitrary name I've selected; it could be any string. Usually, a descriptive phrase is the most practical.)

- A route map named INTERNAL
- A filter list for outgoing updates (filter list 1)
- A filter list for incoming updates (filter list 2)

The configuration applies the peer group to all internal neighbors—RTD, RTE, and RTH.

Members of a peer group inherit all the configuration options of the peer group. Peer group members can also be configured to override configuration options if the options do not affect outgoing updates. In other words, peer group members can be configured to override options that affect incoming policies. The configuration of RTC, for example, also defines a filter list 3 for incoming updates from the neighbor at IP address 172.16.12.1 (RTH). Filter list 3 will override any incoming policies set by the peer group INTERNALMAP for neighbor RTH.

Example 11-16 demonstrates how to configure a BGP peer group named EXTERNALMAP on RTC and apply it to the exterior neighbors in AS3 and AS2.

Example 11-16 *RTC External BGP Peer Group*

```
router bgp 1
 neighbor EXTERNALMAP peer-group
 neighbor EXTERNALMAP route-map SETMED out
 neighbor EXTERNALMAP filter-list 1 out
 neighbor EXTERNALMAP filter-list 2 in
 neighbor 172.16.20.2 remote-as 3
 neighbor 172.16.20.2 peer-group EXTERNALMAP
 neighbor 172.16.20.3 remote-as 2
 neighbor 172.16.20.3 peer-group EXTERNALMAP
 neighbor 172.16.20.3 filter-list 3 in

ip as-path access-list 1 permit ^$
```

In the configuration in Example 11-16, the **neighbor remote-as** router configuration commands are placed outside the **neighbor peer-group** router configuration commands because different external ASs have to be defined. Also note that this configuration defines filter list 3, which can be used to override configuration options for incoming updates from the neighbor at IP address 172.16.20.3 (RTF).

The following two paragraphs apply only to older IOS versions; these are not restrictions of newer versions.

Note that the external BGP neighbors RTA and RTF that belong in the same peer group EXTERNALMAP were taken from the same subnet, 172.16.20.0. This restriction is needed to prevent loss of information. Placing the external neighbors in different subnets could result in RTC's sending updates to its neighbors (RTA and RTF) with a nonconnected next-hop IP address. These updates would be dropped due to the normal EBGP behavior of ignoring routes with nonconnected next hop (remember that **ebgp-multihop** was implemented to override this behavior).

Another restriction that applies is that peer groups should not be set on EBGP neighbors if the router is acting as a transit between those neighbors. If the router (RTC) is passing updates from one external neighbor to the other, placing external neighbors in peer groups might result in routes being mistakenly removed. Note that filter list 1 has been defined to allow AS1's local routes only to be sent to neighbors RTA and RTF. This way, RTC will not act as a transit router between RTA and RTF.

Predefined peer groups can ease configuration tasks (while decreasing error probability) when bringing up new peers. They can also significantly decrease the size of BGP configurations in the router. In addition, BGP UPDATE messages are generated only once for members of a peer group and then are copied to all the peers, potentially preserving a considerable amount of CPU resources versus what would be required to generate each UPDATE individually.

Sources of Routing Updates

Routes can be injected dynamically or statically into BGP. The choice of method depends on the number and stability of routes.

Injecting Information Dynamically into BGP

The following example demonstrates how routing information can be injected dynamically into BGP. Consider Figure 11-4.

Figure 11-4 *Injecting Routes into BGP*

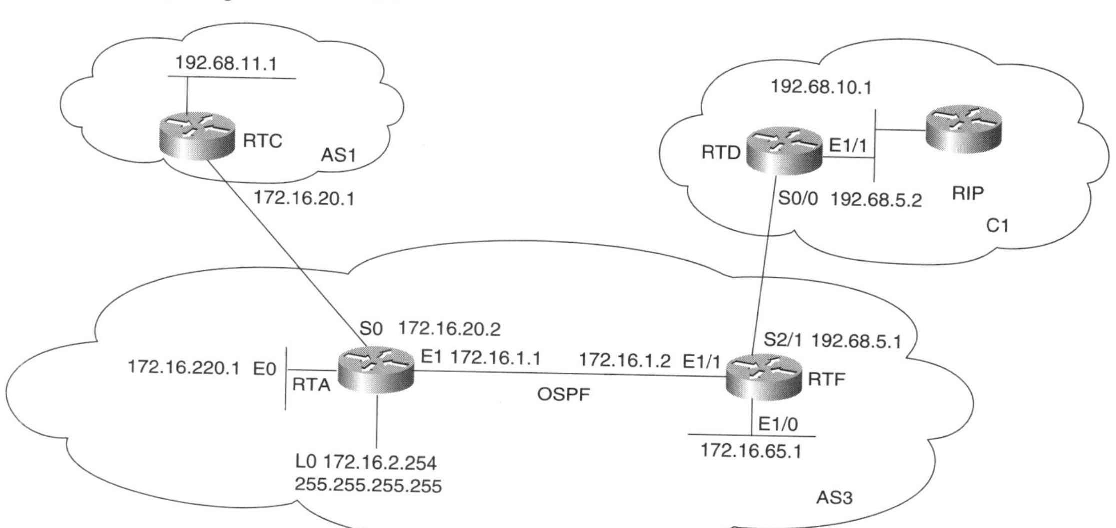

Assume that AS3 is getting Internet connectivity from AS1. AS3 is running OSPF as an IGP inside the AS and is running EBGP with AS1.

On the other hand, AS3 also has one customer, C1, with the following criteria:

- C1 is pointing a default toward AS3.
- C1 advertises all its routes to AS3 via RIP.

RTF is running two routing processes—the OSPF process and the RIP process. RTF will only listen to RIP on its connection to C1 and will redistribute the RIP routes it receives from C1 into OSPF. On the other hand, RTA will run two routing processes—the OSPF process and the BGP process. RTA will inject all its local routes, as well as its customer routes, dynamically into BGP. Example 11-17 illustrates this.

Example 11-17 *RTF Redistribution*

```
interface Ethernet1/0
 ip address 172.16.65.1 255.255.255.192

interface Ethernet1/1
 ip address 172.16.1.2 255.255.255.0

interface Serial2/1
 ip address 192.68.5.1 255.255.255.0

router ospf 10
 redistribute rip subnets
```

continues

Example 11-17 *RTF Redistribution (Continued)*

```
 network 172.16.0.0 0.0.255.255 area 0

router rip
 passive-interface Serial2/1
 network 192.68.5.0
```

RTF's configuration introduces two new commands:

- **passive-interface type number**—This router command disables sending routing updates on the specified interface. In the example, when used with RIP, this command prevents RIP updates from being sent on interface S2/1. This is in case RTF has multiple customers connected that do not need to see each other's networks.

  When used with OSPF, this command disables hello packets from being sent on the specified interface, which therefore prevents link state information from being exchanged on that interface.

- **redistribute protocol** [*process-id*]—The **redistribute** command injects routes from one routing process into another routing process. In this example, RTF is injecting the RIP routes into the OSPF process (OSPF process 10). Numerous extensions of the **redistribute** command exist (such as **subnets**); these extensions will be explained in context.

  The **subnets** keyword is used to make sure that all subnetted information will be injected into the OSPF process. This is required only when redistributing routes into the OSPF protocol. Example 11-18 illustrates this.

Example 11-18 *RTD Redistributing Static Routes into RIP*

```
interface Ethernet1/1
 ip address 192.68.10.1 255.255.255.0

interface Serial0/0
 ip address 192.68.5.2 255.255.255.0

router rip
 redistribute static
 network 192.68.5.0
 network 192.68.10.0
 default-metric 1

ip route 0.0.0.0 0.0.0.0 192.68.5.1
```

Note that RTD has configured a static route pointing a 0/0 default toward RTF. For all destinations that are outside C1, RTD will direct the traffic to RTF. RTD will also redistribute the static default route into the internal RIP domain so that all other routers can follow a default toward AS3. The **default-metric** router command assigns a metric to the routes redistributed into a particular protocol. In this case, the default metric assigns a hop count of 1 to the 0/0 route injected into RIP. Example 11-19 illustrates this.

Example 11-19 *RTA Redistributing OSPF Routes into BGP*

```
interface Ethernet0
 ip address 172.16.220.1 255.255.255.0

interface Ethernet1
 ip address 172.16.1.1 255.255.255.0

interface Serial0
 ip address 172.16.20.2 255.255.255.0

router ospf 10
 passive-interface Serial 0
 network 172.16.0.0 0.0.255.255 area 0

router bgp 3
 redistribute ospf 10 match  external 1 external 2
 neighbor 172.16.20.1 remote-as 1
 no auto-summary
```

RTA has a combination of OSPF routes that belong to AS3 and other external routes that came in from the RIP domain C1. Using the **redistribute** router command, RTA will dynamically inject all these routes into its BGP process. Note that RTA is using the keywords **match external 1 external 2** in conjunction with the **redistribute** router command. This is because OSPF does not inject external OSPF routes into BGP unless it is specifically instructed to do so. This measure was put in for loop avoidance in case the external OSPF information came from BGP.

The output generated in Example 11-20 is a snapshot of what RTA's IP routing table looks like.

Example 11-20 *RTA Routing Table*

```
RTA#show ip route
Codes: C - connected, S - static, I - IGRP, R - RIP, M - mobile, B - BGP
       D - EIGRP, EX - EIGRP external, O - OSPF, IA - OSPF inter area
       N1 - OSPF NSSA external type 1, N2 - OSPF NSSA external type 2
       E1 - OSPF external type 1, E2 - OSPF external type 2, E - EGP
       i - IS-IS, L1 - IS-IS level-1, L2 - IS-IS level-2,
           * - candidate default U - per-user static route, o - ODR
Gateway of last resort is not set
O E2 192.68.5.0/24 [110/20] via 172.16.1.2, 2d13h, Ethernet1
O E2 192.68.10.0/24 [110/20] via 172.16.1.2, 2d13h, Ethernet1
B    192.68.11.0/24 [20/0] via 172.16.20.1, 2d13h
     172.16.0.0/16 is variably subnetted, 5 subnets, 3 masks
C       172.16.2.254/32 is directly connected, Loopback0
C       172.16.220.0/24 is directly connected, Ethernet0
C       172.16.20.0/24 is directly connected, Serial0
C       172.16.1.0/24 is directly connected, Ethernet1
O       172.16.65.0/26 [110/20] via 172.16.1.2, 2d13h, Ethernet1
```

Note in RTA's IP table how networks 192.68.10.0/24 and 192.68.5.0/24 are listed as external OSPF routes (O E2). Dynamic redistribution will cause all these networks to be sent into BGP. The output generated in Example 11-21 shows how RTC's BGP table would look.

Example 11-21 *RTC BGP Routing Table*

```
RTC#show ip bgp
BGP table version is 20, local router ID is 192.68.11.1
Status codes: s suppressed, d damped, h history, * valid, > best,
i - internal Origin codes: i - IGP, e - EGP, ? - incomplete
   Network          Next Hop            Metric LocPrf Weight Path
*> 172.16.1.0/24    172.16.20.2              0             0 3 ?
*> 172.16.2.254/32  172.16.20.2              0             0 3 ?
*> 172.16.20.0/24   172.16.20.2              0             0 3 ?
*> 172.16.65.0/26   172.16.20.2             20             0 3 ?
*> 172.16.220.0/24  172.16.20.2              0             0 3 ?
*> 192.68.5.0       172.16.20.2             20             0 3 ?
*> 192.68.10.0      172.16.20.2             20             0 3 ?
*> 192.68.11.0      0.0.0.0                  0         32768 i
```

Notice that all networks running OSPF in AS3 have become BGP routes in AS1. Usually, not every network that belongs to your AS needs to be sent via BGP. You might be running private or illegal network numbers inside the AS that should not be advertised externally. Also notice how the loopback address 172.16.2.254/32 was injected into BGP. Most providers do not accept advertisements of such long prefixes (for example, /32) and will instruct you to filter them—or, more likely, will filter them on their end. This restriction is put in place to make sure that customers are aggregating their routes as much as possible to contain the growth of the global IP routing tables. Also, the DMZ network 172.16.20.0/24 has been injected into BGP, which is not necessary. This is why redistribution should be accompanied by filtering to specify the exact routes that need to be advertised.

The configuration of RTA in Example 11-22 gives an example of how filtering could be applied.

NOTE From this point forward, due to space limitations, configuration examples will focus on commands that are directly relevant to the discussion at hand. Do not be alarmed if you notice commands that are missing, such as interface commands.

Example 11-22 *Filtering Redistributed Routes*

```
router ospf 10
 passive-interface Serial0
 network 172.16.0.0 0.0.255.255 area 0

router bgp 3
```

Example 11-22 *Filtering Redistributed Routes (Continued)*

```
 redistribute ospf 10 match  external 1 external 2
 neighbor 172.16.20.1 remote-as 1
 neighbor 172.16.20.1 route-map BLOCKROUTES out
 no auto-summary

access-list 1 permit 172.16.2.254 0.0.0.0
access-list 1 permit 172.16.20.0 0.0.0.255

route-map BLOCKROUTES deny 10
 match ip address 1

route-map BLOCKROUTES permit 20
```

Filtering in Example 11-22 was performed with a route map, which specifies a set of actions to be taken in case certain criteria are met. The criteria here are to find a match on the host route 172.16.2.254/32 and the network 172.16.20.0/24 and to prevent them from being sent via BGP. The **access-list 1** will help you find a match on these routes, and **route-map BLOCKROUTES** specifies that they should be denied. The second instance of the route map (20) permits all other routes to be injected into BGP. (Refer to the discussion of filtering in Chapter 6 for more details.)

Example 11-23 demonstrates how RTC's BGP table would look after filtering has been applied. The host route 172.16.2.254/32 and the network 172.16.20.0/24 do not show anymore.

Example 11-23 *RTC BGP Table After Filtering Is Applied*

```
RTC#show ip bgp
BGP table version is 34, local router ID is 192.68.11.1
Status codes: s suppressed, d damped, h history, * valid, > best,
  i - internal Origin codes: i - IGP, e - EGP, ? - incomplete
   Network          Next Hop            Metric LocPrf Weight Path
*> 172.16.1.0/24    172.16.20.2              0             0 3 ?
*> 172.16.65.0/26   172.16.20.2             20             0 3 ?
*> 172.16.220.0/24  172.16.20.2              0             0 3 ?
*> 192.68.5.0       172.16.20.2             20             0 3 ?
*> 192.68.10.0      172.16.20.2             20             0 3 ?
*> 192.68.11.0      0.0.0.0                  0         32768 i
```

To have better control over what is being redistributed from the IGP into BGP, you can use the **network** command. The **network** command is a way to individually list the prefixes that need to be sent via BGP. The **network** command specifies the prefix to be sent out (network and mask). The statement **network 172.16.1.0 mask 255.255.255.0**, for example, specifies that prefix 172.16.1.0/24 should be sent. Networks that fall on a major net boundary (255.0.0.0, 255.255.0.0, or 255.255.255.0) do not need to have the mask included. For example, the statement **network 172.16.0.0** is sufficient to send the prefix

172.16.0.0/16. Such networks are also listed in the BGP routing table without the **/x** notation. For example, the Class C network 192.68.11.0 is equivalent to 192.68.11.0/24.

Considering Figure 11-4, the configuration of RTA in Example 11-24 will specify the networks that will be injected into BGP.

Example 11-24 *RTA Configuration Specifying Networks Injected into BGP*

```
router ospf 10
 passive-interface Serial0
 network 172.16.0.0 0.0.255.255 area 0

router bgp 3
 network 172.16.1.0 mask 255.255.255.0
 network 172.16.65.0 mask 255.255.255.192
 network 172.16.220.0 mask 255.255.255.0
 network 192.68.5.0
 network 192.68.10.0
 neighbor 172.16.20.1 remote-as 1
 no auto-summary
```

Example 11-25 shows what RTC's BGP table would look like.

Example 11-25 *RTC BGP Routing Table*

```
RTC#show ip bgp
BGP table version is 34, local router ID is 192.68.11.1
Status codes: s suppressed, d damped, h history, * valid, > best,
  i - internal Origin codes: i - IGP, e - EGP, i - incomplete
   Network          Next Hop          Metric LocPrf Weight Path
*> 172.16.1.0/24    172.16.20.2            0             0 3 i
*> 172.16.65.0/26   172.16.20.2           20             0 3 i
*> 172.16.220.0/24  172.16.20.2            0             0 3 i
*> 192.68.5.0       172.16.20.2           20             0 3 i
*> 192.68.10.0      172.16.20.2           20             0 3 i
*> 192.68.11.0      0.0.0.0                0         32768 i
```

All routes have been injected into BGP except for 172.16.2.254/32 and 172.16.20.0/24. Note that the table looks similar to the one produced when redistributing the OSPF routes into BGP and applying filters. The only noticeable difference is with the origin code, which is indicated by the **i** at the end of the path information. The **i** origin code indicates that the source of these networks is internal (IGP) to the originating AS. If you look at the previous snapshot of RTC's BGP table, the origin code was **?**, meaning incomplete, which indicates that the origin of these networks is learned by some other means. Anytime routes are injected into BGP via redistribution, the origin code is incomplete, unless otherwise explicitly specified.

The **network** command takes effect only if the prefixes listed are known to the router. In other words, BGP will not blindly advertise prefixes just because they were listed. The router will check for the availability of an exact match of the prefix in the IP routing table before the network is advertised. In Example 11-25, if you list **network 172.16.192.0 mask 255.255.255.0**, that network will not be originated, because it is unknown by the router.

Injecting Information Statically into BGP

Listing prefixes with the **network** command has the same drawbacks as dynamic redistribution. If a route that is listed with the **network** command goes down, BGP will send an update; if the route comes back, BGP will send another update. If this behavior continues, the IGP instability will translate into BGP instabilities. The only way around this is to use a combination of statically defined prefixes in conjunction with the **network** command. This will ensure that the prefixes will always remain in the IP routing tables and will always be advertised.

In the previous example, if you wanted to make sure that the fluctuations of route 192.68.10.0/24 did not translate into fluctuations in the BGP, you would have included in RTA a static route of this form:

```
ip route 192.68.10.0 255.255.255.0 Ethernet1
```

If you use the static approach, the prefix entry will always be present in the IP routing table and will always be advertised, so long as the Ethernet 1 interface is active. The drawback of this approach is that even when a route is down, it will still be advertised by BGP. Considering the gain in network stability compared to the damage that an ill-behaved route or multiple ill-behaved routes can cause, administrators might find this approach very efficient. The RTA configuration in Example 11-26 ensures that 192.68.10.0/24 is always sent.

Example 11-26 *Ensuring That a Route is Always Advertised*

```
router bgp 3
 network 172.16.1.0 mask 255.255.255.0
 network 172.16.65.0 mask 255.255.255.192
 network 172.16.220.0 mask 255.255.255.0
 network 192.68.5.0
 network 192.68.10.0
 neighbor 172.16.20.1 remote-as 1
 no auto-summary

ip route 192.68.10.0 mask 255.255.255.0     Ethernet1
```

Note that RTA itself is originating the 192.68.10.0/24 prefix and is not relying on the advertisement coming from RTF. In case an aggregate is advertised via a static route, it is better to point the static route to null 0 (bit bucket) for loop prevention.

Overlapping Protocols: Backdoors

This example shows how the **backdoor** command can be used to change the EBGP **distance** to have IGP routes favored over EBGP routes for specific network numbers. Figure 11-5 illustrates the topology for this example.

Figure 11-5 *BGP Backdoor Routes*

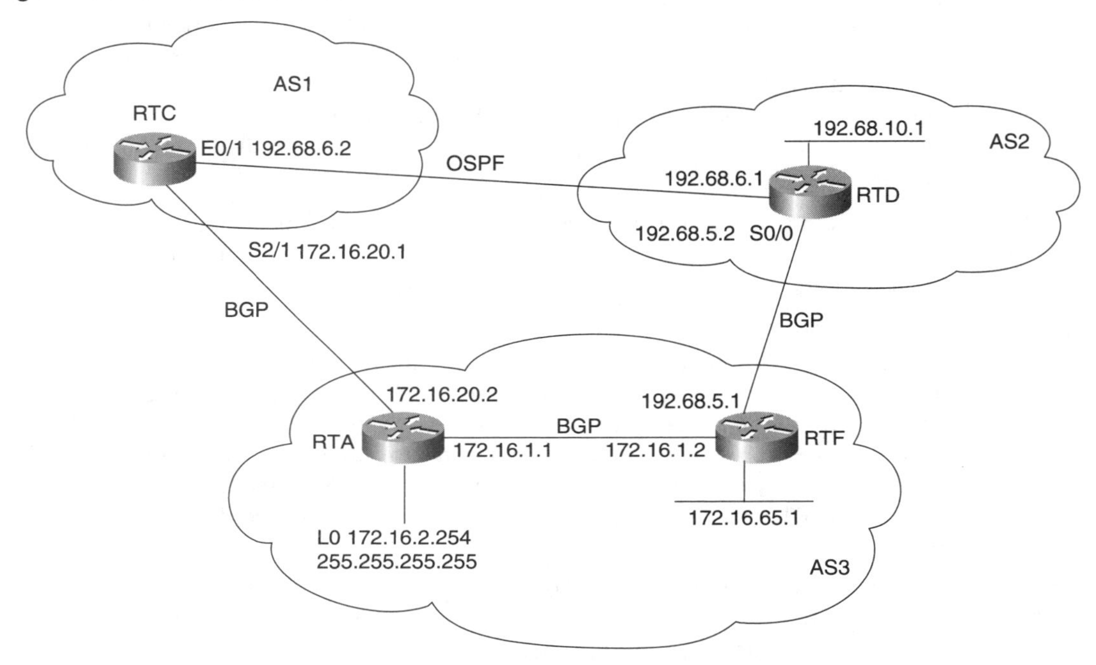

In Figure 11-5, AS2 is running an IGP (OSPF) on the private link between it and AS1, and it is running EBGP with AS3. RTC, in AS1, will receive advertisements about 192.68.10.0/24 from AS3 via EBGP with a distance of 20 and from AS2 via OSPF with a distance of 110. Because the lower distance is preferred, RTC will use the BGP link to AS3 to reach 192.68.10.0/24.

Looking at RTC's IP routing table in Example 11-27 reveals that prefix 192.68.10.0/24 is indeed learned via BGP. RTC will take the longer path via AS3 (next hop 172.16.0.2) to reach 192.68.10.0/24. Note the distance of [20] that the EBGP route has.

Example 11-27 *RTC IP Routing Table*

```
RTC#show ip route
Codes: C - connected, S - static, I - IGRP, R - RIP, M - mobile, B - BGP
       D - EIGRP, EX - EIGRP external, O - OSPF, IA - OSPF inter area
       E1 - OSPF external type 1, E2 - OSPF external type 2, E - EGP
```

Example 11-27 *RTC IP Routing Table (Continued)*

```
       i - IS-IS, L1 - IS-IS level-1, L2 - IS-IS level-2,
         * - candidate default U - per-user static route
Gateway of last resort is not set
C    192.68.6.0/24 is directly connected, Ethernet0/1
B    192.68.10.0/24 [20/0] via 172.16.20.2, 00:21:36
     172.16.0.0/16 is variably subnetted, 3 subnets, 2 masks
C       172.16.20.0/24 is directly connected, Serial2/1
B       172.16.1.0/24 [20/0] via 172.16.20.2, 00:21:37
B       172.16.65.0/26 [20/20] via 172.16.20.2, 00:21:37
```

If you wanted to have RTC prefer the OSPF entry, you would configure RTC as demonstrated in Example 11-28.

Example 11-28 *Configuring RTC to Prefer the OSPF Entry*

```
router bgp 1
  neighbor 172.16.20.2 remote-as 3
  network 192.68.10.0 backdoor
  no auto-summary
```

In Example 11-28, **network 192.68.10.0 backdoor** changes the distance of the BGP route 192.68.10.0/24 from 20 to 200, which makes the OSPF route with a distance of 110 more preferred. Note that **network 192.68.10.0 backdoor** will not cause BGP to generate an advertisement for that network.

The output generated in Example 11-29 shows RTC's new routing table. Note that the 192.68.10.0/24 entry is now learned via OSPF with distance **[110]**, and the private link between AS1 and AS2 will be used.

Example 11-29 *RTC's New Routing Table*

```
RTC#show ip route
Codes: C - connected, S - static, I - IGRP, R - RIP, M - mobile, B - BGP
       D - EIGRP, EX - EIGRP external, O - OSPF, IA - OSPF inter area
       E1 - OSPF external type 1, E2 - OSPF external type 2, E - EGP
       i - IS-IS, L1 - IS-IS level-1, L2 - IS-IS level-2,
         * - candidate default U - per-user static route
Gateway of last resort is not set
C    192.68.6.0/24 is directly connected, Ethernet0/1
O IA 192.68.10.0/24 [110/20] via 192.68.6.1, 00:00:21, Ethernet0/1
     172.16.0.0/16 is variably subnetted, 3 subnets, 2 masks
C       172.16.20.0/24 is directly connected, Serial2/1
B       172.16.1.0/24 [20/0] via 172.16.20.2, 00:29:07
B       172.16.65.0/26 [20/20] via 172.16.20.2, 00:29:07
```

BGP Attributes

In this section, we will work with the network topology illustrated in Figure 11-6 to demonstrate how the different BGP attributes are used.

Figure 11-6 *Applying BGP Attributes*

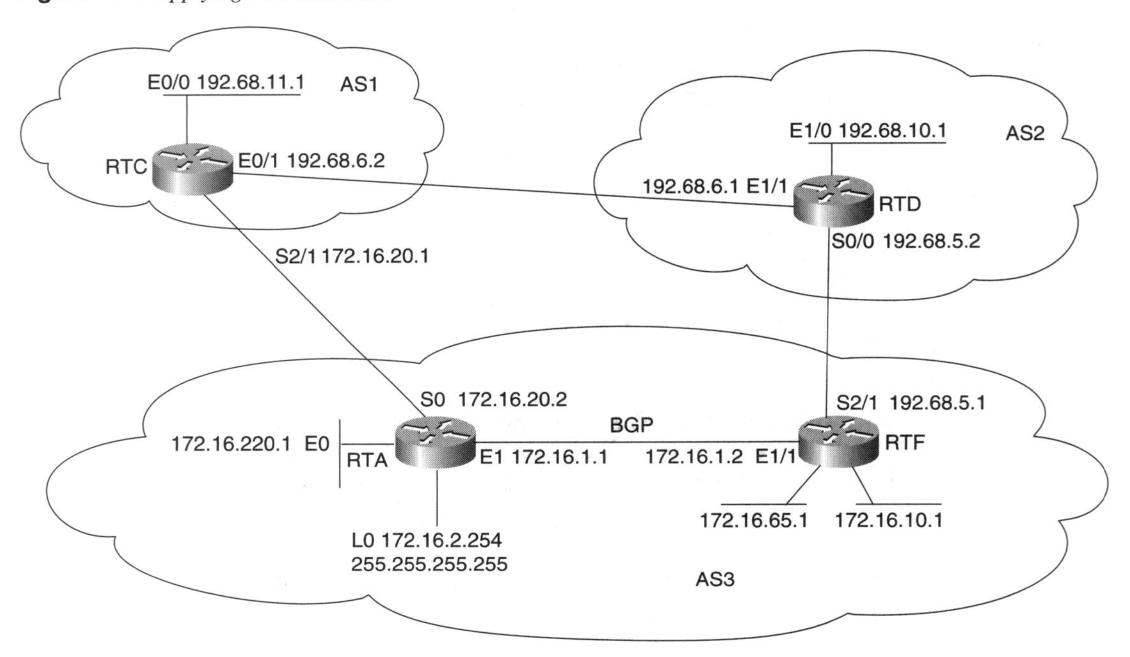

Examples 11-30 through 11-33 are a first run of basic configurations for the routers RTA, RTF, RTC, and RTD illustrated in Figure 11-6. Additional configuration will be added according to the topic under discussion.

Example 11-30 *Basic Configuration for RTA in Figure 11-6*

```
ip subnet-zero

interface Loopback0
 ip address 172.16.2.254 255.255.255.255

interface Ethernet0
 ip address 172.16.220.1 255.255.255.0

interface Ethernet1
 ip address 172.16.1.1 255.255.255.0

interface Serial0
 ip address 172.16.20.2 255.255.255.0
```

Example 11-30 *Basic Configuration for RTA in Figure 11-6 (Continued)*

```
router ospf 10
 passive-interface Serial0
 network 172.16.0.0 0.0.255.255 area 0

router bgp 3
 no synchronization
 network 172.16.1.0 mask 255.255.255.0
 network 172.16.10.0 mask 255.255.255.0
 network 172.16.65.0 mask 255.255.255.192
 network 172.16.220.0 mask 255.255.255.0
 neighbor 172.16.1.2 remote-as 3
 neighbor 172.16.1.2 update-source Loopback0
 neighbor 172.16.20.1 remote-as 1
 neighbor 172.16.20.1 filter-list 10 out
 no auto-summary

ip classless
ip as-path access-list 10 permit ^$
```

Example 11-31 *Basic Configuration for RTF in Figure 11-6*

```
ip subnet-zero

interface Ethernet0/0
 ip address 172.16.10.1 255.255.255.0

interface Ethernet 1/0
 ip address 172.16.65.1 255.255.255.192

interface Ethernet1/1
 ip address 172.16.1.2 255.255.255.0

interface Serial2/1
 ip address 192.68.5.1 255.255.255.0

router ospf 10
 network 172.16.0.0 0.0.255.255 area 0

router bgp 3
 no synchronization
 network 172.16.1.0 mask 255.255.255.0
 network 172.16.10.0 mask 255.255.255.0
 network 172.16.65.0 mask 255.255.255.192
 network 172.16.220.0 mask 255.255.255.0
 neighbor 172.16.2.254  remote-as 3
 neighbor 172.16.2.254 next-hop-self
 neighbor 192.68.5.2 remote-as 2
 neighbor 192.68.5.2 filter-list 10 out
 no auto-summary
```

continues

Example 11-31 *Basic Configuration for RTF in Figure 11-6 (Continued)*

```
ip classless
ip as-path access-list 10 permit ^$
```

Example 11-32 *Basic Configuration for RTC in Figure 11-6*

```
ip subnet-zero

interface Ethernet0/0
 ip address 192.68.11.1 255.255.255.0

interface Ethernet0/1
 ip address 192.68.6.2 255.255.255.0

interface Serial2/1
 ip address 172.16.20.1 255.255.255.0

router bgp 1
 network 192.68.11.0
 neighbor 172.16.20.2 remote-as 3
 neighbor 192.68.6.1 remote-as 2
 no auto-summary

ip classless
```

Example 11-33 *Basic Configuration for RTD in Figure 11-6*

```
ip subnet-zero

interface Ethernet1/0
 ip address 192.68.10.1 255.255.255.0

interface Ethernet1/1
 ip address 192.68.6.1 255.255.255.0

interface Serial0/0
 ip address 192.68.5.2 255.255.255.0

router bgp 2
 network 192.68.10.0
 neighbor 192.68.5.1 remote-as 3
 neighbor 192.68.6.2 remote-as 1
 no auto-summary

ip classless
```

AS3 is assumed to be a nontransit AS. This is why **filter-list 10** is applied to force AS3 to originate its local routes only. Routes learned from AS1 or AS2 will not be propagated outside the AS. Also note that some networks such as 172.16.10.0/24 are advertised via the

network command on both RTA and RTF. This will ensure that a link failure between AS3 and either AS1 or AS2 will not prevent such networks from being advertised.

The NEXT_HOP Attribute

In the next few examples we'll discuss the BGP NEXT_HOP attribute and provide examples of ways to manipulate the NEXT_HOP value.

Example 11-34 shows the BGP table for RTF.

Example 11-34 *BGP Table for RTF*

```
RTF#show ip bgp
BGP table version is 8, local router ID is 192.68.5.1
Status codes: s suppressed, d damped, h history, * valid, > best,
  i - internal Origin codes: i - IGP, e - EGP, ? - incomplete
   Network          Next Hop          Metric LocPrf Weight Path
* i172.16.1.0/24    172.16.2.254           0    100      0 i
*>                  0.0.0.0                0         32768 i
* i172.16.10.0/24   172.16.2.254          20    100      0 i
*>                  0.0.0.0                0         32768 i
* i172.16.65.0/26   172.16.2.254          20    100      0 i
*>                  0.0.0.0                0         32768 i
* i172.16.220.0/24  172.16.2.254           0    100      0 i
*>                  172.16.1.1            20         32768 i
*> 192.68.10.0      192.68.5.2             0                0 2 i
*  192.68.11.0      192.68.5.2                              0 2 1 i
*>i                 172.16.20.1            0    100      0 1 i
```

Network 192.68.11.0/24 is learned via IBGP (note the **i** at the far right) with NEXT_HOP 172.16.20.1, which is the IP address of RTA's external neighbor. The EBGP NEXT_HOP IP address is usually preserved inside the routing domain, which is why it is very important to have an internal route to the NEXT_HOP. Otherwise, the BGP route would be unusable. There are a couple of ways to make sure that you do not have problems reaching the EBGP NEXT_HOP. The first way is to include the network that the next hop belongs to in the IGP. This is illustrated on RTA by including interface serial 0 in the OSPF; this way, RTF would know about 172.16.20.1. Note that even though OSPF is running on RTA interface serial 0, it need not exchange any OSPF hello packets on serial 0—hence the **passive-interface** router command.

The second method is to use the **next-hop-self neighbor** command (see Example 11-31) to force the router to advertise itself, rather than the external peer, as the next hop. In the RTF configuration in Example 11-31, note how the **next-hop-self** command is added at the end of the **neighbor** statement toward RTA. This way, when RTF advertises external networks such as 192.68.10.0/24 toward RTA, it will use itself as the NEXT_HOP. Looking at RTA's BGP table in Example 11-35, the prefix 192.68.10.0/24 is learned via NEXT_HOP

172.16.1.2, which is its internal peer with RTF. Because 172.16.1.2 is part of the OSPF path already, you have no problem reaching it.

Example 11-35 *RTA BGP Table*

```
RTA#show ip bgp
BGP table version is 20, local router ID is 172.16.2.254
Status codes: s suppressed, d damped, h history, * valid, > best,
  i - internal Origin codes: i - IGP, e - EGP, ? - incomplete
   Network          Next Hop            Metric LocPrf Weight Path
* i172.16.1.0/24    172.16.1.2               0    100      0 i
*>                  0.0.0.0                  0         32768 i
* i172.16.10.0/24   172.16.1.2               0    100      0 i
*>                  172.16.1.2              20         32768 i
* i172.16.65.0/26   172.16.1.2               0    100      0 i
*>                  172.16.1.2              20         32768 i
* i172.16.220.0/24  172.16.1.2              20    100      0 i
*>                  0.0.0.0                  0         32768 i
*>i192.68.10.0      172.16.1.2               0    100      0 2 i
*                   172.16.20.1                            0 1 2 i
*> 192.68.11.0      172.16.20.1              0             0 1 i
```

Note in Example 11-35 that 192.68.10.0/24 is actually learned via two different paths, whereas 192.68.11.0/24 is learned via a single path. This might seem misleading, but actually routing is doing the right thing. In this situation, RTF has decided that the best path to reach 192.68.11.0/24 is via RTA (check RTF's BGP table in Example 11-34). This is why RTF will not advertise network 192.68.11.0/24 back to RTA and why RTA will have a single entry for 192.68.11.0/24.

The AS_PATH Attribute

Looking at RTF's BGP table in Example 11-36, you can see the AS_PATH information at the end of each line. Network 192.68.11.0/24 is learned via IBGP with AS_PATH 1 and via EBGP with AS_PATH 2 1. This means that if RTF wanted to reach 192.68.11.0/24 via IBGP, it could go to AS1, and if RTF wanted to reach 192.68.11.0/24 via EBGP, it would have to go via AS2 and then AS1. BGP always prefers the shortest path, which is why the path via IBGP with AS_PATH 1 is preferred. The > at the left indicates that out of the two available paths that BGP has for 192.68.11.0/24, BGP prefers the second one as being the "best" path.

Example 11-36 *RTF BGP Table*

```
RTF#show ip bgp
BGP table version is 8, local router ID is 192.68.5.1
Status codes: s suppressed, d damped, h history, * valid, > best,
  i - internal Origin codes: i - IGP, e - EGP, ? - incomplete
   Network          Next Hop            Metric LocPrf Weight Path
* i172.16.1.0/24    172.16.2.254             0    100      0 i
*>                  0.0.0.0                  0         32768 i
```

Example 11-36 *RTF BGP Table (Continued)*

```
* i172.16.10.0/24   172.16.2.254        20    100      0 i
*>                  0.0.0.0             0          32768 i
* i172.16.65.0/26   172.16.2.254        20    100      0 i
*>                  0.0.0.0             0          32768 i
* i172.16.220.0/24  172.16.2.254        0     100      0 i
*>                  172.16.1.1          20         32768 i
*> 192.68.10.0      192.68.5.2          0              0 2 i
*  192.68.11.0      192.68.5.2                         0 2 1 i
*>i                 172.16.20.1         0     100      0 1 i
```

AS_PATH Manipulation

Considering RTF's BGP table in Example 11-36, RTF has picked the direct path via AS1 to reach 192.68.11.0/24 because it is shorter. The configuration in Example 11-37 shows how the AS_PATH information can be manipulated to make the AS_PATH longer by prepending AS numbers to the path. Considering the network illustrated earlier in Figure 11-6, Example 11-37 prepends two extra AS numbers to the AS_PATH information sent from RTC to RTA to change RTF's decision about reaching 192.68.11.0/24.

Example 11-37 *Manipulating AS_PATH Information by Prepending AS Numbers*

```
router bgp 1
 network 192.68.11.0
 neighbor 172.16.20.2 remote-as 3
 neighbor 172.16.20.2 route-map AddASnumbers out
 neighbor 192.68.6.1 remote-as 2
 no auto-summary

route-map AddASnumbers permit 10
 set as-path prepend 1 1
```

The configuration in Example 11-37 prepends two additional AS_PATH numbers 1 and 1 (1 twice) to the AS_PATH information sent from RTC to RTA. If you look at RTF's BGP table in Example 11-38, you will see that RTF can now reach 192.68.11.0/24 via NEXT_HOP 192.68.5.2—that is, via path 2 1. RTF will prefer this path because it is shorter than the direct path via AS1, which now has three ASs included in the path information (1 1 1).

Example 11-38 *RTF BGP Table After AS_PATH Manipulation*

```
RTF#show ip bgp
BGP table version is 18, local router ID is 192.68.5.1
Status codes: s suppressed, d damped, h history, * valid, > best,
  i - internal Origin codes: i - IGP, e - EGP, ? - incomplete
   Network          Next Hop            Metric LocPrf Weight Path
* i172.16.1.0/24    172.16.2.254             0    100      0 i
*>                  0.0.0.0                  0         32768 i
```

continues

Example 11-38 *RTF BGP Table After AS_PATH Manipulation (Continued)*

```
* i172.16.10.0/24   172.16.2.254          20    100      0 i
*>                  0.0.0.0               0          32768 i
* i172.16.65.0/26   172.16.2.254          20    100      0 i
*>                  0.0.0.0               0          32768 i
* i172.16.220.0/24  172.16.2.254          0     100      0 i
*>                  172.16.1.1            20         32768 i
*> 192.68.10.0      192.68.5.2            0              0 2 i
*> 192.68.11.0      192.68.5.2                           0 2 1 i
* i                 172.16.20.1           0     100      0 1 1 1 i
```

Using Private ASs

The example in this section demonstrates how BGP can be configured to prevent the leakage of private AS numbers into the Internet. Figure 11-7 illustrates the network topology discussed in this section.

Figure 11-7 *Removing Private AS Numbers*

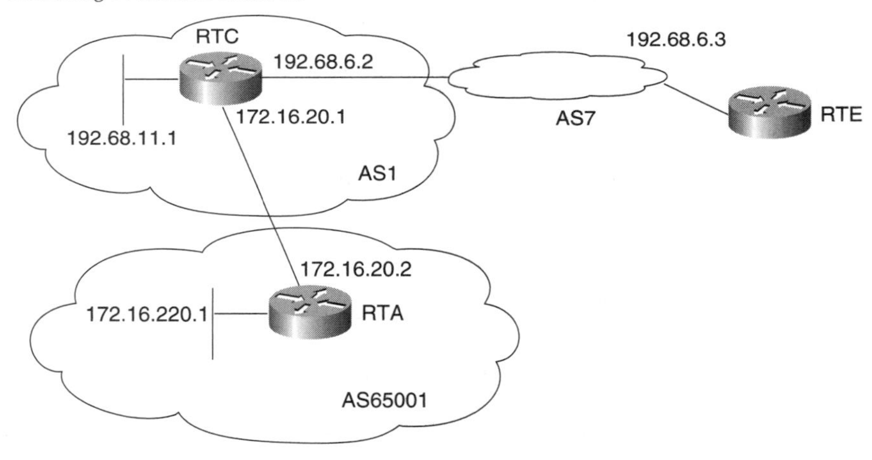

Through the configuration of RTA in Example 11-39 and RTC in Example 11-40, AS1 will prevent private AS number 65001 from being leaked to the Internet when BGP routes are propagated.

Example 11-39 *RTA Configuration to Prevent Leaking Private AS Numbers*

```
router bgp 65001
 network 172.16.220.0 mask 255.255.255.0
 neighbor 172.16.20.1 remote-as 1
 no auto-summary
```

Example 11-40 *RTC Configuration to Prevent Leaking Private AS Numbers*

```
router bgp 1
 network 192.68.11.0 mask 255.255.255.0
 neighbor 172.16.20.2 remote-as 65001
 neighbor 192.68.6.3 remote-as 7
 neighbor 192.68.6.3 remove-private-AS
 no auto-summary
```

Note how the RTC configuration in Example 11-40 uses the **remove-private-AS** keyword in its neighbor connection to AS7. The output in Example 11-41 shows the BGP tables of RTC and RTE.

Example 11-41 *BGP Tables for RTC and RTE*

```
RTC#show ip bgp
BGP table version is 72, local router ID is 192.68.11.1
Status codes: s suppressed, d damped, h history, * valid, > best,
  i - internal Origin codes: i - IGP, e - EGP, ? - incomplete

   Network          Next Hop            Metric LocPrf Weight Path
*> 172.16.220.0/24  172.16.20.2              0             0 65001 i
*> 192.68.11.0      0.0.0.0                  0         32768 i

RTE#show ip bgp
BGP table version is 245, local router ID is 192.68.30.1
Status codes: s suppressed, * valid, > best, i - internal
Origin codes: i - IGP, e - EGP, ? - incomplete

   Network          Next Hop            Metric LocPrf Weight Path
*> 172.16.220.0/24  192.68.6.2                             0 1 i
*> 192.68.11.0      192.68.6.2               0             0 1 i
```

Note that prefix 172.16.220.0/24 has an AS_PATH of 65001 in RTC's BGP table and an AS_PATH of 1 in RTE's BGP table. RTC has stripped the private AS path information when propagating the update to AS7. Note that the **remove-private-AS** command applies to egress routes, and therefore is applied at the egress points of the network.

The LOCAL_PREF Attribute

Setting the local preference (via the LOCAL_PREF attribute) also affects the BGP decision process. If multiple paths for the same prefix are available, the path with the larger local preference value is preferred. LOCAL_PREF is an AS-wide attribute at the highest level of the BGP decision process (it's considered just after the **weight** parameter, which is Cisco-proprietary and local to the router); it is considered before the AS path length. A longer path with a larger local preference is preferred over a shorter path with a smaller local preference. Example 11-42 (still referring to the network in Figure 11-7) configures RTF to have a higher local preference for all BGP updates coming from RTD.

Example 11-42 *Configuring RTF to Have a Higher Local Preference for BGP Updates Originating from RTD*

```
router bgp 3
no synchronization
 network 172.16.1.0 mask 255.255.255.0
 network 172.16.10.0 mask 255.255.255.0
 network 172.16.65.0 mask 255.255.255.192
 network 172.16.220.0 mask 255.255.255.0
 neighbor 172.16.2.254  remote-as 3
 neighbor 172.16.2.254 next-hop-self
 neighbor 192.68.5.2 remote-as 2
 neighbor 192.68.5.2 filter-list 10 out
 neighbor 192.68.5.2 route-map SETLOCAL in
 no auto-summary

ip as-path access-list 10 permit ^$

route-map SETLOCAL permit 10
set local-preference 300
```

route-map SETLOCAL assigns a local preference of 300 (note that the default local preference value is normally 100) for all routes coming from RTD (note the keyword in). Note in Example 11-43 how BGP has decided that prefixes 192.68.10.0/24 and 192.68.11.0/24 can now be reached via NEXT_HOP 192.68.5.2 having a local preference of 300.

Example 11-43 *RTF BGP Table*

```
RTF#show ip bgp
BGP table version is 20, local router ID is 192.68.5.1
Status codes: s suppressed, d damped, h history, * valid, > best,
  i - internal Origin codes: i - IGP, e - EGP, ? - incomplete
   Network          Next Hop           Metric LocPrf Weight Path
*> 172.16.1.0/24    0.0.0.0                 0         32768 i
* i                 172.16.2.254            0    100      0 i
*> 172.16.10.0/24   0.0.0.0                 0         32768 i
* i                 172.16.2.254           20    100      0 i
*> 172.16.65.0/26   0.0.0.0                 0         32768 i
* i                 172.16.2.254           20    100      0 i
*> 172.16.220.0/24  172.16.1.1             20         32768 i
* i                 172.16.2.254            0    100      0 i
*> 192.68.10.0      192.68.5.2              0    300      0 2 i
*> 192.68.11.0      192.68.5.2                   300      0 2 1 i
```

Because the LOCAL_PREF attribute is carried inside the AS, RTF will pass the local preference value to RTA, as illustrated in Example 11-44, which shows RTA's BGP table.

Example 11-44 *RTA BGP Table Reveals the Local Preference Value*

```
RTA#show ip bgp
BGP table version is 43, local router ID is 172.16.2.254
Status codes: s suppressed, d damped, h history, * valid, > best,
  i - internal Origin codes: i - IGP, e - EGP, ? - incomplete
   Network          Next Hop            Metric LocPrf Weight Path
* i172.16.1.0/24    172.16.1.2               0    100      0 i
*>                  0.0.0.0                  0         32768 i
* i172.16.10.0/24   172.16.1.2               0    100      0 i
*>                  172.16.1.2              20         32768 i
* i172.16.65.0/26   172.16.1.2               0    100      0 i
*>                  172.16.1.2              20         32768 i
* i172.16.220.0/24  172.16.1.2              20    100      0 i
*>                  0.0.0.0                  0         32768 i
*>i192.68.10.0      172.16.1.2               0    300      0 2 i
*                   172.16.20.1                            0 1 2 i
*>i192.68.11.0      172.16.1.2                    300      0 2 1 i
*                   172.16.20.1              0             0 1 i
```

Notice how prefix 192.68.11.0/24 is preferred via IBGP with a local preference of 300, even though the AS_PATH via EBGP is shorter. Other prefixes learned via IBGP, such as 172.16.10.0/24, have a default local preference of 100.

The MULTI_EXIT_DISC Attribute

This section demonstrates how metrics can be used by one AS to influence routing decisions of another AS. In Figure 11-8, AS3 is the customer of provider AS1. AS3 wants to generate metrics toward AS1 to influence inbound traffic. In case all BGP attributes are the same, BGP will prefer routes with a lower metric over routes with a higher metric.

Figure 11-8 *Setting the MED Attribute*

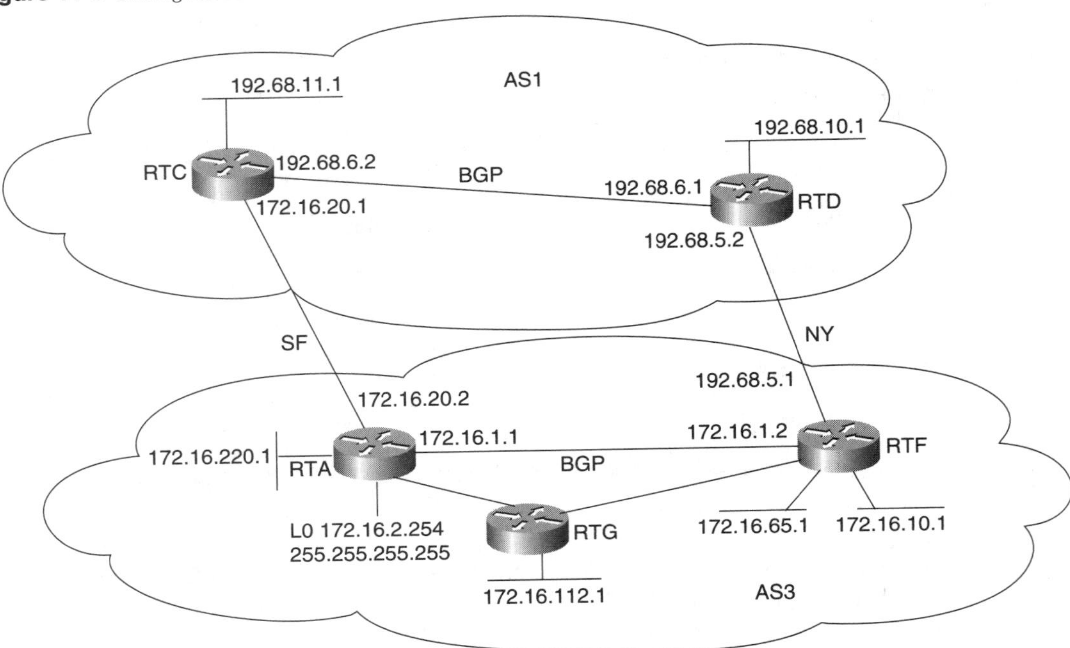

RTA and RTF are running IBGP internally and EBGP with the provider AS1. RTG is an internal non-BGP router, running OSPF only. Assume that RTA and RTF want to send MEDs toward AS1 to achieve the following:

- Incoming traffic toward network 172.16.1.0/24 takes the SF link.
- Incoming traffic toward all other networks should come in by using the border router that can reach these networks with a smaller internal metric. Incoming traffic toward network 172.16.112.0/24, for example, should come in on the SF link if RTA can reach this network with a smaller internal metric than RTF.

Example 11-45 and Example 11-46 show the required configuration for RTA and RTF to satisfy these criteria.

Example 11-45 *Setting the MED Attribute: RTA Configuration*

```
router ospf 10
 passive-interface Serial0
 network 172.16.0.0 0.0.255.255 area 0

router bgp 3
 no synchronization
```

Example 11-45 *Setting the MED Attribute: RTA Configuration (Continued)*

```
 network 172.16.1.0 mask 255.255.255.0
 network 172.16.10.0 mask 255.255.255.0
 network 172.16.65.0 mask 255.255.255.192
 network 172.16.220.0 mask 255.255.255.0
 network 172.16.112.0 mask 255.255.255.0
 neighbor 172.16.1.2 remote-as 3
 neighbor 172.16.1.2 update-source Loopback0
 neighbor 172.16.20.1 remote-as 1
 neighbor 172.16.20.1 filter-list 10 out
 no auto-summary

ip as-path access-list 10 permit ^$
```

Example 11-46 *Setting the MED Attribute: RTF Configuration*

```
router ospf 10
 network 172.16.0.0 0.0.255.255 area 0

router bgp 3
 no synchronization
 network 172.16.1.0 mask 255.255.255.0
 network 172.16.10.0 mask 255.255.255.0
 network 172.16.65.0 mask 255.255.255.192
 network 172.16.220.0 mask 255.255.255.0
 network 172.16.112.0 mask 255.255.255.0
 neighbor 172.16.2.254  remote-as 3
 neighbor 172.16.2.254 next-hop-self
 neighbor 192.68.5.2 remote-as 1
 neighbor 192.68.5.2 route-map SETMETRIC out
 neighbor 192.68.5.2 filter-list 10 out
 no auto-summary

ip as-path access-list 10 permit ^$
access-list 1 permit 172.16.1.0 0.0.0.255

route-map SETMETRIC permit 10
 match ip address 1
 set metric 50

route-map SETMETRIC permit 20
```

The configurations in Example 11-45 and 11-46 will make RTF generate prefix 172.16.1.0/24 with a MED of 50. When AS1 gets the prefix, AS1 will compare a metric of 50 coming from RTF to a metric of 0 coming from RTA and will prefer the SF link. All other networks will be advertised with their internal metrics carried into BGP, and AS1 will choose the entrance that has a smaller metric to the destination. Example 11-47 shows RTD's BGP table after the changes.

Example 11-47 *RTD BGP Table*

```
RTD#show ip bgp
BGP table version is 17, local router ID is 192.68.10.1
Status codes: s suppressed, d damped, h history, * valid, > best,
  i - internal Origin codes: i - IGP, e - EGP, ? - incomplete
   Network          Next Hop            Metric LocPrf Weight Path
*  172.16.1.0/24    192.68.5.1              50             0 3 i
*>i                 192.68.6.2               0    100      0 3 i
*> 172.16.10.0/24   192.68.5.1               0             0 3 i
*> 172.16.65.0/26   192.68.5.1               0             0 3 i
*  172.16.112.0/24  192.68.5.1              84             0 3 i
*>i                 192.68.6.2              74    100      0 3 i
*  172.16.220.0/24  192.68.5.1              20             0 3 i
*>i                 192.68.6.2               0    100      0 3 i
*> 192.68.10.0      0.0.0.0                  0         32768 i
*>i192.68.11.0      192.68.6.2               0    100      0 i
```

Note from the BGP table in Example 11-47 how RTD prefers network 172.16.1.0/24 via NEXT_HOP 192.68.6.2, which is RTC (RTC is using **next-hop-self**). This is because of the lower metric (0 is less than 50). For all other networks, RTD prefers routes that have smaller metrics. Note that 172.16.112.0/24 is learned via metric 74 from RTA and via metric 84 from RTF. RTD will prefer the SF link to reach 172.16.112.0/24.

For BGP learned routes, an AS can also advertise these routes to another AS with the internal IGP metric carried into BGP. This is achieved by using the **set metric-type internal** command as part of a route map toward a neighbor. This would cause BGP routes to carry the internal IGP metric as the BGP MED.

The COMMUNITY Attribute

This section demonstrates how the COMMUNITY attribute can be used to dynamically influence the routing decisions of another AS. With the network illustrated in Figure 11-9, the configuration example in Example 11-48 shows how AS3 can advertise route 172.16.65.0/26 to AS1 and dynamically instructs AS1 not to advertise this route externally. AS3 will assign route 172.16.65.0/26 the COMMUNITY attribute **no-export** when advertising it to AS1.

Figure 11-9 *Setting the COMMUNITY Attribute*

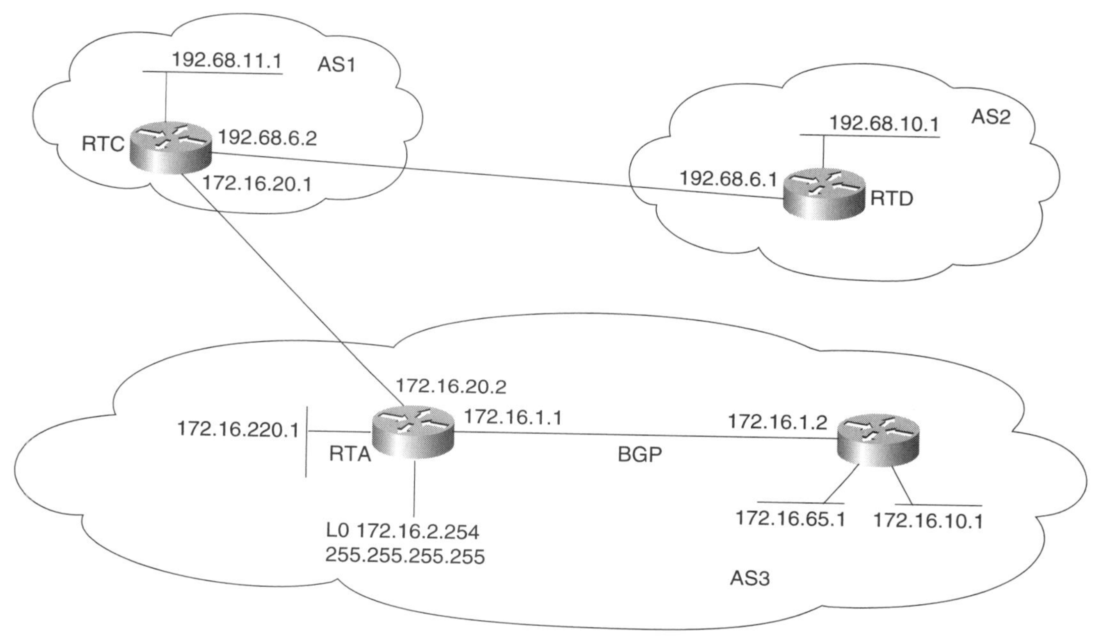

Example 11-48 *RTA Configuration Using the COMMUNITY Attribute*

```
router bgp 3
no synchronization
network 172.16.1.0 mask 255.255.255.0
 network 172.16.10.0 mask 255.255.255.0
 network 172.16.65.0 mask 255.255.255.192
 network 172.16.220.0 mask 255.255.255.0
 neighbor 172.16.1.2 remote-as 3
 neighbor 172.16.1.2 update-source Loopback0
 neighbor 172.16.20.1 remote-as 1
 neighbor 172.16.20.1 send-community
 neighbor 172.16.20.1 route-map SETCOMMUNITY out
 no auto-summary

access-list 1 permit 172.16.65.0 0.0.0.63

route-map SETCOMMUNITY permit 10
match ip address 1
set community no-export

route-map SETCOMMUNITY permit 20
```

Because communities are not propagated to internal or external BGP neighbors by default, the **send-community** option in the **neighbor** router subcommand is required in order for the assigned community to be sent out.

The configuration in Example 11-48 shows that RTA has defined a route map SETCOMMUNITY toward neighbor 172.16.20.1 (RTC). Instance 10 of the route map will match on prefix 172.16.65.0/26 and will set its community attribute to **no-export**. The **send-community** keyword assigned to the neighbor session is required to allow the community attribute to be sent to the specified neighbor. Instance 20 of the route map will allow all other networks to be passed with no change.

Example 11-49 shows RTC's BGP entry for 172.16.65.0/26.

Example 11-49 *RTC BGP Output*

```
RTC#show ip bgp 172.16.65.0 255.255.255.192
BGP routing table entry for 172.16.65.0/26, version 3
Paths: (1 available, best #1, not advertised to EBGP peer)
  3
    172.16.20.2 from 172.16.20.2 (172.16.2.254)
      Origin IGP, metric 20, valid, external, best
      Community: no-export
```

Notice how the entry has been assigned the community **no-export** as an instruction that it is not to be advertised to EBGP peers. RTC will not propagate this route to its external peer RTD. Note that in the RTD BGP table in Example 11-50, RTD does not receive an update about 172.16.65.0/26.

Example 11-50 *RTD BGP Table*

```
RTD#show ip bgp
BGP table version is 22, local router ID is 192.68.10.1
Status codes: s suppressed, d damped, h history, * valid, > best,
  i - internal Origin codes: i - IGP, e - EGP, ? - incomplete
   Network          Next Hop            Metric LocPrf Weight Path
*> 172.16.1.0/24    192.68.6.2                             0 1 3 i
*> 172.16.10.0/24   192.68.6.2                             0 1 3 i
*> 172.16.220.0/24  192.68.6.2                             0 1 3 i
*> 192.68.10.0      0.0.0.0                  0         32768 i
*> 192.68.11.0      192.68.6.2               0             0 1 i
```

BGP-4 Aggregation

The following examples demonstrate different methods of aggregation that are seen on the Internet. The way aggregates are formed and advertised and whether they carry with them more-specific routes will influence traffic patterns and sizes of BGP routing tables. Remember that aggregation applies to routes that exist in the BGP routing table. An aggregate can be sent if at least one more-specific route of that aggregate exists in the BGP table.

Aggregate Only, Suppressing the More-Specific

This section shows how an aggregate can be generated without propagating any of the more-specific routes that fall under the aggregate. In the network illustrated in Figure 11-10, RTA is sending prefixes 172.16.220.0/24, 172.16.1.0/24, 172.16.10.0/24, and 172.16.65.0/26 toward RTC.

Figure 11-10 *BGP Aggregation (Suppressing the Specific Routes)*

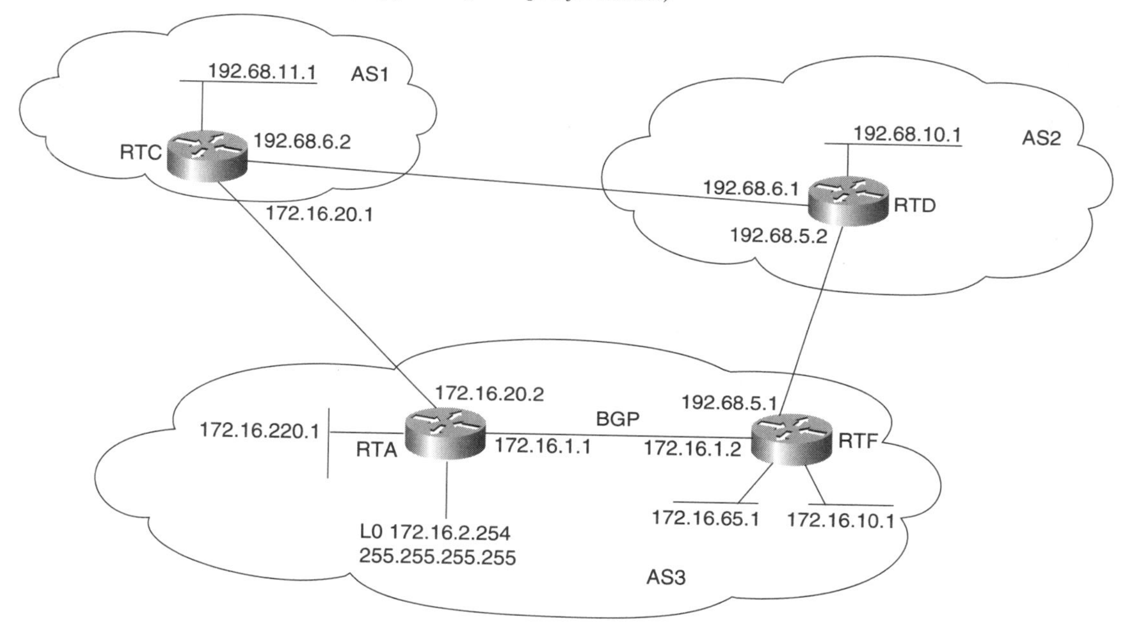

The configuration in Example 11-51 shows how RTA can aggregate all these routes into a single prefix 172.16.0.0/16 and send it to RTC. This of course assumes that AS3 is the sole owner of the class B 172.16.0.0/16. RTF is also doing the same aggregation on its end with a configuration similar to RTA.

Example 11-51 *RTA Configuration: Aggregating Routes into a Single Prefix to Send to RTC*

```
router bgp 3
 no synchronization
 network 172.16.1.0 mask 255.255.255.0
 network 172.16.10.0 mask 255.255.255.0
 network 172.16.65.0 mask 255.255.255.192
 network 172.16.220.0 mask 255.255.255.0
 aggregate-address 172.16.0.0 255.255.0.0 summary-only
 neighbor 172.16.1.2 remote-as 3
 neighbor 172.16.1.2 update-source Loopback0
```

continues

Example 11-51 *RTA Configuration: Aggregating Routes into a Single Prefix to Send to RTC (Continued)*

```
 neighbor 172.16.20.1 remote-as 1
 neighbor 172.16.20.1 filter-list 10 out
 no auto-summary

ip as-path access-list 10 permit ^$
```

RTA's configuration uses the **aggregate-address** command to aggregate all the more-specific routes of 172.16.0.0/16 into a single address.

RTA's BGP table (shown in Example 11-52) indicates that a new aggregate 172.16.0.0/16 has been originated by this router (NEXT_HOP is 0.0.0.0), whereas all the more-specific prefixes have been suppressed (note the **s** at the far left). In this case, the same result could have been achieved by using auto-summarization.

Example 11-52 *RTA BGP Table*

```
RTA#show ip bgp
BGP table version is 14, local router ID is 172.16.2.254
Status codes: s suppressed, d damped, h history, * valid, > best,
  i - internal Origin codes: i - IGP, e - EGP, ? - incomplete
   Network          Next Hop          Metric LocPrf Weight Path
*> 172.16.0.0       0.0.0.0                          32768 i
* i                 172.16.1.2                   100      0 i
s> 172.16.1.0/24    0.0.0.0                0          32768 i
s> 172.16.10.0/24   172.16.1.2            20          32768 i
s> 172.16.65.0/26   172.16.1.2            20          32768 i
s> 172.16.220.0/24  0.0.0.0                0          32768 i
*  192.68.10.0      172.16.20.1                           0 1 2 i
*>i                 172.16.1.2             0     100      0 2 i
*> 192.68.11.0      172.16.20.1            0              0 1 i
```

The output of RTC's BGP table in Example 11-53 shows that the only prefix that was learned from RTA is the aggregate 172.16.0.0/16. Because RTF is also performing the same aggregation, RTC will also learn an aggregate that is originated from RTF (next hop RTD via AS2).

Example 11-53 *RTC BGP Table*

```
RTC#show ip bgp
BGP table version is 22, local router ID is 192.68.11.1
Status codes: s suppressed, d damped, h history, * valid, > best,
  i - internal Origin codes: i - IGP, e - EGP, ? - incomplete
   Network          Next Hop          Metric LocPrf Weight Path
*> 172.16.0.0       172.16.20.2                           0 3 i
*                   192.68.6.1                            0 2 3 i
*> 192.68.10.0      192.68.6.1             0              0 2 i
*> 192.68.11.0      0.0.0.0                0          32768 i
```

Looking at the specific 172.16.0.0/16 aggregate entry, Example 11-54 provides more information about the aggregate itself.

Example 11-54 *RTC BGP Output*

```
RTC#show ip bgp 172.16.0.0
BGP routing table entry for 172.16.0.0/16, version 22
Paths: (2 available, best #1, advertised over EBGP)
  3, (aggregated by 3 172.16.2.254)
    172.16.20.2 from 172.16.20.2 (172.16.2.254)
      Origin IGP, valid, external, atomic-aggregate, best
  2 3, (aggregated by 3 192.68.5.1)
    192.68.6.1 from 192.68.6.1 (192.68.10.1)
      Origin IGP, valid, external, atomic-aggregate
```

Note the presence of the ATOMIC_AGGREGATE attribute, which indicates that the prefix 172.16.0.0/16 is an aggregate. Also note the presence of the **aggregated by 3 172.16.2.254** and **aggregated by 3 192.68.5.1** statements, which represent the AGGREGATOR attribute. The AGGREGATOR attribute (discussed in Chapter 6) indicates the AS number and ROUTER_ID of the router that originated the aggregate—in this case, AS3 and the ROUTER_IDs of RTA and RTF.

Aggregates can also be generated by using static routes, as demonstrated by the configuration for RTA in Example 11-55 and the configuration for RTF in Example 11-56.

Example 11-55 *Generating Aggregates Using Static Routes: RTA Configuration*

```
router bgp 3
 no synchronization
 network 172.16.0.0
 neighbor 172.16.1.2 remote-as 3
 neighbor 172.16.1.2 update-source Loopback0
 neighbor 172.16.20.1 remote-as 1
 neighbor 172.16.20.1 filter-list 10 out
 no auto-summary

ip route 172.16.0.0 255.255.0.0 null0
ip as-path access-list 10 permit ^$
```

Example 11-56 *Generating Aggregates Using Static Routes: RTF Configuration*

```
router bgp 3
 no synchronization
 network 172.16.0.0
 neighbor 172.16.2.254  remote-as 3
 neighbor 172.16.2.254 next-hop-self
 neighbor 192.68.5.2 remote-as 2
 neighbor 192.68.5.2 filter-list 10 out
 no auto-summary

ip route 172.16.0.0 255.255.0.0 null0
ip as-path access-list 10 permit ^$
```

The configuration in Example 11-55 and Example 11-56 places a static instance of 172.16.0.0/16 in the routing table. Note that the static entry is pointing to null0 (bit bucket). If RTA or RTF has no knowledge of the more-specific routes of 172.16.0.0, traffic will be dropped. This is to prevent loops in case RTA or RTF is following defaults to its provider (see "Classless Interdomain Routing (CIDR)" in Chapter 3, "IP Addressing and Allocation Techniques").

Aggregate Plus More-Specific Routes

In some cases, more-specific routes, in addition to the aggregate, need to be passed (leaked) to a neighboring AS. This is usually done in ASs multihomed to a single provider. An AS (the provider) that gets the more-specific routes would be able to make a better decision about which way to reach the route. (You have already seen how an AS receiving different metrics can direct the traffic accordingly.) Figure 11-11 illustrates the topology for this scenario.

Figure 11-11 *More BGP Scenarios*

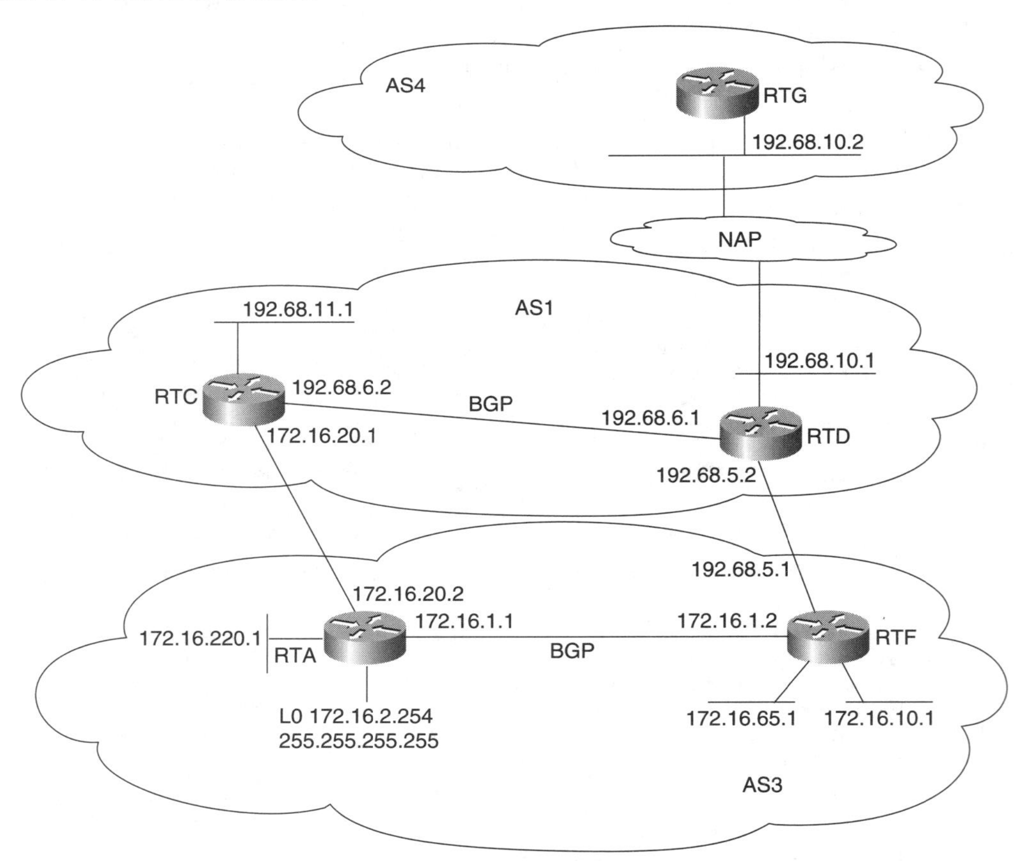

In Figure 11-11, AS3 is multihomed to a single provider, AS1. Through the configurations in Example 11-57 and Example 11-58, RTA and RTF in AS3 can send the aggregate 172.16.0.0/16 and the more-specific routes toward AS1.

Example 11-57 *Multihoming to a Single Provider: RTA Configuration*

```
router bgp 3
 no synchronization
 network 172.16.1.0 mask 255.255.255.0
 network 172.16.10.0 mask 255.255.255.0
 network 172.16.65.0 mask 255.255.255.192
 network 172.16.220.0 mask 255.255.255.0
 aggregate-address 172.16.0.0 255.255.0.0
 neighbor 172.16.1.2 remote-as 3
 neighbor 172.16.1.2 update-source Loopback0
 neighbor 172.16.20.1 remote-as 1
 neighbor 172.16.20.1 filter-list 10 out
 no auto-summary

ip as-path access-list 10 permit ^$
```

Example 11-58 *Multihoming to a Single Provider: RTF Configuration*

```
router bgp 3
 no synchronization
 network 172.16.1.0 mask 255.255.255.0
 network 172.16.10.0 mask 255.255.255.0
 network 172.16.65.0 mask 255.255.255.192
 network 172.16.220.0 mask 255.255.255.0
 aggregate-address 172.16.0.0 255.255.0.0
 neighbor 172.16.2.254  remote-as 3
 neighbor 172.16.2.254 next-hop-self
 neighbor 192.68.5.2 remote-as 1
 neighbor 192.68.5.2 filter-list 10 out
 no auto-summary

ip as-path access-list 10 permit ^$
```

Note that the **aggregate-address** command in both the RTA and RTF configurations does not include the **summary-only** parameter, so both the aggregate and specific routes will be advertised.

RTC's BGP table, shown in Example 11-59, shows that RTC has learned the aggregate 172.16.0.0/16 in addition to the more-specific routes. RTD will also receive the same information.

Example 11-59 *Multihoming to a Single Provider: RTC BGP Table*

```
RTC#show ip bgp
BGP table version is 28, local router ID is 192.68.11.1
Status codes: s suppressed, d damped, h history, * valid, > best,
  i - internal Origin codes: i - IGP, e - EGP, ? - incomplete
   Network          Next Hop            Metric LocPrf Weight Path
* i172.16.0.0       192.68.6.1                    100      0 3 i
*>                  172.16.20.2                            0 3 i
* i172.16.1.0/24    192.68.6.1               0    100      0 3 i
*>                  172.16.20.2              0             0 3 i
* i172.16.10.0/24   192.68.6.1               0    100      0 3 i
*>                  172.16.20.2             20             0 3 i
* i172.16.65.0/26   192.68.6.1               0    100      0 3 i
*>                  172.16.20.2             20             0 3 i
* i172.16.220.0/24  192.68.6.1              20    100      0 3 i
*>                  172.16.20.2              0             0 3 i
*>i192.68.10.0      192.68.6.1               0    100        0 i
*> 192.68.11.0      0.0.0.0                  0         32768 i
```

Using the community **no-export** attribute, RTA and RTF can instruct RTC and RTD not to export the more-specific routes and to send only the aggregate 172.16.0.0/16 toward AS4. This is very useful in controlling routing table expansion, assuming that AS4 can get by using the aggregate route only. Example 11-60 shows the required configuration on RTF to accomplish this; RTA will have the same relative configuration.

Example 11-60 *Suppressing the Export of Specific Routes: RTF Configuration*

```
router bgp 3
 no synchronization
 network 172.16.1.0 mask 255.255.255.0
 network 172.16.10.0 mask 255.255.255.0
 network 172.16.65.0 mask 255.255.255.192
 network 172.16.220.0 mask 255.255.255.0
 aggregate-address 172.16.0.0 255.255.0.0
 neighbor 172.16.2.254 remote-as 3
 neighbor 172.16.2.254 next-hop-self
 neighbor 192.68.5.2 remote-as 1
 neighbor 192.68.5.2 send-community
 neighbor 192.68.5.2 route-map SETCOMMUNITY out
 neighbor 192.68.5.2 filter-list 10 out
 no auto-summary

ip as-path access-list 10 permit ^$
access-list 101 permit ip 172.16.0.0 0.0.255.255 host 255.255.0.0

route-map SETCOMMUNITY permit 10
 match ip address 101
```

Example 11-60 *Suppressing the Export of Specific Routes: RTF Configuration (Continued)*

```
route-map SETCOMMUNITY permit 20
set community no-export
```

In Example 11-60, RTF will use multiple instances of **route-map SETCOMMUNITY** to assign the more-specific routes 172.16.1.0/24, 172.16.220.0/24, 172.16.10.0/24, and 172.16.65.0/26 to **community no-export**, which instructs RTD not to send these routes to exterior ASs such as AS4. On the other hand, the aggregate itself, 172.16.0.0/16, is passed unmodified without any community and will be sent to AS4.

Instance 10 of the route map uses access list 101, which matches on the aggregate 172.16.0.0/16 only. Note how the host 255.255.0.0 part of the access list makes sure that no other entry that starts with 172.16 matches by explicitly specifying the mask to be exactly 255.255.0.0 and nothing else. Instance 10 does not set any community values; hence, the aggregate will be passed as is.

Instance 20 will ensure that all the more-specific routes will have a community **no-export**.

Example 11-61 and Example 11-62 show the required configurations for RTC and RTD.

Example 11-61 *RTC Configuration*

```
router bgp 1
 no synchronization
 network 192.68.11.0
 neighbor 172.16.20.2 remote-as 3
 neighbor 192.68.6.1 remote-as 1
 neighbor 192.68.6.1 next-hop-self
 neighbor 192.68.6.1 send-community
 no auto-summary
```

Example 11-62 *RTD Configuration*

```
router bgp 1
 no synchronization
 network 192.68.10.0
 neighbor 192.68.5.1 remote-as 3
 neighbor 192.68.6.2 remote-as 1
 neighbor 192.68.6.2 next-hop-self
 neighbor 192.68.10.2 remote-as 4
 no auto-summary
```

Note the **send-community** neighbor parameter in RTC's configuration in Example 11-61. Because RTA is also performing the same aggregation, RTD will receive the specific routes from its IBGP session with RTC. If RTC does not propagate the **no-export** community to RTD, RTD will advertise the specific routes to external peers.

Example 11-63 shows selected entries in RTD's BGP table. The first entry indicates that prefix 172.16.220.0/24 is not advertised to EBGP peers. This is because RTA and RTF have tagged this prefix (and all other "specific" routes) with a community value of **no-export**. The second entry indicates that the aggregate itself has been originated by RTA and RTF as is. The aggregate will be passed on to AS4.

Example 11-63 *RTD BGP Output*

```
RTD#show ip bgp 172.16.220.0
BGP routing table entry for 172.16.220.0/24, version 5
Paths: (2 available, best #2, not advertised to EBGP peer)
  3
    192.68.5.1 from 192.68.5.1
      Origin IGP, metric 20, valid, external
      Community: no-export
  3
    192.68.6.2 from 192.68.6.2 (192.68.11.1)
      Origin IGP, metric 0, localpref 100, valid, internal, best
      Community: no-export

RTD#show ip bgp 172.16.0.0
BGP routing table entry for 172.16.0.0/16, version 8
Paths: (2 available, best #1, advertised over IBGP, EBGP)
  3, (aggregated by 3 192.68.5.1)
    192.68.5.1 from 192.68.5.1
      Origin IGP, valid, external, atomic-aggregate, best
  3, (aggregated by 3 172.16.2.254)
    192.68.6.2 from 192.68.6.2 (192.68.11.1)
      Origin IGP, localpref 100, valid, internal, atomic-aggregate
```

Looking at RTG's BGP table in Example 11-64, you will note that only the aggregate 172.16.0.0/16 has been propagated from AS3 to AS4. All the more-specific routes do not show up.

Example 11-64 *RTG BGP Routing Table*

```
RTG#show ip bgp
BGP table version is 14, local router ID is 192.68.10.2
Status codes: s suppressed, d damped, h history, * valid, > best,
  i - internal Origin codes: i - IGP, e - EGP, ? - incomplete
   Network          Next Hop            Metric LocPrf Weight Path
*> 172.16.0.0       192.68.10.1                           0 1 3 i
*> 192.68.10.0      192.68.10.1              0            0 1 i
*> 192.68.11.0      192.68.10.1                           0 1 i
```

Aggregate with a Subset of the More-Specific Routes

Figure 11-12 shows how AS3 can utilize a combination of aggregation and more-specific routes to influence what link AS1 uses to reach AS3's networks.

Figure 11-12 *BGP Aggregates with a Subset of Specific Routes*

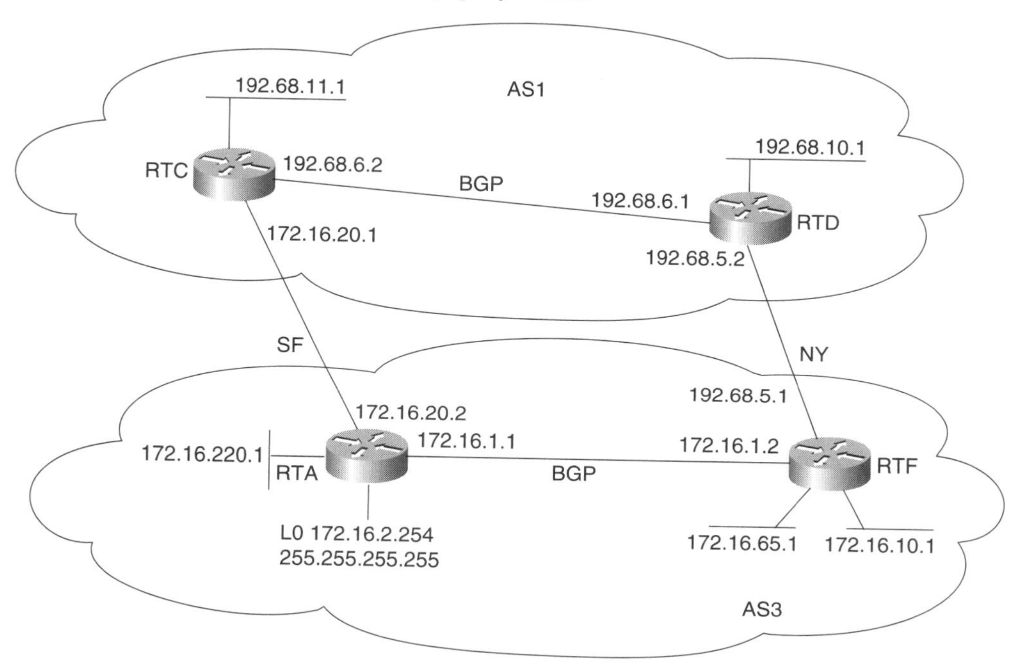

RTA will send over its direct link to AS1 the aggregate 172.16.0.0/16 plus the more-specific routes 172.16.1.0/24, 172.16.10.0/24, and 172.16.65.0/26. RTF will send over its direct link to AS3 the aggregate 172.16.0.0/16 plus the more-specific route 172.16.220.0/24 only. As a result, AS1 is forced to reach 172.16.220.0/24 via RTF and all the other routes in AS3 via RTA.

The *suppress map* is another form of *route map* that can be used to indicate the more-specific routes to be suppressed or the more-specific routes to be allowed. When a route is permitted through the suppress map, the route is suppressed. If the route is not permitted (denied), the route is not suppressed—in other words, it is allowed. Note that the deny logic here does not prevent the route from being advertised; rather, it prevents it from being suppressed. Example 11-65 demonstrates the use of a suppress map.

Example 11-65 *Using a BGP Suppress Map*

```
router bgp 3
 no synchronization
 network 172.16.1.0 mask 255.255.255.0
 network 172.16.10.0 mask 255.255.255.0
 network 172.16.65.0 mask 255.255.255.192
 network 172.16.220.0 mask 255.255.255.0
```

continues

Example 11-65 *Using a BGP Suppress Map (Continued)*

```
 aggregate-address 172.16.0.0 255.255.0.0 suppress-map SUPPRESS
 neighbor 172.16.1.2 remote-as 3
 neighbor 172.16.1.2 update-source Loopback0
 neighbor 172.16.20.1 remote-as 1
 neighbor 172.16.20.1 filter-list 10 out
 no auto-summary

ip as-path access-list 10 permit ^$
access-list 1 permit 172.16.220.0 0.0.0.255
access-list 1 deny any

route-map SUPPRESS permit 10
 match ip address 1
```

RTA's configuration uses a suppress map called SUPPRESS that will prevent 172.16.220.0/24 from being advertised and will enable all other routes. As a result, RTA will announce the aggregate 172.16.0.0/16, plus the more-specific routes 172.16.1.0/24, 172.16.10.0/24, and 172.16.65.0/26. Example 11-66 shows RTA's BGP table. Again, notice how the suppressed entries have the **s** at the far left.

Example 11-66 *RTA's BGP Table*

```
RTA#show ip bgp
BGP table version is 17, local router ID is 172.16.2.254
Status codes: s suppressed, d damped, h history, * valid, > best,
  i - internal Origin codes: i - IGP, e - EGP, ? - incomplete
   Network          Next Hop          Metric LocPrf Weight Path
* i172.16.0.0       172.16.1.2                  100      0 i
*>                  0.0.0.0                          32768 i
*> 172.16.1.0/24    0.0.0.0                0         32768 i
*> 172.16.10.0/24   172.16.1.2            20         32768 i
*> 172.16.65.0/26   172.16.1.2            20         32768 i
s> 172.16.220.0/24  0.0.0.0                0         32768 i
* i192.68.10.0      172.16.1.2             0    100      0 1 i
*>                  172.16.20.1                          0 1 i
* i192.68.11.0      172.16.1.2             0    100      0 1 i
*>                  172.16.20.1            0             0 1 i
```

On the other hand, RTF will use a similar logic to advertise the aggregate, plus the more-specific route 172.16.220.0/24. Example 11-67 shows the configuration for RTF.

Example 11-67 *RTF Configuration*

```
router bgp 3
 no synchronization
 network 172.16.1.0 mask 255.255.255.0
 network 172.16.10.0 mask 255.255.255.0
 network 172.16.65.0 mask 255.255.255.192
 network 172.16.220.0 mask 255.255.255.0
 aggregate-address 172.16.0.0 255.255.0.0 suppress-map ALLOW
```

Example 11-67 *RTF Configuration (Continued)*

```
 neighbor 172.16.2.254 remote-as 3
 neighbor 172.16.2.254 next-hop-self
 neighbor 192.68.5.2 remote-as 1
 neighbor 192.68.5.2 filter-list 10 out
 no auto-summary

ip as-path access-list 10 permit ^$
access-list 1 deny 172.16.220.0 0.0.0.255
access-list 1 permit any

route-map ALLOW permit 10
 match ip address 1
```

RTF's configuration in Example 11-67 includes a suppress map called ALLOW that allows the prefix 172.16.220.0/24 and suppresses everything else. As a result, AS1 will be forced to use RTF to reach 172.16.220.0/24. The naming of the suppress maps SUPPRESS and ALLOW reflects the main function of the route map. In RTA's configuration, it made more sense to suppress a specific entry and allow the rest because the number of routes *to be allowed* is large. In RTF's configuration, it made sense to allow a specific entry and suppress the rest because the number of routes *to be suppressed* is large.

The RTF configuration in Example 11-67 allows the aggregate 172.16.0.0/16 and the more-specific route 172.16.220.0/24 to be advertised; all other more-specific routes will be suppressed. Example 11-68 shows RTF's BGP table.

Example 11-68 *RTF BGP Table*

```
RTF#show ip bgp
BGP table version is 17, local router ID is 192.68.5.1
Status codes: s suppressed, d damped, h history, * valid, > best,
  i - internal Origin codes: i - IGP, e - EGP, ? - incomplete
   Network          Next Hop           Metric LocPrf Weight Path
*> 172.16.0.0       0.0.0.0                           32768 i
* i                 172.16.2.254                100       0 i
s> 172.16.1.0/24    0.0.0.0                 0         32768 i
s i                 172.16.2.254            0   100       0 i
s> 172.16.10.0/24   0.0.0.0                 0         32768 i
s i                 172.16.2.254           20   100       0 i
s> 172.16.65.0/26   0.0.0.0                 0         32768 i
s i                 172.16.2.254           20   100       0 i
*> 172.16.220.0/24  172.16.1.1             20         32768 i
*> 192.68.10.0      192.68.5.2              0             0 1 i
* i                 172.16.20.1                 100       0 1 i
*> 192.68.11.0      192.68.5.2                            0 1 i
* i                 172.16.20.1                 100       0 1 i
```

Given the preceding configuration of RTA and RTF in Example 11-65 and Example 11-67, AS1 will be able to reach 172.16.220.0/24 only via the RTD-RTF link and 172.16.1.0/24,

172.16.65.0/26, and 172.16.10.0/24 via the RTC-RTA link. This is illustrated in RTD's BGP table, shown in Example 11-69.

Example 11-69 *RTD's BGP Table*

```
RTD#show ip bgp
BGP table version is 19, local router ID is 192.68.10.1
Status codes: s suppressed, d damped, h history, * valid, > best,
  i - internal Origin codes: i - IGP, e - EGP, ? - incomplete
   Network          Next Hop          Metric LocPrf Weight Path
* i172.16.0.0       192.68.6.2                  100      0 3 i
*>                  192.68.5.1                           0 3 i
*>i172.16.1.0/24    192.68.6.2             0    100      0 3 i
*>i172.16.10.0/24   192.68.6.2            20    100      0 3 i
*>i172.16.65.0/26   192.68.6.2            20    100      0 3 i
*> 172.16.220.0/24  192.68.5.1            20             0 3 i
*> 192.68.10.0      0.0.0.0                0         32768 i
*>i192.68.11.0      192.68.6.2             0    100      0 i
```

RTD has only one choice to reach 172.16.220.0/24, and that is via the RTD-RTF link. In case of link failure, the aggregate is still advertised via both links, and the route will follow the aggregate.

In certain situations, administrators require that some neighbors receive some of the specific routes already suppressed. Suppression could have been done via the **summary-only** parameter or the **neighbor** command. In this case, Cisco provides a different form of route map called an *unsuppress map* that is applied on a per-neighbor basis. The unsuppress map allows previously suppressed routes to be advertised. For example, if you wanted RTA to prevent 172.16.220.0/24 from being suppressed toward 172.16.1.2 (RTF), you would use the RTA router configuration shown in Example 11-70.

Example 11-70 *RTA Configuration*

```
neighbor 172.16.1.2 unsuppress-map AllowSpecifics

route-map AllowSpecifics permit 10
match ip address 1

access-list 1 permit 172.16.220.0 0.0.0.255
```

The configuration in Example 11-70 allows the advertisement of prefix 172.16.220.0/24 toward RTF.

Loss of Information Inside Aggregates

Aggregation causes loss of granularity. The detailed information that exists in the specific prefixes will be lost when summarized in the form of aggregates. The purpose of an AS_SET is to attempt to preserve the attributes carried in the specific routes in a mathematical SET that gives a better idea of the elements of the aggregate. Figure 11-13 illustrates the network topology for this scenario.

Figure 11-13 *Dealing with Loss of Information with Aggregates*

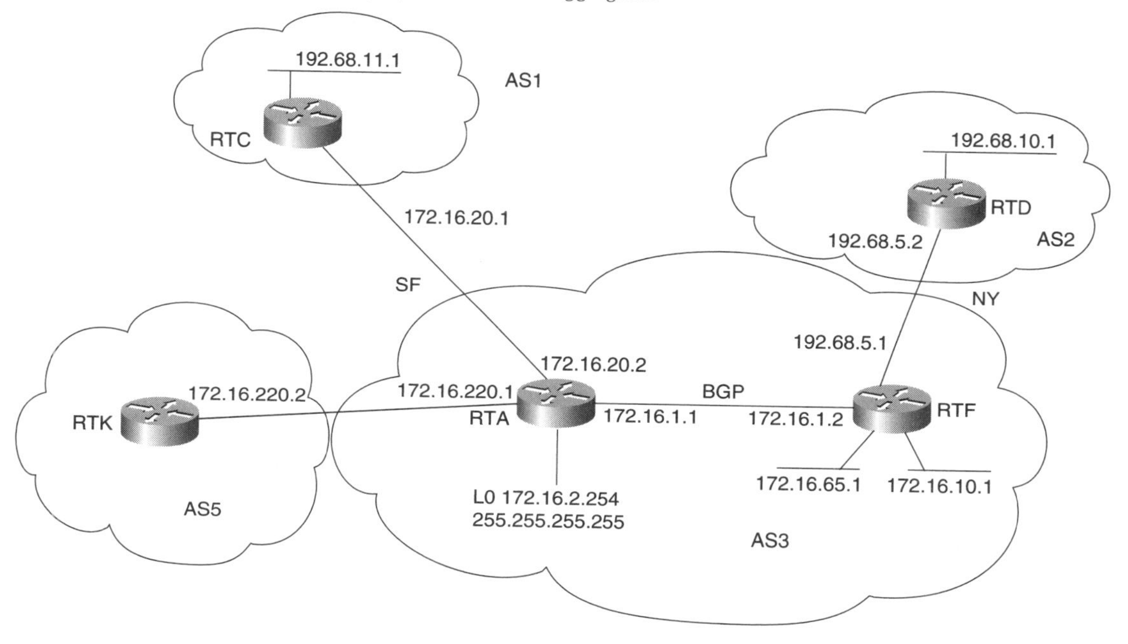

In Figure 11-13, RTA is aggregating prefixes 192.68.10.0/24 and 192.68.11.0/24 coming from AS2 and AS1, respectively. Without AS_SET, the aggregate 192.68.0.0/16 will be considered as having originated from AS3 and will lose all the specific attribute information that the individual prefixes 192.68.10.0/24 and 192.68.11.0/24 have. You will see two configuration possibilities for RTA—first without AS_SET (Example 11-71) and then with AS_SET (Example 11-73). You will see how the aggregate 192.68.0.0/16 will look in both scenarios.

Example 11-71 *RTA Configuration Without AS_SET*

```
router bgp 3
 no synchronization
 network 172.16.1.0 mask 255.255.255.0
 network 172.16.10.0 mask 255.255.255.0
 network 172.16.65.0 mask 255.255.255.192
 network 172.16.220.0 mask 255.255.255.0
 aggregate-address 192.68.0.0 255.255.0.0
 neighbor 172.16.1.2 remote-as 3
 neighbor 172.16.1.2 update-source Loopback0
```

continues

Example 11-71 *RTA Configuration Without AS_SET (Continued)*

```
 neighbor 172.16.20.1 remote-as 1
 neighbor 172.16.20.1 filter-list 10 out
 neighbor 172.16.220.2 remote-as 5
 no auto-summary

ip as-path access-list 10 permit ^$
```

The BGP table for RTK in Example 11-72 shows how the aggregate 192.68.0.0/16 will look when it is received by RTK. Note that the aggregate has lost the individual path information because the AS_PATH consists of AS number 3 only.

Example 11-72 *RTK BGP Table*

```
RTK#show ip bgp
BGP table version is 8, local router ID is 172.16.220.2
Status codes: s suppressed, d damped, h history, * valid, > best,
  i - internal Origin codes: i - IGP, e - EGP, ? - incomplete
   Network          Next Hop            Metric LocPrf Weight Path
*> 172.16.1.0/24    172.16.220.1             0             0 3 i
*> 172.16.10.0/24   172.16.220.1            20             0 3 i
*> 172.16.65.0/26   172.16.220.1            20             0 3 i
*> 172.16.220.0/24  172.16.220.1             0             0 3 i
*> 192.68.0.0/16    172.16.220.1                           0 3 i
*> 192.68.10.0      172.16.220.1                           0 3 2 i
*> 192.68.11.0      172.16.220.1                           0 3 1 i
```

Using the AS_SET concept demonstrated in the configuration in Example 11-73, the aggregate will be sent out from RTA with a SET of the path information.

Example 11-73 *RTA Configuration with AS_SET*

```
router bgp 3
 no synchronization
 network 172.16.1.0 mask 255.255.255.0
 network 172.16.10.0 mask 255.255.255.0
 network 172.16.65.0 mask 255.255.255.192
 network 172.16.220.0 mask 255.255.255.0
 aggregate-address 192.68.0.0 255.255.0.0 as-set
 neighbor 172.16.1.2 remote-as 3
 neighbor 172.16.1.2 update-source Loopback0
 neighbor 172.16.20.1 remote-as 1
 neighbor 172.16.20.1 filter-list 10 out
 neighbor 172.16.220.2 remote-as 5
 no auto-summary

ip as-path access-list 10 permit ^$
```

In the BGP routing table for RTK in Example 11-74, notice how the aggregate 192.68.0.0/16 changes to include a SET {2,1} within its path information. This indicates that the aggregate actually summarizes routes that have passed via ASs 1 or 2. The AS_SET information becomes important in avoiding routing loops because it keeps an indication of where the route has been.

Example 11-74 *RTK BGP Table*

```
RTK#show ip bgp
BGP table version is 12, local router ID is 172.16.220.2
Status codes: s suppressed, d damped, h history, * valid, > best,
  i - internal Origin codes: i - IGP, e - EGP, ? - incomplete

   Network          Next Hop          Metric LocPrf Weight Path
*> 172.16.1.0/24    172.16.220.1           0             0 3 i
*> 172.16.10.0/24   172.16.220.1          20             0 3 i
*> 172.16.65.0/26   172.16.220.1          20             0 3 i
*> 172.16.220.0/24  172.16.220.1           0             0 3 i
*> 192.68.0.0/16    172.16.220.1                         0 3 {2,1} i
*> 192.68.10.0      172.16.220.1                         0 3 2 i
*> 192.68.11.0      172.16.220.1                         0 3 1 i
```

In case the aggregate reaches AS1 or AS2, BGP's loop detection behavior will note the set information and drop the aggregate.

Given that the aggregate with the AS_SET contains information about each individual route that is summarized, changes in the individual route will cause the aggregate to be updated. In the example, if 192.68.11.0/24 goes down, the path information of the aggregate will change from 3 {2,1} to 3 2, and the aggregate will be updated. If the aggregate summarizes tens or hundreds of routes, the aggregate will be constantly oscillating if the routes forming the aggregate are unstable.

Changing the Aggregate's Attributes

In some situations, changing the aggregate's attributes is required. The example in this section shows one scenario in which this could be useful.

As you have already seen, the aggregate can carry information about its individual elements if configured with the AS_SET option. If one or more of the routes forming the AS_SET aggregate are configured with **no-export** community attribute, the aggregate itself will carry the same attribute. This will prevent the aggregate from being exported. To remedy this situation, you can modify the community attribute of the aggregate by using what Cisco calls an **attribute map**, another form of a route map that applies only to aggregates.

In the network depicted in Figure 11-13, RTC tags 192.68.11.0/24 with a community value of **no-export**. If RTA aggregates 192.68.11.0/24 into 192.68.0.0/16 using AS_SET, the aggregate itself will also contain the **no-export** community. Example 11-75 and Example 11-76 show the configurations of RTC and RTA, which are needed to achieve this behavior.

Example 11-75 *RTC Configuration*

```
router bgp 1
 network 192.68.11.0
 neighbor 172.16.20.2 remote-as 3
 neighbor 172.16.20.2 send-community
 neighbor 172.16.20.2 route-map SETCOMMUNITY out
 no auto-summary

access-list 1 permit 192.68.11.0 0.0.0.255

route-map SETCOMMUNITY permit 10
 match ip address 1
 set community no-export

route-map SETCOMMUNITY permit 20
```

Example 11-76 *RTA Configuration*

```
router bgp 3
 no synchronization
 network 172.16.1.0 mask 255.255.255.0
 network 172.16.10.0 mask 255.255.255.0
 network 172.16.65.0 mask 255.255.255.192
 network 172.16.220.0 mask 255.255.255.0
 aggregate-address 192.68.0.0 255.255.0.0 as-set
 neighbor 172.16.1.2 remote-as 3
 neighbor 172.16.1.2 update-source Loopback0
 neighbor 172.16.20.1 remote-as 1
 neighbor 172.16.20.1 filter-list 10 out
 neighbor 172.16.220.2 remote-as 5
 no auto-summary

ip as-path access-list 10 permit ^$
```

Because RTA is performing the aggregation using the AS_SET, the aggregate itself will contain all the elements that the individual routes have—in particular, the community **no-export** coming from prefix 192.68.11.0/24 (originated by RTC). Notice how the BGP table for RTA, shown in Example 11-77, indicates that 192.68.0.0/16 is not to be advertised to EBGP peers.

Example 11-77 *RTA BGP Output*

```
RTA#show ip bgp 192.68.0.0
BGP routing table entry for 192.68.0.0 255.255.0.0, version 22
Paths: (2 available, best #2, not advertised to EBGP peer, advertised over IBGP)
  Local (aggregated by 3 192.68.5.1)
    172.16.1.2 from 172.16.1.2 (192.68.5.1)
      Origin IGP, localpref 100, valid, internal, atomic-aggregate
```

Example 11-77 *RTA BGP Output (Continued)*

```
  {2,1} (aggregated by 3 172.16.2.254)
    0.0.0.0
      Origin IGP, localpref 100, weight 32768, valid, aggregated, local, best
      Community: no-export
```

By using the attribute map, you can manipulate the aggregate attributes. In this example, you can set the community to "none" and allow the aggregate to be advertised to EBGP peers. The configuration for RTA in Example 11-78 defines an attribute map called SET_ATTRIBUTE that sets the community attribute of the aggregate to none.

Example 11-78 *RTA Configuration*

```
router bgp 3
 no synchronization
 network 172.16.1.0 mask 255.255.255.0
 network 172.16.10.0 mask 255.255.255.0
 network 172.16.65.0 mask 255.255.255.192
 aggregate-address 192.68.0.0 255.255.0.0 as-set attribute-map SET_ATTRIBUTE
 neighbor 172.16.1.2 remote-as 3
 neighbor 172.16.1.2 update-source Loopback0
 neighbor 172.16.20.1 remote-as 1
neighbor 172.16.20.1 filter-list 10 out
 neighbor 172.16.220.2 remote-as 5
 no auto-summary

ip as-path access-list 10 permit ^$

route-map SET_ATTRIBUTE permit 10
 set community none
```

Notice how the BGP table in Example 11-79 shows that the aggregate 192.68.0.0/16 is now being advertised to EBGP peers.

Example 11-79 *RTA BGP Output*

```
RTA#show ip bgp 192.68.0.0
BGP routing table entry for 192.68.0.0 255.255.0.0, version 10
Paths: (2 available, best #2, advertised over IBGP, EBGP)
  Local (aggregated by 3 192.68.5.1)
    172.16.1.2 from 172.16.1.2 (192.68.5.1)
      Origin IGP, localpref 100, valid, internal, atomic-aggregate
  {2,1} (aggregated by 3 172.16.2.254)
    0.0.0.0
      Origin IGP, localpref 100, weight 32768, valid, aggregated, local, best
```

Forming the Aggregate Based on a Subset of Specific Routes

Having control over which individual prefixes form the aggregate is very useful in determining which attributes the aggregate will carry. In the previous section, if you could exclude prefix 192.68.11.0/24 from being part of the prefixes that form the aggregate, the aggregate would not inherit the **no-export** community attribute.

The *advertise map* is yet another form of a route map that lets you form the aggregated route based on a limited selection of the more-specific routes. Figure 11-14 illustrates the network topology for this scenario.

Figure 11-14 *Aggregation with Advertise Maps*

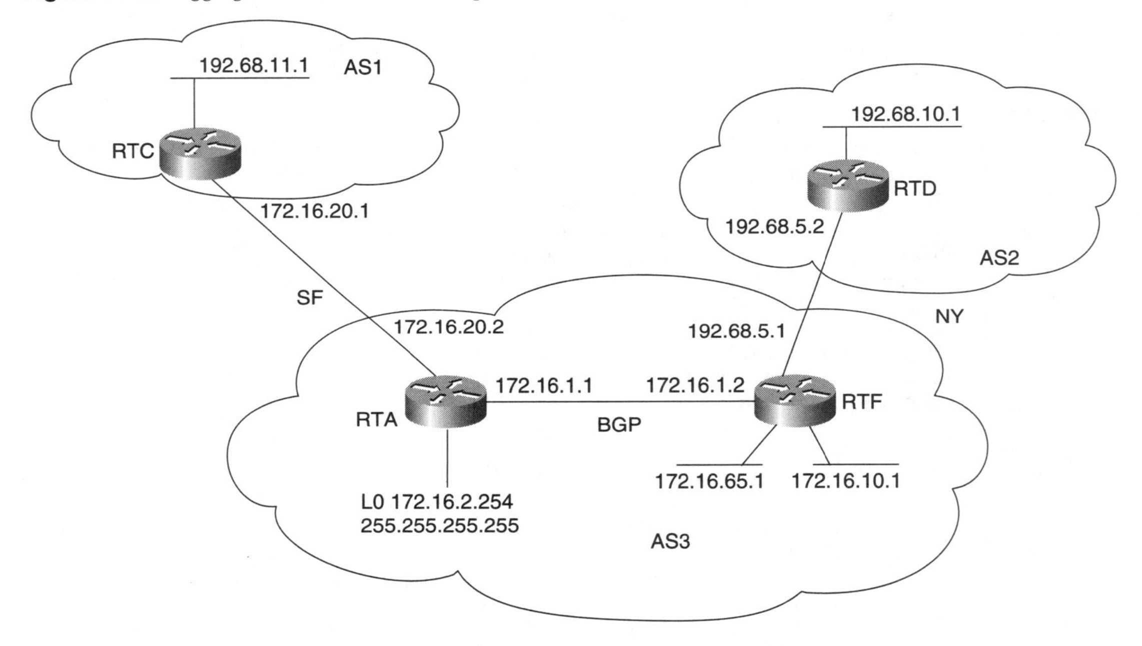

In Figure 11-14, RTA and RTF are getting routes 192.68.11.0/24 and 192.68.10.0/24 from ASs 1 and 2, respectively. If RTA and RTF are to aggregate these routes into 192.68.0.0/16 using the **as-set** option, the aggregate cannot be sent back to either AS1 or AS2, because it contains {1 2} in the AS path. This is due to the normal BGP behavior in detecting loops.

Assume that the required behavior is to have the aggregate 192.68.0.0/16 sent back to AS1 and not to AS2. The solution is to have AS1 not be part of the aggregate's AS_PATH; then, AS1 will not drop the aggregate. This could be achieved by having RTA and RTF form the aggregate based on the 192.68.10.0/24 prefix only, using the **advertise-map** option.

To accomplish this, you would configure RTA as shown in Example 11-80. RTF would have the same relative configuration.

Example 11-80 *RTA Configuration*

```
router bgp 3
 no synchronization
 network 172.16.1.0 mask 255.255.255.0
 network 172.16.10.0 mask 255.255.255.0
 network 172.16.65.0 mask 255.255.255.192
 aggregate-address 192.68.0.0 255.255.0.0 as-set advertise-map
   SELECT_MORE_SPECIF_ROUTES
 neighbor 172.16.1.2 remote-as 3
 neighbor 172.16.1.2 update-source Loopback0
 neighbor 172.16.20.1 remote-as 1
 neighbor 172.16.20.1 filter-list 10 out
 no auto-summary

ip as-path access-list 10 permit ^$

access-list 1 permit 192.68.10.0 0.0.0.255

route-map SELECT_MORE_SPECIF_ROUTES permit 10
 match ip address 1
```

By permitting prefix 192.68.10.0/24, the advertise map causes RTA to base its aggregate calculation on 192.68.10.0/24 only. Thus, 192.68.11.0/24 is not included in the formation of the aggregate.

The **show ip bgp** command output in Example 11-81 illustrates that the aggregate's path information is now 2 and not {1 2}. This means that the aggregate can now be advertised to AS1 because the AS_PATH does not include AS1. AS2 will not be able to receive the aggregate.

Example 11-81 *RTA BGP Output*

```
RTA#show ip bgp 192.68.0.0
BGP routing table entry for 192.68.0.0 255.255.0.0, version 31
Paths: (2 available, best #2, advertised over IBGP)
  2 (aggregated by 3 192.68.5.1)
    172.16.1.2 from 172.16.1.2 (192.68.5.1)
      Origin IGP, localpref 100, valid, internal, atomic-aggregate
  2 (aggregated by 3 172.16.2.254)
    0.0.0.0
      Origin IGP, localpref 100, weight 32768, valid, aggregated,
  local, atomic-aggregate, best
```

Looking Ahead

The BGP attributes are the basic elements in interdomain network design. Combining and manipulating different attributes will result in a unique routing policy for your autonomous system. The next chapter takes what you have learned so far and goes further in showing implementations for major design problems facing every network. That chapter also shows you examples of controlling Internet stability by using route flap dampening, soft reconfiguration, and BGP Route Refresh. We'll also discuss BGP Outbound Route Filter (ORF) capability and Multiprotocol BGP (MBGP). We'll finish with some practical approaches to developing actual routing polices.

This chapter covers the following key topics:

- **Symmetry, redundancy, and load balancing**—Configuration examples for dynamically and statically learned defaults, multihoming to single and multiple providers, load balancing, and customers sharing a backup link.
- **Following defaults inside an AS**—Configuration examples for setting defaults in a variety of architectures. This section examines a particular routing problem assuming a variety of different IGPs.
- **Policy routing**—A configuration example for routing based on source rather than destination.
- **Route reflectors**—A practical example of using route reflectors in conjunction with peer groups.
- **Confederations**—A practical example of how to configure confederations.
- **Controlling route and cache invalidation**—Syntax and a practical example of BGP's soft reconfiguration feature and BGP's Route Refresh capability.
- **BGP Outbound Route Filter (ORF) capability**—BGP ORF is enabled by BGP capabilities and is used to allow a BGP neighbor to "push over" its inbound prefix-list filter. We'll discuss the advantages of BGP ORF, as well as provide configuration guidelines.
- **Route dampening**—Syntax and a practical example of BGP's route dampening feature.

CHAPTER 12

Configuring Effective Internet Routing Policies

Chapter 11, "Configuring Basic BGP Functions and Attributes," covered configuration examples for all the basic functions and attributes of BGP. In this chapter, we will consider examples that address the challenging, potentially conflicting design goals of routing architecture. We will also look at examples designed to help manage growing, complex networks.

Perhaps the most challenging part of configuring your network's routing architecture is determining what your routing policies should be. This step, of course, must come before the actual configuration process, and there is no simple, lockstep method for determining your policies. A careful analysis of network needs, behavior, and potential growth will reveal a unique set of problems and optimal solutions for every network.

Redundancy, Symmetry, and Load Balancing

The examples in this section illustrate the implementation of different route redundancy, symmetry, and load-balancing scenarios. Please remember that these scenarios are not cast in stone. Many variations of these techniques can be used to fit your situation. The examples presented here should guide you to a better understanding of how policies are set. We will first go over a brief implementation of default routes.

Dynamically Learned Defaults

It is important to control defaults in BGP because, if they are originated randomly, they could cause serious problems. Problems occur when a BGP speaker that intends to originate a default to a specific peer floods the default to all its neighbors. Cisco provides a way to target the default toward a specific neighbor.

In Figure 12-1, RTA originates a default route 0.0.0.0/0 toward RTC only. IBGP neighbors, such as RTF, will not get the default.

Figure 12-1 *Dynamically Learned Defaults*

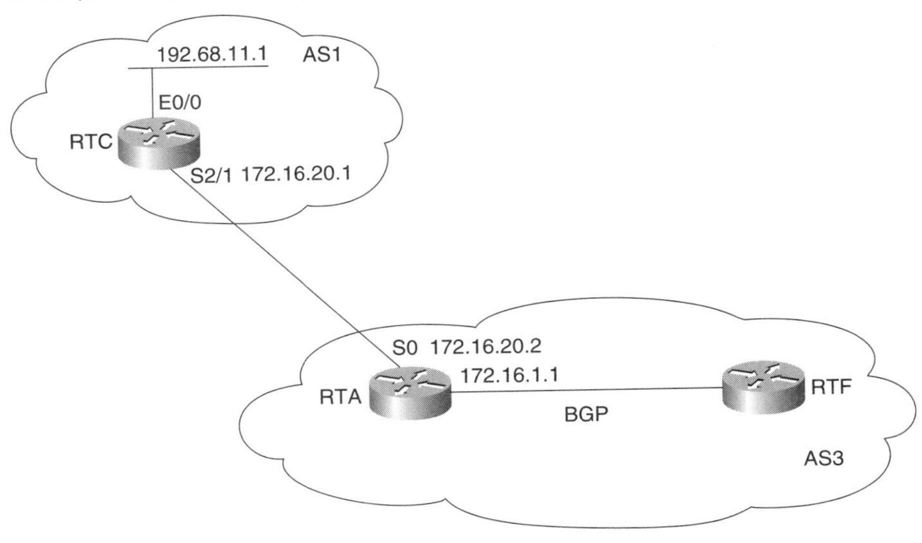

Example 12-1 shows the configuration for RTA.

Example 12-1 *RTA Configuration for Dynamically Learned Defaults*

```
router bgp 3
 no synchronization
 network 172.16.1.0 mask 255.255.255.0
 neighbor 172.16.20.1 remote-as 1
 neighbor 172.16.20.1 default-originate
 no auto-summary
```

The **default-originate** option of the **neighbor** router subcommand will cause 0/0 (the default) to be sent toward RTC. The BGP and IP routing tables of RTC displayed in Example 12-2 illustrate this.

Example 12-2 *BGP/IP Routing Tables for RTC*

```
RTC#show ip bgp
BGP table version is 14, local router ID is 192.68.11.1
Status codes: s suppressed, d damped, h history, * valid, > best,
  i - internal Origin codes: i - IGP, e - EGP, ? - incomplete

  Network          Next Hop     Metric LocPrf Weight Path
*> 0.0.0.0         172.16.20.2                     0 3 i
*> 172.16.1.0/24   172.16.20.2       0             0 3 i
*> 192.68.11.0     0.0.0.0           0         32768 i

RTC#show ip route
```

Example 12-2 *BGP/IP Routing Tables for RTC (Continued)*

```
Codes: C - connected, S - static, I - IGRP, R - RIP, M - mobile, B - BGP
    D - EIGRP, EX - EIGRP external, O - OSPF, IA - OSPF inter area
    E1 - OSPF external type 1, E2 - OSPF external type 2, E - EGP
    i - IS-IS, L1 - IS-IS level-1, L2 - IS-IS level-2,
      * - candidate default U - per-user static route

Gateway of last resort is 172.16.20.2 to network 0.0.0.0

C  192.68.11.0/24 is directly connected, Ethernet0/0
C    172.16.20.0/24 is directly connected, Serial2/1
B*  0.0.0.0/0 [20/0] via 172.16.20.2, 00:04:40
```

The RTC routing table in Example 12-2 indicates that RTC has dynamically learned the 0/0 default from RTA and has set its gateway of last resort to 172.16.20.2, which is RTA.

Defaults can also be originated over all BGP peers by using the **network 0.0.0.0** router command, as long as the router advertising this default already has its own default. You can use the configuration in Example 12-3, assuming that RTA has a default route itself (the default could be created via a static route).

Example 12-3 *Originating Defaults Over All BGP Peers: RTA Configuration*

```
router bgp 3
 no synchronization
 network 0.0.0.0
 network 172.16.1.0 mask 255.255.255.0
 neighbor 172.16.20.1 remote-as 1
 no auto-summary
```

Statically Set Defaults

Instead of dynamically learning the 0/0 default, a router can set its own default statically. Figure 12-2 demonstrates how to accomplish this.

Figure 12-2 *Dealing with the 0/0 Default*

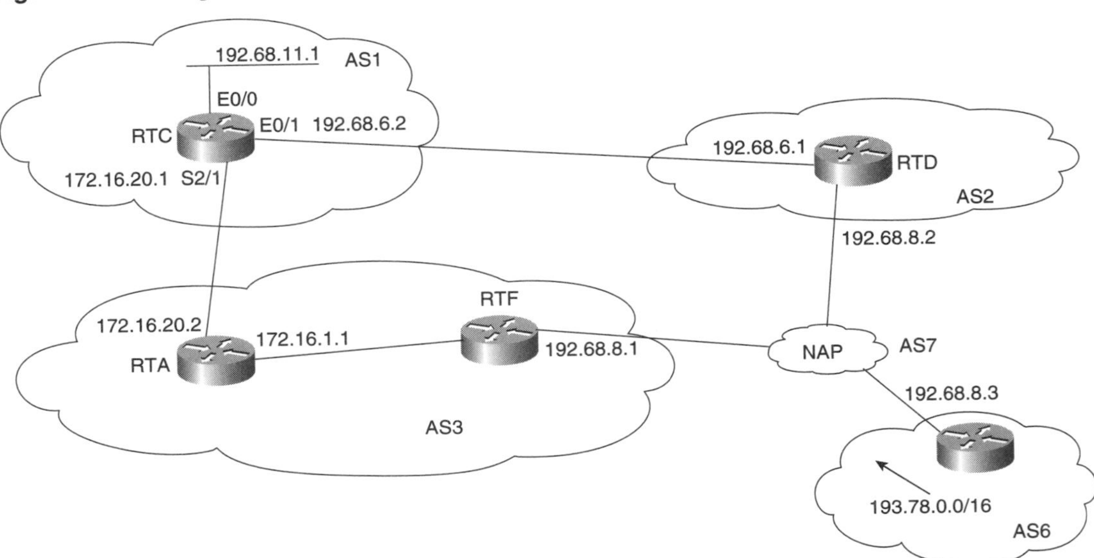

RTC uses the following command:

```
ip route prefix mask {address | interface} [distance]
```

The 0/0 static route can point to a network number, to a gateway address, or to a physical interface as being the default path. The distance is a means of giving preference to the static route in case multiple entries for the same network exist. Routes with a shorter distance are preferred over routes with a longer distance.

The configuration in Example 12-4 shows how RTC can set the default to point toward network 193.78.0.0/16.

Example 12-4 *RTC Configuration: Setting the Default to Point to Network 193.78.0.0/16*

```
router bgp 1
 network 192.68.11.0
 neighbor 172.16.20.2 remote-as 3
 neighbor 192.68.6.1 remote-as 2
 no auto-summary
ip route 0.0.0.0 0.0.0.0 193.78.0.0
```

The BGP table for RTC in Example 12-5 shows that 193.78.0.0/16 has been learned via two paths—the first via AS3 and the second via AS2. BGP prefers the first path as being the best. (BGP attribute manipulation can be used to influence which path BGP will use and hence influence the default path.)

Example 12-5 *RTC BGP Table*

```
RTC#show ip bgp
BGP table version is 8, local router ID is 192.68.11.1
Status codes: s suppressed, d damped, h history, * valid, > best,
  i - internal Origin codes: i - IGP, e - EGP, ? - incomplete

  Network          Next Hop      Metric LocPrf Weight Path
*> 192.68.11.0     0.0.0.0            0         32768 i
*> 193.78.0.0/16   172.16.20.2                      0 3 7 6 i
*                  192.68.6.1                       0 2 7 6 i
```

The IP table for RTC in Example 12-6 shows how the gateway of last resort has been set to follow network 193.78.0.0/16. Recursive lookup in the IP routing table shows that 193.78.0.0/16 can be reached via 172.16.20.2, which is RTA.

Example 12-6 *RTC IP Table*

```
RTC#show ip route
Codes: C - connected, S - static, I - IGRP, R - RIP, M - mobile, B - BGP
    D - EIGRP, EX - EIGRP external, O - OSPF, IA - OSPF inter area
    E1 - OSPF external type 1, E2 - OSPF external type 2, E - EGP
    i - IS-IS, L1 - IS-IS level-1, L2 - IS-IS level-2,
      * - candidate default U - per-user static route
Gateway of last resort is 193.78.0.0 to network 0.0.0.0
C  192.68.6.0/24 is directly connected, Ethernet0/1
C  192.68.11.0/24 is directly connected, Ethernet0/0
B  193.78.0.0/16 [20/0] via 172.16.20.2, 00:32:32
C    172.16.20.0/24 is directly connected, Serial2/1
S*  0.0.0.0/0 [1/0] via 193.78.0.0
```

In case you do not want to follow a single route, you can still use the **ip route 0.0.0.0 0.0.0.0** command to point to multiple networks or IP addresses. The **distance** keyword gives you the ability to prefer one default over another, as demonstrated in Example 12-7.

Example 12-7 *Using* **distance** *to Prefer One Default Over Another: RTC Configuration*

```
router bgp 1
 network 192.68.11.0
 neighbor 172.16.20.2 remote-as 3
 neighbor 192.68.6.1 remote-as 2
 no auto-summary

ip route 0.0.0.0 0.0.0.0 172.16.20.2 40
ip route 0.0.0.0 0.0.0.0 192.68.6.1 50
```

Note how RTC is pointing to two different IP addresses. These could also have been two different network numbers that exist in the IP routing table. The distance of 40 in the first static route will ensure that as long as 172.16.20.2 is available, it will be preferred. In case the route to 172.16.20.2 goes away, the static entry will go with it, and the second entry will kick in. Example 12-8 shows the output of RTC's routing table.

Example 12-8 *RTC Routing Table*

```
RTC#show ip route
Codes: C - connected, S - static, I - IGRP, R - RIP, M - mobile, B - BGP
    D - EIGRP, EX - EIGRP external, O - OSPF, IA - OSPF inter area
    E1 - OSPF external type 1, E2 - OSPF external type 2, E - EGP
    i - IS-IS, L1 - IS-IS level-1, L2 - IS-IS level-2,
      * - candidate default U - per-user static route

Gateway of last resort is 172.16.20.2 to network 0.0.0.0

C  192.68.6.0/24 is directly connected, Ethernet0/1
C  192.68.11.0/24 is directly connected, Ethernet0/0
B  193.78.0.0/16 [20/0] via 172.16.20.2, 00:45:08
C    172.16.20.0/24 is directly connected, Serial2/1
S*  0.0.0.0/0 [40/0] via 172.16.20.2
```

Example 12-9 shows the same output in case the link between RTC and RTA goes down.

Example 12-9 *RTC Routing Table After RTC-RTA Link Failure*

```
RTC#show ip route
Codes: C - connected, S - static, I - IGRP, R - RIP, M - mobile, B - BGP
    D - EIGRP, EX - EIGRP external, O - OSPF, IA - OSPF inter area
    E1 - OSPF external type 1, E2 - OSPF external type 2, E - EGP
    i - IS-IS, L1 - IS-IS level-1, L2 - IS-IS level-2,
      * - candidate default U - per-user static route

Gateway of last resort is 192.68.6.1 to network 0.0.0.0

C  192.68.6.0/24 is directly connected, Ethernet0/1
C  192.68.11.0/24 is directly connected, Ethernet0/0
B  193.78.0.0/16 [20/0] via 192.68.6.1, 00:01:14
S*  0.0.0.0/0 [60/0] via 192.68.6.1
```

Notice that the second static entry with a distance of 60 has now kicked in.

Multihoming to a Single Provider

For the case in which one customer has multiple connections to the same provider, we will look at implementation examples that cover the following:

- Default only, one primary link, and one backup link
- Default, primary, and backup, plus partial routing
- Automatic load balancing

Default Only, One Primary Link, and One Backup Link

In Figure 12-3, AS3 is multihomed to AS1. AS3 is not learning any BGP routes from AS1 and is sending its own routes via BGP. RTA will be running defaults toward AS1, with the NY link being the primary link and the SF link being the secondary link.

Figure 12-3 *Multihoming to a Single Provider (Default Only, One Primary Link, and One Backup Link)*

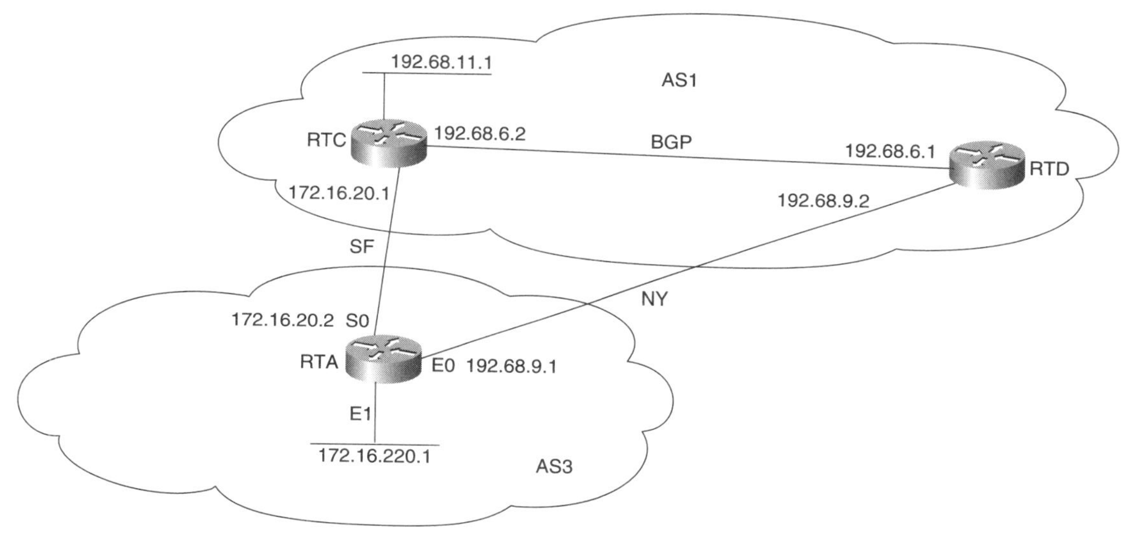

The following policies apply to this network scenario:

- Outbound traffic from AS3 should always go on the NY link unless that link fails, in which case it should switch to the other link.

  This can be achieved by configuring two static routes in RTA pointing the defaults toward the two links. The default via the NY link will be set with a lower distance to be more preferred.

- Inbound traffic toward AS3 should always come on the NY link unless that link fails, in which case it should switch to the other link.

  This can be achieved by having RTA send different metrics toward AS1 on both links, with a lower metric on the NY link. This way, inbound traffic coming from AS1 will always come via the NY link. Other attributes can also be used to accomplish this (that is, BGP communities and associated remote ingress policies).

- Prevent any BGP updates from coming into AS3.

  This can be achieved by having AS3 configure a route map or prefix list that will block all incoming BGP routing updates. Usually, the provider (AS1, in this case) will not send you any updates per your request. Nevertheless, you should always protect your AS against the unknown. The provider could make a mistake and send you all his routes, and your AS would be vulnerable.

Example 12-10 shows the configuration used by RTA with default only, one primary link, and one backup link.

Example 12-10 *Default Only, One Primary Link, and One Backup Link: RTA Configuration*

```
router bgp 3
 network 172.16.220.0 mask 255.255.255.0
 neighbor 172.16.20.1 remote-as 1
 neighbor 172.16.20.1 route-map BLOCK in
 neighbor 172.16.20.1 route-map SETMETRIC1 out
 neighbor 192.68.9.2 remote-as 1
 neighbor 192.68.9.2 route-map BLOCK in
 neighbor 192.68.9.2 route-map SETMETRIC2 out
 no auto-summary

ip route 0.0.0.0 0.0.0.0 172.16.20.1 50
ip route 0.0.0.0 0.0.0.0 192.68.9.2 40

route-map SETMETRIC1 permit 10
 set metric 100

route-map SETMETRIC2 permit 10
 set metric 50

route-map BLOCK deny 10
```

In this configuration, AS3 uses static routes to configure defaults toward AS1. The 0/0 toward RTD is given a distance of 40, lower than the distance of 50 toward RTC. The NY link will act as primary. Alternatively, AS3 could have accepted a single entry from AS1 and configured that entry as the default.

Route maps SETMETRIC1 and SETMETRIC2 are used to set the outbound metric to 50 toward RTD and 100 toward RTC, respectively, thereby manipulating inbound traffic to prefer the NY link.

Route map BLOCK is used to block all incoming BGP updates from AS1.

The RTA IP routing table in Example 12-11 shows how the default route is set. Notice that distance 40 is preferred over distance 50 for the 0/0 route, and the gateway of last resort is pointing to next hop 192.68.9.2.

Example 12-11 *RTA IP Routing Table*

```
RTA#show ip route
Codes: C - connected, S - static, I - IGRP, R - RIP, M - mobile, B - BGP
    D - EIGRP, EX - EIGRP external, O - OSPF, IA - OSPF inter area
    E1 - OSPF external type 1, E2 - OSPF external type 2, E - EGP
    i - IS-IS, L1 - IS-IS level-1, L2 - IS-IS level-2,
    * - candidate default

Gateway of last resort is 192.68.9.2 to network 0.0.0.0

C  192.68.9.0 is directly connected, Ethernet0
   172.16.0.0 255.255.255.0 is subnetted, 2 subnets
C    172.16.220.0 is directly connected, Ethernet1
C    172.16.20.0 is directly connected, Serial0
S*  0.0.0.0 0.0.0.0 [40/0] via 192.68.9.2
```

Example 12-12 shows RTC's BGP table, which reveals that AS3 is always accessed via the RTD-RTA link because of the lower metric 50. Prefix 172.16.220.0/24 can be reached via IBGP and EBGP. The IBGP route has been chosen as the best route. Note in this table that RTC's next hop to reach prefix 172.16.220.0/24 is 192.68.6.1. This is because RTD has configured its neighbor connection with RTC using the **next-hop-self** neighbor command.

Example 12-12 *RTC BGP Table*

```
RTC#show ip bgp
BGP table version is 11, local router ID is 192.68.11.1
Status codes: s suppressed, d damped, h history, * valid, > best,
  i - internal Origin codes: i - IGP, e - EGP, ? - incomplete

  Network           Next Hop       Metric LocPrf Weight Path
*>i172.16.220.0/24  192.68.6.1         50    100      0 3 i
*                   172.16.20.2       100             0 3 i
*> 192.68.11.0      0.0.0.0             0         32768 i
```

Default, Primary, and Backup, Plus Partial Routing

This example shows how traffic can be manipulated in a situation where the AS is accepting partial routing from a single provider and is running defaults toward the provider. Partial routes are usually the provider's local routes and its customers' routes. Figure 12-4 shows AS3 running IBGP internally and running EBGP at two different locations with its provider AS1.

Figure 12-4 *Default, Primary, and Backup, Plus Partial Routing*

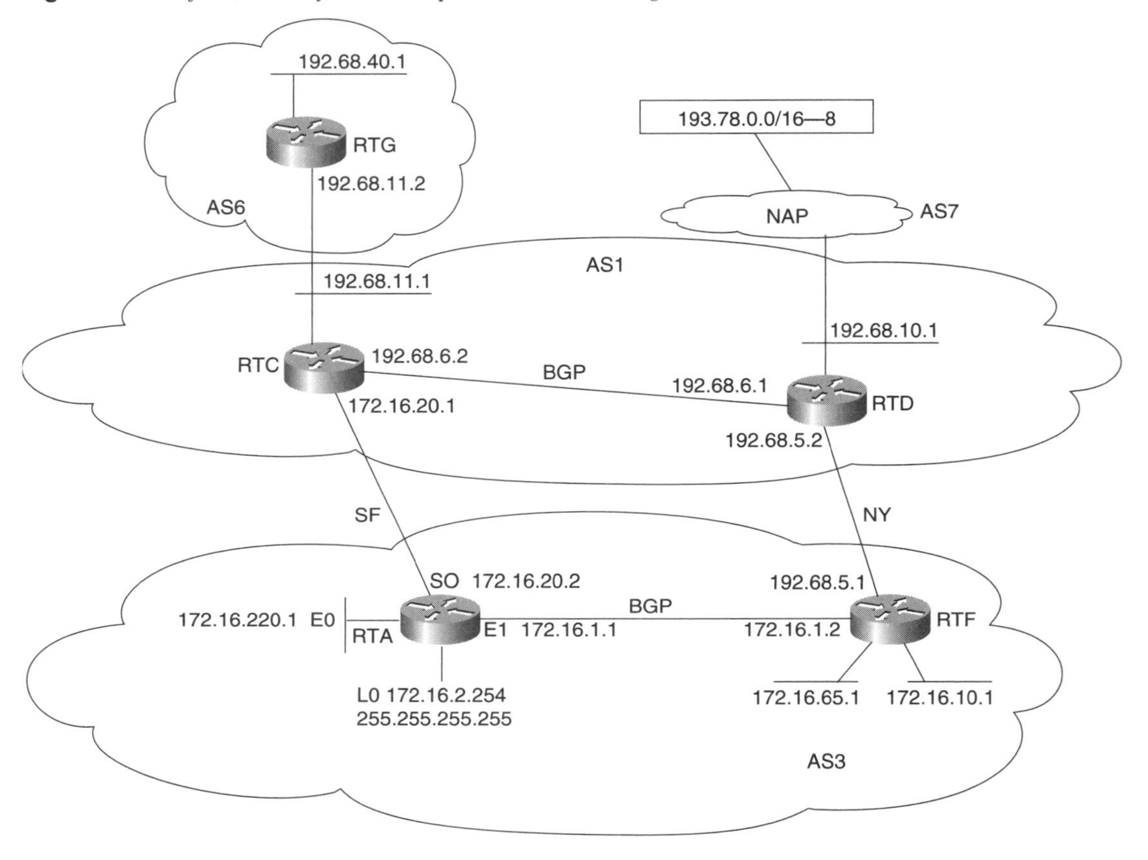

The following policies apply to the network scenario illustrated in Figure 12-4:

- AS3 will accept only AS1's local routes and its customers' routes, such as AS6. AS3 will also accept one route from the Internet to set its default toward the provider AS1.
- For all outbound traffic toward AS1 and AS6 (the partial routes), AS3 should use the SF link. In case of failure, the other link is used.
- For all other outbound traffic toward the Internet, AS3 should use the NY link as the primary link by following a default route. In case of failure, the default via the other link should be used.
- For inbound traffic, AS3 will instruct AS1 to use the SF link for network 172.16.220.0/24.
- For all other inbound traffic, the NY link is the primary.

Example 12-13 and Example 12-14 show partial configurations needed for the BGP configuration in RTA and RTF.

Example 12-13 *Default, Primary, and Backup, Plus Partial Routing: RTA Configuration*

```
router bgp 3
 no synchronization
 network 172.16.1.0 mask 255.255.255.0
 network 172.16.10.0 mask 255.255.255.0
 network 172.16.65.0 mask 255.255.255.192
 network 172.16.220.0 mask 255.255.255.0
 neighbor 172.16.1.2 remote-as 3
 neighbor 172.16.1.2 update-source Loopback0
 neighbor 172.16.1.2 next-hop-self
 neighbor 172.16.20.1 remote-as 1
 neighbor 172.16.20.1 route-map SET_OUTBOUND_TRAFFIC in
 neighbor 172.16.20.1 route-map SET_INBOUND_TRAFFIC out
 neighbor 172.16.20.1 filter-list 10 out
 no auto-summary

ip route 0.0.0.0 0.0.0.0 193.78.0.0
ip as-path access-list 10 permit ^$
ip as-path access-list 4 permit ^1 6$
ip as-path access-list 4 permit ^1$

access-list 2 permit ip 172.16.220.0 0.0.0.255
access-list 101 permit ip 193.78.0.0 0.0.255.255 255.255.0.0 0.0.0.0

route-map SET_OUTBOUND_TRAFFIC permit 10
 match ip address 101
 set local-preference 200

route-map SET_OUTBOUND_TRAFFIC permit 20
 match as-path 4
 set local-preference 300

route-map SET_INBOUND_TRAFFIC permit 10
 match ip address 2
 set metric 200

route-map SET_INBOUND_TRAFFIC permit 20
 set metric 300
```

Example 12-14 *Default, Primary, and Backup, Plus Partial Routing: RTF Configuration*

```
router bgp 3
 no synchronization
 network 172.16.1.0 mask 255.255.255.0
 network 172.16.10.0 mask 255.255.255.0
 network 172.16.65.0 mask 255.255.255.192
 network 172.16.220.0 mask 255.255.255.0
 neighbor 172.16.2.254 remote-as 3
 neighbor 172.16.2.254 next-hop-self
```

continues

Example 12-14 *Default, Primary, and Backup, Plus Partial Routing: RTF Configuration (Continued)*

```
 neighbor 192.68.5.2 remote-as 1
 neighbor 192.68.5.2 route-map SET_OUTBOUND_TRAFFIC in
 neighbor 192.68.5.2 route-map SET_INBOUND_TRAFFIC out
 neighbor 192.68.5.2 filter-list 10 out
 no auto-summary

ip route 0.0.0.0 0.0.0.0 193.78.0.0
ip as-path access-list 10 permit ^$
ip as-path access-list 4 permit ^1 6$
ip as-path access-list 4 permit ^1$

access-list 101 permit ip 193.78.0.0 0.0.255.255 255.255.0.0 0.0.0.0

route-map SET_OUTBOUND_TRAFFIC permit 10
 match ip address 101
 set local-preference 250

route-map SET_OUTBOUND_TRAFFIC permit 20
 match as-path 4
 set local-preference 250

route-map SET_INBOUND_TRAFFIC permit 10
 set metric 250
```

The configuration of RTA in Example 12-13 shows the following:

- Route map SET_OUTBOUND_TRAFFIC is applied on RTA's EBGP session to AS1. This route map will help specify which outbound traffic goes over which link. The first instance (10) will allow only one network, 193.78.0.0/16, to be accepted from the Internet. This network is used to set the default. This will be given a local preference of 200, which is lower than the local preference of 250 coming from RTF. This will cause all traffic toward the Internet to follow the default via the NY link.

  The second instance (20) will set all prefixes coming from AS1 and AS6 with a local preference of 300, which is higher than local preference 250 coming from RTF. This will make the SF link the primary link to reach AS1 and its customer AS6. Note that this route map will allow only partial routes (AS1 and AS6) to be injected into AS3 by specifying the AS_PATH to be either AS1 (^1$) or AS6 (^1 6$).

  Instead of listing all the customers of AS1 one by one as was done in AS path access list 4, a regular expression of the form ^1 ?[0-9]*$ could have been used to identify all the AS paths that start with 1 and that are of length 2—that is, AS1 and its direct customers. The form of the access list would have been **ip as-path access-list 4 permit ^1 ?[0-9]*$** (to enter the **?**, press **Ctrl-V** first).

Be careful, though. In the case where AS1 is directly connected to another major provider with a direct link (rather than via a NAP), the preceding regular expression would also give you the local routes of that second provider.

- Route map SET_INBOUND_TRAFFIC is also applied on RTA's EBGP link to AS1. The first instance (10) will cause prefix 172.16.220.0/24 to be sent with a metric of 200, which is lower than the metric 250 sent by RTF. This will ensure that traffic from AS1 toward this destination will take the SF link. All other updates will be sent with a metric of 300, which is higher than metric 250 sent by RTF. This will cause all other inbound traffic to take the NY link.
- The filter list 10 will prevent AS3 from becoming a transit AS.
- The **ip route 0.0.0.0 0.0.0.0** statement sets the default to 193.78.0.0/16.

RTA's BGP table would have the entries listed in Example 12-15.

Example 12-15 *RTA BGP Table*

```
RTA#show ip bgp
BGP table version is 19, local router ID is 172.16.2.254
Status codes: s suppressed, d damped, h history, * valid, > best,
  i - internal Origin codes: i - IGP, e - EGP, ? - incomplete
  Network          Next Hop      Metric LocPrf Weight Path
* i172.16.1.0/24   172.16.1.2         0    100      0 i
*>                 0.0.0.0            0         32768 i
* i172.16.10.0/24  172.16.1.2         0    100      0 i
*>                 172.16.1.2        20         32768 i
* i172.16.65.0/26  172.16.1.2         0    100      0 i
*>                 172.16.1.2        20         32768 i
* i172.16.220.0/24 172.16.1.2        20    100      0 i
*>                 0.0.0.0            0         32768 i
*> 192.68.10.0     172.16.20.1             300      0 1 i
*> 192.68.11.0     172.16.20.1        0    300      0 1 i
*> 192.68.40.0     172.16.20.1             300      0 1 6 i
*>i193.78.0.0/16   172.16.1.2              250      0 1 7 8 i
*                  172.16.20.1             200      0 1 7 8 i
```

Note how RTA sees only networks that belong to AS1 and its customer AS6 (except for the default route). For network 193.78.0.0/16, which is the default, RTA follows the NY link because of the local preference 250. For traffic toward AS1 and AS6, RTA follows the RTA-RTC link (local preference 300). The IP routing table of RTA in Example 12-16 shows that RTA has set its default to 193.78.0.0/16, which is reachable via 172.16.1.2.

Example 12-16 *RTA IP Routing Table*

```
RTA#show ip route
Codes: C - connected, S - static, I - IGRP, R - RIP, M - mobile, B - BGP
    D - EIGRP, EX - EIGRP external, O - OSPF, IA - OSPF inter area
    N1 - OSPF NSSA external type 1, N2 - OSPF NSSA external type 2
    E1 - OSPF external type 1, E2 - OSPF external type 2, E - EGP
    i - IS-IS, L1 - IS-IS level-1, L2 - IS-IS level-2,
```

continues

Example 12-16 *RTA IP Routing Table (Continued)*

```
       * - candidate default U - per-user static route, o - ODR
Gateway of last resort is 193.78.0.0 to network 0.0.0.0
B  192.68.10.0/24 [20/0] via 172.16.20.1, 00:07:34
B  192.68.11.0/24 [20/0] via 172.16.20.1, 00:07:34
B  192.68.40.0/24 [20/0] via 172.16.20.1, 00:07:34
   172.16.0.0/16 is variably subnetted, 6 subnets, 3 masks
C    172.16.2.254/32 is directly connected, Loopback0
C    172.16.220.0/24 is directly connected, Ethernet0
C    172.16.20.0/24 is directly connected, Serial0
O     172.16.10.0/24 [110/20] via 172.16.1.2, 01:39:52, Ethernet1
C    172.16.1.0/24 is directly connected, Ethernet1
O    172.16.65.0/26 [110/20] via 172.16.1.2, 01:39:52, Ethernet1
S*  0.0.0.0/0 [1/0] via 193.78.0.0
B  193.78.0.0/16 [200/0] via 172.16.1.2, 00:03:07
```

Example 12-17 shows RTD's BGP table.

Example 12-17 *RTD BGP Table*

```
RTD#show ip bgp
BGP table version is 14, local router ID is 192.68.10.1
Status codes: s suppressed, d damped, h history, * valid, > best,
  i - internal Origin codes: i - IGP, e - EGP, ? - incomplete
   Network          Next Hop      Metric LocPrf Weight Path
*> 172.16.1.0/24    192.68.5.1       250              0 3 i
*> 172.16.10.0/24   192.68.5.1       250              0 3 i
*> 172.16.65.0/26   192.68.5.1       250              0 3 i
*>i172.16.220.0/24 192.68.6.2       200   100         0 3 i
*                   192.68.5.1       250              0 3 i
*> 192.68.10.0      0.0.0.0            0          32768 i
*>i192.68.11.0      192.68.6.2         0   100          0 i
*>i192.68.40.0      192.68.6.2         0   100        0 6 i
*> 193.78.0.0/16    192.68.10.2                     0 7 8 i
```

RTD can reach all networks in AS3 via the RTD-RTF direct link, except for prefix 172.16.220.0/24, which can be reached via the RTC-RTA link because of the better metric 200.

Load Balancing with BGP Multipath

Before I begin the load-balancing discussion, it's important for you to understand that actual packet-switching functions performed by the router are entirely dependent upon the enabled Cisco switching mode (that is, CEF per-packet, CEF per-destination, fast switching, process switching, and so on). A detailed discussion of switching modes is beyond the scope of this book, but it is extremely important to understand that it will have a profound effect on load balancing. For additional information on Cisco switching modes, consult the appropriate Cisco documentation or read *Inside Cisco IOS Software Architecture*.

That said, let's begin our load-balancing discussion. Under normal conditions, when a BGP speaker receives identical paths for a prefix from an adjacent AS, only one path will be selected as the best path (normally the one with the lowest BGP ROUTER_ID value) and will be installed in the routing table. If BGP multipath is enabled, multiple paths (up to six) can be installed in the IP routing table.

In Figure 12-5, you can see how the Cisco BGP implementation can do dynamic load balancing for identical paths to the same destination received from the same adjacent autonomous system.

Figure 12-5 *Automatic Load Balancing*

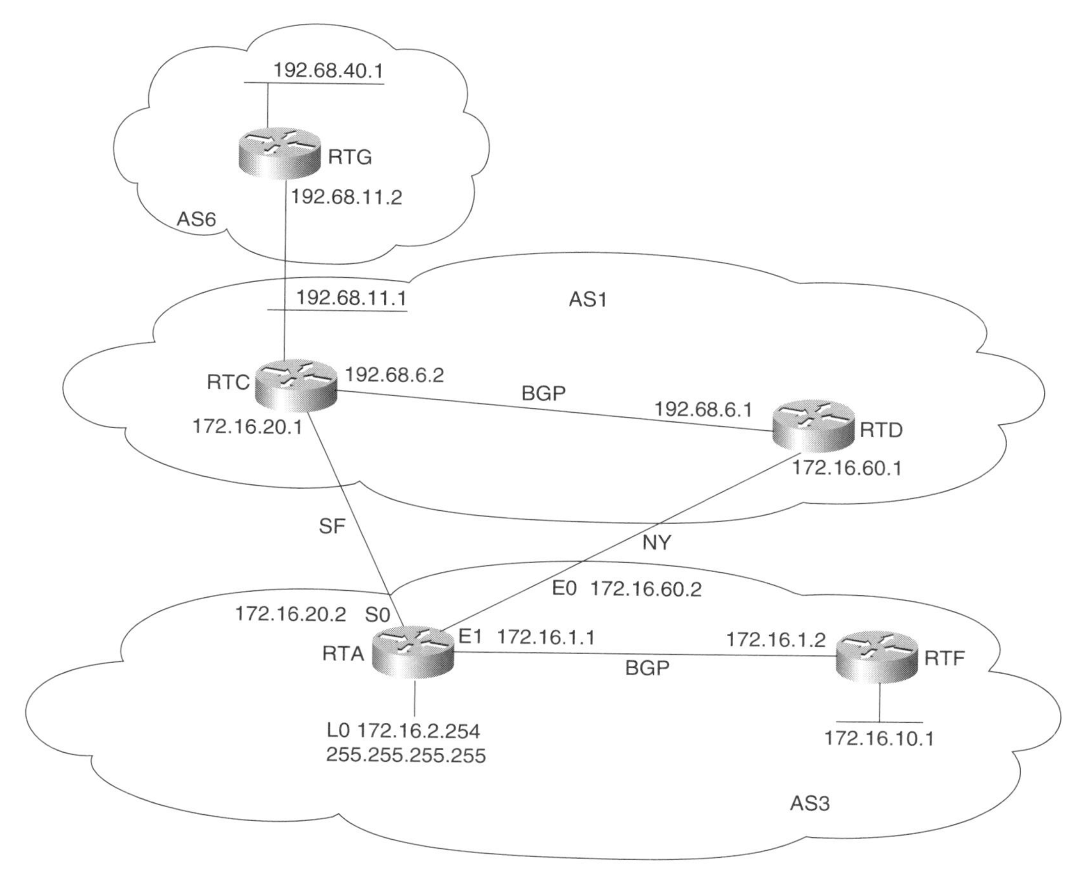

RTA is EBGP peering with routers RTC and RTD in AS1. RTA is receiving identical updates about prefixes 192.68.11.0/24 and 192.68.40.0/24 from two links. You can configure RTA with the **maximum-paths** BGP router subcommand to enable IP routing to load balance among up to six paths. In Example 12-18, the **maximum-paths** number is set to 2.

Example 12-18 *Enabling IP Routing to Load Balance: RTA Configuration*

```
router bgp 3
 no synchronization
 neighbor 172.16.1.2 remote-as 3
 neighbor 172.16.1.2 update-source Loopback0
 neighbor 172.16.20.1 remote-as 1
 neighbor 172.16.20.1 filter-list 10 out
 neighbor 172.16.60.1 remote-as 1
 neighbor 172.16.60.1 filter-list 10 out
 maximum-paths 2
 no auto-summary

ip as-path access-list 10 permit ^$
```

Looking at RTA's BGP table in Example 12-19, you see that RTA has identical path information regarding 192.68.11.0/24 and 192.68.40.0/24. Normally, BGP will pick only one of the entries as the "best" path and give it to the IP routing table.

Example 12-19 *RTA BGP Table*

```
RTA#show ip bgp
BGP table version is 8, local router ID is 172.16.2.254
Status codes: s suppressed, d damped, h history, * valid, > best,
  i - internal Origin codes: i - IGP, e - EGP, ? - incomplete

   Network          Next Hop     Metric LocPrf Weight Path
*>i172.16.10.0/24  172.16.1.2        0    100      0 i
*> 192.68.11.0     172.16.20.1       0             0 1 i
*                  172.16.60.1                     0 1 i
*> 192.68.40.0     172.16.20.1                   0 1 6 i
*                  172.16.60.1                   0 1 6 i
```

Using the **maximum-paths** command will instruct BGP to give all the identical paths (up to six, depending on the configured value) to the IP routing table. Note that the requirement for these paths is that they come from the same AS.

Example 12-20 shows how RTA will keep multiple entries from the same destination in its IP routing table. Note how prefixes 192.68.11.0/24 and 192.68.40.0/24 are learned from both links.

Example 12-20 *RTA IP Routing Table*

```
RTA#show ip route
Codes: C - connected, S - static, I - IGRP, R - RIP, M - mobile, B - BGP
    D - EIGRP, EX - EIGRP external, O - OSPF, IA - OSPF inter area
    N1 - OSPF NSSA external type 1, N2 - OSPF NSSA external type 2
    E1 - OSPF external type 1, E2 - OSPF external type 2, E - EGP
    i - IS-IS, L1 - IS-IS level-1, L2 - IS-IS level-2,
      * - candidate default U - per-user static route, o - ODR

Gateway of last resort is not set

B   192.68.11.0/24 [20/0] via 172.16.60.1, 00:03:20
                   [20/0] via 172.16.20.1, 00:03:18
B   192.68.40.0/24 [20/0] via 172.16.60.1, 00:03:20
                   [20/0] via 172.16.20.1, 00:03:18
    172.16.0.0/16 is variably subnetted, 5 subnets, 2 masks
C     172.16.2.254/32 is directly connected, Loopback0
C     172.16.60.0/24 is directly connected, Ethernet0
C     172.16.20.0/24 is directly connected, Serial0
O      172.16.10.0/24 [110/20] via 172.16.1.2, 00:20:23, Ethernet1
C     172.16.1.0/24 is directly connected, Ethernet1
```

When dealing with IBGP peers, RTA will advertise only a single BGP entry out of the multiple identical entries that have a **next-hop-self**. Because RTA is IBGP peered with RTF, RTA will advertise only one BGP update about 192.68.11.0/24 and 192.68.40.0/24 with a NEXT_HOP of 172.16.2.254 rather than the external NEXT_HOP; this is illustrated in the BGP table in Example 12-21. For external peers, BGP will still pass on the best path as usual.

Example 12-21 *RTF BGP Table*

```
RTF#show ip bgp
BGP table version is 56, local router ID is 172.16.10.1
Status codes: s suppressed, d damped, h history, * valid, > best,
  i - internal Origin codes: i - IGP, e - EGP, ? - incomplete

   Network          Next Hop       Metric LocPrf Weight Path
*> 172.16.10.0/24   0.0.0.0             0         32768 i
*>i192.68.11.0      172.16.2.254        0    100      0 1 i
*>i192.68.40.0      172.16.2.254             100      0 1 6 i
```

Balancing Between Two Routers Sharing Multiple Paths

This section shows how load balancing can be achieved between two routers sharing multiple paths without having routing updates being duplicated over the two paths.

For the scenario in Figure 12-6, you will configure loopback interfaces on RTA and RTC (see Example 12-22 and Example 12-23) and run a single peering session between the two routers. Using static routes, you can point to the loopback interfaces via both of the physical interfaces. This way, the IP routing table will have two paths to reach the NEXT_HOP and will load balance.

Figure 12-6 *Balancing Between Two Routers Sharing Multiple Paths*

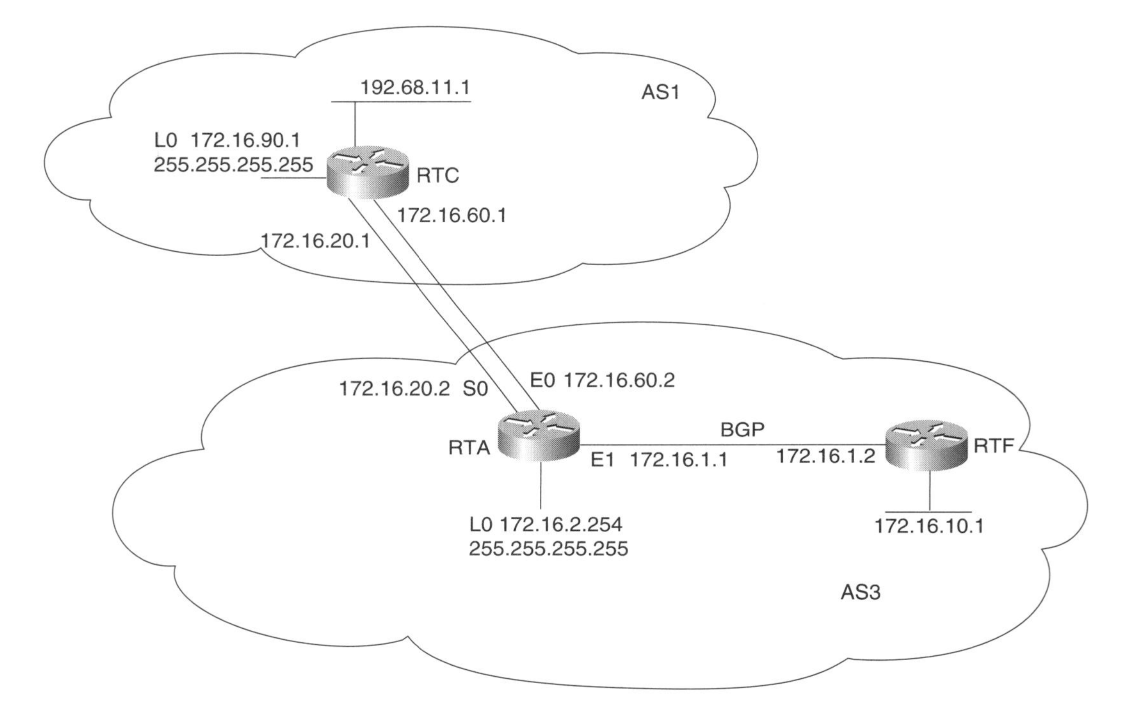

Example 12-22 *Balancing Between Two Routers Sharing Multiple Paths: RTA Configuration*

```
interface Loopback0
 ip address 172.16.2.254 255.255.255.255

router bgp 3
 no synchronization
 neighbor 172.16.1.2 next-hop-self
neighbor 172.16.1.2 remote-as 3
 neighbor 172.16.1.2 update-source Loopback0
 neighbor 172.16.90.1 remote-as 1
neighbor 172.16.90.1 ebgp-multihop 2
 neighbor 172.16.90.1 update-source Loopback0
 no auto-summary
```

Example 12-22 *Balancing Between Two Routers Sharing Multiple Paths: RTA Configuration (Continued)*

```
ip route 172.16.90.1 255.255.255.255 172.16.20.1
ip route 172.16.90.1 255.255.255.255 172.16.60.1
```

Example 12-23 *Balancing Between Two Routers Sharing Multiple Paths: RTC Configuration*

```
interface Loopback0
 ip address 172.16.90.1 255.255.255.255

router bgp 1
 network 192.68.11.0
 neighbor 172.16.2.254 remote-as 3
 neighbor 172.16.2.254 ebgp-multihop 2
 neighbor 172.16.2.254 update-source Loopback0
 no auto-summary

ip route 172.16.2.254 255.255.255.255 172.16.20.2
ip route 172.16.2.254 255.255.255.255 172.16.60.2
```

The output in Example 12-24 shows how RTA is now learning BGP updates from RTC via NEXT_HOP 172.16.90.1, the loopback address. Notice that **update-source** is configured as a BGP **neighbor** parameter. This sets the source IP address of the BGP TCP connection to that of the specified interface. If this weren't specified, the egress interface used to reach the peer would be the source address, and the peer would reject the connection.

Example 12-24 *RTA BGP Table*

```
RTA#show ip bgp
BGP table version is 4, local router ID is 172.16.2.254
Status codes: s suppressed, d damped, h history, * valid, > best,
  i - internal Origin codes: i - IGP, e - EGP, ? - incomplete

  Network          Next Hop       Metric LocPrf Weight Path
*>i172.16.10.0/24  172.16.1.2          0    100      0 i
*> 192.68.11.0     172.16.90.1         0             0 1 i
```

The two static routes in RTA's routing table (see Example 12-25) will provide multiple paths to reach the NEXT_HOP 172.16.90.1, so the router will load balance between the two paths.

Example 12-25 *RTA IP Routing Table*

```
RTA#show ip route
Codes: C - connected, S - static, I - IGRP, R - RIP, M - mobile, B - BGP
    D - EIGRP, EX - EIGRP external, O - OSPF, IA - OSPF inter area
    N1 - OSPF NSSA external type 1, N2 - OSPF NSSA external type 2
    E1 - OSPF external type 1, E2 - OSPF external type 2, E - EGP
    i - IS-IS, L1 - IS-IS level-1, L2 - IS-IS level-2,
      * - candidate default U - per-user static route, o - ODR
```

continues

Example 12-25 *RTA IP Routing Table (Continued)*

```
Gateway of last resort is not set

B  192.68.11.0/24 [20/0] via 172.16.90.1, 00:00:41
   172.16.0.0/16 is variably subnetted, 6 subnets, 2 masks
C     172.16.2.254/32 is directly connected, Loopback0
C     172.16.60.0/24 is directly connected, Ethernet0
C     172.16.20.0/24 is directly connected, Serial0
O     172.16.10.0/24 [110/20] via 172.16.1.2, 02:17:34, Ethernet1
C     172.16.1.0/24 is directly connected, Ethernet1
S     172.16.90.1/32 [1/0] via 172.16.20.1
                     [1/0] via 172.16.60.1
```

Note that all of the preceding load-balancing scenarios deal only with egress traffic flows. Similar configurations are required on the remote side of the connection as well. This will be discussed in the next couple of sections.

Multihoming to Different Providers

For the case of one customer multihomed to multiple providers, we will discuss a scenario in which updates follow a combination of defaults, partial routing, and full routing.

In Figure 12-7, AS3 is multihomed to two different ASs, AS1 and AS2, which in turn exchange routing information and traffic with AS6, as well as one another, via a network access point. AS6, AS2, and AS1 all peer with RTE, which is acting as a route server that has the function of only passing routing updates between all three ASs. The desired policy is as follows:

- AS3 will accept AS1's local and customer routes only via the SF link. All other Internet routes will be accepted via the NY link (primary).
- AS3 will accept a default route from AS1 just in case there is a failure in the NY link.

  AS3 prefers that the SF network 172.16.220.0/24 be reachable by the outside world via the SF link and that the NY networks 172.16.10.0/24 and 172.16.65.0/26 be reachable via the NY link.
- AS3 cannot be a transit network for AS1 and AS2, which means that under no circumstances will AS1 use AS3 to reach AS2.

Figure 12-7 *Multiple Providers (Default, Primary and Backup, Full/Partial)*

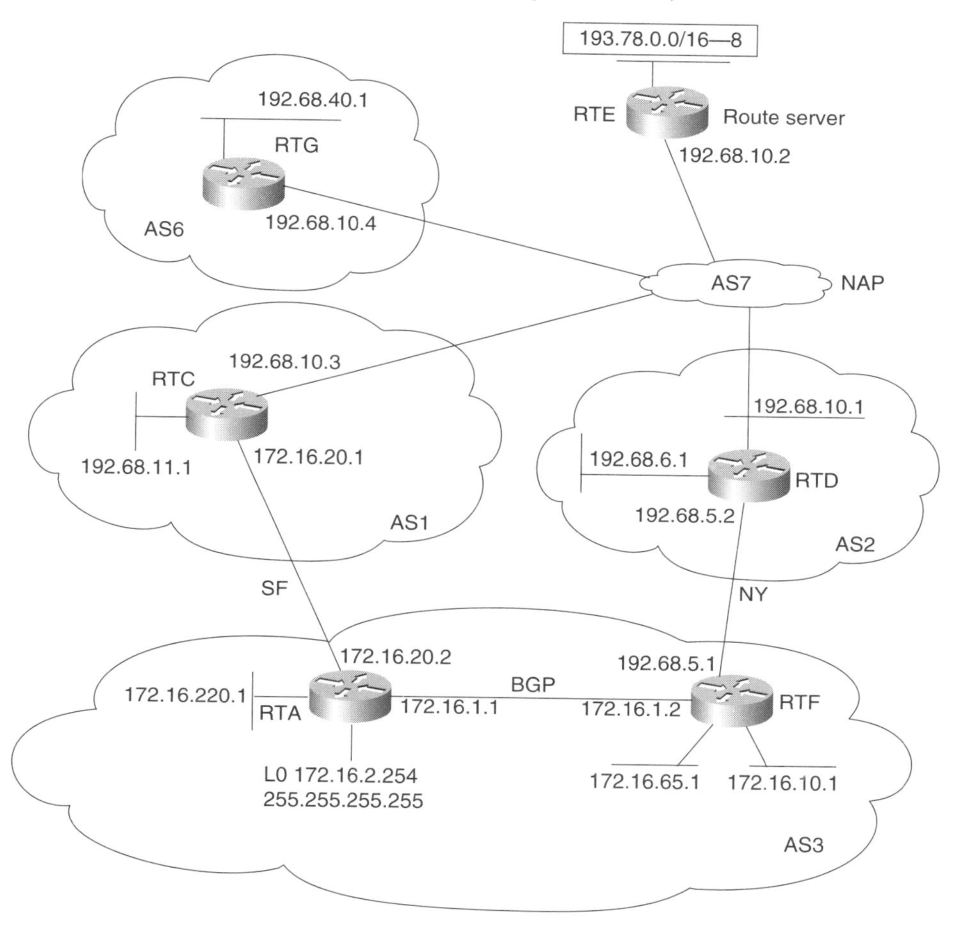

The configurations in Examples 12-26 through 12-29 illustrate how to implement this routing arrangement. Example 12-26 begins with the configuration for RTA.

Example 12-26 *Multiple Providers (Default, Primary and Backup, Full/Partial): RTA Configuration*

```
router bgp 3
 no synchronization
 network 172.16.1.0 mask 255.255.255.0
 network 172.16.10.0 mask 255.255.255.0
 network 172.16.65.0 mask 255.255.255.192
 network 172.16.220.0 mask 255.255.255.0
 neighbor 172.16.1.2 remote-as 3
 neighbor 172.16.1.2 update-source Loopback0
```

continues

Example 12-26 *Multiple Providers (Default, Primary and Backup, Full/Partial): RTA Configuration (Continued)*

```
 neighbor 172.16.1.2 next-hop-self
 neighbor 172.16.20.1 remote-as 1
 neighbor 172.16.20.1 route-map ACCEPT_LOCAL in
 neighbor 172.16.20.1 route-map PREPEND_PATH out
 no auto-summary

ip as-path access-list 1 permit ^1 ?[0-9]*$
ip as-path access-list 2 permit ^$

access-list 1 permit 172.16.65.0 0.0.0.63
access-list 1 permit 172.16.10.0 0.0.0.255

route-map PREPEND_PATH permit 10
 match ip address 1
 set as-path prepend 3

route-map PREPEND_PATH permit 20
 match as-path 2

route-map ACCEPT_LOCAL permit 10
 match as-path 1
```

RTA uses a route map called ACCEPT_LOCAL that accepts partial routes from AS1. The route map will try to match on any path of the form ^1 ?[0-9]*$, which, as already explained, enables AS1's local and customer routes.

RTA defines a route map toward RTC called PREPEND_PATH that will prepend an additional AS number to all NY prefixes (such as 172.16.10.0/24 and 172.16.65.0/26). This will make the AS_PATH length of these prefixes shorter via the NY link. Doing the AS_PATH prepend should always be coordinated with the provider. Your provider might have policies that associate your prefix with the path information. AS1, for example, might have a policy that advertises AS3 to the NAP using the form ^3$, which represents an AS_PATH that starts with 3 and ends with 3. If AS3 starts sending AS_PATH information of the form 3 3 3 3, the provider will drop the routes, because the AS_PATH will not match its policy.

Note that instance 20 of the route map PREPEND_PATH lets AS3's local routes be advertised only. This is done by matching on the local prefixes, with empty AS_PATH information represented by the ^$ regular expression.

In the same manner, Example 12-27 configures RTF to announce the SF prefixes on the NY link with an additional AS in the AS_PATH information. This would make inbound traffic toward these networks preferred via the SF link.

Example 12-27 *Multiple Providers (Default, Primary and Backup, Full/Partial): RTF Configuration*

```
router bgp 3
 no synchronization
 network 172.16.1.0 mask 255.255.255.0
 network 172.16.10.0 mask 255.255.255.0
 network 172.16.65.0 mask 255.255.255.192
 network 172.16.220.0 mask 255.255.255.0
 neighbor 172.16.2.254 remote-as 3
 neighbor 172.16.2.254 next-hop-self
 neighbor 192.68.5.2 remote-as 2
 neighbor 192.68.5.2 route-map PREPEND_PATH out
 no auto-summary

ip as-path access-list 2 permit ^$
access-list 1 permit 172.16.220.0 0.0.0.255

route-map PREPEND_PATH permit 10
 match ip address 1
 set as-path prepend 3

route-map PREPEND_PATH permit 20
 match as-path 2
```

Note that RTF accepts all routes from AS2 and advertises only the local routes (^$), with an extra AS added to the AS_PATH information for the SF route 172.16.220.0/24.

Example 12-28 provides a snapshot of some of the BGP routing tables for RTA.

Example 12-28 *RTA BGP Table*

```
RTA#show ip bgp
BGP table version is 13, local router ID is 172.16.2.254
Status codes: s suppressed, d damped, h history, * valid, > best,
  i - internal Origin codes: i - IGP, e - EGP, ? - incomplete
   Network          Next Hop      Metric LocPrf Weight Path
*> 0.0.0.0          172.16.20.1                      0 1 i
*> 172.16.1.0/24    0.0.0.0            0         32768 i
* i                 172.16.1.2         0    100      0 i
*> 172.16.10.0/24   172.16.1.2        20         32768 i
* i                 172.16.1.2         0    100      0 i
*> 172.16.65.0/26   172.16.1.2        20         32768 i
* i                 172.16.1.2         0    100      0 i
*> 172.16.220.0/24  0.0.0.0            0         32768 i
* i                 172.16.1.2        20    100      0 i
*>i192.68.6.0       172.16.1.2         0    100      0 2 i
*> 192.68.11.0      172.16.20.1        0             0 1 i
*>i193.78.0.0/16     172.16.1.2             100      0 2 7 8 i
```

Note that RTA learns a default (0.0.0.0) from RTC. RTA also learns AS1's local routes (such as 192.68.11.0/24) and can reach those directly via the SF link. For all other routes, RTA will go via the NY link.

On the other hand, inbound traffic will follow the shortest path. The BGP table for RTG in Example 12-29 shows how an outside AS that falls behind the NAP, such as AS6, can reach AS3's networks.

Example 12-29 *RTG BGP Table*

```
RTG#show ip bgp
BGP table version is 9, local router ID is 192.68.40.1
Status codes: s suppressed, d damped, h history, * valid, > best,
  i - internal Origin codes: i - IGP, e - EGP, ? - incomplete
   Network          Next Hop      Metric LocPrf Weight Path
*> 172.16.1.0/24    192.68.10.1                      0 7 2 3 i
*> 172.16.10.0/24   192.68.10.1                      0 7 2 3 i
*> 172.16.65.0/26   192.68.10.1                      0 7 2 3 i
*> 172.16.220.0/24  192.68.10.3                      0 7 1 3 i
*> 192.68.6.0       192.68.10.1                      0 7 2 i
*> 192.68.11.0      192.68.10.3                      0 7 1 i
*> 192.68.40.0      0.0.0.0            0         32768 i
*> 193.78.0.0/16    192.68.10.2                      0 7 8 i
```

Note that the NY prefixes (172.16.10.0/24 and 172.16.65.0/26) can be reached via the NY link (path 7 2 3). The SF prefix 172.16.220.0/24 can be reached via the SF link (path 7 1 3).

Customers of the Same Provider with a Backup Link

Customers of the same provider can, by mutual agreement, interconnect via a private link. The private link will serve as a backup in case the Internet connectivity of any of the customers is broken. The scenario in this section discusses a case in which the private link is used as the primary link between the two ASs and as a backup in case of Internet connectivity failures.

In this example, we will switch roles a bit. In Figure 12-8, AS3 is the provider offering services to two of its customers, AS1 and AS2. AS1 and AS2 agree to use each other as backup in case their links to AS3 fail. In normal conditions, AS1 and AS2 will use the private link only for traffic between AS1 and AS2; for all other Internet traffic, the direct link to the provider AS3 is used.

Figure 12-8 *Backup Private Link Used as Primary*

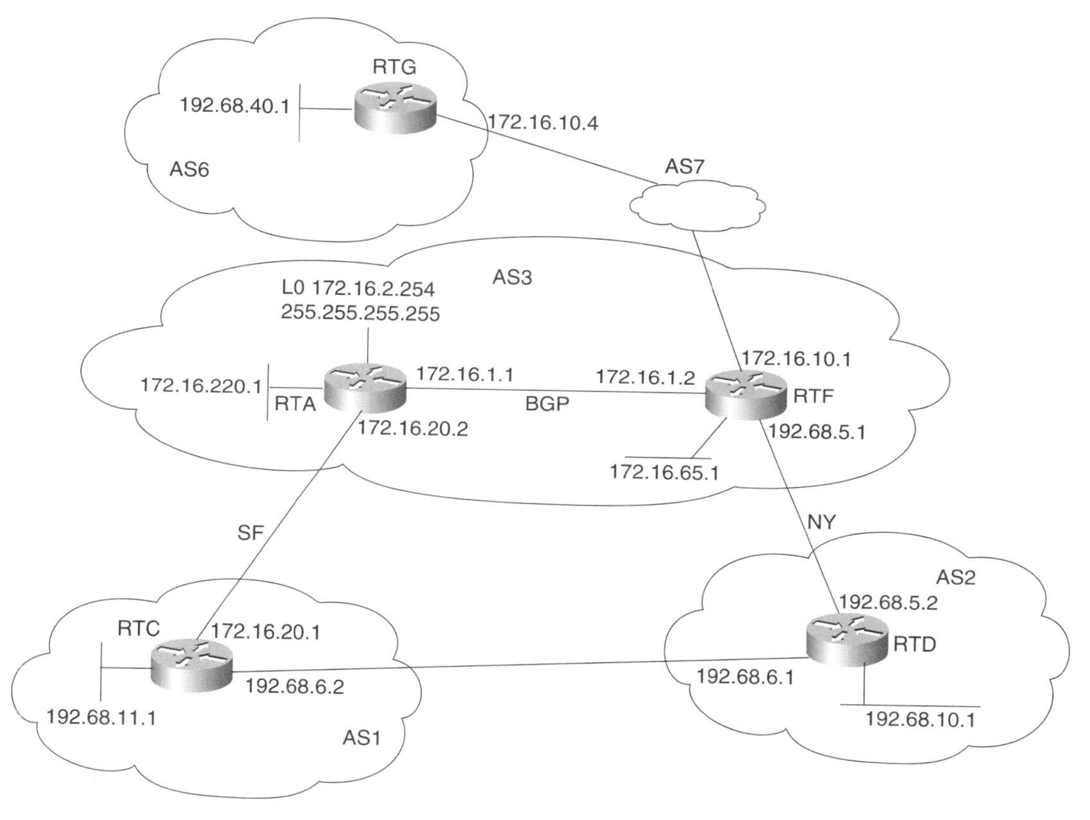

We will assume that AS1 and AS2 are getting full Internet routes. AS1 and AS2 should advertise each other's routes to AS3 because, for the backup behavior to occur, AS3 should be able to reach AS1's networks via AS2 and AS2's networks via AS1. Normally, this scenario is handled automatically by the BGP default behavior. Due to the shortest path rule, AS1 and AS2 will always reach each other's networks over the private link. For the sake of experimenting with setting BGP policies, we will attempt to solve this problem by manipulating the LOCAL_PREF attribute. In Example 12-30, we will concentrate on the router configuration of RTC; RTD's configuration should be similar.

Example 12-30 *Backup Private Link Used as Primary: RTC Configuration*

```
router bgp 1
 network 192.68.11.0
 neighbor 172.16.20.2 remote-as 3
 neighbor 172.16.20.2 route-map PREF_FROM_AS3 in
 neighbor 192.68.6.1 remote-as 2
```

continues

Example 12-30 *Backup Private Link Used as Primary: RTC Configuration (Continued)*

```
 neighbor 192.68.6.1 route-map PREF_FROM_AS2 in
 no auto-summary

ip as-path access-list 1 permit _2_

route-map PREF_FROM_AS3 permit 10
 match as-path 1
 set local-preference 100

route-map PREF_FROM_AS3 permit 20
 set local-preference 300

route-map PREF_FROM_AS2 permit 10
 set local-preference 200
```

The configuration in Example 12-30 shows a route map PREF_FROM_AS2, which sets all updates coming from AS2 with a local preference of 200. The other route map PREF_FROM_AS3 sets all updates coming from AS3 that have AS2 in them with a local preference of 100 (the default); all other updates will have a local preference of 300. Note the regular expression **_2_**, which indicates routes that have passed via AS2. With this configuration, all networks that originated from AS2 or customers of AS2 will be reachable directly via the private link. All other routes will be reachable via the provider AS3. Example 12-31 shows RTC's BGP table.

Example 12-31 *Backup Private Link Used as Primary: RTC BGP Table*

```
RTC#show ip bgp
BGP table version is 11, local router ID is 192.68.11.1
Status codes: s suppressed, d damped, h history, * valid, > best,
  i - internal Origin codes: i - IGP, e - EGP, ? - incomplete

   Network          Next Hop        Metric LocPrf Weight Path
*> 172.16.1.0/24    172.16.20.2          0    300      0 3 i
*                   192.68.6.1                200      0 2 3 i
*> 172.16.10.0/24   172.16.20.2         20    300      0 3 i
*                   192.68.6.1                200      0 2 3 i
*> 172.16.65.0/26   172.16.20.2         20    300      0 3 i
*                   192.68.6.1                200      0 2 3 i
*> 172.16.220.0/24  172.16.20.2          0    300      0 3 i
*                   192.68.6.1                200      0 2 3 i
* 192.68.10.0       172.16.20.2               100      0 3 2 i
*>                  192.68.6.1           0    200      0 2 i
*> 192.68.11.0      0.0.0.0              0         32768 i
*> 192.68.40.0      172.16.20.2               300      0 3 6 i
*                   192.68.6.1                200      0 2 3 6 i
```

Note that prefix 192.68.10.0/24 coming from AS3 has a local preference of 100 because its AS_PATH 3 2 contains 2. All other routes coming from AS3 have a local preference of 300.

Customers of Different Providers with a Backup Link

Providers prefer to use as little configuration as possible when dealing with adding and removing customers, because lots of hacks will reduce scalability. Every time a customer is added or removed, the provider will have to add policies to accommodate the customer's requirement. In the following examples, you will see how an AS can use the COMMUNITY attribute or path manipulation techniques in such a way that a new customer can have the provider dynamically set the customer's policies.

The COMMUNITY Approach

In Figure 12-9, customer AS1 is getting its service from provider AS4. Customer AS2 is getting its service from provider AS3. AS1 and AS2 have a private link that will be used for internal use between the two ASs. For all other traffic, both customers would like to go out via their direct providers—AS1 via AS4 and AS2 via AS3. In case the private link goes down, the customers should be able to talk to one another via the providers. If a link to the provider fails, the other customer should be used to reach the Internet.

Figure 12-9 *Multiple ASs with Multiple Providers*

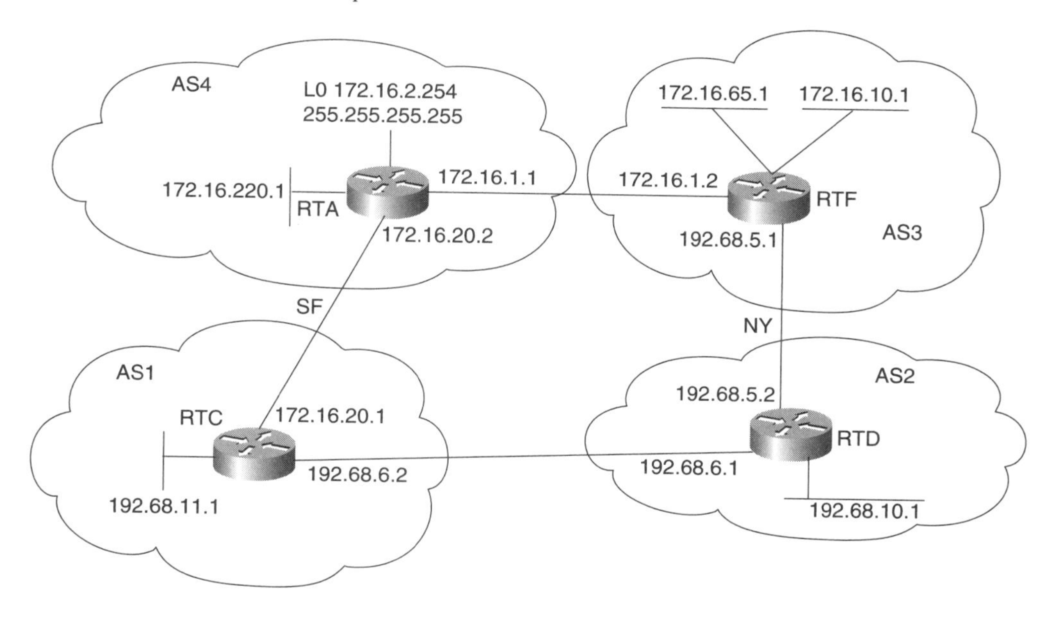

Examples 12-32 through 12-34 show the relevant configuration of RTA, RTC, and RTF, respectively. RTD should be a mirror image of RTC.

Example 12-32 *Backup Links for Multiple ASs with Multiple Providers Via COMMUNITY: RTA Configuration*

```
router bgp 4
 network 172.16.220.0 mask 255.255.255.0
 neighbor 172.16.1.2 remote-as 3
 neighbor 172.16.1.2 route-map CHECK_COMMUNITY in
 neighbor 172.16.20.1 remote-as 1
 neighbor 172.16.20.1 route-map CHECK_COMMUNITY in
 no auto-summary

ip community-list 2 permit 4:40
ip community-list 3 permit 4:60

route-map CHECK_COMMUNITY permit 10
 match community 2
 set local-preference 40

route-map CHECK_COMMUNITY permit 20
 match community 3
 set local-preference 60

route-map CHECK_COMMUNITY permit 30
 set local-preference 100
```

Notice how RTA has configured the route map CHECK_COMMUNITY. The **match community** value statement under the route map correlates with the **ip community-list** *value* list, which states the following:

- Instance 10: For routes with community 4:40, set the local preference to 40.
- Instance 20: For routes with community 4:60, set the local preference to 60.
- Instance 30: For all other routes, set the preference to 100 (default).

Example 12-33 *Backup Links for Multiple ASs with Multiple Providers Via COMMUNITY: RTC Configuration*

```
router bgp 1
 network 192.68.11.0
 neighbor 172.16.20.2 remote-as 4
 neighbor 172.16.20.2 send-community
 neighbor 172.16.20.2 route-map setcommunity out
 neighbor 172.16.20.2 filter-list 10 out
 neighbor 192.68.6.1 remote-as 2
 no auto-summary

ip as-path access-list 2 permit _2_

ip as-path access-list 10 permit ^$
ip as-path access-list 10 permit ^2$

route-map setcommunity permit 10
 match as-path 2
```

Example 12-33 *Backup Links for Multiple ASs with Multiple Providers Via COMMUNITY: RTC Configuration (Continued)*

```
 set community 4:40

route-map setcommunity permit 20
```

Notice the route map **setcommunity**, which is configured toward AS4. The route map states the following:

- Instance 10: For all routes that have passed via AS2 (_2_), set the community to 4:40.
- Instance 20: All other routes will go through and do not have any community set.

RTC also has a **filter-list 10 out** that prevents AS4 from learning about AS3 via AS1. The filter list permits only AS1 and AS2 routes. In case the link between AS4 and AS3 goes down, AS4 cannot use AS1 to reach AS3.

Example 12-34 *Backup Links for Multiple ASs with Multiple Providers Via COMMUNITY: RTF Configuration*

```
router bgp 3
 network 172.16.10.0 mask 255.255.255.0
 network 172.16.65.0 mask 255.255.255.192
 neighbor 172.16.1.1 remote-as 4
 neighbor 172.16.1.1 send-community
 neighbor 172.16.1.1 route-map setcommunity out
 neighbor 192.68.5.2 remote-as 2
 no auto-summary

route-map setcommunity permit 10
 set community 4:60
```

In RTF, the route map **setcommunity**, applied via the BGP **neighbor** command, sets all updates toward AS4 with a community of 4:60.

Consider RTA's BGP table in Example 12-35 to see what you have achieved.

Example 12-35 *Backup Links for Multiple ASs with Multiple Providers Via COMMUNITY: RTA BGP Table*

```
RTA#show ip bgp
BGP table version is 7, local router ID is 172.16.2.254
Status codes: s suppressed, d damped, h history, * valid, > best,
  i - internal Origin codes: i - IGP, e - EGP, ? - incomplete

   Network          Next Hop      Metric LocPrf Weight Path
*> 172.16.10.0/24   172.16.1.2         0     60      0 3 i
*> 172.16.65.0/26   172.16.1.2         0     60      0 3 i
*> 172.16.220.0/24  0.0.0.0            0         32768 i
*> 192.68.10.0      172.16.1.2               60      0 3 2 i
*                   172.16.20.1              40      0 1 2 i
*> 192.68.11.0      172.16.20.1        0    100      0 1 i
```

RTA has dynamically set the local preference for all routes from the provider AS3 to 60. All routes coming from AS2 via AS1 have a preference of 40, and routes local to AS1 have a preference of 100.

For all routes originated by AS1 (customer local routes), such as 192.68.11.0/24, AS4 will go directly to AS1. For routes belonging to AS2 (customer transit routes), such as 192.68.10.0/24, AS4 will use the other provider, AS3. For other routes advertised by the provider (ISP routes), AS4 will go directly to AS3.

The AS_PATH Approach

As an alternative to the COMMUNITY approach, you can manipulate the AS_PATH value to achieve the desired routing shown in Figure 12-9. Also, because LOCAL_PREF is not a transitive attribute, AS_PATH manipulation will affect route selection in not only the adjacent AS, but in downstream ASs as well.

In Example 12-36, RTC will prepend an extra AS entry in its routing updates toward AS4 for all routes received from AS2. AS4 will see AS2's updates with a longer path via AS1 and will go via AS3.

Example 12-36 *Achieving Desired Routing Behavior Via AS_PATH Manipulation: RTC Configuration*

```
router bgp 1
 network 192.68.11.0
 neighbor 172.16.20.2 remote-as 4
 neighbor 172.16.20.2 route-map setpath out
 neighbor 172.16.20.2 filter-list 10 out
 neighbor 192.68.6.1 remote-as 2
 no auto-summary

ip as-path access-list 2 permit _2_

ip as-path access-list 10 permit ^$
ip as-path access-list 10 permit ^2$

route-map setpath permit 10
 match as-path 2
 set as-path prepend 1

route-map setpath permit 20
```

RTC has prepended an additional AS number 1 to its updates toward RTA. Example 12-37 shows how RTA's BGP table will look.

Example 12-37 *Achieving Desired Routing Behavior Via AS_PATH Manipulation: RTC BGP Table*

```
RTA#show ip bgp
BGP table version is 9, local router ID is 172.16.2.254
Status codes: s suppressed, d damped, h history, * valid, > best,
```

Example 12-37 *Achieving Desired Routing Behavior Via AS_PATH Manipulation: RTC BGP Table (Continued)*

```
  i - internal Origin codes: i - IGP, e - EGP, ? - incomplete

   Network          Next Hop       Metric LocPrf Weight Path
*> 172.16.10.0/24   172.16.1.2          0             0 3 i
*> 172.16.65.0/26   172.16.1.2          0             0 3 i
*> 172.16.220.0/24  0.0.0.0             0         32768 i
*> 192.68.10.0      172.16.1.2                        0 3 2 i
*                   172.16.20.1             100       0 1 1 2 i
*> 192.68.11.0      172.16.20.1         0   100       0 1 i
```

Notice how RTA now prefers AS3 to reach prefix 192.68.10.0/24. You must take care to ensure that the provider AS1 is not using any AS_PATH access lists and is accepting only routes of the form ^1$ or ^1 2$ from your AS. Otherwise, AS prepending could result in your provider's filtering your routes. It is always good to coordinate with your provider regarding the changes you want to make.

Following Defaults Inside an AS

The following examples show how border routers can inject defaults inside your AS for your IGP to follow. Figure 12-10 illustrates the following scenario: AS3 is multihomed to two providers, AS1 and AS2. RTA is running EBGP with RTC, and RTF is running EBGP with RTD. Inside AS3, RTA and RTF are running IBGP. You will experiment with two situations: first, RTA and RTF having a direct physical connection, and second, RTA and RTF not having a direct physical connection. The latter scenario is used to demonstrate what could go wrong if your IGP traffic is following a default that conflicts with your BGP policies. Finally, RTG is an interior router that is running an IGP; RTG is following the default route 0/0 to reach networks outside AS3.

Figure 12-10 *Following Defaults Inside the AS; Border Routers Connected*

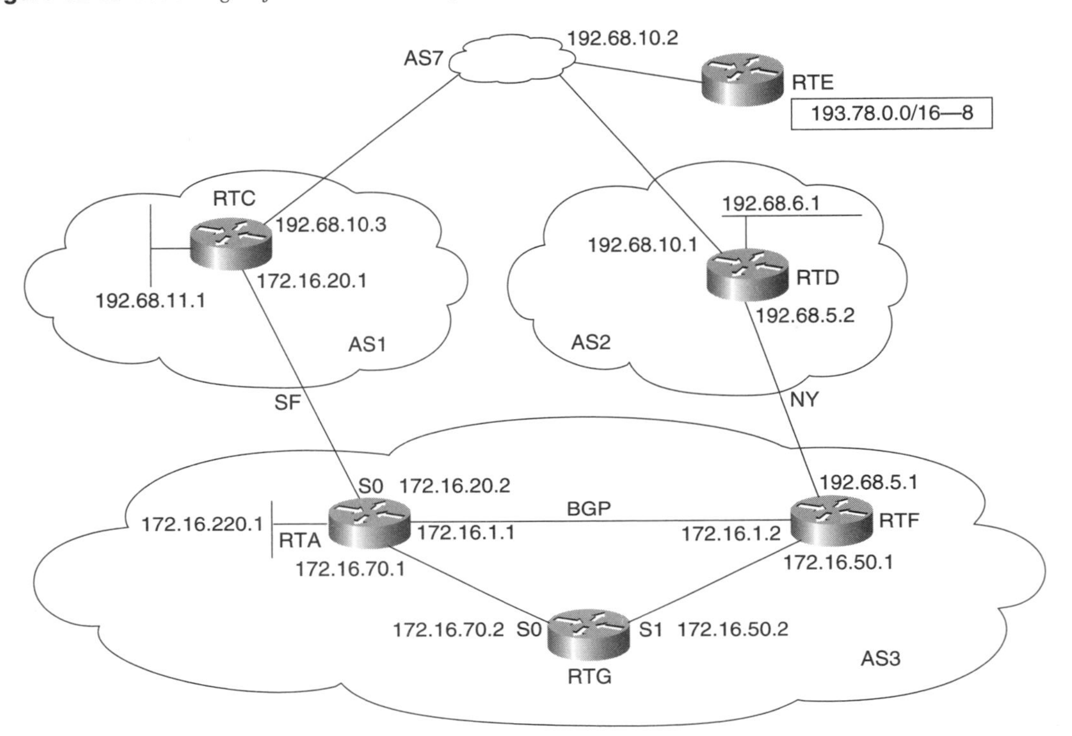

The scenario in which RTA and RTF are directly connected is easy; it is very hard for things to go wrong. As long as RTA and RTF are injecting defaults inside the IGP, traffic that reaches any of the BGP routers will find its way outside the AS. It is important that outbound traffic that reaches a BGP router does not go back to the non-BGP routers to avoid possible routing loops.

In case the border routers are not carrying full routes, they can accept a default to the providers to which they are connected. Both links can be used at the same time, or one link could be used as primary and the second as backup. Whichever policy you use, traffic will find its way out.

In the configurations shown in Example 12-38 and Example 12-39, RTA and RTF are accepting full routes from their respective providers. RTA and RTF are injecting defaults inside the AS (they are not getting any defaults themselves because they carry full routes). You will use OSPF as an IGP (other IGPs will be used in different scenarios later). Notice the presence of the **default-information originate** OSPF subcommand in both configurations.

Example 12-38 *Following Defaults Inside the AS; Border Routers Connected: RTA Configuration*

```
router ospf 10
 passive-interface Serial0
 network 172.16.0.0 0.0.255.255 area 0
 default-information originate always

router bgp 3
 no synchronization
 network 172.16.1.0 mask 255.255.255.0
 network 172.16.70.0 mask 255.255.255.0
 network 172.16.220.0 mask 255.255.255.0
 neighbor 172.16.20.1 remote-as 1
 neighbor 172.16.20.1 filter-list 10 out
 neighbor 172.16.1.2 remote-as 3
 no auto-summary

ip as-path access-list 10 permit ^$
```

Example 12-39 *Following Defaults Inside the AS; Border Routers Connected: RTF Configuration*

```
router ospf 10
 network 172.16.0.0 0.0.255.255 area 0
 default-information originate always

router bgp 3
no synchronization
 network 172.16.1.0 mask 255.255.255.0
 network 172.16.50.0 mask 255.255.255.0
 neighbor 172.16.1.1 remote-as 3
 neighbor 172.16.1.1 next-hop-self
 neighbor 192.68.5.2 remote-as 2
 neighbor 192.68.5.2 filter-list 10 out
 no auto-summary

ip as-path access-list 10 permit ^$
```

Example 12-40 shows the configuration for RTG.

Example 12-40 *Following Defaults Inside the AS; Border Routers Connected: RTG Configuration*

```
router ospf 10
 network 172.16.0.0 0.0.255.255 area 0
```

Note that the RTA and RTF configurations use the **router ospf** subcommand **default-information originate** with the **always** keyword. This command forces OSPF to inject a 0/0 default route into the OSPF domain at all times. The internal router RTG, which is running OSPF only, will receive the default from multiple sources and will follow the shortest internal metric. Routers that are closer (metric-wise) to RTA will use RTA for default; routers closer to RTF will use RTF.

The IP routing table for RTG in Example 12-41 reveals how RTG has set its gateway of last resort to RTA (172.16.70.1), which happens to be at a shorter internal metric than RTF.

Example 12-41 *Following Defaults Inside the AS; Border Routers Connected: RTG IP Routing Table*

```
RTG#show ip route
Codes: C - connected, S - static, I - IGRP, R - RIP, M - mobile, B - BGP
    D - EIGRP, EX - EIGRP external, O - OSPF, IA - OSPF inter area
    N1 - OSPF NSSA external type 1, N2 - OSPF NSSA external type 2
    E1 - OSPF external type 1, E2 - OSPF external type 2, E - EGP
    i - IS-IS, L1 - IS-IS level-1, L2 - IS-IS level-2,
    * - candidate default U - per-user static route, o - ODR
Gateway of last resort is 172.16.70.1 to network 0.0.0.0
   172.16.0.0/16 is subnetted, 5 subnets
O    172.16.220.0/24 [110/74] via 172.16.70.1, 00:03:27, Serial0
C    172.16.50.0/24 is directly connected, Serial1
O    172.16.20.0/24 [110/74] via 172.16.70.1, 00:03:27, Serial0
O    172.16.1.0/24 [110/74] via 172.16.70.1, 00:03:27, Serial0
C    172.16.70.0/24 is directly connected, Serial0
O*E2 0.0.0.0/0 [110/1] via 172.16.70.1, 00:03:27, Serial0
```

BGP Policies Conflicting with the Internal Default

Anytime internal routers are following defaults to reach routes unknown to the AS, you should be careful not to create routing loops. A routing loop occurs when router X follows a default toward router Y, which in turn uses router X to reach the destination. The traffic will end up bouncing between routers X and Y.

The default route 0/0 is injected differently from BGP into the IGP, depending on what IGP you are using. Different scenarios will be considered, utilizing OSPF, RIP, EIGRP, and IS-IS as the IGPs.

In the following scenarios, you will consider the case in which routers RTA and RTF in Figure 12-11 are not directly connected. As you will see, this will make configuration harder and more vulnerable to routing loops. Such configurations could be used in only some restricted cases.

Figure 12-11 *Following Defaults Inside the AS; Border Routers Not Connected*

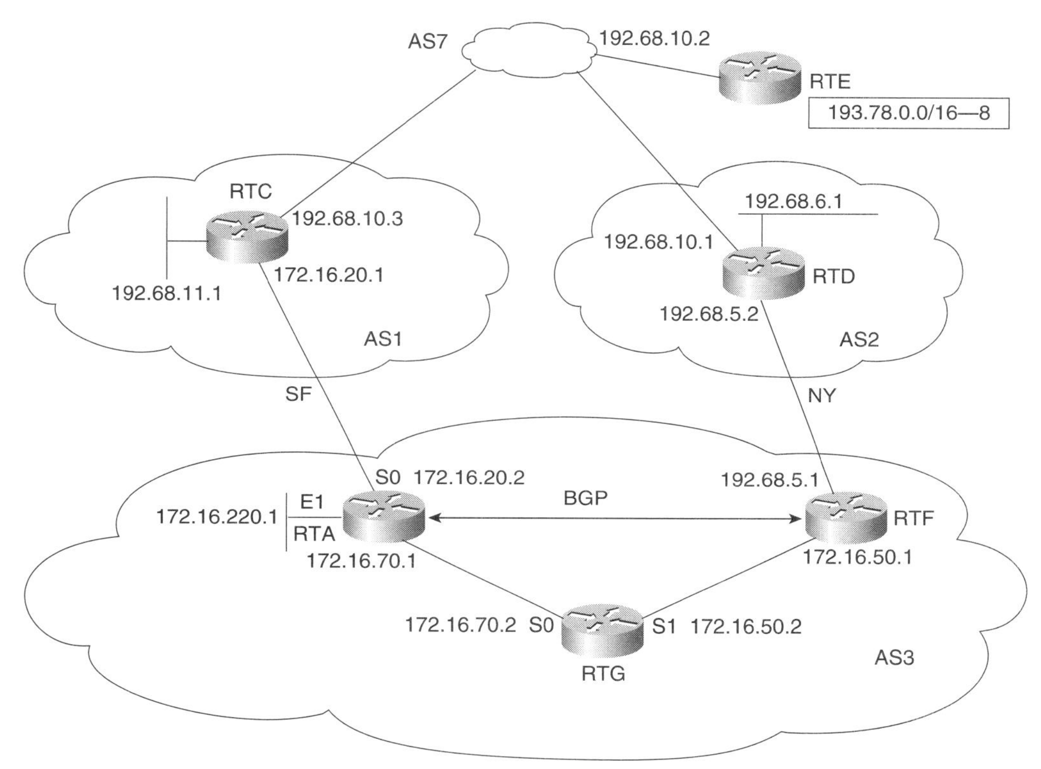

Considering the network topology shown in Figure 12-11, assume that AS3 is setting its policies in a primary/backup environment where the NY link is primary, and the SF link is a backup. As such, RTA learns its IBGP routes with a higher local preference than its EBGP routes and will always direct its traffic toward its IBGP peer, RTF. In case RTG is receiving the 0/0 from both RTA and RTF, RTG must pick the default via RTF (primary); otherwise, a routing loop will occur. The following sequence of events explains why:

Step 1 RTG tries to send traffic to a destination outside AS3.

Step 2 RTG follows the default toward RTA.

Step 3 RTA has its BGP policies set to use RTF as the exit point.

Step 4 To reach RTF, RTA uses RTG as a first hop.

Step 5 RTG receives the traffic destined to the outside destination and forwards it back to RTA, and the loop occurs.

To avoid this situation, you can use any of the following methods:

1. Make sure that RTA does not inject a 0/0 in the IGP unless the primary link goes down. In normal conditions, all traffic will follow the default toward RTF and will be able to exit the AS. In case of a NY link failure, RTA should start sending defaults in the IGP.

   This method works most easily in a primary/backup environment. In cases where the exit point is not defined, it is hard to figure out which router should send the default. In such cases, any border router that receives the traffic should be able to send it on its direct external link.

2. Make sure that the border router (RTA) does not send the traffic back to the internal router (RTG), which already used it (RTA) as the default. This could be done by providing a shorter path (metric-wise) via the BGP routers—for example, by having a direct physical link between RTA and RTF. If RTG uses RTA as default, RTA will use its directly connected link to send the traffic back to RTF.

3. Run a full IBGP mesh between RTA, RTG, and RTF. RTG would learn all routes via BGP.

4. Manipulate the metrics in such a way that the internal router (RTG) always gets a lower metric via the primary.

We used the second method in the previous example. The third method is straightforward and will not be covered. In each of the following scenarios, you will consider a different IGP and use either the first or fourth method to solve the problem. Even though you will use just one method in addressing each case, both methods 1 and 4 can be used with any of the IGPs.

To make the problem easier, you will assume that RTA and RTF are dynamically getting a 0/0 default from their providers (regardless of whether they need it). The following sections experiment with how injecting defaults is treated in a Cisco environment.

Using OSPF as the IGP

You can inject the 0/0 default into OSPF by using the following router command:

```
default-information originate [always] [metric metric-value] [metric-type type-
value] [route-map map-name]
```

The **default-information originate** (without the **always** keyword) will inject a default 0/0 into OSPF only if the router itself has a default. The **always** keyword cannot be used here because, in case of a link failure, the border router would continue to inject a default in the IGP, even though it cannot deliver the traffic anymore. (Remember that there is no direct link between border routers.)

If RTA and RTF in Figure 12-11 are both configured with the router command **default-information originate**, this is what could happen:

Step 1 RTA receives a 0/0 via EBGP and IBGP.

Step 2 Because RTA is preferring everything via RTF (higher local preference), RTA will prefer the 0/0 via IBGP.

Step 3 Because RTA has a default (via BGP), it will start injecting the default into IGP.

You are in a situation in which both routers are generating defaults, and a loop might occur.

You might say that because the NY link is the primary, RTA should not send any defaults. This reasoning will fail, however, because if the NY link goes down, RTF stops, advertising a 0/0 into the IGP. RTA is not sending any defaults either, so traffic cannot exit the AS.

The solution to these problems is to have RTA and RTF inject a default *only* if they have a default themselves and *only* if the default they prefer comes from EBGP. When RTA detects that it is preferring the 0/0 via EBGP rather than IBGP, it will get an indication that there is a problem with the NY link and will start sending the default. This could be achieved by using a route map in conjunction with the **default-information originate** router command, as demonstrated in Example 12-42.

Example 12-42 *Using a Default Only Under Certain Conditions: RTA Configuration*

```
router ospf 10
 passive-interface Serial0
 network 172.16.0.0 0.0.255.255 area 0
 default-information originate route-map SEND_DEFAULT_IF

router bgp 3
no synchronization
 network 172.16.220.0 mask 255.255.255.0
 network 172.16.70.0 mask 255.255.255.0
 neighbor 172.16.20.1 remote-as 1
 neighbor 172.16.20.1 filter-list 10 out
 neighbor 172.16.50.1 remote-as 3
 neighbor 172.16.50.1 route-map setlocalpref in
 no auto-summary

ip as-path access-list 10 permit ^$

access-list 1 permit 0.0.0.0
access-list 2 permit 172.16.20.1

route-map setlocalpref permit 10
 set local-preference 300

route-map SEND_DEFAULT_IF permit 10
 match ip address 1
 match ip next-hop 2
```

Note the route map SEND_DEFAULT_IF that is associated with the **default-information originate** router command. This route map matches on the condition that the 0/0 default (**access-list 1**) has a next hop of 172.16.20.1 (**access-list 2**). This satisfies the condition that the 0/0 is learned via EBGP rather than IBGP. If this is the case, RTA will detect a link failure in NY and will start injecting its own 0/0 into OSPF.

The second route map **setlocalpref** assigns a value of 300 to all the RTA's IBGP routes. This makes all IBGP routes preferred over EBGP routes.

As defined by the configuration in Example 12-43, RTF also originates a default into OSPF only on the condition that RTF is learning the default from its exterior link (NEXT_HOP 192.68.5.2). In case of a NY link failure, RTF will stop advertising a 0/0, even though it might be getting a 0/0 from RTA via IBGP.

Example 12-43 *Stop Advertisement of Default Under Specific Conditions: RTF Configuration*

```
router ospf 10
 network 172.16.0.0 0.0.255.255 area 0
 default-information originate route-map SEND_DEFAULT_IF

router bgp 3
no synchronization
 network 172.16.50.0 mask 255.255.255.0
 neighbor 172.16.70.1 remote-as 3
 neighbor 172.16.70.1 next-hop-self
 neighbor 192.68.5.2 remote-as 2
 neighbor 192.68.5.2 filter-list 10 out
 no auto-summary

ip as-path access-list 10 permit ^$

access-list 1 permit 0.0.0.0
access-list 2 permit 192.68.5.2

route-map SEND_DEFAULT_IF permit 10
 match ip address 1
 match ip next-hop 2
```

As defined in Example 12-44, RTG is running OSPF only and following the 0/0 default for routes outside AS3.

Example 12-44 *Following Default for External Routes: RTG Configuration*

```
router ospf 10
 network 172.16.0.0 0.0.255.255 area 0
```

Example 12-45 shows RTA's IP routing table. Note that RTA prefers the 0/0 default via its IBGP peer RTF with NEXT_HOP 172.16.50.1. Because the NEXT_HOP is different from 172.16.20.1 (the external peer), RTA will not inject any default inside OSPF.

Example 12-45 *RTA IP Routing Table*

```
RTA#show ip route
Codes: C - connected, S - static, I - IGRP, R - RIP, M - mobile, B - BGP
    D - EIGRP, EX - EIGRP external, O - OSPF, IA - OSPF inter area
    N1 - OSPF NSSA external type 1, N2 - OSPF NSSA external type 2
    E1 - OSPF external type 1, E2 - OSPF external type 2, E - EGP
    i - IS-IS, L1 - IS-IS level-1, L2 - IS-IS level-2,
    * - candidate default U - per-user static route, o - ODR

Gateway of last resort is 172.16.50.1 to network 0.0.0.0

B   192.68.6.0/24 [200/0] via 172.16.50.1, 00:03:06
B   192.68.11.0/24 [200/0] via 172.16.50.1, 00:03:06
B   193.78.0.0/16 [200/0] via 172.16.50.1, 00:03:06
    172.16.0.0/16 subnetted, 4 subnets
C     172.16.20.0/24 is directly connected, Serial0
C     172.16.220.0/24 is directly connected, Ethernet1
O     172.16.50.0/24 [110/164] via 172.16.70.2, 02:17:37, Serial1
C     172.16.70.0/24 is directly connected, Serial1
B* 0.0.0.0/0 [200/0] via 172.16.50.1, 00:03:07
```

Example 12-46 shows RTG's IP routing table. Note how RTG sets its default to RTF. Both the BGP policies and the IGP defaults are now in sync.

Example 12-46 *RTG IP Routing Table*

```
RTG#show ip route
Codes: C - connected, S - static, I - IGRP, R - RIP, M - mobile, B - BGP
    D - EIGRP, EX - EIGRP external, O - OSPF, IA - OSPF inter area
    N1 - OSPF NSSA external type 1, N2 - OSPF NSSA external type 2
    E1 - OSPF external type 1, E2 - OSPF external type 2, E - EGP
    i - IS-IS, L1 - IS-IS level-1, L2 - IS-IS level-2,
    * - candidate default U - per-user static route, o - ODR

Gateway of last resort is 172.16.50.1 to network 0.0.0.0

    172.16.0.0/16 is subnetted, 4 subnets
O     172.16.20.0/24 [110/128] via 172.16.70.1, 02:21:04, Serial0
O     172.16.220.0/24 [110/74] via 172.16.70.1, 02:21:04, Serial0
C     172.16.50.0/24 is directly connected, Serial1
C     172.16.70.0/24 is directly connected, Serial0
O*E2 0.0.0.0/0 [110/1] via 172.16.50.1, 00:41:26, Serial1
```

In case the NY link fails, RTA will learn the BGP 0/0 via its external link with next hop 172.16.20.1 and will inject a default into OSPF.

Redistributing the 0/0 from BGP into OSPF via the **redistribute** router command is not allowed or implemented.

Using RIP as the IGP

The Cisco RIP implementation behaves differently from OSPF when dealing with the 0/0 defaults. The BGP-learned 0/0 default is automatically injected into RIP. A **default-metric** router command is required under the RIP process to assign a metric (hop count) to the default. In our example (Figure 12-11), assume that RTA, RTF, and RTG are running RIP. You will set the metric of the 0/0 injected into RIP by RTA in such a way that the internal router (RTG) always prefers RTF.

The configuration for RTA in Example 12-47 will set the 0/0 default metric to 5. Note that no redistribution was necessary to inject the BGP default into RIP.

Example 12-47 *Using RIP as the IGP: RTA Configuration*

```
router rip
 passive-interface Serial0
 network 172.16.0.0
 default-metric 5

router bgp 3
no synchronization
 network 172.16.220.0 mask 255.255.255.0
 network 172.16.70.0 mask 255.255.255.0
 neighbor 172.16.20.1 remote-as 1
 neighbor 172.16.20.1 filter-list 10 out
 neighbor 172.16.50.1 remote-as 3
 neighbor 172.16.50.1 route-map setlocalpref in
 no auto-summary

ip as-path access-list 10 permit ^$

route-map setlocalpref permit 10
 set local-preference 300
```

The configuration for RTF in Example 12-48 will inject the 0/0 into RIP with a hop count of 1.

Example 12-48 *Using RIP as the IGP: RTF Configuration*

```
router rip
network 172.16.0.0
default-metric 1

router bgp 3
no synchronization
 network 172.16.50.0 mask 255.255.255.0
 neighbor 172.16.70.1 remote-as 3
 neighbor 172.16.70.1 next-hop-self
 neighbor 192.68.5.2 remote-as 2
 neighbor 192.68.5.2 filter-list 10 out
 no auto-summary

ip as-path access-list 10 permit ^$
```

The configuration for RTG in Example 12-49 runs RIP only and follows the 0/0 default for routes outside AS3.

Example 12-49 *Using RIP as the IGP: RTG Configuration*

```
router rip
network 172.16.0.0
```

Example 12-50 shows RTG's IP routing table. Note that RTG has set its default to RTF because of the lower metric of 1.

Example 12-50 *RTG IP Routing Table*

```
RTG#show ip route
Codes: C - connected, S - static, I - IGRP, R - RIP, M - mobile, B - BGP
    D - EIGRP, EX - EIGRP external, O - OSPF, IA - OSPF inter area
    N1 - OSPF NSSA external type 1, N2 - OSPF NSSA external type 2
    E1 - OSPF external type 1, E2 - OSPF external type 2, E - EGP
    i - IS-IS, L1 - IS-IS level-1, L2 - IS-IS level-2,
    * - candidate default U - per-user static route, o - ODR

Gateway of last resort is 172.16.50.1 to network 0.0.0.0

   172.16.0.0/16 is subnetted, 4 subnets
R     172.16.220.0/24 [120/1] via 172.16.70.1, 00:00:03, Serial0
C     172.16.50.0/24 is directly connected, Serial1
R     172.16.20.0/24 [120/1] via 172.16.70.1, 00:00:03, Serial0
C     172.16.70.0/24 is directly connected, Serial0
R* 0.0.0.0/0 [120/1] via 172.16.50.1, 00:00:22, Serial1
```

NOTE If more conditions are needed to inject the 0/0 into RIP, redistribution and route maps could be used to inject the default from BGP into RIP.

Using EIGRP as the IGP

BGP-learned defaults are injected into EIGRP via redistribution. The 0/0 metric needs to be converted into an EIGRP-compatible metric by using the **default-metric** router subcommand.

The configuration for RTA in Example 12-51 will inject its default with a high metric in such a way that the internal router (RTG) always gets a lower metric via RTF.

Example 12-51 *Using EIGRP as the IGP: RTA Configuration*

```
router eigrp 1
 redistribute bgp 3 route-map DEFAULT_ONLY
 passive-interface Serial0
 network 172.16.0.0
 default-metric 5 100 250 100 1500

router bgp 3
 no synchronization
 network 172.16.70.0 mask 255.255.255.0
 network 172.16.220.0 mask 255.255.255.0
 neighbor 172.16.20.1 remote-as 1
 neighbor 172.16.20.1 filter-list 10 out
 neighbor 172.16.50.1 remote-as 3
 neighbor 172.16.50.1 route-map setlocalpref in
 no auto-summary

ip as-path access-list 10 permit ^$

access-list 5 permit 0.0.0.0

route-map setlocalpref permit 10
 set local-preference 300

route-map DEFAULT_ONLY permit 10
 match ip address 5
```

RTA uses a route map DEFAULT_ONLY to match on the default route 0/0. Any other updates will be prevented from being redistributed into EIGRP. RTA also sets the metric by using the **default-metric** router subcommand.

In the same manner, the configuration for RTF in Example 12-52 redistributes only the 0/0 into EIGRP using the route map DEFAULT_ONLY.

Example 12-52 *Using EIGRP as the IGP: RTF Configuration*

```
router eigrp 1
 redistribute bgp 3 route-map DEFAULT_ONLY
 network 172.16.0.0
 default-metric 1000 100 250 100 1500

router bgp 3
 no synchronization
 network 172.16.50.0 mask 255.255.255.0
 neighbor 172.16.70.1 remote-as 3
 neighbor 172.16.70.1 next-hop-self
 neighbor 192.68.5.2 remote-as 2
 neighbor 192.68.5.2 filter-list 10 out
 no auto-summary

ip as-path access-list 10 permit ^$

access-list 5 permit 0.0.0.0

route-map DEFAULT_ONLY permit 10
 match ip address 5
```

RTF uses the **default-metric 1000 100 250 100 1500** statement to set its default metric to an EIGRP-compatible metric. Note the bandwidth portion (1000) of the **default-metric** statement in RTF, which is much higher than the bandwidth in RTA (5). This makes the metric from RTF much lower than the one from RTA.

As illustrated by the configuration in Example 12-53, RTG is running EIGRP only and is following the default for all routes outside AS3.

Example 12-53 *Using EIGRP as the IGP: RTG Configuration*

```
router eigrp 1
 network 172.16.0.0
```

Example 12-54 shows RTG's IP routing table. Note that RTG follows the default toward RTF.

Example 12-54 *RTG IP Routing Table*

```
RTG#show ip route
Codes: C - connected, S - static, I - IGRP, R - RIP, M - mobile, B - BGP
       D - EIGRP, EX - EIGRP external, O - OSPF, IA - OSPF inter area
       N1 - OSPF NSSA external type 1, N2 - OSPF NSSA external type 2
       E1 - OSPF external type 1, E2 - OSPF external type 2, E - EGP
    i - IS-IS, L1 - IS-IS level-1, L2 - IS-IS level-2,
      * - candidate default U - per-user static route, o - ODR
```

continues

Example 12-54 *RTG IP Routing Table (Continued)*

```
Gateway of last resort is 172.16.50.1 to network 0.0.0.0

   172.16.0.0/16 is subnetted, 4 subnets
D     172.16.220.0/24 [90/2195456] via 172.16.70.1, 00:12:17, Serial0
C     172.16.50.0/24 is directly connected, Serial1
D     172.16.20.0/24 [90/2681856] via 172.16.70.1, 00:12:17, Serial0
C     172.16.70.0/24 is directly connected, Serial0
D*EX 0.0.0.0/0 [170/3097600] via 172.16.50.1, 00:07:40, Serial1
```

Using IGRP as the IGP

IGRP does not understand the 0.0.0.0 default. To set a default inside IGRP, the **ip default-network** global command needs to be set on RTA and RTF. The default network used needs to be redistributed into IGRP to set the default on the internal routers. A default metric needs to be set for successful redistribution.

As illustrated by the configuration for RTA in Example 12-55, RTA sets network 192.68.6.0/24 (or any other classful network learned via BGP) to be the default network. RTA will redistribute that network only into IGRP.

Example 12-55 *Using IGRP as the IGP: RTA Configuration*

```
router igrp 1
 passive-interface Serial0
 redistribute bgp 3 route-map DEFAULT_ONLY
 network 172.16.0.0
 default-metric 5 100 250 100 1500

router bgp 3
 no synchronization
 network 172.16.70.0 mask 255.255.255.0
 network 172.16.220.0 mask 255.255.255.0
 neighbor 172.16.20.1 remote-as 1
 neighbor 172.16.20.1 filter-list 10 out
 neighbor 172.16.50.1 remote-as 3
 neighbor 172.16.50.1 route-map setlocalpref in
 no auto-summary

ip default-network 192.68.6.0
ip as-path access-list 10 permit ^$

access-list 5 permit 192.68.6.0 0.0.0.255

route-map setlocalpref permit 10
 set local-preference 300

route-map DEFAULT_ONLY permit 10
 match ip address 5
```

As illustrated by the configuration for RTF in Example 12-56, RTF also sets its default, to 192.68.6.0/24, and redistributes the default, with a better metric, into IGRP.

Example 12-56 *Using IGRP as the IGP: RTF Configuration*

```
router igrp 1
 redistribute bgp 3 route-map DEFAULT_ONLY
 network 172.16.0.0
 default-metric 1000 100 250 100 1500

router bgp 3
 no synchronization
 network 172.16.50.0 mask 255.255.255.0
 neighbor 172.16.70.1 remote-as 3
 neighbor 172.16.70.1 next-hop-self
 neighbor 192.68.5.2 remote-as 2
 neighbor 192.68.5.2 filter-list 10 out
 no auto-summary

ip default-network 192.68.6.0
ip as-path access-list 10 permit ^$

access-list 5 permit 192.68.6.0 0.0.0.255

route-map DEFAULT_ONLY permit 10
 match ip address 5
```

As illustrated by the configuration for RTG in Example 12-57, RTG is running IGRP only and is following the default for all routes outside AS3.

Example 12-57 *Using IGRP as the IGP: RTG Configuration*

```
router igrp 1
 network 172.16.0.0
```

Example 12-58 shows the RTG IP routing table. Note that RTG follows the default toward RTF.

Example 12-58 *RTG IP Routing Table*

```
RTG#show ip route
Codes: C - connected, S - static, I - IGRP, R - RIP, M - mobile, B - BGP
       D - EIGRP, EX - EIGRP external, O - OSPF, IA - OSPF inter area
       N1 - OSPF NSSA external type 1, N2 - OSPF NSSA external type 2
       E1 - OSPF external type 1, E2 - OSPF external type 2, E - EGP
        i - IS-IS, L1 - IS-IS level-1, L2 - IS-IS level-2,
          * - candidate default U - per-user static route, o - ODR

Gateway of last resort is 172.16.50.1 to network 192.68.6.0

I*   192.68.6.0/24 [100/8576] via 172.16.50.1, 00:00:32, Serial1
   172.16.0.0/16 is subnetted, 4 subnets
```

continues

Example 12-58 *RTG IP Routing Table (Continued)*

```
I    172.16.220.0/24 [100/8576] via 172.16.70.1, 00:00:32, Serial0
C    172.16.50.0/24 is directly connected, Serial1
I    172.16.20.0/24 [100/10476] via 172.16.70.1, 00:00:32, Serial0
C    172.16.70.0/24 is directly connected, Serial0
```

Using IS-IS as the IGP

IS-IS is similar to OSPF; it uses the **default-information originate** router subcommand.

In the configuration for RTA in Example 12-59, RTA originates a default into IS-IS only on the condition that RTA learns the default from its exterior link.

Example 12-59 *Using IS-IS as the IGP: RTA Configuration*

```
router isis 100
 redistribute connected
 default-information originate route-map SEND_DEFAULT_IF
 net 49.0001.0000.0c00.000a.00

router bgp 3
no synchronization
 network 172.16.220.0 mask 255.255.255.0
 network 172.16.70.0 mask 255.255.255.0
 neighbor 172.16.20.1 remote-as 1
 neighbor 172.16.20.1 filter-list 10 out
 neighbor 172.16.50.1 remote-as 3
 neighbor 172.16.50.1 route-map setlocalpref in
 no auto-summary

ip as-path access-list 10 permit ^$

access-list 1 permit 0.0.0.0
access-list 2 permit 172.16.20.1

route-map SEND_DEFAULT_IF permit 10
 match ip address 1
 match ip next-hop 2
```

In the configuration for RTF in Example 12-60, RTF originates a default into IS-IS on the condition that RTF learns the default from its exterior link.

Example 12-60 *Using IS-IS as the IGP: RTF Configuration*

```
router isis 100
 default-information originate route-map SEND_DEFAULT_IF
 net 49.0001.0000.0c00.000c.00

router bgp 3
no synchronization
 network 172.16.50.0 mask 255.255.255.0
 neighbor 172.16.70.1 remote-as 3
```

Example 12-60 *Using IS-IS as the IGP: RTF Configuration (Continued)*

```
 neighbor 172.16.70.1 next-hop-self
 neighbor 192.68.5.2 remote-as 2
 neighbor 192.68.5.2 filter-list 10 out
 no auto-summary

ip as-path access-list 10 permit ^$

access-list 1 permit 0.0.0.0
access-list 2 permit 192.68.5.2

route-map SEND_DEFAULT_IF permit 10
 match ip address 1
 match ip next-hop 2
```

In the configuration for RTG in Example 12-61, RTG runs IS-IS and follows the 0/0 default for routes outside AS3.

Example 12-61 *Using IS-IS as the IGP: RTG Configuration*

```
router isis 100
 net 49.0001.0000.0c00.000b.00
```

Example 12-62 shows RTG's IP routing table; note how RTG follows the default toward RTF.

Example 12-62 *RTG IP Routing Table*

```
RTG#show ip route
Codes: C - connected, S - static, I - IGRP, R - RIP, M - mobile, B - BGP
       D - EIGRP, EX - EIGRP external, O - OSPF, IA - OSPF inter area
       N1 - OSPF NSSA external type 1, N2 - OSPF NSSA external type 2
       E1 - OSPF external type 1, E2 - OSPF external type 2, E - EGP
        i - IS-IS, L1 - IS-IS level-1, L2 - IS-IS level-2,
          * - candidate default U - per-user static route, o - ODR

Gateway of last resort is 172.16.50.1 to network 0.0.0.0

   172.16.0.0/16 is subnetted, 4 subnets
i L1    172.16.220.0/24 [115/20] via 172.16.70.1, Serial0
i L1    172.16.20.0/24 [115/20] via 172.16.70.1, Serial0
C       172.16.50.0/24 is directly connected, Serial1
C       172.16.70.0/24 is directly connected, Serial0
i*L2 0.0.0.0/0 [115/10] via 172.16.50.1, Serial1
```

Policy Routing

This section demonstrates how policy routing can be used to direct the traffic based on the source IP address rather than the destination IP address. Figure 12-12 shows a router, RTA, that is running BGP with two providers, AS1 and AS2. Internal routers such as RTG and RTF are running IGP only (OSPF) and are following a default route toward RTA.

Figure 12-12 *Policy Routing Scenario*

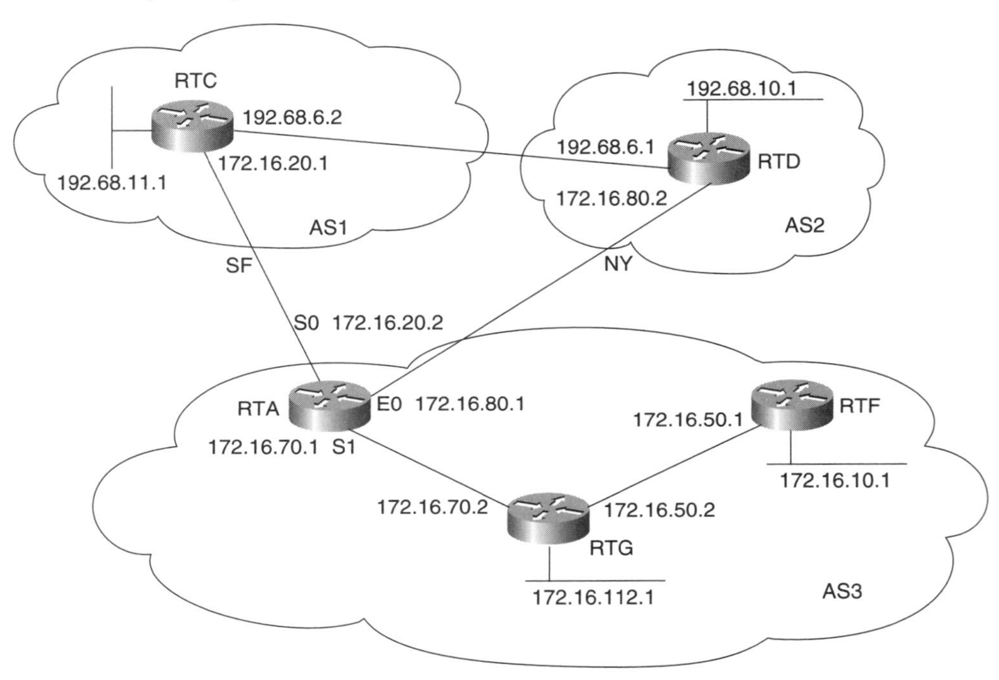

RTA wants to set policy routing in such a way that traffic coming over the serial line S1 from RTG is directed toward AS2 if the source is network 172.16.10.0/24. Traffic coming from RTG with source 172.16.112.0/24 is to be directed toward AS1; in case of a link failure to AS1, the traffic will go to AS2. For all other source IP addresses, follow normal routing.

Example 12-63 shows the configuration for RTA to satisfy the criteria of this policy routing setup.

Example 12-63 *Policy Routing: RTA Configuration*

```
interface Ethernet0
 ip address 172.16.80.1 255.255.255.0

interface Serial1
 ip address 172.16.70.1 255.255.255.0
 ip policy route-map CHECK_SOURCE

router ospf 10
```

Example 12-63 *Policy Routing: RTA Configuration (Continued)*

```
 passive-interface Serial0
 passive-interface Ethernet0
 network 172.16.0.0 0.0.255.255 area 0
 default-information originate always

router bgp 3
 network 172.16.50.0 mask 255.255.255.0
 network 172.16.70.0 mask 255.255.255.0
 network 172.16.10.0 mask 255.255.255.0
 network 172.16.112.0 mask 255.255.255.0
 neighbor 172.16.20.1 remote-as 1
 neighbor 172.16.20.1 filter-list 10 out
 neighbor 172.16.80.2 remote-as 2
 neighbor 172.16.80.2 filter-list 10 out
 no auto-summary

ip as-path access-list 10 permit ^$

access-list 1 permit 172.16.10.0 0.0.0.255
access-list 2 permit 172.16.112.0 0.0.0.255

route-map CHECK_SOURCE permit 10
 match ip address 1
 set ip next-hop 172.16.80.2

route-map CHECK_SOURCE permit 20
 match ip address 2
 set ip next-hop 172.16.20.1 172.16.80.2
```

Policy routing is always applied to the incoming interface. Serial 1 is configured with the interface command **ip policy route-map** *map-name*. This will apply route map CHECK_SOURCE to all Serial 1 incoming traffic. The explanation of the route map follows:

- Instance 10: For all source IP addresses that come from 172.16.10.0/24, set the next hop to 172.16.80.2. If next hop 172.16.80.2 is unreachable, drop the packet.
- Instance 20: For all source IP addresses that come from 172.16.112.0/24, set the next hop to 172.16.20.1. If next hop 172.16.20.1 is unreachable, try sending the traffic to next hop 172.16.80.2.
- For all other source IP addresses, follow normal routing.

The policy routing route maps give you the option of choosing multiple next hops. This is necessary to always have a backup path. For all traffic that does not match the route maps, the router will follow normal routing. To illustrate, a traceroute will be done from RTG to

192.68.10.1 from source IP address 172.16.112.1. Example 12-64 shows RTA's IP routing table.

Example 12-64 *Policy Routing: RTA IP Routing Table*

```
RTA#show ip route
Codes: C - connected, S - static, I - IGRP, R - RIP, M - mobile, B - BGP
       D - EIGRP, EX - EIGRP external, O - OSPF, IA - OSPF inter area
       N1 - OSPF NSSA external type 1, N2 - OSPF NSSA external type 2
       E1 - OSPF external type 1, E2 - OSPF external type 2, E - EGP
        i - IS-IS, L1 - IS-IS level-1, L2 - IS-IS level-2,
          * - candidate default U - per-user static route, o - ODR

Gateway of last resort is not set

B   192.68.10.0/24 [20/0] via 172.16.80.2, 00:30:09
B   192.68.11.0/24 [20/0] via 172.16.20.1, 00:30:14
    172.16.0.0/16 is subnetted, 5 subnets
O       172.16.50.0/24 [110/69] via 172.16.70.2, 00:27:27, Serial1
C       172.16.20.0/24 is directly connected, Serial0
C       172.16.80.0/24 is directly connected, Ethernet0
C       172.16.70.0/24 is directly connected, Serial1
```

Example 12-65 demonstrates a **traceroute** from RTG with a source of 172.16.112.1 and a destination of 192.68.10.1.

Example 12-65 *Policy Routing: RTG* **traceroute**

```
RTG#traceroute
Protocol [ip]:
Target IP address: 192.68.10.1
Source address: 172.16.112.1
Numeric display [n]:
Timeout in seconds [3]:
Probe count [3]:
Minimum Time to Live [1]:
Maximum Time to Live [30]:
Port Number [33434]:
Loose, Strict, Record, Timestamp, Verbose[none]:
Type escape sequence to abort.
Tracing the route to gateway.aeg-aas.de (192.68.10.1)

  1 172.16.70.1 4 msec 4 msec 0 msec
  2 172.16.20.1 4 msec 4 msec 4 msec
  3 192.68.6.1 4 msec 4 msec 4 msec
```

Notice how RTA has taken next hop 172.16.20.1 (the second line in the **traceroute** output) to reach 192.68.10.0/24, even though RTA's routing table indicates that 192.68.10.0/24 should be reached with next hop 172.16.80.2.

This second attempt shows what will happen if Serial 0 is down and next hop 172.16.20.1 is unreachable. The next step is to perform a **traceroute** from RTG with a source of

172.16.112.1 and a destination of 192.68.10.1 while Serial 0 is down, as demonstrated in Example 12-66.

Example 12-66 *Policy Routing: RTG* **traceroute**

```
RTG#traceroute
Protocol [ip]:
Target IP address: 192.68.10.1
Source address: 172.16.112.1
Numeric display [n]:
Timeout in seconds [3]:
Probe count [3]:
Minimum Time to Live [1]:
Maximum Time to Live [30]:
Port Number [33434]:
Loose, Strict, Record, Timestamp, Verbose[none]:
Type escape sequence to abort.
Tracing the route to gateway.aeg-aas.de (192.68.10.1)

 1 172.16.70.1 0 msec 4 msec 4 msec
 2 172.16.80.2 8 msec 4 msec 4 msec
```

The output in Example 12-66 reveals that RTA has taken the alternative next hop 172.16.80.2.

Before implementing any policy-based routing solutions, it's important that you understand the policy routing support and performance implications of the version of IOS and platform you're using. For additional information, consult the appropriate Cisco Command Reference, Configuration Guidelines, and Release Notes for your specific hardware and software versions.

Route Reflectors

This section illustrates a practical use of route reflectors and peer groups. In Figure 12-13, RTG and RTA form a route reflector cluster, where RTG is the route reflector. RTF, RTE, and RTD form another cluster where RTF is the route reflector. RTG and RTF are part of a peer group called REFLECTORS; if there are other route reflectors, all should IBGP peer in a full mesh. RTF puts all its clients in a peer group called CLIENTS, where common policies can be applied.

Figure 12-13 *Route Reflectors*

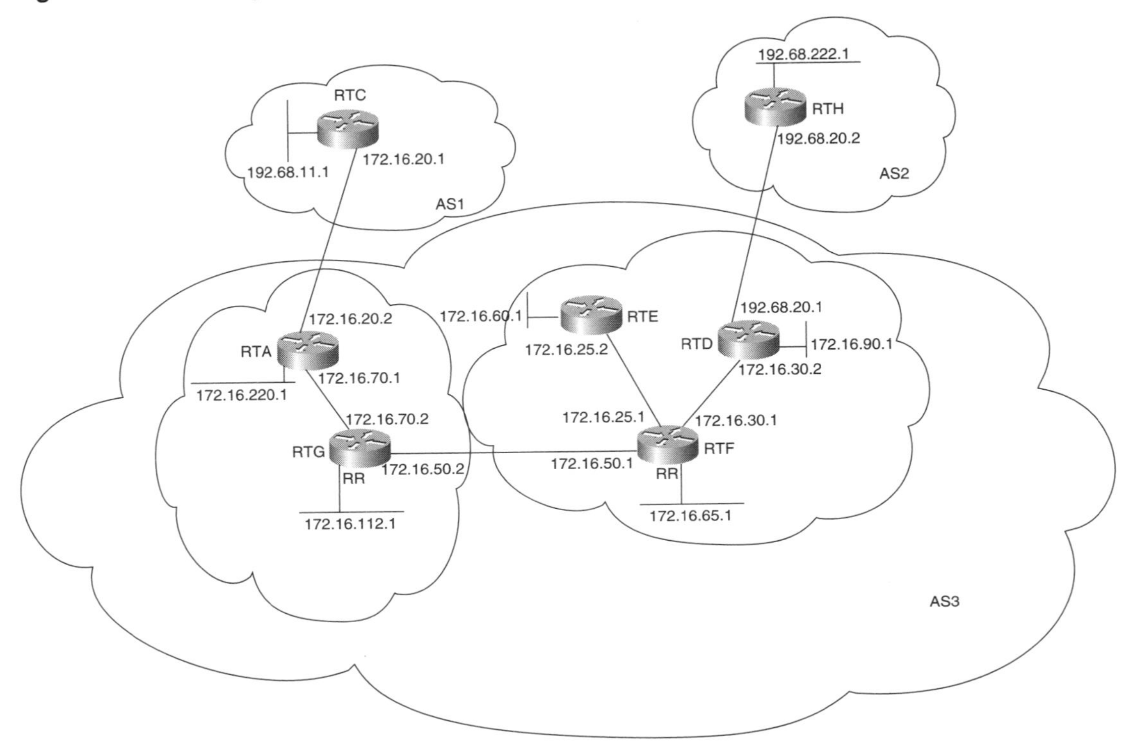

Clients are identified on the route reflector servers by configuring **route-reflector-client** following the **neighbor x.x.x.x** parameter. Traditionally, there was an IOS limitation that required client-to-client reflection to be disabled if the clients were members of a BGP peer group. This is no longer a restriction. Full IBGP mesh will be maintained inside the RTF-RTD-RTE cluster, and the clients will peer only with the associated route reflector. Example 12-67 shows the configuration for RTF.

Example 12-67 *Route Reflectors: RTF Configuration*

```
router bgp 3
 no synchronization
 network 172.16.65.0 mask 255.255.255.192
 network 172.16.50.0 mask 255.255.255.0
 network 172.16.25.0 mask 255.255.255.0
 network 172.16.30.0 mask 255.255.255.0
 neighbor REFLECTORS peer-group
 neighbor REFLECTORS remote-as 3
 neighbor CLIENTS peer-group
```

Example 12-67 *Route Reflectors: RTF Configuration (Continued)*

```
 neighbor CLIENTS remote-as 3
 neighbor CLIENTS route-reflector-client
 neighbor 172.16.25.2 peer-group CLIENTS
 neighbor 172.16.30.2 peer-group CLIENTS
 neighbor 172.16.50.2 peer-group REFLECTORS
 no auto-summary
```

Because RTF provides the only available internal path out of the cluster, RTD and RTE are configured as clients of RTF, and RTF is configured as the route reflector. Together, the three routers comprise what's referred to as a *cluster* in route reflection terminology. From RTD and RTE's perspective, the BGP peering session with RTF is a normal IBGP session. In other words, the client need not be aware that it is a client. (Note that this was one of the requirements for designing route reflection—that the clients need not know that they're clients.) Examples 12-68 through 12-70 show the configurations for RTD, RTG, and RTA, respectively.

Example 12-68 *Route Reflectors: RTD Configuration*

```
router bgp 3
 no synchronization
 network 172.16.90.0 mask 255.255.255.0
 network 172.16.30.0 mask 255.255.255.0
 neighbor 172.16.30.1 remote-as 3
 neighbor 172.16.30.1 next-hop-self
 neighbor 192.68.20.2 remote-as 2
 neighbor 192.68.20.2 filter-list 10 out
 no auto-summary

ip as-path access-list 10 permit ^$
```

Example 12-69 *Route Reflectors: RTG Configuration*

```
router bgp 3
 no synchronization
 network 172.16.112.0 mask 255.255.255.0
 network 172.16.50.0 mask 255.255.255.0
 network 172.16.70.0 mask 255.255.255.0
 neighbor 172.16.50.1 remote-as 3
 neighbor 172.16.70.1 remote-as 3
 neighbor 172.16.70.1 route-reflector-client
 no auto-summary
```

Example 12-70 *Route Reflectors: RTA Configuration*

```
router bgp 3
 no synchronization
 network 172.16.220.0 mask 255.255.255.0
 network 172.16.70.0 mask 255.255.255.0
 neighbor 172.16.20.1 remote-as 1
```

continues

Example 12-70 *Route Reflectors: RTA Configuration (Continued)*

```
 neighbor 172.16.20.1 filter-list 10 out
 neighbor 172.16.70.2 remote-as 3
 neighbor 172.16.70.2 next-hop-self
 no auto-summary

ip as-path access-list 10 permit ^$
```

The BGP table in Example 12-71 shows how RTD sees some of the routes that are being reflected into its own cluster.

Example 12-71 *Route Reflectors: RTD BGP Table*

```
RTD#show ip bgp 172.16.220.0
BGP routing table entry for 172.16.220.0/24, version 52
Paths: (1 available, best #1)
 Local
  172.16.70.1 (metric 192) from 172.16.30.1 (172.16.220.1)
   Origin IGP, metric 0, localpref 100, valid, internal, best
   Originator : 172.16.220.1, Cluster list: 172.16.65.1, 172.16.112.1
```

Note how RTD sees the originator of route 172.16.220.0/24 as 172.16.220.1, which is the ROUTER_ID of RTA. The route also carries a cluster list that contains the ROUTER_IDs of all the route reflectors it passed through.

In the case where multiple route reflectors are configured inside the cluster, all the route reflectors need to be configured with a common CLUSTER_ID. This is needed to detect routing loops that might occur between clusters. For example, if RTE were to be configured as a route reflector, the configurations for RTF and RTE would need the additional router command **bgp cluster-id** *number*. Example 12-72 shows the configuration for RTF.

Example 12-72 *Multiple Route Reflectors: RTF Configuration*

```
router bgp 3
 no synchronization
 network 172.16.65.0 mask 255.255.255.192
 network 172.16.50.0 mask 255.255.255.0
 network 172.16.25.0 mask 255.255.255.0
 network 172.16.30.0 mask 255.255.255.0
 neighbor REFLECTORS peer-group
 neighbor REFLECTORS remote-as 3
 neighbor CLIENTS peer-group
 neighbor CLIENTS remote-as 3
 neighbor CLIENTS route-reflector-client
 neighbor 172.16.25.2 peer-group CLIENTS
 neighbor 172.16.30.2 peer-group CLIENTS
 neighbor 172.16.50.2 peer-group REFLECTORS
 bgp cluster-id 1000
 no auto-summary
```

The CLUSTER_ID is a number identifying the cluster. Each cluster must be assigned a unique value. This is needed in order to avoid looping in case RTF and RTE are both configured as route reflectors in the same cluster. Note that it's good practice to configure a CLUSTER_ID even if you're using a single route reflector. When you configure a CLUSTER_ID, no route reflector clients can be configured on the router. Therefore, if one isn't already defined, you must unconfigure all the existing clients, configure the CLUSTER_ID, and then reconfigure the clients. Therefore, defining the CLUSTER_ID value upon initial configuration is a good idea.

Confederations

For the scenario in Figure 12-14, you want to divide AS3 into two smaller sub-ASs, AS65050 and AS65060. The AS numbers of the sub-ASs are chosen from within the private AS pool range of 64512 to 65535. OSPF is used as the IGP in each sub-AS. The OSPF within AS65050 is running independently of the OSPF in AS65060, which means that the area numbers used in AS65050 can be reused in AS65060. This takes advantage of one of the benefits of BGP—namely, that IGPs in one AS run independently of IGPs in other ASs.

Figure 12-14 *Confederations*

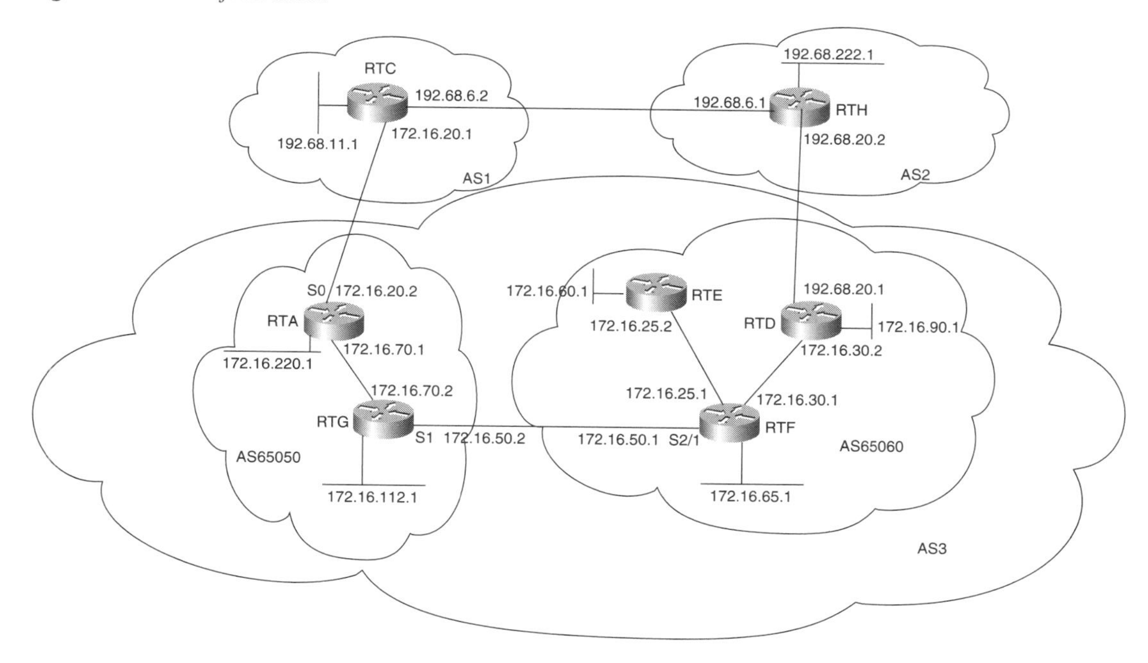

The configuration for RTA in Example 12-73 shows that RTA has all its interfaces in OSPF area 5. RTA is running EBGP with RTC in AS1 and is running IBGP with RTG in AS65050.

Note that RTA uses the **bgp confederation identifier 3** router subcommand to present itself to RTC as being part of confederation 3.

Example 12-73 *Confederations: RTA Configuration*

```
router ospf 10
 passive-interface Serial0
 network 172.16.0.0 0.0.255.255 area 5

router bgp 65050
 no synchronization
 bgp confederation identifier 3
 network 172.16.220.0 mask 255.255.255.0
 network 172.16.70.0 mask 255.255.255.0
 neighbor 172.16.20.1 remote-as 1
 neighbor 172.16.20.1 filter-list 10 out
 neighbor 172.16.70.2 remote-as 65050
 no auto-summary

ip as-path access-list 10 permit ^$
```

As shown in Example 12-74, RTC runs normal EBGP when talking to RTA. According to RTC, RTA belongs to AS3. RTC has no visibility to the sub-ASs inside confederation 3. RTC is also running EBGP with RTH in AS2.

Example 12-74 *Confederations: RTC Configuration*

```
router bgp 1
 network 192.68.11.0
 neighbor 172.16.20.2 remote-as 3
 neighbor 192.68.6.1 remote-as 2
 no auto-summary
```

RTG is the sub-AS65050 border router that is running *confederation EBGP* with router RTF in sub-AS65060. RTG is also running IBGP with RTA. RTG is an OSPF area border router that has a common area 5 with RTA and the rest of its interfaces in area 0. Note how RTG has disabled its OSPF processing on serial 1 (passive-interface Serial1), which is the common interface with RTF. Only EBGP is run on that link. Example 12-75 shows the configuration for RTG.

Example 12-75 *Confederations: RTG Configuration*

```
router ospf 10
 passive-interface Serial1
 network 172.16.70.2 0.0.0.0 area 5
 network 172.16.0.0 0.0.255.255 area 0

router bgp 65050
 no synchronization
 bgp confederation identifier 3
 bgp confederation peers 65060
 network 172.16.112.0 mask 255.255.255.0
```

Example 12-75 *Confederations: RTG Configuration (Continued)*

```
network 172.16.50.0 mask 255.255.255.0
network 172.16.70.0 mask 255.255.255.0
neighbor 172.16.50.1 remote-as 65060
neighbor 172.16.50.1 next-hop-self
neighbor 172.16.70.1 remote-as 65050
no auto-summary
```

RTG also identifies itself as being part of confederation 3 (**bgp confederation identifier 3**). RTG uses the router command **bgp confederation peers 65060** to preserve all the attributes, such as local preference and next hop when traversing the EBGP session to AS65060. This will make the confederation EBGP session with sub-AS65060 look like an IBGP session. The **neighbor 172.16.50.1 next-hop-self** command will set the next-hop address of routes going from RTG to RTF to RTG's IP address. Without this command, the next-hop address of all EBGP routes from AS1 will be sent to RTF with the external next hop 172.16.20.1, which is acceptable only as long as routers in sub-AS65060 can reach it from within the confederation.

As illustrated in Example 12-76, the same configuration that is in RTG applies to RTF, which is the border router of sub-AS65060. RTF is also an area border router in areas 0 and 5. Areas 0 and 5 in AS65060 are totally independent of areas 0 and 5 in AS65050. The two IGPs are shielded from each other by BGP. Full-mesh IBGP sessions are configured between RTE, RTD, and RTF using the peer group SUB_AS_65060.

Example 12-76 *Confederations: RTF Configuration*

```
router ospf 10
 passive-interface Serial2/1
 network 172.16.25.1 0.0.0.0 area 5
 network 172.16.0.0 0.0.255.255 area 0

router bgp 65060
 no synchronization
 bgp confederation identifier 3
 bgp confederation peers 65050
 network 172.16.65.0 mask 255.255.255.192
 network 172.16.50.0 mask 255.255.255.0
 network 172.16.25.0 mask 255.255.255.0
 network 172.16.30.0 mask 255.255.255.0
 neighbor SUB_AS_65060 peer-group
 neighbor SUB_AS_65060 remote-as 65060
 neighbor 172.16.25.2 peer-group SUB_AS_65060
 neighbor 172.16.30.2 peer-group SUB_AS_65060
 neighbor 172.16.50.2 remote-as 65050
 neighbor 172.16.50.2 next-hop-self
```

RTD is a border router for confederation 3. As demonstrated in Example 12-77, RTD is running EBGP with RTH in AS2 and a full IBGP mesh with routers RTE and RTF in sub-AS65060. RTD has all its interfaces in area 0. RTD is not running OSPF on the external link to AS2. This is why the next hop of external updates coming to RTD has to be set to self before the routes are propagated to RTF and RTE.

Example 12-77 *Confederations: RTD Configuration*

```
router ospf 10
 network 172.16.0.0 0.0.255.255 area 0.0.0.0

router bgp 65060
 no synchronization
 bgp confederation identifier 3
 network 172.16.90.0 mask 255.255.255.0
 network 172.16.30.0 mask 255.255.255.0
 neighbor 172.16.25.2 remote-as 65060
 neighbor 172.16.25.2 next-hop-self
 neighbor 172.16.30.1 remote-as 65060
 neighbor 172.16.30.1 next-hop-self
 neighbor 192.68.20.2 remote-as 2
 neighbor 172.16.20.2 filter-list 10 out
 no auto-summary

ip as-path access-list 10 permit ^$
```

As illustrated in Example 12-78, RTE has all its interfaces in OSPF area 5 and is running a full IBGP mesh with RTF and RTD.

Example 12-78 *Confederations: RTE Configuration*

```
router ospf 10
 network 172.16.0.0 0.0.255.255 area 5

router bgp 65060
 no synchronization
 bgp confederation identifier 3
 network 172.16.60.0 mask 255.255.255.0
 network 172.16.25.0 mask 255.255.255.0
 neighbor 172.16.25.1 remote-as 65060
 neighbor 172.16.30.2 remote-as 65060
 no auto-summary
```

As Example 12-79 shows, RTH is a BGP border router in AS2 that is running EBGP with AS1 and AS3. RTH has no visibility to the sub-AS in confederation 3.

Example 12-79 *Confederations: RTH Configuration*

```
router bgp 2
network 192.68.222.0
neighbor 192.68.6.2 remote-as 1
neighbor 192.68.20.1 remote-as 3
no auto-summary
```

Now let's look at some excerpts from the BGP tables.

In Example 12-80, note how RTH sees all routes via two paths—one via AS1 and one via AS3. As you can see, all the sub-ASs are hidden from RTH.

Example 12-80 *Confederations: RTH BGP Table*

```
RTH#show ip bgp
BGP table version is 477, local router ID is 192.68.222.1
Status codes: s suppressed, * valid, > best, i - internal
Origin codes: i - IGP, e - EGP, ? - incomplete

   Network          Next Hop       Metric LocPrf Weight Path
*> 172.16.25.0/24   192.68.20.1                       0 3 i
*                   192.68.6.2                        0 1 3 i
*> 172.16.30.0/24   192.68.20.1         0             0 3 i
*                   192.68.6.2                        0 1 3 i
*> 172.16.50.0/24   192.68.20.1                       0 3 i
*                   192.68.6.2                        0 1 3 i
*> 172.16.60.0/24   192.68.20.1                       0 3 i
*                   192.68.6.2                        0 1 3 i
*> 172.16.70.0/24   192.68.20.1                       0 3 i
*                   192.68.6.2                        0 1 3 i
*> 172.16.90.0/24   192.68.20.1         0             0 3 i
*                   192.68.6.2                        0 1 3 i
*> 172.16.65.0/26   192.68.20.1                       0 3 i
*                   192.68.6.2                        0 1 3 i
*> 172.16.112.0/24  192.68.20.1                       0 3 i
*                   192.68.6.2                        0 1 3 i
*> 172.16.220.0/24  192.68.20.1                       0 3 i
*                   192.68.6.2                        0 1 3 i
*> 192.68.11.0      192.68.6.2          0             0 1 i
*                   192.68.20.1                       0 3 1 i
*> 192.68.222.0     0.0.0.0             0         32768 i
```

Looking at RTA's BGP table in Example 12-81, all the sub-ASs are indicated between parentheses. Any path taken between sub-ASs has a length of 0. Note how prefix 192.68.222.0/24 is learned via two paths—one internal via (65060) 2, and the other external via 1 2. The path length of the internal route via (65060) 2 is considered to be shorter because the sub-ASs are not counted in calculating the path length. This is why the internal path has been chosen over the external path.

Example 12-81 *Confederations: RTA BGP Table*

```
RTA#show ip bgp
BGP table version is 13, local router ID is 172.16.220.1
Status codes: s suppressed, d damped, h history, * valid, > best,
  i - internal Origin codes: i - IGP, e - EGP, ? - incomplete

  Network           Next Hop       Metric LocPrf Weight Path
*>i172.16.25.0/24   172.16.50.1         0    100      0 (65060) i
*>i172.16.30.0/24   172.16.50.1         0    100      0 (65060) i
*>i172.16.50.0/24   172.16.70.2         0    100      0 i
*>i172.16.60.0/24   172.16.50.1         0    100      0 (65060) i
*> 172.16.70.0/24   0.0.0.0             0         32768 i
* i                 172.16.70.2         0    100      0 i
*>i172.16.90.0/24   172.16.50.1         0    100      0 (65060) i
*>i172.16.65.0/26   172.16.50.1         0    100      0 (65060) i
*>i172.16.112.0/24  172.16.70.2         0    100      0 i
*> 172.16.220.0/24  0.0.0.0             0         32768 i
*> 192.68.11.0      172.16.20.1         0             0 1 i
*  192.68.222.0     172.16.20.1                       0 1 2 i
*>i                 172.16.50.1              100      0 (65060) 2 i
```

In the BGP table for RTF in Example 12-82, note how RTF considers all routes coming from sub-AS 65050 to be confederation external routes (confed-external). BGP performs its decision process within a confederation based on the following: EBGP is more preferred than confed-external, which is more preferred than internal.

Example 12-82 *Confederations: RTA BGP Table*

```
RTF#show ip bgp 172.16.220.0
BGP routing table entry for 172.16.220.0/24, version 22
Paths: (1 available, best #1, advertised over IBGP)
 (65050)
  172.16.50.2 from 172.16.50.2 (172.16.112.1)
   Origin IGP, metric 0, localpref 100, valid, confed-external, best
```

Controlling Route and Cache Invalidation

A traditional requirement of BGP was resetting the neighbors' TCP connection in order for a policy change to take effect (**clear ip bgp** [* | *address* | *peer-group*]). Clearing the sessions in this manner restarts the neighbor negotiations from scratch, invalidates the associated portions of the IP forwarding cache, and causes a major impact on the operation of live networks.

The reasoning for this is that, as discussed in Chapter 6, routes learned from a peer are initially populated in the peer's Adj-RIB-In. They are then passed to the Input Policy Engine, modified accordingly, and presented to the BGP decision process. Because an unmodified copy of the route (what was initially stored in the Adj-RIB-In) is usually not available, but is required in order to implement the new policy, one of a few things can happen:

1. The source of the BGP route could manually trigger readvertisement of the route.
2. The entire TCP session could be reset.
3. BGP *soft reconfiguration* can be used to store the peer's Adj-RIB-In in memory.
4. BGP Route Refresh could be used to ask the peer to readvertise its respective Adj-RIB-Out.

As for 1, it's unlikely in the real world that you'll have access to the source router. As for 2, this is the brute-force approach, and it would trigger a great deal of unnecessary instability. As for soft reconfiguration, it's a very nice approach, but it consumes a significant amount of memory. BGP Route Refresh, a very new solution, is by far the most elegant. The following sections discuss 3 and 4.

BGP Soft Reconfiguration

BGP *soft reconfiguration* is one approach that lets policies be configured and activated without resetting the BGP TCP session. This allows new policies to take effect without significantly affecting the network. Soft configuration can be applied in two different ways—inbound and outbound. Use the following EXEC command:

```
clear ip bgp [* | address | peer-group][soft [in|out]]
```

Outbound Soft Reconfiguration

Whenever outbound soft reconfiguration is applied, the new policies are automatically triggered, and appropriate updates (from the Adj-RIB-Out) are generated to enforce the new policy. Outbound soft reconfiguration requires no additional memory. Use the following EXEC command:

```
clear ip bgp [* | address | peer-group] soft out
```

Inbound Soft Reconfiguration

Inbound soft reconfiguration is a bit more involved. All inbound updates (the Adj-RIB-In) from the specified peer are stored in memory unmodified. When a new policy is applied and activated, the stored Adj-RIB-In is again presented to the Input Policy Engine. An additional router subcommand is needed to configure inbound soft reconfiguration:

```
neighbor {address | peer-group} soft-reconfiguration inbound
```

This command is required to start storing the received updates for the specified peer or peer group. The EXEC command used to do the inbound reconfiguration is as follows:

clear ip bgp [* | *address* | *peer-group*] **soft in**

To avoid the memory overhead needed for the inbound soft reconfiguration, the same outcome could be achieved by doing an outbound soft reconfiguration at the other end of the connection, which would force readvertisement of the subsequent Adj-RIB-Out.

If the **in/out** option is not specified (**clear ip bgp** [* | *address* | *peer-group*] **soft**), both inbound and outbound soft reconfiguration will be applied.

The following example demonstrates the difference between clearing a BGP session between two routers without and with the soft configuration BGP feature. While the session is cleared, an output log will be displayed to show the actual session being established and the route updates being exchanged.

Referring still to Figure 12-14, Example 12-83 shows how RTA is configured to send its updates to RTC with a metric of 5000.

Example 12-83 *Inbound Soft Reconfiguration: RTA Configuration*

```
router bgp 65050
 no synchronization
 bgp confederation identifier 3
 network 172.16.220.0 mask 255.255.255.0
 network 172.16.70.0 mask 255.255.255.0
 neighbor 172.16.20.1 remote-as 1
 neighbor 172.16.20.1 soft-reconfiguration inbound
 neighbor 172.16.20.1 filter-list 10 out
 neighbor 172.16.20.1 route-map setmetric out
 neighbor 172.16.70.2 remote-as 65050
 no auto-summary

ip as-path access-list 10 permit ^$

route-map setmetric permit 10
 set metric 5000
```

Note the **neighbor 172.16.20.1 soft-reconfiguration inbound** command in Example 12-83. This is needed only if clearing the session needs to take effect on the inbound—that is, in case you have no control over the neighbor router to clear the session on the outbound.

For this information to take effect, the BGP session would have to be cleared between the two routers, as demonstrated in Example 12-84.

Example 12-84 *Inbound Soft-Reconfiguration: Clearing the BGP Session Between Two Routers*

```
RTA#clear ip bgp 172.16.20.1

BGP: 172.16.20.1 reset requested
BGP: no valid path for 192.68.11.0/24
```

Example 12-84 *Inbound Soft-Reconfiguration: Clearing the BGP Session Between Two Routers (Continued)*

```
BGP: 172.16.20.1 reset by 0x27B740
BGP: 172.16.20.1 went from Established to Idle
BGP: nettable_walker 192.68.11.0/255.255.255.0 no best path selected
BGP: 172.16.20.1 went from Idle to Active
BGP: 172.16.70.2 computing updates, neighbor version 21, table version 23,
  starting at 0.0.0.0
BGP: 172.16.70.2 send UPDATE 192.68.11.0/24 -- unreachable
BGP: 172.16.70.2 1 updates enqueued (average=27, maximum=27)
BGP: 172.16.70.2 update run completed, ran for 0ms, neighbor version 21,
  start version 23, throttled to 23, check point net 0.0.0.0
BGP: scanning routing tables
BGP: 172.16.20.1 went from Active to OpenSent
BGP: 172.16.20.1 went from OpenSent to OpenConfirm
BGP: 172.16.20.1 went from OpenConfirm to Established
BGP: 172.16.20.1 computing updates, neighbor version 0, table version 23,
  starting at 0.0.0.0
BGP: 172.16.20.1 send UPDATE 172.16.25.0/24, next 172.16.20.2, metric 5000, path 3
BGP: 172.16.20.1 send UPDATE 172.16.30.0/24, next 172.16.20.2, path (65060)
BGP: 172.16.20.1 send UPDATE 172.16.50.0/24, next 172.16.20.2, metric 5000, path 3
BGP: 172.16.20.1 send UPDATE 172.16.60.0/24, next 172.16.20.2, path (65060)
BGP: 172.16.20.1 send UPDATE 172.16.70.0/24, next 172.16.20.2, metric 5000, path 3
BGP: 172.16.20.1 send UPDATE 172.16.90.0/24, next 172.16.20.2, path (65060)
BGP: 172.16.20.1 send UPDATE 172.16.65.0/26, next 172.16.20.2, path (65060)
BGP: 172.16.20.1 send UPDATE 172.16.112.0/24, next 172.16.20.2, path
BGP: 172.16.20.1 send UPDATE 172.16.220.0/24, next 172.16.20.2, path
BGP: 172.16.20.1 send UPDATE 192.68.222.0/24, next 172.16.20.2, metric 5000,
  path 3 2
BGP: 172.16.20.1 4 updates enqueued (average=58, maximum=68)
BGP: 172.16.20.1 update run completed, ran for 24ms, neighbor version 0,
  start version 23, throttled to 23, check point net 0.0.0.0
BGP: 172.16.20.1 rcv UPDATE about 192.68.11.0/24, next hop 172.16.20.1,
  path 1 metric 2000
BGP: 172.16.20.1 rcv UPDATE about 192.68.222.0/24, next hop 172.16.20.1,
  path 1 2 metric 2000
BGP: 172.16.20.1 rcv UPDATE about 172.16.25.0/24 -- denied
BGP: 172.16.20.1 rcv UPDATE about 172.16.30.0/24 -- denied
BGP: 172.16.20.1 rcv UPDATE about 172.16.50.0/24 -- denied
BGP: 172.16.20.1 rcv UPDATE about 172.16.60.0/24 -- denied
BGP: 172.16.20.1 rcv UPDATE about 172.16.70.0/24 -- denied
BGP: 172.16.20.1 rcv UPDATE about 172.16.90.0/24 -- denied
BGP: 172.16.20.1 rcv UPDATE about 172.16.65.0/26 -- denied
BGP: 172.16.20.1 rcv UPDATE about 172.16.112.0/24 -- denied
BGP: 172.16.20.1 rcv UPDATE about 172.16.220.0/24 -- denied
BGP: nettable_walker 192.68.11.0/255.255.255.0 calling revise_route
BGP: revise route installing 192.68.11.0/255.255.255.0 -> 172.16.20.1
BGP: 172.16.70.2 computing updates, neighbor version 23, table version 24,
  starting at 0.0.0.0
BGP: NEXT_HOP part 1 net 192.68.11.0/24, neigh 172.16.70.2, next 172.16.20.1
BGP: 172.16.70.2 send UPDATE 192.68.11.0/24, next 172.16.20.1, metric 2000, path 1
BGP: 172.16.70.2 1 updates enqueued (average=59, maximum=59)
BGP: 172.16.70.2 update run completed, ran for 4ms, neighbor version 23,
```

continues

Example 12-84 *Inbound Soft-Reconfiguration: Clearing the BGP Session Between Two Routers (Continued)*

```
  start version 24, throttled to 24, check point net 0.0.0.0
BGP: 172.16.20.1 rcv UPDATE about 172.16.25.0/24 -- withdrawn
BGP: 172.16.20.1 rcv UPDATE about 172.16.30.0/24 -- withdrawn
BGP: 172.16.20.1 rcv UPDATE about 172.16.50.0/24 -- withdrawn
BGP: 172.16.20.1 rcv UPDATE about 172.16.60.0/24 -- withdrawn
BGP: 172.16.20.1 rcv UPDATE about 172.16.70.0/24 -- withdrawn
BGP: 172.16.20.1 rcv UPDATE about 172.16.90.0/24 -- withdrawn
BGP: 172.16.20.1 rcv UPDATE about 172.16.65.0/26 -- withdrawn
BGP: 172.16.20.1 rcv UPDATE about 172.16.112.0/24 -- withdrawn
BGP: 172.16.20.1 rcv UPDATE about 172.16.220.0/24 -- withdrawn
BGP: 172.16.20.1 computing updates, neighbor version 23, table version 24,
  starting at 0.0.0.0
BGP: 172.16.20.1 update run completed, ran for 0ms, neighbor version 23,
  start version 24, throttled to 24, check point net 0.0.0.0
BGP: scanning routing tables
```

Note in the output in Example 12-84 how much overhead is caused by actually killing the TCP session between the two routers and starting over from scratch.

NOTE The overhead introduced would also likely be apparent if you viewed **show process cpu** or **show ip bgp sum** output, which would reveal a high CPU load and a significant change in the number of routes in the BGP table. You would also notice a large number of BGP routes sent and received during this time to all the peers.

The log will show that the BGP peer session is reset, and then the neighbor election goes from Idle to Established, and then the actual routing updates will flow.

In Example 12-85, the same session is cleared by using the soft configuration feature. Note how the metric 5000 was sent without killing the BGP session, and the overhead is much smaller.

Example 12-85 *Inbound Soft Reconfiguration: Clearing the BGP Session Between Two Routers with Soft Configuration*

```
RTA#clear ip bgp 172.16.20.1 soft out
BGP: start outbound soft reconfiguration for 172.16.20.1
BGP: 172.16.20.1 computing updates, neighbor version 0, table version 24,
  starting at 0.0.0.0
BGP: 172.16.20.1 send UPDATE 172.16.25.0/24, next 172.16.20.2, metric 5000, path 3
BGP: 172.16.20.1 send UPDATE 172.16.30.0/24, next 172.16.20.2, metric 5000, path 3
BGP: 172.16.20.1 send UPDATE 172.16.50.0/24, next 172.16.20.2, metric 5000, path 3
BGP: 172.16.20.1 send UPDATE 172.16.60.0/24, next 172.16.20.2, metric 5000, path 3
BGP: 172.16.20.1 send UPDATE 172.16.70.0/24, next 172.16.20.2, metric 5000, path 3
BGP: 172.16.20.1 send UPDATE 172.16.90.0/24, next 172.16.20.2, metric 5000, path 3
BGP: 172.16.20.1 send UPDATE 172.16.65.0/26, next 172.16.20.2, metric 5000, path 3
BGP: 172.16.20.1 send UPDATE 172.16.112.0/24, next 172.16.20.2, metric 5000, path 3
```

Example 12-85 *Inbound Soft Reconfiguration: Clearing the BGP Session Between Two Routers with Soft Configuration (Continued)*

```
BGP: 172.16.20.1 send UPDATE 172.16.220.0/24, next 172.16.20.2, metric 5000, path 3
BGP: 172.16.20.1 send UPDATE 192.68.11.0/24 -- unreachable
BGP: 172.16.20.1 send UPDATE 192.68.222.0/24, next 172.16.20.2, metric 5000,
  path 3 2
BGP: 172.16.20.1 5 updates enqueued (average=52, maximum=68)
BGP: 172.16.20.1 update run completed, ran for 24ms, neighbor version 0,
  start version 24, throttled to 24, check point net 0.0.0.0
BGP: scanning routing tables
```

BGP Route Refresh

BGP Route Refresh capability is enabled by BGP Capabilities (discussed in Chapter 5). During the establishment of the BGP connection, the peers advertise support of the Route Refresh capability. If they support it, they can dynamically request that the peer readvertise its Adj-RIB-Out (which, in reality, is what happens when outbound soft reconfiguration is performed). Because this requires no additional memory for storing the information, it's more efficient than using soft reconfiguration, and it doesn't cause the extra route flapping that a BGP session reset would. When the requestor receives the Adj-RIB-Out, it presents it to the Input Policy Engine (and the new policy).

In the output in Example 12-86, support of the route refresh capability can be verified by examining the **Neighbor capabilities** portion of the **show ip bgp neighbor x.x.x.x** output.

Example 12-86 *BGP Route Refresh Verification*

```
r1#show ip bgp n 1.1.2.2
BGP neighbor is 1.1.2.2,  remote AS 2, external link
  BGP version 4, remote router ID 3.3.3.1
  BGP state = Established, up for 2w0d
  Last read 00:00:15, hold time is 180, keepalive interval is 60 seconds
  Neighbor capabilities:
    Route refresh: advertised and received
    Address family IPv4 Unicast: advertised and received
  Received 20674 messages, 0 notifications, 0 in queue
  Sent 20675 messages, 0 notifications, 0 in queue
  Route refresh request: received 1, sent 2
  Minimum time between advertisement runs is 30 seconds

 For address family: IPv4 Unicast
  BGP table version 6, neighbor version 6
  Index 1, Offset 0, Mask 0x2
  NEXT_HOP is always this router
  Community attribute sent to this neighbor
  1 accepted prefixes consume 36 bytes
  Prefix advertised 4, suppressed 0, withdrawn 0

  Connections established 1; dropped 0
  Last reset never
```

continues

Example 12-86 *BGP Route Refresh Verification (Continued)*

```
Connection state is ESTAB, I/O status: 1, unread input bytes: 0
Local host: 1.1.2.1, Local port: 179
Foreign host: 1.1.2.2, Foreign port: 11000

Enqueued packets for retransmit: 0, input: 0  mis-ordered: 0 (0 bytes)

Event Timers (current time is 0x49ED7420):
Timer          Starts    Wakeups            Next
Retrans         20675          0             0x0
TimeWait            0          0             0x0
AckHold         20674      19530             0x0
SendWnd             0          0             0x0
KeepAlive           0          0             0x0
GiveUp              0          0             0x0
PmtuAger            0          0             0x0
DeadWait            0          0             0x0

iss: 1081723559  snduna: 1082116474  sndnxt: 1082116474     sndwnd:  15567
irs: 1087514066  rcvnxt: 1087906928  rcvwnd:      15605  delrcvwnd:    779

SRTT: 301 ms, RTTO: 621 ms, RTV: 9 ms, KRTT: 0 ms
minRTT: 4 ms, maxRTT: 600 ms, ACK hold: 200 ms
Flags: passive open, nagle, gen tcbs

Datagrams (max data segment is 1460 bytes):
Rcvd: 39791 (out of order: 0), with data: 20674, total data bytes: 392861
Sent: 40473 (retransmit: 0), with data: 20674, total data bytes: 392914
```

Note that route refresh can be supported by only one side of the connection. You can see this by viewing the **advertised** and/or **received** output following the **Route Refresh**: entry.

Example 12-87 shows what you would do to request that a peer readvertise its Adj-RIB-Out.

Example 12-87 *Forcing a Peer to Readvertise Adj-RIB-Out*

```
r1# clear ip bgp 1.1.2.2 soft in
r1#
2w0d: BGP: 1.1.2.2 sending REFRESH_REQ for afi/safi: 1/1
2w0d: BGP: 1.1.2.2 send message type 128, length (incl. header) 23
2w0d: BGP: 1.1.2.2 send message type 4, length (incl. header) 19
2w0d: BGP: 1.1.2.2 rcv message type 4, length (excl. header) 0
```

As you can see from the associated debug output in Example 12-87, this triggers a route refresh request to the peer and a subsequent readvertisement of the peer's Adj-RIB-Out.

As displayed in the **show ip bgp neighbor** output of Example 12-86, there are also counters available to track the number of route refresh requests sent to and received from the peer.

BGP Outbound Request Filter Capability

BGP ORF, enabled by BGP Capabilities (discussed in Chapter 5), helps conserve resources during BGP route update processing. If the ORF capability is advertised by a neighbor during session establishment, this means that the local BGP speaker will allow its neighbor to push over its inbound prefix filter. After it's received, the local BGP speaker installs the filter, in addition to any locally configured outbound filters associated with the neighbor.

Several benefits are associated with BGP ORF:

- The local BGP speaker will no longer consume resources generating routing update messages that will be filtered by the neighbor on input.
- Link bandwidth will not be consumed by the routing updates.
- The neighbor router will not need to consume resources processing routing updates that will be discarded once a filter lookup occurs.

NOTE It's important to understand that the impact of BGP ORF can be quite significant. For example, if a BGP peer were to send a global Internet routing table (more than 75,000 routes today) to a low-end router that is limited in memory, it might cause this router to run out of memory even if the router has inbound filters installed. Also, sending the routes to the neighbor can consume a significant amount of link bandwidth on lower-speed connections.

This is ideal for ISPs with automated route filter-generation tools and routers with lots of BGP peers. Once the filter is generated and deployed to the edge router in the ISPs network, it is pushed over to the customer's router, thereby conserving both customer and ISP resources.

By default, the ORF Capability is not advertised to neighbors. Also, BGP ORF cannot be advertised to a neighbor that's a BGP peer group member.

As a result of varying BGP ORF syntax across different versions of IOS, we've decided to include Appendix C, "BGP Outbound Route Filter (ORF)," that contains the Cisco release notes associated with BGP ORF. For additional information, consult the documentation specific to your version of IOS.

Route Dampening

Route dampening is a mechanism used to minimize the instability caused by route flapping and oscillation over the network. The following is the command used to control route dampening:

bgp dampening [[**route-map** *map-name*] [*half-life-time reuse-value suppress-value maximum-suppress-time*]]

- *half-life-time* is in the range of 1 to 45 minutes. The current default is 15 minutes.
- *reuse-value* is in the range of 1 to 20000. The default is 750.
- *suppress-value* is in the range of 1 to 20000. The default is 2000.
- *maximum-suppress-time* is the maximum duration that a route can be suppressed. The range is 1 to 255. The default is 4 × *half-life-time*.

A route map can be associated with BGP dampening to selectively apply the dampening parameters if certain criteria are found. Sample criteria include matching on a specific IP route, AS_PATH, or community.

Figure 12-15 shows two ASs, AS3 and AS1. RTA in AS3 is running IBGP with RTG in AS3 and EBGP with RTC in AS1. Information coming via EBGP from AS3 is injected into OSPF in AS1.

Figure 12-15 *Route Dampening*

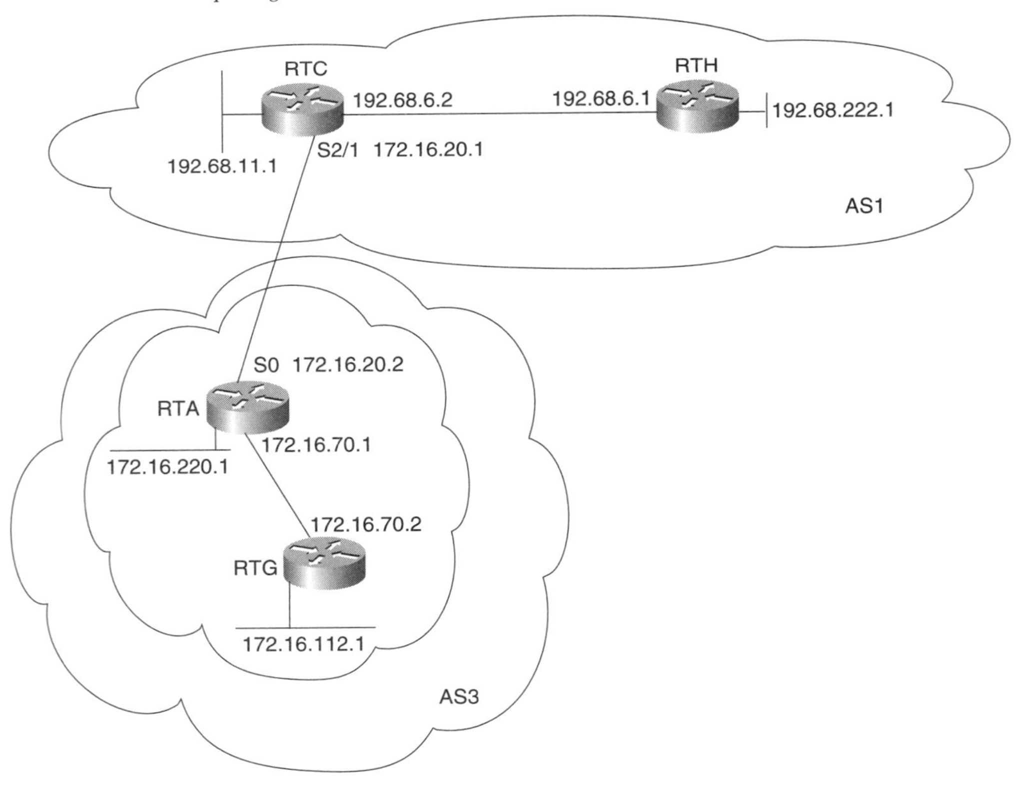

RTC has noticed lots of fluctuations in network 172.16.220.0/24 coming from AS3, causing oscillation in its BGP and consequently in OSPF. The 172.16.220.0/24 keeps showing up and disappearing from RTH's routing table. To rectify the problem, RTC will apply dampening to the BGP by using a route map to selectively dampen route 172.16.220.0/24 only. Example 12-88 and Example 12-89 show the configurations for RTG and RTA, respectively.

Example 12-88 *Route Dampening: RTG Configuration*

```
router bgp 3
 no synchronization
 network 172.16.112.0 mask 255.255.255.0
 neighbor 172.16.70.1 remote-as 3
 no auto-summary
```

Example 12-89 *Route Dampening: RTA Configuration*

```
router bgp 3
 no synchronization
 network 172.16.220.0 mask 255.255.255.0
 network 172.16.70.0 mask 255.255.255.0
 neighbor 172.16.20.1 remote-as 1
 neighbor 172.16.70.2 remote-as 3
 neighbor 172.16.70.2 next-hop-self
 no auto-summary
```

RTC is EBGP peered with RTA, and IBGP peered with RTH. RTC is injecting the BGP routes it receives into OSPF, which is running in AS1. RTC is applying BGP dampening with a route map SELECTIVE_DAMPENING, which applies the dampening parameters to network 172.16.220.0/24 only. All other routes such as 172.16.112.0/24 will not be dampened.

The RTC configuration in Example 12-90 specifies the dampening parameters in the following manner:

- The *half-life-time* is 20 minutes.
- The reuse limit for the penalty is 950.
- Routes will be suppressed if the cumulative penalty exceeds 2500.
- The maximum time a route could be suppressed is 80 minutes.

Example 12-90 *Route Dampening: RTC Configuration*

```
router ospf 10
 redistribute bgp 1 subnets
 network 192.68.0.0 0.0.255.255 area 0

router bgp 1
 bgp dampening route-map SELECTIVE_DAMPENING
```

continues

Example 12-90 *Route Dampening: RTC Configuration (Continued)*

```
 network 192.68.11.0
 neighbor 172.16.20.2 remote-as 3
 neighbor 192.68.6.1 remote-as 1
 no auto-summary

access-list 1 permit 172.16.220.0 0.0.0.255

route-map SELECTIVE_DAMPENING permit 10
 match ip address 1
 set dampening 20 950 2500 80

route-map SELECTIVE_DAMPENING permit 20
```

The output in Example 12-90 shows how RTC treats the flapping route 172.16.220.0/24. A flap is counted anytime the path information changes for a route. The BGP table in Example 12-91 shows the route before any flaps have occurred.

Example 12-91 *Route Dampening: RTC BGP Table Before Route Flapping*

```
RTC#show ip bgp 172.16.220.0
BGP routing table entry for 172.16.220.0/24, version 326
Paths: (1 available, best #1, advertised over IBGP)
 3
  172.16.20.2 from 172.16.20.2 (172.16.220.1)
   Origin IGP, metric 0, valid, external, best
```

The output in Example 12-92 shows the route after one flap. The route is down and is put in the **history** state. The route was given the default penalty of 1000, which has already decayed to 997.

Example 12-92 *Route Dampening: RTC BGP Table After the First Instance of Route Flapping*

```
RTC#show ip bgp 172.16.220.0
BGP routing table entry for 172.16.220.0/24, version 327
Paths: (1 available, no best path, advertised over IBGP)
 3 (history entry)
  172.16.20.2 from 172.16.20.2 (172.16.220.1)
   Origin IGP, metric 0, external
   Dampinfo: penalty 997, flapped 1 times in 00:00:06
```

The output in Example 12-93 shows the route after a second flap (it has come back up again). Another penalty of 1000 has been added, and the cumulative penalty after decay has reached 1454.

Example 12-93 *Route Dampening: RTC BGP Table After the Second Instance of Route Flapping*

```
RTC#show ip bgp 172.16.220.0
BGP routing table entry for 172.16.220.0/24, version 328
Paths: (1 available, best #1, advertised over IBGP)
 3
```

Example 12-93 *Route Dampening: RTC BGP Table After the Second Instance of Route Flapping (Continued)*

```
 172.16.20.2 from 172.16.20.2 (172.16.220.1)
  Origin IGP, metric 0, valid, external, best
  Dampinfo: penalty 1454, flapped 2 times in 00:01:20
```

Example 12-94 shows the route after four flaps. The penalty is now 2851, which exceeds the 2500 limit. The route is now suppressed (dampened) and will not be passed on to RTH. The route will be usable in 31 minutes and 40 seconds. At that time, the penalty will decay to the reuse limit of 950.

Example 12-94 *Route Dampening: RTC BGP Table After Four Instances of Route Flapping*

```
RTC#show ip bgp 172.16.220.0
BGP routing table entry for 172.16.220.0/24, version 329
Paths: (1 available, no best path, advertised over IBGP)
 3, (suppressed due to dampening)
  172.16.20.2 from 172.16.20.2 (172.16.220.1)
   Origin IGP, metric 0, valid, external
   Dampinfo: penalty 2851, flapped 4 times in 00:03:05, reuse in 00:31:40
```

The output in Example 12-95 shows the same route after six flaps. The differences are that the *half-life-time* has been set to 5 minutes instead of 20 minutes, and the *maximum-suppress-time* is 20 minutes instead of 80. With a shorter *half-life-time*, the penalty will be decayed much faster, and the route will be used a lot sooner. Note the reuse time of 8 minutes and 10 seconds.

Example 12-95 *Route Dampening: RTC BGP Table After Six Instances of Route Flapping*

```
RTC#show ip bgp 172.16.220.0
BGP routing table entry for 172.16.220.0/24, version 336
Paths: (1 available, no best path, advertised over IBGP)
 3, (suppressed due to dampening)
  172.16.20.2 from 172.16.20.2 (172.16.220.1)
   Origin IGP, metric 0, valid, external
   Dampinfo: penalty 2939, flapped 6 times in 00:08:21, reuse in 00:08:10
```

Adjusting the dampening timers becomes essential when administrators cannot afford to have a long outage for a specific route. BGP dampening with route maps is a powerful tool to selectively penalize ill-behaved routes in a user-configurable and controlled manner.

Looking Ahead

The Internet has come a long way from the NSFNET backbone to the information highway of the 21st century—and there are no signs of its slowing down. And how could the Internet slow down when thousands of users come online every day, attracted by the most advanced applications technology affords?

Routing protocols have struggled to keep up with the demand, from the early days of EGP to the latest in BGP. BGP started as a simple exterior routing protocol and has evolved into a de facto standard, gluing the Internet together. Indeed, every hook and tweak that BGP can offer has been used, and still it seems that more capabilities are requested every day. As a result, new protocols and new techniques will emerge. Whether they will make routing easier or more complicated, more robust or shakier, is yet to be seen. One thing is certain: Common sense will never go away, and as long as it is the basis of all your designs, you will be the master of your domain.

Because I couldn't possibly cover all the potential benefits and caveats of every BGP-related IOS command, I strongly suggest that you consult the appropriate Cisco documentation or support personnel if a question or problem arises. I have included a current set of IOS BGP configuration parameters in Appendix A, "BGP Command Reference," for additional reference. Appendix B, "References for Further Study," provides references and pointers to interesting online resources, as well as useful books. Appendix C, "BGP Outbound Route Filter (ORF)," contains BGP ORF information. Finally, Appendix D, "Multiprotocol BGP (MBGP)," includes information on Multiprotocol BGP (MBGP).

PART V

Appendixes

The appendixes in this part of the book provide additional references for further reading, an up to date Cisco IOS™ BGP command reference, and information regarding IOS™ modifications intended to provide a more intuitive BGP command line interface.

APPENDIX A

BGP Command Reference

The commands listed in Table A-1 of this appendix are the commands used to configure and monitor Border Gateway Protocol (BGP). For full documentation on complete command syntax (arguments, parameters, and so on), command default settings, command modes, command history, usage guidelines, configuration examples, and lists of related commands, consult the CCO document at www.cisco.com/univercd/cc/td/doc/product/software/ios121/121cgcr/ip_r/iprprt2/1rdbgp.htm#xtocid141910.

Table A-1 *BGP Commands*

Command	Description
aggregate-address	To create an aggregate entry in a BGP routing table, use the **aggregate-address** router configuration command. To disable this function, use the **no** form of this command.
auto-summary (BGP)	To restore the default behavior of automatic summarization of subnet routes into network-level routes, use the **auto-summary** router configuration command. To disable this feature and send subprefix routing information across classful network boundaries, use the **no** form of this command.
bgp always-compare-med	To allow the comparison of the Multi Exit Discriminator (MED) for paths from neighbors in different autonomous systems, use the **bgp always-compare-med** router configuration command. To disallow the comparison, use the **no** form of this command.
bgp bestpath as-path ignore	To prevent the router from considering as-path as a factor in the algorithm for choosing a route, use the **bgp bestpath as-path ignore** router configuration command. To allow the router to consider as-path in choosing a route, use the **no** form of this command.
bgp bestpath med-confed	To enable MED comparison among paths learned from confederation peers, use the **bgp bestpath med-confed** router configuration command. To prevent the software from considering the MED attribute in comparing paths, use the **no** form of this command.

continues

Table A-1 *BGP Commands (Continued)*

Command	Description
bgp bestpath missing-as-worst	To have Cisco IOS software consider a missing MED attribute in a path as having a value of infinity, making the path without a MED value the least desirable path, use the **bgp bestpath missing-as-worst** router configuration command. To return the router to the default (assign a value of 0 to the missing MED), use the **no** form of this command.
bgp client-to-client reflection	To restore route reflection from a BGP route reflector to clients, use the **bgp client-to-client reflection** router configuration command. To disable client-to-client reflection, use the **no** form of this command.
bgp cluster-id	To configure the cluster ID if the BGP cluster has more than one route reflector, use the **bgp cluster-id** router configuration command. To remove the cluster ID, use the **no** form of this command.
bgp confederation identifier	To specify a BGP confederation identifier, use the **bgp confederation identifier** router configuration command. To remove the confederation identifier, use the **no** form of this command.
bgp confederation peers	To configure the autonomous systems that belong to the confederation, use the **bgp confederation peers** router configuration command. To remove an autonomous system from the confederation, use the **no** form of this command.
bgp dampening	To enable BGP route dampening or change various BGP route-dampening factors, use the **bgp dampening** global configuration command. To disable the function or restore the default values, use the **no** form of this command.
bgp default local-preference	To change the default local preference value, use the **bgp default local-preference** router configuration command. To return to the default setting, use the **no** form of this command.
bgp deterministic med	To have Cisco IOS software compare the MED variable when choosing from among routes advertised by the same subautonomous system within a confederation, use the **bgp deterministic med** router configuration command. To disallow the comparison, use the **no** form of this command.
bgp fast-external-fallover	To immediately reset the BGP sessions of any directly adjacent external peers if the link used to reach them goes down, use the **bgp fast-external-fallover** router configuration command. To disable this function, use the **no** form of this command.
bgp log-neighbor-changes	To enable logging of BGP neighbor resets, use the **bgp log-neighbor-changes** router configuration command. To disable the logging of changes in BGP neighbor adjacencies, use the **no** form of this command.
clear ip bgp	To reset a BGP connection using BGP soft reconfiguration, use the **clear ip bgp** EXEC command at the system prompt.
clear ip bgp dampening	To clear BGP route dampening information and unsuppress the suppressed routes, use the **clear ip bgp dampening** EXEC command.

Table A-1 *BGP Commands (Continued)*

Command	Description
clear ip bgp flap-statistics	To clear BGP flap statistics, use the **clear ip bgp flap-statistics** EXEC command.
clear ip bgp peer-group	To remove all the members of a BGP peer group, use the **clear ip bgp peer-group** EXEC command.
clear ip prefix-list	To reset the hit count of the prefix list entries, use the **clear ip prefix-list** router configuration command.
default-information originate (BGP)	To allow the redistribution of network 0.0.0.0 into the BGP, use the **default-information originate** router configuration command. To disable this function, use the **no** form of this command.
default-metric (BGP)	To set default metric values for the Border Gateway Protocol BGP routing protocol, use the **default-metric** router configuration command. To return to the default state, use the **no** form of this command.
distance bgp	To allow the use of external, internal, and local administrative distances that could be a better route to a node, use the **distance bgp** router configuration command. To return to the default values, use the **no** form of this command.
distribute-list in	To filter networks received in updates, use the **distribute-list in** router configuration command. To disable this function, use the **no** form of this command.
distribute-list out	To suppress networks from being advertised in updates, use the **distribute-list out** router configuration command. To disable this function, use the **no** form of this command.
ip as-path access-list	To define a BGP-related access list, use the **ip as-path access-list** global configuration command. To disable use of the access list, use the **no** form of this command.
ip bgp-community new-format	To display BGP communities in the format AA:NN (autonomous system-community number/2-byte number), use the **ip bgp-community new-format** global configuration command. To reenable the previous display format for BGP communities (NN:AA), use the **no** form of this command.
ip community-list	To create a community list for BGP and control access to it, use the **ip community-list** global configuration command. To delete the community-list, use the **no** form of this command.
ip prefix-list	To create an entry in a prefix list, use the **ip prefix-list** global configuration command. To delete the entry, use the **no** form of this command.
ip prefix-list description	To add a text description of a prefix list, use the **ip prefix-list description** global configuration command. To remove the text description, use the **no** form of this command.
ip prefix-list sequence-number	To enable the generation of sequence numbers for entries in a prefix list, use the **ip prefix-list sequence-number** global configuration command.

continues

Table A-1 *BGP Commands (Continued)*

Command	Description
match as-path	To match a BGP autonomous system path access list, use the **match as-path** route-map configuration command. To remove a path list entry, use the **no** form of this command.
match community-list	To match a BGP community, use the **match community-list** route-map configuration command. To remove the community list entry, use the **no** form of this command.
neighbor advertisement-interval	To set the minimum interval between the sending of BGP routing updates, use the **neighbor advertisement-interval** router configuration command. To remove an entry, use the **no** form of this command.
neighbor default-originate	To allow a BGP speaker (the local router) to send the default route 0.0.0.0 to a neighbor for use as a default route, use the **neighbor default-originate** router configuration command. To send no route as a default, use the **no** form of this command.
neighbor description	To associate a description with a neighbor, use the **neighbor description** router configuration command. To remove the description, use the **no** form of this command.
neighbor distribute-list	To distribute BGP neighbor information as specified in an access list, use the **neighbor distribute-list** router configuration command. To remove an entry, use the **no** form of this command.
neighbor ebgp-multihop	To accept and attempt BGP connections to external peers residing on networks that are not directly connected, use the **neighbor ebgp-multihop** router configuration command. To return to the default, use the **no** form of this command.
neighbor filter-list	To set up a BGP filter, use the **neighbor filter-list** router configuration command. To disable this function, use the **no** form of this command.
neighbor maximum-prefix	To control how many prefixes can be received from a neighbor, use the **neighbor maximum-prefix** router configuration command. To disable this function, use the **no** form of this command.
neighbor next-hop-self	To disable next hop processing of BGP updates on the router, use the **neighbor next-hop-self** router configuration command. To disable this feature, use the **no** form of this command.
neighbor password	To enable Message Digest 5 (MD5) authentication on a TCP connection between two BGP peers, use the **neighbor password** router configuration command. To disable this function, use the **no** form of this command.
neighbor peer-group (assigning members)	To configure a BGP neighbor to be a member of a peer group, use the **neighbor peer-group** router configuration command. To remove the neighbor from the peer group, use the **no** form of this command.

Table A-1 *BGP Commands (Continued)*

Command	Description
neighbor peer-group (creating)	To create a BGP peer group, use the **neighbor peer-group** router configuration command. To remove the peer group and all of its members, use the **no** form of this command.
neighbor prefix-list	To distribute BGP neighbor information as specified in a prefix list, use the **neighbor prefix-list** router configuration command. To remove an entry, use the **no** form of this command.
neighbor remote-as	To add an entry to the BGP neighbor table, use the **neighbor remote-as** router configuration command. To remove an entry from the table, use the **no** form of this command.
neighbor route-map	To apply a route map to incoming or outgoing routes, use the **neighbor route-map** router configuration command. To remove a route map, use the **no** form of this command.
neighbor route-reflector-client	To configure the router as a BGP route reflector and configure the specified neighbor as its client, use the **neighbor route-reflector-client** router configuration command. To indicate that the neighbor is not a client, use the **no** form of this command. When all the clients are disabled, the local router is no longer a route reflector.
neighbor send-community	To specify that a "communities" attribute should be sent to a BGP neighbor, use the **neighbor send-community** router configuration command. To remove the entry, use the **no** form of this command.
neighbor shutdown	To disable a neighbor or peer group, use the **neighbor shutdown router** configuration command. To reenable the neighbor or peer group, use the **no** form of this command.
neighbor soft-reconfiguration	To configure the Cisco IOS software to start storing updates, use the **neighbor soft-reconfiguration** router configuration command. To not store received updates, use the **no** form of this command.
neighbor timers	To set the timers for a specific BGP peer or peer group, use the **neighbor timers** router configuration command. To clear the timers for a specific BGP peer or peer group, use the **no** form of this command.
neighbor update-source	To have the Cisco IOS software allow internal BGP sessions to use any operational interface for TCP connections, use the **neighbor update-source** router configuration command. To restore the interface assignment to the closest interface, which is called the *best local address*, use the **no** form of this command.
neighbor version	To configure the Cisco IOS software to accept only a particular BGP version, use the **neighbor version** router configuration command. To use the default version level of a neighbor, use the **no** form of this command.

continues

Table A-1 *BGP Commands (Continued)*

Command	Description
neighbor weight	To assign a weight to a neighbor connection, use the **neighbor weight** router configuration command. To remove a weight assignment, use the **no** form of this command.
network (BGP)	To specify the list of networks for the BGP routing process, use the **network router** configuration command. To remove an entry, use the **no** form of this command.
network backdoor	To specify a backdoor route to a BGP border router that will provide better information about the network, use the **network backdoor** router configuration command. To remove an address from the list, use the **no** form of this command.
network weight	To assign an absolute weight to a BGP network, use the **network weight** router configuration command. To delete an entry, use the **no** form of the command.
router bgp	To configure the BGP routing process, use the **router bgp** global configuration command. To remove a routing process, use the **no** form of this command.
set as-path	To modify an autonomous system path for BGP routes, use the **set as-path** route-map configuration command. To not modify the autonomous system path, use the **no** form of this command.
set comm-list delete	To remove communities from the community attribute of an inbound or outbound update, use the **set comm-list delete** router configuration command. To negate a previous **set comm-list delete** command, use the **no** form of this command.
set community	To set the BGP COMMUNITIES attribute, use the **set community** route-map configuration command. To delete the entry, use the **no** form of this command.
set dampening	To set the BGP route dampening factors, use the **set dampening** route-map configuration command. To disable this function, use the **no** form of this command.
set ip next-hop (BGP)	To indicate where to output packets that pass a match clause of a route map for policy routing, use the **set ip next-hop** route-map configuration command. To delete an entry, use the **no** form of this command.
set metric-type internal	To set the MED value on prefixes advertised to External Border Gateway Protocol (EBGP) neighbors to match the Interior Gateway Protocol (IGP) metric of the next hop, use the **set metric-type internal** route-map configuration command. To return to the default, use the **no** form of this command.
set origin (BGP)	To set the BGP origin code, use the **set origin** route-map configuration command. To delete an entry, use the **no** form of this command.
set weight	To specify the BGP weight for the routing table, use the **set weight** route-map configuration command. To delete an entry, use the **no** form of this command.
show ip bgp	To display entries in the BGP routing table, use the **show ip bgp** EXEC command.

Table A-1 *BGP Commands (Continued)*

Command	Description
show ip bgp cidr-only	To display routes with nonnatural network masks (that is, classless interdomain routing, or CIDR), use the **show ip bgp cidr-only** privileged EXEC command.
show ip bgp community	To display routes that belong to specified BGP communities, use the **show ip bgp community** EXEC command.
show ip bgp community-list	To display routes that are permitted by the BGP community list, use the **show ip bgp community-list** EXEC command.
show ip bgp dampened-paths	To display BGP dampened routes, use the **show ip bgp dampened-paths** EXEC command.
show ip bgp filter-list	To display routes that conform to a specified filter list, use the **show ip bgp filter-list** privileged EXEC command.
show ip bgp flap-statistics	To display BGP flap statistics, use the **show ip bgp flap-statistics** EXEC command.
show ip bgp inconsistent-as	To display routes with inconsistent originating autonomous systems, use the **show ip bgp inconsistent-as** privileged EXEC command.
show ip bgp neighbors	To display information about the TCP and BGP connections to neighbors, use the **show ip bgp neighbors** EXEC command.
show ip bgp paths	To display all the BGP paths in the database, use the **show ip bgp paths** EXEC command.
show ip bgp peer-group	To display information about BGP peer groups, use the **show ip bgp peer-group** EXEC command.
show ip bgp regexp	To display routes matching the regular expression, use the **show ip bgp regexp** privileged EXEC command.
show ip bgp summary	To display the status of all BGP connections, use the **show ip bgp summary** EXEC command.
show ip prefix-list	To display information about a prefix list or prefix list entries, use the **show ip prefix-list** EXEC command.
synchronization	To enable the synchronization between BGP and your Interior Gateway Protocol (IGP) system, use the **synchronization** router configuration command. To enable the Cisco IOS software to advertise a network route without waiting for the IGP, use the **no** form of this command.
table-map	To modify metric and tag values when the IP routing table is updated with BGP learned routes, use the **table-map** router configuration command. To disable this function, use the **no** form of the command.
timers bgp	To adjust BGP network timers, use the **timers bgp** router configuration command. To reset the BGP timing defaults, use the **no** form of this command.

APPENDIX B

References for Further Study

Interesting Organizations

Internet Engineering Task Force (IETF)—www.ietf.org
North American Network Operations Group (NANOG)—www.nanog.org
American Registry for Internet Numbers (ARIN)—www.arin.net
Asian Pacific Network Information Center (APNIC)—www.apnic.net
RIPE Network Coordination Centre (NCC)—www.ripe.net
The Internet Corporation for Assigned Names and Numbers (ICANN)—www.icann.org
Internet Assigned Numbers Authority (IANA)—www.iana.org
Cooperative Association for Internet Data Analysis (CAIDA)—www.caida.org

Research and Education

Next Generation Internet (NGI) Initiative—http://www.ngi.gov
Internet2—www.internet2.edu
Abilene—www.ucaid.edu/abilene/
Very High Speed Backbone Network Service (vBNS)—www.vbns.net
National Science Foundation—www.nsf.gov

Miscellaneous

Exchange Point Information—www.ep.net/
The CIDR Report—www.employees.org/~tbates/cidr-report.html
Asian Pacific Routing Report—www.apnic.net/stats/bgp
Cisco Connection Online (CCO)—www.cisco.com

Books

TCP/IP-Related Sources

Douglas E. Comer, *Internetworking with TCP/IP, Volume 1, Fourth Edition*, April 2000, Prentice Hall; ISBN 0130183806.

Jeff Doyle, *Routing TCP/IP, Volume I*, 1998, Cisco Press; ISBN 1578700418

W. Richard Stevens, *TCP/IP Illustrated, Volume 1*, January 1994, Addison-Wesley Publishing Company; ISBN 0201633469.

W. Richard Stevens and Gary R. Wright, *TCP/IP Illustrated, Volume II*, January 1995, Addison-Wesley Publishing Company; ISBN: 020163354X.

W. Richard Stevens, *TCP/IP Illustrated, Volume III*, January 1996, Addison-Wesley Publishing Company; ISBN: 0201634953.

Routing-Related Sources

C. Huitema, *Routing in the Internet, Second Edition*, 1999, Prentice Hall; ISBN 0130226475,

J. Moy, *OSPF, Anatomy of an Internet Routing Protocol*, 1998, Addison-Wesley Pub Co; ISBN 0201634724.

R. Perlman, *Interconnections, Second Edition*, 1999, Addison-Wesley Pub Co; ISBN 0201634481.

Alvaro Retana, Don Slice, and Russ White, *Advanced IP Network Design*, 1999, Cisco Press; ISBN 1578700973.

J. Stewart, *BGP4: Inter-Domain Routing in the Internet*, 1998, Addison-Wesley Pub Co; ISBN 0201379511.

Internet Request For Comments

RFCs can be obtained from the IETF web server located at www.ietf.org. General background information provided on the two types of RFCs (FYIs and STDs) can be found there as well. The following list documents current RFCs related to BGP.

K. Lougheed and Y. Rekhter, "A Border Gateway Protocol 3 (BGP-3)," RFC 1267, October 1991.

S. Willis and J. Burruss, "Definitions of Managed Objects for the Border Gateway Protocol (Version 3)," RFC 1269, October 1991.

Y. Rekhter, "Experience with the BGP Protocol," RFC 1266, October 1991

Y. Rekhter, "BGP Protocol Analysis," RFC 1265, October 1991.

D. Haskin, "Default Route Advertisement in BGP2 And BGP3 Versions of the Border Gateway Protocol," RFC 1397, January 1993.

K. Varadhan, "BGP OSPF Interaction," RFC 1403, January 1993.
S. Willis, J. Burruss and J. Chu, "Definitions of Managed Objects for the Fourth Version of the Border Gateway Protocol (BGP-4) using SMIv2," RFC 1657, July 1994 .
K. Varadhan, S. Hares and Y. Rekhter, "BGP4/IDRP for IP—OSPF Interaction," RFC 1745, December 1994.
P. Traina, "BGP-4 Protocol Analysis," RFC 1774, March 1995.
P. Traina, "Experience with the BGP-4 Protocol," RFC 1773, March 1995.
Y. Rekhter and T. Li, "A Border Gateway Protocol 4 (BGP-4)," RFC 1771, March 1995.
D. Haskin, "A BGP/IDRP Route Server Alternative to a Full Mesh Routing," RFC 1863, October 1995.
J. Hawkinson and T. Bates, "Guidelines for Creation, Selection, and Registration of an Autonomous System (AS)," RFC 1930, March 1996.
P. Traina, "Autonomous System Confederations for BGP," RFC 1965, June 1996.
T. Bates and R. Chandra, "BGP Route Reflection–An Alternative to Full Mesh IBGP," RFC 1966, June 1996.
E. Chen and T. Bates, "An Application of the BGP Community Attribute in Multi-home Routing," RFC 1998, August 1996.
R. Chandra, P. Traina and T. Li, "BGP Communities Attribute," RFC 1997, August 1996.
J. Stewart, T. Bates, R. Chandra and E. Chen, "Using a Dedicated AS for Sites Homed to a Single Provider," RFC 2270, January 1998.
T. Bates, R. Chandra, D. Katz and Y. Rekhter, "Multiprotocol Extensions for BGP-4," RFC 2283, February 1998.
C. Alaettinoglu, T. Bates, E. Gerich, D. Karrenberg, D. Meyer, M. Terpstra, C. Villamizar, "Routing Policy Specification Language (RSPL)," RFC 2280, January 1998.
A. Heffernan, "Protection of BGP Sessions via the TCP MD5 Signature Option," RFC 2385, August 1998.
C. Villamizar, R. Chandra and R. Govindan, "BGP Route Flap Damping," RFC 2439, November 1998.
E. Chen and J. Stewart, "A Framework for Inter-Domain Route Aggregation," RFC 2519, February 1999.
P. Marques and F. Dupont, "Use of BGP-4 Multiprotocol Extensions for IPv6 Inter-Domain Routing," RFC 2545, March 1999.
C. Alaettinoglu, T. Bates, E. Gerich, D. Karrenberg, D. Meyer, M. Terpstra, C. Villamizar, "Routing Policy Specification Language (RSPL)," RFC 2622, June1999.
C. Alaettinoglu, D. Meyer, C. Orange, M. Prior, J. Schmitz, "Using RPSL in Practice," RFC 2650, August 1999.
C. Alaettinoglu, D. Meyer, S. Murphy, C. Villamizar, "Routing Policy System Security," RFC 2725, December 1999.

B. Aiken, B. Carpenter, I. Foster, C. Lynch, J. Mambretti, R. Moore, J. Strassner, B. Teitelbaum, "Network Policy and Services: A Report of a Workshop on Middleware." RFC 2768, February 2000.

T. Bates, R. Chandra and E. Chen, "BGP Route Reflection–An Alternative to Full Mesh IBGP," RFC 2796, April 2000.

R. Chandra and J. Scudder, "Capabilities Advertisement with BGP-4," RFC 2842, May 2000.

APPENDIX C

BGP Outbound Route Filter (ORF)

Outbound Route Filter (ORF) is a new BGP functionality used to minimize the number of BGP updates sent to a neighbor. This appendix provides information on BGP ORF as it relates to IOS versions 12.0ST and 12.1.

The idea is to push the locally-configured BGP prefix filter to the remote peer so that the remote peer applies this received filter as yet another outbound filter. This results in two benefits:

- The number of prefixes that are sent are reduced and thus leads to a lesser number of BGP updates.
- Less work for the local router which previously used to process all those extra updates. This might mean less transient memory consumption and less attribute and cache creation.

This appendix covers the ORF. The inbound prefix list can be pushed down to the peer acting as its outbound policy.

ORF is defined as a new capability, IOS uses 130 as its code value. The new capability reflects the latest draft which lists all the ORF-types supported as send, receive or both. This means that there is a compatibility issue between routers running these two capabilities. The old knob is accepted only as receive capability.

The local-peer that advertises support for BGP ORF in send-mode will push its inbound prefix list only if it receives the receive-mode BGP ORF capability from the remote-peer. The remote-peer however will wait before sending the first update until it receives a ROUTE-REFRESH request or BGP ORF with IMMEDIATE from the peer. Note that this is done for each address-family (AF) for updates exchanged between the peers depending on the BGP ORF capability advertised.

When to Use BGP ORF

BGP ORF allows one BGP speaker to install its inbound prefix list filter on the remote end, and can be used to reduce the amount of unwanted routing update.

For example, this feature can be used to address the issue of receiving ("unwanted") full routes from multi-homed BGP customers. The customer can simply enable the capability, thus allowing its provider to manage the route filtering, and avoid such unwanted routing updates.

Configuration

The following section provides configuration guidelines that should be used when configuring BGP ORF. BGP ORF is asymmetric in nature and independently configured on each end of the connection.

The steps to configure BGP ORF consist of the following:

1. Enabling the BGP ORF capability as *send-mode*.
2. Enabling the BGP ORF capability as *receive-mode*.
3. Ensure backward compatibility of the old knobs

Enabling the BGP ORF Capability as Send-Mode

The command to enable the BGP ORF capability as send mode is as follows:

```
[no] neighbor x.x.x.x capability orf prefix list send
```

This command is used to configure the local router to advertise the ORF capability with BGP ORF-type (value 128) in send-mode (value 2) during session establishment with the remote peer specified. This command can be used for individual members as well as members of peergroup or the peergroup itself.

The default for this capability is OFF. This is not advertised and has to be turned ON by configuration.

This is available for all address families.

Enabling the BGP ORF Capability as Receive-Mode

The command to enable the BGP ORF capability as send mode is as follows:

```
[no] neighbor x.x.x.x capability orf prefix list receive
```

This command is used to configure the local router to advertise the ORF capability with BGP ORF-type (value 128) in the receive-mode (value 1) during the session establishment with the remote peer specified. This command can be used only for the individual members or for peergroup itself. The command cannot be used for peergroup members.

The default for this capability is OFF. This is not advertised and has to be turned ON by configuration.

BGP ORF support is available for all address families (that is IPv4 unicast, IPv4 multicast, and so on).

Ensuring Backward Compatibility of the Old Knobs

The command to ensure backward compatibility of the old knobs is as follows:

```
[no] neighbor x.x.x.x capability prefix-filter
```

If the preceding knob is configured, the new software accepts this knob as hidden and will advertise it as the new BGP ORF capability in the receive-mode. Note that it will NVGEN in the new format. This means that the remote-peer peering with this before should be upgraded as well to make the ORF work.

If the knob is configured as follows:

```
[no] neighbor x.x.x.x send prefix-filter
```

then the new software accepts this knob as hidden and will advertise it as the new BGP ORF capability in the send-mode. Note that it will NVGEN in the new format. This means that the remote-peer peering with this before should be upgraded as well to make the ORF work.

EXEC Commands

Pushing Out A Prefix List and Receiving a Route Refresh from a Neighbor

The command syntax to push out a prefix list and receive route refresh from a neighbor is as follows (note that any address family can be specified):

```
clear ip bgp x.x.x.x in prefix-filter
clear ip bgp x.x.x.x vrf foo in prefix-filter
clear ip bgp x.x.x.x ipv4 multicast in prefix-filter
```

When the inbound prefix list changes (or is removed), this command can be used to push out the new prefix list, and consequently receive route refresh from the neighbor based on the new prefix list.

The keyword **prefix-filter** will be ignored if the BGP ORF capability has not been received from the neighbor, or if the local speaker has not enabled send-orf for the neighbor.

Without the keyword **prefix-filter**, the command **clear ip bgp** *x.x.x.x* **in** would simply perform the normal route refresh from the neighbor. It does not push out the current inbound prefix list filter to the neighbor. The command is useful when using inbound routing policies other than the prefix list filter such as a route map change.

Displaying the Prefix List Received from a Neighbor

The command syntax to display the prefix list received from a neighbor is as follows:

```
show ip bgp neighbor x.x.x.x received prefix-filter
show ip bgp vpnv4 vrf foo neighbor x.x.x.x received prefix-filter
show ip bgp ipv4 multicast neighbor x.x.x.x received prefix-filter
```

Displaying Changes to the Neighbor BGP Table

Changes to the output of **show ip bgp neighbor** *x.x.x.x* reveal the following information:

```
AF-dependant capabilities:
      Outbound Route Filter (ORF) type (128) Prefix-list:
        Send-mode: advertised, received
    Receive-mode: advertised, received

Outbound Route Filter (ORF): sent, received (2 entries)
First update is deferred until ORF or ROUTE-REFRESH is received
Scheduled to send the Prefix-list filter test
```

Closing Remarks

Even after a BGP speaker pushes its inbound prefix list to the remote end, the speaker will continue to apply the locally defined inbound prefix list filter to received updates.

APPENDIX D

Multiprotocol BGP (MBGP)

With the support of BGP Capabilities (BGPCAP)[1], Multiprotocol BGP (MBGP)[2] defines backward-compatible extensions to BGP-4[3] that allow it to carry routing information for multiple network layer protocols (for example, IPv6, IPX, and so on). Individual network layer protocols are identified by an Address Family (AF), as defined in RFC 1700[4]. These extensions allow a set of BGP peers to exchange reachability information for multiple AFs (for example IPv4, IPv6, IPX) and sub-AFs (for example, unicast or multicast).

NOTE The complete transition plan from the old-style CLI to the new AF-style CLI still has not been completely decided upon within Cisco. For that reason, if you encounter inconsistencies, consult Cisco support personnel or documentation associated with your specific version of IOS.

The Motivation Behind the New Command-Line Interface

With multiple address families, it was quickly realized that the AF topologies would frequently be noncongruent. Also, policies associated with a given session might vary depending on specific AFs. The initial CLI design focused on accommodating only a single AF (IPv4) and its associated sub-AFs (unicast and multicast). Utilizing this design to provide support for additional AFs introduced unnecessary management and policy expression complexities.

It was therefore decided that a new approach would be used—an approach that cleanly separates general session-related parameters from AF-specific parameters. Beyond management aspects alone, this new approach provides several advantages:

- Inbound and outbound policy can be different for each AF.
- A BGP router can be configured as a route reflector for a single AF or multiple AFs.
- No new configuration is required to support "vanilla" BGP (IPv4-unicast).
- Prefixes can be sourced (via redistribution, **aggregate-address** statements, and **network** statements) within any AF independently.

- Peer group functionality will be maintained within the associated AF, because it is relevant for UPDATE generation.

This new model is much more flexible when using multiple AFs. Based on the preceding advantages, the **router bgp** subcommands were divided into three command groups:

1. **Global BGP commands**—These commands affect the operation of BGP global to the router. Examples include **bgp deterministic-med** and **bgp cluster-id**.
2. **Commands to identify the neighbors/peer groups**—These commands define the neighbor or peer group that is accessible from the default routing table by specifying session parameters. Examples include **neighbor 1.2.3.4 remote-as** *as* and **neighbor 1.2.3.4 ebgp-multihop** *ttl.*
3. **Commands per-address family**—Two sets of commands can be per-AF:
   - **Global to per-AF**—These commands are neighbor-independent and modify the behavior of BGP for a specific AF. Prefixes to be sourced (using redistribution, **network**, or **aggregate-address** statements) under this AF fall into this category. Examples include **network 1.2.0.0 mask 255.255.0.0**, **redistribute dvmrp**, and **bgp scan-time**.
   - **AF-specific per-neighbor/peer group**—These commands configure policy for the neighbor(s) or peer groups with distribute lists, prefix lists, or route maps. The neighbors can also be configured as clients of a route reflector, or added as members of a peer group. The neighbor must be explicitly "activated" in order to enable the exchange of Multiprotocol BGP prefixes. Examples include **neighbor 1.2.3.4 filter-list in**, **neighbor peergroup1 route-map foo in**, and **neighbor 1.2.3.4 activate**.

Organizing Command Groups in the New Configuration

There is no ambiguity present for command group 1, so they appear as global BGP configuration parameters. These commands appear only once in the configuration.

There is no ambiguity for command group 2, so they follow command group 1 under the global BGP parameters. BGP neighbors, with an exception to a case in VPN, are defined once in the configuration.

A new submode was introduced under **router bgp** *autonomous-system* configuration mode to define the per-AF commands.

The following output demonstrates the general configuration guidelines when using the new AF-style CLI:

```
router bgp autonomous-system
  address-family afi [sub-afi]
      redistribute protocol
      neighbor 1.2.3.4 activate
...
```

```
  exit-address-family
 exit
```

A neighbor can have different policies applied to a single peer (for example, **route-map** or **prefix-list** statements), one per AF.

For configuring IPv4-unicast BGP (vanilla BGP) policy for neighbors, it is possible to configure them entirely under the command group 2. This is very similar to what we have today (old CLI). The **address-family ipv4 unicast** is implicit, although explicit configuration is recommended.

It is also possible to configure the IPv4-unicast BGP policy using the **address-family** BGP submode. In the **show running-config** output, **address-family ipv4 unicast** is shown, and IPv4-unicast global (global to per-AF) and policy (AF-specific per-neighbor/peer group) commands are listed within the mode.

Under the **address-family** submode, the commands of the global to per-AF group appear first. These are commands that are global to the AF.

Following the global to per-AF commands are the AF-specific per-neighbor/peer group commands. These commands implement the policy to the neighbors for that AF.

Before any policy is defined for a neighbor under an AF, the neighbor should be "activated" for that AF. The command syntax required to activate a neighbor under a specific AF is as follows:

```
router bgp autonomous-system
  address-family afi [sub-afi]
neighbor 1.2.3.4 activate
    ...
  exit-address-family
exit
```

The new configuration structure looks like this:

```
router bgp 1
 no synchronization                          ! Global to BGP
 bgp deterministic-med                       ! Global to BGP
 bgp bestpath med confed                     ! Global to BGP
 neighbor ebgp peer-group                    ! Peer group defn., global to BGP
 neighbor 1.1.1.1 remote-as 2                ! Neighbor defn., global to BGP
 neighbor 2.2.2.2 remote-as 1                ! Neighbor defn., global to BGP
 neighbor 3.3.3.3 remote-as 3                ! Neighbor defn., global to BGP
 !
 address-family ipv4 unicast                 ! Address-family IPv4-unicast
 bgp scan-time 45                            ! Global to IPv4-unicast
 aggregate-address 50.0.0.0 255.255.0.0      ! Global to IPv4-unicast
 neighbor ebgp activate                      ! Activate neighbor for IPv4-unic
 neighbor ebgp route-map ucast-out out       ! Peergroup IPv4-unicast policy
 neighbor 1.1.1.1 activate                   ! Activate neighbor for IPv4-unic
 neighbor 1.1.1.1 peer-group ebgp            ! Neighbor membership - IPv4-unic
 neighbor 1.1.1.1 route-map ucast-in in      ! Neighbor IPv4-unicast policy
 neighbor 2.2.2.2 activate                   ! Activate neighbor for IPv4-unic
 neighbor 2.2.2.2 route-reflector-client     ! RR client - IPv4-unicast
 neighbor 3.3.3.3 activate                   ! Activate neighbor for IPv4-unic
 neighbor 3.3.3.3 peer-group ebgp            ! Neighbor membership - IPv4-unic
 no auto-summary                            ! Disable IPv4-unicast auto aummarization
 exit-address-family                         ! Exit AF sub-mode
 !
```

```
 address-family ipv4 multicast                 ! AF sub-mode
 network 100.0.0.0 mask 255.255.0.0            ! Global to IPv4-multicast
 redistribute dvmrp route-map redist-map       ! Global to IPv4-multicast
 neighbor ebgp activate                        ! Activate neighbor for IPv4-mult
 neighbor 1.1.1.1 peer-group ebgp              ! Neighbor membership - IPv4-mult
 neighbor 1.1.1.1 route-map mcast-in in        ! Neighbor IPv4-multicast polic
 neighbor 3.3.3.3 peer-group ebgp              ! Neighbor membership - IPv4-mult
 exit-address-family                           ! Exit AF sub-mode
exit
```

The following sections provide more information on commands.
Each section addresses two configuration styles:

- **Old style**—The current 12.0S way of configuring BGP.
- **AF style**—The new way of configuring BGP, using **address-family** submode.

The following sections cover configuration guidelines associated with activating a peer, advertising a network, peer groups, route maps, route redistribution, route reflection, and aggregation.

activate

The **activate** command is new to IOS BGP configuration as part of the AF CLI enhancements. It's used to enable (or activate) support of the specified AF for a neighbor. This section discusses the old method used to enable an AF for a neighbor and then provides guidelines for using the new method.

Old Style

The **activate** command was not available in 12.0S. The neighbor was activated for IPv4 BGP automatically. However, if MBGP was enabled, the **nlri** keyword in the **neighbor** command was required:

```
Router(config-router)#neighbor 1.2.3.4 remote-as 10 nlri unicast multicast
```

If the **nlri** keyword was not specified, the router would exchange IPv4 prefixes only. If the **nlri** keyword was specified with the **multicast** option only, only the IPv4 multicast NLRI would be exchanged. This way you could activate only unicast, or only multicast, or both.

AF Style

To enable an AF for the neighbor, the **activate** command is used in BGP router or **address-family** configuration submode. The neighbors that are defined under the BGP router submode are automatically activated for IPv4. For all other AFs, the neighbors must be explicitly activated. To deactivate a neighbor for an AF, use the no form of the command. The following command syntax demonstrates how to enable neighbor 1.2.3.4 to support IPv4 multicast:

```
Router(config-router)#address-family ipv4 multicast
Router(config-router-af)# neighbor 1.2.3.4 activate
```

network

The **network** command can now be specified under a specific AF in order to announce the network under that AF. This section discusses the old and new styles of configuring the **network** command.

Old Style

The old style used the **network** command to advertise a network over BGP. The command used an **nlri** extension to specify if the network was to be advertised as unicast, multicast, or both. The absence of the **nlri** keyword implied IPv4 unicast only. For example:

```
Router(config)#router bgp 10
Router(config-router)#network 2.2.2.0 mask 255.255.255.0
Router(config-router)#network 3.0.0.0 mask 255.0.0.0 nlri multicast
Router(config-router)#network 1.1.0.0 mask 255.255.0.0 nlri unicast multicast
```

AF Style

In this style, the presence of the **address-family** submode obviates the need for the **nlri** keyword. To advertise a network over IPv4, the **network** command has to be specified under BGP router mode. In order for the network to be advertised as multicast NLRI, the **network** command needs to be specified under the **ipv4 multicast** AF submode.

The following commands advertise a network to all the neighbors in the IPv4 address family:

```
Router(config-router)#network 1.1.0.0 mask 255.255.0.0
Router(config-router)#network 2.2.2.0 mask 255.255.255.0
```

To advertise a network in the IPv4 multicast AF, you need to define the network under the IPv4 multicast AF mode:

```
Router(config-router)#address-family ipv4 multicast
Router(config-router-af)#network 1.1.0.0 mask 255.255.0.0
Router(config-router-af)#network 2.2.2.0 mask 255.255.255.0
```

This way, networks can be independently advertised as IPv4 unicast, multicast, or unicast and multicast NLRI.

Peer Groups

Peer groups can now be configured under specific AFs, providing a considerable amount of flexibility over the old style of configuring peer groups. This section discusses both the old and new methods of configuring peer groups.

Old Style

A peer group was defined in the BGP router configuration mode. The **nlri** keyword was used to allow the peer group to exchange multicast prefixes. Using the **nlri** keyword, you could specify unicast and/or multicast. If the **nlri** keyword was not specified, it implied only IPv4 unicast.

The peer group members automatically inherited the unicast and/or multicast capability of the peer group. The following command syntax shows the old method of configuring peer groups:

```
Router(config-router)#router bgp 10
Router(config-router)#neighbor external peer-group nlri unicast multicast
Router(config-router)#neighbor 1.2.3.4 remote-as 20
Router(config-router)#neighbor 1.2.3.4 peer-group external
```

AF Style

The peer group (or its members) is (are) defined under the BGP router mode. However, because we have AF submodes, the need for the **nlri** keyword is obviated. The peer group needs to be activated in the IPv4 multicast AF to enable the exchange of IPv4 multicast prefixes. As with the **neighbor** command, a peer group and its members are activated by default for IPv4 unicast. This behavior can be overridden using the **no** form of the **activate** command. The following command syntax shows how to configure peer groups using the new AF-style CLI:

```
Router(config)#router bgp 10
Router(config-router)#neighbor external peer-group
Router(config-router)#neighbor 1.2.3.4 remote-as 20
Router(config-router)#neighbor 1.2.3.4 peer-group external

Router(config-router)#address-family ipv4 multicast
Router(config-router-af)#neighbor external activate
Router(config-router-af)#neighbor 1.2.3.4 peer-group external
```

Route Maps

The old method of configuring route maps required that all AF policies be contained within a single route map. With the new AF style of configuring route maps, an individual route map can be specified for each AF. This section discusses both the old and new methods of using route maps with multiple AFs.

Old Style

In the old style, a single route map was used to specify policies for all AFs. This route map was then applied as either inbound or outbound for the peer or peer group. Routing policies relating to the two AFs that could be carried in the BGP session (IPv4 unicast and IPv4 multicast) were represented using a single route map by specifying the **match nlri** clause in the route map sequence. The **match nlri** clause in a route map used the following semantics:

```
match nlri multicast            ! Matches only IPv4 multicast
match nlri multicast unicast    ! Matches both IPv4 unicast and multicast
match nlri unicast              ! Matches only IPv4 unicast
match nlri                      ! Unspecified; matches only IPv4 unicast
```

The following example shows how to configure BGP so that any multicast routes from neighbor 1.1.1.1 will be accepted if they match access-list number 1:

```
router bgp 109
  neighbor 1.1.1.1 remote-as 1 nlri unicast multicast
  neighbor 1.1.1.1 route-map filter-mcast in
!
route-map filter-mcast permit 10
  match nlri multicast
  match ip address 1
```

AF Style

One of the important reasons for migrating customer configurations from the old style to the AF style is that routing policies expressed using the **match nlri** keyword in the sequences of a route map soon becomes unmanageable, especially when complicated and differing policies are used for different AFs. Because new IOS supports more than two AFs, it was quickly realized that a more scalable solution was required. A single route map for expressing all policies was seen as overly complex.

The introduction of a new parser mode for each AF facilitated the introduction of a new way of configuring policies on a per-AF basis (that is, a separate route map for each AF associated with a neighbor). Not only can route maps be specified on a per-AF basis, but they can also provide AF-specific filtering rules such as prefix lists, distribution lists, AS_PATH access lists, and so on. With the new style of configuring policies, the keyword **nlri** would no longer be required, and the parser would reject the occurrence of the **match nlri** clause in a route map sequence.

The policy can then be expressed in AF style as follows:

```
router bgp 109
  neighbor 1.1.1.1 remote-as 1
  neighbor 1.1.1.1 route-map filter-ucast in
!
address-family ipv4 multicast
neighbor 1.1.1.1 activate
neighbor 1.1.1.1 route-map filter-mcast in
!
route-map filter-ucast permit 10
  match ip address 1
!
route-map filter-mcast permit 10
  match ip address 2
```

Redistribution

Redistribution is the process of importing routes from one routing protocol to another. When routes are redistributed into BGP using the **redistribute** command, you have to specify the BGP table (Adj-RIB-In, as specified in BGP) into which the routes are to be imported. This BGP table can be either the unicast BGP table or the multicast BGP table.

Old Style

The old style of specifying the table into which a route had to go used the **set nlri** clause in the redistribution route map. The **set nlri** clause in the redistribution route map has the following semantics:

- **set nlri multicast**—Redistributes the matching prefix to the multicast table.
- **set nlri unicast multicast**—Redistributes the matching prefix to both unicast and multicast tables.
- **set nlri unicast**—Redistributes the matching prefix to the unicast table only.
- **set nlri**—Unspecified results in unicast behavior only.

The following example demonstrates redistribution into BGP so that all "connected" prefixes matching access list 1 in the routing table are imported as multicast NLRI:

```
router bgp 109
  redistribute connected route-map mbgp-source-map
  !
route-map mbgp-source-map
  match ip address 1
  set nlri multicast
```

AF Style

With the introduction of AF mode, the AF under which the **redistribute** command is specified determines the table into which the redistributed prefixes are injected. For example, if the **redistribute** statement resides under **address-family ipv4 multicast** mode, the redistributed prefixes are injected as multicast IPv4 NLRI. Hence, the preceding old-style redistribution configuration translates into the following in AF style:

```
router bgp 109
  !
  address-family ipv4 multicast
  redistribute connected route-map mbgp-source-map
  !
route-map mbgp-source-map
  match ip address 1
```

Note that with the introduction of the **redistribute** statement within AF mode, the clause **set nlri** is not required, and the parser would reject the presence of **set nlri** in the route map paragraph.

Route Reflector

Route reflector configuration may now be specified on a per-AF basis, providing a considerable amount of flexibility over the old "centralized" method. This section discusses both old and new styles of configuring route reflection.

Old Style

With the old style, route reflector (RR) client properties were specified globally, and the configuration applied to all AFs negotiated with its clients. The RR knew that it had to reflect routes to and from clients by specifying **route-reflector-client** for a particular neighbor or IBGP peer group. The following is an example in which the IBGP peer 1.1.1.1 is made a route reflector client for both unicast and multicast IPv4 prefixes:

```
router bgp 109
neighbor 1.1.1.1 remote-as 109 nlri unicast multicast
neighbor 1.1.1.1 route-reflector-client
```

AF Style

The AF style of configuring router reflects the fact that a neighbor or peer group is a route reflector client is AF-dependent and is configured in AF mode. In other words, just because a peer is a route reflector client in IPv4 unicast mode does not automatically make it an RR client in IPv4 multicast mode. It must now be specified by explicitly configuring the client in IPv4 multicast AF mode. Thus, the preceding configuration that made 1.1.1.1 a client for both unicast and multicast would now be expressed as follows:

```
router bgp 109
  neighbor 1.1.1.1 remote-as 109
  neighbor 1.1.1.1 route-reflector-client
  !
  address-family ipv4 multicast
  neighbor 1.1.1.1 activate
  neighbor 1.1.1.1 route-reflector-client
```

The new mode gives the operator the flexibility to make a router the route reflector for only certain AFs. As such, the route reflector topologies for different AFs can vary.

Aggregation

Configuring aggregation for single or multiple AFs was complex if varying policies were required. This section provides information on both old and new methods of configuring aggregation.

Old Style

In the old style, a multicast aggregate was configured the same way you configured a unicast aggregate—via the **aggregate-address** command. The **aggregate-address** command was enhanced to specify whether the aggregate address should be applied to unicast or multicast using the **nlri** keyword in the **aggregate-address** command. The following is an example of generating an aggregate in the multicast BGP table:

```
router bgp 109
  aggregate-address 174.0.0.0 255.0.0.0 as-set nlri multicast
```

The **nlri** options that can be specified on an **aggregate-address** command are **unicast**, **multicast**, and **unicast multicast**, which generate aggregates in the BGP table, in the multicast BGP table, or in both, respectively. The absence of the **nlri** keyword in the **aggregate-address** command results in the aggregate's being generated as unicast only.

AF Style

The presence of AF modes for different AFs eliminates the need for the **nlri** keyword in the **aggregate-address** command. The AF mode under which the aggregate is specified determines the table where the aggregated prefix should be generated. Hence, the aggregate displayed in the old-style section can be generated in the AF style as follows:

```
router bgp 109
       !
       address-family ipv4 multicast
       aggregate-address 174.0.0.0 255.0.0.0 as-set
```

List of BGP Commands

Table D-1 lists the BGP commands and the category of each command/subcommand.

Table D-1 *BGP Commands/Subcommands Grouped by Category*

Command/Subcommand	Category
address-family ipv4 unicast	Can appear once under **router bgp** mode
address-family ipv4 multicast	Can appear once under **router bgp** mode
aggregate-address	Per AF
auto-summary	Per AF
bgp always-compare-med	Global to BGP
bestpath	Global to BGP
client-to-client	Per AF
cluster-id	Global to BGP
confederation	Global to BGP

Table D-1 *BGP Commands/Subcommands Grouped by Category (Continued)*

Command/Subcommand	Category
dampening	Per AF
default	Global to BGP
deterministic-med	Global to BGP
fast-external-fallover	Global to BGP
log-neighbor-changes	Global to BGP
redistribute-internal	Global to BGP
router-id	Global to BGP
scan-time	Per AF
default-metric	Global to BGP
distance	Per AF
maximum-paths	Per AF
neighbor	Applied on a per-neighbor basis
activate	Per AF
advertisement-interval	Global to the neighbor (session)
default-originate	Per AF (policy)
description	Global to the neighbor
distribute-list	Per AF (policy)
ebgp-multihop	Global to the neighbor (session)
filter-list	Per AF (policy)
local-as	Global to the neighbor (session)
maximum-prefix	Per AF (policy)
next-hop-self	Global to the neighbor (session)
password	Global to the neighbor (session)
peer-group	Per AF (policy)
prefix-list	Per AF (policy)
remote-as	Global to the neighbor (session)
remove-private-AS	Global to the neighbor (session)
route-map	Per AF (policy)
route-reflector-client	Per AF
send-community	Per AF (policy)

continues

Table D-1 *BGP Commands/Subcommands Grouped by Category (Continued)*

Command/Subcommand	Category
shutdown	Global to the neighbor (session)
soft-reconfiguration	Per AF (policy)
timers	Global to the neighbor (session)
update-source	Global to the neighbor (session)
version	Global to the neighbor (session)
weight	Per AF (policy)
network	Per AF
redistribute	Per AF
synchronization	Per AF
table-map	Per AF
timers	Global to BGP

Upgrading to the AF Style

In order to have a smooth upgrade path, support has been added to parse the old-style 12.0S commands (which had the **nlri** keyword). These commands are as follows:

- **neighbor**
- **network**
- **aggregate**
- **set nlri** and **match nlri** in route maps

The only caveat is that the old-style commands can be used as long as no new features need to be activated. In that event, the old-style BGP commands need to be translated to the new style.

To migrate to the new command set, you must enter the **bgp upgrade-cli** command in router configuration mode:

```
Router(config-router)#bgp upgrade-cli
```

This command will translate the old configuration to the new one. As always, a **wr mem** will need to be done in order to save the new configuration. (Note: The **bgp upgrade-cli** command is not shown in the configuration.)

References

[1]RFC 2842, "Capabilities Advertisement with BGP-4," www.isi.edu/in-notes/rfc2842.txt

[2]RFC 2283, "Multiprotocol Extensions for BGP-4," www.isi.edu/in-notes/rfc2283.txt

[3]RFC 1771, "A Border Gateway Protocol 4 (BGP-4)," www.isi.edu/in-notes/rfc1771.txt

[4]RFC 1700, "Assigned Numbers," www.isi.edu/in-notes/rfc1700.txt

INDEX

Numerics

A

B

C

D

E

F

G

H

I

J-K

L

M

N

O

P

Q-R

S

T

U

V

W-X-Y-Z

CCIE Professional Development

Cisco LAN Switching

Kennedy Clark, CCIE; Kevin Hamilton, CCIE

1-57870-094-9 • **AVAILABLE NOW**

This volume provides an in-depth analysis of Cisco LAN switching technologies, architectures, and deployments, including unique coverage of Catalyst network design essentials. Network designs and configuration examples are incorporated throughout to demonstrate the principles and enable easy translation of the material into practice in production networks.

Advanced IP Network Design

Alvaro Retana, CCIE; Don Slice, CCIE; and Russ White, CCIE

1-57870-097-3 • **AVAILABLE NOW**

Network engineers and managers can use these case studies, which highlight various network design goals, to explore issues including protocol choice, network stability, and growth. This book also includes theoretical discussion on advanced design topics.

Large-Scale IP Network Solutions

Khalid Raza, CCIE; and Mark Turner

1-57870-084-1 • **AVAILABLE NOW**

Network engineers can find solutions as their IP networks grow in size and complexity. Examine all the major IP protocols in-depth and learn about scalability, migration planning, network management, and security for large-scale networks.

Routing TCP/IP, Volume I

Jeff Doyle, CCIE

1-57870-041-8 • **AVAILABLE NOW**

This book takes the reader from a basic understanding of routers and routing protocols through a detailed examination of each of the IP interior routing protocols. Learn techniques for designing networks that maximize the efficiency of the protocol being used. Exercises and review questions provide core study for the CCIE Routing and Switching exam.

www.ciscopress.com

Cisco Career Certifications

CCDA Exam Certification Guide

Anthony Bruno, CCIE & Jacqueline Kim

0-7357-0074-5 • AVAILABLE NOW

CCDA Exam Certification Guide is a comprehensive study tool for DCN Exam #640-441. Written by a CCIE and a CCDA, and reviewed by Cisco technical experts, *CCDA Exam Certification Guide* will help you understand and master the exam objectives. In this solid review on the design areas of the DCN exam, you'll learn to design a network that meets a customer's requirements for perfomance, security, capacity, and scalability.

Designing Cisco Networks

Edited by Diane Teare

1-57870-105-8 • AVAILABLE NOW

Based on the Cisco Systems instructor-led and self-study course available worldwide, *Designing Cisco Networks* will help you understand how to analyze and solve existing network problems while building a framework that supports the functionality, performance, and scalability required from any given environment. Self-assessment through exercises and chapter-ending tests starts you down the path for attaining your CCDA certification.

Interconnecting Cisco Network Devices

Edited by Steve McQuerry

1-57870-111-2 • AVAILABLE NOW

Based on the Cisco course taught worldwide, *Interconnecting Cisco Network Devices* teaches you how to configure Cisco switches and routers in multiprotocol internetworks. ICND is the primary course recommended by Cisco Systems for CCNA #640-507 preparation. If you are pursuing CCNA certification, this book is an excellent starting point for your study.

Building Cisco Remote Access Networks

Catherine Paquet

1-57870-091-4 • AVAILABLE NOW

Based on the actual Cisco BCRAN course, this book teaches you how to design, configure, maintain, and scale a remote access network using Cisco products. *Building Cisco Remote Access Networks* helps you enable and enhance the on-demand connectivity of a small office, home office, or telecommuter site to a Central site. Prepare for CCNP and CCDP certification while learning the fundamentals of remote access networks.

www.ciscopress.com

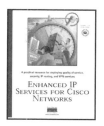

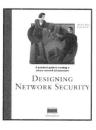

Cisco Press Solutions

EIGRP Network Design Solutions

Ivan Pepelnjak, CCIE

1-57870-165-1 • AVAILABLE NOW

EIGRP Network Design Solutions uses case studies and real-world configuration examples to help you gain an in-depth understanding of the issues involved in designing, deploying, and managing EIGRP-based networks. This book details proper designs that can be used to build large and scalable EIGRP-based networks and documents possible ways each EIGRP feature can be used in network design, implmentation, troubleshooting, and monitoring.

Top-Down Network Design

Priscilla Oppenheimer

1-57870-069-8 • AVAILABLE NOW

Building reliable, secure, and manageable networks is every network professional's goal. This practical guide teaches you a systematic method for network design that can be applied to campus LANs, remote-access networks, WAN links, and large-scale internetworks. Learn how to analyze business and technical requirements, examine traffic flow and Quality of Service requirements, and select protocols and technologies based on performance goals.

Cisco IOS Releases: The Complete Reference

Mack M. Coulibaly

1-57870-179-1 • AVAILABLE NOW

Cisco IOS Releases: The Complete Reference is the first comprehensive guide to the more than three dozen types of Cisco IOS releases being used today on enterprise and service provider networks. It details the release process and its numbering and naming conventions, as well as when, where, and how to use the various releases. A complete map of Cisco IOS software releases and their relationships to one another, in addition to insights into decoding information contained within the software, make this book an indispensable resource for any network professional.

Cisco Systems
Cisco Press

www.ciscopress.com

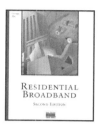

Cisco Press Fundamentals

IP Routing Primer

Robert Wright, CCIE

1-57870-108-2 • **AVAILABLE NOW**

Learn how IP routing behaves in a Cisco router environment. In addition to teaching the core fundamentals, this book enhances your ability to troubleshoot IP routing problems yourself, often eliminating the need to call for additional technical support. The information is presented in an approachable, workbook-type format with dozens of detailed illustrations and real-life scenarios integrated throughout.

Cisco Router Configuration

Allan Leinwand, Bruce Pinsky, Mark Culpepper

1-57870-022-1 • **AVAILABLE NOW**

An example-oriented and chronological approach helps you implement and administer your internetworking devices. Starting with the configuration devices "out of the box;" this book moves to configuring Cisco IOS for the three most popular networking protocols today: TCP/IP, AppleTalk, and Novell Interwork Packet Exchange (IPX). You also learn basic administrative and management configuration, including access control with TACACS+ and RADIUS, network management with SNMP, logging of messages, and time control with NTP.

IP Routing Fundamentals

Mark A. Sportack

1-57870-071-x • **AVAILABLE NOW**

This comprehensive guide provides essential background information on routing in IP networks for network professionals who are deploying and maintaining LANs and WANs daily. Explore the mechanics of routers, routing protocols, network interfaces, and operating systems.

For the latest on Cisco Press resources and Certification and Training guides, or for information on publishing opportunities, visit **www.ciscopress.com**

Cisco Press books are available at your local bookstore, computer store, and online booksellers.